RANGER/EXPLORER/MOUNTAINEER
1991-99 REPAIR MANUAL

Covers all U.S. and Canadian models of Ford Explorer, Ranger, Splash and Mercury Mountaineer; 2 and 4 wheel drive

by **Todd Stidham,** A.S.E.

CHILTON Automotive Books

PUBLISHED BY **HAYNES NORTH AMERICA, Inc.**

Manufactured in USA
© 1999 Haynes North America, Inc.
ISBN 0-8019-9131-5
Library of Congress Catalog Card No. 99-072476
6789012345 9876543210

Haynes Publishing Group
Sparkford Nr Yeovil
Somerset BA22 7JJ England

Haynes North America, Inc
861 Lawrence Drive
Newbury Park
California 91320 USA

ABCDE
FGHIJ
KLM

Contents

Contents

DRIVE TRAIN 7

SUSPENSION AND STEERING 8

BRAKES 9

BODY 10

GLOSSARY

MASTER INDEX

SAFETY NOTICE

Proper service and repair procedures are vital to the safe, reliable operation of all motor vehicles, as well as the personal safety of those performing repairs. This manual outlines procedures for servicing and repairing vehicles using safe, effective methods. The procedures contain many NOTES, CAUTIONS and WARNINGS which should be followed, along with standard procedures to eliminate the possibility of personal injury or improper service which could damage the vehicle or compromise its safety.

It is important to note that repair procedures and techniques, tools and parts for servicing motor vehicles, as well as the skill and experience of the individual performing the work vary widely. It is not possible to anticipate all of the conceivable ways or conditions under which vehicles may be serviced, or to provide cautions as to all possible hazards that may result. Standard and accepted safety precautions and equipment should be used when handling toxic or flammable fluids, and safety goggles or other protection should be used during cutting, grinding, chiseling, prying, or any other process that can cause material removal or projectiles.

Some procedures require the use of tools specially designed for a specific purpose. Before substituting another tool or procedure, you must be completely satisfied that neither your personal safety, nor the performance of the vehicle will be endangered.

Although information in this manual is based on industry sources and is complete as possible at the time of publication, the possibility exists that some car manufacturers made later changes which could not be included here. While striving for total accuracy, the authors or publishers cannot assume responsibility for any errors, changes or omissions that may occur in the compilation of this data.

PART NUMBERS

Part numbers listed in this reference are not recommendations by Haynes North America, Inc. for any product brand name. They are references that can be used with interchange manuals and aftermarket supplier catalogs to locate each brand supplier's discrete part number.

SPECIAL TOOLS

Special tools are recommended by the vehicle manufacturer to perform their specific job. Use has been kept to a minimum, but where absolutely necessary, they are referred to in the text by the part number of the tool manufacturer. These tools can be purchased, under the appropriate part number, from your local dealer or regional distributor, or an equivalent tool can be purchased locally from a tool supplier or parts outlet. Before substituting any tool for the one recommended, read the SAFETY NOTICE at the top of this page.

ACKNOWLEDGMENTS

This publication contains material that is reproduced and distributed under a license from Ford Motor Company. No further reproduction or distribution of the Ford Motor Company material is allowed without the express written permission from Ford Motor Company.

1

GENERAL INFORMATION AND MAINTENANCE

HOW TO USE THIS BOOK

This Chilton's Total Car Care manual is intended to help you learn more about the inner workings of your Ranger, Explorer or Mountaineer while saving you money on its upkeep and operation.

The beginning of the book will likely be referred to the most, since that is where you will find information for maintenance and tune-up. The other sections deal with the more complex systems of your vehicle. Systems (from engine through brakes) are covered to the extent that the average do-it-yourselfer can attempt. This book will not explain such things as rebuilding a differential because the expertise required and the special tools necessary make this uneconomical. It will, however, give you detailed instructions to help you change your own brake pads and shoes, replace spark plugs, and perform many more jobs that can save you money and help avoid expensive problems.

A secondary purpose of this book is a reference for owners who want to understand their vehicle and/or their mechanics better.

Where to Begin

Before removing any bolts, read through the entire procedure. This will give you the overall view of what tools and supplies will be required. So read ahead and plan ahead. Each operation should be approached logically and all procedures thoroughly understood before attempting any work.

If repair of a component is not considered practical, we tell you how to remove the part and then how to install the new or rebuilt replacement. In this way, you at least save labor costs.

Avoiding Trouble

Many procedures in this book require you to "label and disconnect . . ." a group of lines, hoses or wires. Don't be think you can remember where everything goes—you won't. If you hook up vacuum or fuel lines incorrectly, the vehicle may run poorly, if at all. If you hook up electrical wiring incorrectly, you may instantly learn a very expensive lesson.

You don't need to know the proper name for each hose or line. A piece of masking tape on the hose and a piece on its fitting will allow you to assign your own label. As long as you remember your own code, the lines can be reconnected by matching your tags. Remember that tape will dissolve in gasoline or solvents; if a part is to be washed or cleaned, use another method of identification. A permanent felt-tipped marker or a metal scribe can be very handy for marking metal parts. Remove any tape or paper labels after assembly.

Maintenance or Repair?

Maintenance includes routine inspections, adjustments, and replacement of parts which show signs of normal wear. Maintenance compensates for wear or deterioration. Repair implies that something has broken or is not working. A need for a repair is often caused by lack of maintenance. for example: draining and refilling automatic transmission fluid is maintenance recommended at specific intervals. Failure to do this can shorten the life of the transmission/transaxle, requiring very expensive repairs. While no maintenance program can prevent items from eventually breaking or wearing out, a general rule is true: MAINTENANCE IS CHEAPER THAN REPAIR.

Two basic mechanic's rules should be mentioned here. First, whenever the left side of the vehicle or engine is referred to, it means the driver's side. Conversely, the right side of the vehicle means the passenger's side. Second, screws and bolts are removed by turning counterclockwise, and tightened by turning clockwise unless specifically noted.

Safety is always the most important rule. Constantly be aware of the dangers involved in working on an automobile and take the proper precautions. Please refer to the information in this section regarding SERVICING YOUR VEHICLE SAFELY and the SAFETY NOTICE on the acknowledgment page.

Avoiding the Most Common Mistakes

Pay attention to the instructions provided. There are 3 common mistakes in mechanical work:

1. Incorrect order of assembly, disassembly or adjustment. When taking something apart or putting it together, performing steps in the wrong order usually just costs you extra time; however, it CAN break something. Read the entire procedure before beginning. Perform everything in the order in which the instructions say you should, even if you can't see a reason for it. When you're taking apart something that is very intricate, you might want to draw a picture of how it looks when assembled in order to make sure you get everything back in its proper position. When making adjustments, perform them in the proper order. One adjustment possibly will affect another.

2. Overtorquing (or undertorquing). While it is more common for overtorquing to cause damage, undertorquing may allow a fastener to vibrate loose causing serious damage. Especially when dealing with aluminum parts, pay attention to torque specifications and utilize a torque wrench in assembly. If a torque figure is not available, remember that if you are using the right tool to perform the job, you will probably not have to strain yourself to get a fastener tight enough. The pitch of most threads is so slight that the tension you put on the wrench will be multiplied many times in actual force on what you are tightening.

There are many commercial products available for ensuring that fasteners won't come loose, even if they are not torqued just right (a very common brand is Loctite®. If you're worried about getting something together tight enough to hold, but loose enough to avoid mechanical damage during assembly, one of these products might offer substantial insurance. Before choosing a threadlocking compound, read the label on the package and make sure the product is compatible with the materials, fluids, etc. involved.

3. Crossthreading. This occurs when a part such as a bolt is screwed into a nut or casting at the wrong angle and forced. Crossthreading is more likely to occur if access is difficult. It helps to clean and lubricate fasteners, then to start threading the bolt, spark plug, etc. with your fingers. If you encounter resistance, unscrew the part and start over again at a different angle until it can be inserted and turned several times without much effort. Keep in mind that many parts have tapered threads, so that gentle turning will automatically bring the part you're threading to the proper angle. Don't put a wrench on the part until it's been tightened a couple of turns by hand. If you suddenly encounter resistance, and the part has not seated fully, don't force it. Pull it back out to make sure it's clean and threading properly.

Be sure to take your time and be patient, and always plan ahead. Allow yourself ample time to perform repairs and maintenance.

TOOLS AND EQUIPMENT

▶ **See Figures 1 thru 15**

Without the proper tools and equipment it is impossible to properly service your vehicle. It would be virtually impossible to catalog every tool that you would need to perform all of the operations in this book. It would be unwise for the amateur to rush out and buy an expensive set of tools on the theory that he/she may need one or more of them at some time.

The best approach is to proceed slowly, gathering a good quality set of those tools that are used most frequently. Don't be misled by the low cost of bargain tools. It is far better to spend a little more for better quality. Forged wrenches, 6 or 12-point sockets and fine tooth ratchets are by far preferable to their less expensive counterparts. As any good mechanic can tell you, there are few worse experiences than trying to work on a vehicle with bad tools. Your monetary savings will be far outweighed by frustration and mangled knuckles.

Begin accumulating those tools that are used most frequently: those associated with routine maintenance and tune-up. In addition to the normal assortment of screwdrivers and pliers, you should have the following tools:

• Wrenches/sockets and combination open end/box end wrenches in sizes from ⅛ –¾ in. or 3–19mm, as well as a ¹³⁄₁₆ in. or ⅝ in. spark plug socket (depending on plug type).

➡**If possible, buy various length socket drive extensions. Universaljoint and wobble extensions can be extremely useful, but be careful when using them, as they can change the amount of torque applied to the socket.**

• Jackstands for support.
• Oil filter wrench.

- Spout or funnel for pouring fluids.
- Grease gun for chassis lubrication (unless your vehicle is not equipped with any grease fittings)
- Hydrometer for checking the battery (unless equipped with a sealed, maintenance-free battery).
- A container for draining oil and other fluids.
- Rags for wiping up the inevitable mess.

In addition to the above items there are several others that are not absolutely necessary, but handy to have around. These include an equivalent oil absorbent gravel, like cat litter, and the usual supply of lubricants, antifreeze and fluids. This is a basic list for routine maintenance, but only your personal needs and desire can accurately determine your list of tools.

After performing a few projects on the vehicle, you'll be amazed at the other tools and non-tools on your workbench. Some useful household items are: a large turkey baster or siphon, empty coffee cans and ice trays (to store parts), a ball of twine, electrical tape for wiring, small rolls of colored tape for tagging lines or hoses, markers and pens, a note pad, golf tees (for plugging vacuum lines), metal coat hangers or a roll of mechanic's wire (to hold things out of the way), dental pick or similar long, pointed probe, a strong magnet, and a small mirror (to see into recesses and under manifolds).

A more advanced set of tools, suitable for tune-up work, can be drawn up easily. While the tools are slightly more sophisticated, they need not be outrageously expensive. There are several inexpensive tach/dwell meters on the market that are every bit as good for the average mechanic as a professional model. Just be sure that it goes to a least 1200–1500 rpm on the tach scale and that it works on 4, 6 and 8-cylinder engines. The key to these purchases is to make them with an eye towards adaptability and wide range. A basic list of tune-up tools could include:

- Tach/dwell meter.
- Spark plug wrench and gapping tool.
- Feeler gauges for valve adjustment.
- Timing light.

The choice of a timing light should be made carefully. A light which works on the DC current supplied by the vehicle's battery is the best choice; it should

TCCS1200
Fig. 1 All but the most basic procedures will require an assortment of ratchets and sockets

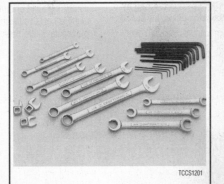
TCCS1201
Fig. 2 In addition to ratchets, a good set of wrenches and hex keys will be necessary

TCCS1202
Fig. 3 A hydraulic floor jack and a set of jackstands are essential for lifting and supporting the vehicle

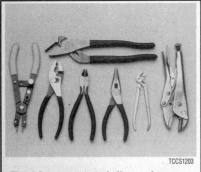
TCCS1203
Fig. 4 An assortment of pliers, grippers and cutters will be handy for old rusted parts and stripped bolt heads

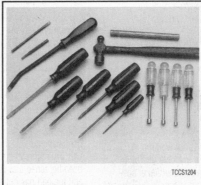
TCCS1204
Fig. 5 Various drivers, chisels and prybars are great tools to have in your toolbox

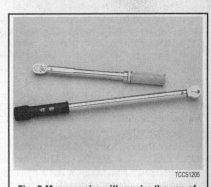
TCCS1205
Fig. 6 Many repairs will require the use of a torque wrench to assure the components are properly fastened

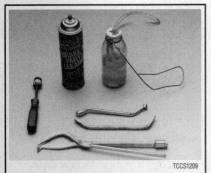
TCCS1209
Fig. 7 Although not always necessary, using specialized brake tools will save time

TCCS1210
Fig. 8 A few inexpensive lubrication tools will make maintenance easier

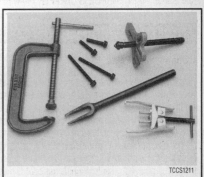
TCCS1211
Fig. 9 Various pullers, clamps and separator tools are needed for many larger, more complicated repairs

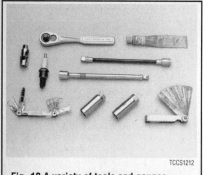

Fig. 10 A variety of tools and gauges should be used for spark plug gapping and installation

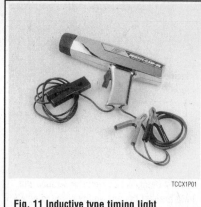

Fig. 11 Inductive type timing light

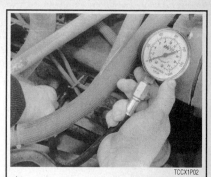

Fig. 12 A screw-in type compression gauge is recommended for compression testing

Fig. 13 A vacuum/pressure tester is necessary for many testing procedures

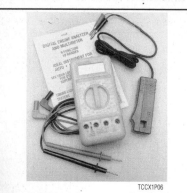

Fig. 14 Most modern automotive multimeters incorporate many helpful features

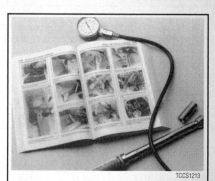

Fig. 15 Proper information is vital, so always have a Chilton Total Car Care manual handy

have a xenon tube for brightness. On any vehicle with an electronic ignition system, a timing light with an inductive pickup that clamps around the No. 1 spark plug cable is preferred.

In addition to these basic tools, there are several other tools and gauges you may find useful. These include:

• Compression gauge. The screw-in type is slower to use, but eliminates the possibility of a faulty reading due to escaping pressure.
• Manifold vacuum gauge.
• 12V test light.
• A combination volt/ohmmeter
• Induction Ammeter. This is used for determining whether or not there is current in a wire. These are handy for use if a wire is broken somewhere in a wiring harness.

As a final note, you will probably find a torque wrench necessary for all but the most basic work. The beam type models are perfectly adequate, although the newer click types (breakaway) are easier to use. The click type torque wrenches tend to be more expensive. Also keep in mind that all types of torque wrenches should be periodically checked and/or recalibrated. You will have to decide for yourself which better fits your pocketbook, and purpose.

Special Tools

Normally, the use of special factory tools is avoided for repair procedures, since these are not readily available for the do-it-yourself mechanic. When it is possible to perform the job with more commonly available tools, it will be pointed out, but occasionally, a special tool was designed to perform a specific function and should be used. Before substituting another tool, you should be convinced that neither your safety nor the performance of the vehicle will be compromised.

Special tools can usually be purchased from an automotive parts store or from your dealer. In some cases special tools may be available directly from the tool manufacturer.

SERVICING YOUR VEHICLE SAFELY

♦ **See Figures 16, 17 and 18**

It is virtually impossible to anticipate all of the hazards involved with automotive maintenance and service, but care and common sense will prevent most accidents.

The rules of safety for mechanics range from "don't smoke around gasoline," to "use the proper tool(s) for the job." The trick to avoiding injuries is to develop safe work habits and to take every possible precaution.

Do's

• Do keep a fire extinguisher and first aid kit handy.
• Do wear safety glasses or goggles when cutting, drilling, grinding or prying, even if you have 20–20 vision. If you wear glasses for the sake of vision, wear safety goggles over your regular glasses.

• Do shield your eyes whenever you work around the battery. Batteries contain sulfuric acid. In case of contact with, flush the area with water or a mixture of water and baking soda, then seek immediate medical attention.
• Do use safety stands (jackstands) for any undervehicle service. Jacks are for raising vehicles; jackstands are for making sure the vehicle stays raised until you want it to come down.
• Do use adequate ventilation when working with any chemicals or hazardous materials. Like carbon monoxide, the asbestos dust resulting from some brake lining wear can be hazardous in sufficient quantities.
• Do disconnect the negative battery cable when working on the electrical system. The secondary ignition system contains EXTREMELY HIGH VOLTAGE. In some cases it can even exceed 50,000 volts.
• Do follow manufacturer's directions whenever working with potentially hazardous materials. Most chemicals and fluids are poisonous.

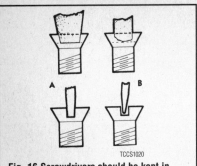

Fig. 16 Screwdrivers should be kept in good condition to prevent injury or damage which could result if the blade slips from the screw

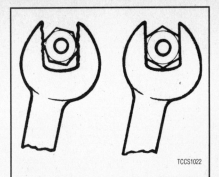

Fig. 17 Using the correct size wrench will help prevent the possibility of rounding off a nut

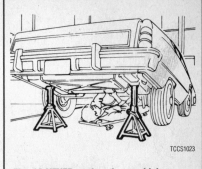

Fig. 18 NEVER work under a vehicle unless it is supported using safety stands (jackstands)

• Do properly maintain your tools. Loose hammerheads, mushroomed punches and chisels, frayed or poorly grounded electrical cords, excessively worn screwdrivers, spread wrenches (open end), cracked sockets, slipping ratchets, or faulty droplight sockets can cause accidents.

• Likewise, keep your tools clean; a greasy wrench can slip off a bolt head, ruining the bolt and often harming your knuckles in the process.

• Do use the proper size and type of tool for the job at hand. Do select a wrench or socket that fits the nut or bolt. The wrench or socket should sit straight, not cocked.

• Do, when possible, pull on a wrench handle rather than push on it, and adjust your stance to prevent a fall.

• Do be sure that adjustable wrenches are tightly closed on the nut or bolt and pulled so that the force is on the side of the fixed jaw.

• Do strike squarely with a hammer; avoid glancing blows.

• Do set the parking brake and block the drive wheels if the work requires a running engine.

Don'ts

• Don't run the engine in a garage or anywhere else without proper ventilation—EVER! Carbon monoxide is poisonous; it takes a long time to leave the human body and you can build up a deadly supply of it in your system by simply breathing in a little at a time. You may not realize you are slowly poisoning yourself. Always use power vents, windows, fans and/or open the garage door.

• Don't work around moving parts while wearing loose clothing. Short sleeves are much safer than long, loose sleeves. Hard-toed shoes with neoprene soles protect your toes and give a better grip on slippery surfaces. Watches and jewelry is not safe working around a vehicle. Long hair should be tied back under a hat or cap.

• Don't use pockets for toolboxes. A fall or bump can drive a screwdriver deep into your body. Even a rag hanging from your back pocket can wrap around a spinning shaft or fan.

• Don't smoke when working around gasoline, cleaning solvent or other flammable material.

• Don't smoke when working around the battery. When the battery is being charged, it gives off explosive hydrogen gas.

• Don't use gasoline to wash your hands; there are excellent soaps available. Gasoline contains dangerous additives which can enter the body through a cut or through your pores. Gasoline also removes all the natural oils from the skin so that bone dry hands will suck up oil and grease.

• Don't service the air conditioning system unless you are equipped with the necessary tools and training. When liquid or compressed gas refrigerant is released to atmospheric pressure it will absorb heat from whatever it contacts. This will chill or freeze anything it touches.

• Don't use screwdrivers for anything other than driving screws! A screwdriver used as an prying tool can snap when you least expect it, causing injuries. At the very least, you'll ruin a good screwdriver.

• Don't use an emergency jack (that little ratchet, scissors, or pantograph jack supplied with the vehicle) for anything other than changing a flat! These jacks are only intended for emergency use out on the road; they are NOT designed as a maintenance tool. If you are serious about maintaining your vehicle yourself, invest in a hydraulic floor jack of at least a 1½ ton capacity, and at least two sturdy jackstands.

FASTENERS, MEASUREMENTS AND CONVERSIONS

Bolts, Nuts and Other Threaded Retainers

▶ **See Figures 19 and 20**

Although there are a great variety of fasteners found in the modern car or truck, the most commonly used retainer is the threaded fastener (nuts, bolts, screws, studs, etc.). Most threaded retainers may be reused, provided that they are not damaged in use or during the repair. Some retainers (such as stretch bolts or torque prevailing nuts) are designed to deform when tightened or in use and should not be reinstalled.

Whenever possible, we will note any special retainers which should be replaced during a procedure. But you should always inspect the condition of a retainer when it is removed and replace any that show signs of damage. Check all threads for rust or corrosion which can increase the torque necessary to achieve the desired clamp load for which that fastener was originally selected. Additionally, be sure that the driver surface of the fastener has not been compromised by rounding or other damage. In some cases a driver surface may become only partially rounded, allowing the driver to catch in only one direction. In many of these occurrences, a fastener may be installed and tightened, but the driver would not be able to grip and loosen the fastener again.

If you must replace a fastener, whether due to design or damage, you must ALWAYS be sure to use the proper replacement. In all cases, a retainer of the same design, material and strength should be used. Markings on the heads of

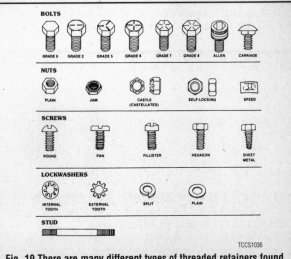

Fig. 19 There are many different types of threaded retainers found on vehicles

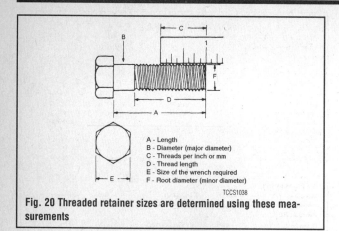

A - Length
B - Diameter (major diameter)
C - Threads per inch or mm
D - Thread length
E - Size of the wrench required
F - Root diameter (minor diameter)

TCCS1038

Fig. 20 Threaded retainer sizes are determined using these measurements

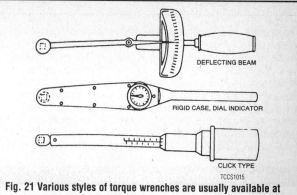

DEFLECTING BEAM

RIGID CASE, DIAL INDICATOR

CLICK TYPE

TCCS1015

Fig. 21 Various styles of torque wrenches are usually available at your local automotive supply store

most bolts will help determine the proper strength of the fastener. The same material, thread and pitch must be selected to assure proper installation and safe operation of the vehicle afterwards.

Thread gauges are available to help measure a bolt or stud's thread. Most automotive and hardware stores keep gauges available to help you select the proper size. In a pinch, you can use another nut or bolt for a thread gauge. If the bolt you are replacing is not too badly damaged, you can select a match by finding another bolt which will thread in its place. If you find a nut which threads properly onto the damaged bolt, then use that nut to help select the replacement bolt.

✳✳ WARNING

Be aware that when you find a bolt with damaged threads, you may also find the nut or drilled hole it was threaded into has also been damaged. If this is the case, you may have to drill and tap the hole, replace the nut or otherwise repair the threads. NEVER try to force a replacement bolt to fit into the damaged threads.

Torque

Torque is defined as the measurement of resistance to turning or rotating. It tends to twist a body about an axis of rotation. A common example of this would be tightening a threaded retainer such as a nut, bolt or screw. Measuring torque is one of the most common ways to help assure that a threaded retainer has been properly fastened.

When tightening a threaded fastener, torque is applied in three distinct areas, the head, the bearing surface and the clamp load. About 50 percent of the measured torque is used in overcoming bearing friction. This is the friction between the bearing surface of the bolt head, screw head or nut face and the base material or washer (the surface on which the fastener is rotating). Approximately 40 percent of the applied torque is used in overcoming thread friction. This leaves only about 10 percent of the applied torque to develop a useful clamp load (the force which holds a joint together). This means that friction can account for as much as 90 percent of the applied torque on a fastener.

TORQUE WRENCHES

♦ See Figure 21

In most applications, a torque wrench can be used to assure proper installation of a fastener. Torque wrenches come in various designs and most automotive supply stores will carry a variety to suit your needs. A torque wrench should be used any time we supply a specific torque value for a fastener. Again, the general rule of "if you are using the right tool for the job, you should not have to strain to tighten a fastener" applies here.

Beam Type

The beam type torque wrench is one of the most popular types. It consists of a pointer attached to the head that runs the length of the flexible beam (shaft) to a scale located near the handle. As the wrench is pulled, the beam bends and the pointer indicates the torque using the scale.

Click (Breakaway) Type

Another popular design of torque wrench is the click type. To use the click type wrench you pre-adjust it to a torque setting. Once the torque is reached, the wrench has a reflex signaling feature that causes a momentary breakaway of the torque wrench body, sending an impulse to the operator's hand.

Pivot Head Type

♦ See Figure 22

Some torque wrenches (usually of the click type) may be equipped with a pivot head which can allow it to be used in areas of limited access. BUT, it must be used properly. To hold a pivot head wrench, grasp the handle lightly, and as you pull on the handle, it should be floated on the pivot point. If the handle comes in contact with the yoke extension during the process of pulling, there is a very good chance the torque readings will be inaccurate because this could alter the wrench loading point. The design of the handle is usually such as to make it inconvenient to deliberately misuse the wrench.

➡**It should be mentioned that the use of any U-joint, wobble or extension will have an effect on the torque readings, no matter what type of wrench you are using. For the most accurate readings, install the socket directly on the wrench driver. If necessary, straight extensions (which hold a socket directly under the wrench driver) will have the least effect on the torque reading. Avoid any extension that alters the length of the wrench from the handle to the head/driving point (such as a crow's foot). U-joint or wobble extensions can greatly affect the readings; avoid their use at all times.**

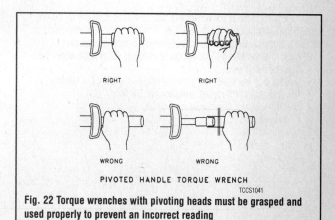

RIGHT

RIGHT

WRONG

WRONG

PIVOTED HANDLE TORQUE WRENCH

TCCS1041

Fig. 22 Torque wrenches with pivoting heads must be grasped and used properly to prevent an incorrect reading

Rigid Case (Direct Reading)

A rigid case or direct reading torque wrench is equipped with a dial indicator to show torque values. One advantage of these wrenches is that they can be held at any position on the wrench without affecting accuracy. These wrenches are often preferred because they tend to be compact, easy to read and have a great degree of accuracy.

TORQUE ANGLE METERS

Because the frictional characteristics of each fastener or threaded hole will vary, clamp loads which are based strictly on torque will vary as well. In most applications, this variance is not significant enough to cause worry. But, in certain applications, a manufacturer's engineers may determine that more precise clamp loads are necessary (such is the case with many aluminum cylinder heads). In these cases, a torque angle method of installation would be specified. When installing fasteners which are torque angle tightened, a predetermined seating torque and standard torque wrench are usually used first to remove any compliance from the joint. The fastener is then tightened the specified additional portion of a turn measured in degrees. A torque angle gauge (mechanical protractor) is used for these applications.

Standard and Metric Measurements

▶ See Figure 23

Throughout this manual, specifications are given to help you determine the condition of various components on your vehicle, or to assist you in their installation. Some of the most common measurements include length (in. or cm/mm), torque (ft. lbs., inch lbs. or Nm) and pressure (psi, in. Hg, kPa or mm Hg). In most cases, we strive to provide the proper measurement as determined by the manufacturer's engineers.

Though, in some cases, that value may not be conveniently measured with what is available in your toolbox. Luckily, many of the measuring devices which are available today will have two scales so the Standard or Metric measurements may easily be taken. If any of the various measuring tools which are available to you do not contain the same scale as listed in the specifications, use the accompanying conversion factors to determine the proper value.

The conversion factor chart is used by taking the given specification and multiplying it by the necessary conversion factor. For instance, looking at the first line, if you have a measurement in inches such as "free-play should be 2 in." but your ruler reads only in millimeters, multiply 2 in. by the conversion factor of 25.4 to get the metric equivalent of 50.8mm. Likewise, if the specification was given only in a Metric measurement, for example in Newton Meters (Nm), then look at the center column first. If the measurement is 100 Nm, multiply it by the conversion factor of 0.738 to get 73.8 ft. lbs.

CONVERSION FACTORS

LENGTH–DISTANCE

Inches (in.)	x 25.4	= Millimeters (mm)	x .0394	= Inches
Feet (ft.)	x .305	= Meters (m)	x 3.281	= Feet
Miles	x 1.609	= Kilometers (km)	x .0621	= Miles

VOLUME

Cubic Inches (in3)	x 16.387	= Cubic Centimeters	x .061	= in3
IMP Pints (IMP pt.)	x .568	= Liters (L)	x 1.76	= IMP pt.
IMP Quarts (IMP qt.)	x 1.137	= Liters (L)	x .88	= IMP qt.
IMP Gallons (IMP gal.)	x 4.546	= Liters (L)	x .22	= IMP gal.
IMP Quarts (IMP qt.)	x 1.201	= US Quarts (US qt.)	x .833	= IMP qt.
IMP Gallons (IMP gal.)	x 1.201	= US Gallons (US gal.)	x .833	= IMP gal.
Fl. Ounces	x 29.573	= Milliliters	x .034	= Ounces
US Pints (US pt.)	x .473	= Liters (L)	x 2.113	= Pints
US Quarts (US qt.)	x .946	= Liters (L)	x 1.057	= Quarts
US Gallons (US gal.)	x 3.785	= Liters (L)	x .264	= Gallons

MASS–WEIGHT

Ounces (oz.)	x 28.35	= Grams (g)	x .035	= Ounces
Pounds (lb.)	x .454	= Kilograms (kg)	x 2.205	= Pounds

PRESSURE

Pounds Per Sq. In. (psi)	x 6.895	= Kilopascals (kPa)	x .145	= psi
Inches of Mercury (Hg)	x .4912	= psi	x 2.036	= Hg
Inches of Mercury (Hg)	x 3.377	= Kilopascals (kPa)	x .2961	= Hg
Inches of Water (H$_2$O)	x .07355	= Inches of Mercury	x 13.783	= H$_2$O
Inches of Water (H$_2$O)	x .03613	= psi	x 27.684	= H$_2$O
Inches of Water (H$_2$O)	x .248	= Kilopascals (kPa)	x 4.026	= H$_2$O

TORQUE

Pounds–Force Inches (in–lb)	x .113	= Newton Meters (N·m)	x 8.85	= in–lb
Pounds–Force Feet (ft–lb)	x 1.356	= Newton Meters (N·m)	x .738	= ft–lb

VELOCITY

Miles Per Hour (MPH)	x 1.609	= Kilometers Per Hour (KPH)	x .621	= MPH

POWER

Horsepower (Hp)	x .745	= Kilowatts	x 1.34	= Horsepower

FUEL CONSUMPTION*

Miles Per Gallon IMP (MPG)	x .354	= Kilometers Per Liter (Km/L)	
Kilometers Per Liter (Km/L)	x 2.352	= IMP MPG	
Miles Per Gallon US (MPG)	x .425	= Kilometers Per Liter (Km/L)	
Kilometers Per Liter (Km/L)	x 2.352	= US MPG	

*It is common to covert from miles per gallon (mpg) to liters/100 kilometers (1/100 km), where mpg (IMP) x 1/100 km = 282 and mpg (US) x 1/100 km = 235.

TEMPERATURE

Degree Fahrenheit (°F)	= (°C x 1.8) + 32
Degree Celsius (°C)	= (°F – 32) x .56

TCCS1044

Fig. 23 Standard and metric conversion factors chart

SERIAL NUMBER IDENTIFICATION

Vehicle Identification Number (VIN)

▶ See Figures 24 and 25

A 17 digit combination of numbers and letters forms the vehicle identification number (VIN). The VIN is stamped on a metal tab that is riveted to the instrument panel close to the windshield. The VIN plate is visible by looking through the windshield on the driver's side. The VIN number is also found on the Safety Compliance Certification Label which is described below.

By looking at the 17 digit VIN number, a variety of information about the vehicle can be determined.

- The 1st digit identifies the country of origin. 1 = USA; 2 = Canada.
- The 2nd digit identifies the manufacturer. F = Ford.
- The 3rd digit identifies the type of vehicle.
- C = Basic (stripped) chassis
- D = Incomplete vehicle
- M = Multi–purpose vehicle
- T = Truck (complete vehicle)

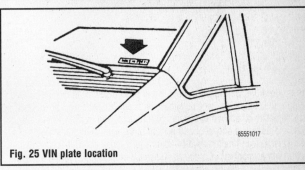

Fig. 25 VIN plate location

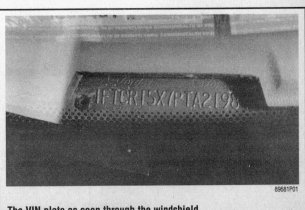

The VIN plate as seen through the windshield

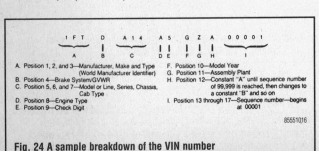

1 FT   D   A 14   A 5   G Z A   00001
     A   B   C   D E   F G H   I

A. Position 1, 2, and 3—Manufacturer, Make and Type (World Manufacturer Identifier)
B. Position 4—Brake System/GVWR
C. Position 5, 6, and 7—Model or Line, Series, Chassis, Cab Type
D. Position 8—Engine Type
E. Position 9—Check Digit
F. Position 10—Model Year
G. Position 11—Assembly Plant
H. Position 12—Constant "A" until sequence number of 99,999 is reached, then changes to a constant "B" and so on
I. Position 13 through 17—Sequence number—begins at 00001

Fig. 24 A sample breakdown of the VIN number

VEHICLE IDENTIFICATION CHART

Engine Code					
Code	Liters	Cu. In. (cc)	Cyl.	Fuel Sys.	Eng. Mfg.
A	2.3	140 (2294)	4	SFI	Ford
C	2.5	152.7 (2500)	4	SFI	Ford
T	2.9	177 (2900)	6	SFI	Ford
U	3.0	183 (2999)	6	SFI	Ford
X	4.0	241 (3949)	6	SFI	Ford
E	4.0	244 (3998)	6	SFI	Ford
P	5.0	302 (4949)	8	SFI	Ford

SFI - Seqeuntial Fuel Injection

Model Year	
Code	Year
M	1991
N	1992
P	1993
R	1994
S	1995
T	1996
V	1997
W	1998
X	1999

89681C51

- The 4th digit identifies the gross vehicle weight rating (GVWR Class) and brake system. For incomplete vehicles, the 4th digit determines the brake system only. All brake systems are hydraulic.

A = up to 3,000 lbs.
B = 3,001–4,000 lbs.
C = 4,001–5,000 lbs.
D = 5,001–6,000 lbs.
E = 6,001–7,000 lbs.
F = 7,001–8,000 lbs.
G = 8,001–8,500 lbs.
H = 8,500–9,000 lbs.
J = 9,001–10,000 lbs.

- The 5th digits identifies the model or line. R = Ranger U = Explorer/Mountaineer.
- The 6th and 7th digits identify chassis and body type.
- The 8th digit identifies the engine.

A = 2.3L 4–cylinder
C = 2.5L 4–cylinder
T = 2.9L 6–cylinder
U = 3.0L 6–cylinder
E = 4.0L SOHC 6–cylinder
X = 4.0L 6–cylinder
P = 5.0L 8–cylinder

- The 9th digit is a check digit.
- The 10th digit identifies the model year.

M = 1991
N = 1992
P = 1993
R = 1994
S = 1995
T = 1996
V = 1997
W = 1998
X = 1999

- The 11th digit identifies the assembly plant.

C = Ontario, Canada
H = Lorain, OH
K = Claycomo, MO
L = Wayne, MI
N = Norfolk, VA
P = St. Paul, MN
T = Edison, NJ
U = Louisville, KY
Z = Hazlewood, MO

- Digits twelve through seventeen make up the sequential serial and warranty number. Digit twelve uses the letter A until the production or sequence of 99,999 units (digits thirteen through seventeen) is reached. Letter A then becomes B for the next production sequence of vehicles.

Vehicle Data

➧ See Figure 26

The vehicle data appears on the Safety Compliance Certification Label on the second and third lines following the identification number. The code set (two

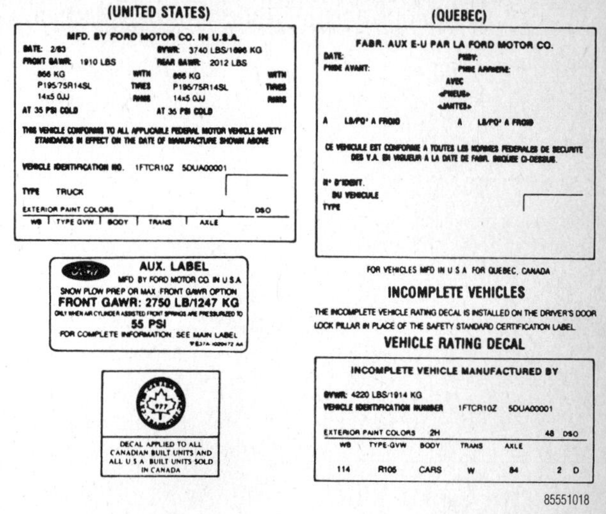

Fig. 26 Vehicle certification labels

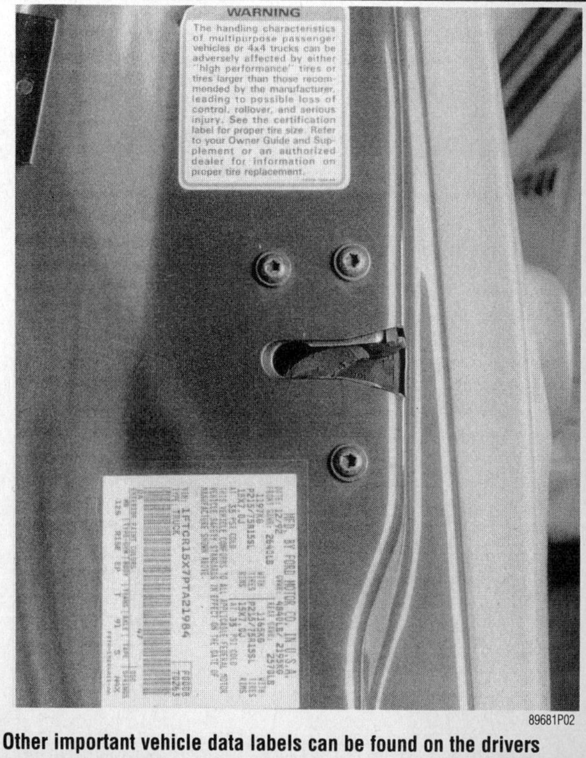

89681P02

Other important vehicle data labels can be found on the drivers door, near the latch

numbers or a number and letter) above COLOR identify the exterior paint color, with two sets of codes designating two tone paint. The three digits under W.N. designate the wheelbase in inches. The letter and three digits under TYPE/G.V.W. designate the truck model within a series and the gross vehicle weight rating. The letters and/or numbers under BODY designate the interior trim, seat and body type. The transmission installed in the vehicle is identified under TRANS by an alphabetical code.

A letter and a number or two numbers under AXLE identify the rear axle ratio and, when required, a letter or number is also stamped after the rear axle code to identify the front axle. The letters and/or numerals under TAPE designate the external body side tape stripe code. The spring usage codes for the vehicle are identified under SPRING.

A two digit number is stamped above D.S.O. to identify the district which originally ordered the vehicle. If the vehicle is built to special order (Domestic Special Order, Foreign Special Order, Limited Production Option or other special order), the complete order number will also appear above D.S.O.

Safety Compliance Certification Label

▶ See Figure 27

The English Safety Compliance Certification Label is affixed to the door latch edge on the driver's side door. The French Safety Compliance Certification Label

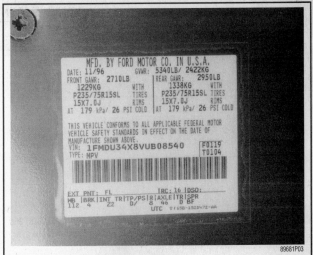

The safety compliance label is found on the drivers door, near the latch

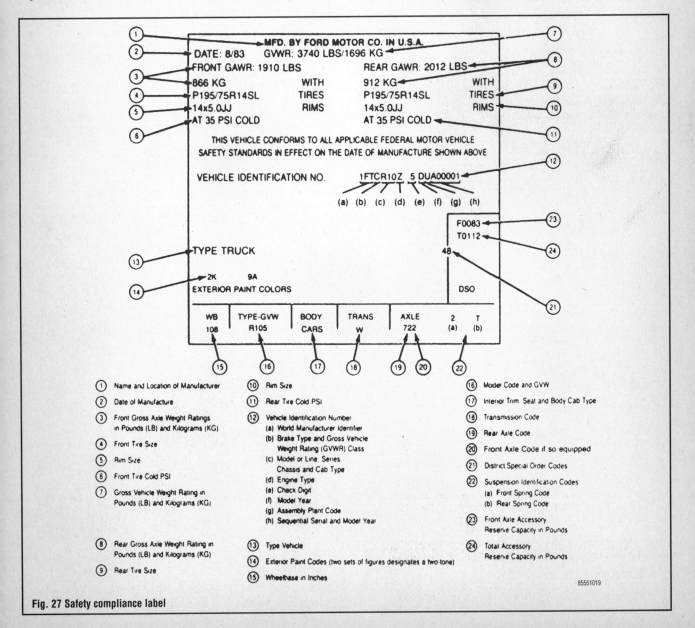

WB	TYPE-GVW	BODY	TRANS	AXLE	2	T
108	R105	CARS	W	722	(a)	(b)

(1) Name and Location of Manufacturer
(2) Date of Manufacture
(3) Front Gross Axle Weight Ratings in Pounds (LB) and Kilograms (KG)
(4) Front Tire Size
(5) Rim Size
(6) Front Tire Cold PSI
(7) Gross Vehicle Weight Rating in Pounds (LB) and Kilograms (KG)
(8) Rear Gross Axle Weight Rating in Pounds (LB) and Kilograms (KG)
(9) Rear Tire Size

(10) Rim Size
(11) Rear Tire Cold PSI
(12) Vehicle Identification Number
  (a) World Manufacturer Identifier
  (b) Brake Type and Gross Vehicle Weight Rating (GVWR) Class
  (c) Model or Line. Series. Chassis and Cab Type
  (d) Engine Type
  (e) Check Digit
  (f) Model Year
  (g) Assembly Plant Code
  (h) Sequential Serial and Model Year
(13) Type Vehicle
(14) Exterior Paint Codes (two sets of figures designates a two-tone)
(15) Wheelbase in Inches

(16) Model Code and GVW
(17) Interior Trim Seat and Body Cab Type
(18) Transmission Code
(19) Rear Axle Code
(20) Front Axle Code if so equipped
(21) District Special Order Codes
(22) Suspension Identification Codes
  (a) Front Spring Code
  (b) Rear Spring Code
(23) Front Axle Accessory Reserve Capacity in Pounds
(24) Total Accessory Reserve Capacity in Pounds

Fig. 27 Safety compliance label

is affixed to the door latch edge on the passenger's side door. The label contains the following information: name of manufacturer, the month and year of manufacture, the certification statement, and the Vehicle Identification number. The label also contains information on Gross Vehicle weight ratings, Wheel and tire data, and additional vehicle data information codes.

Emission Calibration Label

▶ **See Figure 28**

The emission calibration number label is attached to the left side door or the left door post pillar. This label plate identifies the engine calibration number, engine code number and the revision level. These numbers are used to determine if parts are unique to specific engines. The engine codes and calibration are necessary for ordering parts and asking questions related to the engine.

Engine

The engine identification code is a letter located in the eighth digit of the Vehicle Identification Number stamped on a metal tab that is riveted to the instrument panel close to the windshield. Specific engine data is located on a label attached to the timing cover.

CALIBRATION CODE

Use the following to interpret the calibration code from the Emission Calibration Label:

1. MODEL YEAR—This number represents the model year in which the Calibration was first introduced. As shown below, the model year is 1990. (Represented by the Number 0)

2. CALIBRATION DESIGN LEVEL—Represents the design level assigned to the engine (25F).

3. CALIBRATION REVISION LEVEL—Represents the revision level of the calibration (R00). These numbers will advance as revisions occur.

```
0-25F-R00
1  2   3
CALIBRATION CODE
```

Fig. 28 Emission calibration label

ENGINE IDENTIFICATION

Year	Model	Engine Displacement Liters (cc)	Engine Series (ID/VIN)	Fuel System	No. of Cylinders	Engine Type
1991	Ranger	2.3 (2294)	A	SFI	4	OHC
		2.9 (2900)	T	SFI	6	OHV
		3.0 (2999)	U	SFI	6	OHV
		4.0 (3949)	X	SFI	6	OHV
	Explorer	4.0 (3949)	X	SFI	6	OHV
1992	Ranger	2.3 (2294)	A	SFI	4	OHC
		2.9 (2900)	T	SFI	6	OHV
		3.0 (2999)	U	SFI	6	OHV
		4.0 (3949)	X	SFI	6	OHV
	Explorer	4.0 (3949)	X	SFI	6	OHV
1993	Ranger	2.3 (2294)	A	SFI	4	OHC
		3.0 (2999)	U	SFI	6	OHV
		4.0 (3949)	X	SFI	6	OHV
	Explorer	4.0 (3949)	X	SFI	6	OHV
1994	Ranger	2.3 (2294)	A	SFI	4	OHC
		3.0 (2999)	U	SFI	6	OHV
		4.0 (3949)	X	SFI	6	OHV
	Explorer	4.0 (3949)	X	SFI	6	OHV
1995	Ranger	2.3 (2294)	A	SFI	4	OHC
		3.0 (2999)	U	SFI	6	OHV
		4.0 (3949)	X	SFI	6	OHV
	Explorer	4.0 (3949)	X	SFI	6	OHV
1996	Ranger	2.3 (2294)	A	SFI	4	OHC
		3.0 (2999)	U	SFI	6	OHV
		4.0 (3949)	X	SFI	6	OHV
	Explorer	4.0 (3949)	X	SFI	6	OHV
		5.0 (4949)	P	SFI	8	OHV
1997	Ranger	2.3 (2294)	A	SFI	4	OHC
		3.0 (2999)	U	SFI	6	OHV
		4.0 (3949)	X	SFI	6	OHV
	Explorer	4.0 (3949)	X	SFI	6	OHV
		4.0 (3998)	E	SFI	6	OHC
	Mountaineer	4.0 (3998)	X	SFI	6	OHV
		5.0 (4949)	P	SFI	8	OHV
1998	Ranger	2.5 (2500)	C	SFI	4	OHC
		3.0 (2999)	U	SFI	6	OHV
		4.0 (3949)	X	SFI	6	OHV
	Explorer	4.0 (3949)	X	SFI	6	OHV
		4.0 (3998)	E	SFI	6	OHC
	Mountaineer	4.0 (3998)	X	SFI	6	OHV
		5.0 (4949)	P	SFI	8	OHV
1999	Ranger	2.5 (2500)	C	SFI	4	OHC
		3.0 (2999)	U	SFI	6	OHV
		4.0 (3949)	X	SFI	6	OHV
	Explorer	4.0 (3949)	X	SFI	6	OHV
		4.0 (3998)	E	SFI	6	OHC
	Mountaineer	4.0 (3998)	X	SFI	6	OHV
		5.0 (4949)	P	SFI	8	OHV

89681C52

GENERAL ENGINE SPECIFICATIONS

Year	Engine ID/VIN	Engine Displacement Liters (cc)	Fuel System Type	Net Horsepower @ rpm	Net Torque @ rpm (ft. lbs.)	Bore x Stroke (in.)	Compression Ratio	Oil Pressure (lbs. @ rpm)
1991	A	2.3 (2294)	SFI	100@4600	133@2600	3.78x3.13	9.2:1	40–60
	T	2.9 (2900)	SFI	140@4600	170@2600	3.66x2.83	9.0:1	40–60
	U	3.0 (2999)	SFI	145@4800	165@3600	3.50x3.14	9.3:1	40–60
	X	4.0 (3949)	SFI	160@4200	220@2400	3.95x3.32	9.0:1	40–60
1992	A	2.3 (2294)	SFI	100@4600	133@2600	3.78x3.13	9.2:1	40–60
	T	2.9 (2900)	SFI	140@4600	170@2600	3.66x2.83	9.0:1	40–60
	U	3.0 (2999)	SFI	145@4800	165@3600	3.50x3.14	9.3:1	40–60
	X	4.0 (3949)	SFI	160@4200	220@2400	3.95x3.32	9.0:1	40–60
1993	A	2.3 (2294)	SFI	100@4600	133@2600	3.78x3.13	9.2:1	40–60
	U	3.0 (2999)	SFI	145@4800	165@3600	3.50x3.14	9.3:1	40–60
	X	4.0 (3949)	SFI	160@4200	220@2400	3.95x3.32	9.0:1	40–60
1994	A	2.3 (2294)	SFI	100@4600	133@2600	3.78x3.13	9.4:1	40–60
	U	3.0 (2999)	SFI	145@4800	165@3000	3.50x3.14	9.3:1	40–60
	X	4.0 (3949)	SFI	160@4200	220@2400	3.95x3.32	9.0:1	40–60
1995	A	2.3 (2294)	SFI	100@4600	133@2600	3.78x3.13	9.4:1	40–60
	U	3.0 (2999)	SFI	145@4800	165@3000	3.50x3.14	9.3:1	40–60
	X	4.0 (3949)	SFI	160@4200	220@2400	3.95x3.32	9.0:1	40–60
1996	A	2.3 (2294)	SFI	112@4800	135@2400	3.78x3.13	9.4:1	40–60
	U	3.0 (2999)	SFI	147@5000	162@3250	3.50x3.14	9.3:1	40–60
	X	4.0 (3949)	SFI	160@4200	220@3000	3.95x3.32	9.0:1	40–60
	P	5.0 (4949)	SFI	210@4500	280@3500	4.00x3.00	9.0:1	40–60
1997	A	2.3 (2294)	SFI	112@4800	135@2400	3.78x3.13	9.4:1	40–60
	U	3.0 (2999)	SFI	147@5000	162@3250	3.50x3.14	9.3:1	40–60
	X	4.0 (3949)	SFI	160@4200	225@2800	3.95x3.32	9.0:1	40–60
	E	4.0 (3998)	SFI	205@5250	245@3000	3.95x3.31	9.7:1	40–60
	P	5.0 (4949)	SFI	210@4500	280@3500	4.00x3.00	9.0:1	40–60
1998	C	2.5 (2500)	SFI	117@4500	149@2500	3.78x3.40	9.4:1	40–60
	U	3.0 (2999)	SFI	147@5000	162@3250	3.50x3.14	9.3:1	40–60
	X	4.0 (3949)	SFI	160@4200	225@2800	3.95x3.32	9.0:1	40–60
	E	4.0 (3998)	SFI	205@5250	245@3000	3.95x3.31	9.7:1	40–60
	P	5.0 (4949)	SFI	210@4500	280@3500	4.00x3.00	9.0:1	40–60
1999	C	2.5 (2500)	SFI	117@4500	149@2500	3.78x3.40	9.4:1	40–60
	U	3.0 (2999)	SFI	147@5000	162@3250	3.50x3.14	9.3:1	40–60
	X	4.0 (3949)	SFI	160@4200	225@2800	3.95x3.32	9.0:1	40–60
	E	4.0 (3998)	SFI	205@5250	245@3000	3.95x3.31	9.7:1	40–60
	P	5.0 (4949)	SFI	210@4500	280@3500	4.00x3.00	9.0:1	40–60

89681C53

Transmission

The transmission code may be found in two places on the vehicle. One is on the Safety Standard Certification label attached to the left driver's side door lock post. The code appears as a letter in the "Trans" column of the label.

M or D = 5–speed manual transmission
T = 4–speed automatic transmission (A4LD/4R44E/4R55E)
U = 4–speed automatic transmission (4R70W)
D = 5–speed automatic transmission (5R55E)

The other location is on the transmission body itself. On manual transmissions, the identification number is located on a plate attached to the main transmission case. On the plate you find Ford's assigned part number, the serial number and a bar code used for inventory purposes. On automatic transmissions, the identification number is stamped on plate that hangs from the lower left extension housing bolt. The plate identifies when the transmission was built, it's code letter and model number.

➡**There were two types of manual transmissions used from 1991–99: the Misubishi 5-speed, and the Mazda M5OD. The Mitsubishi 5-speed was only used on 1991–92 4X4 Rangers with the 2.9L engine. All other applications used the M5OD transmission.**

Transfer Case

All vehicles can be equipped with a mechanical or electronic shift transfer case. The identification number is stamped on a plate on the side of the case.

Front Drive Axle

The front drive axle on the Ranger, Explorer and Mountaineer can be either the Dana 28 series, or the Dana 35 series. However, there are two versions of the Dana 35 and while both are an Independent Front Suspension (IFS) axles, their differences are drastic. The Mountaineer, 1995–99 Explorers and 1998–99 Ranger use a centrally mounted front differential with unequal length upper and lower control arms and front axle half-shafts. All other models use the twin I-beam style front axle assembly. The identification number is stamped on a plate on the differential housing.

Rear Axle

The rear axle code may be found in two places on the vehicle. One is on the Safety Standard Certification label attached to the left driver's side door lock post. The code appears as a number or letter/number combination in the "Axle" column of the label. The rear axle identification code is also stamped on a metal tag hanging from the axle cover–to–carrier bolt at the 2 o'clock position in the cover bolt circle.

ROUTINE MAINTENANCE AND TUNE-UP

▶ See Figures 29 thru 34

UNDERHOOD MAINTENANCE COMPONENT LOCATIONS

1. Air cleaner housing (conical style)
2. Coolant overflow tank
3. Washer fluid tank
4. Heater hoses
5. Upper radiator hose
6. Engine oil fill cap
7. Spark plug wires
8. Transmission fluid level dipstick
9. Engine oil level dipstick
10. Brake fluid reservoir
11. Power steering reservoir and dipstick
12. Battery
13. Radiator cap
14. Vehicle systems warning labels
15. Serpentine belt routing label
16. Emission and tune-up label
17. Engine air intake hose

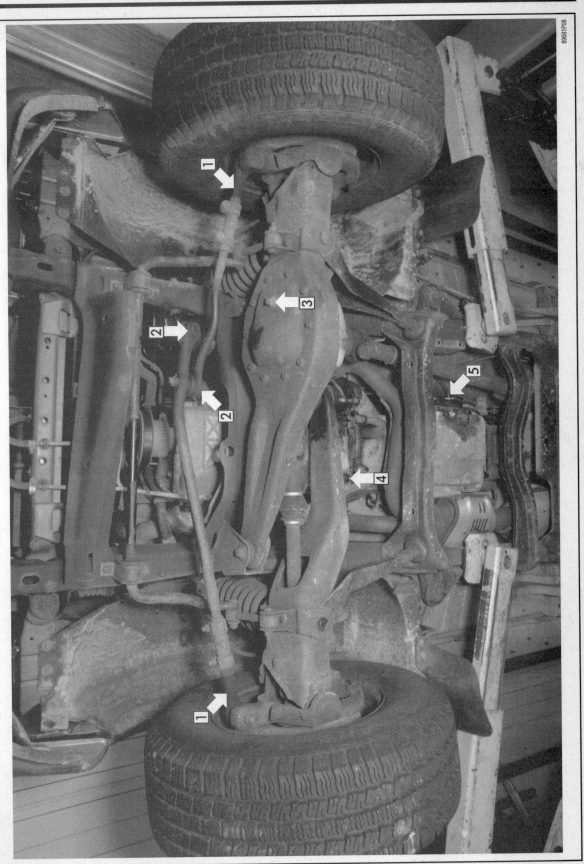

UNDERVEHICLE MAINTENANCE COMPONENT LOCATIONS

1. Outer tie rod end
2. Inner tie rod linkage
3. Front axle oil level check/fill plug
4. Engine oil drain plug
5. Kickdown linkage (automatic)

8968rP08

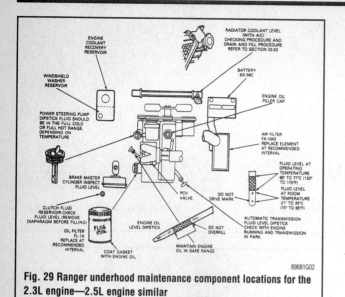

Fig. 29 Ranger underhood maintenance component locations for the 2.3L engine—2.5L engine similar

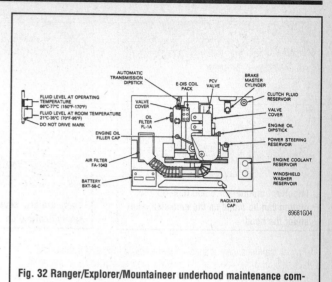

Fig. 32 Ranger/Explorer/Mountaineer underhood maintenance component locations for the 4.0L engine

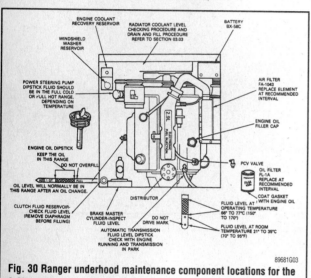

Fig. 30 Ranger underhood maintenance component locations for the 2.9L engine

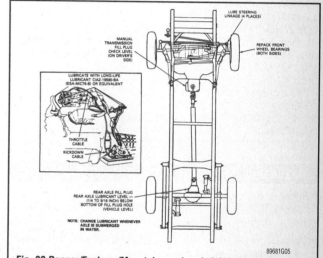

Fig. 33 Ranger/Explorer/Mountaineer chassis lubrication points for two-wheel drive (4x2) models

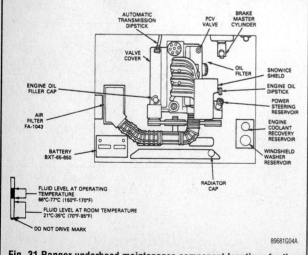

Fig. 31 Ranger underhood maintenance component locations for the 3.0L engine

Fig. 34 Ranger/Explorer/Mountaineer chassis lubrication points for four-wheel drive (4x4) models

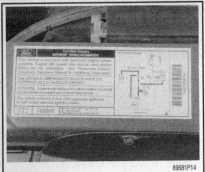

Important maintenance and tune-up information can be found on the emission label under the hood

89681P14

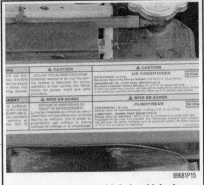

There are also several labels which give safety information . . .

89681P15

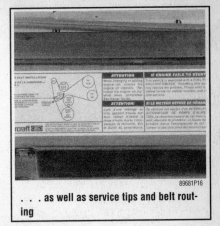

. . . as well as service tips and belt routing

89681P16

Proper maintenance and tune-up is the key to long and trouble-free vehicle life, and the work can yield its own rewards. Studies have shown that a properly tuned and maintained vehicle can achieve better gas mileage than an out-of-tune vehicle. As a conscientious owner and driver, set aside a Saturday morning, say once a month, to check or replace items which could cause major problems later. Keep your own personal log to jot down which services you performed, how much the parts cost you, the date, and the exact odometer reading at the time. Keep all receipts for such items as engine oil and filters, so that they may be referred to in case of related problems or to determine operating expenses. As a do-it-yourselfer, these receipts are the only proof you have that the required maintenance was performed. In the event of a warranty problem, these receipts will be invaluable.

The literature provided with your vehicle when it was originally delivered includes the factory recommended maintenance schedule. If you no longer have this literature, replacement copies are usually available from the dealer. A maintenance schedule is provided later in this section, in case you do not have the factory literature.

Air Cleaner (Element)

The air cleaner is a paper element type. The paper cartridge should be replaced every 30,000 miles, under normal conditions. Under dusty or severe conditions, the filter should be inspected frequently and changed as necessary.

➡Check the air filter more often if the vehicle is operated under severe dusty conditions and replace it as necessary.

REMOVAL & INSTALLATION

▶ See Figures 35, 36 and 37

The Ranger, Explorer and Mountaineer vehicles used two types of air cleaner housings: the square panel and the conical (or canister) type. The square panel type retains the housing cover by bolts or, on later models, bail clips. The conical type utilizes a full circumference clamp around the housing.

1. Loosen the clamp that secures the intake hose assembly to the air cleaner.
2. If necessary, unplug the MAF (Mass Air Flow) and/or IAT (Intake Air Temperature) sensor electrical connector from the air cleaner housing.

➡Some air cleaner assemblies will have enough "give" in the air inlet pipe and sensor wiring harnesses to allow filter replacement without removing or disconnecting these items.

3. Disconnect the hose and inlet tube from the air cleaner.
4. If equipped with the square panel type housing, remove the screws or bail clips attaching the air cleaner cover.
5. If equipped with the conical type housing, unfasten the clamp on the air cleaner body.
6. Seperate the lid from the housing base.
7. Remove the air filter.
8. Installation is the reverse of removal. Don't overtighten the hose clamps! A torque of 12–15 inch lbs. is sufficient.

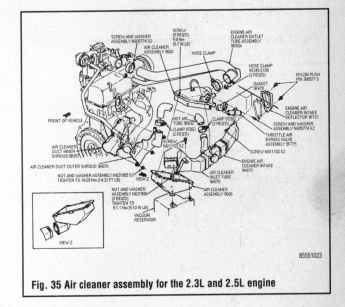

85551023

Fig. 35 Air cleaner assembly for the 2.3L and 2.5L engine

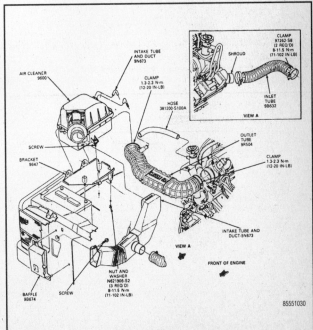

85551030

Fig. 36 Air cleaner assembly for the 3.0L and 4.0L engine—2.9L engine similar

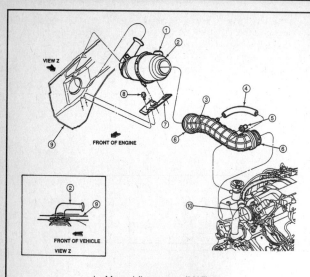

1. Mass airflow sensor (MAF)
2. Air cleaner lid
3. Intake hose
4. Crankcase ventilation hose
5. Intake Air Temperature sensor (IAT)
6. Intake hose clamp
7. Mounting bracket
8. Bracket attaching screws
9. Front fender
10. Throttle body

89681G01

Fig. 37 Conical type air cleaner assembly for the 4.0L engine—other engines similar

Fuel Filter

REMOVAL & INSTALLATION

◆ **See Figures 38, 39, 40 and 41**

Clean all dirt and/or grease from the fuel filter fittings. "Quick Connect" fittings are used on models equipped with a pressurized fuel system. These fittings must be disconnected using the proper procedure or the fittings may be damaged. The fuel filter uses a "hairpin" clip retainer. Spread the two hairpin clip legs about ⅛ in. (3mm) each to disengage it from the fitting, then pull the clip outward. Use finger pressure only; do not use any tools. Push the quick connect fittings onto the filter ends. Ford recommends that the retaining clips be replaced whenever removed. The fuel tubes used on these fuel systems are manufactured in 5/16 in. and 3/8 in. diameters. Each fuel tube takes a different size hairpin clip, so keep this in mind when purchasing new clips. A click will be heard when the hairpin clip snaps into its proper position. Pull on the lines with moderate pressure to ensure proper connection. Start the engine and check for fuel leaks. If the inertia switch (reset switch) was disconnected to relieve the fuel system pressure, cycle the ignition switch from the **OFF** to **ON** position several times to re–charge the fuel system before attempting to start the engine.

➡The inline reservoir type fuel filter should last the life of the vehicle under normal driving conditions. If the filter does need to be replaced, proceed as follows:

✳✳ CAUTION

If the fuel filter is being serviced with the rear of the vehicle higher than the front, or if the tank is pressurized, fuel leakage or siphoning from the tank fuel lines could occur. to prevent this condition, maintain the vehicle front end at or above the level of the rear of vehicle. also, relieve tank pressure by loosening the fuel fill cap. cap should be tightened after pressure is relieved.

89681P71

Loosen the air cleaner cover retaining screws (arrow), then gently lift the assembly up enough . . .

89681P72

. . . to allow the filter to be removed

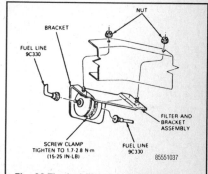

85551037

Fig. 38 The fuel filter is mounted to the drivers side frame rail by a bracket, which also acts as a protective shield

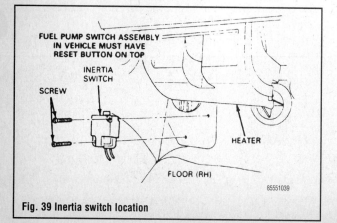

85551039

Fig. 39 Inertia switch location

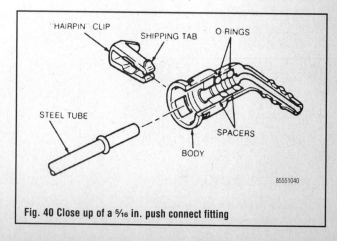

85551040

Fig. 40 Close up of a 5/16 in. push connect fitting

1. Shut the engine off. Depressurize the fuel system as follows:
   a. Disconnect the electrical connector from the inertia switch
   b. Crank the engine for about 15–30 seconds or, if the vehicle starts, until it runs out of fuel.
2. Raise and support the vehicle safely.

3. Detach the fuel lines from both ends of the fuel filter by disengaging both push connect fittings. Install new retainer clips in each push connect fitting.
4. Note which way the **flow** direction arrow points on the old filter.
5. Remove the filter from the bracket by loosening the filter retaining clamp enough to allow the filter to pass through.

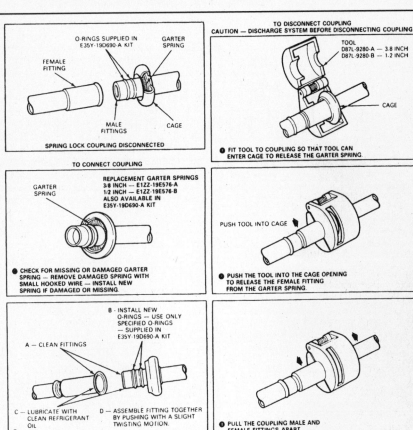

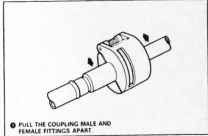

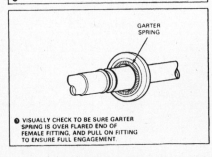

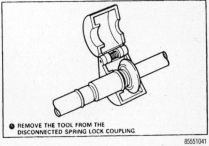

Fig. 41 Installing fuel lines with quick-disconnect couplings—these fittings use a metal garter spring rather than a plastic clip for line retention

Remove the fuel filter mounting bracket retaining nuts . . .

. . . then loosen the filter retaining clamp and slide the bracket assembly back . . .

. . . to provide better access to the push connect fittings (arrows)

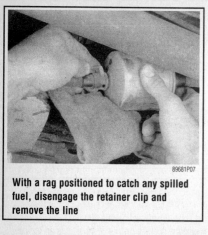

With a rag positioned to catch any spilled fuel, disengage the retainer clip and remove the line

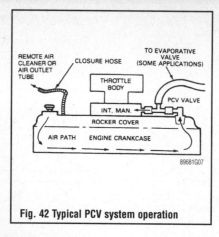

Fig. 42 Typical PCV system operation

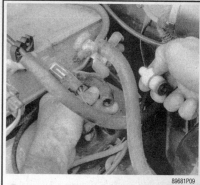

Remove the PCV valve from between the hose and the valve cover grommet

➡ The flow direction arrow should be positioned as installed in the bracket to ensure proper flow of fuel through the replacement filter.

6. Install the filter in the bracket, ensuring proper direction of flow as noted by arrow. Tighten clamp to 15–25 inch lbs.
7. Install the push connect fittings at both ends of the filter.
8. Lower the vehicle.
9. Start the engine and check for leaks.

PCV Valve

INSPECTION

▸ See Figure 42

Check the PCV valve frequently to see if it is free and not gummed up, stuck or blocked. To check the valve, remove it from the engine and shake it. It should rattle. It is possible to clean the PCV valve by soaking it in a solvent and blowing it out with compressed air. This can restore the valve to some level of operating order.

This should be used only in emergency situations. Otherwise, the valve should be replaced at least once a year. Always check PCV valve hose for wear or cracks during service procedure.

REMOVAL & INSTALLATION

Remove the PCV valve by simply disconnecting the vacuum hose from the valve, then pulling the valve from the rocker cover grommet.

Evaporative Canister

▸ See Figure 43

The fuel evaporative emission control canister should be inspected for damage or leaks at the hose fittings. Repair or replace any old or cracked hoses. Replace the canister if it is damaged in any way. The canister is located on the left side radiator support, under the hood.

SERVICING

Ford has designed and tested the evaporative emission components to exceed 120,000 mi. (193,116km) or 10 years of vehicle use. No maintenance or service should be required, except in the case of damage or malfunction. If either condition should exist, simply replace that component.

Battery

PRECAUTIONS

Always use caution when working on or near the battery. Never allow a tool to bridge the gap between the negative and positive battery terminals. Also, be

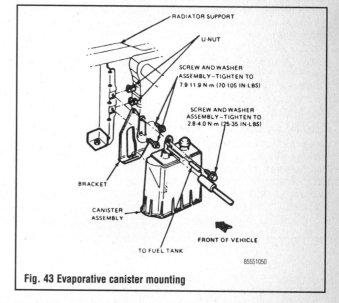

Fig. 43 Evaporative canister mounting

careful not to allow a tool to provide a ground between the positive cable/terminal and any metal component on the vehicle. Either of these conditions will cause a short circuit, leading to sparks and possible personal injury.

Do not smoke or all open flames/sparks near a battery; the gases contained in the battery are very explosive and, if ignited, could cause severe injury or death.

All batteries, regardless of type, should be carefully secured by a battery hold-down device. If not, the terminals or casing may crack from stress during vehicle operation. A battery which is not secured may allow acid to leak, making it discharge faster. The acid can also eat away at components under the hood.

Always inspect the battery case for cracks, leakage and corrosion. A white corrosive substance on the battery case or on nearby components would indicate a leaking or cracked battery. If the battery is cracked, it should be replaced immediately.

GENERAL MAINTENANCE

Always keep the battery cables and terminals free of corrosion. Check and clean these components about once a year.

Keep the top of the battery clean, as a film of dirt can help discharge a battery that is not used for long periods. A solution of baking soda and water may be used for cleaning, but be careful to flush this off with clear water. DO NOT let any of the solution into the filler holes. Baking soda neutralizes battery acid and will de-activate a battery cell.

Batteries in vehicles which are not operated on a regular basis can fall victim to parasitic loads (small current drains which are constantly drawing current from the battery). Normal parasitic loads may drain a battery on a vehicle that is in storage and not used for 6–8 weeks. Vehicles that have additional accessories such as a phone or an alarm system may discharge a battery sooner. If the vehicle is to be stored for longer periods in a secure area and the alarm system is not necessary, the negative battery cable should be disconnected to protect the battery.

Remember that constantly deep cycling a battery (completely discharging and recharging it) will shorten battery life.

BATTERY FLUID

▶ See Figure 44

Check the battery electrolyte level at least once a month, or more often in hot weather or during periods of extended vehicle operation. On non-sealed batteries, the level can be checked either through the case (if translucent) or by removing the cell caps. The electrolyte level in each cell should be kept filled to the split ring inside each cell, or the line marked on the outside of the case.

If the level is low, add only distilled water through the opening until the level is correct. Each cell must be checked and filled individually. Distilled water should be used, because the chemicals and minerals found in most drinking water are harmful to the battery and could significantly shorten its life.

If water is added in freezing weather, the vehicle should be driven several miles to allow the water to mix with the electrolyte. Otherwise, the battery could freeze.

Although some maintenance-free batteries have removable cell caps, the electrolyte condition and level on all sealed maintenance-free batteries must be checked using the built-in hydrometer "eye." The exact type of eye will vary. But, most battery manufacturers, apply a sticker to the battery itself explaining the readings.

➡Although the readings from built-in hydrometers will vary, a green eye usually indicates a properly charged battery with sufficient fluid level. A dark eye is normally an indicator of a battery with sufficient fluid, but which is low in charge. A light or yellow eye usually indicates that electrolyte has dropped below the necessary level. In this last case, sealed batteries with an insufficient electrolyte must usually be discarded.

Checking the Specific Gravity

▶ See Figures 45, 46 and 47

A hydrometer is required to check the specific gravity on all batteries that are not maintenance-free. On batteries that are maintenance-free, the specific gravity is checked by observing the built-in hydrometer "eye" on the top of the battery case.

✳✳ CAUTION

Battery electrolyte contains sulfuric acid. If you should splash any on your skin or in your eyes, flush the affected area with plenty of clear water. If it lands in your eyes, get medical help immediately.

The fluid (sulfuric acid solution) contained in the battery cells will tell you many things about the condition of the battery. Because the cell plates must be kept submerged below the fluid level in order to operate, the fluid level is extremely important. And, because the specific gravity of the acid is an indication of electrical charge, testing the fluid can be an aid in determining if the battery must be replaced. A battery in a vehicle with a properly operating charging system should require little maintenance, but careful, periodic inspection should reveal problems before they leave you stranded.

At least once a year, check the specific gravity of the battery. It should be between 1.20 and 1.26 on the gravity scale. Most auto stores carry a variety of inexpensive battery hydrometers. These can be used on any non-sealed battery to test the specific gravity in each cell.

The battery testing hydrometer has a squeeze bulb at one end and a nozzle at the other. Battery electrolyte is sucked into the hydrometer until the float is lifted from its seat. The specific gravity is then read by noting the position of the float. If gravity is low in one or more cells, the battery should be slowly charged and checked again to see if the gravity has come up. Generally, if after charging, the specific gravity between any two cells varies more than 50 points (0.50), the battery should be replaced, as it can no longer produce sufficient voltage to guarantee proper operation.

CABLES

▶ See Figures 48, 49, 50 and 51

Once a year (or as necessary), the battery terminals and the cable clamps should be cleaned. Loosen the clamps and remove the cables, negative cable first. On top post batteries, the use of a puller specially made for this purpose is recommended. These are inexpensive and available in most parts stores. Side terminal battery cables are secured with a small bolt.

Clean the cable clamps and the battery terminal with a wire brush, until all corrosion, grease, etc., is removed and the metal is shiny. It is especially important to clean the inside of the clamp thoroughly (an old knife is useful here), since a small deposit of oxidation there will prevent a sound connection and inhibit starting or charging. Special tools are available for cleaning these parts, one type for conventional top post batteries and another type for side terminal batteries. It is also a good idea to apply some dielectric grease to the terminal, as this will aid in the prevention of corrosion.

TCCA1G02

Fig. 44 Maintenance-free batteries usually contain a built-in hydrometer to check fluid level

TCCA1P07

Fig. 45 On non-sealed batteries, the fluid level can be checked by removing the cell caps

TCCA1P08

Fig. 46 If the fluid level is low, add only distilled water until the level is correct

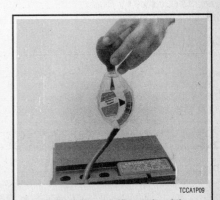

TCCA1P09

Fig. 47 Check the specific gravity of the battery's electrolyte with a hydrometer

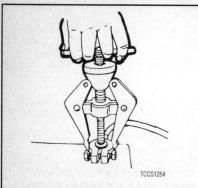

Fig. 48 A special tool is available to pull the clamp from the post

Fig. 49 The underside of this special battery tool has a wire brush to clean post terminals

Fig. 50 Place the tool over the battery posts and twist to clean until the metal is shiny

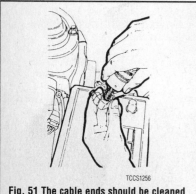

Fig. 51 The cable ends should be cleaned as well

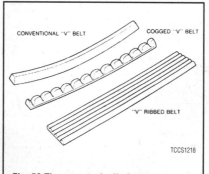

Fig. 52 There are typically 3 types of accessory drive belts found on vehicles today

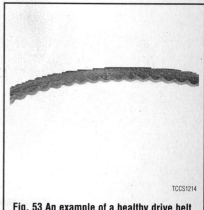

Fig. 53 An example of a healthy drive belt

After the clamps and terminals are clean, reinstall the cables, negative cable last; DO NOT hammer the clamps onto battery posts. Tighten the clamps securely, but do not distort them. Give the clamps and terminals a thin external coating of grease after installation, to retard corrosion.

Check the cables at the same time that the terminals are cleaned. If the cable insulation is cracked or broken, or if the ends are frayed, the cable should be replaced with a new cable of the same length and gauge.

CHARGING

✳✳ CAUTION

The chemical reaction which takes place in all batteries generates explosive hydrogen gas. A spark can cause the battery to explode and splash acid. To avoid personal injury, be sure there is proper ventilation and take appropriate fire safety precautions when working with or near a battery.

A battery should be charged at a slow rate to keep the plates inside from getting too hot. However, if some maintenance-free batteries are allowed to discharge until they are almost "dead," they may have to be charged at a high rate to bring them back to "life." Always follow the charger manufacturer's instructions on charging the battery.

REPLACEMENT

When it becomes necessary to replace the battery, select one with an amperage rating equal to or greater than the battery originally installed. Deterioration and just plain aging of the battery cables, starter motor, and associated wires makes the battery's job harder in successive years. This makes it prudent to install a new battery with a greater capacity than the old.

Belts

➡All 1991–92 engines, except the 4.0L, have manual belt tension adjustment. All 1993–99 engines use a serpentine belt with an automatic adjusting belt tensioner, and no adjustment is possible.

INSPECTION

▶ See Figures 52, 53, 54, 55 and 56

Inspect the belts for signs of glazing or cracking. A glazed belt will be perfectly smooth from slippage, while a good belt will have a slight texture of fabric visible. Cracks will usually start at the inner edge of the belt and run outward. All worn or damaged drive belts should be replaced immediately. It is best to replace all drive belts at one time, as a preventive maintenance measure, during this service operation.

ADJUSTMENT

▶ See Figures 57, 58, 59, 60 and 61

Belt tension can be checked by pressing on the belt at the center point of its longest straight run. The belt should give about 1/4–1/2 in. If the belt is loose, it will slip. If the belt is too tight it will damage bearings in the driven unit. Those units being driven, such as the alternator, power steering pump or compressor, have a bolt which when loosened allows the unit to move for belt adjustment. Sometimes it is necessary to loosen the pivot bolt also, to make the adjustment.

REMOVAL & INSTALLATION

Non-Serpentine

To remove a drive belt, simply loosen the accessory being driven and move it on its pivot point to free the belt. Then, remove the belt. If an idler pulley is

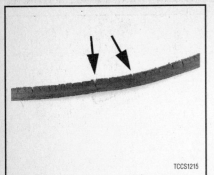

Fig. 54 Deep cracks in this belt will cause flex, building up heat that will eventually lead to belt failure

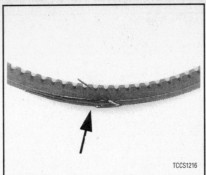

Fig. 55 The cover of this belt is worn, exposing the critical reinforcing cords to excessive wear

Fig. 56 Installing too wide a belt can result in serious belt wear and/or breakage

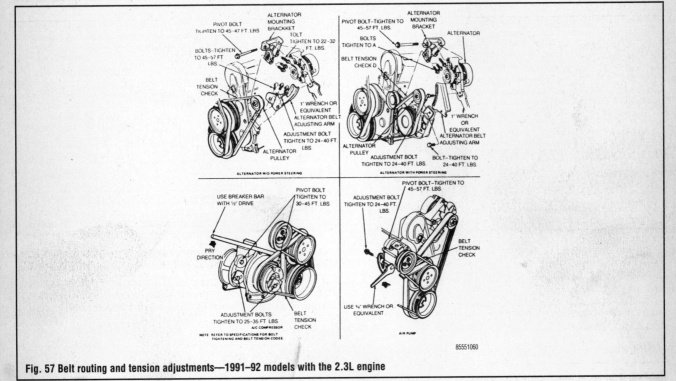

Fig. 57 Belt routing and tension adjustments—1991–92 models with the 2.3L engine

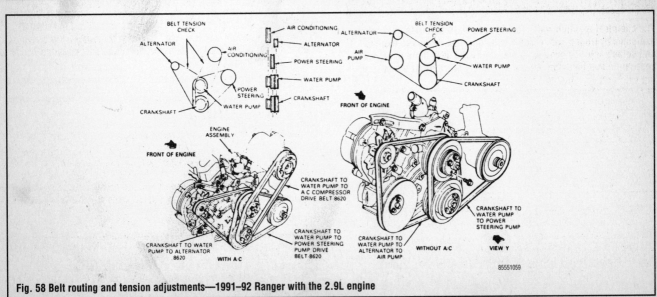

Fig. 58 Belt routing and tension adjustments—1991–92 Ranger with the 2.9L engine

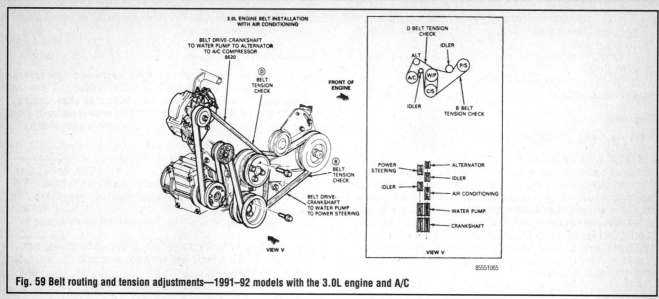

Fig. 59 Belt routing and tension adjustments—1991–92 models with the 3.0L engine and A/C

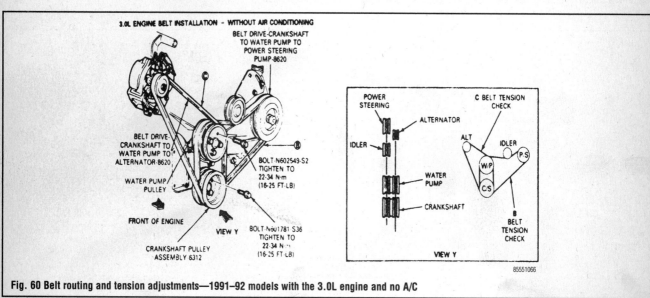

Fig. 60 Belt routing and tension adjustments—1991–92 models with the 3.0L engine and no A/C

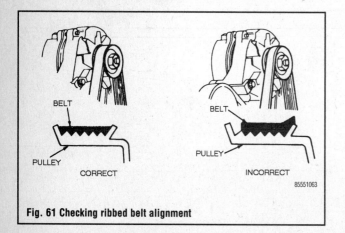

Fig. 61 Checking ribbed belt alignment

used, it is often necessary, only, to loosen the idler pulley to provide enough slack to slip the belt from the pulley.

It is important to note, however, that on engines with many driven accessories, several or all of the belts may have to be removed to get at the one to be replaced.

1. Disconnect the negative battery cable for safety. This will help assure that no one mistakenly cranks the engine over with your hands between the pulleys.

➡Accessories which can be moved will have a slot in its mounting bracket. Some engines utilize a movable idler pulley for tension adjustment. Also, some may have a ½ square hole for using a ½ square drive breaker bar to aid in removal and tensioning.

2. Loosen the mounting bolts for the accessory or idler pulley.
3. Move the accessory to relieve the belt tension enough to allow removal.
4. Remove the belt from the pulleys.

To install:

5. Route the new belt over the pulleys. Insure that the belt is properly seated on all of the pulleys.

➡Insure that the belt is properly seated on all of the pulleys.

6. Move the accessory to apply tension on the belt.

⁂⁂ WARNING

It is not recommended to pry on aluminum or plastic housings as damage to the accessory can occur.

7. When the proper tension is attained, tighten the mounting bolts.

8. Once the belt is installed, take another look at all the pulleys to double check your installation.

9. Connect the negative battery cable, then start and run the engine to check belt operation.

10. Once the engine has reached normal operating temperature, turn the ignition **OFF** and check that the belt tension is within the proper adjustment range.

Serpentine

▶ **See Figures 62, 63, 64, 65 and 66**

All 1993–99 engines utilize one wide-ribbed V-belt to drive the engine accessories such as the water pump, alternator, air conditioner compressor, air pump, etc. Because this belt uses a spring loaded tensioner for adjustment, belt replacement tends to be somewhat easier than it used to be on engines where accessories were pivoted and bolted in place for tension adjustment. Basically, all belt replacement involves is to pivot the tensioner to loosen the belt, then slide the belt off of the pulleys. The two most important points are to pay CLOSE attention to the proper belt routing (since serpentine belts tend to be "snaked" all different ways through the pulleys) and to make sure the V-ribs are properly seated in all the pulleys.

Although belt routing diagrams have been included in this section, the first places you should check for proper belt routing are the labels in your engine compartment. These should include a belt routing diagram which may reflect changes made during a production run.

1. Disconnect the negative battery cable for safety. This will help assure that no one mistakenly cranks the engine over with your hands between the pulleys.

➡**Take a good look at the installed belt and make a note of the routing. Before removing the belt, make sure the routing matches that of the belt routing label or one of the diagrams in this book. If for some reason a diagram does not match (you may not have the original engine or it may have been modified,) carefully note the changes on a piece of paper.**

2. For tensioners equipped with a ½ square hole, insert the drive end of a large breaker bar into the hole. Use the breaker bar to pivot the tensioner away from the drive belt. For tensioners not equipped with this hole, use the proper-sized socket and breaker bar (or a large handled wrench) on the tensioner idler pulley center bolt to pivot the tensioner away from the belt. This will loosen the belt sufficiently that it can be pulled off of one or more of the pulleys. It is usually easiest to carefully pull the belt out from underneath the tensioner pulley itself.

3. Once the belt is off one of the pulleys, gently pivot the tensioner back into position. DO NOT allow the tensioner to snap back, as this could damage the tensioners internal parts.

4. Now finish removing the belt from the other pulleys and remove it from the engine.

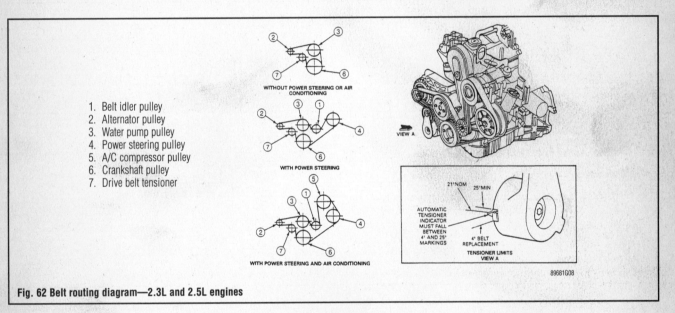

1. Belt idler pulley
2. Alternator pulley
3. Water pump pulley
4. Power steering pulley
5. A/C compressor pulley
6. Crankshaft pulley
7. Drive belt tensioner

Fig. 62 Belt routing diagram—2.3L and 2.5L engines

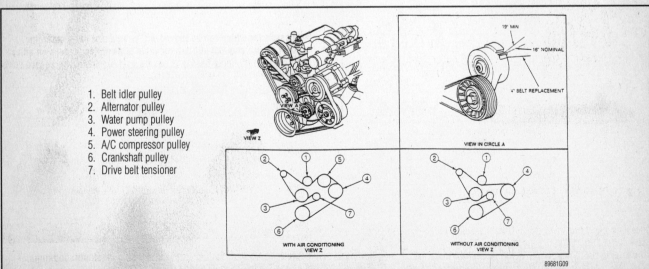

1. Belt idler pulley
2. Alternator pulley
3. Water pump pulley
4. Power steering pulley
5. A/C compressor pulley
6. Crankshaft pulley
7. Drive belt tensioner

Fig. 63 Belt routing diagram—3.0L engines

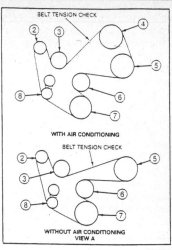

2. Alternator pulley
3. Idler pulley
4. A/C compressor pulley
5. Power steering pulley
6. Water pump pulley
7. Crankshaft pulley
8. Drive belt tensioner

Fig. 64 Belt routing diagram—4.0L engines (VIN code X)

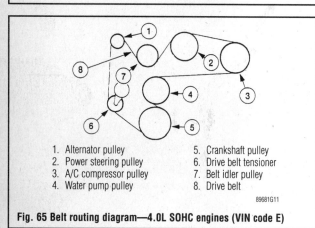

1. Alternator pulley
2. Power steering pulley
3. A/C compressor pulley
4. Water pump pulley
5. Crankshaft pulley
6. Drive belt tensioner
7. Belt idler pulley
8. Drive belt

Fig. 65 Belt routing diagram—4.0L SOHC engines (VIN code E)

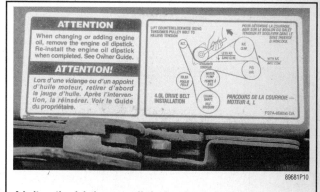

A belt routing label can usually be found under the hood

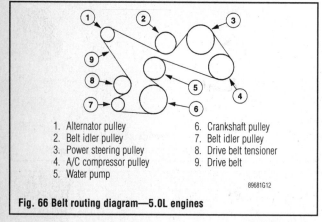

1. Alternator pulley
2. Belt idler pulley
3. Power steering pulley
4. A/C compressor pulley
5. Water pump
6. Crankshaft pulley
7. Belt idler pulley
8. Drive belt tensioner
9. Drive belt

Fig. 66 Belt routing diagram—5.0L engines

Once the tension is relieved, slip the belt off the pulley then slowly release the tensioner

To install:

5. While referring to the proper routing diagram (which you identified earlier), begin to route the belt over the pulleys, leaving whichever pulley you first released it from for last.

6. Once the belt is mostly in place, carefully pivot the tensioner and position the belt over the final pulley. As you begin to allow the tensioner back into contact with the belt, run your hand around the pulleys and make sure the belt is properly seated in the ribs. If not, release the tension and seat the belt.

7. Once the belt is installed, take another look at all the pulleys to double check your installation.

8. Connect the negative battery cable, then start and run the engine to check belt operation.

9. Once the engine has reached normal operating temperature, turn the ignition **OFF** and check that the belt tensioner arrow is within the proper adjustment range.

Timing Belts

INSPECTION

◆ **See Figures 67 thru 75**

➡Only the 2.3L and 2.5L OHC engine uses a rubber timing belt. All other engines use a timing chain, and no periodic inspection is required.

The 2.3L and 2.5L Ranger engine utilizes a timing belt to drive the camshaft from the crankshaft's turning motion and to maintain proper valve timing. Some manufacturer's schedule periodic timing belt replacement to assure optimum engine performance, to make sure the motorist is never stranded should the belt break (as the engine will stop instantly) and for some (manufacturer's with interference motors) to prevent the possibility of severe internal engine damage should the belt break.

Although the 2.3L and 2.5L engine is not listed as an interference motor (it is not listed by the manufacturer as a motor whose valves might contact the pistons if the camshaft was rotated separately from the crankshaft) the first 2 reasons for periodic replacement still apply. Ford does not publish a replacement interval for this motor, but most belt manufacturers recommend intervals anywhere from 45,000 miles (72,500 km) to 90,000 miles (145,000 km). You will have to decide for yourself if the peace of mind offered by a new belt is worth it on higher mileage engines.

But whether or not you decide to replace it, you would be wise to check it periodically to make sure it has not become damaged or worn. Generally speaking, a severely damaged belt will show as engine performance would drop dramatically, but a damaged belt (which could give out suddenly) may not give as much warning. In general, any time the engine timing cover(s) is(are) removed you should inspect the belt for premature parting, severe cracks or missing teeth. Also, an access plug is provided in the upper portion of the timing cover so that camshaft timing can be checked without cover removal. If timing is found to be off, cover removal and further belt inspection or replacement is necessary.

CAMSHAFT TIMING INSPECTION

1. Locate and carefully remove the access plug from the upper portion of the timing cover.

✳✳ WARNING

When turning the engine over by hand, ALWAYS rotate the crankshaft in the proper direction of rotation, otherwise the timing belt might jump one or more teeth due to the configuration of the belt tensioner.

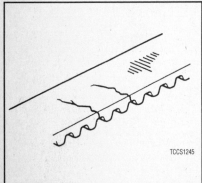

Fig. 67 Do not bend, twist or turn the timing belt inside out. Never allow oil, water or steam to contact the belt

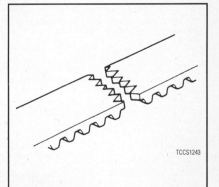

Fig. 68 Check for premature parting of the belt

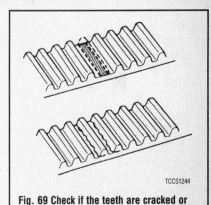

Fig. 69 Check if the teeth are cracked or damaged

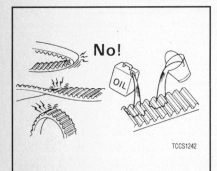

Fig. 70 Look for noticeable cracks or wear on the belt face

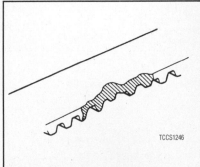

Fig. 71 You may only have damage on one side of the belt; if so, the guide could be the culprit

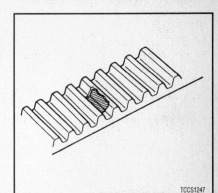

Fig. 72 Foreign materials can get in between the teeth and cause damage

Fig. 73 Inspect the timing belt for cracks, fraying, glazing or damage of any kind

Fig. 74 Damage on only one side of the timing belt may indicate a faulty guide

Fig. 75 ALWAYS replace the timing belt at the interval specified by the manufacturer

2. Turn the engine CLOCKWISE (in the normal direction of rotation) to set the engine at Top Dead Center (TDC) of the No. 1 cylinder by aligning the O mark on the belt cover with the O mark on the crankshaft pulley.

➡If no timing mark is visible through the access cover when the O marks on the crank pulley and cover are aligned, the engine may be on No. 1 exhaust stroke and not the compression stroke (the camshaft is 180° away from No. 1 TDC). If so, the crankshaft must be rotated one full turn to bring the No. 1 piston back to the top and the camshaft around to close the No. 1 intake and exhaust valves.

3. With the O marks aligned, look through the access hole in the cover to assure that the timing mark on the camshaft sprocket aligns with the pointer on the inner belt cover. If the belt timing is incorrect, the timing cover and belt must be removed for further inspection, possible replacement and correct installation. For more details, please refer to Section 3 of this manual.

4. If timing is correct, re-install the access plug.

Hoses

INSPECTION

▶ **See Figures 76, 77, 78 and 79**

Upper and lower radiator hoses along with the heater hoses should be checked for deterioration, leaks and loose hose clamps at least every 15,000 miles (24,000 km). It is also wise to check the hoses periodically in early spring and at the beginning of the fall or winter when you are performing other maintenance. A quick visual inspection could discover a weakened hose which might have left you stranded if it had remained unrepaired.

Whenever you are checking the hoses, make sure the engine and cooling system are cold. Visually inspect for cracking, rotting or collapsed hoses, and replace as necessary. Run your hand along the length of the hose. If a weak or swollen spot is noted when squeezing the hose wall, the hose should be replaced.

REMOVAL & INSTALLATION

✳✳ CAUTION

Never remove the pressure cap while the engine is running, or personal injury from scalding hot coolant or steam may result. If possible, wait until the engine has cooled to remove the pressure cap. If this is not possible, wrap a thick cloth around the pressure cap and turn it slowly to the stop. Step back while the pressure is released from the cooling system. When you are sure all the pressure has been released, use the cloth to turn and remove the cap.

1. Remove the radiator pressure cap.
2. Position a clean container under the radiator and/or engine draincock or plug, then open the drain and allow the cooling system to drain to an appropriate level. For some upper hoses, only a little coolant must be drained. To remove hoses positioned lower on the engine, such as a lower radiator hose, the entire cooling system must be emptied.
3. Loosen the hose clamps at each end of the hose requiring replacement. Clamps are usually either of the spring tension type (which require pliers to squeeze the tabs and loosen) or of the screw tension type (which require screw or hex drivers to loosen). Pull the clamps back on the hose away from the connection.
4. Twist, pull and slide the hose off the fitting, taking care not to damage the neck of the component from which the hose is being removed.

➡If the hose is stuck at the connection, do not try to insert a screwdriver or other sharp tool under the hose end in an effort to free it, as the connection and/or hose may become damaged. Heater connections especially may be easily damaged by such a procedure. If the hose is to be replaced, use a single-edged razor blade to make a slice along the portion of the hose which is stuck on the connection, perpendicular to the end of the hose. Do not cut deep so as to prevent damaging the connection. The hose can then be peeled from the connection and discarded.

Fig. 76 The cracks developing along this hose are a result of age-related hardening

Fig. 77 A hose clamp that is too tight can cause older hoses to separate and tear on either side of the clamp

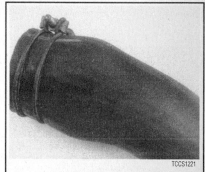

Fig. 78 A soft spongy hose (identifiable by the swollen section) will eventually burst and should be replaced

Fig. 79 Hoses are likely to deteriorate from the inside if the cooling system is not periodically flushed

Squeeze the spring clamp with pliers and slide it away from hose fitting

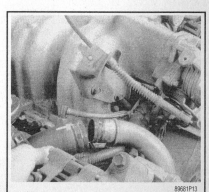

Twist and pull the hose from the fitting to remove it.

5. Clean both hose mounting connections. Inspect the condition of the hose clamps and replace them, if necessary.

To install:

6. Dip the ends of the new hose into clean engine coolant to ease installation.

7. Slide the clamps over the replacement hose, then slide the hose ends over the connections into position.

8. Position and secure the clamps at least ¼ in. (6.35mm) from the ends of the hose. Make sure they are located beyond the raised bead of the connector.

9. Close the radiator or engine drains and properly refill the cooling system with the clean drained engine coolant or a suitable mixture of ethylene glycol coolant and water.

10. If available, install a pressure tester and check for leaks. If a pressure tester is not available, run the engine until normal operating temperature is reached (allowing the system to naturally pressurize), then check for leaks.

✳✳ CAUTION

If you are checking for leaks with the system at normal operating temperature, BE EXTREMELY CAREFUL not to touch any moving or hot engine parts. Once temperature has been reached, shut the engine OFF, and check for leaks around the hose fittings and connections which were removed earlier.

CV-Boots

INSPECTION

▶ **See Figures 80 and 81**

The Mountaineer and 1995–99 Explorer 4-wheel drive models use an Independent Front Suspension (IFS) drive axle which utilizes Constant Velocity (CV) joint equipped axle half-shafts. All other 4-wheel drive front axles are equipped with U-joints, which do not use a rubber boot to protect the joint and retain the grease.

The CV (Constant Velocity) boots should be checked for damage each time the oil is changed and any other time the vehicle is raised for service. These boots keep water, grime, dirt and other damaging matter from entering the CV-joints. Any of these could cause early CV-joint failure which can be expensive to

repair. Heavy grease thrown around the inside of the front wheel(s) and on the brake caliper/drum can be an indication of a torn boot. Thoroughly check the boots for missing clamps and tears. If the boot is damaged, it should be replaced immediately. Please refer to Section 7 for procedures.

Spark Plugs

▶ **See Figures 82 and 83**

A typical spark plug consists of a metal shell surrounding a ceramic insulator. A metal electrode extends downward through the center of the insulator and protrudes a small distance. Located at the end of the plug and attached to the side of the outer metal shell is the side electrode. The side electrode bends in at a 90° angle so that its tip is just past and parallel to the tip of the center electrode. The distance between these two electrodes (measured in thousandths of an inch or hundredths of a millimeter) is called the spark plug gap.

The spark plug does not produce a spark, but instead provides a gap across which the current can arc. The coil produces anywhere from 20,000 to 50,000 volts (depending on the type and application) which travels through the wires to the spark plugs. The current passes along the center electrode and jumps the gap to the side electrode, and in doing so, ignites the air/fuel mixture in the combustion chamber.

SPARK PLUG HEAT RANGE

▶ **See Figure 84**

Spark plug heat range is the ability of the plug to dissipate heat. The longer the insulator (or the farther it extends into the engine), the hotter the plug will operate; the shorter the insulator (the closer the electrode is to the block's cooling passages) the cooler it will operate. A plug that absorbs little heat and remains too cool will quickly accumulate deposits of oil and carbon since it is not hot enough to burn them off. This leads to plug fouling and consequently to misfiring. A plug that absorbs too much heat will have no deposits but, due to the excessive heat, the electrodes will burn away quickly and might possibly lead to preignition or other ignition problems. Preignition takes place when plug tips get so hot that they glow sufficiently to ignite the air/fuel mixture before the actual spark occurs. This early ignition will usually cause a pinging during low speeds and heavy loads.

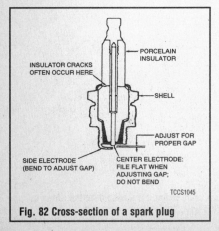

Fig. 80 CV-boots must be inspected periodically for damage

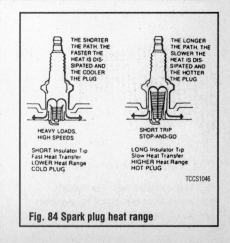

Fig. 81 A torn boot should be replaced immediately

Fig. 82 Cross-section of a spark plug

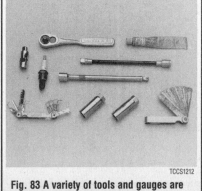

Fig. 83 A variety of tools and gauges are needed for spark plug service

Fig. 84 Spark plug heat range

The general rule of thumb for choosing the correct heat range when picking a spark plug is: if most of your driving is long distance, high speed travel, use a colder plug; if most of your driving is stop and go, use a hotter plug. Original equipment plugs are generally a good compromise between the 2 styles and most people never have the need to change their plugs from the factory-recommended heat range.

REMOVAL & INSTALLATION

▶ **See Figure 85**

➡**Ford recommends replacing standard spark plugs every 30,000 miles (48,000km) and platinum plugs every 60,000 miles (96,000km).**

A set of spark plugs usually requires replacement after about 20,000–30,000 miles (32,000–48,000km), depending on your style of driving. In normal operation plug gap increases about 0.001 in. (0.025mm) for every 2500 miles (4000km). As the gap increases, the plug's voltage requirement also increases. It requires a greater voltage to jump the wider gap and about two to three times as much voltage to fire the plug at high speeds than at idle. The improved air/fuel ratio control of modern fuel injection combined with the higher voltage output of modern ignition systems will often allow an engine to run significantly longer on a set of standard spark plugs, but keep in mind that efficiency will drop as the gap widens (along with fuel economy and power).

When you're removing spark plugs, work on one at a time. Don't start by removing the plug wires all at once, because, unless you number them, they may become mixed up. Take a minute before you begin and number the wires with tape. Also, an anti-seize compound should be used before installing the plugs into the cylinder head.

1. Disconnect the negative battery cable, and if the vehicle has been run recently, allow the engine to thoroughly cool.

2. Carefully twist the spark plug wire boot to loosen it, then pull upward and remove the boot from the plug. Be sure to pull on the boot and not on the wire, otherwise the connector located inside the boot may become separated.

3. Using compressed air, blow any water or debris from the spark plug well to assure that no harmful contaminants are allowed to enter the combustion chamber when the spark plug is removed. If compressed air is not available, use a rag or a brush to clean the area.

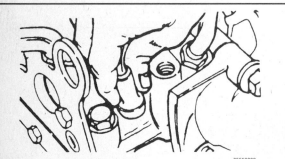

Fig. 85 Always twist and pull on the spark plug boot, never on the wire

➡**Remove the spark plugs when the engine is cold, if possible, to prevent damage to the threads. If removal of the plugs is difficult, apply a few drops of penetrating oil or silicone spray to the area around the base of the plug, and allow it a few minutes to work.**

4. Using a spark plug socket that is equipped with a rubber insert to properly hold the plug, turn the spark plug counterclockwise to loosen and remove the spark plug from the bore.

✳✳ WARNING

Be sure not to use a flexible extension on the socket. Use of a flexible extension may allow a shear force to be applied to the plug. A shear force could break the plug off in the cylinder head, leading to costly and frustrating repairs.

To install:

5. Inspect the spark plug boot for tears or damage. If a damaged boot is found, the spark plug wire must be replaced.

6. Using a wire feeler gauge, check and adjust the spark plug gap. When using a gauge, the proper size should pass between the electrodes with a slight drag. The next larger size should not be able to pass while the next smaller size should pass freely.

➡**Coat the spark plug threads with an anti-seize compound before installing it into the cylinder head.**

7. Carefully thread the plug into the bore by hand. If resistance is felt before the plug is almost completely threaded, back the plug out and begin threading again. In small, hard to reach areas, an old spark plug wire and boot could be used as a threading tool. The boot will hold the plug while you twist the end of the wire and the wire is supple enough to twist before it would allow the plug to crossthread.

✳✳ WARNING

Do not use the spark plug socket to thread the plugs. Always carefully thread the plug by hand or using an old plug wire to prevent the possibility of crossthreading and damaging the cylinder head bore.

8. Carefully tighten the spark plug. If the plug you are installing is equipped with a crush washer, seat the plug, then tighten about ¼ turn to crush the washer. If you are installing a tapered seat plug, tighten the plug to specifications provided by the vehicle or plug manufacturer.

9. Apply a small amount of silicone dielectric compound to the end of the spark plug lead or inside the spark plug boot to prevent sticking, then install the boot to the spark plug and push until it clicks into place. The click may be felt or heard, then gently pull back on the boot to assure proper contact.

INSPECTION & GAPPING

▶ **See Figures 86, 87, 88 and 89**

Check the plugs for deposits and wear. If they are not going to be replaced, clean the plugs thoroughly. Remember that any kind of deposit will decrease the efficiency of the plug. Plugs can be cleaned on a spark plug cleaning machine, which can sometimes be found in service stations, or you can do an acceptable

Remove the spark plug wire from the plug by twisting the boot and pulling outwards. Never pull on the wire

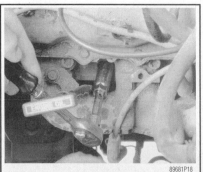

Using the proper size spark plug socket, loosen the plug by rotating it counterclockwise

Once the plug is loose, you should be able to remove it by hand. Compare the plug against the examples given

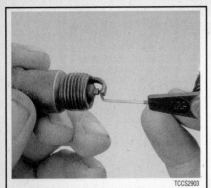

Fig. 86 Checking the spark plug gap with a feeler gauge

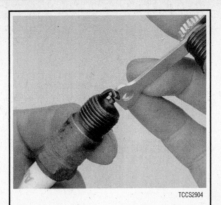

Fig. 87 Adjusting the spark plug gap

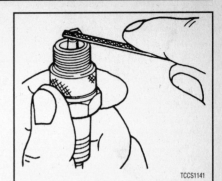

TCCS1141

Fig. 88 If the standard plug is in good condition, the electrode may be filed flat—WARNING: do not file platinum plugs

A **normally worn** spark plug should have light tan or gray deposits on the firing tip.

A **carbon fouled** plug, identified by soft, sooty, black deposits, may indicate an improperly tuned vehicle. Check the air cleaner, ignition components and engine control system.

This spark plug has been **left in the engine too long,** as evidenced by the extreme gap- Plugs with such an extreme gap can cause misfiring and stumbling accompanied by a noticeable lack of power.

An **oil fouled** spark plug indicates an engine with worn poston rings and/or bad valve seals allowing excessive oil to enter the chamber.

A **physically damaged** spark plug may be evidence of severe detonation in that cylinder. Watch that cylinder carefully between services, as a continued detonation will not only damage the plug, but could also damage the engine.

A **bridged** or almost **bridged** spark plug, identified by a build-up between the electrodes caused by excessive carbon or oil build-up on the plug.

TCCA1P40

Fig. 89 Inspect the spark plug to determine engine running conditions

job of cleaning with a stiff brush. If the plugs are cleaned, the electrodes must be filed flat. Use an ignition points file, not an emery board or the like, which will leave deposits. The electrodes must be filed perfectly flat with sharp edges; rounded edges reduce the spark plug voltage by as much as 50%.

Check spark plug gap before installation. The ground electrode (the L-shaped one connected to the body of the plug) must be parallel to the center electrode and the specified size wire gauge (please refer to the Tune-Up Specifications chart for details) must pass between the electrodes with a slight drag.

➡**NEVER adjust the gap on a used platinum type spark plug.**

Always check the gap on new plugs as they are not always set correctly at the factory. Do not use a flat feeler gauge when measuring the gap on a used plug, because the reading may be inaccurate. A round-wire type gapping tool is the best way to check the gap. The correct gauge should pass through the electrode gap with a slight drag. If you're in doubt, try one size smaller and one larger. The smaller gauge should go through easily, while the larger one shouldn't go through at all. Wire gapping tools usually have a bending tool attached. Use that to adjust the side electrode until the proper distance is obtained. Absolutely never attempt to bend the center electrode. Also, be careful not to bend the side electrode too far or too often as it may weaken and break off within the engine, requiring removal of the cylinder head to retrieve it.

Spark Plug Wires

REMOVAL & INSTALLATION

▶ **See Figure 90**

When removing spark plug wires, use great care. Grasp and twist the insulator back and forth on the spark plug to free the insulator. Do not pull on the wire directly as it may become separated from the connector inside the insulator.

To install:

➡**Whenever a high tension wire is removed for any reason form a spark plug, coil or distributor terminal housing, silicone grease must be applied to the boot before it is reconnected. Using a small clean tool, coat the entire interior surface of the boot with Ford silicone grease D7AZ 19A331–A or equivalent.**

1. Install each wire in or on the proper terminal of the coil pack or distributor cap. Be sure the terminal connector inside the insulator is fully seated. The No. 1 terminal is identified on the cap.
2. Remove wire separators from old wire set and install them on new set in approximately same position.
3. Connect wires to proper spark plugs. Be certain all wires are fully seated on terminals.

TESTING

➡**Only test one spark plug wire at a time. When the check is complete return the plug wire to its original location. If the wire is defective and more wires are to be checked, mark the wire as such, return it to its original location, then inspect the other wires. Once all of the wires are**

checked, replace the defective wires one at a time. This will avoid any mix-ups.

With Distributor

▶ **See Figure 91**

1. Remove the distributor cap from the distributor assembly.
2. Visually inspect the spark plug wires for burns, cuts or breaks in the insulation. Check the spark plug boots and the nipples on the distributor cap and coil. Replace any damaged wiring.
3. Inspect the spark plug wires to insure that they are firmly seated on the distributor cap.
4. Disconnect the spark plug wire thought to be defective at the spark plug.
5. Using an ohmmeter, measure the resistance between the distributor cap terminal and the spark plug terminal.

➡**Make certain that a good connection exists between the distributor cap and the spark terminal. Never, under any circumstances, measure resistance by puncturing the spark plug wire.**

6. If the measured resistance is less than 7000 ohms per foot of wire, the wire is good. If the measured resistance is greater than 7000 ohms per foot, the wire is defective and should be replaced.

Without Distributor

1. Visually inspect the spark plug wires for burns, cuts or breaks in the insulation. Check the spark plug boots and the nipples on the coil. Replace any damaged wiring.
2. Inspect the spark plug wires to insure that they are firmly seated on the coil pack.
3. Disconnect the spark plug wire thought to be defective at the spark plug.
4. Using an ohmmeter, measure the resistance between the coil terminal and the spark plug terminal.

➡**Never, under any circumstances, measure resistance by puncturing the spark plug wire.**

5. If the measured resistance is less than 7000 ohms per foot of wire, the wire is good. If the measured resistance is greater than 7000 ohms per foot, the wire is defective and should be replaced.

Distributor Cap and Rotor

➡**1991–92 models with the 2.9L engine, and 1991–94 models with the 3.0L engine use a distributor equipped ignition system. All other models use a distributorless ignition.**

REMOVAL & INSTALLATION

Distributor Cap

1. As a precaution, label all of the spark plug wires with their perspective cylinder number.
2. Loosen the cap hold-down screws.

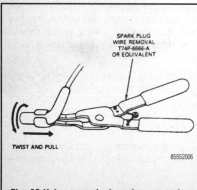

Fig. 90 Using a spark plug wire removal tool

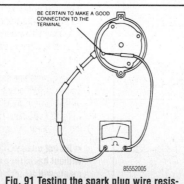

Fig. 91 Testing the spark plug wire resistance through the distributor cap with an ohmmeter

Checking individual plug wire resistance with a digital ohmmeter

3. Remove the cap by lifting straight up to prevent damage to the rotor blade and spring.

➡If the plug wires do not have enough slack to allow cap removal, confirm that they are properly labeled and remove them from the cap.

4. Installation is the reverse of the removal procedure. Note the position of the square alignment locator and tighten the hold-down screws to 18–23 inch pounds (2.0–2.6Nm)

Distributor Rotor

1. Remove the distributor cap.
2. Pull straight up on the rotor to disengage it from the shaft and armature.
3. Installation is the reverse of the removal procedure. Align the locating boss on the rotor with the hole on the armature, then insure that it is fully seated on the shaft.

INSPECTION

Distributor Cap

▶ **See Figure 92**

1. Wash the inside and outside surfaces of the cap with soap and water then dry it with compressed air.
2. Inspect the cap for cracks, broken or worn carbon button, or carbon tracks. Also inspect the cap terminals for dirt and corrosion.
3. Replace the cap if any of the above conditions are observed.

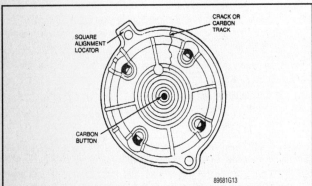

Fig. 92 Inspection points for the distributor cap—note the square alignment locator which limits the cap to one installation position

Distributor Rotor

▶ **See Figure 93**

1. Wash the rotor with soap and water then dry with it compressed air.
2. Inspect the rotor for cracks, carbon tracks, burns or damage to the blade or spring.
3. Replace the rotor if any of the above conditions are observed.

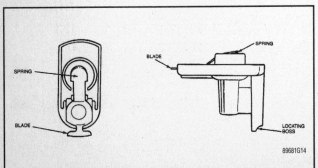

Fig. 93 Inspection points for the distributor rotor—note the locating boss which fits in the armature

Ignition Timing

➡No periodic checking or adjustment of the ignition timing is necessary for any of the vehicles covered by this manual. However, the distributor ignition system used by the 1991–94 2.9L and 3.0L engines does allow for both, should the distributor be removed and installed or otherwise disturbed.

GENERAL INFORMATION

Ignition timing is the measurement, in degrees of crankshaft rotation, of the point at which the spark plugs fire in each of the cylinders. It is measured in degrees before or after Top Dead Center (TDC) of the compression stroke.

Because it takes a fraction of a second for the spark plug to ignite the mixture in the cylinder, the spark plug must fire a little before the piston reaches TDC. Otherwise, the mixture will not be completely ignited as the piston passes TDC and the full power of the explosion will not be used by the engine.

The timing measurement is given in degrees of crankshaft rotation before the piston reaches TDC (BTDC). If the setting for the ignition timing is 5° BTDC, the spark plug must fire 5° before each piston reaches TDC. This only holds true, however, when the engine is at idle speed.

As the engine speed increases, the pistons go faster. The spark plugs have to ignite the fuel even sooner if it is to be completely ignited when the piston reaches TDC. On all engines covered by this manual, spark timing changes are accomplished electronically by the engine and ignition control computers.

If the ignition is set too far advanced (BTDC), the ignition and expansion of the fuel in the cylinder will occur too soon and tend to force the piston down while it is still traveling up. This causes engine ping. If the ignition spark is set too far retarded, after TDC (ATDC), the piston will have already passed TDC and started on its way down when the fuel is ignited. This will cause the piston to be forced down for only a portion of its travel. This will result in poor engine performance and lack of power.

Timing marks consisting of 0 marks or scales can be found on the rim of the crankshaft pulley and the timing cover. The mark(s) on the pulley correspond(s) to the position of the piston in the number 1 cylinder. A stroboscopic (dynamic) timing light is used, which is hooked into the circuit of the No. 1 cylinder spark plug. Every time the spark plug fires, the timing light flashes. By aiming the timing light at the timing marks while the engine is running, the exact position of the piston within the cylinder can be easily read since the stroboscopic flash makes the pulley appear to be standing still. Proper timing is indicated when the mark and scale are in proper alignment.

Because these vehicles utilize high voltage, electronic ignition systems, only a timing light with an inductive pickup should be used. This pickup simply clamps onto the No. 1 spark plug wire, eliminating the adapter. It is not susceptible to cross-firing or false triggering, which may occur with a conventional light, due to the greater voltages produced by electronic ignition.

INSPECTION & ADJUSTMENT

1991–94 2.9L and 3.0L Engines

SETTING INITIAL (BASE) TIMING

➡Specific instructions and specifications for setting initial timing can be found in the Vehicle Emission Control Information (VECI) label in the engine compartment. Because this label contains information regarding any specific calibration requirements for YOUR vehicle, those instructions and specifications should be followed if they differ from the following.

This procedure should not be used as a periodic maintenance adjustment. Timing should only be set after the distributor has been disturbed (removed and re-installed) in some way. If problems are encountered setting the initial timing with this procedure and no mechanical causes are found, follow the spark timing advance check procedure found later in this section.

➡Do not change the ignition timing by the use of a different octane rod without having the proper authority to do so. Federal emission requirements will be affected.

1. Start the engine and allow it to run until it reaches normal operating temperature.

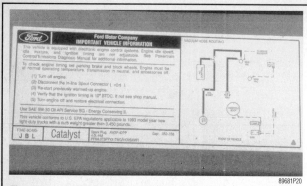

The underhood VECI label is specific to YOUR truck and should be used if it differs from another source

✳✳ CAUTION

NEVER run an engine in a garage or building without proper ventilation. Carbon monoxide will quickly enter the body, excluding oxygen from the blood stream. This condition will cause dizziness, sleepiness and eventually death.

2. Once normal operating temperature has been reached, shut the engine **OFF**.

3. Firmly apply the parking brake and block the drive wheels. Place the transmission in **P** (A/T) or **NEUTRAL** (M/T, as applicable).

4. Make sure heater and A/C, along with all other accessories are in the OFF position.

5. Connect an inductive timing light, such as the Rotunda 059-00006 or equivalent, to the No. 1 spark plug wire, according the tool manufacturer's instructions.

6. Connect a tachometer to the ignition coil connection using an alligator clip. This can be done by inserting the alligator clip into the back of the connector, onto the dark green/yellow dotted wire.

➡**DO NOT allow the alligator clip to accidentally ground to a metal surface while attached to the coil connector as that could permanently damage the ignition coil.**

7. Disconnect the single wire in-line SPOUT connector which connects the control computer (usually terminal 36) to the ignition control module. This will prevent the electronic ignition from advancing the timing during the set procedure.

8. Using a suitable socket or wrench, loosen the distributor hold-down bolt slightly at this time, BUT DO NOT ALLOW THE DISTRIBUTOR TO MOVE or timing will have to be set regardless of the current conditions.

➡**A remote starter must NOT be used to start the vehicle when setting the initial ignition timing. Disconnecting the start wire at the starter relay will cause the ignition control module to revert to Start Mode timing after the vehicle is started. Reconnecting the start wire after the vehicle is running WILL NOT correct the timing.**

9. Start the engine (using the ignition key and NOT a remote starter to assure timing will be set correctly) and allow the engine to return to normal operating temperature.

10. With the engine running at the specified rpm, check the initial timing. If adjustments must be made, rotate the distributor while watching the timing marks. Once proper adjustment has been reached, make sure the distributor is not disturbed until the hold-down bolt can be secured.

11. Reconnect the single wire in-line SPOUT connector and check the timing to verify that the distributor is now advancing beyond the initial setting.

12. Shut the engine **OFF** and tighten the distributor bolt while CAREFULLY holding the distributor from turning. If the distributor moves, you will have to start the engine and reset the timing.

13. Restart the engine and repeat the procedure to check the timing and verify that it did not change

14. Shut the engine **OFF**, then disconnect the tachometer and timing light.

CHECKING SPARK TIMING ADVANCE

Spark timing advance is controlled by the EEC system. This procedure checks the capability of the ignition module to receive the spark timing command from the EEC module. The use of a volt/ohmmeter is required.

1. Turn the ignition switch **OFF**.

2. Disconnect the pin-in-line connector (SPOUT connector) near the TFI module.

3. Start the engine and measure the voltage, at idle, from the SPOUT connector to the distributor base. The reading should equal battery voltage.

4. If the result is okay, the problem lies within the EEC-IV system.

5. If the result was not satisfactory, separate the wiring harness connector from the ignition module. Check for damage, corrosion or dirt. Service as necessary.

6. Measure the resistance between terminal No. 5 and the pin-in-line connector. This test is done at the ignition module connector only. The reading should be less than 5 ohms.

7. If the reading is okay, replace the TFI module.

8. If the result was not satisfactory, service the wiring between the pin in-line connector and the TFI connector.

Except 1991–94 2.9L and 3.0L Engines

These engines utilize a Distributorless Ignition System (DIS). On this system, ignition coil packs fire the spark plugs directly through the spark plug wires. All spark timing and advance is determined by the ignition control module and engine control computer. No ignition timing adjustments are necessary or possible.

Valve Lash

No periodic valve lash adjustments are necessary on these engines. All the engines utilize hydraulic valvetrains to automatically maintain proper valve lash.

Idle Speed and Mixture Adjustments

The engines covered by this manual utilize sophisticated multi-port fuel injection systems in which an engine control computer utilizes information from various sensors to control idle speed and air fuel mixtures. No periodic adjustments are either necessary or possible on these systems. If a problem is suspected, please refer to Sections 4 and 5 of this manual for more information on electronic engine controls and fuel injection.

Air Conditioning System

SYSTEM SERVICE & REPAIR

➡**It is recommended that the A/C system be serviced by an EPA Section 609 certified automotive technician utilizing a refrigerant recovery/recycling machine.**

The do-it-yourselfer should not service his/her own vehicle's A/C system for many reasons, including legal concerns, personal injury, environmental damage and cost.

According to the U.S. Clean Air Act, it is a federal crime to service or repair (involving the refrigerant) a Motor Vehicle Air Conditioning (MVAC) system for money without being EPA certified. It is also illegal to vent R-12 and R-134a refrigerants into the atmosphere. State and/or local laws may be more strict than the federal regulations, so be sure to check with your state and/or local authorities for further information.

➡**Federal law dictates that a fine of up to $25,000 may be levied on people convicted of venting refrigerant into the atmosphere.**

When servicing an A/C system you run the risk of handling or coming in contact with refrigerant, which may result in skin or eye irritation or frostbite. Although low in toxicity (due to chemical stability), inhalation of concentrated refrigerant fumes is dangerous and can result in death; cases of fatal cardiac arrhythmia have been reported in people accidentally subjected to high levels of refrigerant. Some early symptoms include loss of concentration and drowsiness.

TUNE-UP SPECIFICATIONS

Year	Engine ID/VIN	Engine Displacement Liters (cc)	Spark Plugs Gap (in.)	Ignition Timing (deg.)		Fuel Pump (psi)	Idle Speed (rpm)		Valve Clearance	
				MT	AT		MT	AT	In.	Ex.
1991	A	2.3 (2294)	0.044	10B	10B	30–40	①	①	HYD	HYD
	T	2.9 (2900)	0.044	10B	10B	30–40	①	①	HYD	HYD
	U	3.0 (2999)	0.044	10B	10B	30–40	①	①	HYD	HYD
	X	4.0 (3949)	0.054	10B	10B	30–40	①	①	HYD	HYD
1992	A	2.3 (2294)	0.044	10B	10B	30–40	①	①	HYD	HYD
	T	2.9 (2900)	0.044	10B	10B	30–40	①	①	HYD	HYD
	U	3.0 (2999)	0.044	10B	10B	30–40	①	①	HYD	HYD
	X	4.0 (3949)	0.054	10B	10B	30–40	①	①	HYD	HYD
1993	A	2.3 (2294)	0.044	10B	10B	35–45	①	①	HYD	HYD
	U	3.0 (2999)	0.044	10B	10B	35–45	①	①	HYD	HYD
	X	4.0 (3949)	0.054	10B	10B	35–45	①	①	HYD	HYD
1994	A	2.3 (2294)	0.044	10B	10B	35–45	①	①	HYD	HYD
	U	3.0 (2999)	0.044	10B	10B	35–45	①	①	HYD	HYD
	X	4.0 (3949)	0.054	10B	10B	35–45	①	①	HYD	HYD
1995	A	2.3 (2294)	0.044	10B	10B	35–45	①	①	HYD	HYD
	U	3.0 (2999)	0.044	10B	10B	35–45	①	①	HYD	HYD
	X	4.0 (3949)	0.054	10B	10B	35–45	①	①	HYD	HYD
1996	A	2.3 (2294)	0.044	10B	10B	35–45	①	①	HYD	HYD
	U	3.0 (2999)	0.044	10B	10B	35–45	①	①	HYD	HYD
	X	4.0 (3949)	0.054	10B	10B	35–45	①	①	HYD	HYD
	P	5.0 (4949)	0.054	—	10B	35–45	①	①	HYD	HYD
1997	A	2.3 (2294)	0.044	10B	10B	30–45	①	①	HYD	HYD
	U	3.0 (2999)	0.044	10B	10B	30–45	①	①	HYD	HYD
	X	4.0 (3949)	0.054	10B	10B	30–45	①	①	HYD	HYD
	E	4.0 (3998)	0.054	10B	10B	30–45	①	①	HYD	HYD
	P	5.0 (4949)	0.054	—	10B	30–45	①	①	HYD	HYD
1998	C	2.5 (2500)	0.044	10B	10B	30–45	①	①	HYD	HYD
	U	3.0 (2999)	0.044	10B	10B	30–45	①	①	HYD	HYD
	X	4.0 (3949)	0.054	10B	10B	30–45	①	①	HYD	HYD
	E	4.0 (3998)	0.054	10B	10B	30–45	①	①	HYD	HYD
	P	5.0 (4949)	0.054	—	10B	30–45	①	①	HYD	HYD
1999	C	2.5 (2500)	0.044	10B	10B	30–45	①	①	HYD	HYD
	U	3.0 (2999)	0.044	10B	10B	30–45	①	①	HYD	HYD
	X	4.0 (3949)	0.054	10B	10B	30–45	①	①	HYD	HYD
	E	4.0 (3998)	0.054	10B	10B	30–45	①	①	HYD	HYD
	P	5.0 (4949)	0.054	—	10B	30–45	①	①	HYD	HYD

NOTE: The Vehicle Emission Control Information (VECI) label often reflects specification changes made during production.

The label must be used if they differ from those in this chart

B - Before top dead center

HYD - Hydraulic

① Idle speed is electronically controlled and cannot be adjusted

89681C58

➡**Generally, the limit for exposure is lower for R-134a than it is for R-12. Exceptional care must be practiced when handling R-134a.**

Also, some refrigerants can decompose at high temperatures (near gas heaters or open flame), which may result in hydrofluoric acid, hydrochloric acid and phosgene (a fatal nerve gas).

It is usually more economically feasible to have a certified MVAC automotive technician perform A/C system service on your vehicle.

R-12 Refrigerant Conversion

If your vehicle still uses R-12 refrigerant, one way to save A/C system costs down the road is to investigate the possibility of having your system converted to R-134a. The older R-12 systems can be easily converted to R-134a refrigerant by a certified automotive technician by installing a few new components and changing the system oil.

The cost of R-12 is steadily rising and will continue to increase, because it is no longer imported or manufactured in the United States. Therefore, it is often possible to have an R-12 system converted to R-134a and recharged for less than it would cost to just charge the system with R-12.

If you are interested in having your system converted, contact local automotive service stations for more details and information.

PREVENTIVE MAINTENANCE

Although the A/C system should not be serviced by the do-it-yourselfer, preventive maintenance should be practiced to help maintain the efficiency of the vehicle's A/C system. Be sure to perform the following:

• The easiest and most important preventive maintenance for your A/C system is to be sure that it is used on a regular basis. Running the system for five minutes each month (no matter what the season) will help ensure that the seals and all internal components remain lubricated.

➡**Some vehicles automatically operate the A/C system compressor whenever the windshield defroster is activated. Therefore, the A/C system would not need to be operated each month if the defroster was used.**

• In order to prevent heater core freeze-up during A/C operation, it is necessary to maintain proper antifreeze protection. Be sure to properly maintain the engine cooling system.

• Any obstruction of or damage to the condenser configuration will restrict air flow which is essential to its efficient operation. Keep this unit clean and in proper physical shape.

➡**Bug screens which are mounted in front of the condenser (unless they are original equipment) are regarded as obstructions.**

• The condensation drain tube expels any water which accumulates on the bottom of the evaporator housing into the engine compartment. If this tube is obstructed, the air conditioning performance can be restricted and condensation buildup can spill over onto the vehicle's floor.

SYSTEM INSPECTION

Although the A/C system should not be serviced by the do-it-yourselfer, system inspections should be performed to help maintain the efficiency of the vehicle's A/C system. Be sure to perform the following:

The easiest and often most important check for the air conditioning system consists of a visual inspection of the system components. Visually inspect the system for refrigerant leaks, damaged compressor clutch, abnormal compressor drive belt tension and/or condition, plugged evaporator drain tube, blocked condenser fins, disconnected or broken wires, blown fuses, corroded connections and poor insulation.

A refrigerant leak will usually appear as an oily residue at the leakage point in the system. The oily residue soon picks up dust or dirt particles from the surrounding air and appears greasy. Through time, this will build up and appear to be a heavy dirt impregnated grease.

For a thorough visual and operational inspection, check the following:

• Check the surface of the radiator and condenser for dirt, leaves or other material which might block air flow.

• Check for kinks in hoses and lines. Check the system for leaks.

• Make sure the drive belt is properly tensioned. During operation, make sure the belt is free of noise or slippage.

• Make sure the blower motor operates at all appropriate positions, then check for distribution of the air from all outlets.

➡**Remember that in high humidity, air discharged from the vents may not feel as cold as expected, even if the system is working properly. This is because moisture in humid air retains heat more effectively than dry air, thereby making humid air more difficult to cool.**

Windshield Wipers

ELEMENT (REFILL) CARE & REPLACEMENT

▶ **See Figures 94, 95 and 96**

For maximum effectiveness and longest element life, the windshield and wiper blades should be kept clean. Dirt, tree sap, road tar and so on will cause streaking, smearing and blade deterioration if left on the glass. It is advisable to wash the windshield carefully with a commercial glass cleaner at least once a month. Wipe off the rubber blades with the wet rag afterwards. Do not attempt to move wipers across the windshield by hand; damage to the motor and drive mechanism will result.

To inspect and/or replace the wiper blade elements, place the wiper switch in the **LOW** speed position and the ignition switch in the **ACC** position. When the wiper blades are approximately vertical on the windshield, turn the ignition switch to **OFF**.

Examine the wiper blade elements. If they are found to be cracked, broken or torn, they should be replaced immediately. Replacement intervals will vary with usage, although ozone deterioration usually limits element life to about one year. If the wiper pattern is smeared or streaked, or if the blade chatters across the glass, the elements should be replaced. It is easiest and most sensible to replace the elements in pairs.

If your vehicle is equipped with aftermarket blades, there are several different types of refills and your vehicle might have any kind. Aftermarket blades and arms rarely use the exact same type blade or refill as the original equipment.

Regardless of the type of refill used, be sure to follow the part manufacturer's instructions closely. Make sure that all of the frame jaws are engaged as the refill is pushed into place and locked. If the metal blade holder and frame are allowed to touch the glass during wiper operation, the glass will be scratched.

Tires and Wheels

Common sense and good driving habits will afford maximum tire life. Make sure that you don't overload the vehicle or run with incorrect pressure in the tires. Either of these will increase tread wear. Fast starts, sudden stops and sharp cornering are hard on tires and will shorten their useful life span.

➡**For optimum tire life, keep the tires properly inflated, rotate them often and have the wheel alignment checked periodically.**

Inspect your tires frequently. Be especially careful to watch for bubbles in the tread or sidewall, deep cuts or underinflation. Replace any tires with bubbles in the sidewall. If cuts are so deep that they penetrate to the cords, discard the tire. Any cut in the sidewall of a radial tire renders it unsafe. Also look for uneven tread wear patterns that may indicate the front end is out of alignment or that the tires are out of balance.

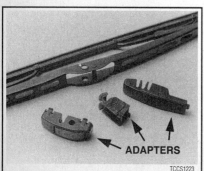

TCCS1223

Fig. 94 Most aftermarket blades are available with multiple adapters to fit different vehicles

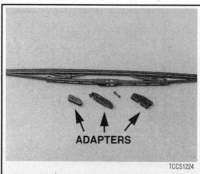

TCCS1224

Fig. 95 Choose a blade which will fit your vehicle, and that will be readily available next time you need blades

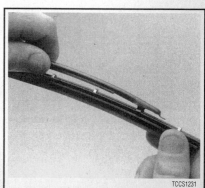

TCCS1231

Fig. 96 When installed, be certain the blade is fully inserted into the backing

TIRE ROTATION

▶ See Figure 97

Tires must be rotated periodically to equalize wear patterns that vary with a tire's position on the vehicle. Tires will also wear in an uneven way as the front steering/suspension system wears to the point where the alignment should be reset.

Rotating the tires will ensure maximum life for the tires as a set, so you will not have to discard a tire early due to wear on only part of the tread. Regular rotation is required to equalize wear.

When rotating "unidirectional tires," make sure that they always roll in the same direction. This means that a tire used on the left side of the vehicle must not be switched to the right side and vice-versa. Such tires should only be rotated front-to-rear or rear-to-front, while always remaining on the same side of the vehicle. These tires are marked on the sidewall as to the direction of rotation; observe the marks when reinstalling the tire(s).

Some styled or "mag" wheels may have different offsets front to rear. In these cases, the rear wheels must not be used up front and vice-versa. Furthermore, if these wheels are equipped with unidirectional tires, they cannot be rotated unless the tire is remounted for the proper direction of rotation.

➡ **The compact or space-saver spare is strictly for emergency use. It must never be included in the tire rotation or placed on the vehicle for everyday use.**

TIRE DESIGN

▶ See Figure 98

For maximum satisfaction, tires should be used in sets of four. Mixing of different brands or types (radial, bias-belted, fiberglass belted) should be avoided. In most cases, the vehicle manufacturer has designated a type of tire on which the vehicle will perform best. Your first choice when replacing tires should be to use the same type of tire that the manufacturer recommends.

When radial tires are used, tire sizes and wheel diameters should be selected to maintain ground clearance and tire load capacity equivalent to the original specified tire. Radial tires should always be used in sets of four.

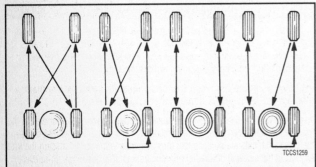

Fig. 97 Common tire rotation patterns for 4 and 5-wheel rotations

Radial tires should never be used on only the front axle.

When selecting tires, pay attention to the original size as marked on the tire. Most tires are described using an industry size code sometimes referred to as P-Metric. This allows the exact identification of the tire specifications, regardless of the manufacturer. If selecting a different tire size or brand, remember to check the installed tire for any sign of interference with the body or suspension while the vehicle is stopping, turning sharply or heavily loaded.

Snow Tires

Good radial tires can produce a big advantage in slippery weather, but in snow, a street radial tire does not have sufficient tread to provide traction and control. The small grooves of a street tire quickly pack with snow and the tire behaves like a billiard ball on a marble floor. The more open, chunky tread of a snow tire will self-clean as the tire turns, providing much better grip on snowy surfaces.

To satisfy municipalities requiring snow tires during weather emergencies, most snow tires carry either an M + S designation after the tire size stamped on the sidewall, or the designation "all-season." In general, no change in tire size is necessary when buying snow tires.

Most manufacturers strongly recommend the use of 4 snow tires on their vehicles for reasons of stability. If snow tires are fitted only to the drive wheels, the opposite end of the vehicle may become very unstable when braking or turning on slippery surfaces. This instability can lead to unpleasant endings if the driver can't counteract the slide in time.

Note that snow tires, whether 2 or 4, will affect vehicle handling in all non-snow situations. The stiffer, heavier snow tires will noticeably change the turning and braking characteristics of the vehicle. Once the snow tires are installed, you must re-learn the behavior of the vehicle and drive accordingly.

➡ **Consider buying extra wheels on which to mount the snow tires. Once done, the "snow wheels" can be installed and removed as needed. This eliminates the potential damage to tires or wheels from seasonal removal and installation. Even if your vehicle has styled wheels, see if inexpensive steel wheels are available. Although the look of the vehicle will change, the expensive wheels will be protected from salt, curb hits and pothole damage.**

TIRE STORAGE

If they are mounted on wheels, store the tires at proper inflation pressure. All tires should be kept in a cool, dry place. If they are stored in the garage or basement, do not let them stand on a concrete floor; set them on strips of wood, a mat or a large stack of newspaper. Keeping them away from direct moisture is of paramount importance. Tires should not be stored upright, but in a flat position.

INFLATION & INSPECTION

▶ See Figures 99 thru 104

The importance of proper tire inflation cannot be overemphasized. A tire employs air as part of its structure. It is designed around the supporting

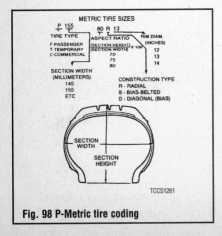

Fig. 98 P-Metric tire coding

Fig. 99 Tires with deep cuts, or cuts which bulge, should be replaced immediately

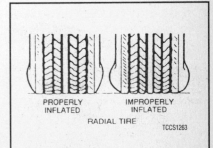

Fig. 100 Radial tires have a characteristic sidewall bulge; don't try to measure pressure by looking at the tire. Use a quality air pressure gauge

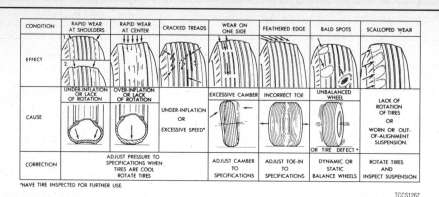

Fig. 101 Common tire wear patterns and causes

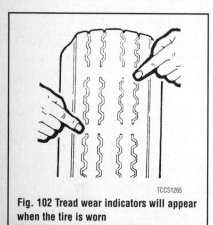

Fig. 102 Tread wear indicators will appear when the tire is worn

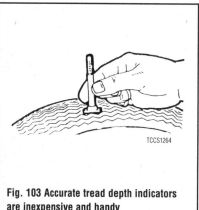

Fig. 103 Accurate tread depth indicators are inexpensive and handy

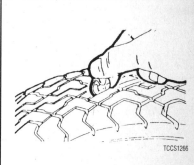

Fig. 104 A penny works well for a quick check of tread depth

strength of the air at a specified pressure. For this reason, improper inflation drastically reduces the tire's ability to perform as intended. A tire will lose some air in day-to-day use; having to add a few pounds of air periodically is not necessarily a sign of a leaking tire.

Two items should be a permanent fixture in every glove compartment: an accurate tire pressure gauge and a tread depth gauge. Check the tire pressure (including the spare) regularly with a pocket type gauge. Too often, the gauge on the end of the air hose at your corner garage is not accurate because it suffers too much abuse. Always check tire pressure when the tires are cold, as pressure increases with temperature. If you must move the vehicle to check the tire inflation, do not drive more than a mile before checking. A cold tire is generally one that has not been driven for more than three hours.

A plate or sticker is normally provided somewhere in the vehicle (door post, hood, tailgate or trunk lid) which shows the proper pressure for the tires. Never counteract excessive pressure build-up by bleeding off air pressure (letting some air out). This will cause the tire to run hotter and wear quicker.

✳✳ CAUTION

Never exceed the maximum tire pressure embossed on the tire! This is the pressure to be used when the tire is at maximum loading, but it is rarely the correct pressure for everyday driving. Con-sult the owner's manual or the tire pressure sticker for the correct tire pressure.

Once you've maintained the correct tire pressures for several weeks, you'll be familiar with the vehicle's braking and handling personality. Slight adjustments in tire pressures can fine-tune these characteristics, but never change the cold pressure specification by more than 2 psi. A slightly softer tire pressure will give a softer ride but also yield lower fuel mileage. A slightly harder tire will give crisper dry road handling but can cause skidding on wet surfaces. Unless you're fully attuned to the vehicle, stick to the recommended inflation pressures.

All automotive tires have built-in tread wear indicator bars that show up as ½ in. (13mm) wide smooth bands across the tire when 1/16 in. (1.5mm) of tread remains. The appearance of tread wear indicators means that the tires should be replaced. In fact, many states have laws prohibiting the use of tires with less than this amount of tread.

You can check your own tread depth with an inexpensive gauge or by using a Lincoln head penny. Slip the Lincoln penny (with Lincoln's head upside-down) into several tread grooves. If you can see the top of Lincoln's head in 2 adjacent grooves, the tire has less than 1/16 in. (1.5mm) tread left and should be replaced. You can measure snow tires in the same manner by using the "tails" side of the Lincoln penny. If you can see the top of the Lincoln memorial, it's time to replace the snow tire(s).

FLUIDS AND LUBRICANTS

Fluid Disposal

Used fluids such as engine oil, transmission fluid, antifreeze and brake fluid are hazardous wastes and must be disposed of properly. Before draining any fluids, consult with the local authorities; in many areas, waste oil, etc. is being accepted as part of recycling programs. A number of service stations and auto parts stores are also accepting waste fluids for recycling.

Be sure of the recycling center's policies before draining any fluids, as many will not accept different fluids that have been mixed together, such as oil and antifreeze.

Oil and Fuel Recommendations

ENGINE OIL

♦ See Figure 105

The recommended oil viscosities for sustained temperatures ranging from below 0°F (–18°C) to above 32°F (0°C) are listed in this Section. They are bro-

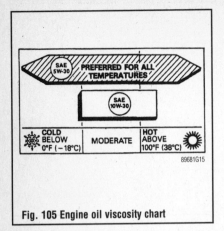

Fig. 105 Engine oil viscosity chart

Look for the API oil identification label when choosing your engine oil

Fig. 106 Typical octane rating label found on the gas pump

ken down into multi–viscosity and single viscosities. Multi–viscosity oils are recommended because of their wider range of acceptable temperatures and driving conditions.

➡Ford recommends that SAE 5W–30 viscosity engine oil should be used for all climate conditions, however, SAE 10W–30 is acceptable for vehicles operated in moderate to hot climates.

When adding oil to the crankcase or changing the oil or filter, it is important that oil of an equal quality to original equipment be used in your truck. The use of inferior oils may void the warranty, damage your engine, or both.

The SAE (Society of Automotive Engineers) grade number of oil indicates the viscosity of the oil (its ability to lubricate at a given temperature). The lower the SAE number, the lighter the oil; the lower the viscosity, the easier it is to crank the engine in cold weather but the less the oil will lubricate and protect the engine in high temperatures. This number is marked on every oil container.

Oil viscosities should be chosen from those oils recommended for the lowest anticipated temperatures during the oil change interval. Due to the need for an oil that embodies both good lubrication at high temperatures and easy cranking in cold weather, multigrade oils have been developed. Basically, a multigrade oil is thinner at low temperatures and thicker at high temperatures. For example, a 10W–40 oil (the W stands for winter) exhibits the characteristics of a 10 weight (SAE 10) oil when the truck is first started and the oil is cold. Its lighter weight allows it to travel to the lubricating surfaces quicker and offer less resistance to starter motor cranking than, say, a straight 30 weight (SAE 30) oil. But after the engine reaches operating temperature, the 10W–40 oil begins acting like straight 40 weight (SAE 40) oil, its heavier weight providing greater lubrication with less chance of foaming than a straight 30 weight oil.

The API (American Petroleum Institute) designations, also found on the oil container, indicates the classification of engine oil used under certain given operating conditions. Only oils designated for use Service SG heavy duty detergent should be used in your truck. Oils of the SG type perform may functions inside the engine besides their basic lubrication. Through a balanced system of metallic detergents and polymeric dispersants, the oil prevents high and low temperature deposits and also keeps sludge and dirt particles in suspension. Acids, particularly sulfuric acid, as well as other by–products of engine combustion are neutralized by the oil. If these acids are allowed to concentrate, they can cause corrosion and rapid wear of the internal engine parts.

✳✳ CAUTION

Non–detergent motor oils or straight mineral oils should not be used in your Ford gasoline engine.

Synthetic Oil

There are many excellent synthetic and fuel–efficient oils currently available that can provide better gas mileage, longer service life, and in some cases better engine protection. These benefits do not come without a few hitches, however; the main one being the price of synthetic oils, which is three or four times the price per quart of conventional oil.

Synthetic oil is not for every truck and every type of driving, so you should consider your engine's condition and your type of driving. Also, check your truck's warranty conditions regarding the use of synthetic oils.

High mileage engines are the wrong candidates for synthetic oil. Older engines with wear have a problem with synthetics: they "use" (consume during operation) more oil as they age. Slippery synthetic oils get past these worn parts easily. If your engine is "using" conventional oil, it will use synthetics much faster. Also, if your truck is leaking oil past old seals you'll have a much greater leak problem with synthetics.

FUEL

◆ **See Figure 106**

All of these trucks must use lead–free gasoline. It is recommended that 1991–99 trucks avoid the use of premium grade gasoline. This is due to the engine control system being calibrated towards the use of regular grade gasoline. The use of premium grades may actually cause driveability problems. Also, Ford recommends that using gasoline with an octane rating lower than 87 can cause persistant and heavy knocking, and may cause internal engine damage.

OPERATION IN FOREIGN COUNTRIES

If you plan to drive your truck outside the United States or Canada, there is a possibility that fuels will be too low in anti–knock quality and could produce engine damage. It is wise to consult with local authorities upon arrival in a foreign country to determine the best fuels available.

Engine

OIL LEVEL CHECK

Check the engine oil level every time you fill the gas tank. The oil level should be above the ADD mark and not above the FULL mark on the dipstick. Make sure that the dipstick is inserted into the crankcase as far as possible and that the vehicle is resting on level ground. Also, allow a few minutes after turn-

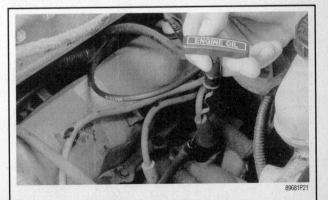

Remove the engine oil dipstick to check the level

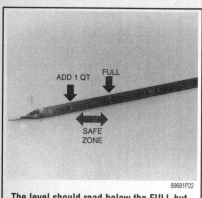

The level should read below the FULL but above the ADD mark

If necessary, remove the fill cap and add the proper amount and grade of oil to correct the level

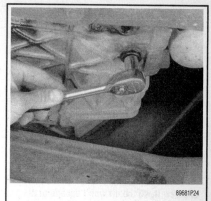

Loosen the oil pan drain plug . . .

ing off the engine for the oil to drain into the pan or an inaccurate reading will result.

1. Open the hood and remove the engine oil dipstick.
2. Wipe the dipstick with a clean, lint–free rag and reinsert it. Be sure to insert it all the way.
3. Pull out the dipstick and note the oil level. It should be between the **FULL** (MAX) mark and the **ADD** (MIN) mark.
4. If the level is below the lower mark, replace the dipstick and add fresh oil to bring the level within the proper range. Do not overfill.
5. Recheck the oil level and close the hood.

➥**Use a multi–grade oil with API classification SG or better.**

OIL & FILTER CHANGE

▶ **See Figures 107 and 108**

➥**The engine oil and oil filter should be changed at the recommended intervals on the Maintenance Chart. Though some manufacturer's have at times recommended changing the filter only at every other oil change, we recommend that you always change the filter with the oil. The benefit of fresh oil is quickly lost if the old filter is clogged and unable to do its job. Also, leaving the old filter in place leaves a significant amount of dirty oil in the system.**

The oil should be changed more frequently if the vehicle is being operated in a very dusty area. Before draining the oil, make sure that the engine is at operating temperature. Hot oil will hold more impurities in suspension and will flow better, allowing the removal of more oil and dirt.

➥**It is usually a good idea to place your ignition key in the box or bag with the bottles of fresh engine oil. In this way it will be VERY HARD to forget to refill the engine crankcase before you go to start the engine.**

1. Raise and support the vehicle safely on jackstands. Make sure the oil drain plug is at the lowest point on the oil pan. If not, you may have to raise the vehicle slightly higher on one jackstand (side) than the other.
2. Before you crawl under the car, take a look at where you will be working and gather all the necessary tools: such as a few wrenches or a strip of sockets, the drain pan, a clean rag, and, if the oil filter is more accessible from underneath the vehicle, you will also want to grab a bottle of oil, the new filter and a filter wrench at this time.

❈❈ CAUTION

The EPA warns that prolonged contact with used engine oil may cause a number of skin disorders, including cancer! You should make every effort to minimize you exposure to used engine oil. Protective gloves should be worn when changing the oil. Wash your hands and any other exposed skin areas as soon as possible after exposure to used engine oil. Soap and water, or waterless hand cleaner should be used.

3. Position the drain pan beneath the oil pan drain plug. Keep in mind that the fast flowing oil, which will spill out as you pull the plug from the pan, will

flow with enough force that it could miss the pan. Position the drain pan accordingly and be ready to move the pan more directly beneath the plug as the oil flow lessens to a trickle.

➥**Some 5.0L engines are equipped with 2 drain plugs (one in front of the crossmember and one behind it, closer to the transmission). Both should be removed to assure proper pan draining, but if the front end is raised and supported on ramps or jackstands, the oil may not fully drain from the front plug. The best way to assure all oil has been drained is to pull the plugs, then remove the jackstands and carefully lower the vehicle (make sure your drain pans are properly positioned because the relative positioning of the drain holes will change as the vehicle is lowered). Once you are sure the front portion of the oil pan has sufficiently drained, raise the vehicle and support it again with jackstands.**

4. Loosen the drain plug with a wrench (or socket and driver), then carefully unscrew the plug with your fingers. Use a rag to shield your fingers from the heat. Push in on the plug as you unscrew it so you can feel when all of the screw threads are out of the hole (and so you will keep the oil from seeping past the threads until you are ready to remove the plug). You can then remove the plug quickly to avoid having hot oil run down your arm. This will also help assure that have the plug in your hand, not in the bottom of a pan of hot oil.

❈❈ CAUTION

Be careful of the oil; when at operating temperature, it is hot enough to cause a severe burn.

5. Allow the oil to drain until nothing but a few drops come out of the drain hole. Check the drain plug to make sure the threads and sealing surface are not damaged. Carefully thread the plug into position and tighten it with a torque wrench to 15–25 ft. lbs. (20–34 Nm). If a torque wrench is not available, snug the drain plug and give a slight additional turn. You don't want the plug to fall out (as you would quickly become stranded), but the pan threads are EASILY stripped from overtighening (and this can be time consuming and/or costly to fix).
6. The oil filter is located on the bottom passenger side of the 4.0L (VIN X and E) engines and the bottom driverside of all other engines; position the drain pan beneath it. To remove the filter, you may need an oil filter wrench since the filter may have been fitted too tightly and/or the heat from the engine may have made it even tighter. A filter wrench can be obtained at any auto parts store and is well-worth the investment. Loosen the filter with the filter wrench. With a rag wrapped around the filter, unscrew the filter from the boss on the side of the engine. Be careful of hot oil that will run down the side of the filter. Make sure that your drain pan is under the filter before you start to remove it from the engine; should some of the hot oil happen to get on you, there will be a place to dump the filter in a hurry and the filter will usually spill a good bit of dirty oil as it is removed.
7. Wipe the base of the mounting boss with a clean, dry cloth. When you install the new filter, smear a small amount of fresh oil on the gasket with your finger, just enough to coat the entire contact surface. When you tighten the filter, rotate it about a half-turn after it contacts the mounting boss (or follow any instructions which are provided on the filter or parts box).

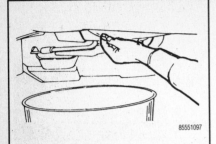

Fig. 107 Unscrew the plug by hand. Keep an inward pressure on the plug as you unscrew it, so the oil won't escape until you pull the plug away

Quickly remove the plug, to help keep the HOT oil off your hands, and allow the oil to drain completely

Use an oil filter wrench to loosen the old filter

Before installing a new oil filter, lightly coat the rubber gasket with clean engine oil

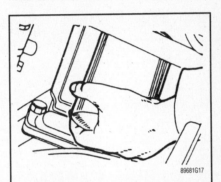

Fig. 108 Always install the new filter by hand (an oil filter wrench will usually lead to overtightening)

Remove the engine oil fill cap and, using a funnel to avoid spills, add the proper amount and grade of oil

❊❊ WARNING

Never operate the engine without engine oil, otherwise SEVERE engine damage will be the result.

8. Remove the jackstands and carefully lower the vehicle, then IMMEDIATELY refill the engine crankcase with the proper amount of oil. DO NOT WAIT TO DO THIS because if you forget and someone tries to start the car, severe engine damage will occur.

9. Refill the engine crankcase slowly, checking the level often. You may notice that it usually takes less than the amount of oil listed in the capacity chart to refill the crankcase. But, that is only until the engine is run and the oil filter is filled with oil. To make sure the proper level is obtained, run the engine to normal operating temperature. While the engine is warming, look under the vehicle for any oil leaks, and if found, shut the engine **OFF** immediately then fix the leak. Shut the engine **OFF**, allow the oil to drain back into the oil pan, and recheck the level. Top off the oil at this time to the fill mark.

➡ **If the vehicle is not resting on level ground, the oil level reading on the dipstick may be slightly off. Be sure to check the level only when the car is sitting level.**

10. Drain your used oil in a suitable container for recycling and clean-up your tools, as you will be needing them again in a couple of thousand more miles (kilometers).

Manual Transmission

FLUID RECOMMENDATION

The lubricant in the transmission should be checked and changed periodically, except when the vehicle has been operated in deep water and water has entered the transmission. When this happens, change the lubricant in the transmission as soon as possible. Use Standard Transmission Lube SAE 80 in the Mitsubishi 5-speed transmission, and Mercon in the Mazda M5OD transmission.

LEVEL CHECK

The fluid level should be checked every six months or 6000 miles (9600 km), whichever comes first.

1. Park the truck on a level surface, turn the engine **OFF**, FIRMLY apply the parking brake and block the drive wheels.

➡ **Ground clearance may make access to the transmission filler plug impossible without raising and supporting the vehicle, BUT, if this is done, the truck MUST be supported at four corners and level. If only the front or rear is supported, an improper fluid level will be indicated. If you are going to place the truck on four jackstands, this might be the perfect opportunity to rotate the tires as well.**

2. Remove the filler plug from the side of the transmission case using a ⅜ in. drive ratchet and extension. The fluid level should be even with the bottom of the filler hole.

3. If additional fluid is necessary, add it through the filler hole using a siphon pump or squeeze bottle.

4. When you are finished, carefully install the filler plug, but DO NOT overtighten it and damage the housing.

DRAIN & REFILL

Under normal conditions, the manufacturer feels that manual transmission fluid should not need to be changed. However, if the truck is driven in deep water (as high as the transmission casing) it is a good idea to replace the fluid. Little harm can come from a fluid change when you have just purchased a used vehicle, especially since the condition of the transmission fluid is usually not known.

If the fluid is to be drained, it is a good idea to warm the fluid first so it will flow better. This can be accomplished by 15–20 miles of highway driving. Fluid which is warmed to normal operating temperature will flow faster, drain more completely and remove more contaminants from the housing.

1. Drive the vehicle to assure the fluid is at normal operating temperature.

2. Raise and support the vehicle securely on jackstands. Remember that the vehicle must be supported level (usually at four points) so the proper amount of fluid can be added.

3. Place a drain pan under the transmission housing, below the drain plug. Remember that the fluid will likely flow with some force at first (arcing outward from the transmission), and will not just drip straight downward into the pan. Position the drain pan accordingly and move it more directly beneath the drain plug as the flow slows to a trickle.

➡To insure that the fill plug is not frozen or rusted in place, remove it from the transmission BEFORE removing the drain plug. It would be unfortunate to drain all of your transmission fluid and then realize that the fill plug is stripped or frozen in place.

4. Remove the fill plug, then the drain plug and allow the transmission fluid to drain out.

➡The transmission drain plug is usually a square receiver which is designed to accept a ⅜ in. driver such as a ratchet or extension.

5. Once the transmission has drained sufficiently, install the drain plug until secure.
6. Fill the transmission to the proper level with the required fluid.
7. Reinstall the filler plug once you are finished.
8. Remove the jackstands and carefully lower the vehicle.

Automatic Transmission

FLUID RECOMMENDATION

Refer to the dipstick to confirm automatic transmission fluid specifications. All transmissions use Mercon® automatic transmission fluid. DO NOT use improper fluids such as Dexron® or gear oil. Use of improper fluids could lead to leaks or transmission damage.

LEVEL CHECK

▶ **See Figure 109**

It is very important to maintain the proper fluid level in an automatic transmission. If the level is either too high or too low, poor shifting operation and

Fig. 109 The transmission dipstick is located near the rear of the engine

internal damage are likely to occur. For this reason, a regular check of the fluid level is essential.

Although it is best to check fluid at normal operating temperature, it can be checked overnight cold, if the ambient temperatures are 50–95°F (21–35°C). If so, refer to the dots on the transmission dipstick instead of the cross-hatched area and level marking lines.

1. Drive the vehicle for 15–20 minutes, allowing the transmission to reach operating temperature.

➡If the car is driven at extended highway speeds, is driven in city traffic in hot weather or is being used to pull a trailer, fluid temperatures will likely exceed normal operating and checking ranges. In these circumstances, give the fluid time to cool (about 30 minutes) before checking the level.

2. Park the car on a level surface, apply the parking brake and leave the engine idling. Make sure the parking brake is FIRMLY ENGAGED. Shift the transmission and engage each gear, then place the selector in **P** (PARK).

3. Open the hood and locate the transmission dipstick. Wipe away any dirt in the area of the dipstick to prevent it from falling into the filler tube. Withdraw the dipstick, wipe it with a clean, lint-free rag and reinsert it until it fully seats.

4. Withdraw the dipstick and hold it horizontally while noting the fluid level. It should be between the upper (FULL) and the lower (ADD) marks.

5. If the level is below the lower mark, use a funnel and add fluid in small quantities through the dipstick filler neck. Keep the engine running while adding fluid and check the level after each small amount. DO NOT overfill as this could lead to foaming and transmission damage or seal leaks.

➡Since the transmission fluid is added through the dipstick tube, if you check the fluid too soon after adding fluid an incorrect reading may occur. After adding fluid, wait a few minutes to allow it to fully drain into the transmission.

DRAIN, PAN/FILTER SERVICE & REFILL

▶ **See Figures 110 and 111**

Transmission Fluid Pan and Filter

Under normal service (moderate highway driving excluding excessive hot or cold conditions), the manufacturer feels that automatic transmission fluid should not need periodic changing. However, if a major service is performed to the transmission, if transmission fluid becomes burnt or discolored through severe usage or if the vehicle is subjected to constant stop-and-go driving in hot weather, trailer towing, long periods of highway use at high speeds, fluid should be changed to prevent transmission damage. A preventive maintenance change is therefore recommended for most vehicles at least every 90,000 miles (145,000 km).

➡Although not a required service, transmission fluid changing can help assure a trouble-free transmission. Likewise, changing the transmission filter at this time is also added insurance.

1. Raise the car and support it securely on jackstands.

➡The torque converters on some transmissions are equipped with drain plugs. Because it may take some time to drain the fluid from the converter, you may wish to follow that procedure at this time, then come back to the pan and filter removal.

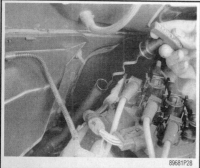

With the engine idling in park (P), remove the Automatic Transmission Fluid (ATF) level dipstick

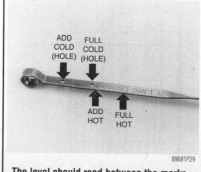

The level should read between the marks. Cold marks (holes) are for below operating temperature checks

If fluid is needed, use a funnel (to avoid spills) and add the required type and amount of ATF

Before removing the transmission fluid pan, insure that the area is clean of dirt and debris

Loosen all of the pan attaching bolts to within a few turns of complete removal

Once the pan is removed, discard the old gasket and insure that the mating surfaces are clean

Inspect this magnet inside of the pan for any large pieces of debris. A light gray coating is normal

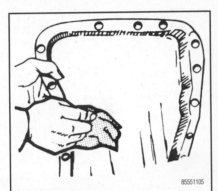

Fig. 110 Clean the pan thoroughly with a safe solvent and allow it to air dry

The transmission filter is secured by a mounting bolt (arrow). Some models may use two bolts

Remove the filter mounting bolt . . .

. . . then pull the filter free from the transmission

Fig. 111 Install a new pan gasket

Fill the transmission with the proper amount of ATF

2. Place a large drain pan under the transmission.

3. Loosen all of the pan attaching bolts to within a few turns of complete removal, then carefully break the gasket seal allowing most of the fluid to drain over the edge of the pan.

✳✳ CAUTION

DO NOT force the pan while breaking the gasket seal. DO NOT allow the pan flange to become bent or otherwise damaged.

4. When fluid has drained to the level of the pan flange, remove the pan bolts and carefully lower the pan doing your best to drain the rest of the fluid into the drain pan.

5. Clean the transmission oil pan thoroughly using a safe solvent, then allow it to air dry. DO NOT use a cloth to dry the pan which might leave behind bits of lint. Discard the old pan gasket.

6. If necessary, remove the Automatic Transmission Fluid (ATF) filter mounting bolts, then remove the filter by pulling it down and off of the valve body. Make sure any gaskets or seals are removed with the old filter. The transmission usually has one round seal and a rectangular gasket.

.7. Install the new oil filter screen making sure all gaskets or seals are in place, then secure using the retaining screws, if applicable.

8. Place a new gasket on the fluid pan, then install the pan to the transmission. Tighten the attaching bolts to 71–119 inch lbs. (8–13 Nm).

9. Add three quarts (six quarts if the torque converter was drained) of fluid to the transmission through the filler tube.

10. Remove the jackstands and carefully lower the vehicle.

11. Start the engine and move the gear selector through all gears in the shift pattern. Allow the engine to reach normal operating temperature.

12. Check the transmission fluid level. Add fluid, as necessary, to obtain the correct level.

Torque Converter

➡**If it is necessary to perform a complete drain and refill, it will be necessary to remove the remaining fluid from the torque converter and the cooler lines.**

1. Remove the converter housing lower cover
2. Rotate the torque converter until the drain plug comes into view.
3. Remove the drain plug and allow the transmission fluid to drain.
4. If necessary disconnect the cooler lines at the transmission and flush them using low pressure, compressed air. Use care when applying air pressure to one of the cooler lines, as fluid will drain, or even shoot, out of the other cooler line.

Transfer Case

FLUID RECOMMENDATION

Use Mercon® automatic transmission fluid when refilling or adding fluid to the transfer case.

LEVEL CHECK

1. Position the vehicle on level ground.
2. Remove the transfer case fill plug (the upper plug) located on the rear of the transfer case. The fluid level should be up to the fill hole.
3. If lubricant doesn't run out when the plug is removed, add lubricant until it does run out.
4. Replace the fill plug.

DRAIN & REFILL

The manufacturer recommends that the transfer case fluid should be changed every 60,000 miles (96,000km). However, if the truck is driven in deep water (as high as the transfer case housing) it is a good idea to replace the fluid. Little harm can come from a fluid change when you have just purchased a used vehi-

cle, especially since the condition of the transfer case fluid is usually not known.

. If the fluid is to be drained, it is a good idea to warm the fluid first so it will flow better. This can be accomplished by 15–20 miles of highway driving. Fluid which is warmed to normal operating temperature will flow faster, drain more completely and remove more contaminants from the housing.

1. Drive the vehicle to assure the fluid is at normal operating temperature.
2. Raise and support the vehicle securely on jackstands. Remember that the vehicle must be supported level (usually at four points) so the proper amount of fluid can be added.
3. Place a drain pan under the transfer case housing, below the drain plug. Remember that the fluid will likely flow with some force at first (arcing outward from the transmission), and will not just drip straight downward into the pan. Position the drain pan accordingly and move it more directly beneath the drain plug as the flow slows to a trickle.

➡**To insure that the fill plug is not frozen or rusted in place, remove it from the transfer case BEFORE removing the drain plug. It would be unfortunate to drain all of your transfer case fluid and then realize that the fill plug is stripped or frozen in place.**

4. Remove the fill plug, then the drain plug and allow the transfer case fluid to drain out.

➡**The transfer case drain plug is usually a square receiver which is designed to accept a ⅜ in. driver such as a ratchet or extension.**

5. Once the transfer case has drained sufficiently, install the drain plug until secure.
6. Fill the transfer case to the proper level with the required fluid.
7. Reinstall the filler plug once you are finished.
8. Remove the jackstands and carefully lower the vehicle.

Front and Rear Drive Axle

FLUID RECOMMENDATION

Use hypoid gear lubricant SAE 80W or 90W.

➡**On models with the front locking differential, add 2 oz. of friction modifier Ford part No. EST–M2C118–A. On models with the rear locking differential, use only locking differential fluid Ford part No. ESP–M2C154–A or its equivalent, and add 4 oz. of friction modifier Ford part No. EST–M2C118–A.**

LEVEL CHECK

The fluid level in the drive axles should be checked at each oil change. Like the manual transmission which is available, the rear axle does not have a dipstick to check fluid level. Instead, a filler plug is located in the side of the housing (or in the side of the cover), at a level just barely above the level to which fluid should fill the housing. To check the fluid level:

1. Make sure the transmission is in **P** (A/T) or in gear on a manual, then FIRMLY set the parking brake and block the drive wheels.

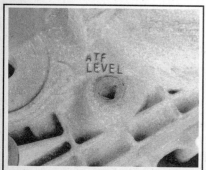
89681P39

The transfer case fill/level check plug is the upper most plug, located on the rear of the case

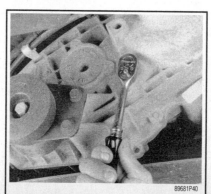
89681P40

Remove the plug using a ⅜ in. drive ratchet

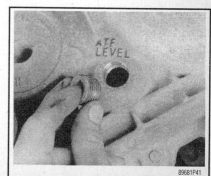
89681P41

Once the plug is removed, fluid should trickle out of the hole. If not, add Mercon ATF fluid until it does

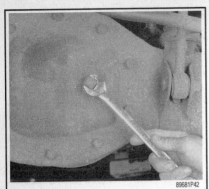

To check the front drive axle fluid level, loosen the fill plug . . .

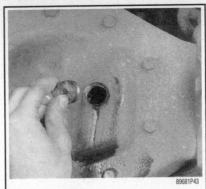

. . . then remove it. Fluid should trickle out of the hole

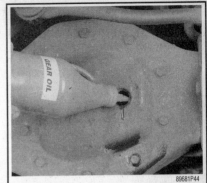

If not, add the proper grade of lubricant until it does

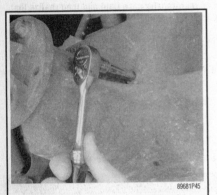

To check the rear drive axle fluid level, loosen the fill plug . . .

. . . then remove it. Fluid should trickle out of the hole

If necessary, add the proper grade of lubricant until fluid trickles out

2. Check under the vehicle to see if there is sufficient clearance for you to access the filler plug on the side of the differential housing. If not you will have to raise and support the vehicle using jackstands at four points to make sure it is completely level. Failure to support the vehicle level will prevent from properly checking or filling the drive axle fluid.

3. Thoroughly clean the area surrounding the fill plug. This will prevent any dirt from entering the housing and contaminating the gear oil.

4. Remove the fill plug and make sure that the gear oil is up to the bottom of the fill hole. If a slight amount of lubricant does not drip out of the hole when the plug is removed, additional lubricant should be added. Use hypoid gear lubricant SAE 80 or 90.

➡ **If the differential is a Traction-Lok limited-slip unit, be sure to use 4 oz. of Ford Friction Modifier C8AZ-19B546-A or equivalent special limited-slip additive with the lubricant.**

5. Once you are finished, install the fill plug, then (if raised) remove the jackstands and lower the vehicle.

DRAIN & REFILL

Drain and refill the drive axle housings every 100,000 miles (160,000 km) or any time the vehicle is driven in high water (up to the axle). Although some fluid can be removed using a suction gun, the best method is to remove the axle housing cover (if equipped) to ensure that all of any present contaminants are removed. As with any fluid change, the oil should be at normal operating temperature to assure the best flow and removal of fluid/contaminants.

➡ **Most front and some rear drive axle assemblies do not have a removable cover for fluid draining. However, these units may have a drain plug instead. Drain plug equipped drive axles can be serviced in the same manner as the manual transmission and/or transfer case. If no drain plug is found, you will need to use a suction gun through the fill hole to remove the fluid. The procedure below is for housing cover equipped axles.**

1. Drive the vehicle until the lubricant reaches normal operating temperature.

2. If necessary for access, raise and support the vehicle safely using jackstands, but be sure that the vehicle is level so you can properly refill the axle when you are finished.

➡ **If a suction gun is used to drain the fluid, remove the fill plug and insert the suction tube into the fill hole until it rests at the lowest most point inside the housing. Operate the suction gun as per the manufacturers directions. When the fluid is completely removed, skip to the differential filling procedure.**

3. Use a wire brush to clean the area around the differential. This will help prevent dirt from contaminating the differential housing while the cover is removed.

4. Position a drain pan under the drive axle.

5. Loosen and remove all but 2 of the housing cover's upper or side retaining bolts. The remaining 2 bolts should then be loosened to within a few turns of complete removal. Use a small prytool to carefully break the gasket seal at the base of the cover and allow the lubricant to drain. Be VERY careful not to force or damage the cover and gasket mating surface.

6. Once most of the fluid has drained, remove the final retaining bolts and separate the cover from the housing.

To fill the differential:

7. Carefully clean the gasket mating surfaces of the cover and axle housing of any remaining gasket or sealer. A putty knife is a good tool to use for this. You may want to cover the differential gears using a rag or piece of plastic to prevent contaminating them with dirt or pieces of the old gasket.

8. Install the housing cover using a new gasket and sealant. Tighten the retaining bolts using a crisscross pattern.

➡ **Make sure the vehicle is level before attempting to add fluid to the drive axle, otherwise an incorrect fluid level will result.**

9. Refill the drive axle housing using the proper grade and quantity of lubricant. Install the filler plug, operate the vehicle and check for any leaks.

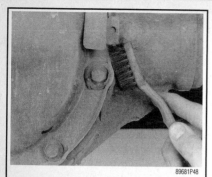

Remove the fill plug, then clean the area around the axle housing cover to prevent dirt from entering it

Loosen and remove all but two of the cover retaining bolts. Don't lose the axle identification tag

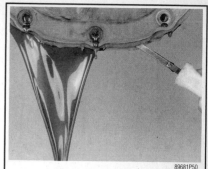

With the remaining bolts loose, carefully pry out on the cover (to break the seal) and allow the fluid to drain

Once most of the fluid has drained, remove the remaining bolts and pull the cover from the housing

Remove any old gasket material from the sealing surfaces then clean them of any residual oil

Cooling System

▶ See Figure 112

✳✳ CAUTION

Never remove the radiator cap under any conditions while the engine is running! Failure to follow these instructions could result in damage to the cooling system and/or personal injury. To avoid having scalding hot coolant or steam blow out of the radiator, use extreme care when removing the radiator cap from a hot radiator. Wait until the engine has cooled, then wrap a thick cloth around the radiator cap and turn it slowly to the first stop. Step back while the pressure is released from the cooling system. When you are sure the pressure has been released, press down on the radiator cap (with the cloth still in position), turn and remove the cap.

FLUID RECOMMENDATIONS

The recommended coolant for all vehicles covered by this manual is a 50/50 mixture of ethylene glycol and water for year-round use. Choose an aluminum compatible, good quality antifreeze with water pump lubricants, rust inhibitors and other corrosion inhibitors along with acid neutralizers.

INSPECTION

▶ See Figures 113 and 114

Any time you have the hood open, glance at the coolant recovery tank to make sure it is properly filled. Top of the cooling system using the recovery tank and its markings as a guideline. If you top off the system, make a note of it to check again soon. A coolant level that consistently drops is usually a sign of a small, hard to detect leak, though in the worst case it could be a sign of an internal engine leak (blown head gasket/cracked block? . . . check the engine oil for coolant contamination). In most cases, you will be able to trace the leak to a loose fitting or damaged hose (and you might solve a problem before it leaves you stranded). Evaporating ethylene glycol antifreeze will leave small, white (salt like) deposits, which can be helpful in tracing a leak.

At least annually or every 12,000 miles (19,000 km), all hoses, fittings and cooling system connections should be inspected for damage, wear or leaks. Hose clamps should be checked for tightness, and soft or cracked hoses should be replaced. Damp spots, or accumulations of rust or dye near hoses or fittings indicate possible leakage. These must be corrected before filling the system with

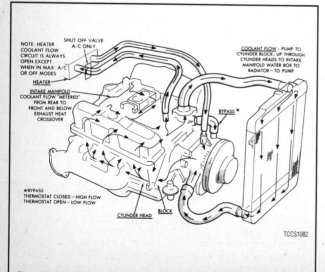

Fig. 112 Cut-away view of a typical cooling system flow

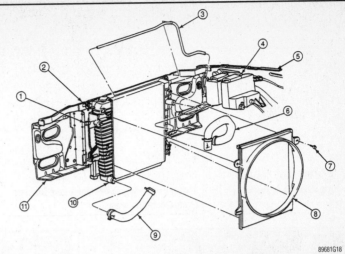

1. U-nut assembly
2. Radiator support
3. Overflow hose
4. Radiator overflow and washer fluid tanks
5. Inner fender
6. Upper radiator hose
7. Shroud attaching screw
8. Fan should
9. Lower radiator hose
10. Radiator
11. Radiator support

89681G18

Fig. 113 Common cooling system components found on all models (not shown is the water pump)—3.0L equipped ranger shown, other models are similar

89681P54

To add coolant, remove the lid from the coolant recovery tank . . .

89681P55

. . . then add enough coolant to attain the proper level as indicated on the tank. Use a funnel to avoid spills

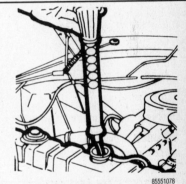

85551078

Fig. 114 Checking antifreeze protection with an inexpensive tester

fresh coolant. The pressure cap should be examined for signs of deterioration and aging. The fan belt and/or other drive belt(s) should be inspected and adjusted to the proper tension. Refer to the information on drive belts found earlier in this section. Finally, if everything looks good, obtain an antifreeze/coolant testing hydrometer in order to check the freeze and boil-over protection capabilities of the coolant currently in your engine. Old or improperly mixed coolant should be replaced.

> ✳✳ **CAUTION**
>
> When draining coolant, keep in mind that cats and dogs are attracted to ethylene glycol antifreeze, and are likely to drink any that is left in an uncovered container or in puddles on the ground. This will prove fatal in sufficient quantity. Always drain coolant into a sealable container. Coolant may be reused unless it is contaminated or several years old.

At least once every 3 years or 36,000 miles (48,000 km), the engine cooling system should be inspected, flushed and refilled with fresh coolant. If the coolant is left in the system too long, it loses its ability to prevent rust and corrosion. If the coolant has too much water, it won't protect against freezing.

If you experience problems with your cooling system, such as overheating or boiling-over, check the simple before expecting the complicated. Make sure the system can fully pressurize (are all the connections tight/is the radiator cap on properly, is the cap seal intact?). Ideally, a pressure tester should be connected to the radiator opening and the system should be pressurized and inspected for leaks. If no obvious problems are found, use a hydrometer antifreeze/coolant tester (available at most automotive supply stores) to check the condition and concentration of the antifreeze in your cooling system. Excessively old coolant or the wrong proportions of water and coolant will hurt the coolant's boiling and freezing points.

Check the Radiator Cap

▶ **See Figure 115**

While you are checking the coolant level, check the radiator cap for a worn or cracked gasket. If the cap doesn't seal properly, fluid will be lost and the engine will overheat. Worn caps should be replaced with new ones.

Clean Radiator of Debris

▶ **See Figure 116**

Periodically, clean any debris—leaves, paper, insects, etc.— from the radiator fins. Pick the large pieces off by hand. The smaller pieces can be washed away with water pressure from a hose.

Carefully straighten any bent radiator fins with a pair of needle-nosed pliers. Be careful; the fins are very soft. Don't wiggle the fins back and forth too much. Straighten them once and try not to move them again.

DRAINING, FLUSHING & REFILLING

▶ **See Figure 117**

> ✳✳ **CAUTION**
>
> When draining coolant, keep in mind that cats and dogs are attracted to ethylene glycol antifreeze, and are likely to drink any that is left in an uncovered container or in puddles on the ground. This will prove fatal in sufficient quantity. Always drain coolant into a sealable container. Coolant may be reused unless it is contaminated or several years old.

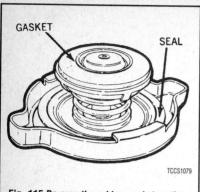

Fig. 115 Be sure the rubber gasket on the radiator cap has a tight seal

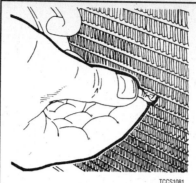

Fig. 116 Periodically remove all debris from the radiator fins

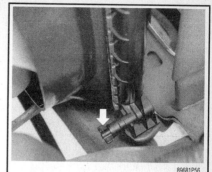

To drain the cooling system, open the radiator petcock (arrow) and allow the coolant to drain into a container

A length of hose (A) can be fitted to the petcock (B) to help direct the flow of the coolant and avoid spills

To refill the system with coolant, remove the radiator cap. NEVER remove the cap if the system is HOT

Use a funnel to avoid spills and fill the radiator with a 50/50 mixture of water/antifreeze

Fig. 117 The system should be pressure checked whenever leakage is suspected and can't be seen

A complete drain and refill of the cooling system at least every 30,000 miles (48,000 km) or 3 years will remove the accumulated rust, scale and other deposits. The recommended coolant for most late model cars is a 50/50 mixture of ethylene glycol and water for year-round use. Choose a good quality antifreeze with water pump lubricants, rust inhibitors and other corrosion inhibitors along with acid neutralizers.

➡ **Before opening the radiator petcock, spray it with some penetrating lubricant.**

1. Drain the existing antifreeze and coolant. Open the radiator and engine drains (petcocks) or disconnect the bottom radiator hose at the radiator outlet. The engine block drain plugs can also be temporarily removed to drain coolant, but they are often hard to get at and it is not really necessary for this procedure.
2. Close the petcock or reconnect the hose (and install any block drain plugs which may have been removed), then fill the system with water.
3. Add a can of quality radiator flush.
4. Idle the engine until the upper radiator hose gets hot.
5. Drain the system again.
6. Repeat this process until the drained water is clear and free of scale.
7. Close all petcocks and connect any loose hoses.

8. If equipped with a coolant recovery system, flush the reservoir with water and leave empty.
9. Determine the capacity of the coolant system, then properly refill the cooling system with a 50/50 mixture of fresh coolant and water, as follows:
    a. Fill the radiator with coolant until it reaches the radiator filler neck seat.
    b. Start the engine and allow it to idle until the thermostat opens (the upper radiator hose will become hot).
    c. Turn the engine **OFF** and refill the radiator until the coolant level is at the filler neck seat.
    d. Fill the engine coolant overflow tank with coolant to the FULL HOT mark, then install the radiator cap.
10. If available, install a pressure tester and check for leaks. If a pressure tester is not available, run the engine until normal operating temperature is reached (allowing the system to naturally pressurize), then check for leaks.

✳✳ CAUTION

If you are checking for leaks with the system at normal operating temperature, BE EXTREMELY CAREFUL not to touch any moving or hot engine parts. Once the temperature has been reached, shut the engine OFF, and check for leaks around the hose fittings and connections which were removed earlier.

11. Check the level of protection with an antifreeze/coolant hydrometer.

Brake Master Cylinder

FLUID RECOMMENDATIONS

✳✳ WARNING

BRAKE FLUID EATS PAINT. Take great care not to splash or spill brake fluid on painted surfaces. Should you spill a small amount on the car's finish, don't panic, just flush the area with plenty of water.

When adding fluid to the system ONLY use fresh DOT 3 brake fluid from a sealed container. DOT 3 brake fluid will absorb moisture when it is exposed to the atmosphere, which will lower its boiling point. A container that has been opened once, closed and placed on a shelf will allow enough moisture to enter over time to contaminate the fluid within. If your brake fluid is contaminated with water, you could boil the brake fluid under hard braking and loose all/some of the brake system. Don't take the risk, buy fresh brake fluid whenever you must add to the system.

LEVEL CHECK

Brake fluid level and condition is a safety related item and it should be checked ANY TIME the hood is opened. Your vehicle should not use brake fluid rapidly (unless there is a leak in the system), but the level should drop slowly in relation to brake pad wear.

The master cylinder reservoir is located under the hood, on the left side firewall. All vehicles covered by this manual should be equipped with a see-through plastic reservoir. This makes checking the level easy and helps reduce the risk of fluid contamination (since you don't have to expose the fluid by opening the cap to check the level). Fluid should be kept near the FULL line or between the MIN and MAX lines, depending on how the reservoir is marked.

If it becomes necessary to add fluid to the system, take a moment to clean the area around the cap and reservoir. Use a clean rag to wipe away dust and dirt which could enter the reservoir after the cover is removed. If the level of the brake fluid is less than half the volume of the reservoir (and the brake pads are not approaching a replacement point), it is advised that you check the brake system for leaks. Leaks in the hydraulic system often occur at the wheel cylinders.

Clutch Master Cylinder

FLUID RECOMMENDATIONS

The hydraulic clutch control system consists of a fluid reservoir, a master cylinder, a slave cylinder and connecting tubing. It uses heavy duty brake fluid meeting DOT 3 specification.

LEVEL CHECK

▶ See Figure 118

The clutch master cylinder reservoir is located under the hood, on the left side firewall. The fluid in the reservoir will slowly increase or rise as the clutch wears. As long as the fluid level is visible at or above the step in the reservoir body, "top-off" is not necessary and should not be done to prevent overflow as well as possible contamination of the fluid while it is exposed.

➡ Before removing the clutch master cylinder reservoir cap, make sure the vehicle is resting on level ground and clean all dirt away from the top of the reservoir.

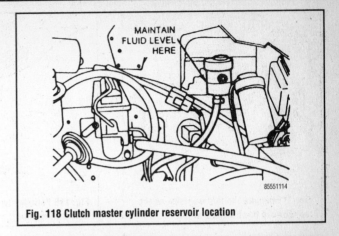

Fig. 118 Clutch master cylinder reservoir location

Power Steering Pump Reservoir

FLUID RECOMMENDATIONS

1991–95 Models

The 1991–95 Ranger/Explorer vehicles use either Type F Automatic Transmission Fluid (ATF) or Ford Premium Power Steering Fluid meeting Ford specification ESW-M2C33-F. Ensure that the fluid added to the power steering pump reservoir is new and clean.

1996–99 Models

The 1996–99 models utilize Mercon® Automatic Transmission Fluid (ATF). Ensure that the fluid added to the power steering pump reservoir is new and clean.

LEVEL CHECK

The level of the power steering fluid should be checked in the reservoir periodically, at least once a year. Fluid is checked using the dipstick which is attached to the reservoir cap. Although the dipstick is equipped with range markings so that you can check the fluid hot or cold, it is recommended that you check the fluid at normal operating temperature (HOT).

✷✷ WARNING

Extensive driving with a low power steering fluid level can damage the power steering pump.

➡ The power steering pump on 1991–95 vehicles requires the use of power steering fluid that meets Ford's specification ESW-M2C33-F, or an equivalent Type F ATF. 1996–99 models require Mercon® ATF.

The brake master cylinder fluid level should be maintained at the MAX mark on the reservoir

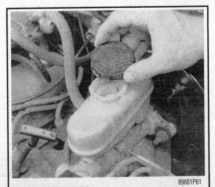

If fluid must be added, thoroughly clean the fill cap area then remove the cap . . .

. . . and add only fresh, clean DOT 3 brake fluid until the proper level is attained

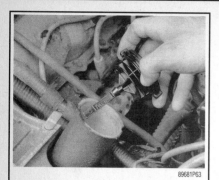

To check power steering fluid level, remove the dipstick attached to the cap and read the level

The level should read between the MAX and MIN marks on the dipstick (HOT marks on opposite side)

Add the proper amount and type of fluid to attain a FULL (MAX) reading on the dipstick

1. Warm the fluid to normal operating temperature by driving for at least one mile, or start the engine and allow it to idle for five minutes.

2. With the engine idling, turn the steering wheel back-and-forth several times from lock-to-lock, then center the wheels and shut the engine **OFF**.

3. Locate the power steering pump reservoir, then remove the cap/dipstick and note the level as indicated by the markings. To be sure of your reading, put the cap back in position, remove it again and double check the level.

4. If the level is below the indicator markings, add fluid to bring it up to the proper level (a funnel is usually very helpful). If you are checking the level after running the engine or driving, make sure you add enough fluid to bring it to the FULL HOT range, but like most automotive fluids, DO NOT overfill.

5. When you are finished, install the dipstick and be sure it is secure.

Manual Steering Gear

The steering gear is factory–filled with steering gear grease. Changing of this lubricant should not be performed and the housing should not be drained, lubricant is not required for the life of the steering gear.

Chassis Greasing

Chassis greasing should be performed every 12 months or 12,000 miles (19,000 km) for most trucks. Greasing can be performed with a commercial pressurized grease gun or at home by using a hand-operated grease gun. Wipe the grease fittings clean before greasing in order to prevent the possibility of forcing any dirt into the component.

There are far less grease points on the modern automotive chassis than there were on trucks of yesteryear. The tie rod ends on these vehicles should be checked and lubricated periodically, and the front suspension should be checked for grease fittings.

A water resistant long life grease that meets Ford's ESA-M1C75-B specification should be used for all chassis greasing applications.

Body Lubrication

Whenever you take care of chassis greasing it is also advised that you walk around the vehicle and give attention to a number of other surfaces which require a variety of lubrication/protection.

HOOD/DOOR LATCH & HINGES

Wipe clean any exposed surfaces of the door hatches and hinges, hood latch and auxiliary catch. Then, treat the surfaces using a multi-purpose grease spray that meets Ford's ESR-M1C159-A specification.

LOCK CYLINDERS

Should be treated with Ford Lock Lubricant, part no. D8AZ-19587-AA or equivalent. Consult your local parts supplier for equivalent lubricants.

DOOR WEATHERSTRIPPING

Spray the door weatherstripping using a silicone lubricant to help pressure the rubber.

THROTTLE VALVE (TV) & KICKDOWN LINKAGE

A water resistant long life grease that meets Ford's ESA-M1C75-B specification should be used for all linkages.

Wheel Bearings

♦ See Figure 119

➡This procedure only covers the repacking (or greasing) of the wheel bearings. For the removal procedures see the appropriate Section for you vehicle. For 4 wheel drive vehicles, see Section 7. For 2 wheel drive vehicles, see Section 8.

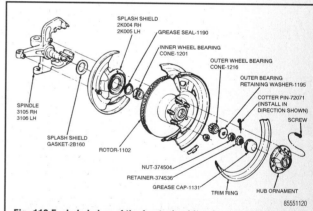

Fig. 119 Exploded view of the front wheel bearings and related components—2WD model shown, 4WD is similar

REPACKING

♦ See Figure 120

It is recommended that the front wheel bearings be cleaned, inspected and repacked every 30,000 miles (48,000km) and as soon as possible if the front hubs have been submerged in water.

➡Sodium based grease is not compatible with lithium based grease. Be careful not to mix the two types. The best way to prevent this is to completely clean all of the old grease from the hub assembly before installing any new grease.

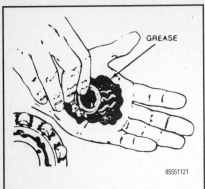

Fig. 120 Packing the wheel bearings with grease

Thoroughly pack the bearing with fresh, high temperature wheel-bearing grease before installation

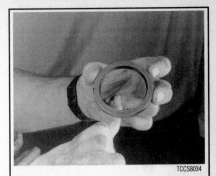

Apply a thin coat of fresh grease to the new bearing grease seal before installing it into the hub

Before handling the bearings there are a few things that you should remember to do and try to avoid.

DO the following:
- Remove all outside dirt from the housing before exposing the bearing.
- Treat a used bearing as gently as you would a new one.
- Work with clean tools in clean surroundings.
- Use clean, dry canvas gloves, or at least clean, dry hands.
- Clean solvents and flushing fluids are a must.
- Use clean paper when laying out the bearings to dry.
- Protect disassembled bearings from rust and dirt. Cover them up.
- Use clean rags to wipe bearings.
- Keep the bearings in oil–proof paper when they are to be stored or are not in use.
- Clean the inside of the housing before replacing the bearing.

Do NOT do the following:
- Don't work in dirty surroundings.
- Don't use dirty, chipped, or damaged tools.
- Try not to work on wooden work benches, or use wooden mallets.
- Don't handle bearings with dirty or moist hands.
- Do not use gasoline for cleaning; use a safe solvent.
- Do not spin–dry bearings with compressed air. They will be damaged.
- Do not spin unclean bearings.
- Avoid using cotton waste or dirty clothes to wipe bearings.
- Try not to scratch or nick bearing surfaces.
- Do not allow the bearing to come in contact with dirt or rust at any time.

➡**4WD vehicles should refer to Section 7 for bearing removal. 2WD vehicles should refer to Section 8 for bearing removal.**

1. Remove the bearing assemblies from the hub.

➡**Do not spin the bearings with compressed air while drying them.**

2. Clean the inner and outer bearings with solvent. Thoroughly clean the hub, bearing cups and spindle. Remove any traces of the old grease. Dry all of the components with a soft, lint-free cloth.

3. Inspect the cups for scratches, pits, excessive wear, and other damage. If found, replace them.
   a. The cups are removed from the hub by driving them out with a drift pin. They are installed in the same manner.
4. If it is determined that the cups are in satisfactory condition and are to remain in the hub, inspect the bearings in the same manner. Replace the bearings if necessary.

➡**When replacing either the bearing or the cup, both parts should be replaced as a unit.**

5. Cover the spindle with a clean cloth, and brush all loose dirt from the dust shield. Carefully remove the cloth to prevent dirt from falling from it.
6. Pack the inside of the hub with wheel bearing grease. Add grease to the hub until the grease is flush with the inside diameter of the bearing cup.
7. Pack the bearing assembly with wheel bearing grease. A bearing packer is desirable for this operation. If a packer is not available, place a large portion of grease into the palm of your hand and sliding the edge of the roller cage through the grease with your other hand, work as much grease in between the rollers as possible.

➡**As an alternate method, place a large portion of grease, and the bearing to be packed, into a sealable heavy plastic bag. Squeeze the bag to force the grease into the bearing. This may reduce the mess usually associated with bearing repacking.**

8. Position the inner bearing cone and roller assembly in the inner cup. Apply a light film of grease to the lips of a new grease seal and install the seal into the hub.
9. Carefully position the hub and rotor assembly onto the spindle. Be careful not to damage the grease seal.
10. Place the outer bearing into position on the spindle and into the bearing cup. Install the adjusting nut finger tight.
11. Adjust the wheel bearings.
12. Install any remaining components which were removed.

TRAILER TOWING

▶ **See Figure 121**

General Recommendations

Your vehicle was primarily designed to carry passengers and cargo. It is important to remember that towing a trailer will place additional loads on your vehicles engine, drivetrain, steering, braking and other systems. However, if you decide to tow a trailer, using the prior equipment is a must.

Local laws may require specific equipment such as trailer brakes or fender mounted mirrors. Check your local laws.

Trailer Weight

The weight of the trailer is the most important factor. A good weight-to-horsepower ratio is about 35:1, 35 lbs. of Gross Combined Weight (GCW) for every horsepower your engine develops. Multiply the engine's rated horsepower by 35 and subtract the weight of the vehicle passengers and luggage. The number remaining is the approximate ideal maximum weight you should tow, although a numerically higher axle ratio can help compensate for heavier weight.

Hitch (Tongue) Weight

Calculate the hitch weight in order to select a proper hitch. The weight of the hitch is usually 9–11% of the trailer gross weight and should be measured with the trailer loaded. Hitches fall into various categories: those that mount on the frame and rear bumper, the bolt-on type, or the weld-on distribution type used for larger trailers. Axle mounted or clamp-on bumper hitches should never be used.

Check the gross weight rating of your trailer. Tongue weight is usually figured as 10% of gross trailer weight. Therefore, a trailer with a maximum gross

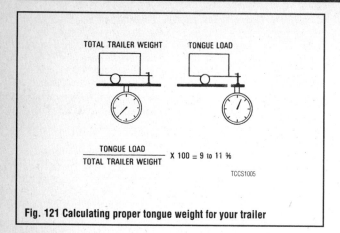

Fig. 121 Calculating proper tongue weight for your trailer

weight of 2000 lbs. will have a maximum tongue weight of 200 lbs. Class I trailers fall into this category. Class II trailers are those with a gross weight rating of 2000–3000 lbs., while Class III trailers fall into the 3500–6000 lbs. category. Class IV trailers are those over 6000 lbs. and are for use with fifth wheel trucks, only.

When you've determined the hitch that you'll need, follow the manufacturer's installation instructions, exactly, especially when it comes to fastener torques. The hitch will subjected to a lot of stress and good hitches come with hardened bolts. Never substitute an inferior bolt for a hardened bolt.

Oil Cooler

Aftermarket engine oil coolers are helpful for prolonging engine oil life and reducing overall engine temperatures. Both of these factors increase engine life. While not absolutely necessary in towing Class I and some Class II trailers, they are recommended for heavier Class II and all Class III towing. Engine oil cooler systems usually consist of an adapter, screwed on in place of the oil filter, a

TOWING THE VEHICLE

➡️**Ford recommends that a flat bed tow service be utilized. If a flat bed tow truck is not available, tow the vehicle with the rear wheels lifted, front hubs unlocked (4WD models) and the steering wheel locked in the straight ahead position using a clamping device designed for towing. DO NOT lock the steering wheel using only the ignition key activated steering lock, as damage to the steering column can occur.**

JUMP STARTING A DEAD BATTERY

▶ **See Figure 122**

Whenever a vehicle is jump started, precautions must be followed in order to prevent the possibility of personal injury. Remember that batteries contain a

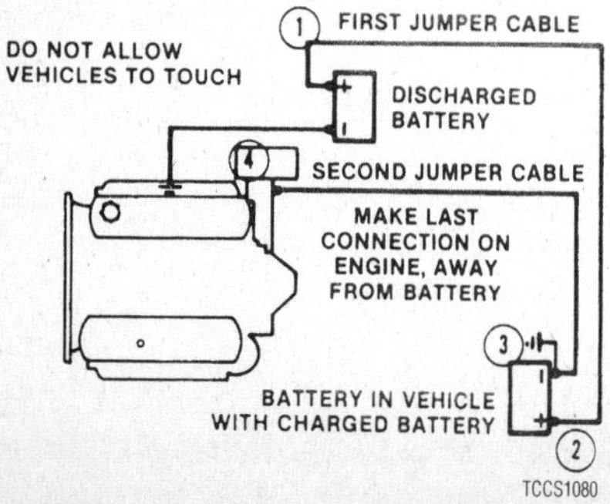

Fig. 122 Connect the jumper cables to the batteries and engine in the order shown

remote filter mounting and a multi-tube, finned heat exchanger, which is mounted in front of the radiator or air conditioning condenser.

TRANSMISSION

An automatic transmission is usually recommended for trailer towing. Modern automatics have proven reliable and, of course, easy to operate, in trailer towing. The increased load of a trailer, however, causes an increase in the temperature of the automatic transmission fluid. Heat is the worst enemy of an automatic transmission. As the temperature of the fluid increases, the life of the fluid decreases.

It is essential, therefore, that you install an automatic transmission cooler. The cooler, which consists of a multi-tube, finned heat exchanger, is usually installed in front of the radiator or air conditioning compressor, and hooked in-line with the transmission cooler tank inlet line. Follow the cooler manufacturer's installation instructions.

Select a cooler of at least adequate capacity, based upon the combined gross weights of the vehicle and trailer.

Cooler manufacturers recommend that you use an aftermarket cooler in addition to, and not instead of, the present cooling tank in your radiator. If you do want to use it in place of the radiator cooling tank, get a cooler at least two sizes larger than normally necessary.

➡️**A transmission cooler can, sometimes, cause slow or harsh shifting in the transmission during cold weather, until the fluid has a chance to come up to normal operating temperature. Some coolers can be purchased with or retrofitted with a temperature bypass valve which will allow fluid flow through the cooler only when the fluid has reached above a certain operating temperature.**

Handling a Trailer

Towing a trailer with ease and safety requires a certain amount of experience. It's a good idea to learn the feel of a trailer by practicing turning, stopping and backing in an open area such as an empty parking lot.

Your truck can be towed forward with the driveshaft connected as long as you do not exceed 35 miles in distance and 50 MPH in speed. Severe damage to the transmission can occur if these limits are exceeded. If your truck has to be towed backward and is a 4WD model, unlock the front axle driving hubs, to prevent the front differential from rotating and place the transfer case in Neutral. Also clamp the steering wheel on all models in the straight ahead position, with a clamping device designed for towing service.

small amount of explosive hydrogen gas which is a by-product of battery charging. Sparks should always be avoided when working around batteries, especially when attaching jumper cables. To minimize the possibility of accidental sparks, follow the procedure carefully.

✳✳ CAUTION

NEVER hook the batteries up in a series circuit or the entire electrical system will go up in smoke, including the starter!

Vehicles equipped with a diesel engine may utilize two 12 volt batteries. If so, the batteries are connected in a parallel circuit (positive terminal to positive terminal, negative terminal to negative terminal). Hooking the batteries up in parallel circuit increases battery cranking power without increasing total battery voltage output. Output remains at 12 volts. On the other hand, hooking two 12 volt batteries up in a series circuit (positive terminal to negative terminal, positive terminal to negative terminal) increases total battery output to 24 volts (12 volts plus 12 volts).

Jump Starting Precautions

• Be sure that both batteries are of the same voltage. Vehicles covered by this manual and most vehicles on the road today utilize a 12 volt charging system.

- Be sure that both batteries are of the same polarity (have the same terminal, in most cases NEGATIVE grounded).
- Be sure that the vehicles are not touching or a short could occur.
- On serviceable batteries, be sure the vent cap holes are not obstructed.
- Do not smoke or allow sparks anywhere near the batteries.
- In cold weather, make sure the battery electrolyte is not frozen. This can occur more readily in a battery that has been in a state of discharge.
- Do not allow electrolyte to contact your skin or clothing.

Jump Starting Procedure

1. Make sure that the voltages of the 2 batteries are the same. Most batteries and charging systems are of the 12 volt variety.
2. Pull the jumping vehicle (with the good battery) into a position so the jumper cables can reach the dead battery and that vehicle's engine. Make sure that the vehicles do NOT touch.
3. Place the transmissions/transaxles of both vehicles in **Neutral** (MT) or **P** (AT), as applicable, then firmly set their parking brakes.

➡If necessary for safety reasons, the hazard lights on both vehicles may be operated throughout the entire procedure without significantly increasing the difficulty of jumping the dead battery.

4. Turn all lights and accessories OFF on both vehicles. Make sure the ignition switches on both vehicles are turned to the **OFF** position.
5. Cover the battery cell caps with a rag, but do not cover the terminals.
6. Make sure the terminals on both batteries are clean and free of corrosion or proper electrical connection will be impeded. If necessary, clean the battery terminals before proceeding.
7. Identify the positive (+) and negative (–) terminals on both batteries.
8. Connect the first jumper cable to the positive (+) terminal of the dead battery, then connect the other end of that cable to the positive (+) terminal of the booster (good) battery.

9. Connect one end of the other jumper cable to the negative (–) terminal on the booster battery and the final cable clamp to an engine bolt head, alternator bracket or other solid, metallic point on the engine with the dead battery. Try to pick a ground on the engine that is positioned away from the battery in order to minimize the possibility of the 2 clamps touching should one loosen during the procedure. DO NOT connect this clamp to the negative (–) terminal of the bad battery.

✳✳ CAUTION

Be very careful to keep the jumper cables away from moving parts (cooling fan, belts, etc.) on both engines.

10. Check to.make sure that the cables are routed away from any moving parts, then start the donor vehicle's engine. Run the engine at moderate speed for several minutes to allow the dead battery a chance to receive some initial charge.
11. With the donor vehicle's engine still running slightly above idle, try to start the vehicle with the dead battery. Crank the engine for no more than 10 seconds at a time and let the starter cool for at least 20 seconds between tries. If the vehicle does not start in 3 tries, it is likely that something else is also wrong or that the battery needs additional time to charge.
12. Once the vehicle is started, allow it to run at idle for a few seconds to make sure that it is operating properly.
13. Turn ON the headlights, heater blower and, if equipped, the rear defroster of both vehicles in order to reduce the severity of voltage spikes and subsequent risk of damage to the vehicles' electrical systems when the cables are disconnected. This step is especially important to any vehicle equipped with computer control modules.
14. Carefully disconnect the cables in the reverse order of connection. Start with the negative cable that is attached to the engine ground, then the negative cable on the donor battery. Disconnect the positive cable from the donor battery and finally, disconnect the positive cable from the formerly dead battery. Be careful when disconnecting the cables from the positive terminals not to allow the alligator clips to touch any metal on either vehicle or a short and sparks will occur.

JACKING

♦ **See Figures 123 and 124**

It is very important to be careful about running the engine, on vehicles equipped with limited slip differentials, while the vehicle is up on a jack. This is because if the drive train is engaged, power is transmitted to the wheel with the best traction and the vehicle will drive off the jack, resulting in possible damage or injury.

Jack the truck from under the axles, radius arms, or spring hangers and the frame. Be sure and block the diagonally opposite wheel to prevent the vehicle from moving. Place jackstands under the vehicle at the points mentioned above when you are going to work under the vehicle.

✳✳ CAUTION

On models equipped with an under chassis mounted spare tire, remove the tire, wheel or tire carrier from the vehicle before it is placed in a high lift position in order to avoid sudden weight release from the chassis.

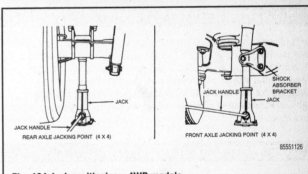

Fig. 124 Jack positioning—4WD models

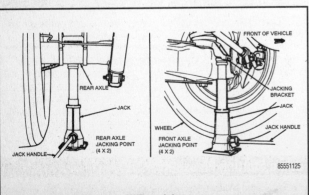

Fig. 123 Jack positioning—2WD models

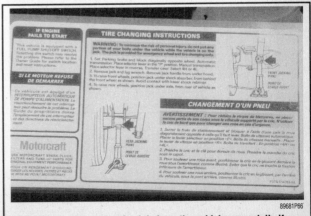

Always follow any instruction labels on the vehicle, especially if they differ from another source

When raising the vehicle on a hoist, position the front end adapters under the center of the lower suspension arm or the spring supports as near to the wheels as practical. The rear hoist adapters should be placed under the spring mounting pads or the rear axle housing. Be careful not to touch the rear shock absorber mounting brackets.

Lift the front by positioning the jack under the lower front shock absorber mount

Lift the rear by positioning the jack under the rear spring mount on the axle

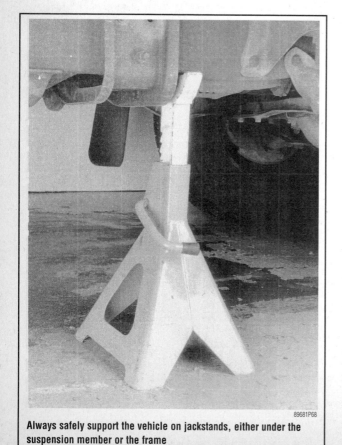

Always safely support the vehicle on jackstands, either under the suspension member or the frame

The jackstand can be positioned under the spring-to-frame mount

CAPACITIES

Year	Model	Engine ID/VIN	Engine Displacement Liters (cc)	Engine Oil with Filter (qts.)	Transmission Man. ①	Transmission Auto. ②	Transfer Case (pts.)	Drive Axle Front (pts.)	Drive Axle Rear (pts.)	Fuel Tank (gal.)	Cooling System wo/AC (qts.)	Cooling System w/AC (qts.)
1991	Ranger	A	2.3 (2294)	5.0	5.6	9.7 ⑥	2.5	3.5	5.0	16.3 ③	6.5	7.2
		T	2.9 (2900)	5.0	④	9.7 ⑥	2.5	3.5	5.0	16.3 ③	7.2	7.8
		U	3.0 (2999)	5.0	5.6	9.7 ⑥	2.5	3.5	5.0	16.3 ③	9.5	10.2
		X	4.0 (3949)	5.0	5.6	9.7 ⑥	2.5	3.5	5.0	16.3 ③	7.8	8.6
	Explorer	X	4.0 (3949)	5.0	5.6	9.7 ⑥	2.5	3.5	5.3	19.3	7.8	8.6
1992	Ranger	A	2.3 (2294)	5.0	5.6	9.7 ⑥	2.5	3.5	5.0	⑤	6.5	7.2
		T	2.9 (2900)	5.0	④	9.7 ⑥	2.5	3.5	5.0	⑤	7.2	7.8
		U	3.0 (2999)	4.5	5.6	9.7 ⑥	2.5	3.5	5.0	⑤	9.5	10.2
		X	4.0 (3949)	5.0	5.6	9.7 ⑥	2.5	3.5	5.0	⑤	7.8	8.6
	Explorer	X	4.0 (3949)	5.0	5.6	9.7 ⑥	2.5	3.5	5.3	19.3	7.8	8.6
1993	Ranger	A	2.3 (2294)	5.0	5.6	9.7 ⑥	2.5	3.5	5.0	⑤	6.5	7.2
		U	3.0 (2999)	4.5	5.6	9.7 ⑥	2.5	3.5	5.0	⑤	9.5	10.2
		X	4.0 (3949)	5.0	5.6	9.7 ⑥	2.5	3.5	5.0	⑤	7.8	8.6
	Explorer	X	4.0 (3949)	5.0	5.6	9.7 ⑥	2.5	3.5	5.3	19.3	7.8	8.6
1994	Ranger	A	2.3 (2294)	5.0	5.6	9.7 ⑥	2.5	3.5	5.0	⑤	6.5	7.2
		U	3.0 (2999)	4.5	5.6	9.7 ⑥	2.5	3.5	5.0	⑤	9.5	10.2
		X	4.0 (3949)	5.0	5.6	9.7 ⑥	2.5	3.5	5.0	⑤	7.8	8.6
	Explorer	X	4.0 (3949)	5.0	5.6	9.7 ⑥	2.5	3.5	5.3	19.3	7.8	8.6
1995	Ranger	A	2.3 (2294)	5.0	5.6	9.7 ⑥	2.5	3.5	5.0	⑤	6.5	7.2
		U	3.0 (2999)	4.5	5.6	9.7 ⑥	2.5	3.5	5.0	⑤	9.5	10.2
		X	4.0 (3949)	5.0	5.6	9.7 ⑥	2.5	3.5	5.0	⑤	7.8	8.6
	Explorer	X	4.0 (3949)	5.0	5.6	9.7 ⑥	2.5	3.5	5.3	19.3	7.8	8.6
1996	Ranger	A	2.3 (2294)	5.0	5.6	9.5 ⑥	2.5	3.5	5.0	⑤	6.5	7.2
		U	3.0 (2999)	4.5	5.6	9.5 ⑥	2.5	3.5	5.0	⑤	9.5	10.2
		X	4.0 (3949)	5.0	5.6	9.5 ⑥	2.5	3.5	5.0	⑤	7.8	8.6
	Explorer	X	4.0 (3949)	5.0	5.6	9.5 ⑥	2.5	3.5	5.3	⑤	7.8	8.6
		P	5.0 (4949)	5.0	5.6	13.9	2.5	3.5	5.5	⑤	12.8	12.8
1997	Ranger	A	2.3 (2294)	5.0	5.6	9.5 ⑥	2.5	3.5	5.0	⑤	6.5	7.2
		U	3.0 (2999)	4.5	5.6	9.5 ⑥	2.5	3.5	5.0	⑤	9.5	10.2
		X	4.0 (3998)	5.0	5.6	9.5 ⑥	2.5	3.5	5.0	⑤	7.8	8.6
	Explorer	X	4.0 (3949)	5.0	5.6	9.5 ⑥	2.5	3.5	5.3	⑤	7.8	8.6
		E	4.0 (3998)	5.0	5.6	9.5 ⑥	2.5	3.5	5.5	⑤	8.1	8.1
	Mountaineer	X	4.0 (3949)	5.0	5.6	9.5 ⑥	2.5	3.5	5.3	⑤	7.8	8.6
		P	5.0 (4949)	5.0	5.6	13.9	2.5	3.5	5.5	⑤	13.5	13.5
1998	Ranger	C	2.5 (2500)	5.0	5.6	9.5 ⑥	2.5	3.5	5.0	⑤	6.5	7.2
		U	3.0 (2999)	4.5	5.6	9.5 ⑥	2.5	3.5	5.0	⑤	9.5	10.2
		X	4.0 (3998)	5.0	5.6	9.5 ⑥	2.5	3.5	5.0	⑤	7.8	8.6
	Explorer	X	4.0 (3949)	5.0	5.6	9.5 ⑥	2.5	3.5	5.3	⑤	7.8	8.6
		E	4.0 (3998)	5.0	5.6	9.5 ⑥	2.5	3.5	5.5	⑤	8.1	8.1
	Mountaineer	X	4.0 (3949)	5.0	5.6	9.5 ⑥	2.5	3.5	5.3	⑤	7.8	8.6
		P	5.0 (4949)	5.0	5.6	13.9	2.5	3.5	5.5	⑤	13.5	13.5
1999	Ranger	C	2.5 (2500)	5.0	5.6	9.5 ⑥	2.5	3.5	5.0	⑤	6.5	7.2
		U	3.0 (2999)	4.5	5.6	9.5 ⑥	2.5	3.5	5.0	⑤	9.5	10.2
		X	4.0 (3998)	5.0	5.6	9.5 ⑥	2.5	3.5	5.0	⑤	7.8	8.6
	Explorer	X	4.0 (3949)	5.0	5.6	9.5 ⑥	2.5	3.5	5.3	⑤	7.8	8.6
		E	4.0 (3998)	5.0	5.6	9.5 ⑥	2.5	3.5	5.5	⑤	8.1	8.1
	Mountaineer	X	4.0 (3949)	5.0	5.6	9.5 ⑥	2.5	3.5	5.3	⑤	7.8	8.6
		P	5.0 (4949)	5.0	5.6	13.9	2.5	3.5	5.5	⑤	13.5	13.5

① All measurements given are in pints (pts.)
② All Meaurements given are in quarts (qts.)
③ 19.6 gallon tank was optional
④ Mistubishi 5-speed: 4.8
   Mazda 5-speed: 5.6

⑤ Ranger with standard wheelbase: 16.3
   Ranger with long wheelbase: 19.6
   Explorer/Mountaineer with 2-doors: 19
   Explorer/Mountaineer with 4-doors: 22

⑥ Measurement given is for 4x2 vehicles
   for 4x4 vehicles, add 0.3 pts.

89681C54

MANUFACTURER RECOMMENDED MAINTENANCE INTERVALS

TO BE SERVICED	VEHICLE MILEAGE INTERVAL (x1000)																															
	5	10	15	20	25	30	35	40	45	50	55	60	65	70	75	80	85	90	95	100	105	110	115	120	125	130	135	140	145	150	155	160
Change engine oil and filter ①	✓	✓	✓	✓	✓	✓	✓	✓	✓	✓	✓	✓	✓	✓	✓	✓	✓	✓	✓	✓	✓	✓	✓	✓	✓	✓	✓	✓	✓	✓	✓	✓
Adjust clutch	✓	✓	✓	✓	✓	✓	✓	✓	✓	✓	✓	✓	✓	✓	✓	✓	✓	✓	✓	✓	✓	✓	✓	✓	✓	✓	✓	✓	✓	✓	✓	✓
Rotate tires and check air pressure	✓		✓		✓		✓		✓		✓		✓		✓		✓		✓		✓		✓		✓		✓		✓		✓	
Inspect engine cooling system ②			✓			✓			✓			✓			✓			✓			✓			✓			✓			✓		
Change ATF and filter						✓						✓						✓						✓						✓		
Replace air cleaner element						✓						✓						✓						✓						✓		
Replace spark plugs												✓												✓								
Inspect exhaust heat shields						✓						✓						✓						✓						✓		
Inspect brake pads and rotors						✓						✓						✓						✓						✓		
Replace PCV valve ③						✓						✓						✓						✓						✓		
Inspect accessory drive belt												✓												✓								
Change engine coolant and flush the cooling system						✓						✓						✓						✓						✓		

① The engine oil and filter should be changed every 5,000 miles (8,000 km) or 6 months, whichever occurs first.
② Perform this service every 15,000 miles (24,000 km) or 12 months, whichever occurs first.
③ On the 5.0L engine, this includes replacing the crankcase emission air filter.

89681C06

MANUFACTURER RECOMMENDED SEVERE MAINTENANCE INTERVALS ①

TO BE SERVICED	VEHICLE MILEAGE INTERVAL (x1000)																															
	3	6	9	12	15	18	21	24	27	30	33	36	39	42	45	48	51	54	57	60	63	66	69	72	75	78	81	84	87	90	93	96
Change engine oil and filter ②	✓	✓	✓	✓	✓	✓	✓	✓	✓	✓	✓	✓	✓	✓	✓	✓	✓	✓	✓	✓	✓	✓	✓	✓	✓	✓	✓	✓	✓	✓	✓	✓
Adjust clutch		✓		✓		✓		✓		✓		✓		✓		✓		✓		✓		✓		✓		✓		✓		✓		✓
Rotate tires and check air pressure		✓			✓			✓			✓			✓			✓			✓			✓			✓			✓			✓
Inspect engine cooling system				✓						✓					✓					✓					✓					✓		
Change ATF and filter														✓														✓				
Replace air cleaner element ③										✓										✓										✓		
Replace spark plugs—except 5.0L engine																				✓												
Replace spark plugs—5.0L engine										✓										✓										✓		
Inspect exhaust heat shields										✓										✓										✓		
Inspect brake pads and rotors										✓										✓										✓		
Replace PCV valve																				✓												
Inspect accessory drive belt																				✓												
Change engine coolant and flush the cooling system																✓														✓		

① If a vehicle is operated under any of the following conditions it is considered severe service:
  - Extremely dusty areas.
  - 50% or more of the vehicle operation is in 90°F (32°C) or higher temperatures, or constant operation in temperatures below 32°F (0°C).
  - Prolonged idling (vehicle operation in stop-and-go traffic).
  - Frequent short running periods (engine does not warm to normal operating temperature).
  - Police, taxi, delivery usage or trailer towing usage.
② Change the engine oil every 3,000 miles or 3 months, whichever occurs first.
③ On 5.0L engines, replace the crankcase emission air filter as well.

89681C07

ENGLISH TO METRIC CONVERSION: MASS (WEIGHT)

Current mass measurement is expressed in pounds and ounces (lbs. & ozs.). The metric unit of mass (or weight) is the kilogram (kg). Even although this table does not show conversion of masses (weights) larger than 15 lbs, it is easy to calculate larger units by following the data immediately below.

To convert ounces (oz.) to grams (g): multiply th number of ozs. by 28
To convert grams (g) to ounces (oz.): multiply the number of grams by .035

To convert pounds (lbs.) to kilograms (kg): multiply the number of lbs. by .45
To convert kilograms (kg) to pounds (lbs.): multiply the number of kilograms by 2.2

lbs	kg	lbs	kg	oz	kg	oz	kg
0.1	0.04	0.9	0.41	0.1	0.003	0.9	0.024
0.2	0.09	1	0.4	0.2	0.005	1	0.03
0.3	0.14	2	0.9	0.3	0.008	2	0.06
0.4	0.18	3	1.4	0.4	0.011	3	0.08
0.5	0.23	4	1.8	0.5	0.014	4	0.11
0.6	0.27	5	2.3	0.6	0.017	5	0.14
0.7	0.32	10	4.5	0.7	0.020	10	0.28
0.8	0.36	15	6.8	0.8	0.023	15	0.42

ENGLISH TO METRIC CONVERSION: TEMPERATURE

To convert Fahrenheit (°F) to Celsius (°C): take number of °F and subtract 32; multiply result by 5; divide result by 9

To convert Celsius (°C) to Fahrenheit (°F): take number of °C and multiply by 9; divide result by 5; add 32 to total

Fahrenheit (F)	Celsius (C)			Fahrenheit (F)	Celsius (C)			Fahrenheit (F)	Celsius (C)		
°F	°C	°C	°F	°F	°C	°C	°F	°F	°C	°C	°F
−40	−40	−38	−36.4	80	26.7	18	64.4	215	101.7	80	176
−35	−37.2	−36	−32.8	85	29.4	20	68	220	104.4	85	185
−30	−34.4	−34	−29.2	90	32.2	22	71.6	225	107.2	90	194
−25	−31.7	−32	−25.6	95	35.0	24	75.2	230	110.0	95	202
−20	−28.9	−30	−22	100	37.8	26	78.8	235	112.8	100	212
−15	−26.1	−28	−18.4	105	40.6	28	82.4	240	115.6	105	221
−10	−23.3	−26	−14.8	110	43.3	30	86	245	118.3	110	230
−5	−20.6	−24	−11.2	115	46.1	32	89.6	250	121.1	115	239
0	−17.8	−22	−7.6	120	48.9	34	93.2	255	123.9	120	248
1	−17.2	−20	−4	125	51.7	36	96.8	260	126.6	125	257
2	−16.7	−18	−0.4	130	54.4	38	100.4	265	129.4	130	266
3	−16.1	−16	3.2	135	57.2	40	104	270	132.2	135	275
4	−15.6	−14	6.8	140	60.0	42	107.6	275	135.0	140	284
5	−15.0	−12	10.4	145	62.8	44	112.2	280	137.8	145	293
10	−12.2	−10	14	150	65.6	46	114.8	285	140.6	150	302
15	−9.4	−8	17.6	155	68.3	48	118.4	290	143.3	155	311
20	−6.7	−6	21.2	160	71.1	50	122	295	146.1	160	320
25	−3.9	−4	24.8	165	73.9	52	125.6	300	148.9	165	329
30	−1.1	−2	28.4	170	76.7	54	129.2	305	151.7	170	338
35	1.7	0	32	175	79.4	56	132.8	310	154.4	175	347
40	4.4	2	35.6	180	82.2	58	136.4	315	157.2	180	356
45	7.2	4	39.2	185	85.0	60	140	320	160.0	185	365
50	10.0	6	42.8	190	87.8	62	143.6	325	162.8	190	374
55	12.8	8	46.4	195	90.6	64	147.2	330	165.6	195	383
60	15.6	10	50	200	93.3	66	150.8	335	168.3	200	392
65	18.3	12	53.6	205	96.1	68	154.4	340	171.1	205	401
70	21.1	14	57.2	210	98.9	70	158	345	173.9	210	410
75	23.9	16	60.8	212	100.0	75	167	350	176.7	215	414

TCCS1C01

ENGLISH TO METRIC CONVERSION: LENGTH

To convert inches (ins.) to millimeters (mm): multiply number of inches by 25.4

To convert millimeters (mm) to inches (ins.): multiply number of millimeters by .04

Inches		Decimals	Milli-meters	Inches to millimeters		Inches		Decimals	Milli-meters	Inches to millimeters	
				inches	mm					inches	mm
	1/64	0.051625	0.3969	0.0001	0.00254		33/64	0.515625	13.0969	0.6	15.24
1/32		0.03125	0.7937	0.0002	0.00508	17/32		0.53125	13.4937	0.7	17.78
	3/64	0.046875	1.1906	0.0003	0.00762		35/64	0.546875	13.8906	0.8	20.32
1/16		0.0625	1.5875	0.0004	0.01016	9/16		0.5625	14.2875	0.9	22.86
	5/64	0.078125	1.9844	0.0005	0.01270		37/64	0.578125	14.6844	1	25.4
3/32		0.09375	2.3812	0.0006	0.01524	19/32		0.59375	15.0812	2	50.8
	7/64	0.109375	2.7781	0.0007	0.01778		39/64	0.609375	15.4781	3	76.2
1/8		0.125	3.1750	0.0008	0.02032	5/8		0.625	15.8750	4	101.6
	9/64	0.140625	3.5719	0.0009	0.02286		41/64	0.640625	16.2719	5	127.0
5/32		0.15625	3.9687	0.001	0.0254	21/32		0.65625	16.6687	6	152.4
	11/64	0.171875	4.3656	0.002	0.0508		43/64	0.671875	17.0656	7	177.8
3/16		0.1875	4.7625	0.003	0.0762	11/16		0.6875	17.4625	8	203.2
	13/64	0.203125	5.1594	0.004	0.1016		45/64	0.703125	17.8594	9	228.6
7/32		0.21875	5.5562	0.005	0.1270	23/32		0.71875	18.2562	10	254.0
	15/64	0.234375	5.9531	0.006	0.1524		47/64	0.734375	18.6531	11	279.4
1/4		0.25	6.3500	0.007	0.1778	3/4		0.75	19.0500	12	304.8
	17/64	0.265625	6.7469	0.008	0.2032		49/64	0.765625	19.4469	13	330.2
9/32		0.28125	7.1437	0.009	0.2286	25/32		0.78125	19.8437	14	355.6
	19/64	0.296875	7.5406	0.01	0.254		51/64	0.796875	20.2406	15	381.0
5/16		0.3125	7.9375	0.02	0.508	13/16		0.8125	20.6375	16	406.4
	21/64	0.328125	8.3344	0.03	0.762		53/64	0.828125	21.0344	17	431.8
11/32		0.34375	8.7312	0.04	1.016	27/32		0.84375	21.4312	18	457.2
	23/64	0.359375	9.1281	0.05	1.270		55/64	0.859375	21.8281	19	482.6
3/8		0.375	9.5250	0.06	1.524	7/8		0.875	22.2250	20	508.0
	25/64	0.390625	9.9219	0.07	1.778		57/64	0.890625	22.6219	21	533.4
13/32		0.40625	10.3187	0.08	2.032	29/32		0.90625	23.0187	22	558.8
	27/64	0.421875	10.7156	0.09	2.286		59/64	0.921875	23.4156	23	584.2
7/16		0.4375	11.1125	0.1	2.54	15/16		0.9375	23.8125	24	609.6
	29/64	0.453125	11.5094	0.2	5.08		61/64	0.953125	24.2094	25	635.0
15/32		0.46875	11.9062	0.3	7.62	31/32		0.96875	24.6062	26	660.4
	31/64	0.484375	12.3031	0.4	10.16		63/64	0.984375	25.0031	27	690.6
1/2		0.5	12.7000	0.5	12.70						

ENGLISH TO METRIC CONVERSION: TORQUE

To convert foot-pounds (ft. lbs.) to Newton-meters: multiply the number of ft. lbs. by 1.3

To convert inch-pounds (in. lbs.) to Newton-meters: multiply the number of in. lbs. by .11

in lbs	N-m	in lbs	N-m	in lbs	N-m	in lbs	N-m	in lbs	N-m
0.1	0.01	1	0.11	10	1.13	19	2.15	28	3.16
0.2	0.02	2	0.23	11	1.24	20	2.26	29	3.28
0.3	0.03	3	0.34	12	1.36	21	2.37	30	3.39
0.4	0.04	4	0.45	13	1.47	22	2.49	31	3.50
0.5	0.06	5	0.56	14	1.58	23	2.60	32	3.62
0.6	0.07	6	0.68	15	1.70	24	2.71	33	3.73
0.7	0.08	7	0.78	16	1.81	25	2.82	34	3.84
0.8	0.09	8	0.90	17	1.92	26	2.94	35	3.95
0.9	0.10	9	1.02	18	2.03	27	3.05	36	4.0

ENGLISH TO METRIC CONVERSION: TORQUE

Torque is now expressed as either foot-pounds (ft./lbs.) or inch-pounds (in./lbs.). The metric measurement unit for torque is the Newton-meter (Nm). This unit—the Nm—will be used for all SI metric torque references, both the present ft./lbs. and in./lbs.

ft lbs	N-m	ft lbs	N-m	ft lbs	N-m	ft lbs	N-m
0.1	0.1	33	44.7	74	100.3	115	155.9
0.2	0.3	34	46.1	75	101.7	116	157.3
0.3	0.4	35	47.4	76	103.0	117	158.6
0.4	0.5	36	48.8	77	104.4	118	160.0
0.5	0.7	37	50.7	78	105.8	119	161.3
0.6	0.8	38	51.5	79	107.1	120	162.7
0.7	1.0	39	52.9	80	108.5	121	164.0
0.8	1.1	40	54.2	81	109.8	122	165.4
0.9	1.2	41	55.6	82	111.2	123	166.8
1	1.3	42	56.9	83	112.5	124	168.1
2	2.7	43	58.3	84	113.9	125	169.5
3	4.1	44	59.7	85	115.2	126	170.8
4	5.4	45	61.0	86	116.6	127	172.2
5	6.8	46	62.4	87	118.0	128	173.5
6	8.1	47	63.7	88	119.3	129	174.9
7	9.5	48	65.1	89	120.7	130	176.2
8	10.8	49	66.4	90	122.0	131	177.6
9	12.2	50	67.8	91	123.4	132	179.0
10	13.6	51	69.2	92	124.7	133	180.3
11	14.9	52	70.5	93	126.1	134	181.7
12	16.3	53	71.9	94	127.4	135	183.0
13	17.6	54	73.2	95	128.8	136	184.4
14	18.9	55	74.6	96	130.2	137	185.7
15	20.3	56	75.9	97	131.5	138	187.1
16	21.7	57	77.3	98	132.9	139	188.5
17	23.0	58	78.6	99	134.2	140	189.8
18	24.4	59	80.0	100	135.6	141	191.2
19	25.8	60	81.4	101	136.9	142	192.5
20	27.1	61	82.7	102	138.3	143	193.9
21	28.5	62	84.1	103	139.6	144	195.2
22	29.8	63	85.4	104	141.0	145	196.6
23	31.2	64	86.8	105	142.4	146	198.0
24	32.5	65	88.1	106	143.7	147	199.3
25	33.9	66	89.5	107	145.1	148	200.7
26	35.2	67	90.8	108	146.4	149	202.0
27	36.6	68	92.2	109	147.8	150	203.4
28	38.0	69	93.6	110	149.1	151	204.7
29	39.3	70	94.9	111	150.5	152	206.1
30	40.7	71	96.3	112	151.8	153	207.4
31	42.0	72	97.6	113	153.2	154	208.8
32	43.4	73	99.0	114	154.6	155	210.2

TCCS1C03

ENGLISH TO METRIC CONVERSION: FORCE

Force is presently measured in pounds (lbs.). This type of measurement is used to measure spring pressure, specifically how many pounds it takes to compress a spring. Our present force unit (the pound) will be replaced in SI metric measurements by the Newton (N). This term will eventually see use in specifications for electric motor brush spring pressures, valve spring pressures, etc.

To convert pounds (lbs.) to Newton (N): multiply the number of lbs. by 4.45

lbs	N	lbs	N	lbs	N	oz	N
0.01	0.04	21	93.4	59	262.4	1	0.3
0.02	0.09	22	97.9	60	266.9	2	0.6
0.03	0.13	23	102.3	61	271.3	3	0.8
0.04	0.18	24	106.8	62	275.8	4	1.1
0.05	0.22	25	111.2	63	280.2	5	1.4
0.06	0.27	26	115.6	64	284.6	6	1.7
0.07	0.31	27	120.1	65	289.1	7	2.0
0.08	0.36	28	124.6	66	293.6	8	2.2
0.09	0.40	29	129.0	67	298.0	9	2.5
0.1	0.4	30	133.4	68	302.5	10	2.8
0.2	0.9	31	137.9	69	306.9	11	3.1
0.3	1.3	32	142.3	70	311.4	12	3.3
0.4	1.8	33	146.8	71	315.8	13	3.6
0.5	2.2	34	151.2	72	320.3	14	3.9
0.6	2.7	35	155.7	73	324.7	15	4.2
0.7	3.1	36	160.1	74	329.2	16	4.4
0.8	3.6	37	164.6	75	333.6	17	4.7
0.9	4.0	38	169.0	76	338.1	18	5.0
1	4.4	39	173.5	77	342.5	19	5.3
2	8.9	40	177.9	78	347.0	20	5.6
3	13.4	41	182.4	79	351.4	21	5.8
4	17.8	42	186.8	80	355.9	22	6.1
5	22.2	43	191.3	81	360.3	23	6.4
6	26.7	44	195.7	82	364.8	24	6.7
7	31.1	45	200.2	83	369.2	25	7.0
8	35.6	46	204.6	84	373.6	26	7.2
9	40.0	47	209.1	85	378.1	27	7.5
10	44.5	48	213.5	86	382.6	28	7.8
11	48.9	49	218.0	87	387.0	29	8.1
12	53.4	50	224.4	88	391.4	30	8.3
13	57.8	51	226.9	89	395.9	31	8.6
14	62.3	52	231.3	90	400.3	32	8.9
15	66.7	53	235.8	91	404.8	33	9.2
16	71.2	54	240.2	92	409.2	34	9.4
17	75.6	55	244.6	93	413.7	35	9.7
18	80.1	56	249.1	94	418.1	36	10.0
19	84.5	57	253.6	95	422.6	37	10.3
20	89.0	58	258.0	96	427.0	38	10.6

TCCS1C04

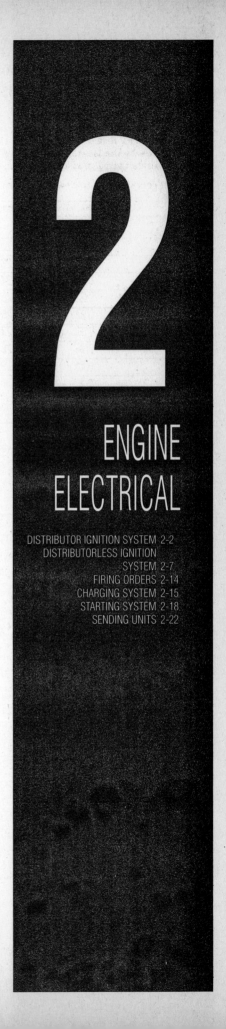

2

ENGINE
ELECTRICAL

DISTRIBUTOR IGNITION SYSTEM

➡For information on understanding electricity and troubleshooting electrical circuits, please refer to Section 6 of this manual.

General Information

▶ **See Figure 1**

Only the 1991–92 2.9L and the 1991–94 3.0L engines are equipped with the distributor ignition system. The distributor ignition system consists of the following components:
- Ignition Control Module (ICM)
- Distributor
- Camshaft Position (CMP) sensor
- Ignition coil

The distributor ignition system designed by Ford has two distinct configurations. The first configuration is known as the distributor mounted system, because the ICM is mounted directly on the distributor housing. The second configuration is known as a remote mount system, since the ICM is mounted on the front fender apron.

The distributor used by this system is sealed and houses the CMP sensor. The distributor does not utilize vacuum or centrifugal advance mechanisms; the ignition timing is automatically controlled by the Powertrain Control Module (PCM) and the ICM.

Ford calls this electronic ignition the Thick Film Integrated-IV (TFI-IV) ignition system. The TFI module is also known as the Ignition Control Module (ICM) which reports engine position and rpm to the PCM. The PCM then determines the proper spark timing and advance, and returns a reference signal to tell the TFI module to switch the coil, thereby by creating a spark. The PCM used on these vehicles is referred to by Ford as the Electronic Engine Control-IV (EEC-IV) module.

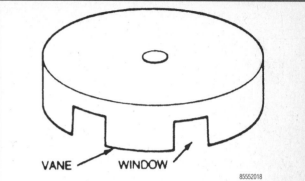

Fig. 2 The rotary armature has open areas called windows and tabs called vanes

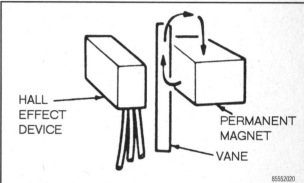

Fig. 3 The vane interrupts the magnetic field passing through the Hall effect device

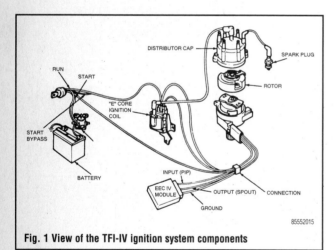

Fig. 1 View of the TFI-IV ignition system components

SYSTEM OPERATION

▶ **See Figures 2 and 3**

The CMP sensor, housed inside the distributor, responds to a rotating metallic shutter mounted on the distributor shaft. This rotating shutter produces a digital Profile Ignition Pick-up (PIP) signal, which is used by the PCM and ICM to provide base timing information, determine engine speed (rpm) and crankshaft position. The distributor shaft rotates at one-half crankshaft speed, therefore the shutter rotates once for every two crankshaft revolutions.

The ICM functions in either one of two modes: push start or Computer Controlled Dwell (CCD). The push start mode allows for increased dwell, or coil on time, when starting the engine. During this mode, the ICM determines when to turn on the ignition coil based on engine speed information. The coil is turned off, thereby firing, whenever a rising edge of a SPark OUTput (SPOUT) signal is

received. The SPOUT signal is generated by the PCM, and provides spark timing information to the ICM. During the push start mode, the SPOUT signal only indicates the timing for coil firing; the falling edge of the SPOUT signal is ignored. Despite the name, the push start mode is also enabled during engine starting with the ignition key.

➡**Do not attempt to push start a vehicle equipped with an automatic transmission.**

During the CCD mode, both edges of the SPOUT signal are utilized. The leading edge of the SPOUT signal is used by the ICM in the same manner as during the push start mode. The falling edge of the signal is generated to control the timing for turning the ignition coil on (the ICM no longer controls this function as during the push start mode). During the CCD mode, the coil on time, or dwell, is entirely controlled by the PCM through the SPOUT signal.

In the event that the SPOUT signal from the PCM is disrupted, the ICM will use the PIP signal from the CMP to fire the ignition coil, which results in a fixed spark angle and dwell.

Diagnosis and Testing

SERVICE PRECAUTIONS

- Always turn the key **OFF** and isolate both ends of a circuit whenever testing for shorts or continuity.
- Never measure voltage or resistance directly at the processor connector.
- Always disconnect solenoids and switches from the harness before measuring for continuity, resistance or energizing by way of a 12-volt source.
- When disconnecting connectors, inspect for damaged or pushed-out pins, corrosion, loose wires, etc. Service if required.

PRELIMINARY CHECKS

1. Visually inspect the engine compartment to ensure that all vacuum lines and spark plug wires are properly routed and securely connected.

2. Examine all wiring harness and connectors for insulation damage, burned, overheated, loose or broken conditions. Ensure that the ICM is securely fastened to the front fender apron.

3. Be certain that the battery is fully charged and that all accessories are OFF during the diagnosis.

TEST PROCEDURES

➡**Perform the test procedures in the order in which they are presented here.**

Ignition Coil Secondary Voltage Test

CRANK MODE

▶ **See Figure 4**

1. Connect a spark tester between the ignition coil wire and a good engine ground.
2. Crank the engine and check for spark at the tester.
3. Turn the ignition switch **OFF.**
4. If no spark occurs, check the following:
   a. Inspect the ignition coil for damage or carbon tracking.
   b. Check that the distributor shaft is rotating when the engine is being cranked.
   c. If the results in Steps a and b are okay, go to Module Test.
5. If a spark did occur, check the distributor cap and rotor for damage or carbon tracking. Go to the Ignition Coil Secondary Voltage (Run Mode) Test.

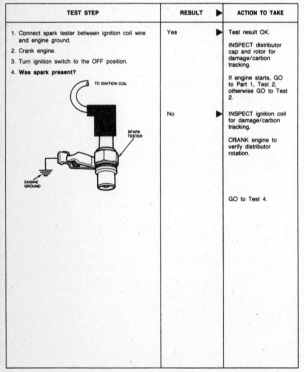

TEST STEP	RESULT ▶	ACTION TO TAKE
1. Connect spark tester between ignition coil wire and engine ground. 2. Crank engine. 3. Turn ignition switch to the OFF position. 4. **Was spark present?**	Yes ▶	Test result OK. INSPECT distributor cap and rotor for damage/carbon tracking. If engine starts, GO to Part 1, Test 2, otherwise GO to Test 2.
	No ▶	INSPECT ignition coil for damage/carbon tracking. CRANK engine to verify distributor rotation. GO to Test 4.

85552022

Fig. 4 Secondary coil voltage test 1 chart—crank mode check

RUN MODE

▶ **See Figures 5, 6 and 7**

1. Fully apply the parking brake. Place the gear shift lever in Neutral (manual transmission) or Park (automatic transmission).

TEST STEP	RESULT ▶	ACTION TO TAKE
1. Place the transmission shift lever in the PARK (A/T) or NEUTRAL (M/T) position and set the parking brake. ⚠ **CAUTION** **Failure to perform this step may result in the vehicle moving when the starter is subsequently engaged during the test.** 2. Disconnect wire at S terminal of starter relay. 3. Attach remote starter switch. 4. Turn ignition switch to the RUN position. 5. Crank the engine using remote starter switch. 6. Turn ignition switch to the OFF position. 7. Remove remote starter switch. 8. Reconnect wire to S terminal of starter relay. 9. **Was spark present?**	Yes ▶	Test result OK. Problem is not in the ignition system.
	No ▶	GO to Test 3.

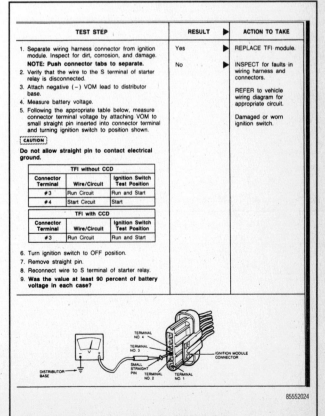

85552023

Fig. 5 Secondary coil voltage test 2 chart—run mode check

TEST STEP	RESULT ▶	ACTION TO TAKE
1. Separate wiring harness connector from ignition module. Inspect for dirt, corrosion, and damage. **NOTE: Push connector tabs to separate.** 2. Verify that the wire to the S terminal of starter relay is disconnected. 3. Attach negative (–) VOM lead to distributor base. 4. Measure battery voltage. 5. Following the appropriate table below, measure connector terminal voltage by attaching VOM to small straight pin inserted into connector terminal and turning ignition switch to position shown.	Yes ▶	REPLACE TFI module.
	No ▶	INSPECT for faults in wiring harness and connectors. REFER to vehicle wiring diagram for appropriate circuit. Damaged or worn ignition switch.

⚠ **CAUTION**

Do not allow straight pin to contact electrical ground.

TFI without CCD		
Connector Terminal	Wire/Circuit	Ignition Switch Test Position
#3	Run Circuit	Run and Start
#4	Start Circuit	Start

TFI with CCD		
Connector Terminal	Wire/Circuit	Ignition Switch Test Position
#3	Run Circuit	Run and Start

6. Turn ignition switch to OFF position.
7. Remove straight pin.
8. Reconnect wire to S terminal of starter relay.
9. Was the value at least 90 percent of battery voltage in each case?

85552024

Fig. 6 Wiring harness test 3 chart—voltage check

TEST STEP	RESULT ▶	ACTION TO TAKE
1. Place the transmission shift lever in the PARK (A/T) or NEUTRAL (M/T) position and set the parking brake. **CAUTION** **Failure to perform this step may result in the vehicle moving when the starter is subsequently engaged during the test.** 2. Disconnect the harness connector from the TFI module and connect the TFI tester. 3. Connect the red lead from the tester to the positive (+) side of the battery. 4. Disconnect the wire at the S terminal of the starter relay, and attach remote starter switch. 5. Crank the engine using the remote starter switch and note the status of the two LED lamps. 6. Remove the tester and remote starter switch. 7. Reconnect the wire to the starter relay and the connector to the TFI. 8. **Did the PIP light blink?**	Yes ▶ No ▶	GO to Test 6. REMOVE distributor cap and VERIFY rotation. If OK, GO to Test 5.

85552025

Fig. 7 Distributor hall effect test 4 chart

2. Disconnect the **S** terminal wire at the starter relay. Attach a remote starter switch.

3. Turn the ignition switch to the **RUN** position.

4. Using the remote starter switch, crank the engine and check for spark.

5. Turn the ignition switch **OFF**.

6. If no spark occurred, the problem lies with the wiring harness. Inspect the wiring harness for short circuits, open circuits and other defects.

7. If a spark did occur, the problem is not in the ignition system.

ICM Test

▶ See Figures 8 and 9

1. Remove the ICM from the distributor or the front fender apron.

2. Measure the resistance between the ICM terminals as shown below:

    a. GND—PIP IN: should be greater than 500 ohms.

    b. PIP PWR—PIP IN: should be less than 2,000 ohms.

    c. PIP PWR—TFI PWR: should be less than 200 ohms.

    d. GND—IGN GND: should be less than 2 ohms.

    e. PIP IN—PIP: should be less than 200 ohms.

3. If any of these checks failed, replace the ICM with a new one.

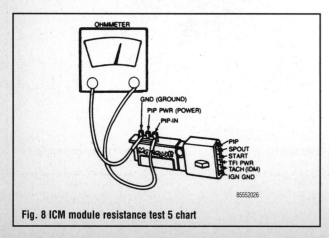

Fig. 8 ICM module resistance test 5 chart

TEST STEP	RESULT ▶	ACTION TO TAKE
1. Use status of Tach light from Test 4. 2. **Did the Tach light blink?**	Yes ▶ No ▶	GO to Test 7. REPLACE TFI module and CHECK for spark using the method described in Test 1. If spark was not present REPLACE the coil also.

8555227A

Fig. 9 ICM module test 6 chart

System Test

▶ See Figure 10

1. Disconnect the pin-in-line connector near the ICM.

2. Crank the engine

3. Turn the ignition switch **OFF**.

4. If a spark did occur, check the PIP and ignition ground wires for continuity. If okay, the problem is not in the ignition system.

5. If no spark occurs, check the voltage at the positive (+) terminal of the ignition coil with the ignition switch in **RUN**.

6. If the reading is not within battery voltage, check for a worn or damaged ignition switch.

7. If the reading is within battery voltage, check for faults in the wiring between the coil and TFI module terminal No. 2 or any additional wiring or components connected to that circuit.

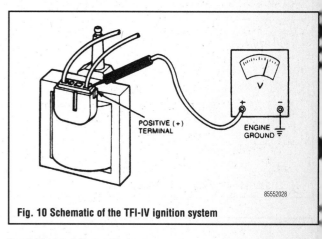

Fig. 10 Schematic of the TFI-IV ignition system

Spark Timing Advance Test

Spark timing advance is controlled by the EEC system. This procedure checks the capability of the ignition module to receive the spark timing command from the EEC module. The use of a volt/ohmmeter is required.

1. Turn the ignition switch **OFF**.

2. Disconnect the pin-in-line connector (SPOUT connector) near the TFI module.

3. Start the engine and measure the voltage, at idle, from the SPOUT connector to the distributor base. The reading should equal battery voltage.

4. If the result is okay, the problem lies within the EEC-IV system.

5. If the result was not satisfactory, separate the wiring harness connector from the ignition module. Check for damage, corrosion or dirt. Service as necessary.

6. Measure the resistance between terminal No. 5 and the pin-in-line connector. This test is done at the ignition module connector only. The reading should be less than 5 ohms.

7. If the reading is okay, replace the TFI module.

8. If the result was not satisfactory, service the wiring between the pin inline connector and the TFI connector.

Ignition Coil

TESTING

Ignition Coil and Secondary Wire

▶ **See Figure 11**

1. Disconnect the ignition coil connector and check for dirt, corrosion or damage.
2. Substitute a known-good coil and check for spark using the spark tester.

➡**Dangerous high voltage may be present when performing this test. Do not hold the coil while performing this test.**

3. Crank the engine and check for spark.
4. Turn the ignition switch **OFF**.
5. If a spark did occur, measure the resistance of the ignition coil wire, replace it if the resistance is greater than 7000 ohms per foot. If the readings are within specification, replace the ignition coil.
6. If no spark occurs, the problem is not the coil.

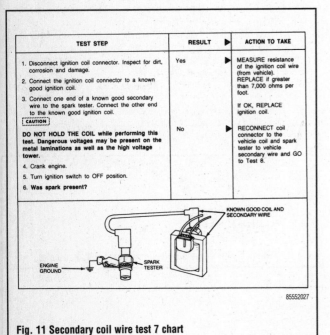

TEST STEP	RESULT ▶	ACTION TO TAKE
1. Disconnect ignition coil connector. Inspect for dirt, corrosion and damage. 2. Connect the ignition coil connector to a known good ignition coil. 3. Connect one end of a known good secondary wire to the spark tester. Connect the other end to the known good ignition coil. **CAUTION** **DO NOT HOLD THE COIL while performing this test. Dangerous voltages may be present on the metal laminations as well as the high voltage tower.** 4. Crank engine. 5. Turn ignition switch to OFF position. 6. **Was spark present?**	Yes No	▶ MEASURE resistance of the ignition coil wire (from vehicle). REPLACE if greater than 7,000 ohms per foot. If OK, REPLACE ignition coil. ▶ RECONNECT coil connector to the vehicle coil and spark tester to vehicle secondary wire and GO to Test 8.

85552027

Fig. 11 Secondary coil wire test 7 chart

Ignition Coil Supply Voltage

▶ **See Figure 12**

1. Remove the/coil connector.
2. Attach the negative (–) lead from a Volt/ohmmeter to the distributor base.
3. Measure the battery voltage.
4. Turn the ignition switch to the **RUN** position.
5. Measure the voltage at the positive (+) terminal of the ignition coil. If the reading is at least 90% of battery voltage, check the ignition coil connector for dirt, corrosion and damage. Check the ignition coil terminals for dirt, corrosion and damage; if no problem is found, replace the ignition coil. If the reading is less than 90% of battery voltage, check the wiring between the ignition coil and ignition switch, or for a worn or damaged ignition switch.

Ignition Coil Primary Resistance Test

▶ **See Figure 13**

1. Turn the ignition switch off, then disconnect the ignition coil connector.
2. Check for dirt, corrosion or damage.
3. Use an ohmmeter to measure the resistance from the positive (+) to negative (–) terminals of the ignition coil.
4. If the reading is between 0.3–1.0 ohms the ignition coil is OK; continue on to the Ignition Coil Secondary Resistance Test. If the reading is less than 0.3 ohms or greater than 1.0 ohms , replace the ignition coil.

Ignition Coil Secondary Resistance Test

▶ **See Figure 14**

1. Use an ohmmeter to measure the resistance between the negative (–) terminal to the high voltage terminal of the ignition coil.
2. If the reading is between 6,500–11,500 ohms, the ignition coil is OK. If the reading is less than 6500 ohms or more than 11,500 ohms , replace the ignition coil.

REMOVAL & INSTALLATION

1. Disconnect the negative battery cable.
2. Label and detach all wiring from the ignition coil.
3. Remove the ignition coil-to-bracket bolts, then remove the ignition coil.
4. If necessary, at this time the radio ignition interference capacitor can be removed from the ignition coil.

To install:

5. If necessary, install the radio interference capacitor onto the ignition coil. Tighten the mounting bolt to 25–35 inch lbs. (2.8–4.0 Nm).
6. Position the ignition coil onto the mounting bracket, then install and tighten the mounting bolts to 25–35 inch lbs. (2.8–4.0 Nm).
7. Attach all wiring to the ignition coil, then connect the negative battery cable.

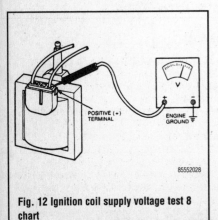

POSITIVE (+) TERMINAL
ENGINE GROUND

85552028

Fig. 12 Ignition coil supply voltage test 8 chart

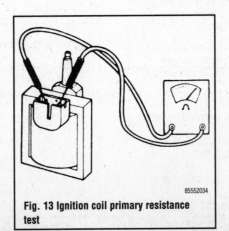

85552034

Fig. 13 Ignition coil primary resistance test

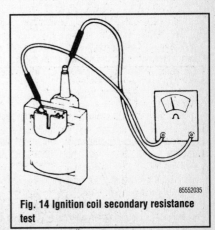

85552035

Fig. 14 Ignition coil secondary resistance test

Ignition Control Module (ICM)

REMOVAL & INSTALLATION

Remote Mounted Module

▶ **See Figure 15**

1. Disconnect the negative battery cable.
2. Label and detach all wiring from the ICM.
3. Remove the ICM/heatsink-to-fender apron bolts, then remove the ICM/heatsink.
4. If necessary, at this time the ICM can be removed from the heat sink.

To install:

5. Apply an approximately 1⁄32 in. (0.80mm) thick layer of silicone dielectric compound (D7AZ-19A331-A or equivalent) to the base plate of the ICM.
6. Install the ICM onto the heat sink. Tighten the mounting bolts to 15–35 inch lbs. (1.7–4.0 Nm).
7. Position the ICM onto the right-hand, front fender apron, then install and tighten the mounting bolts to 90–120 inch lbs. (10–14 Nm).
8. Attach all wiring to the ICM, then connect the negative battery cable.

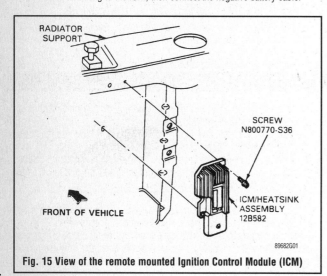

Fig. 15 View of the remote mounted Ignition Control Module (ICM)

Distributor Mounted Module

1. Disconnect the negative battery cable.
2. Remove the distributor assembly from the engine.
3. Place the distributor on the workbench and remove the module retaining screws. Pull the right side of the module down the distributor mounting flange and back up to disengage the module terminal from the connector in the distributor base. The module may be pulled toward the flange and away from the distributor.

➡ **Do not attempt to lift the module from the mounting surface, except as explained above. The pins will break at the distributor module connector.**

To install:

4. Coat the base plate of the TFI ignition module uniformly with 1⁄32 inch of silicone dielectric compound WA–10 or equivalent.
5. Position the module on the distributor base mounting flange. Carefully position the module toward the distributor bowl and engage the three connector pins securely.
6. Install the retaining screws. Tighten to 15–35 inch lbs (1.7–4.0 Nm), starting with the upper right screw.
7. Install the distributor into the engine. Install the cap and wires.
8. Reconnect the negative battery cable.
9. Recheck the initial timing. Adjust if necessary.

Distributor

REMOVAL & INSTALLATION

▶ **See Figures 16 and 17**

1. Rotate the engine until the No. 1 piston is on Top Dead Center (TDC) of its compression stroke.
2. Disconnect the negative battery cable. Disconnect the vehicle wiring harness connector from the distributor. Before removing the distributor cap, mark the position of the No. 1 wire tower on the cap for reference.

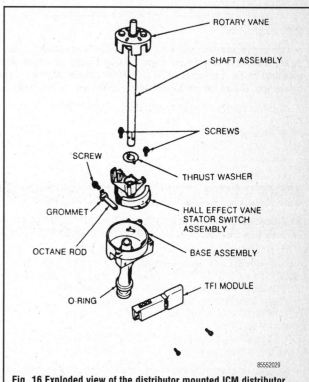

Fig. 16 Exploded view of the distributor mounted ICM distributor

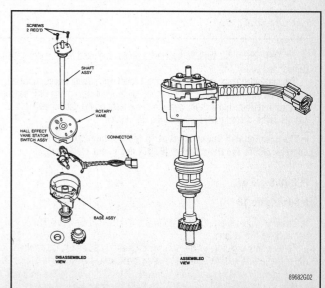

Fig. 17 Example of the remote mounted ICM distributor

3. Loosen the distributor cap hold-down screws and remove the cap. Matchmark the position of the rotor to the distributor housing. Position the cap and wires out of the way.

4. Scribe a mark in the distributor body and the engine block to indicate the position of the distributor in the engine.

5. Remove the distributor hold-down bolt and clamp.

➡**Some engines may be equipped with a security-type distributor hold-down bolt. If this is the case, use distributor wrench T82L–12270–A or equivalent, to remove the retaining bolt and clamp.**

6. Remove the distributor assembly from the engine. Be sure not to rotate the engine while the distributor is removed.

To install:

7. Make sure that the engine is still with the No. 1 piston up on TDC of its compression stroke.

➡**If the engine was disturbed while the distributor was removed, it will be necessary to remove the No. 1 spark plug and rotate the engine clockwise until the No. 1 piston is on the compression stroke. Align the timing pointer with TDC on the crankshaft damper or flywheel, as required.**

8. Check that the O-ring is installed and in good condition on the distributor body.

9. On all vehicles:

a. Rotate the distributor shaft so the rotor points toward the mark on the distributor housing made previously.

b. Rotate the rotor slightly so the leading edge of the vane is centered in the vane switch state assembly.

c. Rotate the distributor in the block to align the leading edge of the vane with the vane switch stator assembly. Make certain the rotor is pointing to the No. 1 mark on the distributor base.

➡**If the vane and vane switch stator cannot be aligned by rotating the distributor in the cylinder block, remove the distributor enough to just disengage the distributor gear from the camshaft gear. Rotate the rotor enough to engage the distributor gear on another tooth of the camshaft gear. Repeat Step 9 if necessary.**

10. Install the distributor hold-down clamp and bolt(s); tighten them slightly.

11. Attach the vehicle wiring harness connector to the distributor.

12. Install the cap and wires. Install the No. 1 spark plug, if removed.

13. Recheck the initial timing.

14. Tighten the hold-down clamp and recheck the timing. Adjust if necessary.

Camshaft Position (CMP) Sensor

For Camshaft Position (CMP) sensor procedures, please refer to Section 4 in this manual.

DISTRIBUTORLESS IGNITION SYSTEM

General Information

The distributorless ignition system used by 1991–94 2.3L and 4.0L, and all 1995–99 engines is referred to as the Electronic Ignition (EI) system. It eliminates the conventional distributor by utilizing multiple ignition coils instead. The EI system consists of the following components:

- Crankshaft Position (CKP) sensor
- Ignition Control Module (ICM) (EEC-IV systems only)
- Ignition coil(s)
- The spark angle portion of the Powertrain Control Module (PCM)
- Related wiring

➡**The function of the ICM was incorporated into the PCM beginning with the EEC-V system; otherwise the newer system operates in the same manner.**

SYSTEM OPERATION

The CKP sensor is a variable reluctance sensor, mounted near the crankshaft damper and pulley.

The crankshaft damper has a 36 minus 1 tooth wheel (data wheel) mounted on it. When this wheel rotates the magnetic field (reluctance) of the CKP sensor changes in relationship with the passing of the teeth on the data wheel. This change in the magnetic field is called the CKP signal.

➡**The base ignition timing is set at 10 (plus or minus 2 degrees) degrees Before Top Dead Center (BTDC) and is not adjustable.**

EEC-IV Systems

▶ **See Figure 18**

The CKP signal is sent to the ICM, where it is used to create the Profile Ignition Pick-up (PIP) signal.

The one missing tooth on the data wheel creates one large space between two of the teeth. The ICM utilizes this large space as a reference to help determine base ignition timing and engine speed (rpm), and to synchronize the ignition coils for the proper spark timing sequence.

The PIP signal is sent from the ICM to the PCM, which will use the PIP signal to determine base ignition timing and rpm calculations.

The ICM also receives the Spark Angle Word (SAW) signal from the PCM, which is used by the ICM to calculate the proper spark timing advance. Once all of the signals are calculated, the ICM determines the proper ON and OFF timing for the ignition coils.

The 4.0L engine utilizes one ignition coil pack, which contains three separate ignition coils. Each ignition coil fires two spark plugs simultaneously. One of the two plugs being fired is on the compression stroke (this plug uses most of the voltage) and the other plug is on the exhaust stroke (this plug uses very little of the voltage). Since these two plugs are connected in series, the firing voltage of one plug is negative (with respect to ground) and the other plug is positive.

If, for some reason, a fault arises in the EI system, the Failure Mode Effects Management (FMEM) portion of the ICM maintains vehicle operation. If the ICM stops receiving the SAW input signal, it will directly fire the ignition coils based on the CKP signal. This condition results in a fixed timing of 10 degrees BTDC.

EEC-V Systems

The CKP signal is sent to the PCM, which uses the signal to determine base ignition timing and rpm calculations.

The one missing tooth on the data wheel creates one large space between two of the teeth. The PCM utilizes this large space as a reference to help determine base ignition timing and engine speed (rpm), and to synchronize the ignition coils for the proper spark timing sequence.

All engines, except the 2.3L, 2.5L and 5.0L engines, utilize one ignition coil pack, which contains three separate ignition coils, whereas the 2.3L, 2.5L and 5.0L engines use two separate ignition coil packs, each of which contains two ignition coils. Each ignition coil fires two spark plugs simultaneously. One of the two plugs being fired is on the compression stroke (this plug uses most of the voltage) and the other plug is on the exhaust stroke (this plug uses very little of the voltage). Since these two plugs are connected in series, the firing voltage of one plug is negative (with respect to ground) and the other plug is positive.

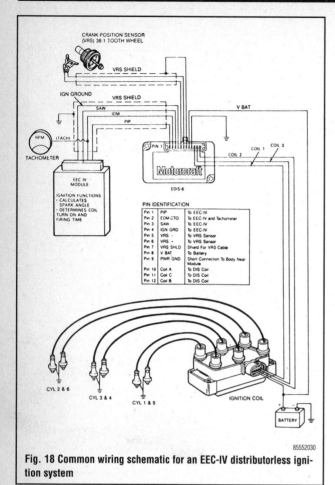

Fig. 18 Common wiring schematic for an EEC-IV distributorless ignition system

Diagnosis and Testing

SERVICE PRECAUTIONS

- Always turn the ignition key **OFF** and isolate both ends of a circuit whenever testing for shorts or continuity.
- Never measure voltage or resistance directly at the processor connector.
- Always disconnect solenoids and switches from the harness before measuring for continuity, resistance or energizing by way of a 12-volt source.
- When disconnecting connectors, inspect for damaged or pushed-out pins, corrosion, loose wires, etc. Service if required.

PRELIMINARY CHECKS

1. Visually inspect the engine compartment to ensure that all vacuum lines and spark plug wires are properly routed and securely connected.
2. Examine all wiring harnesses and connectors for insulation damage, burned, overheated, loose or broken connections.
3. Be certain that the battery is fully charged and that all accessories are **OFF** during the diagnosis.

GENERAL SYSTEM TEST

▶ **See Figures 19 thru 30**

This is a general system test for a no-start condition. Use the accompanying flow charts for this test. For ignition coil testing refer to the ignition coil procedures.

➡ Most Digital Volt Ohmmeters (DVOMs) used today belong to a class referred to as ìaveraging.î Some averaging DVOMs include the Rotunda® 007–00001, the Fluke® 70, 20 series and the Fluke® 88. Recently a new class of DVOMs, referred to as True RMS DVOMs (such as: the Fluke® 87, 8060A, 8062A, etc.), are being used. True RMS DVOMs should not be used for the tests presented here. They may display different voltage readings depending on whether the DVOM is first turned on and then the test leads are attached, or if the leads are attached first, then the DVOM is turned on. Also they may not auto range to the same range during each test, and some show different values depending on the range selected.

Ignition Coil Pack(s)

TESTING

Primary and Secondary Circuit Tests

1. Turn the ignition switch **OFF**, disconnect the battery, then detach the wiring harness connector from the ignition coil to be tested.
2. Check for dirt, corrosion or damage on the terminals.

PRIMARY RESISTANCE

▶ **See Figures 31 and 32**

1. Use an ohmmeter to measure the resistance between the following terminals on the ignition coil, and note the resistance:

Except 2.3L, 2.5L and 5.0L engines
- B+ to Coil 1
- B+ to Coil 2
- B+ to Coil 3

2.3L, 2.5L and 5.0L engines
- B+ to Coil 1
- B+ to Coil 2

or,
- B+ to Coil 3
- B+ to Coil 4

The resistance between all of these terminals should have been between 0.3–1.0 ohms. If the resistance was more or less than this value, the coil should be replaced with a new one.

SECONDARY RESISTANCE

▶ **See Figures 31 and 32**

1. Measure, using the ohmmeter, and note the resistance between each corresponding coil terminal and the two spark plug wire towers on the ignition coil. The coil terminals and plug wires towers are grouped as follows:

Except 2.3L, 2.5L and 5.0L engines
- Terminal 3 (coil 1)—spark plugs 1 and 5
- Terminal 2 (coil 3)—spark plugs 2 and 6
- Terminal 1 (coil 2)—spark plugs 3 and 4

2.3L, 2.5L engines—right-hand coil pack
- Terminal 1 (coil 2)—spark plugs 2 and 3
- Terminal 3 (coil 1)—spark plugs 1 and 4

2.3L, 2.5L engines—left-hand coil pack
- Terminal 1 (coil 4)—spark plugs 2 and 3
- Terminal 3 (coil 3)—spark plugs 1 and 4

5.0L engines—right-hand coil pack
- Terminal 1 (coil 2)—spark plugs 3 and 5
- Terminal 3 (coil 1)—spark plugs 1 and 6

5.0L engines—left-hand coil pack
- Terminal 1 (coil 4)—spark plugs 2 and 8
- Terminal 3 (coil 3)—spark plugs 4 and 7

If the resistance for all of the readings was between 6,500–11,500 ohms, the ignition coils are OK. If any of the readings was less than 6,500 ohms or more than 11,500 ohms, replace the corresponding coil pack.

TEST STEP	RESULT	▶	ACTION TO TAKE
A1 PERFORM EEC-IV QUICK TEST			
• perform EEC-IV Quick Test.	Yes	▶	GO to **A2** .
• Has Quick Test been performed?	No	▶	GO to Section 14 first and perform Quick Test.
A2 CHECK FOR SPARK DURING CRANK			
• Using a Neon Bulb Spark Tester (OTC D 89P-6666-A), check for spark at all spark plug wires while cranking.	Yes	▶	GO to **A3** .
• **Was spark present on ALL spark plug wires and consistent (one spark per crankshaft revolution)?**	No	▶	GO to **A10** .
A3 CHECK PIP AT EDIS MODULE			
• Key off.	Yes	▶	GO to **A4** .
• Install EDIS diagnostic cable to breakout box.	No	▶	GO to **A7** .
• Use EDIS 6 overlay.			
• Connect LED test lamp between J43 (PIP E) and J7 (GND).			
• **Does the LED test lamp blink continuously during crank?**			
A4 CHECK PIP CONTINUITY TO EEC			
• Key off.	Yes	▶	GO to **A5** .
• Disconnect the EEC processor.	No	▶	SERVICE open circuit. RECONNECT the EEC processor and RERUN Quick Test.
• **Is the resistance between J43 (PIP E) and Pin 56 (PIP) of the EEC connector less than 5 ohms?**			
A5 CHECK IGND AT EDIS			
• Key off.	Yes	▶	GO to **A6** .
• **Is the resistance between J47 (IGND E) and J7 (BAT–) less than 5 ohms?**	No	▶	REPLACE EDIS module and RERUN Quick Test.

85552040

Fig. 19 Test A—no start, part 1

TEST STEP	RESULT	▶	ACTION TO TAKE
A10 DETERMINE MISSING SPARK PATTERN			
• Is spark missing from BOTH cylinder 1 and 5 plug wires?	Yes	▶	GO to **A12** .
or	No	▶	GO to **A11** .
• Is spark missing from BOTH cylinder 2 and 6 plug wires?			
or			
• Is spark missing from BOTH cylinder 3 and 4 plug wires?			
A11 CHECK PLUGS AND WIRES			
• Check spark plug wires for insulation damage, looseness, shorting or other damage.	Yes	▶	REINSTALL plugs and wires. GO to **A12** .
• Remove and check spark plugs for damage, wear, carbon deposits and proper plug gap.	No	▶	SERVICE or REPLACE damaged component. RERUN Quick Test.
• **Are spark plugs and wires OK?**			
A12 CHECK VBAT C AT COIL			
• Key off.	Yes	▶	GO to **A13** .
• Install EDIS diagnostic cable to breakout box.	No	▶	SERVICE open circuit. RECONNECT the EEC processor and RERUN Quick Test.
• Use EDIS 6 overlay.			
• Connect the LED test lamp between J5 (VBAT C) and J7 (BAT-).			
• Key On.			
• **Is the LED test lamp on and bright?**			
A13 CHECK COIL FOR FAILURE			
• Connect LED test lamp between J7 (BAT-) to each coil - J3, J6 and J10, one at a time.	Yes	▶	GO to **A14** .
• Key on.	No	▶	REPLACE Coil pack. RERUN Quick Test.
• **Is the LED test lamp on and bright?**			
A14 CHECK GND CONTINUITY TO EDIS MODULE			
• Key off.	Yes	▶	GO to **A15** .
• **Is the resistance between J27 (GND E) and J7 (BAT-) less than 5 ohms?**	No	▶	SERVICE open circuit. RECONNECT EEC and RERUN Quick Test.

85552042

Fig. 21 Test A—no start, part 3

TEST STEP	RESULT	▶	ACTION TO TAKE
A6 CHECK IGND CONTINUITY TO EEC			
• Key off.	Yes	▶	REPLACE EDIS module. RUN Quick Test.
• **Is the resistance between J47 (IGND E) and Pin 16 (IGN GND) of the EEC connector less than 5 ohms?**	No	▶	SERVICE open circuit. RECONNECT EEC and RERUN Quick Test.
A7 CHECK PIP AT EDIS MODULE/ISOLATE EEC			
• Key off.	Yes	▶	REPLACE EEC processor. RERUN Quick Test.
• Disconnect the EEC processor.	No	▶	GO to **A8** .
• Crank the engine.			
• **Does the LED test lamp blink continuously during crank?**			
A8 CHECK PIP CIRCUIT FOR SHORT TO GROUND			
• Key off.	Yes	▶	PIP is shorted to ground in harness. CHECK connectors, SERVICE or REPLACE harness. RERUN Quick Test.
• Disconnect the EDIS module from the EDIS diagnostic cable.			
• Disconnect the HEGO sensor.	No	▶	GO to **A9** .
• **Is the resistance between J43 (PIP E) and J7 (BAT–) less than 5 ohms?**			
A9 CHECK PIP CIRCUIT FOR SHORT TO POWER			
• **Is the resistance between J43 (PIP E) and J51 (VBAT E) less than 5 ohms?**	Yes	▶	PIP is shorted to power in harness. CHECK connectors, SERVICE or REPLACE harness. RUN Quick Test.
	No	▶	REPLACE EDIS module. RERUN Quick Test.

85552041

Fig. 20 Test A—no start, part 2

TEST STEP	RESULT	▶	ACTION TO TAKE
A15 CHECK GND IN EDIS MODULE			
• Key off.	Yes	▶	GO to **A16** .
• **Is the resistance between J27 (GND E) and J47 (IGND E) less than 5 ohms?**	No	▶	REPLACE EDIS module. RERUN Quick Test.
A16 CHECK VBAT E AT EDIS MODULE			
• Connect the LED test lamp between J51 (VBAT E) and J7 (BAT-).	Yes	▶	GO to **A17** .
• Key on.	No	▶	SERVICE open circuit. RECONNECT the EEC processor and RERUN Quick Test.
• **Is the LED test lamp on and bright?**			
A17 CHECK VRS AMPLITUDE AT EDIS MODULE			
• **Is the A/C voltage between J35 (VRS+ E) and J48 (VRS- E) more than 1 volt when the engine is cranked?**	Yes	▶	GO to **A18** .
	No	▶	GO to **A19** .
A18 CHECK VRS BIAS AT EDIS MODULE			
• Key on.	Yes	▶	REPLACE EDIS module. RERUN Quick Test.
• **Is the DC voltage between J35 (VRS+ E) and J27 (GND E) between 1.0 and 2.0 volts?**	No	▶	GO to **A28** .
A19 CHECK VRS CRANKING VOLTAGE AT EDIS			
• Key off.	Yes	▶	REPLACE EDIS module. RERUN Quick Test.
• Disconnect the EDIS module from the EDIS diagnostic cable.	No	▶	GO to **A20** .
• **Is the A/C voltage more than 1 volt when the engine is cranked?**			
A20 CHECK VRS CRANKING VOLTAGE AT SENSOR			
• Key off.	Yes	▶	GO to **A22** .
• Disconnect the VRS engine harness from the EDIS diagnostic cable.	No	▶	GO to **A21** .
• **Is the A/C voltage between J32 (VRS- S) and J31 (VRS+ S) more than 1 volt when the engine is cranked?**			

85552043

Fig. 22 Test A—no start, part 4

TEST STEP		RESULT	▶	ACTION TO TAKE
A21	CHECK VR SENSOR AND CRANKSHAFT WHEEL			
• Check the crankshaft data wheel for damage. • Check the air gap. • Is the air gap correct and is the crankshaft data wheel OK?		Yes	▶	REPLACE VR sensor. RERUN Quick Test.
		No	▶	REPAIR or REPLACE bad parts. SET air gap.
A22	CHECK VRS+ CIRCUIT FOR OPEN			
• Key off. • Reconnect the EDIS diagnostic cable. • Is the resistance between J35 (VRS+ E) and J31 (VRS+ S) less than 5 ohms?		Yes	▶	GO to A23 .
		No	▶	SERVICE open circuit in VRS+ harness. RERUN Quick Test.
A23	CHECK VRS- CIRCUIT FOR OPEN			
• Key off. • Is the resistance between J32 (VRS- S) and J48 (VRS – E) less than 5 ohms?		Yes	▶	GO to A24 .
		No	▶	SERVICE open circuit in VRS- harness. RERUN Quick Test.
A24	CHECK VRS- CIRCUIT FOR SHORT TO POWER			
• Key off. • Disconnect the HEGO sensor. • Is the resistance between J48 (VRS- E) and J51 (VBAT E) greater than 10K ohms?		Yes	▶	GO to A25 .
		No	▶	SERVICE short circuit in VRS- harness. RERUN Quick Test.
A25	CHECK VRS- CIRCUIT FOR SHORT TO GROUND			
• Is the resistance between J48 (VRS- E) and J7 (BAT-) greater than 10K ohms?		Yes	▶	GO to A26 .
		No	▶	SERVICE short circuit in VRS- harness. RERUN Quick Test.

85552044

Fig. 23 Test A—no start, part 5

TEST STEP		RESULT	▶	ACTION TO TAKE
A31	CHECK VRS- CIRCUIT FOR SHORT TO POWER			
• Is the resistance between J48 (VRS- E) and J51 (VBAT E) greater than 10K ohms?		Yes	▶	GO to A32 .
		No	▶	SERVICE short circuit in VRS- harness. RERUN Quick Test.
A32	CHECK VRS- CIRCUIT FOR SHORT TO GROUND			
• Is the resistance between J48 (VRS- E) and J7 (BAT-) less than 5 ohms?		Yes	▶	SERVICE short circuit in VRS- harness. RERUN Quick Test.
		No	▶	REPLACE EDIS module. RERUN Quick Test.

85552046

Fig. 25 Test A—no start, part 7

TEST STEP		RESULT	▶	ACTION TO TAKE
A26	CHECK VRS+ CIRCUIT FOR SHORT TO GROUND			
• Is the resistance between J35 (VRS+ E) and J7 (BAT-) greater than 10K ohms?		Yes	▶	GO to A27 .
		No	▶	SERVICE short circuit in VRS+ harness. RERUN Quick Test.
A27	CHECK VRS+ CIRCUIT FOR SHORT TO POWER			
• Is the resistance between J35 (VRS+ E) and J51 (VBAT E) greater than 10K ohms?		Yes	▶	VRS+ is shorted to VRS-. SERVICE short in harness. RERUN Quick Test.
		No	▶	SERVICE short circuit in VRS+ harness. RERUN Quick Test.
A28	CHECK VRS BIAS AT EDIS MODULE			
• Key off. • Disconnect the VR sensor from the EDIS diagnostic cable. • Key on. • Is the DC voltage between J35 (VRS+ E) and J7 (BAT-) between 1.0 and 2.0 volts?		Yes	▶	REPLACE VR sensor. RERUN Quick Test.
		No	▶	GO to A29 .
A29	CHECK VRS+ CIRCUIT FOR SHORT TO POWER			
• Key off. • Disconnect the EDIS module from the EDIS diagnostic cable. • Disconnect the HEGO sensor. • Is the resistance between J35 (VRS+ E) and J51 (VBAT E) greater than 10K ohms?		Yes	▶	GO to A30 .
		No	▶	VRS+ is shorted to power in harness. CHECK connectors, SERVICE or REPLACE harness. RERUN Quick Test.
A30	CHECK VRS+ CIRCUIT FOR SHORT TO GROUND			
• Is the resistance between J35 (VRS+ E) and J7 (BAT-) greater than 10K ohms?		Yes	▶	GO to A31 .
		No	▶	SERVICE short circuit in VRS+ harness. RERUN Quick Test.

85552045

Fig. 24 Test A—no start, part 6

TEST STEP		RESULT	▶	ACTION TO TAKE
B1	CHECK IDM CONTINUITY TO EEC			
• Key off. • Install EDIS diagnostic cable to breakout box. • Use EDIS 6 overlay. • Disconnect the EEC processor. • Is the resistance between J41 (IDM E) and Pin 4 (IDM) of the EEC connector less than 5 ohms?		Yes	▶	GO to B2 .
		No	▶	SERVICE open in IDM circuit. RERUN Quick Test.
B2	CHECK IDM CIRCUIT FOR SHORT TO GROUND			
• Key off. • Disconnect the EDIS module from the EDIS diagnostic cable. • Disconnect the HEGO sensor. • Is the resistance between J41 (IDM E) and J7 (BAT-) greater than 10K ohms?		Yes	▶	GO to B3 .
		No	▶	IDM is shorted to ground in harness. CHECK connectors, SERVICE or REPLACE harness. RERUN Quick Test.
B3	CHECK IDM CIRCUIT FOR SHORT TO POWER			
• Is the resistance between J41 (IDM E) and J51 (VBAT E) greater than 10K ohms?		Yes	▶	REPLACE EDIS module. RECONNECT EEC processor. RERUN Quick Test. If fault persists, REPLACE EEC processor and RERUN Quick Test.
		No	▶	IDM is shorted to power in harness. CHECK connectors, SERVICE or REPLACE harness. RERUN Quick Test.

85552047

Fig. 26 Test B—code 16, memory code 18 and/or "Check Engine Light On" IDM failure

TEST STEP	RESULT	▶	ACTION TO TAKE
C1 CHECK FOR COIL SIGNALS AT EDIS			
• Key off. • Install EDIS diagnostic cable to breakout box. • Use the EDIS-6 overlay. • Key on. • Connect LED test lamp from J51 (VBAT E) to each coil - J53, J54 and J55, one at a time. • **Does the lamp turn on brightly for each coil?**	Yes	▶	GO to [C6] .
	No	▶	GO to [C2] .
C2 CHECK EDIS COIL AT CRANK			
• Crank engine. • **Does lamp blink at each coil during crank?**	Yes	▶	GO to [C3] .
	No	▶	GO to [C4] .
C3 CHECK COIL CONTINUITY TO EDIS MODULE			
• Key off. • Disconnect EDIS module from the EDIS diagnostic cable. • Disconnect the coil pack from the EDIS diagnostic cable. • **Is the resistance between J3 and J53, J6 and J55, J10 and J54 less than 5 ohms?**	Yes	▶	REPLACE coil pack. RERUN Quick Test.
	No	▶	SERVICE open circuit in coil harness. RERUN Quick Test.
C4 CHECK COIL FOR SHORT TO POWER			
• Key off. • Disconnect the coil pack from the EDIS diagnostic cable. • Crank the engine. • **Does lamp blink at any coil during crank?**	Yes	▶	REPLACE coil pack. RERUN Quick Test.
	No	▶	GO to [C5] .
C5 CHECK COIL CIRCUITS FOR SHORT TO POWER			
• Key off. • HEGO disconnected. • Disconnect EDIS module from EDIS diagnostic cable. • **Is the resistance between J51 (VBAT E) and each coil - J3, J6 and J10 - greater than 10K ohms?**	Yes	▶	REPLACE EDIS module. RERUN Quick Test.
	No	▶	SERVICE short to power in coil harness RERUN Quick Test.

85552048

Fig. 27 Test C—memory code 45 and/or "Check Engine Light On" coil failure, part 1

TEST STEP	RESULT	▶	ACTION TO TAKE
C6 CHECK COIL FOR SHORT TO GROUND			
• Key off. • Disconnect the coil pack from the EDIS diagnostic cable. • Key on. • Connect LED test lamp from J7 (BAT-) to each coil - J53, J54 and J55, one at a time. • **Does the lamp turn on for each coil?**	Yes	▶	GO to [C7] .
	No	▶	REPLACE coil pack. RERUN Quick Test.
C7 CHECK COIL CIRCUITS FOR SHORT TO GROUND			
• Key off. • Disconnect the EDIS module from the EDIS diagnostic cable. • Key on. • Connect LED test lamp from J7 (BAT-) to each coil - J53, J54 and J55, one at a time. • **Does the lamp turn on for each coil?**	Yes	▶	SERVICE short circuit in coil harness. RERUN Quick Test.
	No	▶	REPLACE EDIS module. RERUN Quick Test.

85552049

Fig. 28 Test C—memory code 45 and/or "Check Engine Light On" coil failure, part 2

TEST STEP	RESULT	▶	ACTION TO TAKE
D1 CHECK FOR SPARK AT WIRES			
• Engine on. • Using a Neon Bulb Spark Tester (OTC D 89P-6666-A), check for spark at all spark plug wires. • **Was spark present on ALL spark plug wires and consistent (one spark per crankshaft revolution)?**	Yes	▶	GO to [D2] .
	No	▶	GO to [D6] .
D2 CHECK TIMING WITH TIMING LIGHT			
• Install timing light. • Start engine and warm to normal engine temperature. • Transmission out of gear. • **Is the spark angle greater than 19 degrees BTDC?**	Yes	▶	REFER to engine diagnostics in Shop Manual.
	No	▶	GO to [D3] .
D3 CHECK SAW CONTINUITY TO EEC			
• Key off. • Install EDIS diagnostic cable but do not connect the EDIS module or coil pack to the cable. • Connect the cable to the breakout box. • Use the EDIS 6 overlay. • Disconnect the EEC processor. • **Is the resistance between J45 (SAW E) and Pin 36 (SAW) of the EEC connector less than 5 ohms?**	Yes	▶	GO to [D4] .
	No	▶	SERVICE open in SAW circuit. RECONNECT the EEC processor and RERUN Quick Test.
D4 CHECK SAW CIRCUIT FOR SHORT TO GROUND			
• Key off. • HEGO disconnected. • **Is the resistance between J45 (SAW E) and J7 (BAT -) greater than 10K ohms?**	Yes	▶	GO to [D5] .
	No	▶	SAW is shorted to ground in harness. CHECK connectors, SERVICE or REPLACE harness. RERUN Quick Test.

85552050

Fig. 29 Test D—engine running with code 18, SAW failure, part 1

TEST STEP	RESULT	▶	ACTION TO TAKE
D5 CHECK SAW CIRCUIT FOR SHORT-TO-POWER			
• **Is the resistance between J45 (SAW E) and J51 (VBAT E) greater than 10K ohms?**	Yes	▶	REPLACE EDIS module. RECONNECT EEC processor. RERUN Quick Test. If fault persists, REPLACE EEC processor and RERUN Quick Test.
	No	▶	SAW is shorted to ground in harness. CHECK connectors, SERVICE or REPLACE harness. RERUN Quick Test.
D6 CHECK PLUGS AND WIRES			
• Check spark plug wires for insulation damage, looseness, shorting or other damage. • Remove and check spark plugs for damage, wear, carbon deposits and proper plug gap. • **Are spark plugs and wires OK?**	Yes	▶	REPLACE coil pack.
	No	▶	SERVICE or REPLACE damaged component. RERUN Quick Test.

85552051

Fig. 30 Test D—engine running with code 18, SAW failure, part 2

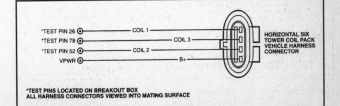

*TEST PINS LOCATED ON BREAKOUT BOX
ALL HARNESS CONNECTORS VIEWED INTO MATING SURFACE

89682G25

Fig. 31 Engine ignition coil harness connections—3.0L and 4.0L engines

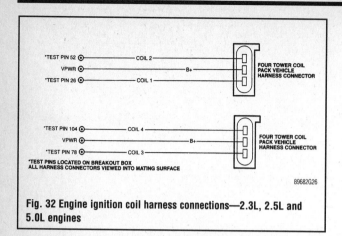

Fig. 32 Engine ignition coil harness connections—2.3L, 2.5L and 5.0L engines

➡On 2.3L, 2.5L and 5.0L engines, if one coil pack is found to be defective, the other pack does not need to be replaced.

REMOVAL & INSTALLATION

▶ See Figures 33, 34, 35, 36 and 37

➡All engines, except the 2.3L, 2.5L and 5.0L engines, utilizes one coil pack containing three separate coils. The 2.3L, 2.5L and 5.0L engines use two coil packs containing two separate coils each.

1. Disconnect the negative battery cable.
2. Unplug the electrical harness connector from the ignition coil pack.
3. Label and remove the spark plug wires from the ignition coil terminal towers by squeezing the locking tabs to release the coil boot retainers.
4. Remove the coil pack mounting screws and remove the coil pack.

To install:

5. Install the coil pack and the retaining screws. Tighten the retaining screws to 40–62 inch lbs. (4.5–7 Nm).

➡Be sure to place some dielectric compound into each spark plug boot prior to installation of the spark plug wire.

6. Attach the spark plug wires and electrical harness connector to the coil pack.
7. Connect the negative battery cable.

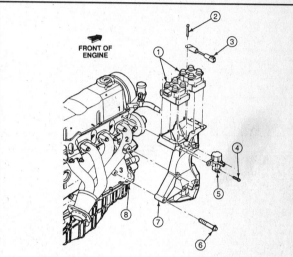

1. Ignition coil packs
2. Coil-to-bracket mounting bolt
3. Radio ignition interference capacitor
4. Screw
5. EGR control
6. Bracket-to-engine mounting bolt
7. Mounting bracket
8. Cylinder block

Fig. 34 1992–99 ignition coil mounting for the 2.3L, 2.5L engine

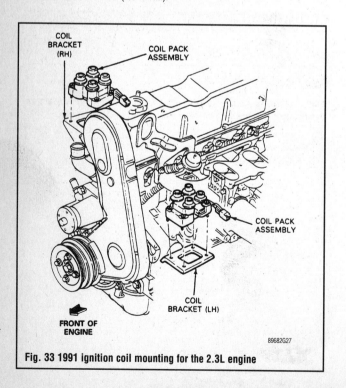

Fig. 33 1991 ignition coil mounting for the 2.3L engine

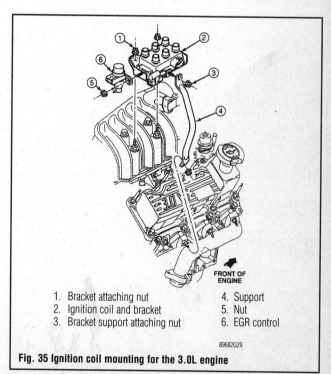

1. Bracket attaching nut
2. Ignition coil and bracket
3. Bracket support attaching nut
4. Support
5. Nut
6. EGR control

Fig. 35 Ignition coil mounting for the 3.0L engine

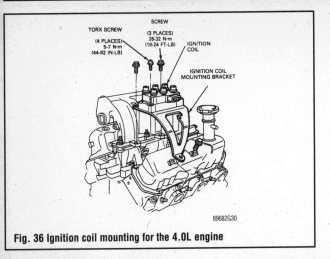

Fig. 36 Ignition coil mounting for the 4.0L engine

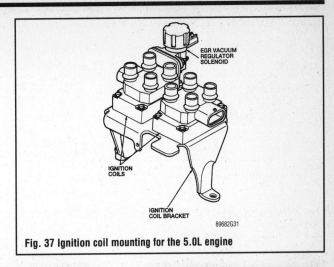

Fig. 37 Ignition coil mounting for the 5.0L engine

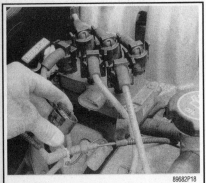

To remove the coil pack, unplug the electrical harness connector from it

Label the spark plug wires according to their position on the coil pack

Remove the plug wires from the coil by squeezing the lock tabs (arrows) and pulling straight up

Remove the coil retaining screws . . . .

. . . then remove the coil pack from its mounting bracket

Ignition Control Module (ICM)

REMOVAL & INSTALLATION

♦ See Figures 38, 39 and 40

➡ Only the EEC-IV ignition systems use an external ICM. EEC-V systems have incorperated the ICM into the Power Control Module (PCM).

1. Disconnect the negative battery cable.
2. Detach the wiring harness connector(s) from the ICM.
3. Remove the mounting bolts, then remove the ICM.

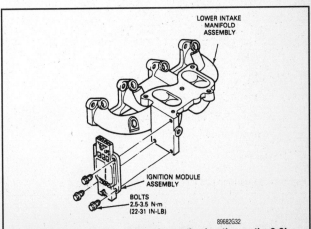

Fig. 38 Ignition control module and mounting location on the 2.3L, 2.5L engine

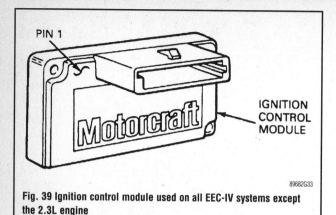

Fig. 39 Ignition control module used on all EEC-IV systems except the 2.3L engine

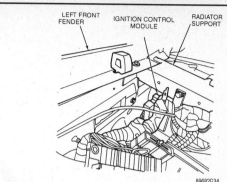

Fig. 40 Ignition control module mounting on all EEC-IV systems except the 2.3L engine

To install:

4. Position the ICM onto the inner fender apron and install the mounting bolts. Tighten the bolts to 22–31 inch lbs (2.5–3.5 Nm).
5. Attach the wiring harness connector(s) to the ICM.
6. Connect the negative battery cable.

Camshaft Position (CMP) and Crankshaft Position (CKP) Sensors

For procedures on these sensors, please refer to Section 4 in this manual.

FIRING ORDERS

▶ See Figures 41, 42, 43, 44 and 45

➥To avoid confusion, remove and tag the spark plug wires one at a time, for replacement.

If a distributor is not keyed for installation with only one orientation, it could have been removed previously and rewired. The resultant wiring would hold the correct firing order, but could change the relative placement of the plug towers in relation to the engine. For this reason it is imperative that you label all wires before disconnecting any of them. Also, before removal, compare the current wiring with the accompanying illustrations. If the current wiring does not match, make notes in your book to reflect how your engine is wired.

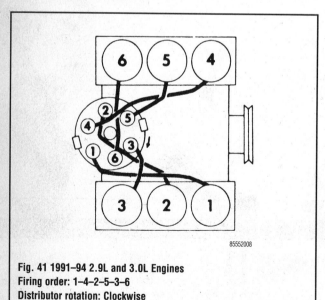

Fig. 41 1991–94 2.9L and 3.0L Engines
Firing order: 1–4–2–5–3–6
Distributor rotation: Clockwise

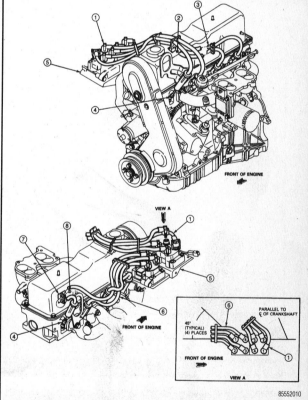

Fig. 42 2.3L, 2.5L Engines
Firing order: 1–3–4–2
Distributorless ignition

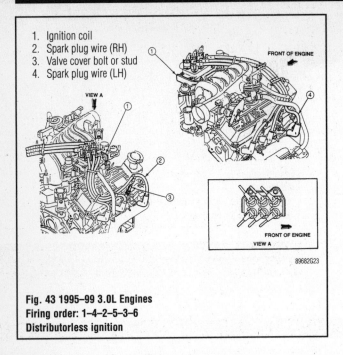

1. Ignition coil
2. Spark plug wire (RH)
3. Valve cover bolt or stud
4. Spark plug wire (LH)

Fig. 43 1995–99 3.0L Engines
Firing order: 1–4–2–5–3–6
Distributorless ignition

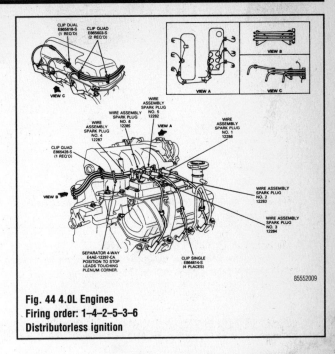

Fig. 44 4.0L Engines
Firing order: 1–4–2–5–3–6
Distributorless ignition

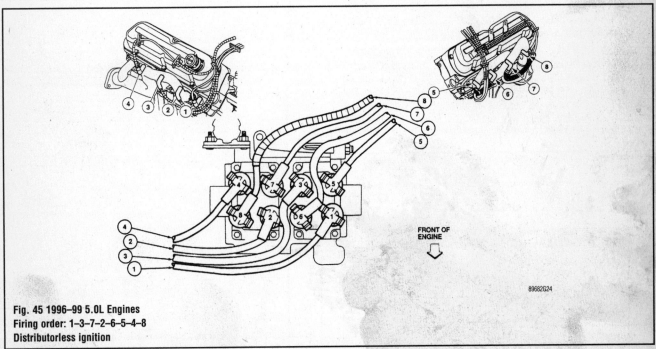

Fig. 45 1996–99 5.0L Engines
Firing order: 1–3–7–2–6–5–4–8
Distributorless ignition

CHARGING SYSTEM

General Information

▶ See Figure 46

The charging system is a negative (-) ground system which consists of an alternator, a regulator, a charge indicator, a storage battery, wiring connecting the components, and fuse link wire.

The alternator is belt-driven from the engine. Energy is supplied from the alternator/regulator system to the rotating field through two brushes to two slip-rings. The slip-rings are mounted on the rotor shaft and are connected to the field coil. This energy supplied to the rotating field from the battery is called excitation current and is used to initially energize the field to begin the genera-

tion of electricity. Once the alternator starts to generate electricity, the excitation current comes from its own output rather than the battery.

The alternator produces power in the form of alternating current. The alternating current is rectified by 6 diodes into direct current. The direct current is used to charge the battery and power the rest of the electrical system.

When the ignition key is turned **ON**, current flows from the battery, through the charging system indicator light on the instrument panel, to the voltage regulator, and to the alternator. Since the alternator is not producing any current, the alternator warning light comes on. When the engine is started, the alternator begins to produce current and turns the alternator light off. As the alternator turns and produces current, the current is divided in two ways: one part to the battery to charge the battery and power the electrical components of the vehicle,

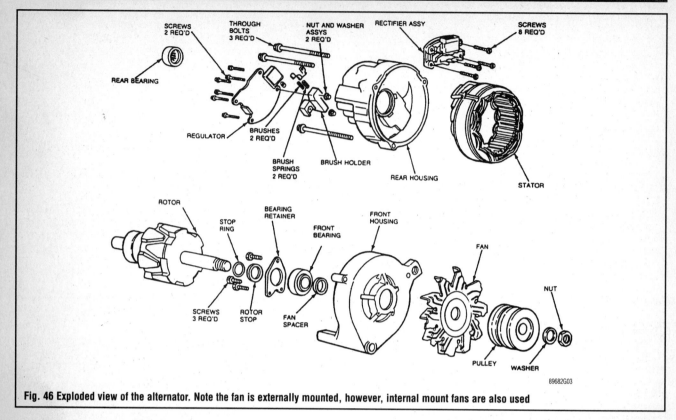

Fig. 46 Exploded view of the alternator. Note the fan is externally mounted, however, internal mount fans are also used

and one part is returned to the alternator to enable it to increase its output. In this situation, the alternator is receiving current from the battery and from itself. A voltage regulator is wired into the current supply to the alternator to prevent it from receiving too much current, which, in turn, would cause it to produce too much current. Conversely, if the voltage regulator does not allow the alternator to receive enough current, the battery will not be fully charged and will eventually drain.

The battery is connected to the alternator at all times, whether the ignition key is turned **ON** or not. If the battery were shorted to ground, the alternator would also be shorted. This would damage the alternator. To prevent this, a fuse link is installed in the wiring between the battery and the alternator. If the battery is shorted the fuse link melts, protecting the alternator.

Alternator Precautions

To prevent damage to the alternator and regulator, the following precautions should be taken when working with the electrical system.
• Never reverse the battery connections.
• Booster batteries for starting must be connected properly: positive-to-positive and negative-to-ground.
• Disconnect the battery cables before using a fast charger; the charger has a tendency to force current through the diodes in the opposite direction for which they were designed. This burns out the diodes.
• Never use a fast charger as a booster for starting the vehicle.
• Never disconnect the voltage regulator while the engine is running.
• Avoid long soldering times when replacing diodes or transistors. Prolonged heat is damaging to AC generators.
• Do not use test lamps of more than 12 volts (V) for checking diode continuity.
• Do not short across or ground any of the terminals on the AC generator.
• The polarity of the battery, generator, and regulator must be matched and considered before making any electrical connections within the system.
• Never operate the alternator on an open circuit. make sure that all connections within the circuit are clean and tight.
• Disconnect the battery terminals when performing any service on the electrical system. This will eliminate the possibility of accidental reversal of polarity.
• Disconnect the battery ground cable if arc welding is to be done on any part of the vehicle.

Alternator

TESTING

General Information

There are many possible ways in which the charging system can malfunction. Often the source of a problem is difficult to diagnose, requiring special equipment and a good deal of experience. This is usually not the case, however, where the charging system fails completely and causes the dash board warning light to come on or the battery to discharge. To troubleshoot a complete system failure, only two pieces of equipment are needed: a test light, to determine that current is reaching a certain point and a current indicator (ammeter), to determine the direction of the current flow and its measurement in amps. This test works under three assumptions:
1. The battery is known to be good and fully charged.
2. The alternator belt is in good condition and adjusted to the proper tension.
3. All connections in the system are clean and tight.

➡**In order for the current indicator to give a valid reading, the vehicle must be equipped with battery cables which are of the same gauge size and quality as original equipment battery cables.**

Before commencing with the following tests, turn off all electrical components on the vehicle. Make sure the doors of the vehicle are closed. If the vehicle is equipped with a clock, disconnect the clock by removing the lead wire from the rear of the clock.

Battery No-Load Test

1. Ensure that the ignition switch is turned **OFF**.
2. Connect a tachometer to the engine by following the manufacturer's instructions.
3. Using a Digital Volt Ohmmeter (DVOM) measure the voltage across the positive (+) and negative (-) battery terminals. Note the voltage reading for future reference.

Ensure that all electrical components on the vehicle are turned off. Be sure the doors of the vehicle are closed. If the vehicle is equipped with a clock, disconnect the clock by removing the lead wire from the rear of the clock.

4. Start the engine and have an assistant run it at 1500 rpm.

5. Read the voltage across the battery terminals again. The voltage should now be between 14.1–14.7 volts.

   a. If the voltage increase is less than 2.5 volts over the base voltage measured in Step 3, perform the Battery Load test.

   b. If there was no voltage increase, or the voltage increase was greater than 2.5 volts, perform the Alternator Load and No-Load tests.

Battery Load Test

1. With the engine running, turn the air conditioner ON (if equipped) or the blower motor on high speed and the headlights on high beam.

2. Have your assistant increase the engine speed to approximately 2000 rpm.

3. Read the voltage across the battery terminals again.

   a. If the voltage increase is 0.5 volts over the base voltage measured in Battery No-Load test Step 3, the charging system is working properly. If your problem continues, there may be a problem with the battery.

   b. If the voltage does not increase as indicated, perform the Alternator Load and No-Load tests.

Alternator Load Test

✳✳ WARNING

Do NOT use a normal Digital Volt Ohmmeter (DVOM) for this test; your DVOM will be destroyed by the large amounts of amperage from the car's battery. Use a tester designed for charging system analysis, such as the Rotunda Alternator, Regulator, Battery and Starter Motor Tester 010–00725 (ARBST) or equivalent.

1. Switch the tester to the ammeter setting.

2. Attach the positive (+) and negative (-) leads of the tester to the battery terminals.

3. Connect the current probe to the **B+** terminal on the alternator.

4. Start the engine and have an assistant run the engine at 2000 rpm. Adjust the tester load bank to determine the output of the alternator. Alternator output should be within ten percent of the alternator's output rating; if so, continue with the Alternator No-Load test. If the output is not within ten percent of the alternator's output rating, there is a problem in the charging system. Have the system further tested by a Ford qualified automotive technician.

Alternator No-Load Test

1. Using the same tester as in the Alternator Load Test, switch the tester to the voltmeter function.

2. Connect the voltmeter positive (+) lead to the alternator **B+** terminal and the negative (-) lead to a good engine ground.

3. Turn all of the electrical accessories off and shut the doors.

4. While an assistant operates the engine at 2000 rpm, check the alternator output voltage. The voltage should be between 13.0–15.0 volts. If the alternator does not produce voltage within this range there is a problem in the charging system. Have the system further tested by a Ford qualified automotive technician.

REMOVAL & INSTALLATION

1. Disconnect the negative battery cable.

2. Remove the accessory drive belt.

3. Label and disengage all of the wiring connectors from the alternator. To disconnect push-on type terminals, disengage the lock tab and pull straight off.

4. Remove the alternator bolts, then remove the alternator from the engine

To install:

5. Position the alternator on the engine.

6. Install the alternator mounting bolts. On 3.8L and 5.0L engines, tighten the upper bolt to 16–21 ft. lbs. (21–29 Nm) and the lower bolt to 30–40 ft. lbs. (40–55 Nm). On 4.6L engines, tighten both bolts to 15–22 ft. lbs. (20–30 Nm).

7. On 4.6L engines, install the alternator mounting bracket and bolts. Tighten the bolts to 71–106 inch lbs. (8–12 Nm).

After disconnecting the battery and removing the drive belt, unplug the single wire connector . . .

. . . then the multi-wire connector from the back of the alternator—integral regulator units lack the single wire

If the push-on connectors are difficult to remove, use a small pick to disengage the connector latch

Unbolt the battery (B+) lead from the back of the alternator . . .

. . . then remove the alternator mounting bolts

Remove the alternator from its mounting bracket

8. Install the accessory drive belt. Ensure that the drive belt is properly installed on the pulleys before starting the engine.

9. Attach all engine wiring harness connectors to the alternator.

10. Connect the negative battery cable.

Voltage Regulator

REMOVAL & INSTALLATION

1991–95 models with non-integral type regulator

▶ **See Figures 47, 48 and 49**

1. Disconnect the negative battery cable.

2. Remove 4 Torx® head screws holding the voltage regulator to the alternator rear housing. Remove the regulator, with the brush and terminal holder attached.

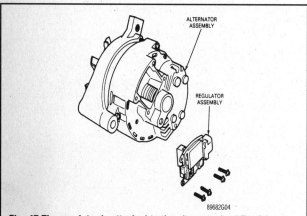

Fig. 47 The regulator is attached to the alternator by 4 Torx® head screws

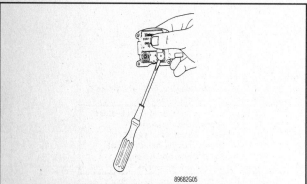

Fig. 48 Holding the regulator in one hand, break off the tab covering the A screw to expose the brush holder retaining screws

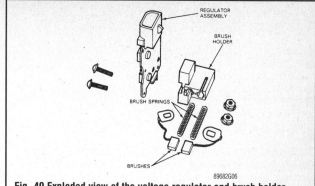

Fig. 49 Exploded view of the voltage regulator and brush holder assembly

3. Hold the regulator in one hand and pry off the cap covering the **A** terminal screw head with a small prybar.

4. Remove 2 Torx® head screws retaining the regulator to the brush holder. Separate the regulator from the brush holder.

To install:

5. Install the brush holder on the regulator with 2 retaining screws. Tighten the screws to 25–35 inch lbs. (2.8–4.0 Nm).

6. Install the cap on the head of the **A** terminal screw.

7. Depress the brushes into the holder and hold the brushes in position by inserting a standard size paper clip, or equivalent tool, through both the location hole in the regulator and through the holes in the brushes.

8. Install the regulator/brush holder assembly and remove the paper clip. Install the attaching screws and tighten to 20–30 inch lbs. (2.3–3.4 Nm).

9. Connect the negative battery cable.

1995–99 models with integral type regulator

▶ **See Figure 50**

The internal voltage regulator used on alternators used with these vehicles is not removable or, in any other way, serviceable. If the voltage regulator is found to be defective, a new alternator must be installed.

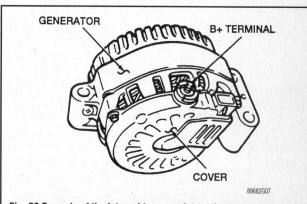

Fig. 50 Example of the integral type regulator alternator

STARTING SYSTEM

General Information

The starting system is designed to rotate the engine at a speed fast enough for the engine to start. The starting system is comprised of the following components:

• Permanent magnet gear-reduction starter motor with a solenoid-actuated drive

• Battery

• Remote control starter switch (part of the ignition switch)

• Park/Neutral Position (PNP) or Manual Lever Position (MLP) switch (on 1994 automatic transmission models) or Transmission Range (TR) sensor (on 1995–99 automatic transmission models)

• Clutch Pedal Position (CPP) switch (on manual transmission models)

• Starter relay

• Heavy circuit wiring

Heavy cables, connectors and switches are utilized by the starting system because of the large amount of amperage this system is required to handle while cranking the engine. For premium starter motor function, the resistance in the starting system must be kept to an absolute minimum.

A discharged or faulty battery, loose or corroded connections, or partially broken cables will result in slower-than-normal cranking speeds. The amount of damage evident may even prevent the starter motor from rotating the engine at all.

Vehicles equipped with a manual transmission are equipped with a Clutch Pedal Position (CPP) switch in the starter circuit, which is designed to prevent the starter motor from operating unless the clutch pedal is depressed. Vehicles equipped with automatic transmissions are equipped with either a Park/Neutral Position (PNP) switch, a Manual Lever Position (MLP) switch or a Transmission Range (TR) sensor in the starter circuit. These switches prevent the starter motor from functioning unless the transmission range selector lever is in Neutral (**N**) or Park (**P**).

The starter motor is a 12 volt assembly, which has the starter solenoid mounted on the drive end-housing. The starter solenoid energizes when the relay contacts are closed. When the solenoid energizes, the starter drive engages with the flywheel ring gear, rotating the crankshaft and starting the engine. An overrunning clutch in the starter drive assembly protects the starter motor from excessive speed when the engine starts.

Starter

TESTING

▶ See Figures 51 and 52

Use the charts to help locate and diagnose starting system problems. Remember that the starter uses large amounts of current during operation, so use all appropriate precautions during testing.

System Inspection

CAUTION: When disconnecting the plastic hardshell connector at the solenoid "S" terminal, grasp the plastic connector and pull lead off. DO NOT pull separately on lead wire.

WARNING: WHEN SERVICING STARTER OR PERFORMING OTHER UNDERHOOD WORK IN THE VICINITY OF THE STARTER, BE AWARE THAT THE HEAVY GAUGE BATTERY INPUT LEAD AT THE STARTER SOLENOID IS "ELECTRICALLY HOT" AT ALL TIMES.

A protective cap or boot is provided over this terminal on all carlines and must be replaced after servicing. Be sure to disconnect battery negative cable before servicing starter.

1. Inspect starting system for loose connections.

2. If system does not operate properly, note condition and continue diagnosis using the symptom chart.

WARNING: WHEN WORKING IN AREA OF THE STARTER, BE CAREFUL TO AVOID TOUCHING HOT EXHAUST COMPONENTS.

CONDITION	POSSIBLE SOURCE	ACTION
Starter solenoid does not pull-in and starter does not crank (Audible click may or may not be heard).	• Open fuse. • Low battery. • Inoperative fender apron relay. • Open circuit or high resistance in external feed circuit to starter solenoid. • Inoperative starter.	• Check fuse continuity. • Refer to appropriate battery section in this manual. • Go to Evaluation Procedure 2. • Go to Test A. • Replace starter. See removal and installation procedure.
Unusual starter noise during starter overrun.	• Starter not mounted flush (cocked). • Noise from other components. • Ring gear tooth damage or excessive ring gear runout. • Defective starter.	• Realign starter on transmission bell housing. • Investigate other powertrain accessory noise contributors. • Refer to appropriate engine section in this manual. • Replace starter. See removal and installation procedure.
Starter cranks but engine does not start.	• Problem in fuel system. • Problem in ignition system. • Engine related concern.	• Refer to appropriate fuel system section in this manual. • Refer to appropriate ignition system section in this manual. • Refer to appropriate engine section in this manual.
Starter cranks slowly.	• Low battery. • High resistance or loose connections in starter solenoid battery feed or ground circuit. • Ring gear runout excessive. • Inoperative starter.	• Refer to appropriate battery section in this manual. • Check that all connections are secure. • Refer to appropriate engine section in this manual. • Replace Starter. See removal and installation procedure.
Starter remains engaged and runs with engine.	• Shorted ignition switch. • Battery cable touching solenoid 'S' terminal (inoperative or mispositioned cable). • Inoperative starter.	• Refer to appropriate ignition system section in this manual. • Replace or relocate cable and replace starter. • Replace starter. See removal and installation procedure.

89682G08

Fig. 51 Starter system inspection chart

Evaluation Procedure 1

NOTE: Hoist vehicle (if necessary) to access starter solenoid terminals.

CAUTION: Remove plastic safety cap on starter solenoid and disconnect hardshell connector at solenoid 'S' terminal

CHECK STARTER MOTOR — TEST A

TEST STEP		RESULT	▶	ACTION TO TAKE
A1	CHECK FOR VOLTAGE TO STARTER			
	• Key OFF. Transmission in Park or Neutral. • Check for voltage between starter B+ terminal and starter drive housing. • Is voltage OK? (12-12.45V)	Yes ▶ No ▶		GO to **A2**. CHECK wire connections between battery and starter solenoid and the ground circuit for open or short.
A2	CHECK STARTER MOTOR			
	• Key OFF. Transmission in Park or Neutral. • Connect one end of a jumper wire to the starter B+ terminal and momentarily touch the other end to solenoid 'S' terminal. • Does starter crank?	Yes ▶ No ▶		CHECK connections from output of fender apron relay to 'S' terminal for open or short. Defective starter. REPLACE starter.

Evaluation Procedure 2

CHECK FENDER APRON RELAY — TEST B

TEST STEP		RESULT	▶	ACTION TO TAKE
B1	CHECK FENDER APRON RELAY			
	• Key in START. Transmission in Park or Neutral. • Is case ground OK?	Yes ▶ No ▶		GO to **B2**. SERVICE ground. GO to **B2**.
B2	CHECK VOLTAGE AT FENDER APRON RELAY START TERMINAL			
	• Key in START. Transmission in Park or Neutral. • Check for voltage between fender apron relay start terminal and case ground. • Is voltage OK? (12-12.45 V)	Yes ▶ No ▶		GO to **B3**. Open circuit or high resistance exists in external circuit wiring or components. Check the following: ● All circuit connections including plastic hardshell connector at solenoid 'S' terminal to make sure it is not broken or distorted. ● Ignition switch. ● Neutral switch or manual lever position sensor. ● Anti-theft contact.
B3	CHECK OUTPUT TERMINAL VOLTAGE			
	• Key in START. Transmission in Park or Neutral. • Check for voltage at output terminal of fender relay. • Is voltage OK?	Yes ▶ No ▶		REFER to Starter System Diagnosis in this section. Defective fender apron relay. REMOVE and REPLACE relay.

89682G09

Fig. 52 Starter system evaluation procedure chart

REMOVAL & INSTALLATION

▶ **See Figure 53**

1. Disconnect the negative battery cable.
2. Raise the front of the vehicle and install jackstands beneath the frame. Firmly apply the parking brake and place blocks in back of the rear wheels.
3. Tag and disconnect the wiring at the starter.

※※ WARNING

When detaching the hardshell connector at the S-terminal, grasp the plastic shell to pull it off. Do not pull on the wire itself. Ensure to pull the connector straight off to prevent damage to the connector and S-terminal. If any part of the connector is damaged, replace the damaged component.

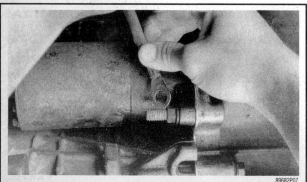

Disconnect all wires connected to the starter, including this ground wire on the starter mountning bolt stud

89682P07

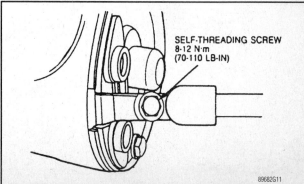

SELF-THREADING SCREW
8-12 N·m
(70-110 LB-IN)

89682G11

Fig. 53 Some starters use a self-threading bolt to hold the starter cable

Remove the starter motor (arrow) mounting bolts . . .

4. Remove the starter mounting bolts and remove the starter.

To install:

5. Position the starter motor against the engine and install the mounting bolts. Tighten the mounting bolts to 15–19 ft. lbs. (21–27 Nm).

6. Install the starter solenoid connector by pushing it straight on. Ensure that the connector locks in position with a notable click.

Install the starter cable nut to the starter solenoid B-terminal. Tighten the nut to 80–123 inch lbs. (9–14 Nm).

7. Connect any remaining wiring to the starter motor.

8. Lower the front of the vehicle and remove the wheel blocks.

9. Connect the negative battery cable.

RELAY REPLACEMENT

1. Disconnect the negative battery cable from the battery.
2. If necessary, remove the power distribution box cover.
3. Disconnect the positive battery cable from the battery terminal.

. . . then remove the starter—be careful, the starter motor can be quite heavy

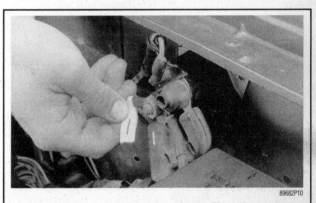

Label all of the wires on the starter relay before removing them

Also remove any protective caps

Remove the push-on connectors by pulling them straight off

Remove the cable securing nuts . . .

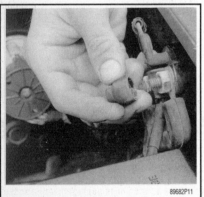

. . . then remove all of the cables from the relay

Remove the relay-to-fender apron attaching screws . . .

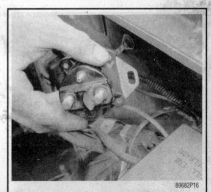

. . . then remove the relay from the fender

4. Remove the nut securing the positive battery cable to the relay.
5. Remove the positive cable and any other wiring under that cable.
6. Label and remove the push-on wires from the front of the relay.
7. Remove the nut and disconnect the cable from the starter side of the relay.
8. Remove the relay mounting bolts and remove the relay.

To install:

9. Install the relay and mounting bolts. Tighten the mounting bolts until snug.
10. Attach all wiring to the relay.
11. If equipped, install the power distribution box cover.
12. Connect the positive (+) cable to the battery.
13. Connect the negative (-) cable to the battery.

SENDING UNITS

➡This section describes the operating principles of sending units, warning lights and gauges. Sensors which provide information to the Electronic Control Module (ECM) are covered in Section 4 of this manual.

Instrument panels contain a number of indicating devices (gauges and warning lights). These devices are composed of two separate components. One is the sending unit, mounted on the engine or other remote part of the vehicle, and the other is the actual gauge or light in the instrument panel.

Several types of sending units exist, however most can be characterized as being either a pressure type or a resistance type. Pressure type sending units convert liquid pressure into an electrical signal which is sent to the gauge. Resistance type sending units are most often used to measure temperature and use variable resistance to control the current flow back to the indicating device. Both types of sending units are connected in series by a wire to the battery (through the ignition switch). When the ignition is turned **ON**, current flows from the battery through the indicating device and on to the sending unit.

Coolant Temperature Sender

The coolant temperature sender is located in the following positions:
- 2.3L, 2.5L engine—left side rear of the engine, below the cylinder head
- 3.0L engine—top front of the engine, on the intake manifold
- 2.9L and 4.0L engine—top left front of the engine, on the intake manifold
- 4.0L SOHC engine—top front of the engine, on the intake manifold
- 5.0L engine—top front of the engine, on the left-hand side of the camshaft synchronizer

TESTING

▸ **See Figures 54 and 55**

Before going to the trouble of removing the sender from the engine block and testing it, perform the tests presented in the accompanying chart to ensure that it is the sender malfunctioning, and not another part of the circuit.

1. Remove the coolant temperature sender from the engine block.
2. Attach an ohmmeter to the sender unit as follows:
   a. Attach one lead to the metal body of the sender unit (near the sender unit's threads).
   b. Attach the other lead to the sender unit's wiring harness connector terminal.
3. With the leads still attached, place the sender unit in a pot of cold water so that neither of the leads is immersed in the water. The portion of the sender unit which normally makes contact with the engine coolant should be submerged.
4. Measure and note the resistance.
5. Slowly heat the pot up (on the stove) to 190–210° F (88–99° C) and observe the resistance of the sender unit. The resistance should evenly and steadily decrease as the water temperature increases. The resistance should not jump drastically or decrease erratically.
6. If the sender unit did not function as described, replace the sender unit with a new one.

REMOVAL & INSTALLATION

▸ **See Figure 56**

❊❊ CAUTION

Ensure that the engine is cold prior to opening the cooling system or removing the sender from the engine. The cooling system on a hot engine is under high pressures, and released hot coolant or steam can cause severe burns.

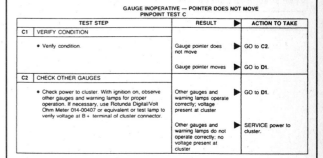

Temperature Gauge System
CAUTION: Do not apply 12-volts or ground directly to the temperature sender terminal. This voltage will damage the sender.

1. Verify that the engine-to-body ground strap is secure. A poor ground can cause high temperature gauge indication.

2. Idle the engine, with all accessories off, until the thermostat opens and the engine coolant temperature stabilizes. The temperature gauge pointer should indicate in the lower half of the normal band. If the coolant temperature does not stabilize, check the cooling system for proper function.

GAUGE INOPERATIVE — POINTER DOES NOT MOVE
PINPOINT TEST C

	TEST STEP	RESULT ▶	ACTION TO TAKE
C1	VERIFY CONDITION		
	● Verify condition.	Gauge pointer does not move	▶ GO to **C2**.
		Gauge pointer moves	▶ GO to **D1**.
C2	CHECK OTHER GAUGES		
	● Check power to cluster. With ignition on, observe other gauges and warning lamps for proper operation. If necessary, use Rotunda Digital/Volt Ohm Meter 014-00407 or equivalent or test lamp to verify voltage at B+ terminal of cluster connector.	Other gauges and warning lamps operate correctly; voltage present at cluster	▶ GO to **D1**.
		Other gauges and warning lamps do not operate correctly; no voltage present at cluster	▶ SERVICE power to cluster.

GAUGE INACCURATE
PINPOINT TEST D

	TEST STEP	RESULT ▶	ACTION TO TAKE
D1	TEST BOX CHECK		
	● Insert Instrument Gauge, System Tester, Rotunda 021-00055 or equivalent in sender circuit. Disconnect connector at sender and connect tester to cluster side of connector. Set tester to LOW (73 ohms).	Gauge reads C	▶ GO to **D2**.
		Pointer does not move	▶ GO to **D3**.
D2	TEST BOX CHECK		
	● Set tester to HIGH (10 ohms).	Gauge reads H	▶ REPLACE sender.
		Gauge does not read H	▶ GO to **D3**.
D3	CHECK SENDER WIRING		
	● Check sender circuit wiring for shorts or open with ohmmeter, using Rotunda Digital Volt/Ohm Meter 014-00407, or equivalent.	(OK) ▶ REPLACE gauge.	
		(OK) ▶ SERVICE wiring.	

89682G13

Fig. 54 Temperature gauge diagnostic chart

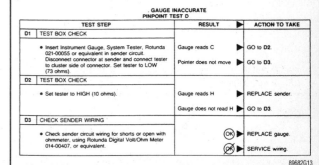

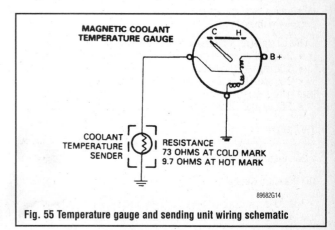

MAGNETIC COOLANT TEMPERATURE GAUGE

COOLANT TEMPERATURE SENDER

RESISTANCE
73 OHMS AT COLD MARK
9.7 OHMS AT HOT MARK

89682G14

Fig. 55 Temperature gauge and sending unit wiring schematic

1. Disconnect the negative battery cable.
2. Remove the radiator cap to relieve any system pressure.
3. Disconnect the wiring at the sender.
4. Remove the coolant temperature sender from the engine.

To install:

5. Coat the threads on the sender with Teflon® tape or electrically conductive sealer, then install the sender. Tighten the sender to 107–143 inch lbs. (12–16 Nm).

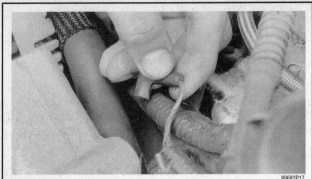

The sending unit uses a push-on wire connector. To remove, simply pull straight up from the sender

89682P17

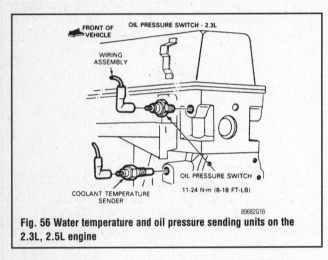

Fig. 56 Water temperature and oil pressure sending units on the 2.3L, 2.5L engine

89682G16

6. Attach the wiring to the sender and connect the negative battery cable.

7. If necessary, add antifreeze to replace any lost coolant, then install the radiator cap.

Oil Pressure Sender and Switch

➥Oil pressure senders are used for oil pressure gauges, whereas the oil pressure switches are used for vehicles equipped only with a low oil pressure warning lamp.

The oil pressure senders/switches are located as follows:
- 2.3L, 2.5L engine—Left side rear of the engine, in the cylinder head
- 3.0L engine—Behind the right cylinder head, in the engine block
- 2.9L and 4.0L engines—Left side front of the engine, below the cylinder head in the engine block
- 5.0L engines—Left-hand front of the engine, below the rocker arm cover

TESTING

♦ **See Figures 57 and 58**

Oil Pressure Sender

Use the accompanying diagnostic chart to help pinpoint oil pressure sender and oil pressure gauge malfunctioning.

Oil Pressure Switch

1. To test the oil pressure switch, open the hood and locate the switch.

2. Disconnect the wire from the switch. Attach one end of a jumper wire to the terminal on the end of the wire, then touch the other end of the jumper wire to a good engine ground (any bare metal engine surface). Have an assistant observe the instrument gauge cluster while you do this and tell you if the low

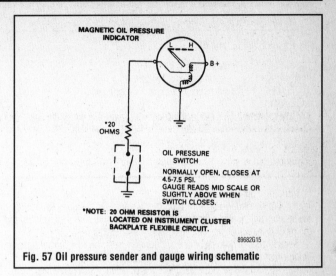

Fig. 57 Oil pressure sender and gauge wiring schematic

89682G15

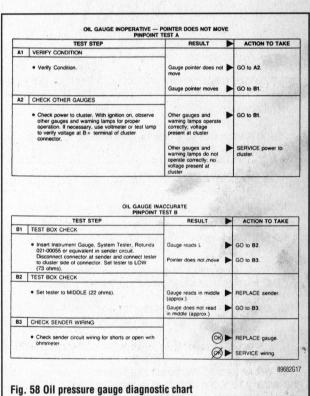

Fig. 58 Oil pressure gauge diagnostic chart

89682G17

oil warning lamp illuminates or not; the low oil warning lamp should illuminate.

  a. If the lamp does not illuminate, skip to Step 3.

  b. If the lamp does illuminate, replace the switch with a new one.

3. Before jumping to any bad conclusions, try a different area for grounding the jumper wire on the engine. If the lamp still does not illuminate, touch the jumper wire end to the negative (-) battery post.

  a. If the lamp illuminates, the problem lies with the engine not being properly grounded.

  b. If the lamp does not illuminate, skip to Step 4.

4. Connect the original wire to the oil pressure switch. While sitting in the vehicle, turn the ignition switch to the **ON** position without actually starting the engine. Observe the other lights on the instrument cluster.

  a. If all of the other lights illuminate when turning the ignition switch **ON**, the oil pressure switch is defective and must be replaced.

  b. If none of the other lights illuminate, there is a problem with power supply to the instrument cluster and gauges.

REMOVAL & INSTALLATION

▶ See Figures 56, 59 and 60

1. Disconnect the negative battery cable.
2. Disconnect the wiring at the sender/switch.
3. Remove the oil pressure sender/switch from the engine.
   To install:
4. Coat the threads with electrically conductive sealer and thread the unit into place. Tighten the sender/switch to 10–18 ft. lbs (13–24 Nm).
5. Attach the wiring to the sender/switch and connect the negative battery cable.

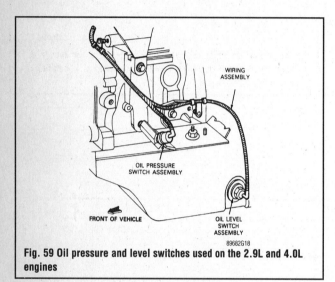

Fig. 59 Oil pressure and level switches used on the 2.9L and 4.0L engines

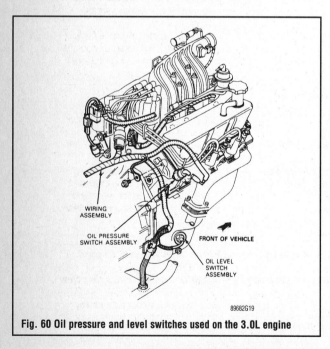

Fig. 60 Oil pressure and level switches used on the 3.0L engine

Low Oil Level Sensor

▶ See Figures 59 and 60

The low oil level sensor is located in the engine oil pan on all models

TESTING

▶ See Figures 61 and 62

Use the accompanying diagnostic chart to help pinpoint low oil level sensor malfunctioning.

➡**The ignition switch should be turned OFF for a minimum of 5 minutes between checks to ensure that the electronic relay, which has a 5 minute timer, has reset.**

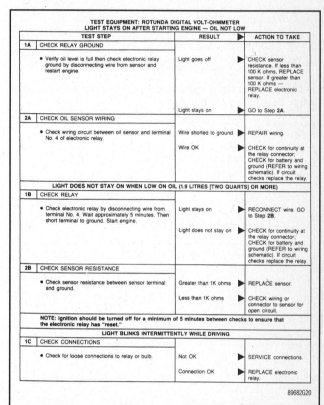

Fig. 61 Low oil level indicator diagnostic chart

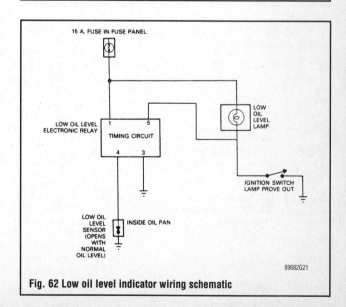

Fig. 62 Low oil level indicator wiring schematic

REMOVAL & INSTALLATION

◆ **See Figure 63**

➡**Always install a new gasket whenever the oil level sensor is removed**

1. Turn the engine **OFF**.
2. Raise the front of the vehicle and install jackstands beneath the frame. Firmly apply the parking brake and place blocks in back of the rear wheels.
3. Drain at least 2 quarts (1.9 liters) of engine oil out of the pan.
4. Disconnect the sensor wiring.
5. Remove the sensor from the oil pan using a 1 in. (26mm) socket or wrench. Discard the old gasket.

To install:

6. Install a new gasket onto the sensor.

➡**When installing the new gasket, the flange faces the sensor and the words ìpansideî should face the oil pan.**

7. Install the sensor and gasket assembly into the oil pan. Tighten the sensor to 13–20 ft. lbs. (17–27 Nm).
8. Connect the electrical wire to the sensor.
9. Lower the front of the vehicle and remove the wheel blocks.

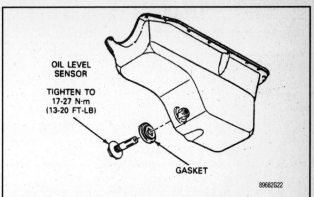

Fig. 63 Typical low oil level sensor mounting—note: the sensor is constantly submerged in oil, therefore, drain some oil out of the engine before removing it

10. Refill the crankcase to the proper level.
11. Start the engine and check for leaks.

Troubleshooting Basic Starting System Problems

Problem	Cause	Solution
Starter motor rotates engine slowly	• Battery charge low or battery defective	• Charge or replace battery
	• Defective circuit between battery and starter motor	• Clean and tighten, or replace cables
	• Low load current	• Bench-test starter motor. Inspect for worn brushes and weak brush springs.
	• High load current	• Bench-test starter motor. Check engine for friction, drag or coolant in cylinders. Check ring gear-to-pinion gear clearance.
Starter motor will not rotate engine	• Battery charge low or battery defective	• Charge or replace battery
	• Faulty solenoid	• Check solenoid ground. Repair or replace as necessary.
	• Damaged drive pinion gear or ring gear	• Replace damaged gear(s)
	• Starter motor engagement weak	• Bench-test starter motor
	• Starter motor rotates slowly with high load current	• Inspect drive yoke pull-down and point gap, check for worn end bushings, check ring gear clearance
	• Engine seized	• Repair engine
Starter motor drive will not engage (solenoid known to be good)	• Defective contact point assembly	• Repair or replace contact point assembly
	• Inadequate contact point assembly ground	• Repair connection at ground screw
	• Defective hold-in coil	• Replace field winding assembly
Starter motor drive will not disengage	• Starter motor loose on flywheel housing	• Tighten mounting bolts
	• Worn drive end busing	• Replace bushing
	• Damaged ring gear teeth	• Replace ring gear or driveplate
	• Drive yoke return spring broken or missing	• Replace spring
Starter motor drive disengages prematurely	• Weak drive assembly thrust spring	• Replace drive mechanism
	• Hold-in coil defective	• Replace field winding assembly
Low load current	• Worn brushes	• Replace brushes
	• Weak brush springs	• Replace springs

Troubleshooting Basic Charging System Problems

Problem	Cause	Solution
Noisy alternator	• Loose mountings • Loose drive pulley • Worn bearings • Brush noise • Internal circuits shorted (High pitched whine)	• Tighten mounting bolts • Tighten pulley • Replace alternator • Replace alternator • Replace alternator
Squeal when starting engine or accelerating	• Glazed or loose belt	• Replace or adjust belt
Indicator light remains on or ammeter indicates discharge (engine running)	• Broken belt • Broken or disconnected wires • Internal alternator problems • Defective voltage regulator	• Install belt • Repair or connect wiring • Replace alternator • Replace voltage regulator/alternator
Car light bulbs continually burn out—battery needs water continually	• Alternator/regulator overcharging	• Replace voltage regulator/alternator
Car lights flare on acceleration	• Battery low • Internal alternator/regulator problems	• Charge or replace battery • Replace alternator/regulator
Low voltage output (alternator light flickers continually or ammeter needle wanders)	• Loose or worn belt • Dirty or corroded connections • Internal alternator/regulator problems	• Replace or adjust belt • Clean or replace connections • Replace alternator/regulator

TCCS2C02

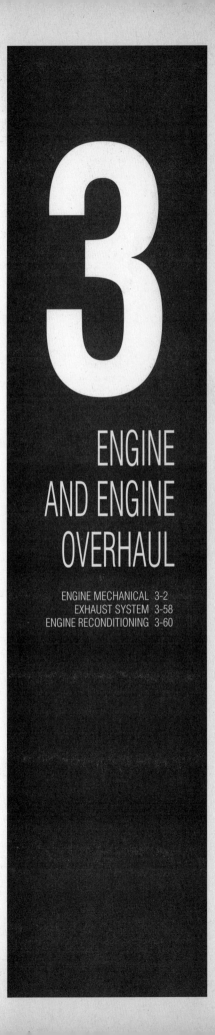

3

ENGINE
AND ENGINE
OVERHAUL

ENGINE MECHANICAL

Engine

REMOVAL & INSTALLATION

▶ **See Figures 1, 2, 3, 4 and 5**

In the process of removing the engine, you will come across a number of steps which call for the removal of a separate component or system, such as "disconnect the exhaust system" or "remove the radiator." In most instances, a detailed removal procedure can be found elsewhere in this manual.

It is virtually impossible to list each individual wire and hose which must be disconnected, simply because so many different model and engine combinations have been manufactured. Careful observation and common sense are the best possible approaches to any repair procedure.

Removal and installation of the engine can be made easier if you follow these basic points:
- If you have to drain any of the fluids, use a suitable container.
- Always tag any wires or hoses and, if possible, the components they came from before disconnecting them.
- Because there are so many bolts and fasteners involved, store and label the retainers from components separately in muffin pans, jars or coffee cans. This will prevent confusion during installation.
- After unbolting the transmission or transaxle, always make sure it is properly supported.
- If it is necessary to disconnect the air conditioning system, have this service performed by a qualified technician using a recovery/recycling station. If the system does not have to be disconnected, unbolt the compressor and set it aside.
- When unbolting the engine mounts, always make sure the engine is properly supported. When removing the engine, make sure that any lifting devices are properly attached to the engine. It is recommended that if your engine is supplied with lifting hooks, your lifting apparatus be attached to them.
- Lift the engine from its compartment slowly, checking that no hoses, wires or other components are still connected.
- After the engine is clear of the compartment, place it on an engine stand or workbench.
- After the engine has been removed, you can perform a partial or full teardown of the engine using the procedures outlined in this manual.

➥**On vehicles equipped with air conditioning, it is vital to refer to Section 1 prior to performing this procedure. On 1991–93 models, it is not necessary to have the A/C system evacuated since the A/C compressor can be unbolted from the engine, and positioned out of the way, without disconnecting any of the refrigerant lines.**

1. On 1994–99 models equipped with air conditioning, have the system discharged and evacuated by a MVAC, EPA-certified, automotive technician. Have the A/C compressor removed from the engine.
2. Disconnect the negative battery cable.
3. Remove the hood.
4. Remove the air intake tube and the accessory drive belt.

✳✳ CAUTION

When draining engine coolant, keep in mind that cats and dogs are attracted to ethylene glycol antifreeze and could drink any that is left in an uncovered container or in puddles on the ground. This will prove fatal in sufficient quantity. Always drain coolant into a sealable container. Coolant should be reused unless it is contaminated or is several years old.

5. Drain the cooling system.
6. Remove the cooling fan, shroud, radiator and all cooling system hoses.
7. On all models except the 1996 Explorer with the 5.0L engine and all 1997–99 Explorer/Mountaineer models, label and detach all engine wiring and vacuum hoses which will interfere with engine removal. Position the wire harness out of the way.
8. On 1996 Explorers with the 5.0L engine and all 1997–99 Explorer/Mountaineer models, the engine wiring harness is removed with the engine. Only label and detach the harness connectors from components which must be removed. Also unplug the harness at the main bulkhead (firewall), transmission and PCM connections.
9. On 1991–93 models equipped with air conditioning, unbolt the A/C compressor from the engine without disconnecting the refrigerant lines and position it out of the way.
10. Unbolt the power steering pump from the engine and position it out of the way. The fluid lines do not have to be disconnected.
11. Detach the accelerator and transmission control cables from the throttle body, and the control cablesí mounting bracket from the engine.
12. Release fuel system pressure, then disconnect the fuel supply and return lines from the engine.
13. Remove any remaining mounting brackets and/or drive belt tensioners.
14. Raise the vehicle and safely support it on jackstands.

✳✳ CAUTION

The EPA warns that prolonged contact with used engine oil may cause a number of skin disorders, including cancer! You should make every effort to minimize your exposure to used engine oil. Protective gloves should be worn when changing the oil. Wash your hands and any other exposed skin areas as soon as possible after exposure to used engine oil. Soap and water, or waterless hand cleaner should be used.

15. Drain the engine oil and remove the oil filter.
16. Detach the exhaust system from the exhaust manifolds.
17. Remove the starter motor and starter motor wiring from the engine.
18. Label and detach any under vehicle engine wiring, which will interfere with engine removal.
19. On vehicles equipped with automatic transmissions, matchmark the position of the torque converter to the flywheel. Remove the bolts.
20. Remove all of the engine-to-transmission bolts.

➥**All Ford engines use a plate between the engine and the transmission. Some models may have a smaller, removable, flywheel/flexplate**

21. If equipped, remove the transmission oil cooler line retainers-to-engine bolts.
22. Remove the front engine support insulator-to-crossmember retaining fasteners.
23. If equipped, remove the engine damper mounting bracket from the engine. The bracket may use two TORX® bolts for the lower mounting points.
24. Partially lower the vehicle and support it with jackstands in the new position.
25. Support the transmission with a floor jack.
26. Using a engine crane or hoist, lift the engine out of the vehicle. Be sure to lift the engine slowly and check often that nothing (such as wires, hoses, etc.) will cause the engine to hang up on the vehicle.
27. At this point, the engine can be installed on an engine stand.
   To install:

➥**Lightly oil all bolts and stud threads, except those specifying special sealant, prior to installation.**

28. Using the hoist or engine crane, slowly and carefully position the engine in the vehicle. Make sure the exhaust manifolds are properly aligned with the exhaust pipes.
29. Align the engine to the transmission and install two engine-to-transmission bolts.

➥**Seat the left-hand side, front engine support insulator locating pin prior to the right-hand side, front engine support insulator.**

30. Lower the engine onto the front engine support insulators.
31. Detach the engine crane or hoist from the engine.
32. Remove the floor jack from beneath the transmission fluid pan.
33. Tighten the two installed engine-to-transmission bolts, then raise and securely support the vehicle on jackstands.
34. Install and tighten the remaining engine-to-transmission bolts.
35. The remainder of installation is the reverse of the removal procedure. Be sure to tighten the fasteners to the values presented in the torque specification chart.

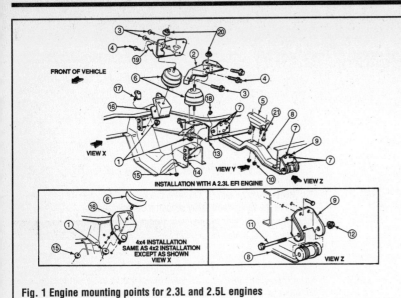

1. Lower support insulator nut
2. Engine-to-insulator bracket—LH
3. Engine bracket mounting bolt
4. Engine bracket mounting stud
5. Rear engine support insulator
6. Front engine support insulator
7. Bracket-to-frame rivet
8. Rear engine support
9. Rear engine support bracket
10. Attaching nut
11. Bolt
12. Nut
13. Insulator-to-frame bracket—LH
14. Bolt and retainer assembly
15. Nut
16. Insulator-to-frame bracket—RH
17. Bolt and retainer
18. Nut
19. Engine-to-insulator bracket—RH
20. Nut
21. Screw and washer

89683G01

Fig. 1 Engine mounting points for 2.3L and 2.5L engines

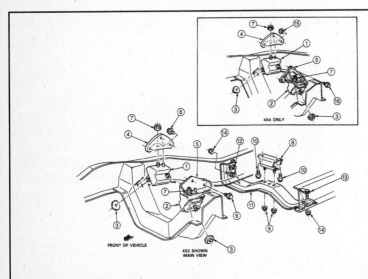

1. Front engine support insulator—RH
2. Front engine support insulator—LH
3. Nut and washer
4. Engine-to-insulator—RH
5. Engine-to-insulator—LH
6. Screw and washer
7. Nut
8. Rear engine support insulator
9. Nut and washer
10. Screw and washer
11. Rear engine support
12. Bolt and retainer
13. Bolt and retainer
14. Nut
15. Screw and washer
16. Screw and washer

89683G02

Fig. 2 Engine mounting points for 3.0L engines

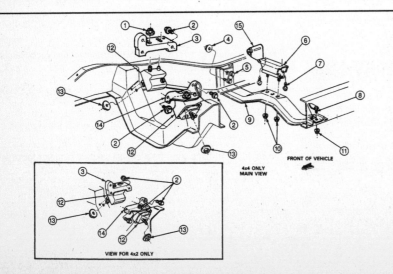

1. Nut and washer
2. Screw and washer
3. Engine-to-insulator bracket
4. Nut
5. Bolt and retainer
6. Rear engine support insulator
7. Screw and washer
8. Bolt and retainer
9. Rear crossmember
10. Nut
11. Nut
12. Front engine support insulator
13. Nut and washer
14. Engine-to-insulator bracket
15. Exhaust hanger

89683G03

Fig. 3 Engine mounting points 4.0L engines

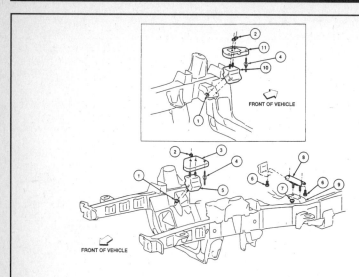

1. Nut and washer
2. Nut and washer
3. Engine-to-insulator bracket—RH
4. Stud bolt
5. Front engine support insulator—RH
6. Bolt
7. Nut and washer
8. Rear engine support insulator
9. Rear crossmember
10. Front engine support insulator—LH
11. Engine-to-insulator bracket—LH

89683G04

Fig. 4 Engine mounting points 5.0L engines

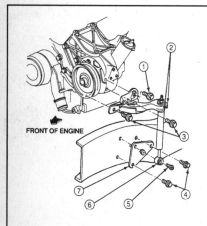

1. Bolt
2. Engine damper and upper mount
3. Bolts
4. Bolts
5. Lower damper mounting bolt
6. Engine damper lower mount
7. Lower damper mounting bracket

89683G05

Fig. 5 Engine damper mounting for 4.0L engines

✴✴ WARNING

Do NOT start the engine without first filling it with the proper type and amount of clean engine oil, and installing a new oil filter. Otherwise, severe engine damage will result.

36. Fill the crankcase with the proper type and quantity of engine oil. If necessary, adjust the transmission and/or throttle linkage.
37. Install the air intake duct assembly.
38. Connect the negative battery cable, then fill and bleed the cooling system.
39. Bring the engine to normal operating temperature, then check for leaks.
40. Stop the engine and check all fluid levels.
41. Install the hood, aligning the marks that were made during removal.
42. If equipped, have the A/C system properly leak-tested, evacuated and charged by a MVAC-trained, EPA-certified, automotive technician.

Valve Rocker Arm Cover

REMOVAL & INSTALLATION

2.3L and 2.5L Engines

▶ See Figure 6

➡**To service the valve cover on the 2.3L and 2.5L engine, the throttle body assembly and EGR supply tube must first be removed. Refer to the necessary service procedures.**

1. Disconnect the negative battery cable.
2. Unplug any electrical connections on the air intake hose, then remove the hose.
3. Remove any splash shielding from around the throttle body.
4. Remove the throttle body assembly from the intake manifold.
5. Label and disconnect any electrical connections, including spark plug cables, that will interfere with the removal of the valve cover.
6. If necessary, remove the EGR supply tube.
7. Remove the valve cover retaining bolts and remove the valve cover.

➡**A gentle tap with a soft hammer may help to break the seal on the gasket.**

✴✴ WARNING

Never pry between the valve cover and the cylinder head. Damage to the machined sealing surface, or distortion to the valve cover could occur, resulting in an oil leak.

8. Remove the valve cover gasket from the cover.
To install:
9. Thoroughly clean the gasket mating surfaces on the cover and the cylinder head.
10. Install a new gasket to the valve cover.

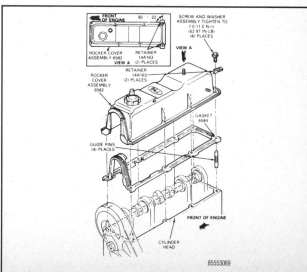

85553069

Fig. 6 Exploded view of the 2.3L and 2.5L engine rocker arm cover

11. Place the valve cover onto the cylinder head and install all of the retaining bolts finger-tight.

12. Alternately tighten the bolts to the proper specification.

13. If removed, install the EGR supply tube.

14. Install any electrical connections which were removed.

15. Install the throttle body to the intake manifold.

16. Install any splash shielding removed from around the throttle body.

17. Install the air intake hose and attach the wire harness connections which were removed.

18. Reconnect the negative battery cable.

19. Start the engine and check for leaks.

2.9L Engines

▶ See Figure 7

1. Disconnect the negative battery cable. Remove the air cleaner and attaching parts. Label each spark plug wire prior to its removal in order to ease the installation of the wires on the correct spark plugs.

2. Remove the spark plug wires.

3. Remove the PCV valve and hose.

4. Remove the rocker arm cover attaching screws and the load distribution washers (patch pieces). Be sure the washers are installed in their original position.

5. Detach the transmission fluid level indicator tube and bracket from the valve cover.

6. Disconnect the vacuum line at the canister purge solenoid and disconnect the line routed from the canister to the purge solenoid (disconnect the power brake booster hose, if so equipped).

7. With a light plastic hammer, tap the rocker arm covers to break the seal.

8. Remove the rocker arm covers.

To install:

9. Clean all gasket material from the cylinder heads and rocker arm cover gasket surfaces.

10. Install the rocker arm covers, using new gaskets and install the attaching screw and rocker arm cover reinforcement pieces.

11. Attach the transmission fluid level indicator tube and the bracket to the rocker arm cover.

12. After ensuring all rocker arm cover reinforcement washers are installed in their original position, tighten the rocker arm cover screws to the proper specification.

13. Install the spark plug wires.

14. Install the PCV valve and hose.

15. Install the engine oil fill cap.

16. Connect the vacuum line at the canister purge (connect the power brake hose, if so equipped) solenoid and connect the line routed from canister to the purge solenoid.

17. Install the air cleaner and the attaching parts.

18. Reconnect the negative battery cable. Start the engine and check for oil leaks.

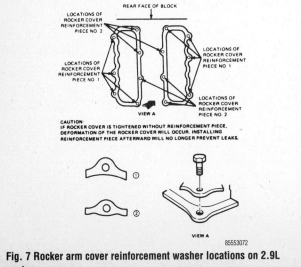

Fig. 7 Rocker arm cover reinforcement washer locations on 2.9L engines

3.0L Engine

▶ See Figure 8

➡The valve covers installed on the 3.0L engine incorporate integral (built in) gaskets which should last the life of the vehicle. Replacement gaskets are available if required.

1. Disconnect the negative battery cable. Disconnect the ignition wires from the spark plugs, but leave them attached to their wire looms.

2. Remove the ignition wire separators from the rocker arm cover attaching bolt studs with the wires attached, then lay the wires out of the way.

3. If the left hand cover is being removed, remove the throttle body assembly, the PCV valve and fuel injector harness stand–offs. If the right hand cover is being removed, remove the engine harness connectors, fuel injector harness stand–offs and air cleaner closure hose from the oil fill adapter.

4. Using caution, slide a sharp thin blade knife between the cylinder head gasket surface and the valve cover gasket at the four RTV junctions. CUT ONLY THE RTV SEALER AND AVOID CUTTING THE INTEGRAL GASKET.

5. Remove the integral gasket from the valve cover gasket channel. Note bolt/stud fasteners locations before removing gasket for correct installation. Clean gasket channel and remove any traces of RTV sealant.

To install:

6. Align fastener holes, lay new gasket onto channel and install by hand. Install gasket to each fastener, seat fastener against cover and at the same time roll gasket around fastener collar. If installed correctly all fasteners will be secured by gasket and not fall out.

7. Install valve cover to the engine, lightly oil all bolts and stud threads. Apply a bead of RTV sealant at the cylinder head to intake manifold rail step (two places per rail).

8. Place the valve cover on the cylinder head and install attaching bolts and studs. Tighten the attaching bolts to specifications.

9. Install all remaining components in reverse order of removal procedure. Connect the ignition wires to the spark plugs and reconnect the negative battery cable. Start the engine and run to normal operating temperature, then check for oil and vacuum leaks.

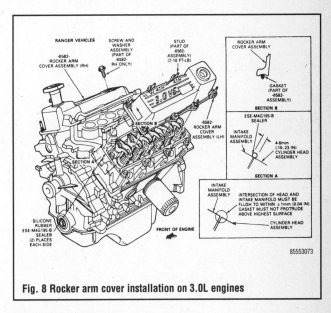

Fig. 8 Rocker arm cover installation on 3.0L engines

4.0L Engine (VIN X)

▶ See Figure 9

➡Failure to install new valve cover gaskets and valve cover reinforcement pieces will result in oil leaks.

1. Disconnect the negative battery cable. Tag and remove the spark plug wires.

2. Disconnect and remove the fuel supply and return lines. See Section 5.

3. For left valve cover removal, remove the upper intake manifold.

4. For right valve cover removal, remove the air inlet duct and hose to oil fill tube and the alternator. Drain the cooling system and remove the upper radi-

ator hose from the engine. Remove the EDIS ignition coil and bracket assembly. Remove the A/C low pressure hose bracket if so equipped. Remove the PCV valve hose and breather.

5. Remove the valve cover bolts and load distribution pieces. The washers must be installed in their original positions, so keep track of them.

6. Remove the valve cover. It will probably be necessary to tap the cover loose with a plastic or rubber mallet.

7. Remove the valve cover gaskets.

To install:

8. Clean all gasket material from the cover and head.

9. Installation is the reverse of removal. Always use a new gasket coated with sealer. If any of the RTV silicone gasket material was removed from the mating area of the head(s) and intake manifold, replace it. Torque the bolts to 3–5 ft. lbs.

10. Reconnect the negative battery cable. Start the engine and run to normal operating temperature and check for oil and fuel leaks.

4.0L SOHC Engine (VIN E)

➡**Always use new gaskets when installing the valve covers.**

RIGHT HAND COVER

1. Disconnect the negative battery cable.
2. Remove the upper intake manifold.

✳✳ CAUTION

When draining the coolant, keep in mind that cats and dogs are attracted by ethylene glycol antifreeze, and are quite likely to drink any that is left in an uncovered container or in puddles on the ground. This will prove fatal in sufficient quantity. Always drain the coolant into a sealable container. Coolant should be reused unless it is contaminated or several years old.

To remove the valve cover, first disconnect the crankcase breather vent tube

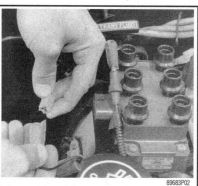
Label and unplug any electrical connections . . .

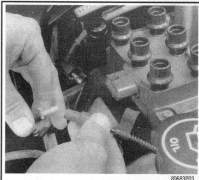
. . . as well as vacuum fittings which will inhibit valve cover removal

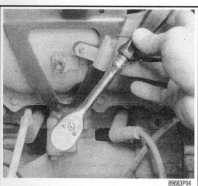
Remove the coil pack mounting bracket attaching bolts . . .

. . . then remove the coil pack and bracket from the engine

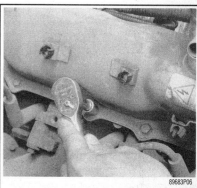
Remove the valve cover hold-down bolts . . .

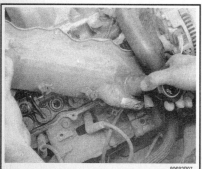
. . . then remove the cover from the engine. A slight tap with a soft-faced hammer helps to break the seal

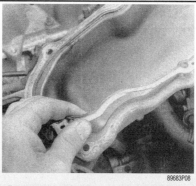
Remove the old valve cover gasket and discard

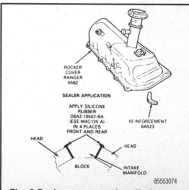
Fig. 9 Rocker arm cover installation on 4.0L engines

3. Drain the cooling system until the coolant is below the upper radiator hose.

4. Remove the upper radiator hose and the connector tube behind the alternator.

5. Remove the bolts securing the heater hose bracket and the transmission dipstick tube.

6. Label and disconnect the spark plug cables from their plugs and wire looms.

7. Remove the valve cover hold-down bolts and remove the cover from the engine. Discard the old valve cover gasket.

➡A gentle tap with a soft hammer may help to break the seal on the gasket.

✳✳ WARNING

Never pry between the valve cover and the cylinder head. Damage to the machined sealing surface, or distortion to the valve cover could occur, resulting in an oil leak.

To install:

8. Thoroughly clean the mating surfaces of the engine and cover.

9. Install a new gasket to the cover and place the cover in position on the engine.

10. Install all of the hold-down bolts and tighten to specifications.

11. Attach the spark plug cables to their wire looms and plugs.

12. Install the upper radiator hose assembly and the tube securing bolt.

13. Install the upper intake manifold.

14. Refill the cooling system and run the engine.

15. Connect the negative battery cable.

16. Allow the engine to reach normal operating temperature (upper radiator hose hot) and check for leaks.

LEFT HAND COVER

1. Disconnect the negative battery cable.

2. Remove the upper intake manifold.

3. Remove the two fuel line upper bracket bolts.

4. Detach the Camshaft Position (CMP) sensor electrical connection.

5. Disconnect the wire harness from the Differential Pressure Feedback (DPFE) transducer, which is mounted to the valve cover.

6. Label and detach the two vacuum lines connected to the DPFE transducer.

7. Disconnect the engine electrical multi-plug and remove it from the valve cover.

8. Detach the wire harness connections on the coil pack.

9. Label and remove the spark plug cables from the coil pack.

10. Remove the valve cover hold-down bolts and remove the valve cover. Discard the old valve cover gasket.

➡A gentle tap with a soft hammer may help to break the seal on the gasket.

✳✳ WARNING

Never pry between the valve cover and the cylinder head. Damage to the machined sealing surface, or distortion to the valve cover could occur, resulting in an oil leak.

To install:

11. Thoroughly clean the mating surfaces of the engine and cover.

12. Install a new gasket to the cover and place the cover in position on the engine.

13. Install all of the hold-down bolts and tighten to specifications.

14. Attach the spark plug cables to the coil pack.

15. Attach the wire harness connections to the coil pack.

16. Install and connect the engine electrical multi-plug to the valve cover.

17. Attach the vacuum lines and electrical connections to the DPFE transducer.

18. Connect the CMP sensor harness.

19. Install the two fuel line upper bracket bolts.

20. Install the upper intake manifold.

21. Connect the negative battery cable.

22. Allow the engine to reach normal operating temperature (upper radiator hose hot) and check for leaks.

5.0L Engines

♦ **See Figure 10**

➡To remove the valve covers, the upper intake manifold must be removed. Obtain a new gasket for the intake assembly before removing it. If only the right-hand valve cover is to be removed, the intake manifold can remain on the engine, however, you will need to remove the throttle body assembly from the upper intake manifold.

1. Disconnect the negative battery cable.

✳✳ CAUTION

When draining the coolant, keep in mind that cats and dogs are attracted by ethylene glycol antifreeze, and are quite likely to drink any that is left in an uncovered container or in puddles on the ground. This will prove fatal in sufficient quantity. Always drain the coolant into a sealable container. Coolant should be reused unless it is contaminated or several years old.

2. Drain the cooling system until the coolant level is below the intake manifold.

3. Remove the upper intake manifold.

4. Label and remove the spark plug wires from the coil packs.

5. Detach the coil pack electrical connections and remove them from the engine.

6. Remove any remaining wires or lines which will interfere with valve cover removal.

7. Remove the valve cover hold-down bolts and remove the covers.

➡A gentle tap with a soft hammer may help to break the seal on the gasket.

✳✳ WARNING

Never pry between the valve cover and the cylinder head. Damage to the machined sealing surface, or distortion to the valve cover could occur, resulting in an oil leak.

To install:

8. Clean all gasket mating surfaces. Install a new gasket to the cylinder head and position the cover on the engine.

➡Ensure that the stamping and chamfered edge of the steel carrier of the gasket are facing up when installed.

9. Install all of the hold-down bolts and tighten to specifications in the sequence given.

10. Connect all wires and lines disconnected from the engine.

11. Install the coil packs and the spark plug wires to the coils.

12. Install the upper intake manifold.

13. Refill the cooling system.

14. Connect the negative battery cable.

15. Allow the engine to reach normal operating temperature (upper radiator hose hot) and check for leaks.

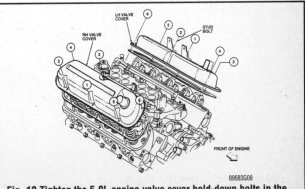

Fig. 10 Tighten the 5.0L engine valve cover hold-down bolts in the sequence shown

Rocker Arms

REMOVAL & INSTALLATION

2.3L, 2.5L and 4.0L SOHC (VIN E) Engines

▶ **See Figure 11**

➡**A special tool is required to compress the valve spring.**

1. Remove the valve cover and associated parts as required.
2. Rotate the camshaft so that the base circle of the cam is against the cam follower you intend to remove.

➡**If removing more than one cam follower, label them so they can be returned to their original position.**

3. Using special tool T88T-6565-BH (for 2.3L and 2.5L engines), T97T-6565-A (for 4.0L engines) or equivalent, depress the valve spring, as necessary, a000nd slide the cam follower over the lash adjuster and out from under the camshaft.
4. Install the cam follower in the reverse order of removal. Lubricate the followers with SAE 50W engine oil meeting Ford specification WSE-M2C908-A1 and API SG prior to installing.

3.0L and 5.0L Engines

▶ **See Figures 12 and 13**

1. Remove the rocker arm covers.
2. Remove the single retaining bolt at each rocker arm.
3. The rocker arm and pushrod may then be removed from the engine. Keep all rocker arms and pushrods in order so they may be installed in their original locations.
4. Installation is the reverse of removal. Lubricate the rocker arm assemblies with SAE 50W engine oil. Insure that the fulcrums are properly seated into the

cylinder head (3.0L engines) or the fulcrum guide (5.0L engines). Tighten the rocker arm fulcrum bolts to specifications.

Rocker Arm Shaft Assembly

REMOVAL & INSTALLATION

▶ **See Figures 14 and 15**

➡**This procedure applies only to 2.9L and 4.0L (VIN X) engines.**

1. Remove the valve rocker arm covers.
2. Remove the rocker arm shaft stand attaching bolts by loosening the bolts two turns at a time, in sequence (from the end of shaft to middle shaft).
3. Lift off the rocker arm and shaft assembly. If equipped, remove the oil baffle.

To install:

4. If equipped, loosen the valve lash adjusting screws a few turns. Apply engine oil to the assembly to provide the initial lubrication.
5. If equipped, install the oil baffle.
6. Install rocker arm shaft assembly to the cylinder head and guide adjusting screws on to the pushrods.
7. Install and tighten rocker arm stand attaching bolts to specification, two turns at a time, in sequence (from middle of shaft to the end of shaft).
8. Adjust the valve lash to the cold specified setting. Refer to Section 1 under Valve Lash Adjustment for procedures.
9. Install the valve rocker arm covers.

DISASSEMBLY & REASSEMBLY

1. Remove the spring washer and pin from each end of the valve rocker arm shaft.
2. Slide the rocker arms, springs and rocker arm shaft supports off the shaft. Be sure to mark the parts for re–assembly in the same locations.

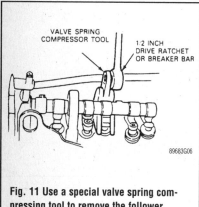

Fig. 11 Use a special valve spring compressing tool to remove the follower

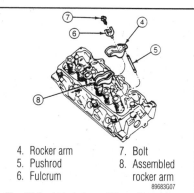

4. Rocker arm
5. Pushrod
6. Fulcrum
7. Bolt
8. Assembled rocker arm

Fig. 12 Exploded view of the valve rocker arms used on the 3.0L engines

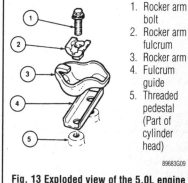

1. Rocker arm bolt
2. Rocker arm fulcrum
3. Rocker arm
4. Fulcrum guide
5. Threaded pedestal (Part of cylinder head)

Fig. 13 Exploded view of the 5.0L engine rocker arm assembly

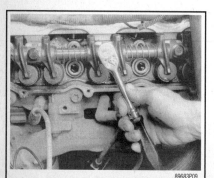

To remove the rocker shaft, first remove the valve cover, then loosen the shaft retaining bolts . . .

. . . and remove the assembly from the cylinder head

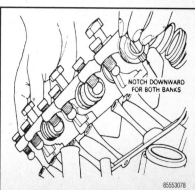

Fig. 14 Rocker arm shaft assembly installation on the 2.9L engine

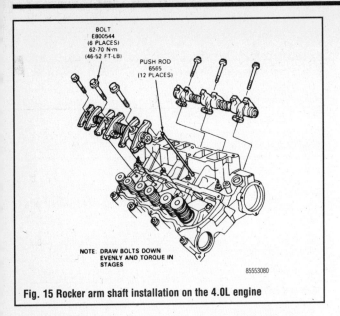

Fig. 15 Rocker arm shaft installation on the 4.0L engine

3. If it is necessary to remove the plugs from each end of the shaft, drill or pierce the plug on one end. Use a steel rod to knock out the plug on the opposite end. Working from the open end, knock out the remaining plug.

4. The oil holes in the rocker arm shaft must point down when the shaft is installed. This position of the shaft can be recognized by a notch on the front face of the shaft.

5. If the plugs were removed from the shaft, use a blunt tool and install a plug, cup side out, in each end of the shaft.

6. Install a spring washer and pin on one end of the shaft, coat the rocker arm shaft with heavy engine oil and install the parts in the same sequence they were removed.

Thermostat

REMOVAL & INSTALLATION

2.3L and 2.5L Engines

▶ See Figure 16

1. Drain the cooling system below the level of the coolant outlet housing.

❊❊ CAUTION

When draining the coolant, keep in mind that cats and dogs are attracted by ethylene glycol antifreeze, and are quite likely to drink any that is left in an uncovered container or in puddles on the ground. This will prove fatal in sufficient quantity. Always drain the coolant into a sealable container. Coolant should be reused unless it is contaminated or several years old.

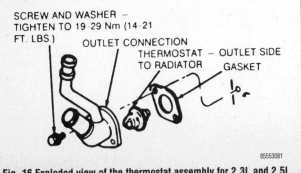

Fig. 16 Exploded view of the thermostat assembly for 2.3L and 2.5L engines

2. Disconnect the heater return hose at the thermostat housing located on the left front lower side of engine.

3. Remove the coolant outlet housing retaining bolts and slide the housing with the hose attached to one side.

4. Remove the thermostat from the outlet.

5. Remove the gasket from the engine block and clean both mating surfaces.

➡**It is good practice to check the operation of a new thermostat before it is installed in an engine. Place the thermostat in a pan of boiling water. If it does not open more than ¼ in., do not install it in the engine.**

To install:

6. Coat a new gasket with water resistant sealer and position it on the outlet of the engine. The gasket must be in place before the thermostat is installed.

7. Install the thermostat with the bridge (opposite end from the spring) inside the elbow connection and turn it clockwise to lock it in position, with the bridge against the flats cast into the elbow connection.

8. Position the elbow connection onto the mounting surface of the outlet, so that the thermostat flange is resting on the gasket and install the retaining bolts.

9. Connect the heater hose to the thermostat housing.

10. Fill the radiator and operate the engine until it reaches operating temperature. Check the coolant level and adjust as necessary.

3.0L Engine

▶ See Figure 17

1. Drain the cooling system.

❊❊ CAUTION

When draining the coolant, keep in mind that cats and dogs are attracted by ethylene glycol antifreeze, and are quite likely to drink any that is left in an uncovered container or in puddles on the ground. This will prove fatal in sufficient quantity. Always drain the coolant into a sealable container. Coolant should be reused unless it is contaminated or several years old.

2. Disconnect the battery ground cable.

3. Remove the upper radiator hose.

4. Remove the thermostat housing bolts.

5. Remove the housing and thermostat as an assembly.

6. Remove the thermostat from the housing.

To install:

7. Clean all gasket material from the housing and engine.

8. Turn the thermostat clockwise into the housing until the thermostat bridge is perpendicular to the mounting holes.

9. Position the housing on the engine, using a new gasket coated with sealer. Tighten the bolts to 19 ft. lbs. (26 Nm).

10. Install the hose, fill and bleed the cooling system, connect the battery ground cable and start the engine. Check for leaks.

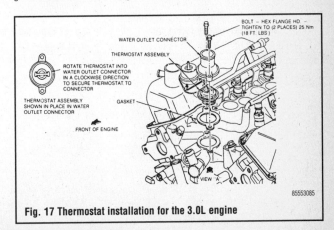

Fig. 17 Thermostat installation for the 3.0L engine

2.9L and 4.0L Engines

▶ See Figure 18

1. Drain the cooling system.

❈❈ CAUTION

When draining the coolant, keep in mind that cats and dogs are attracted by ethylene glycol antifreeze, and are quite likely to drink any that is left in an uncovered container or in puddles on the ground. This will prove fatal in sufficient quantity. Always drain the coolant into a sealable container. Coolant should be reused unless it is contaminated or several years old.

2. Disconnect the battery ground.
3. Remove the air cleaner duct assembly.

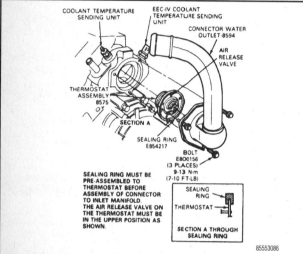

Fig. 18 Exploded view of the thermostat housing for the 4.0L engine—2.9L engine is similar

4. Remove the upper radiator hose.
5. Remove the 3 thermostat housing attaching bolts.
6. Remove the thermostat housing. You may have to tap it loose with a plastic mallet or your hand.
7. Pull the thermostat from the intake manifold.

To install:

❈❈ WARNING

Do not use a sharp metal tool for scraping. Damage to the sealing surfaces could result and cause a leak.

8. Clean all mating surfaces thoroughly.
9. Make sure that the sealing ring is properly installed on the thermostat rim. Position the thermostat in the housing making sure that the air release valve is in the **up** (12 o'clock) position.
10. Coat the mating surfaces of the housing and engine with an adhesive type sealer. Position the new gasket on the thermostat and place the housing on the engine. Tighten the bolts to specification.

5.0L Engine

♦ **See Figures 19 and 20**

1. Drain the cooling system.

❈❈ CAUTION

When draining the coolant, keep in mind that cats and dogs are attracted by ethylene glycol antifreeze, and are quite likely to drink any that is left in an uncovered container or in puddles on the ground. This will prove fatal in sufficient quantity. Always drain the coolant into a sealable container. Coolant should be reused unless it is contaminated or several years old.

2. Disconnect the battery ground.
3. Remove the upper radiator hose.

To remove the thermostat, first remove the upper radiator hose, then the three attaching screws

Pull the thermostat housing from the intake manifold . . .

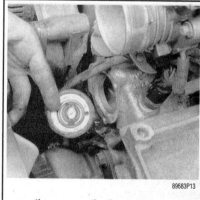

. . . then remove the thermostat

Ensure that the sealing ring is properly seated. Install the thermostat with the release valve facing upwards

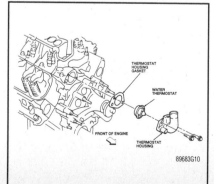

Fig. 19 Exploded view of the 5.0L engine thermostat and related components

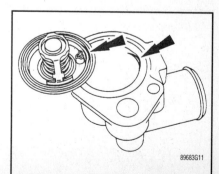

Fig. 20 Align the air bleed hole on the thermostat with the notch in the housing, which is also the 12 o'clock position

4. Remove the 2 thermostat housing attaching bolts.
5. Loosen the bypass hose at the water pump.
6. Remove the thermostat housing. You may have to tap it loose with a plastic mallet or your hand.

To install:

✳✳ WARNING

Do not use a sharp metal tool for scraping. Damage to the sealing surfaces could result and cause a leak.

7. Clean all mating surfaces thoroughly.
8. Position the thermostat in the housing making sure that the air release valve is in the **up** (12 o'clock) position.
9. Coat the mating surfaces of the housing and engine with an adhesive type sealer. Position the new gasket on the engine and place the housing on the engine. Tighten the bolts to specifications.

Intake Manifold

The engines covered by this manual utilize an upper and lower intake manifold assembly. If necessary, only the upper intake manifold may be removed by following the intake manifold procedure up to that point. Obviously, installation would also begin at the upper intake steps.

REMOVAL & INSTALLATION

✳✳ WARNING

Anytime the upper or lower intake manifold has been removed, cover all openings with a rag or a sheet of plastic to prevent dirt and debris from falling into the engine.

2.3L and 2.5L Engines

♦ See Figures 21 thru 28

The intake manifold is a two–piece (upper and lower) aluminum casting. Runner lengths are tuned to optimize engine torque and power output. The manifold provides mounting flanges for the air throttle body assembly, fuel supply manifold, accelerator control bracket and the EGR valve and supply tube. A vacuum fitting is installed to provide vacuum to various engine accessories. Pockets for the fuel injectors are machined to prevent both air and fuel leakage. The following procedure is for the removal of the intake manifold with the fuel charging assembly attached.

1. Make sure the ignition is off, then drain the coolant from the radiator (engine cold).

✳✳ CAUTION

When draining the coolant, keep in mind that cats and dogs are attracted by ethylene glycol antifreeze, and are quite likely to drink any that is left in an uncovered container or in puddles on the ground. This will prove fatal in sufficient quantity. Always drain the

coolant into a sealable container. Coolant should be reused unless it is contaminated or several years old.

2. Disconnect the negative battery cable and secure it out of the way.
3. Remove the fuel filler cap to vent tank pressure. Release the pressure from the fuel system at the fuel pressure relief valve using EFI pressure gauge T80L–9974–A or equivalent. The fuel pressure relief valve is located on the fuel line in the upper right hand corner of the engine compartment. Remove the valve cap to gain access to the valve.
4. Label and unplug any electrical connectors related to the intake manifold assemblies being removed.
5. Tag and disconnect the vacuum lines at the upper intake manifold vacuum tree, at the EGR valve and at the fuel pressure regulator and canister purge line as necessary.
6. Remove the throttle linkage shield and disconnect the throttle linkage and speed control cable (if equipped). Unbolt the accelerator cable from the bracket and position the cable out of the way.
7. Disconnect the air intake hose, air bypass hose and crankcase vent hose.
8. Disconnect the PCV hose from the fitting on the underside of the upper intake manifold.
9. Loosen the clamp on the coolant bypass line at the lower intake manifold and disconnect the hose.
10. Disconnect the EGR tube from the EGR valve by removing the flange nut.
11. Remove the upper intake manifold retaining nuts. Remove the upper intake manifold and throttle body assembly.

➡If you only need to remove the upper intake manifold, stop at this point. Otherwise, continue with the procedure to also remove the lower intake manifold.

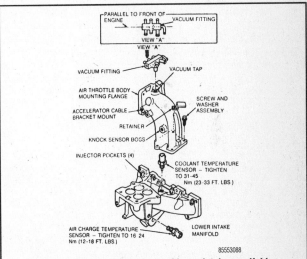

Fig. 21 Exploded view of the upper and lower intake manifold assemblies on the 2.3L and 2.5L engine

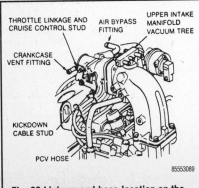

Fig. 22 Linkage and hose location on the 2.3L and 2.5L engine

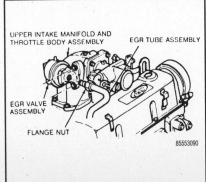

Fig. 23 Disconnect the EGR valve supply tube

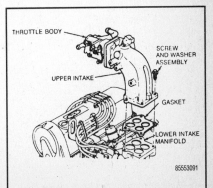

Fig. 24 Upper intake manifold removal on the 2.3L and 2.5L engine

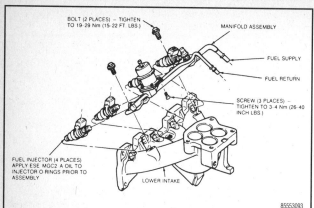

BOLT (2 PLACES) – TIGHTEN TO 19-29 Nm (15-22 FT. LBS)

MANIFOLD ASSEMBLY

FUEL SUPPLY

FUEL RETURN

SCREW (3 PLACES) – TIGHTEN TO 3-4 Nm (26-40 INCH LBS.)

FUEL INJECTOR (4 PLACES) APPLY ESE MGC2 A OIL TO INJECTOR O-RINGS PRIOR TO ASSEMBLY

LOWER INTAKE

85553093

Fig. 25 Fuel supply manifold and connections on the 2.3L and 2.5L engine. The injectors do not need to be removed unless a new manifold is being installed

12. Disengage the push connect fitting at the fuel supply manifold and fuel return lines. Disconnect the fuel return line from the fuel supply manifold.

13. Remove the engine oil dipstick bracket retaining bolt.

14. Unplug the electrical connectors from all four fuel injectors and move the harness aside.

15. Remove the four bottom retaining bolts from the lower manifold. The front two bolts also secure an engine lifting bracket. Once the bolts are removed, remove the lower intake manifold.

16. Clean and inspect the mounting faces of the lower intake manifold and cylinder head. Both surfaces must be clean and flat. If the intake manifold upper or lower section is being replaced, it will be necessary to transfer components from the old to the new part.

To install:

17. To install, first clean and oil the manifold bolt threads. Install a new lower manifold gasket.

18. Position the lower manifold assembly to the head and install the engine lifting bracket. Install the four top manifold retaining bolts finger-tight. Install the four remaining manifold bolts and tighten to 12–15 ft. lbs. (single plug 2.3L engines) or 15–22 ft. lbs. (2.3L and 2.5L twin plug engines), following the sequence illustrated.

19. Engage the four electrical connectors to the injectors.

20. Install the engine oil dipstick, then connect the fuel return and supply lines to the fuel supply manifold.

➡The following procedures are for installing the upper intake manifold.

21. Make sure the gasket surfaces of the upper and lower intake manifolds are clean. Place a gasket on the lower intake manifold assembly, then place the upper intake manifold in position.

22. Install the retaining bolts and tighten in sequence to 15–22 ft. lbs.

23. Connect the EGR tube to the EGR valve and tighten it to 18 ft. lbs.

24. Connect the coolant bypass line and tighten the clamp. Connect the PCV system hose to the fitting on the underside of the upper intake manifold.

25. If removed, install the vacuum tee on the upper intake manifold. Use Teflon® tape on the threads and tighten to 12–18 ft. lbs. Reconnect the vacuum lines to the tee, the EGR valve and the fuel pressure regulator and canister purge line as necessary.

26. Hold the accelerator cable bracket in position on the upper intake manifold and install the retaining bolt. Tighten the bolt to 10–15 ft. lbs.

27. Install the accelerator cable to the bracket.

28. Position a new gasket on the fuel charging assembly air throttle body mounting flange. Install the air throttle body to the fuel charging assembly. Install two retaining nuts and two bolts and tighten to 15–25 ft. lbs.

29. Connect the accelerator and speed control cable (if equipped), then install the throttle linkage shield.

30. Reconnect any electrical harness plugs which were removed.

31. Connect the air intake hose, air bypass hose and crankcase ventilation hose.

32. Reconnect the negative battery cable. Refill the cooling system to specifications and pressurize the fuel system by turning the ignition switch on and off (without starting the engine) at least six times. Leaving the ignition on for at least five seconds each time.

33. Start the engine and let it idle while checking for fuel, coolant and vacuum leaks. Correct as necessary. Road test the vehicle for proper operation.

2.9L Engine

▸ **See Figure 29**

1. Disconnect battery negative cable.

2. Remove air cleaner air intake duct from throttle body.

3. Disconnect throttle cable and bracket assembly.

4. Disconnect EGR tube at EGR valve.

5. Label and disconnect all vacuum hoses from fittings on upper intake manifold.

6. Detach the electrical connections at throttle body, EGR pressure sensor, intake manifold upper and lower and distributor. Also disconnect fuel injector subharness from main EEC harness.

7. Remove upper intake manifold (plenum) assembly.

➡**If you only need to remove the upper intake manifold, stop at this point. Otherwise, continue with the procedure to also remove the lower intake manifold.**

8. Drain coolant. Remove the upper radiator and heater supply hoses from intake manifold.

✷✷ CAUTION

When draining the coolant, keep in mind that cats and dogs are attracted by ethylene glycol antifreeze, and are quite likely to drink any that is left in an uncovered container or in puddles on the ground. This will prove fatal in sufficient quantity. Always drain the coolant into a sealable container. Coolant should be reused unless it is contaminated or several years old.

9. Remove distributor cap and spark plug wires as an assembly.

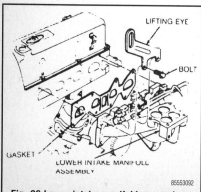

LIFTING EYE

BOLT

GASKET

LOWER INTAKE MANIFOLD ASSEMBLY

85553092

Fig. 26 Lower intake manifold removal on the 2.3L and 2.5L engine

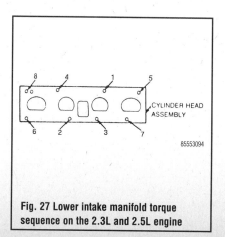

8 4 1 5

CYLINDER HEAD ASSEMBLY

6 2 3 7

85553094

Fig. 27 Lower intake manifold torque sequence on the 2.3L and 2.5L engine

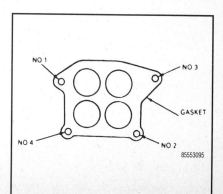

NO 1

NO 3

GASKET

NO 4

NO 2

85553095

Fig. 28 Upper intake manifold torque sequence on the 2.3L and 2.5L engine

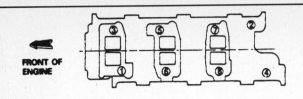

STEP	DESCRIPTION	N·m	lb-ft
1	Tighten manifold retaining bolts and nuts in sequence to	4-8	3-6
2	Tighten manifold retaining bolts and nuts in sequence to	8-15	6-11
3	Tighten manifold retaining bolts and nuts in sequence to	15-21	11-15
4	Tighten manifold retaining bolts and nuts in sequence to	21-25	15-18

89683G12

Fig. 29 Intake manifold tightening sequence and procedure for the 2.9L engine

10. Observe and mark the location of the distributor rotor and housing so ignition timing can be maintained at reassembly. Remove distributor hold-down screw and clamp and lift out distributor.

11. Remove rocker arm covers.

12. Remove intake manifold attaching bolts and nuts. Note length of manifold attaching bolts during removal so that they may be installed in their original positions. Tap manifold lightly with a plastic mallet to break gasket seal. Lift off manifold.

13. Remove all old gasket material and sealing compound.

To install:

14. Apply sealing compound to the joining surfaces. Place the intake manifold gasket in position. Ensure the tab on the right hand bank cylinder head gasket fits into the cutout of the manifold gasket.

15. Apply sealing compound to the attaching bolt bosses on the intake manifold and position the intake manifold. Follow the tightening sequence and tighten the bolts to specifications.

16. Install distributor so that rotor and housing are in the same position marked at removal.

17. Install distributor clamp and attaching bolts.

18. Replace rocker arm cover gasket, and install rocker arm valve covers using the procedure under Rocker Arm Cover and Rocker Arm.

19. Install distributor cap. Coat the inside of each spark plug wire connector with silicone grease with a small screwdriver, and install the wires. Connect distributor wiring harness.

➡The following procedures are for installing the upper intake manifold.

20. Apply sealing compound to the joining surfaces of the upper and lower intake manifolds. Install the upper intake manifold gaskets.

21. Install upper intake manifold (plenum) assembly. Tighten the bolts in two steps to specifications.

22. Connect all vacuum hoses to fittings on upper intake manifold.

23. Engage electrical connections at throttle body, EGR pressure sensor, intake manifolds sub harness to EEC main harness.

24. Install and adjust throttle linkage bracket assembly and cover.

25. Connect hoses from water outlet to radiator, and bypass hose from thermostat housing rear cover to intake manifold.

26. Connect battery negative cable.

27. Refill and bleed the cooling system.

28. Recheck ignition timing and reset engine idle speed to specification.

29. Run engine at fast idle and check for coolant and oil leaks.

3.0L Engine

♦ See Figures 30, 31 and 32

➡The throttle body is cast integral to the upper intake manifold. To remove the upper intake manifold, refer to Section 5 for throttle body removal.

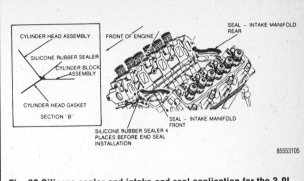

85553105

Fig. 30 Silicone sealer and intake end seal application for the 3.0L engine

1. Drain the cooling system (with the engine cold).

✳✳ CAUTION

When draining the coolant, keep in mind that cats and dogs are attracted by ethylene glycol antifreeze, and are quite likely to drink any that is left in an uncovered container or in puddles on the ground. This will prove fatal in sufficient quantity. Always drain the coolant into a sealable container. Coolant should be reused unless it is contaminated or several years old.

2. Disconnect the battery ground cable.

3. Depressurize the fuel system and remove the air intake throttle body as outlined in Section 5.

4. Disconnect the fuel return and supply lines.

5. Remove the fuel injector wiring harness from the engine.

6. Disconnect the upper radiator hose.

7. Disconnect the water outlet heater hose.

8. If equipped with distributor ignition, disconnect the distributor cap with the spark plug wires attached. Matchmark and remove the distributor assembly.

9. If equipped with distributorless ignition, Label and remove the spark plug wires from the coil pack, then remove the coil pack.

10. Remove the valve covers. Loosen retaining nut from cylinder #3 intake valve and rotate rocker arm fulcrum away from valve retainer. Remove the pushrod.

11. Remove the intake manifold attaching bolts and studs (Torx® socket required).

12. Lift the intake manifold off the engine. Use a plastic mallet to tap lightly around the intake manifold to break it loose, if necessary. Do not pry between the manifold and cylinder head with any sharp instrument. The manifold can be removed with the fuel rails and injectors in place.

13. Remove the manifold side gaskets and end seals and discard. If the manifold is being replaced, transfer the fuel injector and fuel rail components to the new manifold on a clean workbench. Clean all gasket mating surfaces.

To install:

14. First lightly oil all attaching bolts and stud threads. The intake manifold, cylinder head and cylinder block mating surfaces should be clean and free of old silicone rubber sealer. Use a suitable solvent to clean these areas.

15. Apply silicone rubber sealer (D6AZ-19562-A or equivalent) to the intersection of the cylinder block assembly and head assembly at four corners as illustrated.

➡When using silicone rubber sealer, assembly must occur within 15 minutes after sealer application. After this time, the sealer may start to set-up and its sealing effectiveness may be reduced. In high temperature/humidity conditions, the RTV will start to skin over in about 5 minutes.

16. Install the front intake manifold seal and rear intake manifold seal, then secure them with retaining features.

17. Position the intake manifold gaskets in place and insert the locking tabs over the tabs on the cylinder head gaskets.

18. Apply silicone rubber sealer over the gasket in the same places as in Step 14.

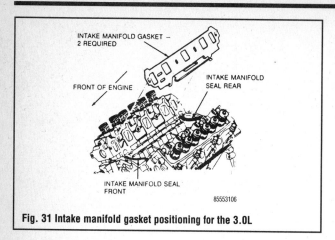

Fig. 31 Intake manifold gasket positioning for the 3.0L

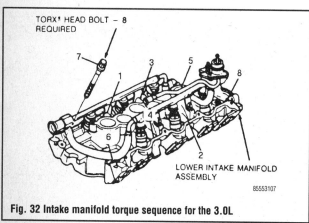

Fig. 32 Intake manifold torque sequence for the 3.0L

19. Carefully lower the intake manifold into position on the cylinder block and cylinder heads to prevent smearing the silicone sealer and causing gasketing voids.

20. Install the retaining bolts. Tighten in two stages, using the sequence illustrated, first to 11 ft. lbs., then to 18 ft. lbs.

21. If installing a new manifold, install fuel supply rail and injectors. Refer to the necessary service procedures.

22. Install #3 cylinder intake valve pushrod. Apply oil to pushrod and fulcrum prior to installation. Rotate the crankshaft to place the lifter on the heel position or base circle of camshaft. Tighten to 8 ft. lbs. to seat fulcrum in cylinder head. Final bolt torque is 24 ft. lbs.

23. Install valve covers, fuel injector harness, throttle body assembly, hose and electrical connections.

24. If equipped with distributor ignition, install the distributor assembly, using the matchmarks made earlier to insure correct alignment. Install the distributor cap and spark plug wires.

25. If equipped with distributorless ignition, install the coil pack then install the spark plug wires to their original locations.

26. Install coolant hoses. Connect all vacuum lines. Reconnect fuel lines. Install fuel line safety clips.

27. Fill and bleed cooling system. If any engine coolant accidentally spilled into the engine while the intake was off, change engine oil and filter.

28. Install air cleaner hose. Connect battery ground cable. Start engine and check for coolant, oil, fuel and vacuum leaks.

29. If equipped with distributor ignition, verify base initial timing as outlined. Check and adjust engine idle as necessary.

4.0L Engine (VIN X)

♦ See Figures 33 and 34

The intake manifold is a 4–piece assembly, consisting of the upper intake manifold, the throttle body, the fuel supply manifold, and the lower intake manifold.

1. Disconnect the battery ground cable.
2. Remove the weather shield.

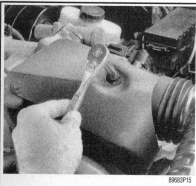

Begin the intake removal by unbolting the throttle linkage weather shield . . .

. . . then remove the air intake duct from the throttle body

Disconnect the throttle linkage, then unbolt and remove the cable bracket

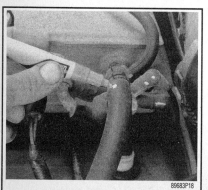

Label all of the electrical and vacuum connections on the intake manifold . . .

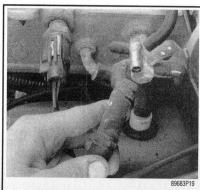

. . . then disconnect the vacuum lines . . .

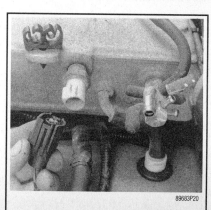

. . . and the electrical harness plugs

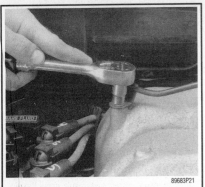

Also, ensure that any brackets which are bolted to the manifold are unfastened

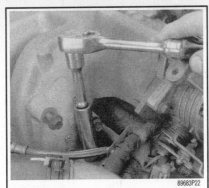

Remove the upper intake manifold attaching bolts . . .

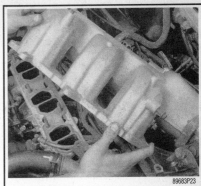

. . . then lift the manifold from the engine

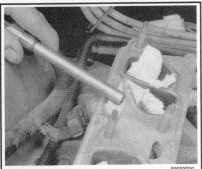

Stuff rags into the intake runners, then remove the old upper intake gasket; use care when scraping

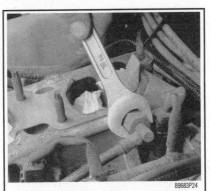

Disconnect the fuel supply and return lines from the injector fuel rail

Label all of the electrical connections on the lower intake manifold . . .

. . . then disconnect them. Next, remove the valve covers

Remove the lower intake manifold attaching bolts . . .

. . . then lift the manifold from the engine

Remove the old intake gasket from the cylinder heads and engine block

3. Remove the air cleaner intake duct.
4. Disconnect the throttle cable and bracket.
5. Tag and unplug all vacuum lines connected to the manifold.
6. Tag and disconnect all electrical wires attached to the upper manifold assembly.
7. Relieve the fuel system pressure.
8. Tag and remove the spark plug wires.
9. Remove the EDIS ignition coil and bracket.
10. Remove the 6 attaching nuts and lift off the upper manifold.

➡ If you only need to remove the upper intake manifold, stop at this point. Otherwise, continue with the procedure to also remove the lower intake manifold.

11. Disconnect the fuel supply and return lines from the injector fuel rail.
12. Label and disconnect all of the electrical connections on the lower manifold assembly.

13. Remove the valve covers.
14. Remove the lower intake manifold bolts. Tap the manifold lightly with a plastic mallet and remove it.
15. Clean all surfaces of old gasket material.
To install:
16. Apply RTV silicone gasket material at the junction points of the heads and manifold.

➡**This material will set within 15 minutes, so work quickly!**

17. Install new manifold gaskets and again apply the RTV material.
18. Position the manifold and install the nuts hand-tight. Tighten the nuts in 4 stages, using the sequence shown, to 18 ft. lbs.
19. Once again, apply RTV material to the manifold/head joints.
20. Install the valve covers using new gaskets.

➡**The following procedures are for installing the upper intake manifold.**

21. Position a new gasket and install the upper manifold. Tighten the nuts to 18 ft. lbs.
22. Install the EDIS coil.
23. Connect the fuel and return lines.
24. Install the throttle body.
25. Connect all wires.
26. Connect all vacuum lines.
27. Connect the throttle linkage.
28. Install the weather shield.
29. Install the air cleaner and duct.
30. Fill and bleed the cooling system.
31. Connect the battery ground.
32. Run the engine and check for leaks.

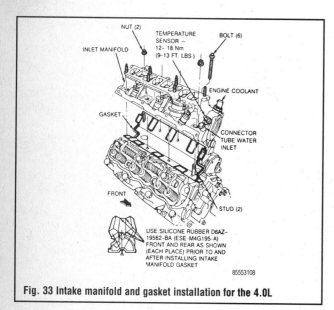

Fig. 33 Intake manifold and gasket installation for the 4.0L

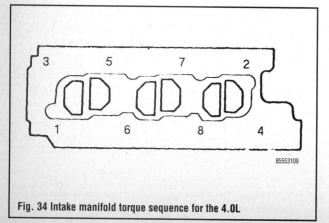

Fig. 34 Intake manifold torque sequence for the 4.0L

4.0L SOHC Engine (VIN E)

1. Disconnect the negative battery cable.
2. Remove the air cleaner-to-intake tube.
3. Remove the accelerator splash shield.
4. Disconnect the accelerator and, if equipped with cruise control, speed control cables from the throttle control cam.
5. Remove the accelerator cable retaining bracket from the upper intake manifold.
6. Label and disconnect all vacuum and electrical connections on the intake manifold.
7. Remove the eight upper intake manifold attaching bolts.
8. Lift up on the manifold and remove both fuel Vapor Management Valve (VMV) hoses.
9. Remove the upper intake manifold.

➡**If you only need to remove the upper intake manifold, stop at this point. Otherwise, continue with the procedure to also remove the lower intake manifold.**

10. Remove the 12 lower manifold attaching bolts.
11. Remove the lower intake manifold from the engine.
To install:
12. Install the lower intake manifold to the engine.
13. Install the attaching bolts. Tighten to specification in several steps.

➡**Ford does not specify a sequence, but it is recommended that you start tightening in the middle and work you way out to the ends. Repeat the tightening sequence several times until the bolts will no longer turn at the specified torque.**

➡**The following procedures are for installing the upper intake manifold.**

14. Install the upper manifold.
15. Attach both VMV hoses to the manifold.
16. Install the attaching bolts and tighten to specification. See the note above.
17. Attach any vacuum and electrical connections that were removed.
18. Connect the accelerator cable bracket to the intake and the cable (or cables if equipped with cruise control) to the throttle cam.
19. Install the accelerator splash shield.
20. Install the air cleaner-to-intake supply tube.
21. Connect the negative battery cable. Run the engine until normal operating temperature is reached and check for vacuum leaks.

5.0L Engine

◆ See Figures 35 thru 40

➡**To remove the lower intake manifold on the 5.0L engine, the camshaft synchronizer, which houses the Camshaft Position (CMP) sensor, must be removed. Refer to Section 4 before starting this procedure as there are special tools necessary. If the tools are not available and you remove the CMP, the fuel injectors will not remain timed to the engine and the vehicle will not run.**

1. Disconnect the negative battery cable.
2. Drain the cooling system.

❊❊ CAUTION

When draining the coolant, keep in mind that cats and dogs are attracted by ethylene glycol antifreeze, and are quite likely to drink any that is left in an uncovered container or in puddles on the ground. This will prove fatal in sufficient quantity. Always drain the coolant into a sealable container. Coolant should be reused unless it is contaminated or several years old.

3. Remove the air cleaner outlet tube.
4. Disconnect the crankcase ventilation hose from the throttle body.
5. Remove the throttle body shield then disengage the cables from the throttle shaft.
6. Label and disconnect any electrical components or vacuum lines attached to the upper intake manifold.
7. Remove the accelerator cable brackets from the manifold and position aside.
8. If equipped, disconnect the EGR spacer (or throttle body) coolant hoses.

9. Label and remove the spark plug wires from the coil packs.
10. Disconnect the ignition coil wiring harness plug.
11. Unbolt and remove the coil packs from the engine.
12. Remove the intake cover plate to gain access to the two long upper intake manifold attaching bolts.
13. Remove any wires or loom holders from the upper manifold.
14. Loosen and remove the upper intake manifold attaching bolts in the sequence given.
15. Remove the upper manifold and its gasket.

➡️**If you only need to remove the upper intake manifold, stop at this point. Otherwise, continue with the procedure to also remove the lower intake manifold.**

✳️ CAUTION

Fuel lines on fuel injected vehicles will remain pressurized after the engine is shut off. Fuel pressure must be relieved before servicing the fuel system.

16. Properly relieve the fuel system pressure then disconnect the fuel supply and return lines from the fuel supply manifold.
17. Disconnect the heater hoses from the hot water tube. Also remove the tube from the lower manifold.
18. Label and disconnect any electrical components, sensors or vacuum lines connected to the lower manifold.
19. Disconnect the upper radiator hose from the water outlet.
20. Loosen the water pump bypass hose clamp at the pump.
21. Remove the rear engine ground strap.
22. Remove the camshaft synchronizer with the Camshaft Position (CMP) sensor installed. Refer to Section 4.
23. Loosen and remove the lower manifold attaching bolts in the sequence given.
24. Remove the lower manifold and its gasket from the engine.

To install:
25. Ensure that all of the gasket mating surfaces are clean and free or grease, oil or dirt. Also ensure that the EGR passages in the manifolds and heads are clear.
26. Apply a 1/16 in. (1.6mm) bead of silicone sealer to the points where the cylinder block rails meet the cylinder heads.
27. Position new seals on the cylinder block and new gaskets on the cylinder heads with the gaskets interlocked with the seal tabs. Make sure the holes in the gaskets are aligned with the holes in the cylinder heads.
28. Apply a 1/16 in. (1.6mm) bead of sealer to the outer end of each intake manifold seal for the full width of the seal. Make sure the silicone sealer will not fall into the engine and possibly block oil passages.
29. Using guide pins to ease installation, carefully lower the intake manifold into position on the cylinder block and cylinder heads. Also, ensure that the water pump bypass hose is installed at the same time.
30. Install the lower manifold attaching bolts and tighten, in sequence shown, to specification in two steps as follows:
   a. Tighten all bolts to 5–10 ft. lbs. (6–14 Nm).
   b. Tighten all bolts to 23–25 ft. lbs. (31–34 Nm).
31. Install the camshaft synchronizer. Refer to Section 4.

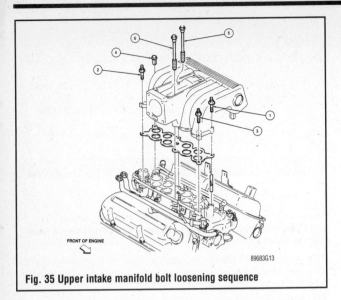

Fig. 35 Upper intake manifold bolt loosening sequence

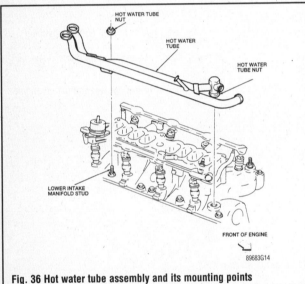

Fig. 36 Hot water tube assembly and its mounting points

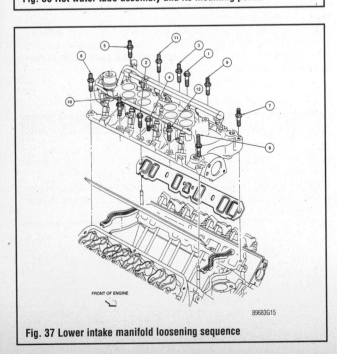

Fig. 37 Lower intake manifold loosening sequence

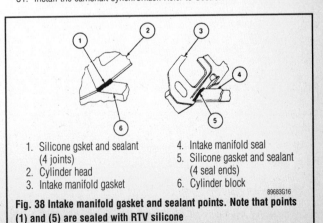

1. Silicone gsket and sealant (4 joints)
2. Cylinder head
3. Intake manifold gasket
4. Intake manifold seal
5. Silicone gasket and sealant (4 seal ends)
6. Cylinder block

Fig. 38 Intake manifold gasket and sealant points. Note that points (1) and (5) are sealed with RTV silicone

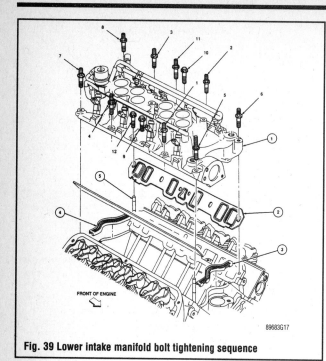

Fig. 39 Lower intake manifold bolt tightening sequence

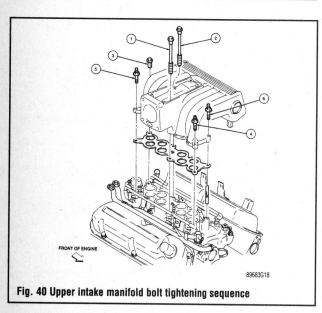

Fig. 40 Upper intake manifold bolt tightening sequence

32. Install the rear engine ground strap.
33. Tighten the water pump bypass hose clamp at the water pump.
34. Install the upper radiator hose to the water outlet.
35. Connect any electrical components or vacuum lines which were removed from the lower manifold.
36. Install the hot water tube to the engine, and connect the heater hose to the tube.
37. Connect the fuel lines, then temporarily connect the negative battery cable. Cycle the ignition to pressurize the fuel system and check for leaks. Turn the ignition key back and forth (from **ON** to **OFF**) at least 6 times, leaving the key **ON** for 5 seconds each time. If no leaks are found, disconnect the negative battery cable and continue the installation.

➡**The following procedures are for installing the upper intake manifold.**

38. Install the upper intake manifold using a new gasket. Tighten the attaching bolts in the sequence given to the proper specification.
39. Install the intake cover plate.
40. Install the ignition coils to the engine and connect the harness plug and spark plug wires to them.

41. If equipped, install the EGR spacer (throttle body) coolant hoses.
42. Install the accelerator cable brackets and cables to the intake and throttle shaft.
43. Connect any electrical components or vacuum lines removed from the upper manifold.
44. Install the throttle body shield.
45. Install the air cleaner outlet tube to the throttle body.
46. Refill and bleed the cooling system.
47. Connect the negative battery cable then start and run the engine until it reaches normal operating temperatures. Check for leaks.

Exhaust Manifold

REMOVAL & INSTALLATION

✳ CAUTION

Allow the engine to cool before attempting to remove the manifolds. Serious injury can result from contact with hot exhaust manifolds.

2.3L and 2.5L Engines

▶ **See Figure 41**

1. Disconnect the negative battery cable.
2. Remove the air cleaner outlet tube.
3. Remove the EGR transducer lines at the tube. Loosen and remove the EGR valve-to-exhaust manifold tube.
4. Disconnect the exhaust pipe from the exhaust manifold.
5. Remove the two nuts securing the lifting bracket/transducer mount, and remove the bracket.
6. Remove the exhaust manifold mounting bolts/nuts and remove the manifold.
7. Install the exhaust manifold in the reverse order. Torque the manifold in sequence in two steps, first 5–7 ft. lbs. and then 16–23 ft. lbs.

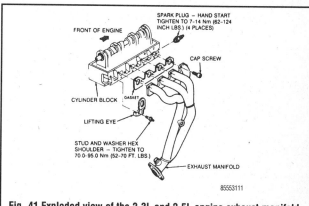

Fig. 41 Exploded view of the 2.3L and 2.5L engine exhaust manifold

2.9L Engines

▶ **See Figure 42**

1. Disconnect the attaching nuts from the muffler inlet pipe.
2. Remove the manifold attaching bolts.
3. Lift the manifold from the cylinder head.

To install:
4. Position the manifold on the heads and install and tighten the attaching bolts to specification.
5. Install and tighten the inlet pipe attaching nuts.

3.0L Engine

▶ **See Figure 43**

1. Disconnect the negative battery cable. Raise and safely support the vehicle as necessary.

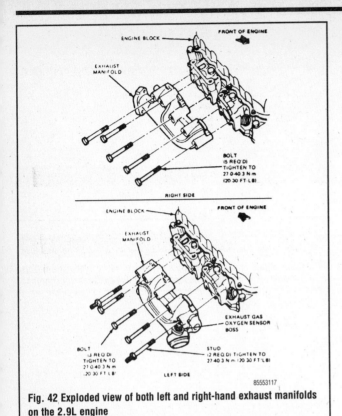

Fig. 42 Exploded view of both left and right-hand exhaust manifolds on the 2.9L engine

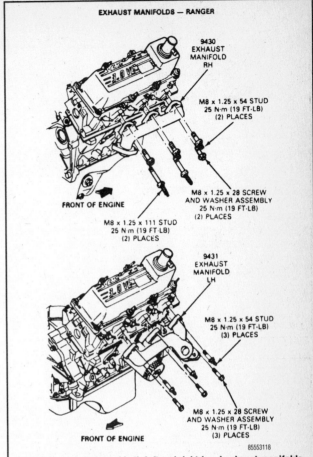

Fig. 43 Exploded view of both left and right-hand exhaust manifolds on the 3.0L engine

2. Remove the spark plugs.

3. If removing the left side exhaust manifold remove the oil level indicator tube retaining nut, rotate the dipstick assembly out of the way. Also, if equipped, loosen the EGR tube flare nut at the valve and remove the tube bolt at the manifold.

4. Remove the manifold to exhaust pipe attaching nuts, then separate the exhaust pipe from the manifold.

5. Remove the exhaust manifold attaching bolts and the manifold.

To install:

6. Clean all gasket mating surfaces.

7. Lightly oil all bolt and stud threads before installation. If a new manifold is being installed, the oxygen sensor will have to be transferred to the new part.

8. Position the exhaust manifold on the cylinder head and install the manifold attaching bolts. Tighten them to 18 ft. lbs.

9. Connect (replace gasket if so equipped) the exhaust pipe to the manifold, then tighten the attaching nuts to 30 ft. lbs. TIGHTEN BOTH NUTS IN EQUAL AMOUNTS TO CORRECTLY SEAT INLET PIPE FLANGE.

10. If installing the left side manifold, install the oil tube dipstick assembly (apply sealer to the tube) as necessary. Also reattach the EGR tube and components if removed.

11. Install the spark plugs.

12. Connect the negative battery cable. Start the engine and check for leaks.

4.0L Engine (VIN X)

▶ See Figures 44 and 45

1. Disconnect the negative battery cable. Remove the oil level indicator tube bracket.

2. Raise and safely support the vehicle.

3. Remove the exhaust pipe–to–manifold bolts.

4. Lower the vehicle.

5. If removing the left-hand manifold, disconnect the power steering pump hoses.

6. If removing the right-hand manifold, remove the hot air intake shroud which is bolted around the manifold.

7. Unbolt and remove the manifold.

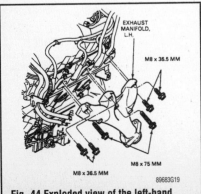

Fig. 44 Exploded view of the left-hand exhaust manifold on the 4.0L engine

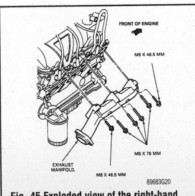

Fig. 45 Exploded view of the right-hand exhaust manifold on the 4.0L engine

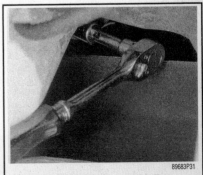

To remove the exhaust manifold, first remove the exhaust pipe-to-manifold bolts from underneath

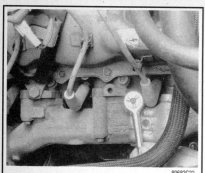

Unbolt the hot air intake shroud, which wraps around the manifold and covers some of the attaching bolts

Remove the shroud . . .

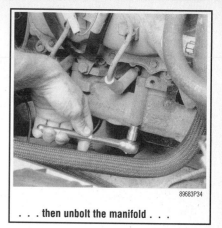

. . . then unbolt the manifold . . .

. . . and lift it from the engine

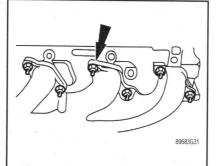

Fig. 46 The 4.0L SOHC engine exhaust manifold is retained by six nuts. Always use new nuts when installing the manifold

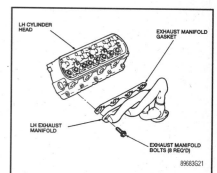

Fig. 47 Example of the 5.0L engine exhaust manifold. Left-hand manifold shown, right-hand manifold is similar

8. Clean and lightly oil all fastener threads.
9. Installation is the reverse of removal. Replace all gaskets if so equipped. Torque the manifold bolts to 19 ft. lbs.; the exhaust pipe nuts to 20 ft. lbs. TIGHTEN BOTH EXHAUST RETAINING NUTS IN EQUAL AMOUNTS TO CORRECTLY SEAT INLET PIPE FLANGE.
10. If installing the left-hand manifold, reconnect the power steering pump hoses, then fill and bleed the system.
11. Connect the negative battery cable and run the engine to check for leaks.

4.0L SOHC Engine (VIN E)

▶ See Figure 46

➡When installing the exhaust manifold, always use a new gasket and attaching nuts.

1. Disconnect the negative battery cable.
2. Raise and safely support the vehicle.
3. Remove the exhaust inlet pipe-to-manifold attaching bolts.
4. Lower the vehicle.
5. For removing the left-hand manifold, proceed as follows:
   a. Disconnect the hoses from the Differential Pressure Feedback EGR (DPFE) transducer, which is mounted to the valve cover.
   b. Disconnect the EGR tube from the manifold and the valve and remove the tube.
6. Remove the six manifold-to-engine attaching nuts.
7. Remove the manifold and the gasket. Discard the old gasket.

To install:

8. Clean the gasket mating surfaces.
9. Position the exhaust manifold and new gasket to the cylinder head and install new attaching nuts. Tighten the nuts to 15–18 ft. lbs. (20–25 Nm).
10. For installing the left-hand manifold, proceed as follows:
    a. Position and install the EGR tube to the manifold and the valve.
    b. Connect the two hoses to the DPFE transducer.
11. Raise and safely support the vehicle.

12. Install the exhaust inlet pipe-to-manifold attaching bolts and tighten to 25–32 ft. lbs. (34–46 Nm).
13. Lower the vehicle and reconnect the negative battery cable.
14. Start the engine and check for leaks.

5.0L Engine

▶ See Figure 47

➡When installing the manifolds, always use new gaskets.

1. Disconnect the negative battery cable.
2. Remove the accessory drive belt.
3. For the right-hand manifold, proceed as follows:
   a. Drain the cooling system.
   b. Disconnect the alternator wires.
   c. Remove the drive belt tensioner.
   d. Disconnect the heater hot water tube from the water pump.
   e. Remove the alternator bracket bolts and then remove the assembly.
4. For the left-hand manifold, proceed as follows:
   a. Remove A/C compressor bolts and position it off to the side.
   b. Remove the oil level indicator tube nut and tube.
5. Raise and safely support the vehicle.
6. Remove the exhaust inlet pipe-to-manifold bolts.
7. Lower vehicle to a suitable height to access the manifold-to-engine attaching bolts.

➡Access to the manifold-to-engine bolts is through the wheel well opening.

8. Remove the pushpins securing the fender apron, and remove it for access to the manifold attaching bolts.
9. Label and disconnect the spark plug wires from the side of the engine whose manifold is to be removed.
10. Remove the exhaust manifold attaching bolts.
11. Lower the vehicle and remove the manifold.
12. Discard the old gasket.

To install:

13. Clean the gasket mating surfaces. Inspect the manifold for cracks and damaged gasket mating surfaces. Replace if damaged.

14. Position the exhaust manifold and gasket to the cylinder head and install all of the bolts finger-tight.

15. For installing the left-hand manifold, proceed as follows:

    a. Position the A/C compressor to its bracket and install the attaching bolts. Tighten the bolts to 16–21 ft. lbs. (21–29 Nm).

    b. Install the drive belt.

16. For installing the right-hand manifold, proceed as follows:

    a. Install generator bracket to the cylinder head.

    b. Connect heater hot water tube to the water pump.

    c. Install the drive belt tensioner. Tighten the bolts to 15–22 ft. lbs. (20–30 Nm).

    d. Connect the alternator wires.

    e. Install the accessory drive belt.

    f. Refill the cooling system.

17. Raise and safely support the vehicle to allow access to the exhaust manifold-to-engine attaching bolts.

18. Tighten the exhaust manifold bolts to 26–35 ft. lbs. (35–44 Nm).

19. Connect the spark plug wires to the plugs.

20. Install the fender apron and its pushpins.

21. Raise and safely support the vehicle to allow access to the exhaust inlet-to-manifold pipe fasteners.

22. Install the inlet pipe bolts to the exhaust manifold and tighten to 26–33 ft. lbs. (34–46 Nm).

23. Lower the vehicle.

24. If installing the left-hand manifold, install the oil level indicator tube and its securing nut.

25. Connect the negative battery cable, start the engine and check for leaks.

Radiator

REMOVAL & INSTALLATION

▶ **See Figures 48 and 49**

1. Drain the cooling system. Remove the overflow tube from the coolant recovery bottle and from the radiator.

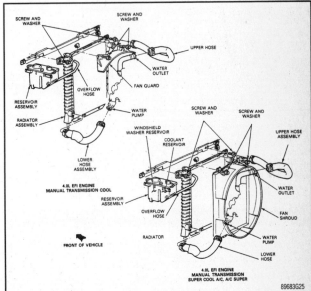

Fig. 48 Exploded view of the 2.3L and 2.5L engine radiator and related components

Fig. 49 Exploded view of the 4.0L engine radiator and related components—2.9L and 3.0L engines are similar

To remove the radiator, first remove the air intake tube, then unbolt the shroud and position it over the fan

Disconnect the upper and lower hoses from the radiator

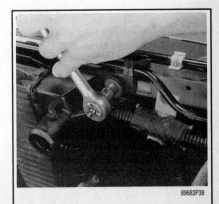

Remove the radiator retaining bolts . . .

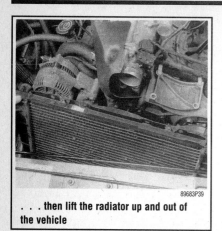

. . . then lift the radiator up and out of the vehicle

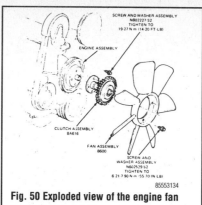

Fig. 50 Exploded view of the engine fan for the 2.3L and 2.5L engine

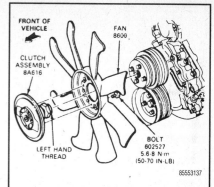

Fig. 51 Exploded view of the engine fan for the 2.9L and 3.0L engines

✳ CAUTION

When draining the coolant, keep in mind that cats and dogs are attracted by ethylene glycol antifreeze, and are quite likely to drink any that is left in an uncovered container or in puddles on the ground. This will prove fatal in sufficient quantity. Always drain the coolant into a sealable container. Coolant should be reused unless it is contaminated or several years old.

2. If necessary, remove the air cleaner outlet tube from the throttle body.

3. Remove the retaining bolts at the top of the shroud, and position the shroud over the fan, clear of the radiator.

4. If equipped with the 5.0L engine, remove the engine fan and the radiator shroud from the vehicle.

5. If equipped with an automatic transmission, disconnect the transmission cooling lines from the bottom of the radiator.

6. Disconnect the upper and lower hoses from the radiator.

7. Remove the radiator retaining bolts or the upper supports and lift the radiator from the vehicle.

8. Install the radiator in the reverse order of removal. Fill the cooling system and check for leaks. On automatic transmission equipped vehicles, run the engine until normal operating temperature is reached, then check the transmission fluid level. Correct as needed.

Engine Fan

REMOVAL & INSTALLATION

➡**Refer to exploded view illustration before starting this service procedure.**

✳ WARNING

The following procedures for removing the fan clutch gives the factory recommended loosening and tightening directions for the fan hub nut. However, it has been our experience that certain aftermarket parts manufacturers have changed this to enable use of universal fit parts. We recommend trying the factory direction first, then, if the nut doesn't seem to be moving, reverse the direction. Placing too much load on the water pump snout will break it.

2.3L and 2.5L Engines

♦ See Figure 50

➡**The 2.3L and 2.5L engine does not use a fan hub nut. It is retained by four bolts which also secure the pump pulley to the water pump.**

1. If not equipped with A/C, disconnect the overflow tube from the fan guard, then unbolt and remove the guard.

2. If equipped with A/C, disconnect the overflow tube from the shroud, remove the mounting screws and lift the shroud off the brackets. Place the shroud behind the fan.

3. Remove the 4 clutch/fan assembly-to-pulley screws and remove the clutch/fan assembly. Vehicles equipped with A/C should remove the clutch/fan and shroud together.

4. If necessary, remove the fan-to-clutch bolts to separate the fan from the clutch.

5. Installation is the reverse of removal. Torque the fan-to-clutch screws to 55–70 inch lbs. (6–8 Nm); the fan/clutch assembly-to-pulley bolts to 12–18 ft. lbs. (16–24 Nm).

2.9L and 3.0L Engines

♦ See Figure 51

1. If necessary, remove the air cleaner outlet tube.

2. Using Strap Wrench D79L-6731-A and Fan Clutch Nut Wrench T83T-6312-B, or their equivalents, loosen the large nut attaching the clutch to the water pump hub.

➡**According to the manufacturer, the nut uses LH threads and is loosened clockwise.**

3. Remove the two upper fan shroud retaining bolts. If the overflow hose is routed through the fan shroud, remove it from the shroud.

4. Lift up on the fan shroud to disengage the lower mounting clips.

5. Remove the fan/clutch assembly and the fan shroud together.

6. If necessary, remove the fan-to-clutch bolts to separate the fan from the clutch.

To install:

7. Installation is the reverse of removal. Torque the fan-to-clutch bolts to 55–70 inch lbs. (6–8 Nm); the hub nut to 30–100 ft. lbs. (41–135 Nm) for 1991–95 models and 34–46 ft. lbs. (46–63 Nm) for 1996–99 models. Don't forget, the nut uses LH threads and is tightened counterclockwise.

4.0L Engine (VIN X)

♦ See Figure 52

1. If necessary, remove the air cleaner outlet tube.

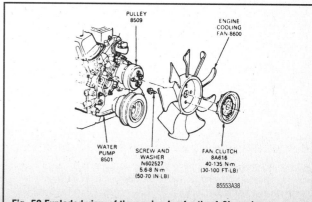

Fig. 52 Exploded view of the engine fan for the 4.0L engine

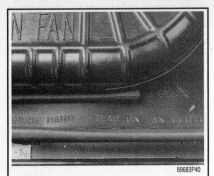

89683P40

Before attempting to unfasten the engine fan, check the fan shroud for indications of normal or reverse threads

89683P41

Remove the air intake tube. You will need these specialized tools to unfasten the fan clutch nut

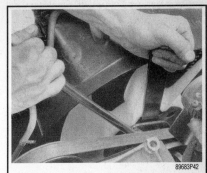

89683P42

Using the special tools, loosen the fan clutch nut in the direction indicated on the shroud.

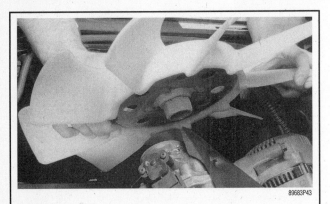

89683P43

Remove the fan and clutch assembly from the vehicle

➡ **According to the manufacturer, the nut uses RH threads and is loosened counterclockwise.**

2. Using Fan Clutch Pulley Holder T84T–6312–C and Fan Clutch Nut Wrench T84T–6312–D, or their equivalents, loosen the large nut attaching the clutch to the water pump hub.

➡ **Some models have enough room between the shroud and the engine to remove the fan without unbolting the shroud.**

3. Remove the two upper fan shroud retaining bolts. If the overflow hose is routed through the fan shroud, remove it from the shroud.
4. Lift up on the fan shroud to disengage the lower mounting clips.
5. Remove the fan/clutch assembly and the fan shroud together.
6. If necessary, remove the fan-to-clutch bolts to separate the fan from the clutch.

To install:
7. Installation is the reverse of removal. Torque the fan-to-clutch bolts to 55–70 inch lbs. (6–8 Nm); the hub nut to 30–100 ft. lbs. (41–135 Nm) for 1991–95 models and 34–46 ft. lbs. (46–63 Nm) for 1996–99 models. Don't forget, the nut uses RH threads and is tightened clockwise.

4.0L SOHC (VIN E) and 5.0L Engines

1. If necessary, remove the air cleaner outlet tube.
2. Using Fan Clutch Pulley Holder T84T–6312–C and Fan Clutch Nut Wrench T84T–6312–D for the 4.0L engine, or Holder T96T-6312-A and Wrench T96T-6312-B for the 5.0L engine, loosen the large nut attaching the clutch to the water pump hub.

✷✷ WARNING

The manufacturer does not specify a loosening or tightening direction. Using extreme care, try loosening the nut in one direction first. If it does not move, change directions. Applying too much force to the end of the water pump will break it.

3. Remove the two upper fan shroud retaining bolts. If the overflow hose is routed through the fan shroud, remove it from the shroud.
4. Lift up on the fan shroud to disengage the lower mounting clips.
5. Remove the fan/clutch assembly and the fan shroud together.
6. If necessary, remove the fan-to-clutch bolts to separate the fan from the clutch.

To install:
7. Installation is the reverse of removal. Torque the fan-to-clutch bolts to 14–19 ft. lbs. (19–26 Nm); the hub nut to 34–46 ft. lbs. (46–63 Nm). Tighten the nut in the reverse direction of removal.

Water Pump

REMOVAL & INSTALLATION

2.3L and 2.5L Engines

▶ **See Figure 53**

1. Disconnect the negative battery cable.
2. Drain the cooling system.

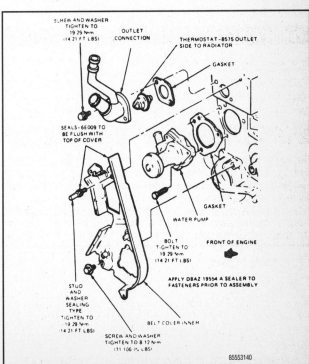

85553140

Fig. 53 Exploded view of the water pump and related parts for the 2.3L and 2.5L engine

※※ CAUTION

When draining engine coolant, keep in mind that cats and dogs are attracted to ethylene glycol antifreeze and could drink any that is left in an uncovered container or in puddles on the ground. This will prove fatal in sufficient quantity. Always drain coolant into a sealable container. Coolant should be reused unless it is contaminated or is several years old.

3. Remove the two bolts that retain the fan shroud and position the shroud back over the fan.

4. Remove the four bolts that retain the cooling fan. Remove the fan and shroud.

5. Loosen and remove the accessory drive belt. Earlier models may have two drive belts, remove them both.

6. Remove the water pump pulley and, if necessary, the vent hose to the emissions canister.

7. Remove the heater hose at the water pump.

8. Remove the timing belt cover. Remove the lower radiator hose from the water pump.

9. Remove the water pump mounting bolts and the water pump. Clean all gasket mounting surfaces.

10. Install the water pump in the reverse order of removal. Coat the threads of the mounting bolts with sealer before installation.

2.9L Engines

1. Drain the coolant from the radiator and remove the lower hose and the return hose from the water inlet housing.

※※ CAUTION

When draining the coolant, keep in mind that cats and dogs are attracted by ethylene glycol antifreeze, and are quite likely to drink any that is left in an uncovered container or in puddles on the ground. This will prove fatal in sufficient quantity. Always drain the coolant into a sealable container. Coolant should be reused unless it is contaminated or several years old.

2. Using Tools T83T–6312–A and B remove the fan and clutch assembly from the front of the water pump.

➡See the engine fan removal procedure in this section.

3. Loosen the alternator mounting bolts and remove the alternator belt.

4. Remove the water pump pulley.

5. Remove the bolts retaining the water pump assembly and remove the water pump, water inlet housing, and the thermostat from the front cover.

6. Before installing the water pump, clean the gasket surfaces on the front cover and on the water pump assembly. Apply gasket sealer to both sides of the new gasket and install the water pump in the reverse order of removal.

3.0L Engine

♦ See Figures 54 and 55

1. Disconnect the battery ground cable.

2. Drain the cooling system.

※※ CAUTION

When draining the coolant, keep in mind that cats and dogs are attracted by ethylene glycol antifreeze, and are quite likely to drink any that is left in an uncovered container or in puddles on the ground. This will prove fatal in sufficient quantity. Always drain the coolant into a sealable container. Coolant should be reused unless it is contaminated or several years old.

3. Remove the engine fan.

4. Loosen the 4 water pump pulley bolts.

5. Remove the accessory drive belts.

6. Remove the water pump pulley.

7. Remove the alternator adjusting arm and throttle body brace.

8. Remove the lower radiator hose.

9. Disconnect the heater hose at the pump.

10. Rotate the belt adjuster out of the way.

11. Remove the water pump attaching bolts. Note their location for installation.

12. Remove the pump and discard the gasket.

13. Thoroughly clean the pump and engine mating surfaces.

To install:

14. Using an adhesive type sealer, position a new gasket on the timing cover.

15. Position the water pump and start the bolts. When all the bolts are started, torque them to specifications. Refer to the necessary illustration.

16. Install the lower hose and connect the radiator hose.

17. Install the pulley and hand-tighten the 4 bolts.

18. Install the alternator adjusting arm and brace.

19. Install the belts and tension them. See Section 1.

20. Tighten the 4 pulley bolts to 19 ft. lbs.

21. Install the fan.

22. Fill and bleed the cooling system.

23. Connect the battery ground cable. Run the engine and check for leaks.

4.0L Engine (VIN X)

1. Disconnect the negative battery cable.

2. Drain the cooling system.

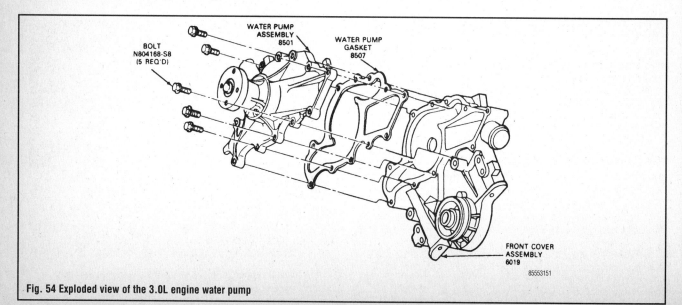

Fig. 54 Exploded view of the 3.0L engine water pump

BOLT N804168-S8 (5 REQ'D)

WATER PUMP ASSEMBLY 8501

WATER PUMP GASKET 8507

FRONT COVER ASSEMBLY 6019

85553151

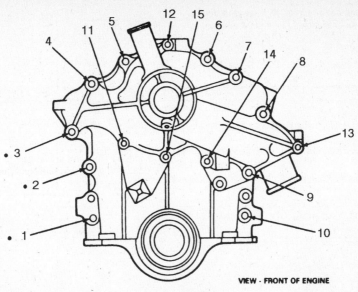

FRONT COVER, WATER PUMP — FASTENER CHART

VIEW - FRONT OF ENGINE

Fastener and Hole No.	Fasteners			
	Part No.	Size	N-m	Ft-Lb
• 1	N804215	M8 x 1.25 x 72.25	25	19
• 2	N804215	M8 x 1.25 x 72.25	25	19
• 3	N606547-S8	M8 x 1.25 x 70.0	25	19
4	N606547-S8	M8 x 1.25 x 70.0	25	19
5	N605909-S8	M8 x 1.25 x 42.0	25	19
6	N804154-S8	M8 x 1.25 x 99.3	25	19
7	N606547-S8	M8 x 1.25 x 70.0	25	19
8	N606547-S8	M8 x 1.25 x 70.0	25	19
9	N606547-S8	M8 x 1.25 x 70.0	25	19
10	N605909-S8	M8 x 1.25 x 42.0	25	19
11	N804168-S8	M6 x 1.0 x 25.0	10	7
12	N804168-S8	M6 x 1.0 x 25.0	10	7
13	N804168-S8	M6 x 1.0 x 25.0	10	7
14	N804168-S8	M6 x 1.0 x 25.0	10	7
15	N804168-S8	M6 x 1.0 x 25.0	10	7

NOTE: •Apply Pipe Sealant with Teflon D8AZ-19554-A (ESG-M4G194-A) Sealer to Fastener Threads

85553152

Fig. 55 3.0L engine water pump and front cover fastener chart

※※ CAUTION

When draining the coolant, keep in mind that cats and dogs are attracted by ethylene glycol antifreeze, and are quite likely to drink any that is left in an uncovered container or in puddles on the ground. This will prove fatal in sufficient quantity. Always drain the coolant into a sealable container. Coolant should be reused unless it is contaminated or several years old.

3. Remove the fan and fan clutch assembly.

➡See the engine fan removal procedure in this section.

4. Remove the lower radiator hose from the water pump.
5. On 1997–99 Explorer/Mountaineer models, remove the radiator.
6. Loosen the water pump pulley attaching bolts.
7. Except 1997–99 Explorer/Mountaineer models, loosen the alternator mounting bolts and remove the belt. On vehicles with air conditioning, remove the tensioner pulley, alternator and bracket.
8. Except 1997–99 Explorer/Mountaineer models, remove the A/C compressor and power steering pump mounting bracket, without disconnecting the lines, and set off to the side.
9. Remove the water pump pulley.

89683P44

To service the water pump, first drain the cooling system, then remove the engine fan/clutch . . .

. . . and the fan shroud from the vehicle

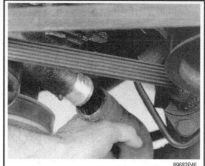

Remove the lower radiator hose from the water pump. Position a drain pan underneath to catch any coolant

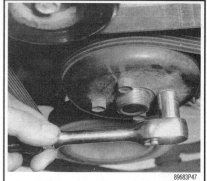

Loosen the water pump pulley attaching bolts . . .

. . . before removing the accessory drive belt . . .

. . . then with the drive belt out of the way, finish removing the water pump pulley

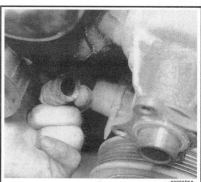

Remove the heater hose connection at the water pump

Remove all of the water pump attaching bolts . . .

. . . then remove the pump from the engine

Remove all traces of the old gasket before installing the pump

10. Disconnect the heater hose at the pump.
11. Remove the attaching bolts and remove the water pump.
To install:
12. Clean the mounting surfaces of the pump and front cover thoroughly. Remove all traces of gasket material.
13. Apply adhesive gasket sealer to both sides of a new gasket and place gasket on the pump.
14. Position the pump on the cover and install the bolts finger–tight. When all bolts are in place, torque them to 72–108 inch lbs. (8.5–12 Nm).
15. Install the pulley.
16. On vehicles with air conditioning, install the alternator, bracket and tensioner pulley.
17. Install the A/C compressor and power steering pump mounting bracket.
18. Install and adjust the drive belt.
19. Connect the hoses and tighten the clamps.
20. Install the fan and clutch assembly.

21. Fill and bleed the cooling system.
22. Connect the negative battery cable, then start the engine and check for leaks.

4.0L SOHC Engine (VIN E)

1. Disconnect the negative battery cable.
2. Drain the cooling system.

❋❋ CAUTION

When draining the coolant, keep in mind that cats and dogs are attracted by ethylene glycol antifreeze, and are quite likely to drink any that is left in an uncovered container or in puddles on the ground. This will prove fatal in sufficient quantity. Always drain the coolant into a sealable container. Coolant should be reused unless it is contaminated or several years old.

3. Remove the fan and fan clutch assembly.

➡**See the engine fan removal procedure in this section.**

4. Remove the radiator.
5. Loosen the water pump pulley attaching bolts.
6. Remove the accessory drive belt and the idler pulley.
7. Slide the bypass hose clamp back, away from the pump.
8. Disconnect the heater hose at the pump.
9. Remove the lower radiator hose.
10. Remove the water pump pulley.
11. Remove all of the water pump attaching bolts. Pay attention to the locations of any stud bolts.
12. Remove the water pump.

To install:

13. Clean the mounting surfaces of the pump and front cover thoroughly. Remove all traces of gasket material.
14. Apply adhesive gasket sealer to both sides of a new gasket and place the gasket on the pump.
15. Position the pump on the cover, while connecting the bypass hose to the pump, and install the bolts finger–tight. When all bolts are in place, torque them to 72–108 inch lbs. (6–9 ft. lbs. or 8.5–12 Nm).
16. Position the bypass hose clamp back to its original position.
17. Install the water pump pulley and its attaching bolts. Snug the bolts.
18. Connect the lower radiator and heater hoses to the water pump.
19. Install the belt idler pulley.
20. Lift the accessory drive belt tensioner and install the belt.
21. Securely tighten the water pump pulley attaching bolts.
22. Install the radiator and the engine fan.
23. Refill and bleed the cooling system.
24. Connect the negative battery cable, start the engine and check for leaks.

5.0L Engine

◗ **See Figure 56**

1. Disconnect the negative battery cable.
2. Drain the cooling system.

✳✳ CAUTION

When draining the coolant, keep in mind that cats and dogs are attracted by ethylene glycol antifreeze, and are quite likely to drink any that is left in an uncovered container or in puddles on the ground. This will prove fatal in sufficient quantity. Always drain the coolant into a sealable container. Coolant should be reused unless it is contaminated or several years old.

3. Remove the fan/clutch assembly and shroud.

➡**See the engine fan removal procedure in this section.**

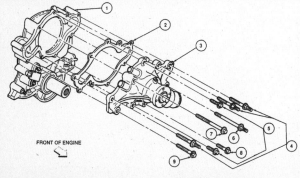

FRONT OF ENGINE

1. Engine front cover
2. Water pump housing gasket
3. Water pump
4. Water pump stud bolts
5. Water pump bolts
6. Water pump stud bolt
7. Water pump bolt
8. Water pump bolt
9. Water pump bolt

89683G26

Fig. 56 Exploded view of the 5.0L water pump

4. Loosen the water pump pulley attaching bolts.
5. Remove the accessory drive belt.
6. Remove the water bypass hose from the pump.
7. Disconnect the heater hose at the pump.
8. Remove the engine control sensor wiring harness brackets and position the harness out of the way.
9. Remove the water pump pulley.
10. Remove all of the water pump attaching bolts. Pay attention to the locations of any stud bolts.
11. Pull the water pump away from the front cover, then disconnect the lower radiator hose from the pump
12. Lift the water pump from the vehicle.

To install:

13. Clean the mounting surfaces of the pump and front cover thoroughly. Remove all traces of gasket material.
14. Apply adhesive gasket sealer to both sides of a new gasket and place the gasket on the pump.
15. Install the lower radiator hose to the water pump.
16. Position the pump on the cover and install the bolts finger–tight. When all bolts are in place, torque them to 15–21 ft. lbs. (20–28 Nm).
17. Position the engine control sensor wiring harness and install the retaining nuts.
18. Install the water pump pulley and its attaching bolts. Snug the bolts.
19. Install the heater and water bypass hoses to the water pump.
20. Lift the accessory drive belt tensioner and install the belt.
21. Securely tighten the water pump pulley attaching bolts.
22. Install the engine fan/clutch assembly and the shroud.
23. Refill and bleed the cooling system.
24. Connect the negative battery cable, start the engine and check for leaks.

Cylinder Head

REMOVAL & INSTALLATION

➡**Before installing the cylinder heads, have them cleaned and professionally checked. If there is a problem, generally, it will not go away by simply installing new gaskets. Cylinder heads can and do warp, which is the major cause of gasket failure. This is usually due to overheating.**

2.3L and 2.5L Engine

◗ **See Figure 57**

1. Disconnect the negative battery cable.
2. Drain cooling system.

✳✳ CAUTION

When draining the coolant, keep in mind that cats and dogs are attracted by ethylene glycol antifreeze, and are quite likely to drink any that is left in an uncovered container or in puddles on the ground. This will prove fatal in sufficient quantity. Always drain the coolant into a sealable container. Coolant should be reused unless it is contaminated or several years old.

3. Remove air cleaner assembly.
4. Remove the heater hose-to-valve cover retaining screws.
5. Remove the spark plugs.
6. Label and disconnect all of the upper engine components and alternator wiring harnesses.
7. Label and remove the spark plug wires.
8. Disconnect the Exhaust Gas Oxygen (EGO) sensor at the exhaust manifold.
9. Disconnect required vacuum hoses.
10. Remove dipstick tube and bracket.
11. Remove rocker retaining bolts and remove cover.
12. Remove intake manifold retaining bolts.
13. Loosen alternator retaining bolts and remove belt from the pulley. Remove mounting bracket retaining bolts to the head.
14. Disconnect the upper radiator hose at both ends and remove from the vehicle.

15. Remove the timing belt cover bolts and remove the cover. For power steering-equipped vehicles, unbolt the power steering pump bracket and position it off to the side.

16. Loosen the timing belt idler retaining bolts. Position idler in the unloaded position and tighten the retaining bolts.

17. Remove the timing belt from the cam pulley and auxiliary pulley.

18. Remove four nuts and/or stud bolts retaining heat stove to exhaust manifold.

19. Remove the eight exhaust manifold retaining bolts.

20. Remove the timing belt idler and two bracket bolts.

21. Remove the timing belt idler spring stop from the cylinder head.

22. Disconnect the oil sending unit lead wire.

23. Remove the cylinder head retaining bolts.

24. Remove the cylinder head.

25. Clean the cylinder head, intake manifold and exhaust manifold gasket surfaces.

26. Blow oil out of the cylinder head bolt block hoses.

27. Clean valve cover gasket surface on the head.

28. Check cylinder head for flatness.

To install:

29. Position head gasket on the block.

30. Clean rocker arm cover (cam cover).

31. Install valve cover gasket to the valve cover.

32. Position cylinder head to block.

33. Install cylinder head retaining bolts and tighten to specifications.

34. Connect oil sending unit lead wires.

35. Install the timing belt idler spring stop to the cylinder head.

36. Position the timing belt idler to the cylinder head, and install its retaining bolts.

37. Install the eight exhaust manifold retaining bolts and/or stud bolts.

38. Install four nuts and/or stud bolts retaining heat stove to exhaust manifold.

39. Align the cam gear with pointer.

40. Align the crank pulley (TDC) with the pointer on the timing belt cover.

41. Position the timing belt to the pulleys (cam and auxiliary).

42. Loosen idler retaining bolts to tension the belt, then rotate the engine and check timing alignment.

43. Adjust belt tensioner and tighten retaining bolts.

44. Install the timing belt cover and its four retaining bolts.

45. Connect the upper radiator hose to the engine and radiator and tighten the retaining clamps.

46. Position the alternator bracket to cylinder head and install its retainers.

47. If removed, position the power steering pump bracket to the engine and install its attaching bolts.

48. Install the accessory drive belt and, if necessary, adjust the belt tension using Belt Tension Gauge Rotunda 021–00045 or equivalent.

49. Position the intake manifold to the cylinder head, and install its retaining bolts.

50. Install the rocker arm covers and retaining bolts.

51. Install the spark plugs.

52. Install the dipstick tube and bracket.

53. Connect the appropriate vacuum hoses.

54. Connect all of the upper engine components and alternator wiring harnesses.

55. Position and connect the spark plug wires.

56. Install the heater hose-to-valve cover retaining screws.

57. Fill and bleed the cooling system.

58. Install the air cleaner.

59. Connect the negative battery cable.

60. Start the engine and check for leaks.

2.9L Engines

▶ See Figures 58 and 59

➡ According to the manufacturer, you must use new cylinder head bolts when installing the heads.

1. Disconnect the battery ground cable.

2. Drain the radiator coolant.

�֎�֎ CAUTION

When draining the coolant, keep in mind that cats and dogs are attracted by ethylene glycol antifreeze, and are quite likely to drink any that is left in an uncovered container or in puddles on the ground. This will prove fatal in sufficient quantity. Always drain the coolant into a sealable container. Coolant should be reused unless it is contaminated or several years old.

3. Remove the intake tube from the throttle body and disconnect the throttle linkage and cover.

4. Remove the distributor.

5. Remove the radiator hose and the by-pass hose from the thermostat housing and intake manifold.

6. Remove the rocker arm covers and the rocker arm shafts.

7. Depressurize the fuel system and remove the fuel line from the fuel rail.

8. Remove the intake manifold.

9. Remove and label the pushrods in order to keep them in sequence for proper assembly.

10. Remove the exhaust manifolds.

11. Remove the cylinder head attaching bolts. Remove the cylinder heads and discard the head gaskets.

To install:

12. Clean the cylinder heads, intake manifold, valve rocker arm cover and cylinder block gasket surfaces.

13. Place the cylinder head gaskets in position on the cylinder block.

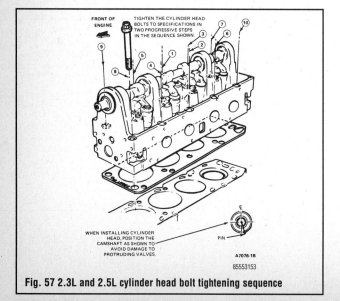

Fig. 57 2.3L and 2.5L cylinder head bolt tightening sequence

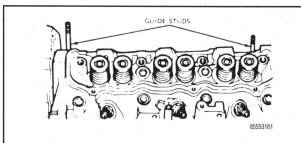

Fig. 58 Cylinder head alignment studs on the 2.9L engine

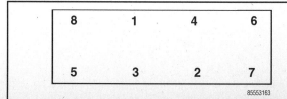

Fig. 59 Cylinder head torque sequence for the 2.9L engine

➡**Gaskets are marked with the words FRONT and TOP for correct positioning. Left and right cylinder head gaskets are not interchangeable. Use new cylinder head bolts.**

14. Install the fabricated alignment dowels in the cylinder block and install the cylinder head assemblies on the cylinder block, one at a time.

15. Remove the alignment dowels and install new cylinder head attaching bolts. Tighten the bolts to specification following the torque sequence.

16. Install the intake manifold.

17. Install the exhaust manifolds.

18. Apply Lubriplate®, or equivalent, to both ends of the pushrods and install the pushrods.

19. Install oil baffles and rocker arms.

20. Install the distributor.

21. Adjust the valves as described in Section 1 under Valve Lash adjustment.

22. Install the rocker arm covers.

23. Connect the fuel line to the fuel rail.

24. Install the distributor cap with spark plug wires attached. Coat the inside of each spark plug boot with silicone lubricant and install them on the spark plug.

25. Install the throttle linkage and air cleaner intake tube.

26. Fill the cooling system according to instructions on the underhood decal and bleed the cooling system.

27. Connect the battery ground cable.

28. Operate the engine at fast idle and check for oil, fuel and coolant leaks.

29. If necessary, check and adjust the ignition timing.

3.0L Engine

▶ **See Figures 60, 61 and 62**

➡**According to the manufacturer, you must use new cylinder head bolts when installing the heads.**

1. Drain the cooling system (engine cold) into a clean container and save the coolant for reuse.

✳✳ CAUTION

When draining the coolant, keep in mind that cats and dogs are attracted by ethylene glycol antifreeze, and are quite likely to drink any that is left in an uncovered container or in puddles on the ground. This will prove fatal in sufficient quantity. Always drain the coolant into a sealable container. Coolant should be reused unless it is contaminated or several years old.

2. Disconnect the battery ground cable.

3. Remove the air cleaner.

4. Relieve fuel pressure. Disconnect fuel lines as necessary. Mark vacuum line location and remove lines.

5. Disconnect upper and lower radiator hoses—position out of the way.

6. Label and remove the ignition wires from the spark plugs and locating studs.

7. If equipped, mark the distributor housing to block and note rotor position. Remove the distributor.

8. Remove coil assembly.

9. Remove the throttle body. See Section 5.

10. Remove the accessory drive belt.

11. If the left-hand cylinder head is being removed:

a. Remove the power steering pump and bracket assembly. DO NOT disconnect the hoses. Tie the assembly out of the way.

b. Remove the engine oil dipstick and tube. Rotate or remove tube assembly.

c. Remove the fuel line retaining bracket bolt from the front of cylinder head.

12. If the right-hand head is being removed:

a. Disconnect alternator electrical harnesses.

b. Remove belt tensioner assembly.

c. Remove the alternator and bracket.

d. Remove hose from valve cover to oil fill adapter.

13. Remove the spark plugs.

14. Remove the exhaust manifold(s).

15. Remove the rocker arm covers as previously described.

16. Loosen rocker arm fulcrum retaining bolts enough to allow the rocker arm to be lifted off the pushrod and rotate to one side.

➡**Regardless of which cylinder head is being removed, the #3 cylinder intake valve pushrod must be removed to allow removal of the intake manifold.**

17. Remove the pushrods, keeping them in order so they may be installed in their original locations.

18. Remove the intake manifold as outlined. Refer to the necessary service procedure.

19. Loosen the cylinder head attaching bolts in reverse of the torque sequence, then remove the bolts and lift off the cylinder head(s). Remove and discard the old cylinder head gasket(s).

To install:

20. Clean the cylinder heads, intake manifold, valve rocker arm cover and cylinder block gasket surfaces of all traces of old gasket material and/or sealer.

21. Lightly oil all bolt and stud bolt threads except those specifying special sealant. Position the new head gasket(s) on the cylinder block, using the dowels for alignment. The dowels should be replaced if damaged.

22. Position the cylinder head(s) on the block and install new attaching bolts. Tighten the head bolts in sequence to 59 ft. lbs. Back off all bolts one full turn (360 degrees). Retighten the cylinder head bolts in sequence, in two steps to 37 ft. lbs. Final tighten to 68 ft. lbs.

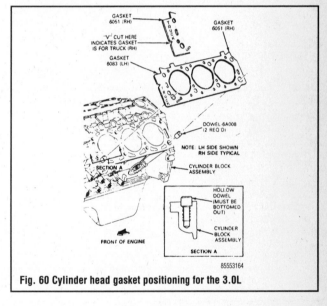

Fig. 60 Cylinder head gasket positioning for the 3.0L

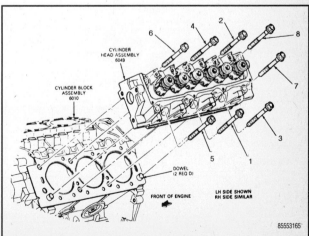

Fig. 61 Cylinder head installation & bolt torque sequence for the 3.0L

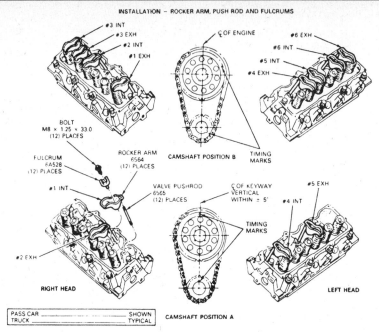

INSTALLATION – ROCKER ARM, PUSH ROD AND FULCRUMS

ASSEMBLY PROCEDURE

1. ROTATE CAMSHAFT TO POSITION "A" AS SHOWN.
2. INSTALL PUSH RODS (6565) (12) PLACES- PUSH RODS MUST BE SEATED PROPERLY ON TAPPET ASSEMBLY
3. INSTALL ROCKER ARMS (6564), FULCRUMS (6A528) AND BOLTS IN LOCATIONS AS SPECIFIED IN CAMSHAFT POSITION "A", TORQUE BOLTS TO 11 N·m AS REQ'D TO SEAT FULCRUMS IN CYLINDER HEAD
4. ROTATE CRANKSHAFT 120° TO POSITION "B"
5. INSTALL ROCKER ARMS (6564), FULCRUMS (6A528), AND BOLTS IN LOCATIONS AS SPECIFIED IN CAMSHAFT POSITION "B", TORQUE BOLTS TO 11 N·m AS REQ'D TO SEAT FULCRUMS IN CYLINDER HEAD

NOTE: FULCRUMS MUST BE FULLY SEATED IN CYLINDER HEADS AND PUSH RODS MUST BE FULLY SEATED IN ROCKER ARM SOCKETS PRIOR TO FINAL TORQUE.
6. APPLY ESE-M2C39-F OIL TO ROCKER ARM ASSEMBLIES.
7. FINAL TORQUE BOLTS TO 32.0 N·m (CAMSHAFT MAY BE IN ANY POSITION).

NOTE: CAMSHAFT POSITIONS "A" AND "B" ARE REQUIRED TO PLACE TAPPET ASSEMBLY ON BASE CIRCLE OF CAMSHAFT LOBE TO CHECK COLLAPSED TAPPET GAP.

FULCRUM AND BOLT MUST BE FULLY SEATED AFTER FINAL TORQUE

4.69-2.15 WITH TAPPET FULLY COLLAPSED ON BASE CIRCLE OF CAM LOBE AFTER ASSEMBLY REF. QUALITY AUDIT ONLY.

CYL. NO.	CAMSHAFT POSITION	
	A	B
	SET GAP OF VALVES NOTED	
1	INT.	EXH.
2	EXH.	INT.
3	NONE	INT.-EXH.
4	INT.	EXH.
5	EXH.	INT.
6	NONE	INT.-EXH.

85553167

Fig. 62 Valve rocker arm installation procedure and collapsed lifter gap clearance check for the 3.0L engine

23. Install intake manifold as outlined.

24. Dip each pushrod in heavy engine oil then install the pushrods in their original locations.

25. For each valve, rotate the crankshaft until the tappet rests on the heel (base circle) of the camshaft lobe before tightening the fulcrum attaching bolts. Position the rocker arms over the pushrods. Install the fulcrums (tighten to 8 ft. lbs. to seat fulcrum) and then tighten the fulcrum attaching bolts to 24 ft. lbs. (32 Nm). Refer to the necessary illustration for details if necessary.

✳✳ WARNING

The fulcrums must be fully seated in the cylinder head and pushrods must be seated in the rocker arm sockets prior to final tightening.

26. Lubricate all rocker arm assemblies with heavy engine oil. If the original valve train components are being installed, a valve clearance check is not required. If, however, a component has been replaced, the valve clearance should be checked.

27. Install the exhaust manifold(s).

28. Install the dipstick tube and spark plugs.

29. Position the rocker arm cover with a new gasket on the cylinder head and install the retaining bolts. Note the location of the spark plug wire routing clip stud bolts.

30. Install the injector harness.

31. If equipped, install the distributor.

32. Install the ignition coil assembly.

33. Install the spark plug wires.

34. Install the throttle body and new gasket. Refer to the necessary service procedures.

35. If the left hand cylinder head was removed, perform the following:
   a. Install the fuel line retaining bracket bolt to the front of cylinder head. Torque to 26 ft. lbs.
   b. Install the engine oil dipstick and tube assembly.
   c. Install the power steering pump and bracket assembly.

36. If the right hand cylinder head was removed, perform the following:
   a. Install hose from valve cover to oil fill adapter.
   b. Install the alternator and bracket.
   c. Install belt tensioner assembly.
   d. Reconnect alternator electrical harnesses.

37. Install the accessory drive belt.

38. Connect fuel lines. Install fuel line safety clips.

39. Install all radiator hoses. Connect vacuum lines.

40. Drain and change engine oil.

41. Install the air cleaner.
42. Fill and bleed the cooling system.
43. Connect the battery ground cable.
44. Start the engine and check for leaks. If equipped with distributor ignition, verify base ignition timing.

4.0L Engine (VIN X)

▶ See Figures 63 and 64

1. Drain the cooling system (engine cold) into a clean container and save the coolant for reuse.

✳✳ CAUTION

When draining the coolant, keep in mind that cats and dogs are attracted by ethylene glycol antifreeze, and are quite likely to drink any that is left in an uncovered container or in puddles on the ground. This will prove fatal in sufficient quantity. Always drain the coolant into a sealable container. Coolant should be reused unless it is contaminated or several years old.

2. Disconnect the battery ground cable.
3. Remove the air cleaner.
4. Remove the rocker arm covers as previously described.
5. Remove the upper and lower intake manifolds as described earlier.

6. If the left cylinder head is being removed:
   a. Remove the accessory drive belt.
   b. Remove the air conditioning compressor.
   c. Remove the power steering pump and bracket assembly. DO NOT disconnect the hoses. Tie the assembly out of the way.
   d. Remove the spark plugs.
7. If the right head is being removed:
   a. Remove the accessory drive belt.
   b. Remove the alternator and bracket.
   c. Remove the EDIS ignition coil and bracket.
   d. Remove the spark plugs.
8. Remove the exhaust manifold(s).
9. Remove the rocker shaft assembly.
10. Remove the pushrods, keeping them in order so they may be installed in their original locations.
11. Loosen the cylinder head attaching bolts in reverse of the torque sequence, then remove the bolts and discard them. They cannot be reused.
12. Lift off the cylinder head(s).
13. Remove and discard the old cylinder head gasket(s).

To install:
14. Clean the cylinder heads, intake manifolds, valve rocker arm cover and cylinder block gasket surfaces of all traces of old gasket material and/or sealer. Refer to the following overhaul procedures for cylinder head component removal, valve replacement, resurfacing, etc.
15. Lightly oil all bolt and stud bolt threads except those specifying special sealant. Position the new head gasket(s) on the cylinder block, using the dowels for alignment. The dowels should be replaced if damaged.

➡ The cylinder head(s) and intake manifold are torqued alternately and in sequence, to assure a correct fit and gasket crush.

16. Position the cylinder head(s) on the block.
17. Apply a bead of RTV silicone gasket material to the mating joints of the head and block at the 4 corners. Install the intake manifold gasket and again apply the sealer.

After removing the intake manifold, loosen the accessory mounting bracket bolts . . .

. . . then remove the bracket and accessory

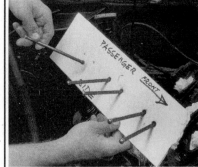

Remove the rocker shafts and, keeping them in order, the pushrods

Loosen and remove the cylinder head attaching bolts . . .

. . . then lift the cylinder head from the engine

Remove and discard the old cylinder head gasket

With rags placed in the cylinder bores, scrape the gasket mating surfaces clean

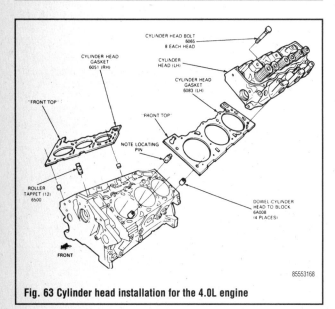

Fig. 63 Cylinder head installation for the 4.0L engine

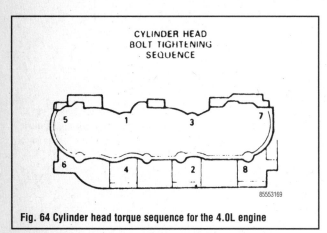

Fig. 64 Cylinder head torque sequence for the 4.0L engine

➡**This sealer sets within 15 minutes, so work quickly!**

18. Install the lower intake manifold and install the bolts and nuts for the manifold and head(s). Tighten all fasteners finger–tight.

19. Tighten the intake manifold fasteners, in sequence, to 36–72 inch lbs.

✻✻ WARNING

Do not re–use the old head bolts. ALWAYS use new head bolts!

20. Torque the head bolts, in sequence, to 59 ft. lbs.
21. Tighten the intake manifold fasteners, in sequence, to 6–11 ft. lbs.

22. Tighten the head bolts, in sequence, an additional 80–85 degrees tighter. 85 degrees is a little less than ¼ turn, ¼ turn would equal 90 degrees.

23. Torque the intake manifold fasteners, in sequence, to 11–15 ft. lbs.; then, in sequence, to 15–18 ft. lbs.

24. Dip each pushrod in heavy engine oil then install the pushrods in their original locations.

25. Install the rocker shaft assembly(ies) and tighten the bolts to 46–52 ft. lbs., front to rear, in several equal stages.

26. Apply another bead of RTV sealer at the 4 corners where the intake manifold and heads meet.

27. Install the valve covers, using new gaskets coated with sealer. Torque the bolts to 36–60 inch lbs. After 2 minutes, re–torque the cover bolts.

28. Install the upper intake manifold. Torque the nuts to 15–18 ft. lbs.
29. Install the exhaust manifold(s).
30. Install the spark plugs and wires.
31. If the left head was removed, install the power steering pump, compressor and drive belt.
32. If the right head was removed, install the EDIS coil and bracket, alternator and bracket, and the drive belt.
33. Install the air cleaner.
34. Fill the cooling system. See Section 1.

➡**At this point, it's a good idea to change the engine oil. Coolant contamination of the engine oil often occurs during cylinder head removal.**

35. Connect the battery ground cable.
36. Start the engine and check for leaks.

4.0L SOHC Engine (VIN E)

◆ **See Figures 65 thru 75**

➡**If only one cylinder head is to be removed, only follow the procedures which apply. The following tools, or their equivalents are absolutely necessary to properly perform this procedure:**

- Cam chain tensioner tool T97T-6K254-A
- Cam gear removal tool T97T-6256-F
- Cam gear torque adapter T97T-6256-G
- Camshaft gear positioning/holding tool T97T-6256-B
- Camshaft gear positioning/holding tool adapter T97T-6256-A
- Camshaft holding tool T97T-6256-C
- Crankshaft holding tool T97T-6303-A
- Camshaft holding tool adapter T97T-6256-D

1. Disconnect the negative battery cable.
2. Drain the cooling system.

✻✻ CAUTION

When draining engine coolant, keep in mind that cats and dogs are attracted to ethylene glycol antifreeze and could drink any that is left in an uncovered container or in puddles on the ground. This will prove fatal in sufficient quantity. Always drain coolant into a sealable container. Coolant should be reused unless it is contaminated or is several years old.

3. Remove the upper and lower intake manifolds.
4. Remove the engine fan/clutch assembly and the shroud.
5. Remove the top radiator hose and connecting tube.
6. Disengage the accessory drive belt.
7. Disconnect the alternator electrical harness, then unbolt the bracket from the engine and remove it, alternator and all.
8. Unbolt the air conditioner compressor/power steering mounting bracket and position it off to the side.
9. Label and disconnect the complete engine wire harness, including injectors, sensors, etc., from the engine and position it out of the way.
10. Disconnect the EGR valve supply tube, then remove the valve.
11. Remove the heater hose bracket from the engine and disconnect the transmission dipstick tube.
12. Disconnect both heater hoses from the engine.
13. Remove the thermostat housing bypass hose.
14. Remove the thermostat housing assembly from the engine.
15. Label and disconnect the spark plug wires from the plugs.
16. Remove the fuel line upper bracket bolts.

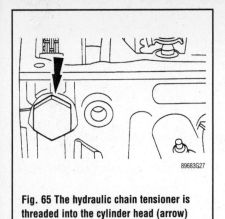

Fig. 65 The hydraulic chain tensioner is threaded into the cylinder head (arrow)

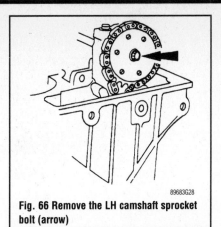

Fig. 66 Remove the LH camshaft sprocket bolt (arrow)

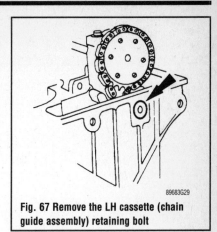

Fig. 67 Remove the LH cassette (chain guide assembly) retaining bolt

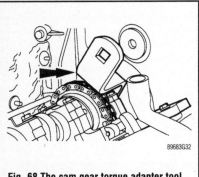

Fig. 68 The cam gear torque adapter tool (arrow) is necessary for the removal of the RH camshaft sprocket bolt

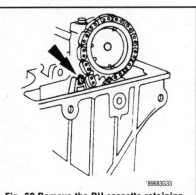

Fig. 69 Remove the RH cassette retaining bolt (arrow)

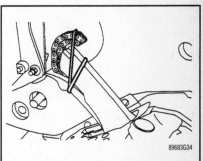

Fig. 70 Remove the RH camshaft sprocket and fasten a rubber band around the chain and the cassette to prevent the chain from dropping into the engine

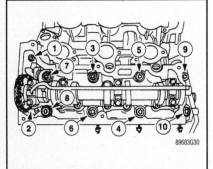

Fig. 71 Cylinder head bolt loosening and tightening sequence for the 4.0L SOHC engine

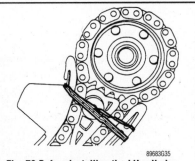

Fig. 72 Before installing the LH cylinder head, fasten a rubber band around the chain and cassette to keep the sprocket from being disturbed

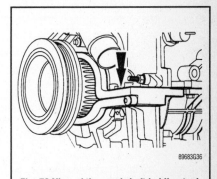

Fig. 73 View of the crankshaft holding tool (arrow) installed to the crankshaft pulley with its stop tight against the engine block

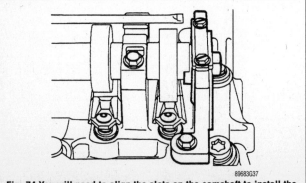

Fig. 74 You will need to align the slots on the camshaft to install the camshaft holding tool to the cylinder head

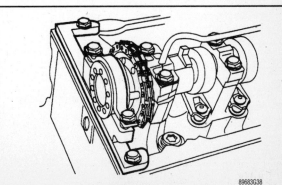

Fig. 75 With the camshaft gear positioning/holding tool installed, the sprocket bolt can be properly tightened

17. Remove the fuel injection supply manifold.
18. Remove both valve covers.
19. Remove the six fuel injectors.
20. Remove the crankcase vent separator spring steel clip, then remove the separator.
21. Remove the engine oil dipstick and tube.
22. Raise and safely support the vehicle.
23. Unbolt both exhaust pipe inlets from the exhaust manifolds.
24. Lower the vehicle.
25. Remove the LH hydraulic chain tensioner and the camshaft sprocket bolt.
26. Remove the LH cassette (chain guide) retaining bolt.
27. Remove the eight 12 mm and two 8 mm bolts, in sequence, from the LH cylinder head.
28. Remove the cylinder head and discard the old gasket.

✳✳ WARNING

The RH exhaust manifold must be removed before the RH cylinder head to avoid breaking the camshaft cassette.

29. Remove the RH exhaust manifold.
30. Remove the RH hydraulic chain tensioner. Access to the tensioner is through the RH fender well.

✳✳ WARNING

The RH camshaft sprocket bolt uses left-hand threads.

31. Use the cam gear torque adapter tool to remove the RH camshaft sprocket bolt.
32. Remove the RH cassette retaining bolt.

✳✳ WARNING

You must remove the camshaft sprocket from the chain and cassette to gain clearance to remove the cylinder head and avoid breaking the cassette.

➡**Hold the chain to the cassette with a rubber band to aid removal and prevent the chain from falling into the cylinder block.**

33. Remove the RH camshaft sprocket from the cassette.
34. Remove the eight 12mm and two 8mm bolts, in sequence, from the RH cylinder head.
35. Remove the cylinder head and discard the old gasket.
To install:
36. Thoroughly clean all gasket mating surfaces. Remove all traces of old gasket material, oil, grease or dirt.
37. Insure that the rubber band is holding the RH chain to the cassette.
38. Install the RH cylinder head gasket.
39. Position the RH cylinder head to the engine block and install the attaching bolts. Tighten the bolts in three stages: first tighten to 26 ft. lbs. (35 Nm), second, rotate 90°, third, rotate an additional 90°.
40. Install a rubber band to the LH cassette to hold the chain and sprocket in place.
41. Install the LH cylinder head gasket.
42. Position the LH cylinder head to the engine block and install the attaching bolts. Tighten the bolts in three stages: first tighten to 26 ft. lbs. (35 Nm), second, rotate 90°, third, rotate an additional 90°.
43. Install the RH camshaft sprocket in the cassette.
44. Loosely install the RH camshaft sprocket bolt.

➡**The camshaft sprocket must turn freely on the camshaft, DO NOT tighten the bolt.**

45. Install the RH cassette retaining bolt.
46. Loosely install the LH camshaft sprocket bolt.

➡**The camshaft sprocket must turn freely on the camshaft, DO NOT tighten the bolt.**

47. Install the LH cassette retaining bolt.
48. To properly time the left-hand cylinder head camshaft, proceed as follows:

a. Use the camshaft chain tensioner tool and install it into the LH cylinder head.
b. Rotate the crankshaft one revolution.
c. Position the crankshaft at top dead center of number one cylinder and install the crankshaft holding tool.

➡**The crankshaft holding tool must firmly contact the cylinder block.**

d. Position the camshaft timing slots to properly fit the camshaft holding tool and position the toll on the LH cylinder head.

➡**The camshaft timing slots are off-center and below the center-line of the camshaft.**

e. Install the camshaft gear positioning/holding tool on the LH cylinder head.
f. Ensure that the bolts on the camshaft gear positioning/holding tool are tight, then tighten the LH camshaft sprocket bolts to 63 ft. lbs. (85 Nm).
g. Remove the camshaft chain tensioner tool.
h. Install the LH hydraulic camshaft tensioner and tighten to 35–39 ft. lbs. (47–53 Nm).
i. Remove the camshaft gear positioning/holding tool, camshaft holding tool and the crankshaft holding tool.
49. To properly time the right-hand cylinder head camshaft, proceed as follows:

a. Use the camshaft chain tensioner tool and install it into the RH cylinder head.

➡**Access to the chain tensioner is through the fender well.**

b. Rotate the crankshaft one revolution.
c. Position the crankshaft at top dead center of number one cylinder and install the crankshaft holding tool.

➡**The crankshaft holding tool must firmly contact the cylinder block.**

d. Position the camshaft timing slots to properly fit the camshaft holding tool and position the tool on the RH cylinder head.

➡**The camshaft timing slots are off-center and below the center-line of the camshaft.**

e. Install the camshaft gear positioning/holding tool on the RH cylinder head.
f. Install the camshaft gear removal tool on the RH cylinder head.

✳✳ WARNING

The RH camshaft sprocket bolt uses left-hand threads.

g. Ensure that the bolts on the camshaft gear positioning/holding tool are tight, then tighten the RH camshaft sprocket bolts to 63 ft. lbs. (85 Nm).
h. Remove the camshaft chain tensioner tool.
i. Install the RH hydraulic camshaft tensioner and tighten to 35–39 ft. lbs. (47–53 Nm).
j. Remove the camshaft gear positioning/holding tool, camshaft holding tool and the crankshaft holding tool.
50. Install the RH exhaust manifold.
51. Rasie and safely support the vehicle.
52. Install the exhaust inlet pipes to the manifolds.
53. Lower the vehicle.
54. Install the engine oil dipstick and tube.
55. Install the crankcase vent separator and the spring clip.
56. Lubricate the injector o-rings with SAE 50W oil and install them.
57. Install both valve covers.
58. Install the fuel injection supply manifold.
59. Tighten the upper fuel line bracket.
60. Install the spark plug wires to the plugs.
61. Install the thermostat housing assembly.
62. Install the thermostat bypass hose.
63. Connect both heater hoses to the engine and install the mounting bracket.
64. Install the EGR valve and connect the supply tube.
65. Position the engine wiring harness and connect all of the electrical plugs which were removed.
66. Position both engine accessory brackets to the engine and install the attaching bolts.

67. Attach the alternator electrical connections.
68. Install the accessory drive belt, top radiator hose and tube, as well as the engine fan/clutch assembly and shroud.
69. Install the lower and upper intake manifolds.
70. Refill and bleed the cooling system.
71. Connect the negative battery cable then start and run the engine. Check for leaks.

5.0L Engine

▶ **See Figure 76**

➡**According to the manufacturer, you must use new cylinder head bolts when installing the head(s).**

1. Disconnect the negative battery cable.
2. Drain the cooling system.

☀ CAUTION

When draining engine coolant, keep in mind that cats and dogs are attracted to ethylene glycol antifreeze and could drink any that is left in an uncovered container or in puddles on the ground. This will prove fatal in sufficient quantity. Always drain coolant into a sealable container. Coolant should be reused unless it is contaminated or is several years old.

3. Remove one or both valve covers.
4. Remove the upper and lower intake manifolds.
5. Remove the accessory drive belt.
6. If the LH cylinder head is being removed, proceed as follows:
   a. Remove the A/C compressor/power steering mounting bracket and position it out of the way.
   b. Remove the engine oil dipstick and tube.
7. If the RH cylinder head is being removed, proceed as follows:
   a. Disconnect the alternator electrical harness.
   b. Unbolt the alternator mounting bracket and remove it from the engine.
8. Remove the exhaust manifolds from the engine.
9. Loosen the rocker arm bolts so that the rockers can be rotated to the side.
10. Remove the pushrods, keeping them in order so that they can be installed to their original locations.
11. Remove and discard the cylinder head bolts. Lift the cylinder head from the engine and discard the old gasket.

To install:

12. Thoroughly clean all of the gasket mating surfaces.
13. Position a new cylinder head gasket to the engine block, then install the cylinder head.
14. Install new cylinder head bolts and tighten in three steps:
    a. Tighten all bolts in sequence to 25–37 ft. lbs. (34–47 Nm).
    b. Tighten all bolts in sequence to 45–55 ft. lbs. (61–75 Nm).
    c. Tighten all bolts an additional 85–95° (¼ turn).
15. Ensure that the oil passages within the pushrods are clear and install them in the engine.

➡**Lubricate the ends of the pushrods with SAE 50W engine oil.**

16. Thoroughly coat the rocker arms with SAE 50W engine oil and rotate them back to their proper positions. tighten the attaching bolts to 18–25 ft. lbs. (24–34 Nm).

17. Install the exhaust manifolds.
18. If the RH cylinder head was removed, proceed as follows:
    a. Attach the alternator mounting bracket and to the engine.
    b. Connect the alternator electrical harness.
19. If the LH cylinder head was removed, proceed as follows:
    a. Install the engine oil dipstick and tube.
    b. Install the A/C compressor/power steering mounting bracket to the engine.
20. Install the lower and upper intake manifolds.
21. Install the one or both valve covers.
22. Refill and bleed the cooling system.
23. Connect the negative battery cable, then start and run the engine. Check for leaks.

Oil Pan

REMOVAL & INSTALLATION

2.3L and 2.5L Engines

▶ **See Figure 77**

1. Disconnect the battery ground cable.
2. Remove the engine assembly from vehicle.

☀ CAUTION

Do NOT turn the engine assembly upside down with the oil pan still attached. Sludge and debris in the oil pan will fall into the cylinders, pistons and connecting rods, possibly causing rapid wear. Sludge may also plug the engine oil pickup screen.

3. Mount the engine assembly on an engine stand with the engine mounted in the upright position.
4. Remove the oil pan mounting bolts.
5. Remove the oil pan from the engine.
6. Remove and discard the oil pan gasket. Thoroughly clean all gasket mating surfaces.

To install:

➡**Wait no longer than 4 minutes after applying silicone gasket sealant to install the oil pan.**

7. Apply a 0.24 inch (6mm) bead of silicone gasket sealant in six places; on both sides of the rear main cap and front cover humps and along the seams for the cover-to-engine block.
8. Position and press into place the new oil pan gasket onto the oil pan mounting flange.
9. Using a straight edge, line up the oil pan to the engine block.
10. Install the oil pan mounting bolts. The 2 long bolts are installed in the two rear pan holes (holes 15 and 18 shown in the illustration) near the flywheel.

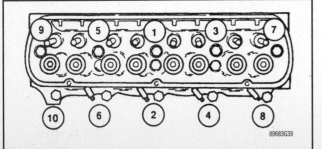

Fig. 76 Cylinder head bolt tightening sequence for the 5.0L engine

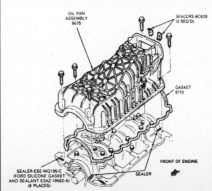

Fig. 77 Oil pan on the 1994 2.3L engine—1995—99 engines similar

11. Tighten the oil pan bolts, in sequence, to 124–141 inch lbs. (14–16 Nm).

12. Install the engine assembly into the vehicle.

13. Connect the negative battery cable. Fill the engine with the proper amount and type of engine oil. Add all necessary fluids and be sure that all components are installed/connected correctly.

2.9L Engines

▶ **See Figures 78 and 79**

1. Disconnect the battery ground cable.
2. Remove the carburetor air cleaner assembly.
3. Remove the fan shroud and position it over the fan.
4. Remove the distributor cap with the wires still attached, and position it forward of the dash panel.
5. Remove the distributor and cover the opening with a clean rag.
6. Remove the nuts attaching the front engine mounts to the cross member.
7. Remove the engine oil dipstick tube.
8. Raise the truck on a hoist and support with jackstands.
9. Drain the engine crankcase and remove the oil filter.

✳✳ CAUTION

The EPA warns that prolonged contact with used engine oil may cause a number of skin disorders, including cancer! You should make every effort to minimize your exposure to used engine oil. Protective gloves should be worn when changing the oil. Wash your hands and any other exposed skin areas as soon as possible after exposure to used engine oil. Soap and water, or waterless hand cleaner should be used.

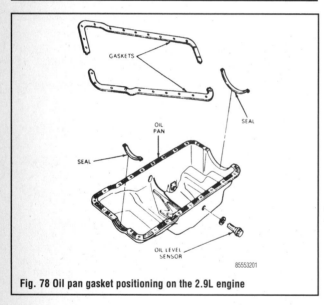

Fig. 78 Oil pan gasket positioning on the 2.9L engine

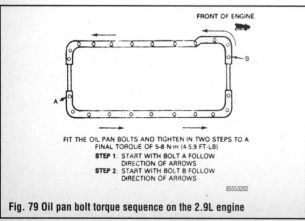

Fig. 79 Oil pan bolt torque sequence on the 2.9L engine

10. Remove the transmission fluid filler tube and plug the hole in the pan, On automatic transmission models.

11. Disconnect the muffler inlet pipes.

12. If equipped with an oil cooler, disconnect the bracket and lower the cooler.

13. Remove the starter motor.

14. On automatic transmission models, position the cooler lines out of the way.

15. Disconnect the front stabilizer bar and position it forward.

16. Position a jack under the engine and raise the engine until it touches the dash panel. Install wooden blocks between the front motor mounts and the no. 2 crossmember.

17. Lower the engine onto the blocks and remove the jack.

18. Remove the oil pan attaching bolts and lower the pan assembly.

19. Installation is the reverse of the removal procedure

3.0L Engine

▶ **See Figure 80**

1. Disconnect the negative battery cable.
2. Remove the oil level dipstick.
3. Remove the fan shroud. Leave the fan shroud over the fan assembly.
4. Remove the motor mount nuts from the frame.

✳✳ WARNING

On models equipped with distributor ignition, failure to remove the distributor will damage or break it when the engine is lifted.

5. If equipped, mark and remove the distributor assembly from the engine.
6. Raise and support the vehicle safely. Remove the oil level sensor wire.
7. Drain the engine oil from the crankcase into a suitable container and dispose of it properly.

✳✳ CAUTION

The EPA warns that prolonged contact with used engine oil may cause a number of skin disorders, including cancer! You should make every effort to minimize your exposure to used engine oil. Protective gloves should be worn when changing the oil. Wash your hands and any other exposed skin areas as soon as possible after exposure to used engine oil. Soap and water, or waterless hand cleaner should be used.

8. Remove the starter motor from the engine.
9. Remove the transmission inspection cover.
10. Remove the right hand axle I—Beam. The brake caliper must be removed and secured out of the way. Refer to the necessary service procedures.
11. Remove the oil pan attaching bolts, using a suitable lifting device, raise the engine about 2 inches. Remove the oil pan from the engine block.

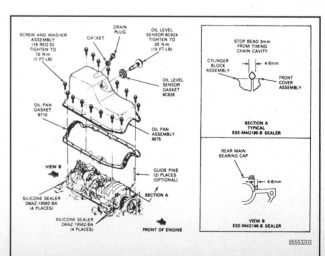

Fig. 80 Oil pan installation for the 3.0L engine

➡Oil pan fits tightly between the transmission spacer plate and oil pump pickup tube. Use care when removing the oil pan from the engine.

12. Clean all gasket surfaces on the engine and oil pan. Remove all traces of old gasket and/or sealer.

To install:

13. Apply a 4mm bead of RTV sealer to the junctions of the rear main bearing cap and block, and the front cover and block. The sealer sets in 15 minutes, so work quickly!

14. Apply adhesive to the gasket mating surfaces and install oil pan gasket.

15. Install the oil pan on the engine block.

16. Tighten the pan bolts EVENLY to 9 ft. lbs. working from the center to the end position on the oil pan.

17. Install low–oil level sensor connector. Lower engine assembly to original position.

18. Install right hand axle I–Beam. Install the brake caliper. Refer to the necessary service procedures.

19. Install transmission inspection cover. Install starter motor.

20. Lower the vehicle and install the fan shroud.

21. Install motor mount retaining nuts. If removed, install distributor assembly.

22. Replace the oil level dipstick. Connect the battery ground. Fill crankcase with the correct amount of new engine oil. Start engine and check for leaks.

23. If equipped with distributor ignition, check the base ignition timing.

4.0L Engine (VIN X)

▶ **See Figures 81 and 82**

➡Review the complete service procedure before starting this repair.

1. Disconnect the negative battery cable. Remove the complete engine assembly from the vehicle. Refer to the necessary service procedures in this section.

2. Mount the engine on a suitable engine stand with oil pan facing up.

3. Remove the oil pan attaching bolts (note location of 2 spacers) and remove the pan from the engine block.

4. Remove the oil pan gasket and crankshaft rear main bearing cap wedge seal.

5. Clean all gasket surfaces on the engine and oil pan. Remove all traces of old gasket and/or sealer.

To install:

6. Install a new crankshaft rear main bearing cap wedge seal. The seal should fit snugly into the sides of the rear main bearing cap.

7. Position the oil pan gasket to the engine block and place the oil pan in correct position on the 4 locating studs.

8. Tighten the oil pan retaining bolts EVENLY to 5–7 ft. lbs.

9. The transmission bolts to the engine and oil pan. There are 2 spacers on the rear of the oil pan to allow proper mating of the transmission and oil pan. If

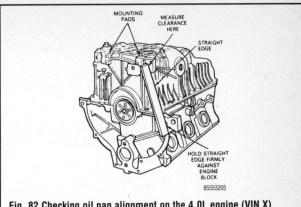

Fig. 82 Checking oil pan alignment on the 4.0L engine (VIN X)

these spacers were lost, or the oil pan was replaced, you must determine the proper spacers to install. To do this:

a. With the oil pan installed, place a straightedge across the machined mating surface of the rear of the block, extending over the oil pan–to–transmission mounting surface.

b. Using a feeler gauge, measure the gap between the oil pan mounting pad and the straightedge.

c. Repeat the procedure for the other side.

d. Select the spacers as follows:

- Gap = 0.011–0.020 in.; spacer = 0.010 in.
- Gap = 0.021–0.029 in.; spacer = 0.020 in.
- Gap = 0.030–0.039 in.; spacer = 0.030 in.

➡Failure to use the correct spacers will result in damage to the oil pan and oil leakage.

10. Install the selected spacers to the mounting pads on the rear of the oil pan before bolting the engine and transmission together. Install the engine assembly in the vehicle.

11. Connect the negative battery cable. Start the engine and check for leaks.

4.0L SOHC Engine (VIN E)

▶ **See Figure 83**

➡The 4.0L SOHC engine does not use an oil pan in the conventional sense. There is a separate access panel that unbolts from what would be considered the oil pan (which is now known as the ladder frame).

1. Disconnect the negative battery cable.

2. Raise and safely support the vehicle.

3. Drain the engine oil.

4. Remove the ten oil pan bolts and remove the pan.

5. Installation is the reverse of removal. Clean the gasket mating surfaces and install a new gasket. Tighten the pan bolts to 6–7.4 ft. lbs. (8–10 Nm). Refill the engine with clean oil.

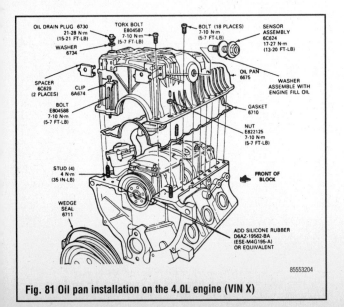

Fig. 81 Oil pan installation on the 4.0L engine (VIN X)

1. Oil pan
2. Tube assembly oil pickup
3. Ladder frame

Fig. 83 Exploded view of the 4.0L SOHC engine oil pan assembly

5.0L Engine

▶ See Figure 84

➡The oil pan cannot be removed with the engine in the vehicle.

1. Remove the engine.
2. Drain the engine oil.
3. Remove the oil pan bolts.
4. Remove the oil pan and gasket.
5. Installation is the reverse of removal. Use RTV sealer at the four corners of the block and pan. Tighten the four oil pan end attaching bolts to 12–18 ft. lbs. (16–25 Nm) and the 18 oil pan bolts to 110–144 inch lbs. (13–16 Nm).

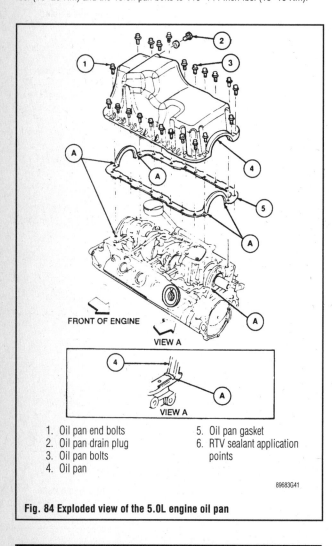

1. Oil pan end bolts
2. Oil pan drain plug
3. Oil pan bolts
4. Oil pan
5. Oil pan gasket
6. RTV sealant application points

89683G41

Fig. 84 Exploded view of the 5.0L engine oil pan

Oil Pump

REMOVAL & INSTALLATION

Except 4.0L SOHC (VIN E), 5.0L, 1995–97 2.3L and 1998–99 2.5L Engines

▶ See Figures 85, 86 and 87

➡The oil pumps are not serviceable. If defective, they must be replaced.

1. Follow the service procedures under Oil Pan Removal and remove the oil pan assembly.
2. Remove the oil pick-up and tube assembly from the pump.
3. Remove the oil pump retainer bolts and remove the oil pump.

To install:

4. Prime the oil pump with clean engine oil by filling either the inlet or outlet port with clean engine oil. Rotate the pump shaft to distribute the oil within the pump body.

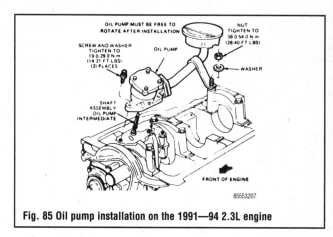

Fig. 85 Oil pump installation on the 1991—94 2.3L engine

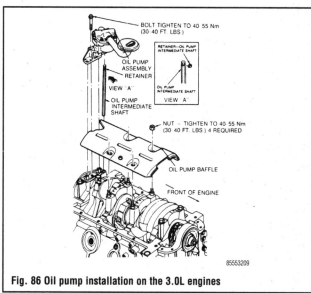

Fig. 86 Oil pump installation on the 3.0L engines

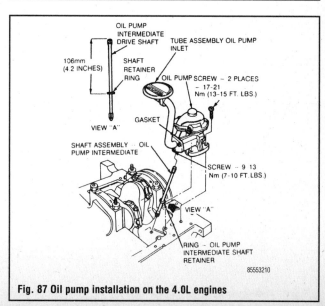

Fig. 87 Oil pump installation on the 4.0L engines

5. Install the pump and tighten the mounting bolts to:
- 14–21 ft. lbs. (19–29 Nm) on 1991–94 2.3L engines
- 6–10 ft. lbs. (8–14 Nm) on 2.9L engines
- 30–40 ft. lbs. (41–54 Nm) on 3.0L engines
- 13–15 ft. lbs. (18–20 Nm) on 4.0L engines

✳✳ WARNING

Do not force the oil pump if it does not seat readily. The oil pump driveshaft may be misaligned with the distributor or shaft assembly. If the pump is tightened down with the driveshaft misaligned, damage to the pump could occur. To align, rotate the intermediate driveshaft into a new position.

6. Install the oil pick-up and tube assembly to the pump. If there is a gasket between the pump and the pick-up, use a new gasket when installing.
7. Install the oil pan as previously described.

1995—97 2.3L and 1998–99 2.5L Engines

➥The oil pump is located on the front of the engine and is turned by the timing belt.

1. Disconnect the negative battery cable.
2. Remove the timing belt.
3. Detach the camshaft position sensor (CMP) electrical connector.
4. Remove the oil pump sprocket bolt and sprocket.

➥Use a prybar or drift through one of the holes in the pump sprocket to keep it from turning while loosening the bolt.

5. Unbolt the camshaft position sensor.
6. Remove the four bolts retaining the oil pump to the engine block.
7. Remove the oil pump from the front of the engine and discard the pump-to-block gasket.
8. Inspect the oil pump and O-rings and replace as necessary. Clean all gasket mating surfaces thoroughly.

9. Installation is the reverse of the removal procedure, however note the following:
   a. Prime the oil pump and with 8 ounces (236ml) of new engine oil and lubricate the O-rings with same.
   b. Use a new pump-to-block gasket.
   c. Tighten the oil pump bolts to 89—123 inch lbs. (10—14 Nm), the camshaft position sensor bolts to 45—61 inch lbs. (5—7 Nm) and the oil pump sprocket bolt to 30—40 ft. Lbs. (40—55 Nm).

4.0L SOHC (VIN E) and 5.0L Engines

▶ See Figures 88 thru 93

➥The oil pump cannot be removed with the engine in the vehicle.

1. Remove the engine.
2. Remove the oil pan.
3. Unbolt the oil pick-up tube.
4. On the 4.0L engine, remove the eight ladder frame bolts which were under the oil pan.
5. On the 4.0L engine, remove the two rear outer ladder frame bolts.
6. On the 4.0L engine, remove the seven LH and the eight RH ladder frame bolts.
7. On the 4.0L engine, lift the ladder frame from the engine.
8. Remove the two oil pump attaching bolts and the pump.
9. Installation is the reverse of removal. Submerge the pump in clean engine oil to prime it. Tighten the pump attaching bolts to 13–15 ft. lbs. (17–21 Nm) for the 4.0L engine and 23–31 ft. lbs. (30–43 Nm) for the 5.0L engine.

Crankshaft Damper

REMOVAL & INSTALLATION

1. Disconnect the negative battery cable for safety.
2. Remove the engine fan/clutch assembly and shroud.

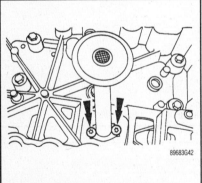

Fig. 88 Remove the two oil pick-up attaching bolts (arrows)—4.0L engine shown

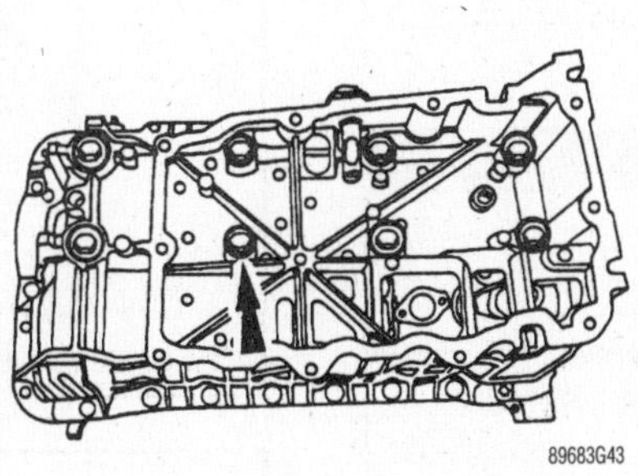

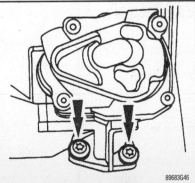

Fig. 89 On the 4.0L engine, remove the eight ladder frame bolts in the oil pan area

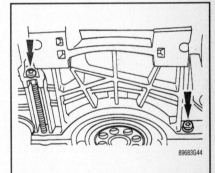

Fig. 90 The two rear ladder frame bolts (arrows) on the 4.0L engine use TORX® drive fasteners

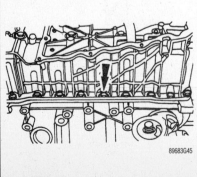

Fig. 91 View of the side ladder frame bolts (arrow) on the 4.0L engine

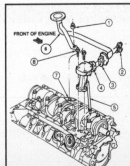

Fig. 92 Remove the two oil pump attaching bolts—4.0L engine shown

1. Oil pick-up attaching nut
2. Oil pick-up-to-pump bolts
3. Oil pick-up gasket
4. Oil pump
5. Oil pump driveshaft
6. Oil pick-up assembly
7. Pick-up nut attaching stud

Fig. 93 Exploded view of the 5.0L engine oil pump and pick-up assembly

With the engine fan and shroud removed, unbolt the crankshaft damper from the crankshaft

89683P61

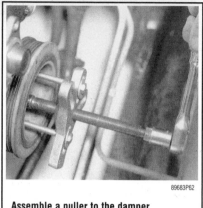

89683P62

Assemble a puller to the damper . . .

89683P63

. . . then tighten the center bolt to remove the damper from the crankshaft

3. Remove the accessory drive belt.
4. If equipped, unbolt the crankshaft pulley from the damper.
5. Remove the damper-to-crankshaft snout attaching bolt.
6. Assemble a puller to the damper and remove it.

To install:

7. Inspect the front cover seal and replace if necessary.
8. Apply multi-purpose grease to the front cover seal rubbing surface.
9. Apply a small amount of RTV sealant to the damper keyway groove.
10. Align the groove with the crankshaft keyway and install the damper.

✸✸ WARNING

Never hammer on the damper to install it.

11. Use a crankshaft damper installation tool to press the damper onto the crankshaft.
12. Install the damper-to-crankshaft snout and tighten to specifications.
13. Install the crankshaft pulley and the accessory drive belt.
14. Install the engine fan/clutch assembly and the shroud.
15. Connect the negative battery cable. Run the engine and check for oil leaks.

Timing Belt and Cover

This procedure applies to the 2.3L and 2.5L engine only.

TROUBLESHOOTING

Should the camshaft drive belt/timing belt jump timing by a tooth or two, the engine could still run; but very poorly. To visually check for correct timing of the crankshaft, auxiliary shaft, and the camshaft follow this procedure:

➡There is an access plug provided in the cam drive belt cover so that the camshaft timing cam be checked without moving the drive belt cover.

1. Remove the access plug.
2. Turn the crankshaft until the timing marks on the crankshaft indicate TDC.
3. Make sure that the timing mark on the camshaft drive sprocket is aligned with the pointer on the inner belt cover.

➡Never turn the crankshaft of any of the overhead cam engines in the opposite direction of normal rotation. Backward rotation of the crankshaft may cause the timing belt to slip and alter the timing.

REMOVAL & INSTALLATION

▶ **See Figures 94, 95 and 96**

1. Rotate the engine so that No. 1 cylinder is at TDC on the compression stroke. Check that the timing marks are aligned on the camshaft and crankshaft pulleys. An access plug is provided in the cam belt cover so that the camshaft timing can be checked without removal of the cover or any other parts. Set the crankshaft to TDC by aligning the timing mark on the crank pulley with the TDC

mark on the belt cover. Look through the access hole in the belt cover to make sure that the timing mark on the cam drive sprocket is lined up with the pointer on the inner belt cover.

➡Always turn the engine in the normal direction of rotation. Backward rotation may cause the timing belt to jump time, due to the arrangement of the belt tensioner.

2. Drain cooling system. Remove the upper radiator hose as necessary. Remove the fan blade and water pump pulley bolts.

✸✸ CAUTION

When draining the coolant, keep in mind that cats and dogs are attracted by ethylene glycol antifreeze, and are quite likely to drink

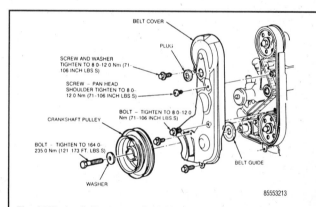

85553213

Fig. 94 Timing belt cover on the 2.3L and 2.5L engine

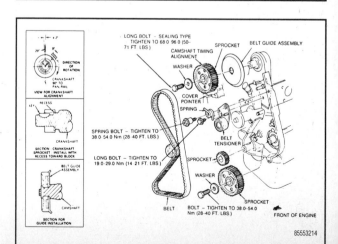

85553214

Fig. 95 Timing belt assembly on the 2.3L and 2.5L engine

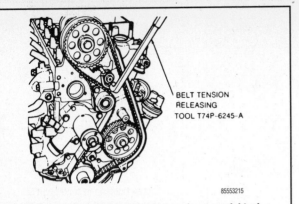

Fig. 96 Releasing the timing belt tensioner using a special tool

any that is left in an uncovered container or in puddles on the ground. This will prove fatal in sufficient quantity. Always drain the coolant into a sealable container. Coolant should be reused unless it is contaminated or several years old.

3. Loosen the alternator retaining bolts and remove the drive belt from the pulleys. Remove the water pump pulley.

4. Loosen and position the power steering pump mounting bracket and position it aside.

5. Remove the four timing belt outer cover retaining bolts and remove the cover. Remove the crankshaft pulley and belt guide.

6. Loosen the belt tensioner pulley assembly, then position a camshaft belt adjuster tool (T74P–6254–A or equivalent) on the tension spring rollpin and retract the belt tensioner away from the timing belt. Tighten the adjustment bolt to lock the tensioner in the retracted position.

7. Remove the timing belt.

To install:

8. Install the new belt over the crankshaft sprocket and then counterclockwise over the auxiliary and camshaft sprockets, making sure the lugs on the belt properly engage the sprocket teeth on the pulleys. Be careful not to rotate the pulleys when installing the belt.

9. Release the timing belt tensioner pulley, allowing the tensioner to take up the belt slack. If the spring does not have enough tension to move the roller against the belt (belt hangs loose), it might be necessary to manually push the roller against the belt and tighten the bolt.

➡ **The spring cannot be used to set belt tension; a wrench must be used on the tensioner assembly.**

10. Rotate the crankshaft two complete turns by hand (in the normal direction of rotation) to remove the slack from the belt, then tighten the tensioner adjustment and pivot bolts to specifications. Refer to the necessary illustrations. Make sure the belt is seated properly on the pulleys and that the timing marks are still in alignment when No. 1 cylinder is again at TDC/compression.

11. Install the crankshaft pulley and belt guide.

12. Install the timing belt cover.

13. Install the water pump pulley and fan blades. Install upper radiator hose if necessary. Refill the cooling system.

14. Position the alternator and drive belts, then adjust and tighten it to specifications.

15. Start the engine and check the ignition timing. Adjust the timing, if necessary.

Timing Chain Cover & Oil Seal

REMOVAL & INSTALLATION

2.9L Engines

➡ **See Figures 97, 98 and 99**

1. Disconnect the negative battery cable.
2. Remove the oil pan as described under Oil Pan removal and installation.
3. Drain the coolant. Remove the radiator.

✳✳ **CAUTION**

When draining the coolant, keep in mind that cats and dogs are attracted by ethylene glycol antifreeze, and are quite likely to drink any that is left in an uncovered container or in puddles on the ground. This will prove fatal in sufficient quantity. Always drain the coolant into a sealable container. Coolant should be reused unless it is contaminated or several years old.

4. Remove the A/C compressor and the power steering bracket, if so equipped, and position them out of the way. DO NOT disconnect the A/C refrigerant lines.

5. Remove the alternator, drive belt(s) and, if equipped, the Thermactor pump.

6. Remove the fan.

7. Remove the water pump and the heater and radiator hoses.

8. Remove the drive pulley from the crankshaft.

9. Remove the front cover retaining bolts. If necessary, tap the cover lightly with a plastic hammer to break the gasket seal. Remove the front cover. If the front cover plate gasket needs replacement, remove the two screws and remove the plate. If necessary, remove the guide sleeves from the cylinder block.

10. If the front cover oil seal needs replacement use the following procedure:

a. Support the front cover to prevent damage while driving out the seal.

b. Drive out the seal from front cover with Front Cover Aligner, T74P–6019–A, or equivalent.

c. Support the front cover to prevent damage while installing the seal.

d. Coat the new front cover oil seal with Lubriplate® or equivalent. Install the new seal in the front cover.

To install:

11. Clean the front cover mating surfaces of gasket material. Apply sealer to the gasket surfaces on the cylinder block and back side of the front cover plate. Install the guide sleeves, with new seal rings, with the chamfered end toward the front cover, if removed. Position the gasket and the front cover plate on the cylinder block. Temporarily install the four front cover screws to position the

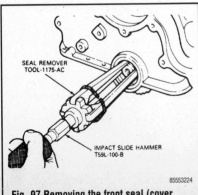
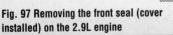

Fig. 97 Removing the front seal (cover installed) on the 2.9L engine

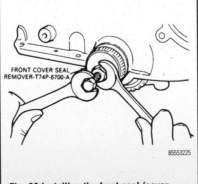

Fig. 98 Installing the front seal (cover installed) on the 2.9L engine

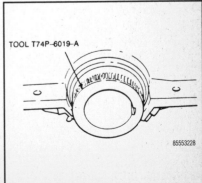

Fig. 99 Front cover alignment tool on the 2.9L engine

gasket and cover plate in plate. Install and tighten the two cover plate attaching bolts, then remove the four screws that were temporarily installed.

12. Apply gasket sealer to the front cover gasket surface. Place the gasket in position on the front cover.

13. Place the front cover on the engine and start all the retaining screws two or three turns. Center the cover by inserting Front Cover Aligner, Tool T74P–6019–A, or equivalent in oil seal.

14. Torque the front cover attaching screws to 13–16 ft. lbs.

15. Install the belt drive pulley.

16. Install the oil pan as described under Oil Pan removal and installation.

17. Install the water pump, heater hose, A/C compressor, alternator, Thermactor pump and drive belt(s). Adjust drive belt tension.

18. Fill and bleed the cooling system.

19. Connect the negative batter cable.

20. Operate the engine at fast idle speed and check for coolant and oil leaks.

3.0L Engine

▶ **See Figures 100 and 101**

➡The A/C system must be discharged to remove the front cover. Have the A/C refrigerant reclaimed by a MVAC certified shop. The front seal can be serviced with the engine in the vehicle. Remove the crankshaft damper, then follow the seal replacement procedure under installation.

1. Disconnect the negative battery cable.
2. Drain the cooling system and crankcase.

✳✳ CAUTION

When draining the coolant, keep in mind that cats and dogs are attracted by ethylene glycol antifreeze, and are quite likely to drink any that is left in an uncovered container or in puddles on the ground. This will prove fatal in sufficient quantity. Always drain the coolant into a sealable container. Coolant should be reused unless it is contaminated or several years old.

3. Remove the cooling fan.

4. Loosen the water pump pulley bolts. Loosen and remove the accessory drive belts. Remove the water pump pulley.

5. Remove the alternator adjusting arm and brace assembly. Remove the heated air intake duct from the engine.

6. Remove the upper motor mount retaining nuts. Remove the A/C compressor upper bolts, then remove the front cover front nuts on vehicles with automatic transmission and A/C.

7. Raise the vehicle. Remove the A/C compressor bolts and bracket if so equipped and position the assembly aside.

8. Remove the crankshaft pulley and damper assembly. Remove the oil pan. Refer to the necessary service procedures in this section.

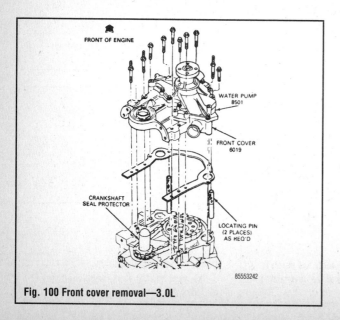

Fig. 100 Front cover removal—3.0L

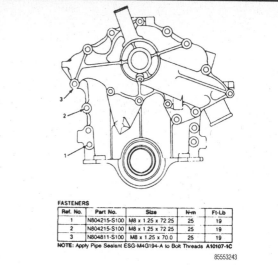

FASTENERS				
Ref. No.	Part No.	Size	N-m	Ft-Lb
1	N804215-S100	M8 x 1.25 x 72.25	25	19
2	N804215-S100	M8 x 1.25 x 72.25	25	19
3	N804811-S100	M8 x 1.25 x 70.0	25	19

NOTE: Apply Pipe Sealant ESG-M4G194-A to Bolt Threads A10107-1C

Fig. 101 Front cover bolt installation chart—3.0L

➡According to the manufacturer, you must remove the water pump to remove the cover. However, we have found that on some models and/or years the water pump can be left bolted to the cover, thereby reducing some of the labor. Try removing the cover with the water pump attached first.

9. Lower the vehicle. Remove the lower radiator hose. Remove the water pump.

10. If necessary, remove the crankshaft position sensor.

11. Remove the timing cover to cylinder block attaching bolts. Carefully remove the timing cover from the cylinder block.

12. Inspect the oil seal. If the seal needs replacing, follow the procedures under installation.

To install:

13. Clean timing cover and oil pan sealing surfaces. Clean and inspect all parts. The camshaft retaining bolt has a drilled oil passage for timing chain assembly lubrication. Clean oil passage with solvent. Do not replace with standard bolt.

14. Install timing cover assembly. Install retaining bolts with pipe sealant and tighten as outlined. Refer to the necessary illustration.

15. If the front seal needs to be replaced, proceed as follows:

    a. Using Front Cover Seal Removal Tool T70P-6B070-A, or its equivalent, remove the front seal.

    b. Lubricate the engine front cover and oil seal lip inner lip with engine oil.

    c. Using Crankshaft Seal Replacer/Cover Aligner T82L-6316-A, or its equivalent, install the new seal into the front cover.

16. If necessary, install the crankshaft position sensor.

17. Install oil pan and water pump. Refer to the necessary procedures in this section.

18. Install crankshaft damper and pulley assembly.

19. Install drive belt components. Install drive belts and adjust.

20. Fill crankcase. Refill and bleed cooling system. Connect the negative battery cable. Start engine check for coolant, oil and exhaust leaks.

4.0L Engine (VIN X)

▶ **See Figure 102**

➡Review the complete service procedure before starting this repair. Refer to the necessary service procedures in this section. The front seal can be serviced with the engine in the vehicle. Remove the crankshaft damper, then follow the seal replacement procedure under installation.

1. Disconnect the negative battery cable. Remove/lower the oil pan.
2. Drain the cooling system.

✳✳ CAUTION

When draining the coolant, keep in mind that cats and dogs are attracted by ethylene glycol antifreeze, and are quite likely to drink

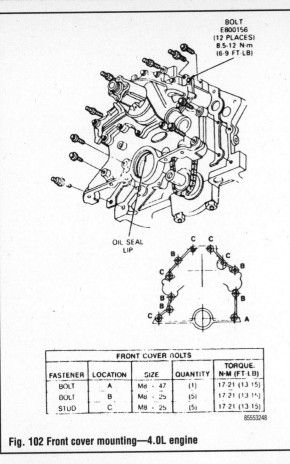

BOLT
E800156
(12 PLACES)
8.5-12 N·m
(6-9 FT·LB)

OIL SEAL
LIP

FRONT COVER BOLTS

FASTENER	LOCATION	SIZE	QUANTITY	TORQUE. N·M (FT·LB)
BOLT	A	M8 · 47	(1)	17-21 (13-15)
BOLT	B	M8 · 25	(5)	17-21 (13-15)
STUD	C	M8 · 25	(5)	17-21 (13-15)

85553248

Fig. 102 Front cover mounting—4.0L engine

any that is left in an uncovered container or in puddles on the ground. This will prove fatal in sufficient quantity. Always drain the coolant into a sealable container. Coolant should be reused unless it is contaminated or several years old.

3. Remove the engine fan and shroud.
4. Remove the air conditioning compressor and position it out of the way. DO NOT disconnect the refrigerant lines!
5. Remove the power steering pump and position it out of the way. DO NOT disconnect the hoses!
6. Remove the alternator.

89683P64

To remove the front cover, remove the fan, shroud and unbolt the front cover-to-accessory bracket brace . . .

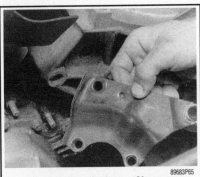

89683P65

. . . then remove the brace. Also remove the damper and any other obstructions to the cover

89683P66

Remove the front cover attaching bolts

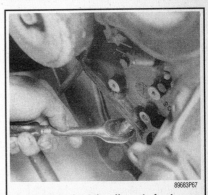

89683P67

Don't forget about the oil pan-to-front cover attaching bolts!

89683P68

Remove the old gaskets and thoroughly clean all of the mating surfaces

89683P69

Place the cover on a bench and carefully knock the old seal out of the cover using a hammer and punch

89683P70

Use an ordinary seal driver, and seat a new seal into the cover at the same position as the old one

7. Remove the water pump.
8. Remove the drive pulley/damper from the crankshaft.
9. Remove the crankshaft timing sensor.
10. Remove the front cover attaching bolts. It may be necessary to tap the cover loose with a plastic mallet.
11. Inspect the oil seal. If the seal needs replacing, follow the procedures under installation.

To install:

12. Thoroughly clean all of the gasket and sealing surfaces and remove all traces of the old gaskets, oil, grease and/or dirt. Use new gaskets and apply a thin layer of sealant/adhesive to them.

➡If the specialized tools aren't available, the front seal can be replaced using normal hand tools. Before installing the cover, use a punch to carefully knock the old seal out of the cover, and a seal driver to seat the new seal.

13. Install the front cover and attaching bolts. Refer to the necessary illustration.
14. If the front seal needs to be replaced, proceed as follows:
   a. Using Front Cover Seal Removal Tool T74P-6700-A, or its equivalent, remove the front seal.
   b. Lubricate the engine front cover and oil seal lip inner lip with engine oil.
   c. Using Crankshaft Seal Replacer/Cover Aligner T88T-6701-A, or its equivalent, install the new seal into the front cover.
15. Install the crankshaft timing sensor.
16. Install the drive pulley/damper.
17. Install the water pump.
18. Install the fan.
19. Install the alternator.
20. Install the power steering pump.
21. Install the air conditioning compressor.
22. Install the oil pan.
23. Fill the cooling system.
24. Fill the crankcase with the proper grade and amount of engine oil. Connect the negative battery cable. Start the engine and check for leaks, then road-test the vehicle for proper operation.

4.0L SOHC Engine (VIN E)

➡According to the manufacturer, the engine must be removed in order to service the front cover. However, the front seal can be serviced with the engine in the vehicle. Remove the crankshaft damper, then follow the seal replacement procedure under installation.

1. Remove the engine from the vehicle.
2. Remove the oil pan and ladder frame.

➡For ladder frame removal procedures, refer to the oil pump removal and installation procedure in this section.

3. Remove the water pump.
4. Remove the crankshaft pulley and damper.
5. Remove the front cover attaching bolts and remove the cover.
6. Inspect the oil seal. If the seal needs replacing, follow the procedures under installation.

To install:

7. Thoroughly clean all gasket mating surfaces. Use new gaskets and coat them with a sealer/adhesive.
8. Install the front cover and tighten all of the bolts.
9. If the front seal needs to be replaced, proceed as follows:
   a. Using Front Cover Seal Removal Tool T74P-6700-A, or its equivalent, remove the front seal.
   b. Lubricate the engine front cover and oil seal inner lip with engine oil.
   c. Using Crankshaft Seal Replacer/Cover Aligner T88T-6701-A, or its equivalent, install the new seal into the front cover.
10. Install the crankshaft damper and pulley. Install a new crankshaft pulley bolt and tighten to specifications

✳✳ WARNING

Never hammer on the damper. Use an appropriate damper installation tool to press the damper onto the crankshaft snout.

11. Install the water pump.
12. Install the ladder frame and oil pan.
13. Install the engine into the vehicle.
14. Run the engine and check for leaks.

5.0L Engine

◆ **See Figures 103 and 104**

➡According to the manufacturer, the engine must be removed in order to service the front cover. However, the front seal can be serviced with the engine in the vehicle. Remove the crankshaft damper, then follow the seal replacement procedure under installation.

1. Remove the engine from the vehicle.
2. Remove the water pump by-pass hose.
3. Remove the Crankshaft Position Sensor (CPS).
4. Remove the crankshaft pulley and damper.
5. Remove the oil pan.

➡The front cover and the water pump are removed as an assembly.

6. Remove the front cover attaching bolts and remove the cover.
7. Inspect the oil seal. If the seal needs replacing, follow the procedures under installation.

To install:

8. Thoroughly clean all gasket mating surfaces. Use new gaskets and coat them with a sealer/adhesive.
9. Install the front cover/water pump assembly and tighten all of the bolts.
10. If the front seal needs to be replaced, proceed as follows:
   a. Using Front Cover Seal Removal Tool T70P-6B070-B, or its equivalent, remove front seal.
   b. Lubricate the engine front cover and oil seal lip inner lip with engine oil.
   c. Using Crankshaft Seal Replacer/Cover Aligner T88T-6701-A, or its equivalent, install the new seal into the front cover.
11. Install the oil pan.
12. Install the crankshaft damper and pulley.

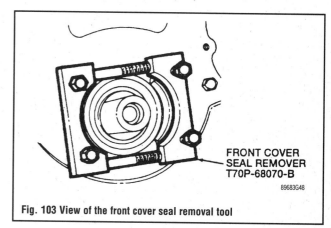

**FRONT COVER
SEAL REMOVER
T70P-68070-B**

89683G48

Fig. 103 View of the front cover seal removal tool

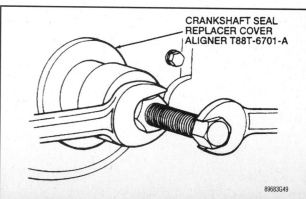

**CRANKSHAFT SEAL
REPLACER COVER
ALIGNER T88T-6701-A**

89683G49

Fig. 104 Using the seal replacer tool to install a new front seal

❊❊ WARNING

Never hammer on the damper. Use an appropriate damper installation tool to press the damper onto the crankshaft snout.

13. Install the Crankshaft Position Sensor (CPS) and the water pump bypass hose.
14. Install the engine into the vehicle.
15. Run the engine and check for leaks.

Timing Chain and Gears

REMOVAL & INSTALLATION

2.9L Engine

1. Drain the cooling system and crankcase. Remove the oil pan and radiator.

❊❊ CAUTION

When draining the coolant, keep in mind that cats and dogs are attracted by ethylene glycol antifreeze, and are quite likely to drink any that is left in an uncovered container or in puddles on the ground. This will prove fatal in sufficient quantity. Always drain the coolant into a sealable container. Coolant should be reused unless it is contaminated or several years old.

2. Remove the cylinder front cover and water pump, drive belt, and camshaft timing gear.
3. Use the clutch aligner T71P–P–7137–H or equivalent and remove the crankshaft sprocket.
   To install:
4. Align the keyway in the gear with the key, then slide the gear onto the shaft, making sure that it seats tight against the spacer.

➡**Feed the timing chain around the crankshaft sprocket and then around the camshaft sprocket. Install the camshaft sprocket together with timing chain as an assembly. Align all necessary timing marks.**

5. Check the camshaft end play. Refer to checking camshaft. If not within specifications, replace the thrust plate.
6. Align the keyway in the crankshaft gear with key in the crankshaft, and align the timing marks. Install the gear, using a crankshaft sprocket replacer tool.
7. Install the cylinder front cover following the procedures in this section. Install the oil pan and radiator.
8. Fill and bleed the cooling system and crankcase.
9. Start the engine and adjust the ignition timing.
10. Operate the engine at fast idle and check all hose connections and gaskets for leaks.

3.0L Engine

▶ **See Figures 105 and 106**

1. Disconnect the negative battery cable.
2. Drain the cooling system and crankcase.

❊❊ CAUTION

When draining the coolant, keep in mind that cats and dogs are attracted by ethylene glycol antifreeze, and are quite likely to drink any that is left in an uncovered container or in puddles on the ground. This will prove fatal in sufficient quantity. Always drain the coolant into a sealable container. Coolant should be reused unless it is contaminated or several years old.

3. Remove the timing cover.
4. Rotate crankshaft until No. 1 piston is at TDC and timing marks are aligned in the correct position.
5. Remove the camshaft sprocket retaining bolt and washer. Check timing chain deflection for excessive wear.
6. Slide sprockets and timing chain forward and remove as assembly.
   To install:
7. Clean timing cover and oil pan sealing surfaces. Clean and inspect all parts. The camshaft retaining bolt has a drilled oil passage for timing chain assembly lubrication. Clean oil passage with solvent. Do not replace with standard bolt.
8. Slide sprockets and timing chain on as assembly with timing marks in the correct location. Install camshaft retaining bolt and washer. Torque bolt to 46 ft. lbs. Lubricate the timing chain assembly.
9. Install timing cover assembly. Install retaining bolts with pipe sealant and tighten as outlined.
10. Refill and bleed cooling system. Connect the negative battery cable. Start engine check for coolant, oil and exhaust leaks.

4.0L Engine (VIN X)

▶ **See Figures 107 and 108**

➡**Review the complete service procedure before starting this repair. Refer to the necessary service procedures in this section.**

1. Disconnect the negative battery cable.
2. Drain the cooling system.

❊❊ CAUTION

When draining the coolant, keep in mind that cats and dogs are attracted by ethylene glycol antifreeze, and are quite likely to drink any that is left in an uncovered container or in puddles on the ground. This will prove fatal in sufficient quantity. Always drain the coolant into a sealable container. Coolant should be reused unless it is contaminated or several years old.

3. Remove the front cover.
4. Remove the radiator.

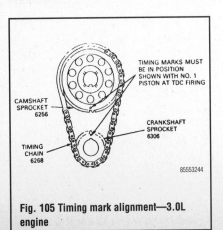

Fig. 105 Timing mark alignment—3.0L engine

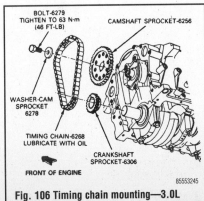

Fig. 106 Timing chain mounting—3.0L engine

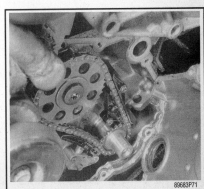

To remove the timing chain and sprockets, first remove the engine front cover

5. Rotate the engine by hand until the No.1 cylinder is at TDC compression, and the timing marks are aligned.

6. Remove the lower tensioner bolt and install a holding clip in the bolt hole and the slot on the rubbing block.

Unbolt and remove the tensioner.

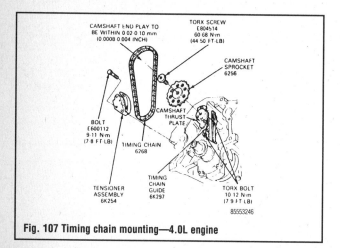

Fig. 107 Timing chain mounting—4.0L engine

7. Remove the camshaft sprocket bolt and sprocket retaining key.

8. Remove the camshaft and crankshaft sprockets with the timing chain.

9. If necessary, remove the chain guide.

To install:

10. Install the timing chain guide. Make sure the pin of the guide is in the hole in the block. Tighten the bolts to 84–96 inch lbs.

11. Align the timing marks on the crankshaft and camshaft sprockets and install the sprockets and chain.

12. Install the camshaft sprocket bolt and sprocket retaining key. Make sure that the timing marks are still aligned.

13. Install the tensioner with the clip in place to keep it retracted.

14. Install the crankshaft key. Make sure the timing marks are still aligned.

15. Make sure the tensioner side of the chain is held inward and the other side is straight and tight.

16. Install the camshaft sprocket bolt and tighten it to 50 ft. lbs.

17. Remove the tensioner clip.

18. Check camshaft end-play.

19. Install the front cover.

20. Install the radiator.

21. Fill the cooling system.

22. Fill the crankcase to the proper level. Connect the negative battery cable. Start engine check for leaks and roadtest the vehicle for proper operation.

Remove the tensioner lower attaching bolt . . .

. . . and install a holding clip in the bolt hole and the slot on the rubbing block

Unbolt and remove the tensioner

A close-up view of a homemade holding clip . . .

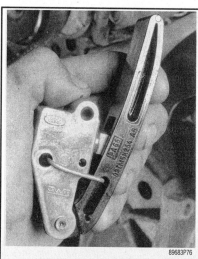

. . . and its proper positioning on the tensioner

Loosen the camshaft sprocket bolt . . .

89683P78

. . . then remove it

89683P79

Remove the camshaft sprocket and chain

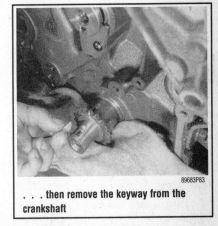

89683P80

If necessary, unbolt the chain guide attaching bolts . . .

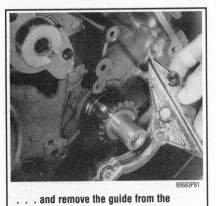

89683P81

. . . and remove the guide from the engine

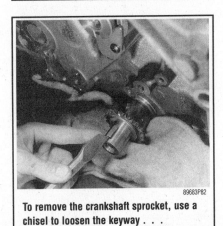

89683P82

To remove the crankshaft sprocket, use a chisel to loosen the keyway . . .

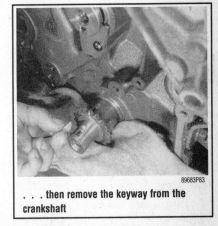

89683P83

. . . then remove the keyway from the crankshaft

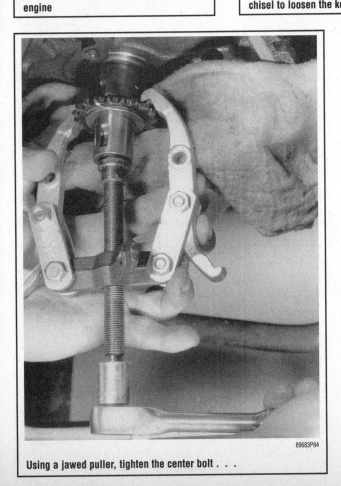

89683P84

Using a jawed puller, tighten the center bolt . . .

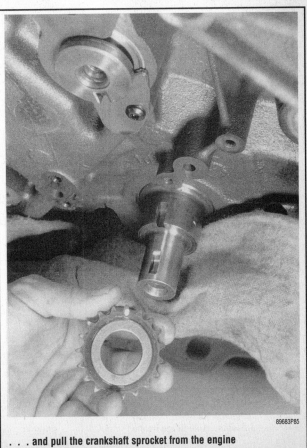

89683P85

. . . and pull the crankshaft sprocket from the engine

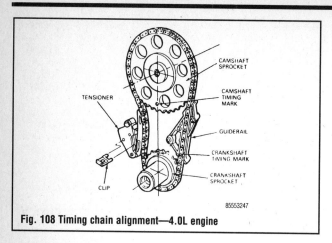

Fig. 108 Timing chain alignment—4.0L engine

4.0L SOHC Engine (VIN E)

▶ See Figures 109 thru 114

On the 4.0L SOHC engine, there are four chains which are used to time the camshafts and balance the engine. There is a jackshaft mounted in the middle of the engine block. The two camshafts are connected to the jackshaft by two chains. The jackshaft is connected to the crankshaft by a third chain. Also, a balance shaft assembly is chain driven off of the crankshaft and timed to the rotation of the engine.

In order to remove either of the camshaft timing or balance shaft chains, the jack shaft chain and sprockets must first be removed. Once the jackshaft chain is removed, the left-hand camshaft and the balance shaft chain can be serviced. In order to remove the right-hand camshaft chain, the jackshaft must be removed. Additionally, in order to service either camshaft chain assembly, the cylinder heads must be removed.

➡**According to the manufacturer, the engine must be removed in order to service the timing chain and sprocket assemblies.**

1. Remove the engine from the vehicle.
2. Remove the oil pan and ladder frame.

➡**For ladder frame removal procedures, refer to the oil pump removal and installation procedure in this section.**

3. Remove the front cover attaching bolts and remove the cover.
4. Remove the cylinder heads
5. Install a pin in the jackshaft tensioner to hold it in the locked position.
6. Loosen and remove the jackshaft sprocket bolt.
7. Remove the jackshaft sprocket and chain assembly.
8. Remove the left-hand front cassette retaining bolt and remove the cassette (chain and tensioner assembly).
9. Position the engine to gain access to the rear of the engine. Ensure that the flywheel is removed.
10. Remove the rear jackshaft plug from the back of the engine block.
11. Remove the right-hand rear cassette retaining bolt and spacer.
12. Loosen and remove the rear jackshaft sprocket bolt, then remove the cassette (chain and tensioner assembly).
13. If the balance shaft chain is to be serviced, do it before installing the timing chains.

To install:

14. Thoroughly clean all gasket mating surfaces. Use new gaskets and coat them with a sealer/adhesive.
15. Install the right-hand rear cassette and the sprocket-to-jackshaft bolt.
16. Install the rear cassette retaining bolt.
17. Install the rear jackshaft plug.
18. Install the front cassette and its retaining bolt.
19. Position jackshaft sprocket and chain on the engine and remove the tensioner pin.
20. Install the jackshaft sprocket bolt and tighten in two stages.
    a. Stage 1: 32–35 ft. lbs. (43–47 Nm)
    b. Stage 2: Turn an additional 65–75°
21. Install the cylinder heads. Time the chains as outlined in the cylinder head procedure.
22. Install the front cover and tighten all of the bolts.

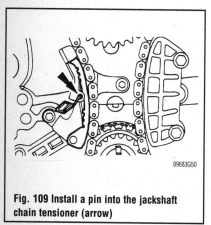

Fig. 109 Install a pin into the jackshaft chain tensioner (arrow)

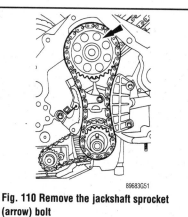

Fig. 110 Remove the jackshaft sprocket (arrow) bolt

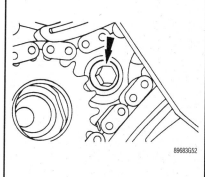

Fig. 111 View of the left-hand front cassette retaining bolt (arrow)

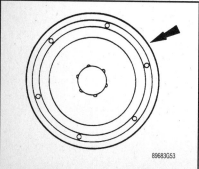

Fig. 112 The rear jackshaft plug (arrow) must be removed from the back of the engine block

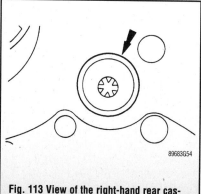

Fig. 113 View of the right-hand rear cassette retaining bolt

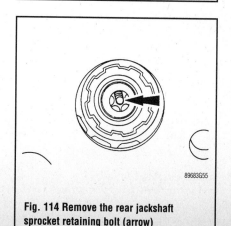

Fig. 114 Remove the rear jackshaft sprocket retaining bolt (arrow)

23. Install the ladder frame and oil pan.
24. Install the engine into the vehicle.
25. Run the engine and check for leaks.

5.0L Engine

♦ **See Figure 115**

1. Remove the engine front cover.
2. Rotate the engine until the No. 1 piston is at TDC. Align the timing marks on the camshaft sprocket to the crankshaft sprocket.
3. Remove the camshaft sprocket retaining bolt.
4. Slide the crankshaft and camshaft sprockets and chain forward until all three components are removed.

To install:

5. Position the crank and camshaft sprockets and chain assembly to the engine.
6. Ensure that the timing marks on the two sprockets are aligned.
7. Install the camshaft sprocket bolt and washer. Tighten to 40–45 ft. lbs. (54–61 Nm).
8. Install the front cover.
9. Start the engine and check for leaks.

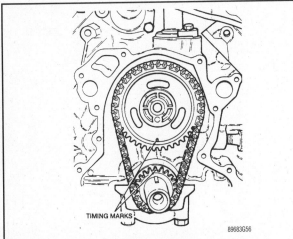

Fig. 115 Timing chain assembly alignment marks on the 5.0L engine

TIMING CHAIN DEFLECTION

1. Remove the timing chain tensioner.
2. Rotate the crankshaft counterclockwise (as viewed from the front of the engine) to take up the slack on the left hand side of the chain.
3. Mark a reference point on a block approximately at mid–point of the chain. Measure from this point to the chain.
4. Rotate the crankshaft in the opposite direction to take up the slack on the right hand side of the chain. Force the left hand side of the chain out with your fingers and measure the distance between the reference point and the chain. The deflection is the difference between the two measurements.
5. If the deflection measurement exceeds specification, replace the timing chain and sprockets.
6. If the wear on the tensioner face exceeds 1.5mm, replace the tensioner.
7. When installing the crankshaft sprocket, fill the keyway chamfer cavity with EOAZ–19554–AA Threadlock and Sealer or equivalent, flush with the front face of the sprocket.

Camshaft and Auxiliary Shaft Sprockets and Seals

This procedure applies to 2.3L and 2.5L engines only.

REMOVAL & INSTALLATION

The cylinder front cover, camshaft and auxiliary shaft seals are replaced in the same manner with the same tools after the respective gear has been removed. Always use a new attaching bolt when replacing the camshaft sprocket or use new Teflon® sealing tape on the threads of the old bolt. To remove the sprockets, first remove the timing cover and belt, then use tool T74P–6256–B, or equivalent to remove its retaining bolt and pull the cam drive sprocket. The same tool is used in exactly the same manner to remove the auxiliary shaft sprocket, as well as to hold the sprockets while the attaching bolts are installed and tightened.

A front cover seal remover tool T74P–6700–B or equivalent is used to remove all the seals. When positioning this tool, make sure that the jaws are gripping the thin edge of the seal very tightly before operating the jack–screw portion of the tool.

To install the seals, a cam and auxiliary shaft seal replacer T74P–6150–A or equivalent with a stepped, threaded arbor is used. The tool acts as a press, using the internal threads of the various shafts as a pilot.

Camshafts, Bearings and Lifters

REMOVAL & INSTALLATION

2.3L and 2.5L Engine

♦ **See Figure 116**

➡**The following procedure covers camshaft removal and installation with the cylinder head on or off the engine. If the cylinder head has been removed, follow Steps 7–9 then skip to Step 12.**

1. Drain the cooling system. Remove the air cleaner assembly and disconnect the negative battery cable.

✳✳ CAUTION

When draining the coolant, keep in mind that cats and dogs are attracted by ethylene glycol antifreeze, and are quite likely to drink any that is left in an uncovered container or in puddles on the ground. This will prove fatal in sufficient quantity. Always drain the coolant into a sealable container. Coolant should be reused unless it is contaminated or several years old.

2. Remove the spark plug wires from the plugs, disconnect the retainer from the valve cover and position the wires out of the way. Disconnect rubber vacuum lines as necessary.
3. Remove all drive belts. Remove the alternator mounting bracket–to–cylinder head mounting bolts, position bracket and alternator out of the way.
4. Disconnect and remove the upper radiator hose. Disconnect the radiator shroud.
5. Remove the fan blades and water pump pulley and fan shroud. Remove cam belt and valve covers.
6. Align engine timing marks at TDC for No. 1 cylinder. Remove cam drive belt.
7. Remove the rocker arms (camshaft followers).
8. Remove the camshaft drive gear and belt guide using a suitable puller. Remove the front oil seal with a sheet metal screw and slide hammer.
9. Remove the camshaft retainer located on the rear mounting stand by unbolting the two bolts.
10. Jack up the front of the vehicle and support on jackstands. Remove the front motor mount bolts. Disconnect the lower radiator hose from the radiator. Disconnect and plug the automatic transmission cooler lines.
11. Position a piece of wood on a floor jack and raise the engine carefully as far as it will go. Place blocks of wood between the engine mounts and cross-member pedestals.
12. Remove the camshaft by carefully withdrawing toward the front of the engine. Caution should be used to prevent damage to cam bearings, lobes and journals.
13. Check the camshaft journals and lobes for wear. Inspect the cam bearings, if worn (unless the proper bearing installing tool is on hand), the cylinder head must be removed for new bearings to be installed by a machine shop.
14. Camshaft installation is in the reverse order of service removal procedure. Coat the camshaft with a heavy SF (or better) grade oil before sliding it into the cylinder head. Install a new front seal. Apply a coat of sealer or teflon tape to the cam drive gear bolt before installation. After any procedure requiring

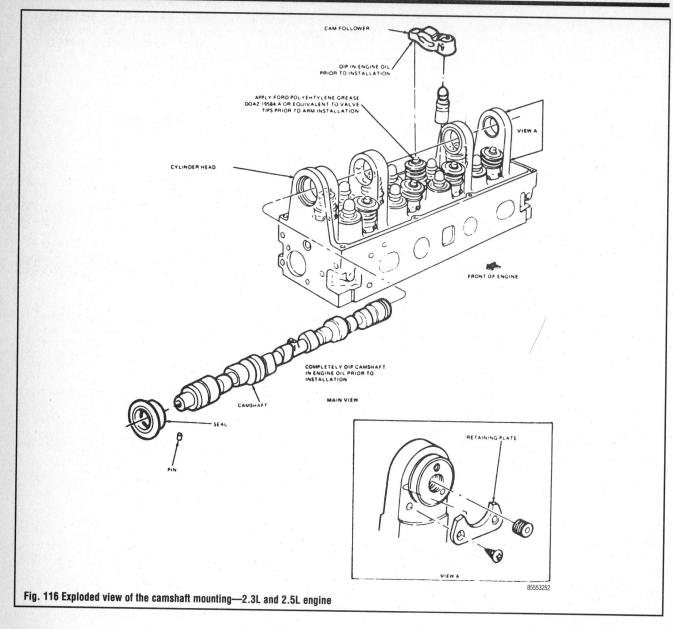

Fig. 116 Exploded view of the camshaft mounting—2.3L and 2.5L engine

removal of the rocker arms, each lash adjuster must be fully collapsed after assembly, then released. This must be done before the camshaft is turned.

15. Refill cooling system. Start engine and check for leaks. Roadtest the vehicle for proper operation.

2.9L Engines

▶ See Figure 117

1. Disconnect the battery ground cable from the battery.
2. Drain the oil from the crankcase.

✳✳ CAUTION

The EPA warns that prolonged contact with used engine oil may cause a number of skin disorders, including cancer! You should make every effort to minimize your exposure to used engine oil. Protective gloves should be worn when changing the oil. Wash your hands and any other exposed skin areas as soon as possible after exposure to used engine oil. Soap and water, or waterless hand cleaner should be used.

3. Remove the radiator, fan and spacer, drive belt and pulley.

4. Label and remove the spark plug wires from the spark plugs.
5. Remove the distributor cap with spark plug wires as an assembly.
6. Disconnect the distributor wiring harness and remove the distributor.
7. Remove the alternator.
8. Remove the intake manifold as described earlier.
9. Remove the rocker arm covers and rocker arm and shaft assemblies as described in this section. Label and remove the push rods and the tappets, so they can be reinstalled in the same location.
10. Remove the oil pan as described in this section.
11. Remove the crankshaft damper.
12. Remove the engine front cover and water pump as an assembly.
13. Remove the camshaft gear attaching bolt and washer, and slide gear and chain off camshaft.
14. Remove the camshaft thrust plate.
15. Carefully remove the camshaft from the block, avoiding any damage to the camshaft bearings.
16. Remove the camshaft drive gear and spacer ring.

To install:

17. Oil the camshaft journals with a heavy SF grade (or better) engine oil and apply Lubriplate® or equivalent lubricant to the cam lobes. Install the spacer ring with the chamfered side toward the camshaft. Insert the camshaft key.

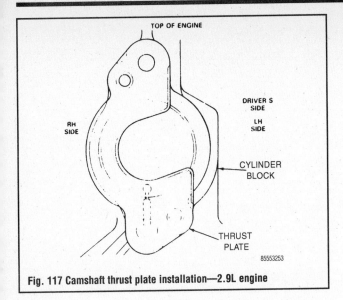

Fig. 117 Camshaft thrust plate installation—2.9L engine

18. Install the camshaft in the block, carefully avoiding damage to the bearing surfaces.

19. Install the thrust plate so that it covers the main oil gallery.

20. Check the camshaft end play. The spacer ring and thrust plate are available in two thicknesses to permit adjusting the end play.

21. Install camshaft gear as described under timing gear removal and installation.

22. Install the engine front cover and water pump as an assembly.

23. Install the crankshaft pulley and secure with washer and attaching bolt. Torque the bolt to 85–96 ft. lbs.

24. Install the oil pan, as described in this section.

25. Position the tappets in their original locations. Apply Lubriplate® or equivalent to both ends of the push rods.

➡**Install the push rods in same location as removed.**

26. Install the intake manifold, as described earlier.

27. Install the oil baffles and rocker arm and shaft assemblies. Tighten the rocker arm stand bolts to 43–50 ft. lbs. Adjust the valves and install the valve rocker arm covers.

28. Install the water pump pulley, fan spacer, fan, and drive belt. Adjust the belt tension.

29. Install the alternator.

30. Install the distributor, distributor wiring harness and distributor cap and plug wires. Connect the plug wires to the spark plugs. Refer to Distributor removal and installation in this manual.

➡**Before installing plug wires, coat inside of each boot with silicone lubricant using a small screwdriver.**

31. Install the radiator.

32. Fill the cooling system to the proper level with a 50;BS50 mix of antifreeze and bleed cooling system.

33. Fill the crankcase with oil.

34. Connect the battery ground cable to the battery.

35. Run the engine and check and adjust the engine timing and idle speed.

36. Run the engine at fast idle speed and check for coolant, fuel, vacuum and oil leaks.

3.0L Engine

♦ See Figures 118 and 119

1. Disconnect the negative battery cable.
2. Remove the air cleaner hoses.
3. Remove the fan and spacer, and shroud.
4. Drain the cooling system. Remove the radiator.

❋❋ CAUTION

When draining the coolant, keep in mind that cats and dogs are attracted by ethylene glycol antifreeze, and are quite likely to drink any that is left in an uncovered container or in puddles on the ground. This will prove fatal in sufficient quantity. Always drain the coolant into a sealable container. Coolant should be reused unless it is contaminated or several years old.

5. Remove the condenser.
6. Relieve the fuel system pressure.
7. Remove the fuel lines at the fuel supply manifold.
8. Tag and disconnect all vacuum hoses in the way.
9. Tag and disconnect all wires in the way.
10. Remove the engine front cover and water pump.
11. Remove the alternator.
12. Remove the power steering pump and secure it out of the way. DO NOT disconnect the hoses!
13. Remove the air conditioning compressor and secure it out of the way. DO NOT disconnect the hoses!
14. Remove the throttle body. See Section 5.
15. Remove the fuel injection harness. See Section 5.
16. Drain the engine oil into a suitable container and dispose of it properly.

❋❋ CAUTION

The EPA warns that prolonged contact with used engine oil may cause a number of skin disorders, including cancer! You should make every effort to minimize your exposure to used engine oil. Protective gloves should be worn when changing the oil. Wash your hands and any other exposed skin areas as soon as possible after exposure to used engine oil. Soap and water, or waterless hand cleaner should be used.

17. Turn the engine by hand to 0 BTDC of the power stroke on No. 1 cylinder.
18. Disconnect the spark plug wires from the plugs.
19. If equipped, remove the distributor cap with the spark plug wires as an assembly.
20. If equipped, matchmark the rotor, distributor body and engine. Disconnect the distributor wiring harness and remove the distributor.
21. Remove the rocker arm covers.
22. Remove the intake manifold as previously described.
23. Loosen the rocker arm bolts enough to pivot the rocker arms out of the way and remove the pushrods. Identify them for installation. They must be installed in their original positions!
24. Remove the tappets. Identify them for installation.
25. Remove the crankshaft pulley/damper.
26. Remove the starter.
27. Remove the oil pan as previously described.
28. Turn the engine by hand until the timing marks align at TDC of the power stroke on No.1 piston.
29. Check the camshaft end-play. If excessive, you'll have to replace the thrust plate.
30. Remove the camshaft gear attaching bolt and washer, then slide the gear off the camshaft.
31. Remove the camshaft thrust plate.
32. Carefully slide the camshaft out of the engine block, using caution to avoid any damage to the camshaft bearings.

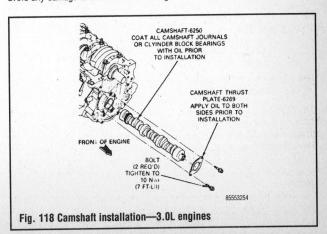

Fig. 118 Camshaft installation—3.0L engines

To install:

33. Oil the camshaft journals and cam lobes with heavy SG engine oil (50W). Install the spacer ring with the chamfered side toward the camshaft, then insert the camshaft key.

34. Install the camshaft in the block, using caution to avoid any damage to the camshaft bearings.

35. Install the thrust plate. Tighten the attaching screws to 84 inch lbs.

36. Rotate the camshaft and crankshaft as necessary to align the timing marks. Install the camshaft gear and chain. Tighten the attaching bolt to 46 ft. lbs.

37. Coat the tappets with 50W engine oil and place them in their original locations.

38. Apply 50W engine oil to both ends of the pushrods. Install the pushrods in their original locations.

39. Pivot the rocker arms into position. Tighten the fulcrum bolts to 8 ft. lbs.

40. Rotate the engine until both timing marks are at the tops of their sprockets and aligned. Tighten the following fulcrum bolts to 18 ft. lbs.:
- No.1 intake
- No.2 exhaust
- No.4 intake
- No.5 exhaust

41. Rotate the engine until the camshaft timing mark is at the bottom of the sprocket and the crankshaft timing mark is at the top of the sprocket, and both are aligned. Tighten the following fulcrum bolts to 18 ft. lbs.:
- No.1 exhaust
- No.2 intake
- No.3 intake and exhaust
- No.4 exhaust
- No.5 intake
- No.6 intake and exhaust

42. Now, tighten all the bolts to 24 ft. lbs.

43. Turn the engine by hand to 0 BTDC of the power stroke on No. 1 cylinder.

44. Install the engine front cover and water pump assembly.

45. Install the oil pan.

46. Install the crankshaft damper/pulley and tighten the retaining bolt to 107 ft. lbs.

47. Install the intake manifold and tighten the mounting bolts to the specifications and in the sequence described under Intake Manifold removal and installation.

48. Install the valve covers.

49. Install the injector harness.

50. If equipped, install the distributor.

51. Install the cap and wires.

52. Install the throttle body.

53. Install the alternator.

54. Install the power steering pump.

55. Install the compressor.

56. Connect all wires.

57. Connect all vacuum lines.

58. Install the radiator and condenser.

59. Install the fan and clutch.

60. Install the fuel lines.

61. Install the starter.

62. Refill the cooling system.

63. Replace the oil filter and refill the crankcase with the specified amount of engine oil.

64. Reconnect the battery ground cable.

65. Start the engine and check the ignition timing and idle speed. Adjust if necessary. Run the engine at fast idle and check for coolant, fuel, vacuum or oil leaks.

4.0L Engine (VIN X)

◆ **See Figures 120 and 121**

1. Disconnect the negative battery cable.
2. Drain the engine oil into a suitable container and dispose of it properly.

✳✳ CAUTION

The EPA warns that prolonged contact with used engine oil may cause a number of skin disorders, including cancer! You should make every effort to minimize your exposure to used engine oil. Protective gloves should be worn when changing the oil. Wash your hands and any other exposed skin areas as soon as possible after exposure to used engine oil. Soap and water, or waterless hand cleaner should be used.

3. Drain the cooling system.

✳✳ CAUTION

When draining the coolant, keep in mind that cats and dogs are attracted by ethylene glycol antifreeze, and are quite likely to drink any that is left in an uncovered container or in puddles on the ground. This will prove fatal in sufficient quantity. Always drain the coolant into a sealable container. Coolant should be reused unless it is contaminated or several years old.

4. Remove the radiator.
5. Remove the condenser.
6. Remove the fan and spacer, and shroud.
7. Remove the air cleaner hoses.
8. Tag and remove the spark plug wires.
9. Remove the EDIS ignition coil and bracket.
10. Remove the crankshaft pulley/damper.
11. Remove the clamp. bolt and oil pump drive from the rear of the block.
12. Remove the alternator.
13. Relieve the fuel system pressure.
14. Remove the fuel lines at the fuel supply manifold.
15. Remove the upper and lower intake manifolds as previously described.
16. Remove the rocker arm covers.
17. Remove the rocker shaft assemblies.
18. Remove the pushrods. Identify them for installation. They must be installed in their original positions!
19. Remove the tappets. Identify them for installation.
20. Remove the oil pan as previously described.
21. Remove the engine front cover and water pump.
22. Place the timing chain tensioner in the retracted position and install the retaining clip.
23. Turn the engine by hand until the timing marks align at TDC of the power stroke on No.1 piston.
24. Check the camshaft end-play. If excessive, you'll have to replace the thrust plate.
25. Remove the camshaft gear attaching bolt and washer, then slide the gear off the camshaft.
26. Remove the camshaft thrust plate.
27. Carefully slide the camshaft out of the engine block, using caution to avoid any damage to the camshaft bearings.

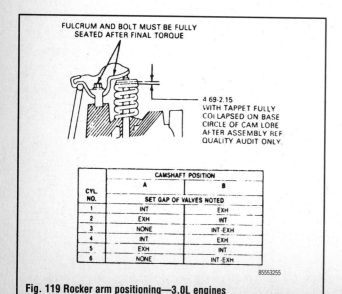

FULCRUM AND BOLT MUST BE FULLY
SEATED AFTER FINAL TORQUE

4 69-2.15
WITH TAPPET FULLY
COLLAPSED ON BASE
CIRCLE OF CAM LOBE
AFTER ASSEMBLY REF.
QUALITY AUDIT ONLY.

CYL. NO.	CAMSHAFT POSITION	
	A	B
	SET GAP OF VALVES NOTED	
1	INT	EXH
2	EXH	INT
3	NONE	INT·EXH
4	INT	EXH
5	EXH	INT
6	NONE	INT·EXH

85553255

Fig. 119 Rocker arm positioning—3.0L engines

To install:

28. Oil the camshaft journals and cam lobes with a heavy (50W) SG grade (or better) engine oil.

29. Install the camshaft in the block, using caution to avoid any damage to the camshaft bearings.

30. Install the thrust plate. Make sure that it covers the main oil gallery. Tighten the attaching screws to 96 inch lbs.

31. Rotate the camshaft and crankshaft as necessary to align the timing marks. Install the camshaft gear and chain. Tighten the attaching bolt to 50 ft. lbs.

32. Remove the clip from the chain tensioner.

33. Install the engine front cover and water pump assembly. Refer to the necessary service procedures in this Section.

34. Install the crankshaft damper/pulley and tighten the retaining bolt to 107 ft. lbs.

35. Install the oil pan.

36. Coat the tappets with 50W engine oil and place them in their original locations.

37. Apply 50W engine oil to both ends of the pushrods. Install the pushrods in their original locations.

38. Install the upper and lower intake manifolds.

39. Install the rocker shaft assemblies.

40. Install the valve covers.

41. Install the fan and clutch.

42. Install the fuel lines.

43. Install the oil pump drive.

44. Install the alternator.

45. Install the EDIS coil and plug wires. Coat the inside of each wire boot with silicone lubricant.

46. Install the radiator and condenser.

47. Refill the cooling system.

48. Replace the oil filter and refill the crankcase with the specified amount of engine oil.

49. Reconnect the battery ground cable.

50. Start the engine and check the ignition timing and idle speed. Adjust if necessary. Run the engine at fast idle and check for coolant, fuel, vacuum or oil leaks.

4.0L SOHC Engine (VIN E)

▶ See Figures 122 and 123

LEFT-HAND CAMSHAFT

1. Disconnect the negative battery cable for safety.
2. Remove the LH valve cover.
3. Remove the LH hydraulic camshaft tensioner.
4. Remove the camshaft sprocket bolt.

➡**When removing the followers, label them so that they may be returned to their original positions.**

5. Using the Valve Spring Compressor Tool ST1330-A, or its equivalent, remove the camshaft roller followers.

6. Remove the camshaft bearing cap bolts and the oil rail.

7. Remove the camshaft.

To install:

8. Lubricate all of the moving parts with SAE 50W engine oil.

9. Install the camshaft onto the cylinder head.

10. Position the oil rail and install the bearing caps and bolts. Tighten the bolts in two stages.

    a. Stage 1: 53.5 inch lbs. (6 Nm)

    b. Stage 2: 11–12.5 ft. lbs. (15–17 Nm)

11. Install the camshaft followers in the same manner as removal.

12. Install the camshaft sprocket bolt. Do not tighten the bolt.

13. Refer to the steps in the cylinder head removal and installation procedure to properly time the camshaft.

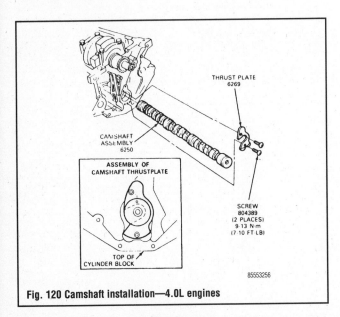

Fig. 120 Camshaft installation—4.0L engines

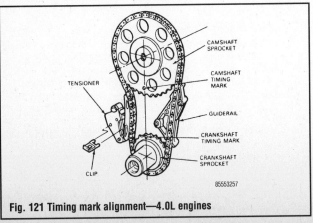

Fig. 121 Timing mark alignment—4.0L engines

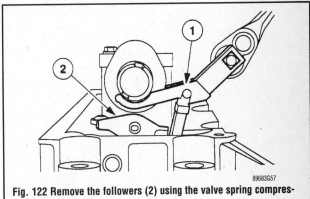

Fig. 122 Remove the followers (2) using the valve spring compressor tool (1)

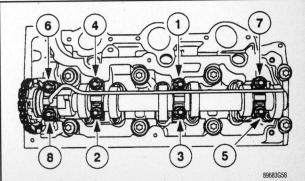

Fig. 123 4.0L SOHC camshaft bearing cap bolt loosening and tightening sequence

14. Install the valve cover.
15. Connect the negative battery cable.
16. Start the engine and check for leaks.

RIGHT-HAND CAMSHAFT

1. Disconnect the negative battery cable for safety.
2. Remove the RH valve cover.
3. Remove the RH hydraulic camshaft tensioner.

➡**The RH camshaft sprocket bolt uses left-hand threads.**

4. Using the Cam Gear Torque Adapter Tool T97T-6256-F, or its equivalent, remove the camshaft sprocket bolt.

➡**When removing the followers, label them so that they may be returned to their original positions.**

5. Using the Valve Spring Compressor Tool ST1330-A, or its equivalent, remove the camshaft roller followers.
6. Remove the camshaft bearing cap bolts and the oil rail.
7. Remove the camshaft.
To install:
8. Lubricate all of the moving parts with SAE 50W engine oil.
9. Install the camshaft onto the cylinder head.
10. Position the oil rail and install the bearing caps and bolts. Tighten the bolts in two stages.
   a. Stage 1: 53.5 inch lbs. (6 Nm)
   b. Stage 2: 11–12.5 ft. lbs. (15–17 Nm)
11. Install the camshaft followers in the same manner as removal.
12. Install the camshaft sprocket bolt. Do not tighten the bolt.
13. Refer to the steps in the cylinder head removal and installation procedure to properly time the camshaft.
14. Install the valve cover.
15. Connect the negative battery cable.
16. Start the engine and check for leaks.

5.0L Engine

▶ **See Figure 124**

1. Disconnect the negative battery cable.
2. Remove the timing chain cover.
3. Remove the camshaft sprocket and chain assembly.
4. Remove the upper and lower intake manifolds.
5. Remove both valve covers.
6. Loosen the rocker arm bolts and rotate the rocker arms to the side.
7. Remove the pushrods in sequence so that they may be installed to their original positions.
8. Remove all of the lifters, also keeping them in order.
9. Remove the camshaft thrust plate bolts and the plate.

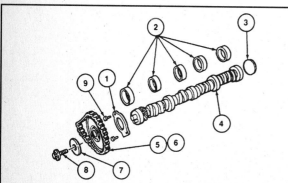

1. Camshaft thrust plate
2. Camshaft bearing
3. Camshaft rear bearing cover
4. Camshaft
5. Timing chain
6. Camshaft sprocket
7. Camshaft sprocket washer
8. Camshaft sprocket bolt
9. Camshaft thrust plate bolt

89683G59

Fig. 124 Exploded view of the camshaft and its related components on the 5.0L engine

10. Withdraw the camshaft from the engine, taking care not to damage the bearings or lobes and journals.
To install:
11. Apply SAE 50W engine oil to the camshaft lobes and journals.
12. Carefully install the camshaft into position in the cylinder block.
13. Apply SAE 50W engine oil to the camshaft thrust plate.
14. Position the thrust plate with the groove toward the block and install the retaining bolts. Tighten to 9–12 ft. lbs. (13–16 Nm).
15. Apply SAE 50W engine oil to the valve tappets and install them. If reusing the old lifters, place them in their original positions.
16. Install the pushrods to their original positions.
17. Reposition the rocker arms and tighten them as outlined earlier in this Section.
18. Install the valve covers, the lower and the upper intake manifolds.
19. Install the camshaft sprocket and chain assembly. Ensure that the timing marks on the cam and crankshaft sprockets are aligned.
20. Install the timing chain cover.
21. Connect the negative battery cable. Start the engine and check for leaks.

INSPECTION

Camshaft Lobe Lift

▶ **See Figure 125**

2.3L, 2.5L AND 4.0L SOHC (VIN E) ENGINES

Check the lift of each lobe in consecutive order and make a note of the readings. Camshaft assembly specifications are sometimes modified by Ford after production. Refer to a local reputable machine shop as necessary.
1. Remove the air cleaner and the valve rocker arm cover.
2. Measure the distance between the major (A–A) and minor (B–B) diameters of each cam lobe with a Vernier caliper and record the readings. The difference in the readings on each cam diameter is the lobe lift.
3. If the readings do not meet specifications, replace the camshaft and all rocker arms.
4. Install the valve rocker arm cover and the air cleaner.

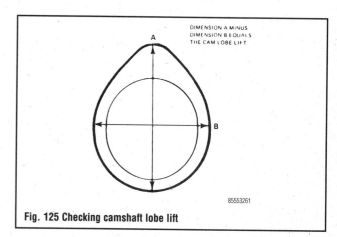

DIMENSION A MINUS
DIMENSION B EQUALS
THE CAM LOBE LIFT

85553261

Fig. 125 Checking camshaft lobe lift

2.9L, 3.0L, 4.0L (VIN X) AND 5.0L ENGINES

Check the lift of each lobe in consecutive order and make a note of the reading. Camshaft assembly specifications are sometimes modify by Ford after production. Refer to a local reputable machine shop as necessary.
1. Remove the fresh air inlet tube and the air cleaner. Remove the heater hose and crankcase ventilation hoses. Remove valve rocker arm cover(s).
2. Remove the rocker arm stud nut or fulcrum bolts, fulcrum seat and rocker arm.
3. Make sure the push rod is in the valve tappet socket. Install a dial indicator D78P–4201–B (or equivalent) so that the actuating point of the indicator is in the push rod socket (or the indicator ball socket adapter Tool 6565–AB is on the end of the push rod) and in the same plane as the push rod movement.
4. Disconnect the I terminal and the S terminal at the starter relay. Install an auxiliary starter switch between the battery and S terminals of the starter relay. Crank the engine with the ignition switch off. Turn the crankshaft over until the

tappet is on the base circle of the camshaft lobe. At this position, the push rod will be in its lowest position.

5. Zero the dial indicator. Continue to rotate the crankshaft slowly until the push rod is in the fully raised position.

6. Compare the total lift recorded on the dial indicator with the specification. To check the accuracy of the original indicator reading, continue to rotate the crankshaft until the indicator reads zero. If the lift on any lobe is below specified wear limits, the camshaft and the valve tappet operating on the worn lobe(s) must be replaced.

7. Remove the dial indicator and auxiliary starter switch.

8. Install the rocker arm, fulcrum seat and stud nut or fulcrum bolts.

9. Install the valve rocker arm covers and the air cleaner.

Camshaft End Play

2.3L AND 2.5L ENGINES

▶ **See Figure 126**

Remove the camshaft drive belt cover. Push the camshaft toward the rear of the engine. Install a dial indicator so that the indicator point is on the camshaft sprocket attaching screw or gear hub. Zero the dial indicator. Position a prybar between the camshaft sprocket or gear and the cylinder head. Pull the camshaft forward and release it. Compare the dial indicator reading with specifications. If the end play is excessive, replace the thrust plate at the rear of the cylinder head. Remove the dial indicator and install the camshaft drive belt cover. The camshaft end-play specification is 0.001–0.007 inch and the service limit is 0.003 inch. Camshaft specifications are sometimes modified by Ford after production.

2.9L, 3.0L, 4.0L AND 5.0L ENGINES

▶ **See Figure 127**

1. Push the camshaft toward the rear of the engine. Install a dial indicator (Tool D78P–4201–C or equivalent so that the indicator point is on the camshaft sprocket attaching screw.

2. Zero the dial indicator. Position a prybar between the camshaft gear and the block. Pull the camshaft forward and release it. Compare the dial indicator reading with the specification. The camshaft end-play specification is 0.0008–0.004 inch and the service limit is 0.009 inch (0.007 inch on 3.0L engine). Camshaft specifications are sometimes modified by Ford after production.

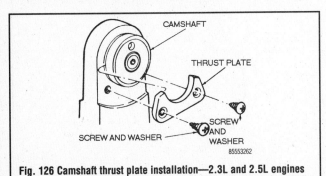

Fig. 126 Camshaft thrust plate installation—2.3L and 2.5L engines

3. If the end play is excessive, check the spacer for correct installation before it is removed. If the spacer is correctly installed, replace the thrust plate.

➡ **The spacer ring and thrust plate are available in two thicknesses to permit adjusting the end play.**

4. Remove the dial indicator.

BEARING REMOVAL & INSTALLATION

If excessive camshaft wear is found, or if the engine is completely rebuilt, the camshaft bearings should be replaced. Use these service repair procedures as a guide.

2.3L and 2.5L Engines

▶ **See Figure 128**

1. Remove the head and place it on a work stand.

2. Remove the camshaft.

3. Using a tool such as Bearing Replacer T71P–6250–A, remove the bearings.

4. Coat the new bearings with clean 50W engine oil and install them with the tool.

2.9L Engines

▶ **See Figures 129 and 130**

1. Remove the engine and place it on a work stand.

2. Remove the flywheel.

3. Remove the camshaft.

4. Using a sharp punch and hammer, drive a hole in the rear bearing bore plug and pry it out.

5. Using the special tools and instructions in Cam Bearing Replacer Kit T71P–6250–A, or their equivalents, remove the bearings.

6. To remove the front and rear bearings, use the special adapter tube T72C–6250, or equivalent.

To install:

7. Following the instructions in the tool kit, install the bearings. Make sure that you follow the instructions carefully. Failure to use the correct expanding collets can cause severe bearing damage!

➡ **Make sure that the oil holes in the bearings and block are aligned!**

8. Install a new bearing bore plug coated with sealer.

9. Install the camshaft.

10. Install the flywheel.

11. Install the engine.

3.0L, 4.0L (VIN X) and 5.0L Engines

▶ **See Figure 130**

1. Remove the engine and place it on a work stand.

2. Remove the flywheel.

3. Remove the camshaft.

4. Using a sharp punch and hammer, drive a hole in the rear bearing bore plug and pry it out.

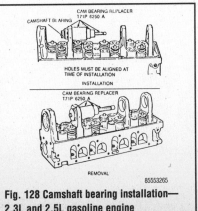

Fig. 128 Camshaft bearing installation—2.3L and 2.5L gasoline engine

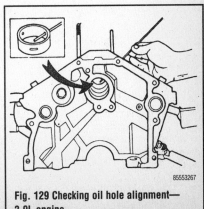

Fig. 129 Checking oil hole alignment—2.9L engine

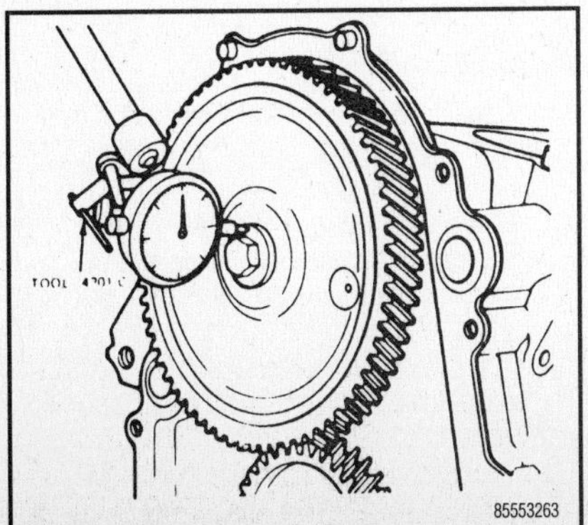

Fig. 127 Checking camshaft end-play—2.9L engines

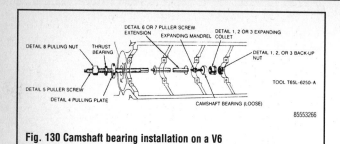

Fig. 130 Camshaft bearing installation on a V6

5. Using the special tools and instructions in Cam Bearing Replacer Kit T65L–6250–A, or their equivalents, remove the bearings.

6. To remove the front bearing, install the tool from the rear of the block.

To install:

7. Following the instructions in the tool kit, install the bearings. Make sure that you follow the instructions carefully. Failure to use the correct expanding collets can cause severe bearing damage!

➡**Make sure that the oil holes in the bearings and block are aligned! Make sure that the front bearing is installed 0.51–0.89mm below the face of the block.**

8. Install a new bearing bore plug coated with sealer.

9. Install the camshaft.
10. Install the flywheel.
11. Install the engine.

4.0L SOHC Engine (VIN E)

The bearings are integral with the cylinder heads and are not replaceable. If the bearing surfaces are damaged, a new cylinder head will have to be installed.

Auxiliary Shaft

REMOVAL & INSTALLATION

2.3L and 2.5L Engines

▶ **See Figure 131**

1. Remove the camshaft drive belt cover.
2. Remove the drive belt. Remove the auxiliary shaft sprocket. A puller may be necessary to remove the sprocket.
3. Remove the distributor and fuel pump.
4. Remove the auxiliary shaft cover and thrust plate.
5. Withdraw the auxiliary shaft from block.

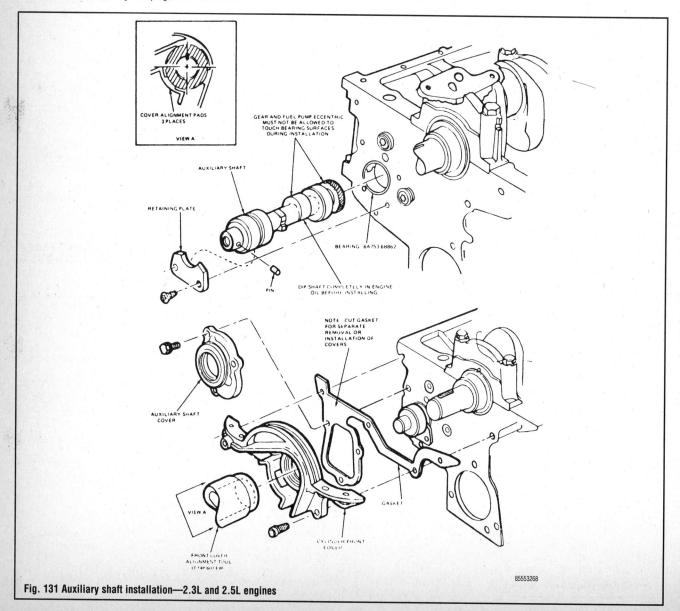

Fig. 131 Auxiliary shaft installation—2.3L and 2.5L engines

➡️The distributor drive gear and the fuel pump eccentric on the auxiliary shaft must not be allowed to touch the auxiliary shaft bearings during removal and installation. Completely coat the shaft with oil before sliding it into place.

6. Slide the auxiliary shaft into the housing and insert the thrust plate to hold the shaft.

7. Install a new gasket and auxiliary shaft cover.

➡️The auxiliary shaft cover and cylinder front cover share a gasket. Cut off the old gasket around the cylinder cover and use half of the new gasket on the auxiliary shaft cover.

8. Fit a new gasket into the fuel pump and install the pump.
9. Insert the distributor and install the auxiliary shaft sprocket.
10. Align the timing marks and install the drive belt.
11. Install the drive belt cover.
12. Check the ignition timing.

Rear Main Oil Seal

REMOVAL & INSTALLATION

▶ **See Figures 132, 133 and 134**

If the crankshaft rear oil seal replacement is the only operation being performed, it can be done in the vehicle as detailed in the following procedure. If the oil seal is being replaced in conjunction with a rear main bearing replacement, the engine must be removed from the vehicle and installed on a work stand.

1. Remove the starter.
2. Remove the transmission from the vehicle, following the procedures in Section 7.
3. On a manual shift transmission, remove the pressure plate and cover assembly and the clutch disc following the procedure in Section 7.
4. Remove the flywheel attaching bolts and remove the flywheel and engine rear cover plate.

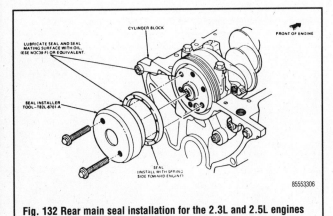

Fig. 132 Rear main seal installation for the 2.3L and 2.5L engines

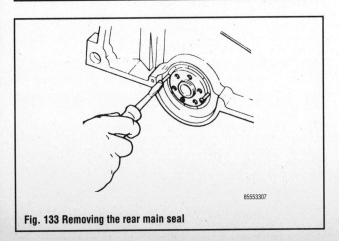

Fig. 133 Removing the rear main seal

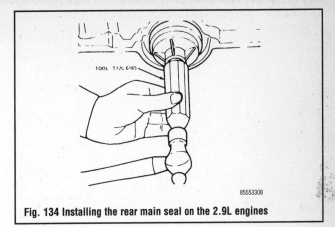

Fig. 134 Installing the rear main seal on the 2.9L engines

5. Use an awl to punch two holes in the crankshaft rear oil seal. Punch the holes on opposite sides of the crankshaft and just above the bearing cap to cylinder block split line. Install a sheet metal screw in each hole. Use two large screwdrivers or small pry bars and pry against both screws at the same time to remove the crankshaft rear oil seal. It may be necessary to place small blocks of wood against the cylinder block to provide a fulcrum point for the pry bars. Use caution throughout this procedure to avoid scratching or otherwise damaging the crankshaft oil seal surface.

To install:

6. Clean the oil seal recess in the cylinder block and main bearing cap.
7. Clean, inspect and polish the rear oil seal rubbing surface on the crankshaft. Coat a new oil seal and the crankshaft with a light film of engine oil. Start the seal in the recess with the seal lip facing forward and install it with a seal driver. Keep the tool, T82L–6701–A (4–cyl. engines) or T72C–6165 (6–cyl. engine) straight with the centerline of the crankshaft and install the seal until the tool contacts the cylinder block surface. Remove the tool and inspect the seal to be sure it was not damaged during installation.
8. Install the engine rear cover plate. Position the flywheel on the crankshaft flange. Coat the threads of the flywheel attaching bolts with oil–resistant sealer and install the bolts. Tighten the bolts in sequence across from each other to the specifications listed in the torque chart in this section.
9. On a manual shift transmission, install the clutch disc and the pressure plate assembly following the procedure in Section 7.
10. Install the transmission, following the procedure in Section 7.

Flywheel and Ring Gear

REMOVAL & INSTALLATION

▶ **See Figures 135, 136 and 137**

1. Remove the transmission, following procedures in Section 7.
2. On a manual shift transmission, remove the clutch pressure plate and cover assembly and clutch disc, following the procedures in Section 7.

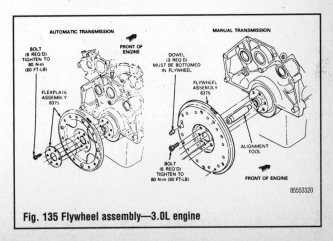

Fig. 135 Flywheel assembly—3.0L engine

3. Remove the flywheel attaching bolts and remove the flywheel.

To install:

4. Position the flywheel on the crankshaft flange. Coat the threads of the flywheel attaching bolts with Loctite® or equivalent and install the bolts. Tighten the bolts in sequence across from each other to specifications.

5. On a manual shift transmission, install the clutch disc and pressure plate and cover assembly following the procedures in Section 7.

6. Install the transmission following the procedure in Section 7.

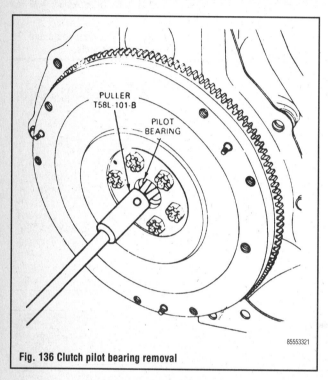

Fig. 136 Clutch pilot bearing removal

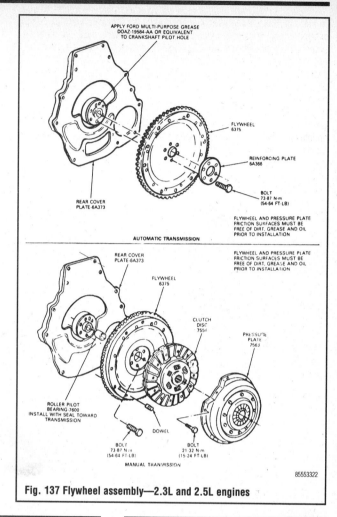

Fig. 137 Flywheel assembly—2.3L and 2.5L engines

Lock the flywheel in place and remove the retaining bolts . . .

. . . then remove the flywheel from the crankshaft

Upon installation, apply a thread-locking compound to the flywheel bolts

EXHAUST SYSTEM

Inspection

▶ See Figures 138 thru 144

➥Safety glasses should be worn at all times when working on or near the exhaust system. Older exhaust systems will almost always be covered with loose rust particles which are more than a nuisance and could injure your eye.

✻✻✻ CAUTION

DO NOT perform exhaust repairs or inspection with the engine or exhaust hot. Allow the system to cool completely. Exhaust systems are noted for sharp edges, flaking metal and rusted bolts. Gloves and eye protection are required. A healthy supply of penetrating oil and rags is highly recommended.

Your vehicle must be raised and supported safely at four points to inspect the exhaust system properly. Start the inspection at the exhaust manifold where the header pipe is attached and work your way to the back of the vehicle. On dual exhaust systems, remember to inspect both sides of the vehicle. Check the complete exhaust system for open seams, holes, loose connections, or other deterioration which could permit exhaust fumes to seep into the passenger compartment. Inspect all mounting brackets and hangers for deterioration, some may have rubber O-rings that can become overstretched and non-supportive (and should be replaced if worn). Many technicians use a pointed tool to poke up into the exhaust system at rust spots to see whether or not they crumble. Most models have heat shield(s) covering certain parts of the exhaust system, it is often necessary to remove these shields to visually inspect those components.

REPLACEMENT

▶ **See Figures 145, 146 and 147**

There are basically two types of exhaust systems. One is the flange type where the component ends are attached with bolts and a gasket in-between. The other exhaust system is the slip joint type. These components slip into one another using clamps to retain them together.

❊❊ CAUTION

Allow the exhaust system to cool sufficiently before spraying a solvent exhaust fasteners. Some solvents are highly flammable and could ignite when sprayed on hot exhaust components.

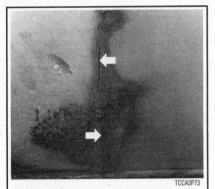

Fig. 138 Cracks in the muffler are a guaranteed leak

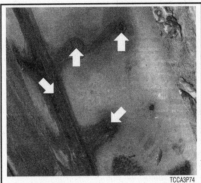

Fig. 139 Check the muffler for rotted spot welds and seams

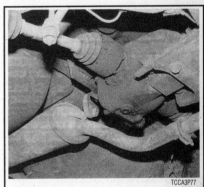

Fig. 140 Make sure the exhaust does contact the body or suspension

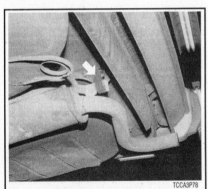

Fig. 141 Check for overstretched or torn exhaust hangers

Fig. 142 Example of a badly deteriorated exhaust pipe

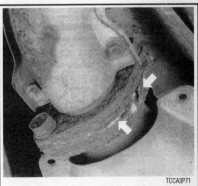

Fig. 143 Inspect flanges for gaskets that have deteriorated and need replacement

Fig. 144 Some systems, like this one, use large O-rings (donuts) in between the flanges

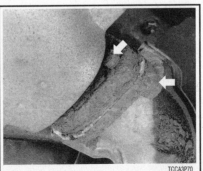

Fig. 145 Nuts and bolts will be extremely difficult to remove when deteriorated with rust

Fig. 146 Example of a flange type exhaust system joint

Fig. 147 Example of a common slip joint type system

Before removing any component of the exhaust system, ALWAYS squirt a liquid rust dissolving agent onto the fasteners for ease of removal. A lot of knuckle skin will be saved by following this rule. It may even be wise to spray the fasteners and allow them to sit overnight.

❊❊ CAUTION

Do NOT perform exhaust repairs or inspection with the engine or exhaust hot. Allow the system to cool. Exhaust systems are noted for sharp edges, flaking metal and rusted bolts. Gloves and eye protection are required.

ENGINE RECONDITIONING

Determining Engine Condition

Anything that generates heat and/or friction will eventually burn or wear out (for example, a light bulb generates heat, therefore its life span is limited). With this in mind, a running engine generates tremendous amounts of both; friction is encountered by the moving and rotating parts inside the engine and heat is created by friction and combustion of the fuel. However, the engine has systems designed to help reduce the effects of heat and friction and provide added longevity. The oiling system reduces the amount of friction encountered by the moving parts inside the engine, while the cooling system reduces heat created by friction and combustion. If either system is not maintained, a break-down will be inevitable. Therefore, you can see how regular maintenance can affect the service life of your vehicle. If you do not drain, flush and refill your cooling system at the proper intervals, deposits will begin to accumulate in the radiator, thereby reducing the amount of heat it can extract from the coolant. The same applies to your oil and filter; if it is not changed often enough it becomes laden with contaminates and is unable to properly lubricate the engine. This increases friction and wear.

There are a number of methods for evaluating the condition of your engine. A compression test can reveal the condition of your pistons, piston rings, cylinder bores, head gasket(s), valves and valve seats. An oil pressure test can warn you of possible engine bearing, or oil pump failures. Excessive oil consumption, evidence of oil in the engine air intake area and/or bluish smoke from the tailpipe may indicate worn piston rings, worn valve guides and/or valve seals. As a general rule, an engine that uses no more than one quart of oil every 1000 miles is in good condition. Engines that use one quart of oil or more in less than 1000 miles should first be checked for oil leaks. If any oil leaks are present, have them fixed before determining how much oil is consumed by the engine, especially if blue smoke is not visible at the tailpipe.

COMPRESSION TEST

▶ **See Figure 148**

A noticeable lack of engine power, excessive oil consumption and/or poor fuel mileage measured over an extended period are all indicators of internal engine wear. Worn piston rings, scored or worn cylinder bores, blown head gaskets, sticking or burnt valves, and worn valve seats are all possible culprits. A check of each cylinder's compression will help locate the problem.

1. Raise and support the vehicle safely, as necessary for access. Remember that some longer exhaust pipes may be difficult to wrestle out from under the vehicle if it is not supported high enough.

2. If you haven't already, apply a generous amount of penetrating oil or solvent to any rusted fasteners.

3. On flange joints, carefully loosen and remove the retainers at the flange. If bolts or nuts are difficult to break loose, apply more penetrating liquid and give it some additional time to set. If the fasteners still will not come loose an impact driver may be necessary to jar it loose (and keep the fastener from breaking).

➡**When unbolting the headpipe from the manifold, make sure that the bolts are free before trying to remove them. If you snap a stud in the exhaust manifold, the stud will have to be removed with a bolt extractor, which often means removal of the manifold itself.**

4. On slip joint components, remove the mounting U-bolts from around the exhaust pipe you are extracting from the vehicle. Don't be surprised if the U-bolts break while removing the nuts.

5. Loosen the exhaust pipe from any mounting brackets retaining it to the floor pan and separate the components. Slight twisting and turning may be required to remove the component completely from the vehicle. You may need to tap on the component with a rubber mallet to loosen it. If all else fails, use a hacksaw to separate the parts. An oxy-acetylene cutting torch may be faster but the sparks are DANGEROUS near the fuel tank, and at the very least, accidents could happen, resulting in damage to the under-vehicle parts, not to mention yourself.

6. When installing exhaust components, you should loosely position all components before tightening any of the joints. Once you are certain that the system is run correctly, begin tightening the fasteners at the front of the vehicle and work your way back.

➡**A screw-in type compression gauge is more accurate than the type you simply hold against the spark plug hole. Although it takes slightly longer to use, it's worth the effort to obtain a more accurate reading.**

1. Make sure that the proper amount and viscosity of engine oil is in the crankcase, then ensure the battery is fully charged.

2. Warm-up the engine to normal operating temperature, then shut the engine **OFF**.

3. Disable the ignition system.

4. Label and disconnect all of the spark plug wires from the plugs.

5. Thoroughly clean the cylinder head area around the spark plug ports, then remove the spark plugs.

6. Set the throttle plate to the fully open (wide-open throttle) position. You can block the accelerator linkage open for this, or you can have an assistant fully depress the accelerator pedal.

7. Install a screw-in type compression gauge into the No. 1 spark plug hole until the fitting is snug.

❊❊ WARNING

Be careful not to crossthread the spark plug hole.

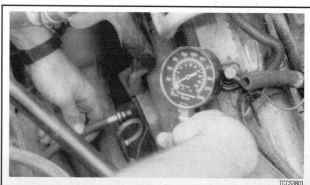

Fig. 148 A screw-in type compression gauge is more accurate and easier to use without an assistant

8. According to the tool manufacturer's instructions, connect a remote starting switch to the starting circuit.

9. With the ignition switch in the **OFF** position, use the remote starting switch to crank the engine through at least five compression strokes (approximately 5 seconds of cranking) and record the highest reading on the gauge.

10. Repeat the test on each cylinder, cranking the engine approximately the same number of compression strokes and/or time as the first.

11. Compare the highest readings from each cylinder to that of the others. The indicated compression pressures are considered within specifications if the lowest reading cylinder is within 75 percent of the pressure recorded for the highest reading cylinder. For example, if your highest reading cylinder pressure was 150 psi (1034 kPa), then 75 percent of that would be 113 psi (779 kPa). So the lowest reading cylinder should be no less than 113 psi (779 kPa).

12. If a cylinder exhibits an unusually low compression reading, pour a tablespoon of clean engine oil into the cylinder through the spark plug hole and repeat the compression test. If the compression rises after adding oil, it means that the cylinder's piston rings and/or cylinder bore are damaged or worn. If the pressure remains low, the valves may not be seating properly (a valve job is needed), or the head gasket may be blown near that cylinder. If compression in any two adjacent cylinders is low, and if the addition of oil doesn't help raise compression, there is leakage past the head gasket. Oil and coolant in the combustion chamber, combined with blue or constant white smoke from the tailpipe, are symptoms of this problem. However, don't be alarmed by the normal white smoke emitted from the tailpipe during engine warm-up or from cold weather driving. There may be evidence of water droplets on the engine dipstick and/or oil droplets in the cooling system if a head gasket is blown.

OIL PRESSURE TEST

Check for proper oil pressure at the sending unit passage with an externally mounted mechanical oil pressure gauge (as opposed to relying on a factory installed dash-mounted gauge). A tachometer may also be needed, as some specifications may require running the engine at a specific rpm.

1. With the engine cold, locate and remove the oil pressure sending unit.

2. Following the manufacturer's instructions, connect a mechanical oil pressure gauge and, if necessary, a tachometer to the engine.

3. Start the engine and allow it to idle.

4. Check the oil pressure reading when cold and record the number. You may need to run the engine at a specified rpm, so check the specifications.

5. Run the engine until normal operating temperature is reached (upper radiator hose will feel warm).

6. Check the oil pressure reading again with the engine hot and record the number. Turn the engine **OFF**.

7. Compare your hot oil pressure reading to specification. If the reading is low, check the cold pressure reading against the chart. If the cold pressure is well above the specification, and the hot reading was lower than the specification, you may have the wrong viscosity oil in the engine. Change the oil, making sure to use the proper grade and quantity, then repeat the test.

Low oil pressure readings could be attributed to internal component wear, pump related problems, a low oil level, or oil viscosity that is too low. High oil pressure readings could be caused by an overfilled crankcase, too high of an oil viscosity or a faulty pressure relief valve.

Buy or Rebuild?

Now if you have determined that your engine is worn out, you must make some decisions. The question of whether or not an engine is worth rebuilding is largely a subjective matter and one of personal worth. Is the engine a popular one, or is it an obsolete model? Are parts available? Will it get acceptable gas mileage once it is rebuilt? Is the car it's being put into worth keeping? Would it be less expensive to buy a new engine, have your engine rebuilt by a pro, rebuild it yourself or buy a used engine from a salvage yard? Or would it be simpler and less expensive to buy another car? If you have considered all these matters, and have still decided to rebuild the engine, then it is time to decide how you will rebuild it.

➡The editors at Chilton feel that most engine machining should be performed by a professional machine shop. Think of it as an assurance that the job has been done right the first time. There are many expensive and specialized tools required to perform such tasks as boring and honing an engine block or having a valve job done on a cylinder head. Even inspecting the parts requires expensive micrometers and gauges to properly measure wear and clearances. A machine shop can deliver to you clean, and ready to assemble parts, saving you time and aggravation. Your maximum savings will come from performing the removal, disassembly, assembly and installation of the engine and purchasing or renting only the tools required to perform these tasks.

A complete rebuild or overhaul of an engine involves replacing all of the moving parts (pistons, rods, crankshaft, camshaft, etc.) with new ones and machining the non-moving wearing surfaces of the block and heads. Unfortunately, this may not be cost effective. For instance, your crankshaft may have been damaged or worn, but it can be machined undersize for a minimal fee.

So although you can replace everything inside the engine, it is usually wiser to replace only those parts which are really needed, and, if possible, repair the more expensive ones. Later in this section, we will break the engine down into its two main components: the cylinder head and the engine block. We will discuss each component, and the recommended parts to replace during a rebuild on each.

Engine Overhaul Tips

Most engine overhaul procedures are fairly standard. In addition to specific parts replacement procedures and specifications for your individual engine, this section is also a guide to acceptable rebuilding procedures. Examples of standard rebuilding practice are given and should be used along with specific details concerning your particular engine.

Competent and accurate machine shop services will ensure maximum performance, reliability and engine life. In most instances it is more profitable for the do-it-yourself mechanic to remove, clean and inspect the component, buy the necessary parts and deliver these to a shop for actual machine work.

Much of the assembly work (crankshaft, bearings, piston rods, and other components) is well within the scope of the do-it-yourself mechanic's tools and abilities. You will have to decide for yourself the depth of involvement you desire in an engine repair or rebuild.

TOOLS

The tools required for an engine overhaul or parts replacement will depend on the depth of your involvement. With a few exceptions, they will be the tools found in a mechanic's tool kit (see Section 1 of this manual). More in-depth work will require some or all of the following:
- A dial indicator (reading in thousandths) mounted on a universal base
- Micrometers and telescope gauges
- Jaw and screw-type pullers
- Scraper
- Valve spring compressor
- Ring groove cleaner
- Piston ring expander and compressor
- Ridge reamer
- Cylinder hone or glaze breaker
- Plastigage®
- Engine stand

The use of most of these tools is illustrated in this section. Many can be rented for a one-time use from a local parts jobber or tool supply house specializing in automotive work.

Occasionally, the use of special tools is called for. See the information on Special Tools and the Safety Notice in the front of this book before substituting another tool.

OVERHAUL TIPS

Aluminum has become extremely popular for use in engines, due to its low weight. Observe the following precautions when handling aluminum parts:
- Never hot tank aluminum parts (the caustic hot tank solution will eat the aluminum.)
- Remove all aluminum parts (identification tag, etc.) from engine parts prior to the tanking.
- Always coat threads lightly with engine oil or anti-seize compounds before installation, to prevent seizure.
- Never overtighten bolts or spark plugs especially in aluminum threads.

When assembling the engine, any parts that will be exposed to frictional contact must be prelubed to provide lubrication at initial start-up. Any product specifically formulated for this purpose can be used, but engine oil is not recommended as a prelube in most cases.

When semi-permanent (locked, but removable) installation of bolts or nuts is desired, threads should be cleaned and coated with Loctite® or another similar, commercial non-hardening sealant.

CLEANING

▶ **See Figures 149 thru 152**

Before the engine and its components are inspected, they must be thoroughly cleaned. You will need to remove any engine varnish, oil sludge and/or carbon deposits from all of the components to insure an accurate inspection. A crack in the engine block or cylinder head can easily become overlooked if hidden by a layer of sludge or carbon.

Most of the cleaning process can be carried out with common hand tools and readily available solvents or solutions. Carbon deposits can be chipped away using a hammer and a hard wooden chisel. Old gasket material and varnish or sludge can usually be removed using a scraper and/or cleaning solvent. Extremely stubborn deposits may require the use of a power drill with a wire brush. If using a wire brush, use extreme care around any critical machined surfaces (such as the gasket surfaces, bearing saddles, cylinder bores, etc.). Use of a wire brush is NOT RECOMMENDED on any aluminum components. Always follow any safety recommendations given by the manufacturer of the tool and/or solvent.

※※ CAUTION

Always wear eye protection during any cleaning process involving scraping, chipping or spraying of solvents.

An alternative to the mess and hassle of cleaning the parts yourself is to drop them off at a local garage or machine shop. They should have the necessary equipment to properly clean all of the parts for a nominal fee.

Remove any oil galley plugs, freeze plugs and/or pressed-in bearings and carefully wash and degrease all of the engine components including the fasteners and bolts. Small parts such as the valves, springs, etc., should be placed in a metal basket and allowed to soak. Use pipe cleaner type brushes, and clean all passageways in the components.

Use a ring expander and remove the rings from the pistons. Clean the piston ring grooves with a special tool or a piece of broken ring. Scrape the carbon off of the top of the piston. You should never use a wire brush on the pistons. After preparing all of the piston assemblies in this manner, wash and degrease them again.

※※ WARNING

Use extreme care when cleaning around the cylinder head valve seats. A mistake or slip may cost you a new seat.

When cleaning the cylinder head, remove carbon from the combustion chamber with the valves installed. This will avoid damaging the valve seats.

REPAIRING DAMAGED THREADS

▶ **See Figures 153, 154, 155, 156 and 157**

Several methods of repairing damaged threads are available. Heli-Coil® (shown here), Keenserts® and Microdot® are among the most widely used. All involve basically the same principle—drilling out stripped threads, tapping the hole and installing a prewound insert—making welding, plugging and oversize fasteners unnecessary.

Two types of thread repair inserts are usually supplied: a standard type for most inch coarse, inch fine, metric course and metric fine thread sizes and a spark lug type to fit most spark plug port sizes. Consult the individual tool manufacturer's catalog to determine exact applications. Typical thread repair kits will contain a selection of prewound threaded inserts, a tap (corresponding to the outside diameter threads of the insert) and an installation tool. Spark plug inserts usually differ because they require a tap equipped with pilot threads and a combined reamer/tap section. Most manufacturers also supply blister-packed

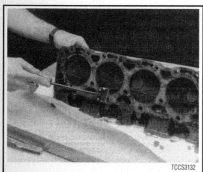

Fig. 149 Use a gasket scraper to remove the old gasket material from the mating surfaces

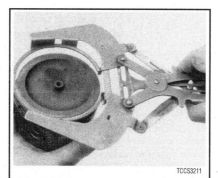

Fig. 150 Before cleaning and inspection, use a ring expander tool to remove the piston rings

Fig. 151 Clean the piston ring grooves using a ring groove cleaner tool, or . . .

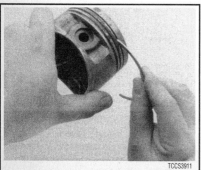

Fig. 152 . . . use a piece of an old ring to clean the grooves. Be careful, the ring can be quite sharp

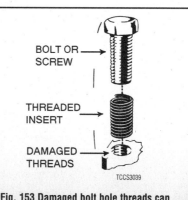

Fig. 153 Damaged bolt hole threads can be replaced with thread repair inserts

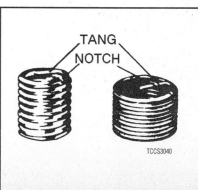

Fig. 154 Standard thread repair insert (left), and spark plug thread insert

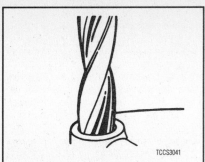

Fig. 155 Drill out the damaged threads with the specified size bit. Be sure to drill completely through the hole or to the bottom of a blind hole

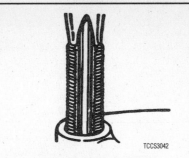

Fig. 156 Using the kit, tap the hole in order to receive the thread insert. Keep the tap well oiled and back it out frequently to avoid clogging the threads

Fig. 157 Screw the insert onto the installer tool until the tang engages the slot. Thread the insert into the hole until it is ¼–½ turn below the top surface, then remove the tool and break off the tang using a punch

thread repair inserts separately in addition to a master kit containing a variety of taps and inserts plus installation tools.

Before attempting to repair a threaded hole, remove any snapped, broken or damaged bolts or studs. Penetrating oil can be used to free frozen threads. The offending item can usually be removed with locking pliers or using a screw/stud extractor. After the hole is clear, the thread can be repaired as shown in the kit manufacturer's instructions.

Engine Preparation

To properly rebuild an engine, you must first remove it from the vehicle, then disassemble and diagnose it. Ideally you should place your engine on an engine stand. This affords you the best access to the engine components. Remove the flywheel or flexplate before installing the engine to the stand.

Now that you have the engine on a stand, and assuming that you have drained the oil and coolant from the engine, itís time to strip it of all but the necessary components. Before you start disassembling the engine, you may want to take a moment to draw some pictures, or fabricate some labels or containers to mark the locations of various components and the bolts and/or studs which fasten them. Modern day engines use a lot of little brackets and clips which hold wiring harnesses and such, and these holders are often mounted on studs and/or bolts that can be easily mixed up. The manufacturer spent a lot of time and money designing your vehicle, and they wouldnít have wasted any of it by haphazardly placing brackets, clips or fasteners on the vehicle. If itís present when you disassemble it, put it back when you assemble, you will regret not remembering that little bracket which holds a wire harness out of the path of a rotating part.

You should begin by unbolting any accessories still attached to the engine, such as the water pump, power steering pump, alternator, etc. Then, unfasten any manifolds (intake or exhaust) which were not removed during the engine removal procedure. Finally, remove any covers remaining on the engine such as the rocker arm, front or timing cover and oil pan. Some front covers may require the vibration damper and/or crank pulley to be removed beforehand. The idea is to reduce the engine to the bare necessities of cylinder head(s), valve train, engine block, crankshaft, pistons and connecting rods, plus any other ëin blockí components such as oil pumps, balance shafts and auxiliary shafts.

Finally, remove the cylinder head(s) from the engine block and carefully place on a bench. Disassembly instructions for each component follow later in this section.

Cylinder Head

There are two basic types of cylinder heads used on todayís automobiles: the Overhead Valve (OHV) and the Overhead Camshaft (OHC). The latter can also be broken down into two subgroups: the Single Overhead Camshaft (SOHC) and the Dual Overhead Camshaft (DOHC). Generally, if there is only a single camshaft on a head, it is just referred to as an OHC head. Also, an engine with an OHV cylinder head is also known as a pushrod engine.

Most cylinder heads these days are made of an aluminum alloy due to its light weight, durability and heat transfer qualities. However, cast iron was the material of choice in the past, and is still used on many vehicles. Whether made from aluminum or iron, all cylinder heads have valves and seats. Some use two valves per cylinder, while the more hi-tech engines will utilize a multi-valve

configuration using 3, 4 and even 5 valves per cylinder. When the valve contacts the seat, it does so on precision machined surfaces, which seals the combustion chamber. All cylinder heads have a valve guide for each valve. The guide centers the valve to the seat and allows it to move up and down within it. The clearance between the valve and guide can be critical. Too much clearance and the engine may consume oil, lose vacuum and/or damage the seat. Too little, and the valve can stick in the guide causing the engine to run poorly if at all, and possibly causing severe damage. The last component all automotive cylinder heads have are valve springs. The spring holds the valve against its seat. It also returns the valve to this position when the valve has been opened by the valve train or camshaft. The spring is fastened to the valve by a retainer and valve locks (sometimes called keepers). Aluminum heads will also have a valve spring shim to keep the spring from wearing away the aluminum.

An ideal method of rebuilding the cylinder head would involve replacing all of the valves, guides, seats, springs, etc. with new ones. However, depending on how the engine was maintained, often this is not necessary. A major cause of valve, guide and seat wear is an improperly tuned engine. An engine that is running too rich, will often wash the lubricating oil out of the guide with gasoline, causing it to wear rapidly. Conversely, an engine which is running too lean will place higher combustion temperatures on the valves and seats allowing them to wear or even burn. Springs fall victim to the driving habits of the individual. A driver who often runs the engine rpm to the redline will wear out or break the springs faster then one that stays well below it. Unfortunately, mileage takes it toll on all of the parts. Generally, the valves, guides, springs and seats in a cylinder head can be machined and re-used, saving you money. However, if a valve is burnt, it may be wise to replace all of the valves, since they were all operating in the same environment. The same goes for any other component on the cylinder head. Think of it as an insurance policy against future problems related to that component.

Unfortunately, the only way to find out which components need replacing, is to disassemble and carefully check each piece. After the cylinder head(s) are disassembled, thoroughly clean all of the components.

DISASSEMBLY

Except the 2.3 and 4.0L SOHC (VIN E) Engines

◆ See Figures 158 thru 163

Before disassembling the cylinder head, you may want to fabricate some containers to hold the various parts, as some of them can be quite small (such as keepers) and easily lost. Also keeping yourself and the components organized will aid in assembly and reduce confusion. Where possible, try to maintain a components original location; this is especially important if there is not going to be any machine work performed on the components.

1. If you havenít already removed the rocker arms and/or shafts, do so now.
2. Position the head so that the springs are easily accessed.
3. Use a valve spring compressor tool, and relieve spring tension from the retainer.

➡**Due to engine varnish, the retainer may stick to the valve locks. A gentle tap with a hammer may help to break it loose.**

4. Remove the valve locks from the valve tip and/or retainer. A small magnet may help in removing the locks.

Fig. 158 When removing an OHV valve spring, use a compressor tool to relieve the tension from the retainer

Fig. 159 A small magnet will help in removal of the valve locks

Fig. 160 Be careful not to lose the small valve locks (keepers)

Fig. 161 Remove the valve seal from the valve stem—O-ring type seal shown

Fig. 162 Removing an umbrella/positive type seal

Fig. 163 Invert the cylinder head and withdraw the valve from the valve guide bore

5. Lift the valve spring, tool and all, off of the valve stem.

6. If equipped, remove the valve seal. If the seal is difficult to remove with the valve in place, try removing the valve first, then the seal. Follow the steps below for valve removal.

7. Position the head to allow access for withdrawing the valve.

➡**Cylinder heads that have seen a lot of miles and/or abuse may have mushroomed the valve lock grove and/or tip, causing difficulty in removal of the valve. If this has happened, use a metal file to carefully remove the high spots around the lock grooves and/or tip. Only file it enough to allow removal.**

8. Remove the valve from the cylinder head.

9. If equipped, remove the valve spring shim. A small magnetic tool or screwdriver will aid in removal.

10. Repeat Steps 3 though 9 until all of the valves have been removed.

2.3L, 2.5L and 4.0L SOHC (VIN E) Engines

▶ **See Figures 164 thru 176**

Whether it is a single or dual overhead camshaft cylinder head, the disassembly procedure is relatively unchanged. One aspect to pay attention to is careful labeling of the parts on the dual camshaft cylinder head. There will be an intake camshaft and followers as well as an exhaust camshaft and followers and they must be labeled as such. In some cases, the components are identical and could easily be installed incorrectly. DO NOT MIX THEM UP! Determining which is which is very simple; the intake camshaft and components are on the same side of the head as was the intake manifold. Conversely, the exhaust camshaft and components are on the same side of the head as was the exhaust manifold.

Most cylinder heads with rocker arm-type camshaft followers are easily disassembled using a standard valve spring compressor. However, certain models may not have enough open space around the spring for the standard tool and may require you to use a C-clamp style compressor tool instead.

1. If not already removed, remove the rocker arms and/or shafts and the camshaft. If applicable, also remove the hydraulic lash adjusters. Mark their positions for assembly.

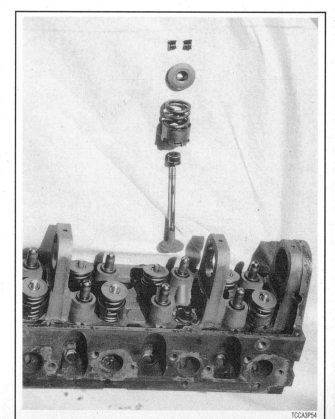

Fig. 164 Exploded view of a valve, seal, spring, retainer and locks from an OHC cylinder head

2. Position the cylinder head to allow access to the valve spring.

3. Use a valve spring compressor tool to relieve the spring tension from the retainer.

➡ **Due to engine varnish, the retainer may stick to the valve locks. A gentle tap with a hammer may help to break it loose.**

4. Remove the valve locks from the valve tip and/or retainer. A small magnet may help in removing the small locks.

5. Lift the valve spring, tool and all, off of the valve stem.

6. If equipped, remove the valve seal. If the seal is difficult to remove with the valve in place, try removing the valve first, then the seal. Follow the steps below for valve removal.

7. Position the head to allow access for withdrawing the valve.

➡ **Cylinder heads that have seen a lot of miles and/or abuse may have mushroomed the valve lock grove and/or tip, causing difficulty in removal of the valve. If this has happened, use a metal file to carefully remove the high spots around the lock grooves and/or tip. Only file it enough to allow removal.**

8. Remove the valve from the cylinder head.

9. If equipped, remove the valve spring shim. A small magnetic tool or screwdriver will aid in removal.

10. Repeat Steps 3 though 9 until all of the valves have been removed.

INSPECTION

Now that all of the cylinder head components are clean, it's time to inspect them for wear and/or damage. To accurately inspect them, you will need some specialized tools:
- A 0–1 in. micrometer for the valves
- A dial indicator or inside diameter gauge for the valve guides
- A spring pressure test gauge

If you do not have access to the proper tools, you may want to bring the components to a shop that does.

Fig. 165 Example of a multi-valve cylinder head. Note how it has 2 intake and 2 exhaust valve ports

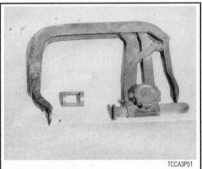

Fig. 166 C-clamp type spring compressor and an OHC spring removal tool (center) for cup type followers

Fig. 167 The 4.0L SOHC engine cylinder heads retain the camshaft using bolt-on bearing caps

Fig. 168 Example of the shaft mounted rocker arms on some OHC heads

Fig. 169 Another example of the rocker arm type OHC head. This model uses a follower under the camshaft

Fig. 170 Before the camshaft can be removed, all of the followers must first be removed . . .

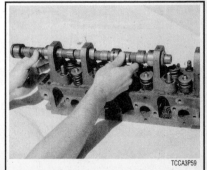

Fig. 171 . . . then the camshaft can be removed by sliding it out (shown), or unbolting a bearing cap (not shown)

Fig. 172 Compress the valve spring . . .

Fig. 173 . . . then remove the valve locks from the valve stem and spring retainer

Fig. 174 Remove the valve spring and retainer from the cylinder head

Fig. 175 Remove the valve seal from the guide. Some gentle prying or pliers may help to remove stubborn ones

Fig. 176 All aluminum and some cast iron heads will have these valve spring shims. Remove all of them as well

Fig. 177 Valve stems may be rolled on a flat surface to check for bends

Valves

▶ See Figures 177 and 178

The first thing to inspect are the valve heads. Look closely at the head, margin and face for any cracks, excessive wear or burning. The margin is the best place to look for burning. It should have a squared edge with an even width all around the diameter. When a valve burns, the margin will look melted and the edges rounded. Also inspect the valve head for any signs of tulipping. This will show as a lifting of the edges or dishing in the center of the head and will usually not occur to all of the valves. All of the heads should look the same, any that seem dished more than others are probably bad. Next, inspect the valve lock grooves and valve tips. Check for any burrs around the lock grooves, especially if you had to file them to remove the valve. Valve tips should appear flat, although slight rounding with high mileage engines is normal. Slightly worn valve tips will need to be machined flat. Last, measure the valve stem diameter with the micrometer. Measure the area that rides within the guide, especially towards the tip where most of the wear occurs. Take several measurements along its length and com-

pare them to each other. Wear should be even along the length with little to no taper. If no minimum diameter is given in the specifications, then the stem should not read more than 0.001 in. (0.025mm) below the unworn portion of the stem. Any valves that fail these inspections should be replaced.

Springs, Retainers and Valve Locks

▶ See Figures 179 and 180

The first thing to check is the most obvious, broken springs. Next check the free length and squareness of each spring. If applicable, insure to distinguish between intake and exhaust springs. Use a ruler and/or carpenter's square to measure the length. A carpenter's square should be used to check the springs for squareness. If a spring pressure test gauge is available, check each springs rating and compare to the specifications chart. Check the readings against the specifications given. Any springs that fail these inspections should be replaced.

The spring retainers rarely need replacing, however they should still be checked as a precaution. Inspect the spring mating surface and the valve lock

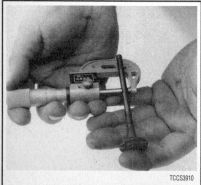

Fig. 178 Use a micrometer to check the valve stem diameter

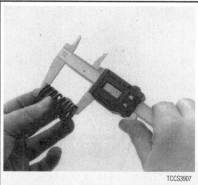

Fig. 179 Use a caliper to check the valve spring free-length

Fig. 180 Check the valve spring for squareness on a flat surface; a carpenter's square can be used

retention area for any signs of excessive wear. Also check for any signs of cracking. Replace any retainers that are questionable.

Valve locks should be inspected for excessive wear on the outside contact area as well as on the inner notched surface. Any locks which appear worn or broken and its respective valve should be replaced.

Cylinder Head

There are several things to check on the cylinder head: valve guides, seats, cylinder head surface flatness, cracks and physical damage.

VALVE GUIDES

▶ See Figure 181

Now that you know the valves are good, you can use them to check the guides, although a new valve, if available, is preferred. Before you measure anything, look at the guides carefully and inspect them for any cracks, chips or breakage. Also if the guide is a removable style (as in most aluminum heads), check them for any looseness or evidence of movement. All of the guides should appear to be at the same height from the spring seat. If any seem lower (or higher) from another, the guide has moved. Mount a dial indicator onto the spring side of the cylinder head. Lightly oil the valve stem and insert it into the cylinder head. Position the dial indicator against the valve stem near the tip and zero the gauge. Grasp the valve stem and wiggle towards and away from the dial indicator and observe the readings. Mount the dial indicator 90 degrees from the initial point and zero the gauge and again take a reading. Compare the two readings for an out of round condition. Check the readings against the specifications given. An Inside Diameter (I.D.) gauge designed for valve guides will give you an accurate valve guide bore measurement. If the I.D. gauge is used, compare the readings with the specifications given. Any guides that fail these inspections should be replaced or machined.

VALVE SEATS

A visual inspection of the valve seats should show a slightly worn and pitted surface where the valve face contacts the seat. Inspect the seat carefully for severe pitting or cracks. Also, a seat that is badly worn will be recessed into the cylinder head. A severely worn or recessed seat may need to be replaced. All cracked seats must be replaced. A seat concentricity gauge, if available, should be used to check the seat run-out. If run-out exceeds specifications the seat must be machined (if no specification is available given use 0.002 in. or 0.051mm).

CYLINDER HEAD SURFACE FLATNESS

▶ See Figures 182 and 183

After you have cleaned the gasket surface of the cylinder head of any old gasket material, check the head for flatness.

Place a straightedge across the gasket surface. Using feeler gauges, determine the clearance at the center of the straightedge and across the cylinder head at several points. Check along the centerline and diagonally on the head surface. If the warpage exceeds 0.003 in. (0.076mm) within a 6.0 in. (15.2cm) span, or 0.006 in. (0.152mm) over the total length of the head, the cylinder head must be resurfaced. After resurfacing the heads of a V-type engine, the intake manifold flange surface should be checked, and if necessary, milled proportionally to allow for the change in its mounting position.

CRACKS AND PHYSICAL DAMAGE

Generally, cracks are limited to the combustion chamber, however, it is not uncommon for the head to crack in a spark plug hole, port, outside of the head or in the valve spring/rocker arm area. The first area to inspect is always the hottest: the exhaust seat/port area.

A visual inspection should be performed, but just because you donít see a crack does not mean it is not there. Some more reliable methods for inspecting for cracks include Magnaflux®, a magnetic process or Zyglo®, a dye penetrant. Magnaflux® is used only on ferrous metal (cast iron) heads. Zyglo® uses a spray on fluorescent mixture along with a black light to reveal the cracks. It is strongly recommended to have your cylinder head checked professionally for cracks, especially if the engine was known to have overheated and/or leaked or consumed coolant. Contact a local shop for availability and pricing of these services.

Physical damage is usually very evident. For example, a broken mounting ear from dropping the head or a bent or broken stud and/or bolt. All of these defects should be fixed or, if unrepairable, the head should be replaced.

Camshaft and Followers

Inspect the camshaft(s) and followers as described earlier in this section.

REFINISHING & REPAIRING

Many of the procedures given for refinishing and repairing the cylinder head components must be performed by a machine shop. Certain steps, if the inspected part is not worn, can be performed yourself inexpensively. However, you spent a lot of time and effort so far, why risk trying to save a couple bucks if you might have to do it all over again?

Valves

Any valves that were not replaced should be refaced and the tips ground flat. Unless you have access to a valve grinding machine, this should be done by a machine shop. If the valves are in extremely good condition, as well as the valve seats and guides, they may be lapped in without performing machine work.

It is a recommended practice to lap the valves even after machine work has been performed and/or new valves have been purchased. This insures a positive seal between the valve and seat.

LAPPING THE VALVES

➡ Before lapping the valves to the seats, read the rest of the cylinder head section to insure that any related parts are in acceptable enough condition to continue. Also, remember that before any valve seat machining and/or lapping can be performed, the guides must be within factory recommended specifications.

1. Invert the cylinder head.
2. Lightly lubricate the valve stems and insert them into the cylinder head in their numbered order.

Fig. 181 A dial gauge may be used to check valve stem-to-guide clearance; read the gauge while moving the valve stem

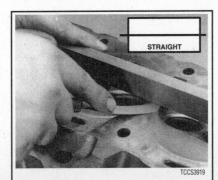

Fig. 182 Check the head for flatness across the center of the head surface using a straightedge and feeler gauge

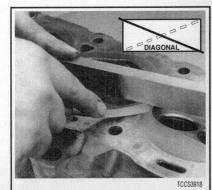

Fig. 183 Checks should also be made along both diagonals of the head surface

3. Raise the valve from the seat and apply a small amount of fine lapping compound to the seat.

4. Moisten the suction head of a hand-lapping tool and attach it to the head of the valve.

5. Rotate the tool between the palms of both hands, changing the position of the valve on the valve seat and lifting the tool often to prevent grooving.

6. Lap the valve until a smooth, polished circle is evident on the valve and seat.

7. Remove the tool and the valve. Wipe away all traces of the grinding compound and store the valve to maintain its lapped location.

❋❋ WARNING

Do not get the valves out of order after they have been lapped. They must be put back with the same valve seat with which they were lapped.

Springs, Retainers and Valve Locks

There is no repair or refinishing possible with the springs, retainers and valve locks. If they are found to be worn or defective, they must be replaced with new (or known good) parts.

Cylinder Head

Most refinishing procedures dealing with the cylinder head must be performed by a machine shop. Read the sections below and review your inspection data to determine whether or not machining is necessary.

VALVE GUIDE

➡**If any machining or replacements are made to the valve guides, the seats must be machined.**

Unless the valve guides need machining or replacing, the only service to perform is to thoroughly clean them of any dirt or oil residue.

There are only two types of valve guides used on automobile engines: the replaceable-type (all aluminum heads) and the cast-in integral-type (most cast iron heads). There are four recommended methods for repairing worn guides.

• Knurling
• Inserts
• Reaming oversize
• Replacing

Knurling is a process in which metal is displaced and raised, thereby reducing clearance, giving a true center, and providing oil control. It is the least expensive way of repairing the valve guides. However, it is not necessarily the best, and in some cases, a knurled valve guide will not stand up for more than a short time. It requires a special knurlizer and precision reaming tools to obtain proper clearances. It would not be cost effective to purchase these tools, unless you plan on rebuilding several of the same cylinder head.

Installing a guide insert involves machining the guide to accept a bronze insert. One style is the coil-type which is installed into a threaded guide. Another is the thin-walled insert where the guide is reamed oversize to accept a split-sleeve insert. After the insert is installed, a special tool is then run through the guide to expand the insert, locking it to the guide. The insert is then reamed to the standard size for proper valve clearance.

Reaming for oversize valves restores normal clearances and provides a true valve seat. Most cast-in type guides can be reamed to accept an valve with an oversize stem. The cost factor for this can become quite high as you will need to purchase the reamer and new, oversize stem valves for all guides which were reamed. Oversizes are generally 0.003–0.030 in. (0.076–0.762mm), with 0.015 in. (0.381mm) being the most common.

To replace cast-in type valve guides, they must be drilled out, then reamed to accept replacement guides. This must be done on a fixture which will allow centering and leveling off of the original valve seat or guide, otherwise a serious guide-to-seat misalignment may occur making it impossible to properly machine the seat.

Replaceable-type guides are pressed into the cylinder head. A hammer and a stepped drift or punch may be used to install and remove the guides. Before removing the guides, measure the protrusion on the spring side of the head and record it for installation. Use the stepped drift to hammer out the old guide from the combustion chamber side of the head. When installing, determine whether or not the guide also seals a water jacket in the head, and if it does, use the recommended sealing agent. If there is no water jacket, grease the valve guide and

its bore. Use the stepped drift, and hammer the new guide into the cylinder head from the spring side of the cylinder head. A stack of washers the same thickness as the measured protrusion may help the installation process.

VALVE SEATS

➡**Before any valve seat machining can be performed, the guides must be within factory recommended specifications. If any machining occurred or if replacements were made to the valve guides, the seats must be machined.**

If the seats are in good condition, the valves can be lapped to the seats, and the cylinder head assembled. See the valves section for instructions on lapping.

If the valve seats are worn, cracked or damaged, they must be serviced by a machine shop. The valve seat must be perfectly centered to the valve guide, which requires very accurate machining.

CYLINDER HEAD SURFACE

If the cylinder head is warped, it must be machined flat. If the warpage is extremely severe, the head may need to be replaced. In some instances, it may be possible to straighten a warped head enough to allow machining. In either case, contact a professional machine shop for service.

➡**Any OHC cylinder head that shows excessive warpage should have the camshaft bearing journals align bored after the cylinder head has been resurfaced.**

❋❋ WARNING

Failure to align bore the camshaft bearing journals could result in severe engine damage including but not limited to: valve and piston damage, connecting rod damage, camshaft and/or crankshaft breakage.

Certain cracks can be repaired in both cast iron and aluminum heads. For cast iron, a tapered threaded insert is installed along the length of the crack. Aluminum can also use the tapered inserts, however welding is the preferred method. Some physical damage can be repaired through brazing or welding. Contact a machine shop to get expert advice for your particular dilemma.

ASSEMBLY

The first step for any assembly job is to have a clean area in which to work. Next, thoroughly clean all of the parts and components that are to be assembled. Finally, place all of the components onto a suitable work space and, if necessary, arrange the parts to their respective positions.

Except the 2.3L, 2.5L and 4.0L SOHC (VIN E) Engines

1. Lightly lubricate the valve stems and insert all of the valves into the cylinder head. If possible, maintain their original locations.

2. If equipped, install any valve spring shims which were removed.

3. If equipped, install the new valve seals, keeping the following in mind:

• If the valve seal presses over the guide, lightly lubricate the outer guide surfaces.

• If the seal is an O-ring type, it is installed just after compressing the spring but before the valve locks.

4. Place the valve spring and retainer over the stem.

5. Position the spring compressor tool and compress the spring.

6. Assemble the valve locks to the stem.

7. Relieve the spring pressure slowly and insure that neither valve lock becomes dislodged by the retainer.

8. Remove the spring compressor tool.

9. Repeat Steps 2 through 8 until all of the springs have been installed.

2.3L, 2.5L and 4.0L SOHC (VIN E) Engines

1. Lightly lubricate the valve stems and insert all of the valves into the cylinder head. If possible, maintain their original locations.

2. If equipped, install any valve spring shims which were removed.

3. If equipped, install the new valve seals, keeping the following in mind:

• If the valve seal presses over the guide, lightly lubricate the outer guide surfaces.

- If the seal is an O-ring type, it is installed just after compressing the spring but before the valve locks.
  4. Place the valve spring and retainer over the stem.
  5. Position the spring compressor tool and compress the spring.
  6. Assemble the valve locks to the stem.
  7. Relieve the spring pressure slowly and insure that neither valve lock becomes dislodged by the retainer.
  8. Remove the spring compressor tool.
  9. Repeat Steps 2 through 8 until all of the springs have been installed.
  10. Install the camshaft(s), rockers, shafts and any other components that were removed for disassembly.

Engine Block

GENERAL INFORMATION

A thorough overhaul or rebuild of an engine block would include replacing the pistons, rings, bearings, timing belt/chain assembly and oil pump. For OHV engines also include a new camshaft and lifters. The block would then have the cylinders bored and honed oversize (or if using removable cylinder sleeves, new sleeves installed) and the crankshaft would be cut undersize to provide new wearing surfaces and perfect clearances. However, your particular engine may not have everything worn out. What if only the piston rings have worn out and the clearances on everything else are still within factory specifications? Well, you could just replace the rings and put it back together, but this would be a very rare example. Chances are, if one component in your engine is worn, other components are sure to follow, and soon. At the very least, you should always replace the rings, bearings and oil pump. This is what is commonly called a "freshen up".

Cylinder Ridge Removal

Because the top piston ring does not travel to the very top of the cylinder, a ridge is built up between the end of the travel and the top of the cylinder bore.

Pushing the piston and connecting rod assembly past the ridge can be difficult, and damage to the piston ring lands could occur. If the ridge is not removed before installing a new piston or not removed at all, piston ring breakage and piston damage may occur.

➡It is always recommended that you remove any cylinder ridges before removing the piston and connecting rod assemblies. If you know that new pistons are going to be installed and the engine block will be bored oversize, you may be able to forego this step. However, some ridges may actually prevent the assemblies from being removed, necessitating its removal.

There are several different types of ridge reamers on the market, none of which are inexpensive. Unless a great deal of engine rebuilding is anticipated, borrow or rent a reamer.
  1. Turn the crankshaft until the piston is at the bottom of its travel.
  2. Cover the head of the piston with a rag.
  3. Follow the tool manufacturers instructions and cut away the ridge, exercising extreme care to avoid cutting too deeply.
  4. Remove the ridge reamer, the rag and as many of the cuttings as possible. Continue until all of the cylinder ridges have been removed.

DISASSEMBLY

▶ **See Figures 184 and 185**

The engine disassembly instructions following assume that you have the engine mounted on an engine stand. If not, it is easiest to disassemble the engine on a bench or the floor with it resting on the bell housing or transmission mounting surface. You must be able to access the connecting rod fasteners and turn the crankshaft during disassembly. Also, all engine covers (timing, front, side, oil pan, whatever) should have already been removed. Engines which are seized or locked up may not be able to be completely disassembled, and a core (salvage yard) engine should be purchased.

Except the 2.3L, 2.5L and 4.0L SOHC (VIN E) Engines

If not done during the cylinder head removal, remove the pushrods and lifters, keeping them in order for assembly. Remove the timing gears and/or tim-

ing chain assembly, then remove the oil pump drive assembly and withdraw the camshaft from the engine block. Remove the oil pick-up and pump assembly. If equipped, remove any balance or auxiliary shafts. If necessary, remove the cylinder ridge from the top of the bore. See the cylinder ridge removal procedure earlier in this section.

2.3L, 2.5L and 4.0L SOHC (VIN E) Engines

If not done during the cylinder head removal, remove the timing chain/belt and/or gear/sprocket assembly. Remove the oil pick-up and pump assembly and, if necessary, the pump drive. If equipped, remove any balance or auxiliary shafts. If necessary, remove the cylinder ridge from the top of the bore. See the cylinder ridge removal procedure earlier in this section.

All Engines

Rotate the engine over so that the crankshaft is exposed. Use a number punch or scribe and mark each connecting rod with its respective cylinder number. The cylinder closest to the front of the engine is always number 1. However, depending on the engine placement, the front of the engine could either be the flywheel or damper/pulley end. Generally the front of the engine faces the front of the vehicle. Use a number punch or scribe and also mark the main bearing caps from front to rear with the front most cap being number 1 (if there are five caps, mark them 1 through 5, front to rear).

✴✴ WARNING

Take special care when pushing the connecting rod up from the crankshaft because the sharp threads of the rod bolts/studs will score the crankshaft journal. Insure that special plastic caps are installed over them, or cut two pieces of rubber hose to do the same.

Again, rotate the engine, this time to position the number one cylinder bore (head surface) up. Turn the crankshaft until the number one piston is at the bottom of its travel, this should allow the maximum access to its connecting rod. Remove the number one connecting rods fasteners and cap and place two lengths of rubber hose over the rod bolts/studs to protect the crankshaft from damage. Using a sturdy wooden dowel and a hammer, push the connecting rod up about 1 in. (25mm) from the crankshaft and remove the upper bearing insert. Continue pushing or tapping the connecting rod up until the piston rings are out of the cylinder bore. Remove the piston and rod by hand, put the upper half of the bearing insert back into the rod, install the cap with its bearing insert installed, and hand-tighten the cap fasteners. If the parts are kept in order in this manner, they will not get lost and you will be able to tell which bearings came form what cylinder if any problems are discovered and diagnosis is necessary. Remove all the other piston assemblies in the same manner. On V-style engines, remove all of the pistons from one bank, then reposition the engine with the other cylinder bank head surface up, and remove that banks piston assemblies.

The only remaining component in the engine block should now be the crankshaft. Loosen the main bearing caps evenly until the fasteners can be turned by hand, then remove them and the caps. Remove the crankshaft from the engine block. Thoroughly clean all of the components.

Fig. 184 Place rubber hose over the connecting rod studs to protect the crankshaft and cylinder bores from damage

TCCS3803

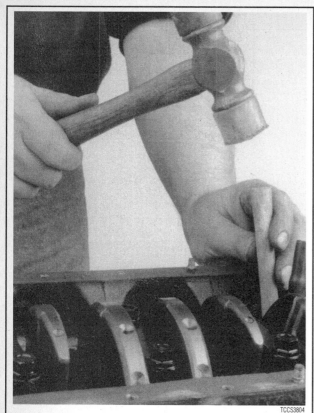

Fig. 185 Carefully tap the piston out of the bore using a wooden dowel

INSPECTION

Now that the engine block and all of its components are clean, itís time to inspect them for wear and/or damage. To accurately inspect them, you will need some specialized tools:

• Two or three separate micrometers to measure the pistons and crankshaft journals
• A dial indicator
• Telescoping gauges for the cylinder bores
• A rod alignment fixture to check for bent connecting rods

If you do not have access to the proper tools, you may want to bring the components to a shop that does.

Generally, you shouldnít expect cracks in the engine block or its components unless it was known to leak, consume or mix engine fluids, it was severely overheated, or there was evidence of bad bearings and/or crankshaft damage. A visual inspection should be performed on all of the components, but just because you donít see a crack does not mean it is not there. Some more reliable methods for inspecting for cracks include Magnaflux®, a magnetic process or Zyglo®, a dye penetrant. Magnaflux® is used only on ferrous metal (cast iron). Zyglo® uses a spray on fluorescent mixture along with a black light to reveal the cracks. It is strongly recommended to have your engine block checked professionally for cracks, especially if the engine was known to have overheated and/or leaked or consumed coolant. Contact a local shop for availability and pricing of these services.

Engine Block

ENGINE BLOCK BEARING ALIGNMENT

Remove the main bearing caps and, if still installed, the main bearing inserts. Inspect all of the main bearing saddles and caps for damage, burrs or high spots. If damage is found, and it is caused from a spun main bearing, the block will need to be align-bored or, if severe enough, replacement. Any burrs or high spots should be carefully removed with a metal file.

Place a straightedge on the bearing saddles, in the engine block, along the centerline of the crankshaft. If any clearance exists between the straightedge and the saddles, the block must be align-bored.

Align-boring consists of machining the main bearing saddles and caps by means of a flycutter that runs through the bearing saddles.

DECK FLATNESS

The top of the engine block where the cylinder head mounts is called the deck. Insure that the deck surface is clean of dirt, carbon deposits and old gasket material. Place a straightedge across the surface of the deck along its centerline and, using feeler gauges, check the clearance along several points. Repeat the checking procedure with the straightedge placed along both diagonals of the deck surface. If the reading exceeds 0.003 in. (0.076mm) within a 6.0 in. (15.2cm) span, or 0.006 in. (0.152mm) over the total length of the deck, it must be machined.

CYLINDER BORES

▶ See Figure 186

The cylinder bores house the pistons and are slightly larger than the pistons themselves. A common piston-to-bore clearance is 0.0015–0.0025 in. (0.0381mm–0.0635mm). Inspect and measure the cylinder bores. The bore should be checked for out-of-roundness, taper and size. The results of this inspection will determine whether the cylinder can be used in its existing size and condition, or a rebore to the next oversize is required (or in the case of removable sleeves, have replacements installed).

The amount of cylinder wall wear is always greater at the top of the cylinder than at the bottom. This wear is known as taper. Any cylinder that has a taper of 0.0012 in. (0.305mm) or more, must be rebored. Measurements are taken at a number of positions in each cylinder: at the top, middle and bottom and at two points at each position; that is, at a point 90 degrees from the crankshaft centerline, as well as a point parallel to the crankshaft centerline. The measurements are made with either a special dial indicator or a telescopic gauge and micrometer. If the necessary precision tools to check the bore are not available, take the block to a machine shop and have them mike it. Also if you donít have the tools to check the cylinder bores, chances are you will not have the necessary devices to check the pistons, connecting rods and crankshaft. Take these components with you and save yourself an extra trip.

For our procedures, we will use a telescopic gauge and a micrometer. You will need one of each, with a measuring range which covers your cylinder bore size.

1. Position the telescopic gauge in the cylinder bore, loosen the gauges lock and allow it to expand.

➡ Your first two readings will be at the top of the cylinder bore, then proceed to the middle and finally the bottom, making a total of six measurements.

2. Hold the gauge square in the bore, 90 degrees from the crankshaft centerline, and gently tighten the lock. Tilt the gauge back to remove it from the bore.

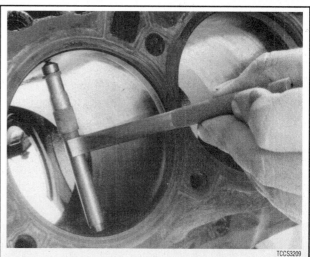

Fig. 186 Use a telescoping gauge to measure the cylinder bore diameter—take several readings within the same bore

3. Measure the gauge with the micrometer and record the reading.

4. Again, hold the gauge square in the bore, this time parallel to the crankshaft centerline, and gently tighten the lock. Again, you will tilt the gauge back to remove it from the bore.

5. Measure the gauge with the micrometer and record this reading. The difference between these two readings is the out-of-round measurement of the cylinder.

6. Repeat steps 1 through 5, each time going to the next lower position, until you reach the bottom of the cylinder. Then go to the next cylinder, and continue until all of the cylinders have been measured.

The difference between these measurements will tell you all about the wear in your cylinders. The measurements which were taken 90 degrees from the crankshaft centerline will always reflect the most wear. That is because at this position is where the engine power presses the piston against the cylinder bore the hardest. This is known as thrust wear. Take your top, 90 degree measurement and compare it to your bottom, 90 degree measurement. The difference between them is the taper. When you measure your pistons, you will compare these readings to your piston sizes and determine piston-to-wall clearance.

Crankshaft

Inspect the crankshaft for visible signs of wear or damage. All of the journals should be perfectly round and smooth. Slight scores are normal for a used crankshaft, but you should hardly feel them with your fingernail. When measuring the crankshaft with a micrometer, you will take readings at the front and rear of each journal, then turn the micrometer 90 degrees and take two more readings, front and rear. The difference between the front-to-rear readings is the journal taper and the first-to-90 degree reading is the out-of-round measurement. Generally, there should be no taper or out-of-roundness found, however, up to 0.0005 in. (0.0127mm) for either can be overlooked. Also, the readings should fall within the factory specifications for journal diameters.

If the crankshaft journals fall within specifications, it is recommended that it be polished before being returned to service. Polishing the crankshaft insures that any minor burrs or high spots are smoothed, thereby reducing the chance of scoring the new bearings.

Pistons and Connecting Rods

PISTONS

▶ See Figure 187

The piston should be visually inspected for any signs of cracking or burning (caused by hot spots or detonation), and scuffing or excessive wear on the skirts. The wrist pin attaches the piston to the connecting rod. The piston should move freely on the wrist pin, both sliding and pivoting. Grasp the connecting rod securely, or mount it in a vise, and try to rock the piston back and forth along the centerline of the wrist pin. There should not be any excessive play evident between the piston and the pin. If there are C-clips retaining the pin in the piston then you have wrist pin bushings in the rods. There should not be any excessive play between the wrist pin and the rod bushing. Normal clearance for the wrist pin is approx. 0.001–0.002 in. (0.025mm–0.051mm).

Fig. 187 Measure the piston's outer diameter, perpendicular to the wrist pin, with a micrometer

TCCS3210

Use a micrometer and measure the diameter of the piston, perpendicular to the wrist pin, on the skirt. Compare the reading to its original cylinder measurement obtained earlier. The difference between the two readings is the piston-to-wall clearance. If the clearance is within specifications, the piston may be used as is. If the piston is out of specification, but the bore is not, you will need a new piston. If both are out of specification, you will need the cylinder rebored and oversize pistons installed. Generally if two or more pistons/bores are out of specification, it is best to rebore the entire block and purchase a complete set of oversize pistons.

CONNECTING ROD

You should have the connecting rod checked for straightness at a machine shop. If the connecting rod is bent, it will unevenly wear the bearing and piston, as well as place greater stress on these components. Any bent or twisted connecting rods must be replaced. If the rods are straight and the wrist pin clearance is within specifications, then only the bearing end of the rod need be checked. Place the connecting rod into a vice, with the bearing inserts in place, install the cap to the rod and torque the fasteners to specifications. Use a telescoping gauge and carefully measure the inside diameter of the bearings. Compare this reading to the rods original crankshaft journal diameter measurement. The difference is the oil clearance. If the oil clearance is not within specifications, install new bearings in the rod and take another measurement. If the clearance is still out of specifications, and the crankshaft is not, the rod will need to be reconditioned by a machine shop.

➡**You can also use Plastigage® to check the bearing clearances. The assembling section has complete instructions on its use.**

Camshaft

Inspect the camshaft and lifters/followers as described earlier in this section.

Bearings

All of the engine bearings should be visually inspected for wear and/or damage. The bearing should look evenly worn all around with no deep scores or pits. If the bearing is severely worn, scored, pitted or heat blued, then the bearing, and the components that use it, should be brought to a machine shop for inspection. Full-circle bearings (used on most camshafts, auxiliary shafts, balance shafts, etc.) require specialized tools for removal and installation, and should be brought to a machine shop for service.

Oil Pump

➡**The oil pump is responsible for providing constant lubrication to the whole engine and so it is recommended that a new oil pump be installed when rebuilding the engine.**

Completely disassemble the oil pump and thoroughly clean all of the components. Inspect the oil pump gears and housing for wear and/or damage. Insure that the pressure relief valve operates properly and there is no binding or sticking due to varnish or debris. If all of the parts are in proper working condition, lubricate the gears and relief valve, and assemble the pump.

REFINISHING

▶ See Figure 188

Almost all engine block refinishing must be performed by a machine shop. If the cylinders are not to be rebored, then the cylinder glaze can be removed with a ball hone. When removing cylinder glaze with a ball hone, use a light or penetrating type oil to lubricate the hone. Do not allow the hone to run dry as this may cause excessive scoring of the cylinder bores and wear on the hone. If new pistons are required, they will need to be installed to the connecting rods. This should be performed by a machine shop as the pistons must be installed in the correct relationship to the rod or engine damage can occur.

Pistons and Connecting Rods

▶ See Figure 189

Only pistons with the wrist pin retained by C-clips are serviceable by the home-mechanic. Press fit pistons require special presses and/or heaters to remove/install the connecting rod and should only be performed by a machine shop.

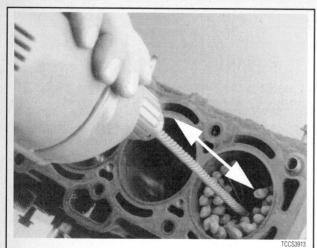

Fig. 188 Use a ball type cylinder hone to remove any glaze and provide a new surface for seating the piston rings

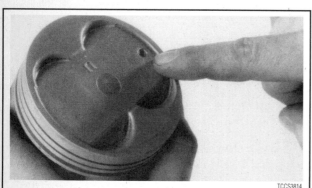

Fig. 189 Most pistons are marked to indicate positioning in the engine (usually a mark means the side facing the front)

All pistons will have a mark indicating the direction to the front of the engine and the must be installed into the engine in that manner. Usually it is a notch or arrow on the top of the piston, or it may be the letter F cast or stamped into the piston.

C-CLIP TYPE PISTONS

1. Note the location of the forward mark on the piston and mark the connecting rod in relation.
2. Remove the C-clips from the piston and withdraw the wrist pin.

➡ Varnish build-up or C-clip groove burrs may increase the difficulty of removing the wrist pin. If necessary, use a punch or drift to carefully tap the wrist pin out.

3. Insure that the wrist pin bushing in the connecting rod is usable, and lubricate it with assembly lube.
4. Remove the wrist pin from the new piston and lubricate the pin bores on the piston.
5. Align the forward marks on the piston and the connecting rod and install the wrist pin.
6. The new C-clips will have a flat and a rounded side to them. Install both C-clips with the flat side facing out.
7. Repeat all of the steps for each piston being replaced.

ASSEMBLY

Before you begin assembling the engine, first give yourself a clean, dirt free work area. Next, clean every engine component again. The key to a good assembly is cleanliness.

Mount the engine block into the engine stand and wash it one last time using water and detergent (dishwashing detergent works well). While washing it, scrub

the cylinder bores with a soft bristle brush and thoroughly clean all of the oil passages. Completely dry the engine and spray the entire assembly down with an anti-rust solution such as WD-40® or similar product. Take a clean lint-free rag and wipe up any excess anti-rust solution from the bores, bearing saddles, etc. Repeat the final cleaning process on the crankshaft. Replace any freeze or oil galley plugs which were removed during disassembly.

Crankshaft

◆ **See Figures 190, 191, 192 and 193**

1. Remove the main bearing inserts from the block and bearing caps.
2. If the crankshaft main bearing journals have been refinished to a definite undersize, install the correct undersize bearing. Be sure that the bearing inserts and bearing bores are clean. Foreign material under inserts will distort bearing and cause failure.
3. Place the upper main bearing inserts in bores with tang in slot.

➡ **The oil holes in the bearing inserts must be aligned with the oil holes in the cylinder block.**

4. Install the lower main bearing inserts in bearing caps.
5. Clean the mating surfaces of block and rear main bearing cap.
6. Carefully lower the crankshaft into place. Be careful not to damage bearing surfaces.
7. Check the clearance of each main bearing by using the following procedure:

  a. Place a piece of Plastigage® or its equivalent, on bearing surface across full width of bearing cap and about ¼ in. off center.

  b. Install cap and tighten bolts to specifications. Do not turn crankshaft while Plastigage® is in place.

  c. Remove the cap. Using the supplied Plastigage® scale, check width of Plastigage® at widest point to get maximum clearance. Difference between readings is taper of journal.

  d. If clearance exceeds specified limits, try a 0.001 in. or 0.002 in. undersize bearing in combination with the standard bearing. Bearing clearance must be within specified limits. If standard and 0.002 in. undersize bearing

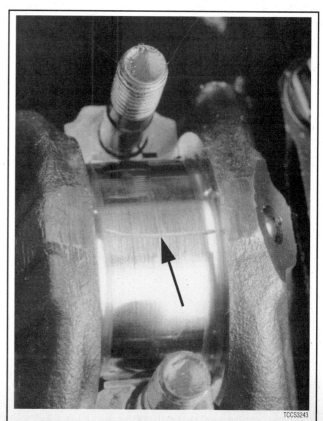

Fig. 190 Apply a strip of gauging material to the bearing journal, then install and torque the cap

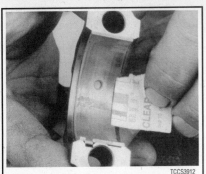

Fig. 191 After the cap is removed again, use the scale supplied with the gauging material to check the clearance

Fig. 192 A dial gauge may be used to check crankshaft end-play

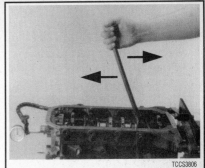

Fig. 193 Carefully pry the crankshaft back and forth while reading the dial gauge for end-play

does not bring clearance within desired limits, refinish crankshaft journal, then install undersize bearings.

8. After the bearings have been fitted, apply a light coat of engine oil to the journals and bearings. Install the rear main bearing cap. Install all bearing caps except the thrust bearing cap. Be sure that main bearing caps are installed in original locations. Tighten the bearing cap bolts to specifications.

9. Install the thrust bearing cap with bolts finger-tight.

10. Pry the crankshaft forward against the thrust surface of upper half of bearing.

11. Hold the crankshaft forward and pry the thrust bearing cap to the rear. This aligns the thrust surfaces of both halves of the bearing.

12. Retain the forward pressure on the crankshaft. Tighten the cap bolts to specifications.

13. Measure the crankshaft end-play as follows:

a. Mount a dial gauge to the engine block and position the tip of the gauge to read from the crankshaft end.

b. Carefully pry the crankshaft toward the rear of the engine and hold it there while you zero the gauge.

c. Carefully pry the crankshaft toward the front of the engine and read the gauge.

d. Confirm that the reading is within specifications. If not, install a new thrust bearing and repeat the procedure. If the reading is still out of specifications with a new bearing, have a machine shop inspect the thrust surfaces of the crankshaft, and if possible, repair it.

14. Install the rear main seal.

15. Rotate the crankshaft so as to position the first rod journal to the bottom of its stroke.

Pistons and Connecting Rods

▶ See Figures 194, 195, 196 and 197

1. Before installing the piston/connecting rod assembly, oil the pistons, piston rings and the cylinder walls with light engine oil. Install connecting rod bolt protectors or rubber hose onto the connecting rod bolts/studs. Also perform the following:

a. Select the proper ring set for the size cylinder bore.

b. Position the ring in the bore in which it is going to be used.

c. Push the ring down into the bore area where normal ring wear is not encountered.

d. Use the head of the piston to position the ring in the bore so that the ring is square with the cylinder wall. Use caution to avoid damage to the ring or cylinder bore.

e. Measure the gap between the ends of the ring with a feeler gauge. Ring gap in a worn cylinder is normally greater than specification. If the ring gap is greater than the specified limits, try an oversize ring set.

f. Check the ring side clearance of the compression rings with a feeler gauge inserted between the ring and its lower land according to specification. The gauge should slide freely around the entire ring circumference without binding. Any wear that occurs will form a step at the inner portion of the lower land. If the lower lands have high steps, the piston should be replaced.

2. Unless new pistons are installed, be sure to install the pistons in the cylinders from which they were removed. The numbers on the connecting rod and bearing cap must be on the same side when installed in the cylinder bore. If a connecting rod is ever transposed from one engine or cylinder to another, new bearings should be fitted and the connecting rod should be numbered to correspond with the new cylinder number. The notch on the piston head goes toward the front of the engine.

3. Install all of the rod bearing inserts into the rods and caps.

4. Install the rings to the pistons. Install the oil control ring first, then the second compression ring and finally the top compression ring. Use a piston ring expander tool to aid in installation and to help reduce the chance of breakage.

5. Make sure the ring gaps are properly spaced around the circumference of the piston. Fit a piston ring compressor around the piston and slide the piston and connecting rod assembly down into the cylinder bore, pushing it in with the wooden hammer handle. Push the piston down until it is only slightly below the top of the cylinder bore. Guide the connecting rod onto the crankshaft bearing journal carefully, to avoid damaging the crankshaft.

6. Check the bearing clearance of all the rod bearings, fitting them to the crankshaft bearing journals. Follow the procedure in the crankshaft installation above.

Fig. 194 Checking the piston ring-to-ring groove side clearance using the ring and a feeler gauge

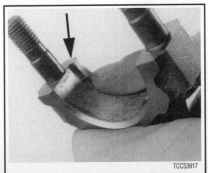

Fig. 195 The notch on the side of the bearing cap matches the tang on the bearing insert

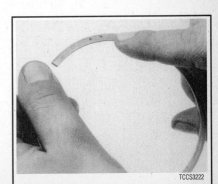

Fig. 196 Most rings are marked to show which side of the ring should face up when installed to the piston

Fig. 197 Install the piston and rod assembly into the block using a ring compressor and the handle of a hammer

7. After the bearings have been fitted, apply a light coating of assembly oil to the journals and bearings.

8. Turn the crankshaft until the appropriate bearing journal is at the bottom of its stroke, then push the piston assembly all the way down until the connecting rod bearing seats on the crankshaft journal. Be careful not to allow the bearing cap screws to strike the crankshaft bearing journals and damage them.

9. After the piston and connecting rod assemblies have been installed, check the connecting rod side clearance on each crankshaft journal.

10. Install the auxiliary/balance shaft(s)/assembly(ies).

11. Prime and install the oil pump and the oil pump intake tube.

Except the 2.3L, 2.5L and 4.0L SOHC (VIN E) Engines

CAMSHAFT, LIFTERS AND TIMING ASSEMBLY

1. Install the camshaft.
2. Install the lifters/followers into their bores.
3. Install the timing gears/chain assembly.

CYLINDER HEAD(S)

1. Install the cylinder head(s) using new gaskets.
2. Assemble the rest of the valve train (pushrods and rocker arms and/or shafts).

2.3L, 2.5L and 4.0L SOHC (VIN E) Engines

CYLINDER HEAD(S)

1. Install the cylinder head(s) using new gaskets.
2. Install the timing sprockets/gears and the belt/chain assemblies.

Engine Covers and Components

Install the timing cover(s) and oil pan. Refer to your notes and drawings made prior to disassembly and install all of the components that were removed. Install the engine into the vehicle.

Engine Start-up and Break-in

STARTING THE ENGINE

Now that the engine is installed and every wire and hose is properly connected, go back and double check that all coolant and vacuum hoses are connected. Check that your oil drain plug is installed and properly tightened. If not already done, install a new oil filter onto the engine. Fill the crankcase with the proper amount and grade of engine oil. Fill the cooling system with a 50/50 mixture of coolant/water.

1. Connect the vehicle battery.
2. Start the engine. Keep your eye on your oil pressure indicator; if it does not indicate oil pressure within 10 seconds of starting, turn the vehicle **OFF**.

✳✳ WARNING

Damage to the engine can result if it is allowed to run with no oil pressure. Check the engine oil level to make sure that it is full. Check for any leaks and if found, repair the leaks before continuing. If there is still no indication of oil pressure, you may need to prime the system.

3. Confirm that there are no fluid leaks (oil or other).
4. Allow the engine to reach normal operating temperature (the upper radiator hose will be hot to the touch).
5. At this point any necessary checks or adjustments can be performed, such as ignition timing.
6. Install any remaining components or body panels which were removed.

BREAKING IT IN

Make the first miles on the new engine, easy ones. Vary the speed but do not accelerate hard. Most importantly, do not lug the engine, and avoid sustained high speeds until at least 100 miles. Check the engine oil and coolant levels frequently. Expect the engine to use a little oil until the rings seat. Change the oil and filter at 500 miles, 1500 miles, then every 3000 miles past that.

KEEP IT MAINTAINED

Now that you have just gone through all of that hard work, keep yourself from doing it all over again by thoroughly maintaining it. Not that you may not have maintained it before, heck you could have had one to two hundred thousand miles on it before doing this. However, you may have bought the vehicle used, and the previous owner did not keep up on maintenance. Which is why you just went through all of that hard work. See?

ENGINE SPECIFICATIONS—2.3L ENGINE

Description	English	Metric
Type	Inline Single Overhead Camshaft (SOHC)	
Displacement	140 cu. in.	2.3L (2294cc)
Number of Cylinders	4	
Bore	3.780 in.	96.012mm
Stroke	3.126 in.	79.400mm
Compression ratio		
1991-93	9.2:1	
1994-97	9.4:1	
Valve lash (clearance)	Hydraulic	
Cylinder head		
Cylinder head-to-engine block surface warpage	0.003 in. (6 in. span)	0.0762mm (152.4mm span)
Valve seat width		
Intake valves	0.068-0.088 in.	1.727-2.235mm
Exhaust valve	0.070-0.090 in.	1.778-2.286mm
Valve seat angle—Intake and exhaust valves	45°	
Valve guide bore diameter—Intake and exhaust valves	0.3433-0.3443 in.	8.720-8.745mm
Valves, valve springs and camshaft		
Camshaft journal diameter (No.1-4)	1.7713-1.7720 in.	44.9910-45.0088mm
Camshaft-to-bearing clearance	0.001-0.003 in.	0.0254-0.0762mm
Camshaft thrust clearance	0.001-0.007 in.	0.0254-0.1778mm
Camshaft lobe lift		
Intake and exhaust valves		
1991-94	0.2381 in.	6.0477mm
1995-97	0.2163 in.	5.4940mm
Camshaft runout	0.005 in.	0.127mm
Camshaft follower (rocker) ratio	1.86:1	
Valve stem diameter		
Intake valves	0.2746-0.2754 in.	6.9748-6.9951mm
Exhaust valves	.2736-.2744 in.	6.9494-6.9697mm
Valve guide-to-valve stem clearance		
Intake valves	0.0010-0.0027 in.	0.0254-0.0686mm
Exhaust valves	0.0015-0.0032 in.	0.0381-0.08128mm
Valve face angle limit	44°	
Valve head diameter		
Intake valve	1.723-1.747 in.	43.764-44.374mm
Exhaust valve	1.490-1.510 in.	37.846-38.354mm
Valve head radial runout	0.002 in.	0.0508mm
Valve spring free length (approximate)	2.02 in.	51.308mm
Valve spring preload—Intake and exhaust valves	57-63 lbs. @ 1.56 in.	25.9-28.6 kg @ 39.62mm
Valve spring squareness	0.078 in.	1.9812mm
Valve spring installed height	1.54-1.56 in.	39.116-39.624mm
Engine block		
Engine block-to-cylinder head surface warpage	0.003 in. (6 in. span)	0.0762mm (152.4mm span)
Standard cylinder bore	3.7795-3.7801 in.	95.9993-96.0145mm
Cylinder bore out-of-round and taper	0.0015/0.010	
Cylinder bore-to-piston clearance	0.0024-0.0034 in.	0.061-0.086mm
Pistons		
Standard piston diameter	3.7883-3.7793 in.	95.969-95.994mm
Piston ring groove width		
Top compression ring	0.0598-0.0606 in.	1.5182-1.5392mm
Second compression ring	0.0598-0.0606 in.	1.5182-1.5392mm
Oil ring	0.1193-0.1203 in.	3.030-3.056mm
Piston pin diameter	0.9121-0.9122 in.	23.167-23.170mm

89683C01

ENGINE SPECIFICATIONS—2.3L ENGINE

Description	English	Metric
Piston rings		
Thickness		
Top compression ring	0.058-0.059 in.	1.46-1.49mm
Second compression ring	0.058-0.059 in.	1.46-1.49mm
Side clearance		
Top compression ring	0.0016-0.0033 in.	0.041-0.084mm
Second compression ring	0.0016-0.0033 in.	0.041-0.084mm
End-gap		
Top compression ring	0.008-0.016 in.	0.20-0.41mm
Second compression ring	0.013-0.019 in.	0.33-0.48mm
Oil ring	0.010-0.030 in.	0.33-0.76mm
Crankshaft and connecting rods		
Crankshaft main journal diameter	2.2051-2.2059 in.	56.0095-56.0298mm
Main bearing-to-journal clearance (oil clearance)	0.0008-0.0026 in.	0.02032-0.06604mm
Crankshaft journal out-of-round and taper	0.0006 in.	0.01524mm
Crankshaft thrust play	0.004-0.008 in.	0.1016-0.2032mm
Crankshaft runout	0.005 in.	0.127mm
Flywheel runout	0.005 in.	0.127mm
Connecting rod journal diameter	2.0464-2.0472 in.	51.9786-51.9989mm
Connecting rod journal-to-connecting rod clearance	0.0008-0.0026 in.	0.02032-0.06604mm
Connecting rod small end bore inside diameter	0.9104-0.9112 in.	23.124-23.144mm
Connecting rod journal out-of-round and taper	0.0006 in.	0.01524mm
Connecting rod big end side clearance	0.0035-0.0115 in.	0.0889-0.2921mm
Connecting rod twist	0.003 in.	0.0762mm
Connecting rod bend	0.0015 in.	0.0381mm

89683C02

ENGINE SPECIFICATIONS—2.5L ENGINE

Description	English	Metric
Type	Inline Single Overhead Camshaft (SOHC)	
Displacement	152.7 cu. in.	2.5L (2500cc)
Number of Cylinders	4	
Bore	3.780 in.	96.012mm
Stroke	3.402 in.	86.410mm
Compression ratio	9.4:1	
Valve lash (clearance)	Hydraulic	
Cylinder head		
Cylinder head-to-engine block surface warpage	0.003 in. (6 in. span)	0.0762mm (152.4mm span)
Valve seat width		
Intake valves	0.068-0.088 in.	1.727-2.235mm
Exhaust valve	0.070-0.090 in.	1.778-2.286mm
Valve seat angle—Intake and exhaust valves	44.75°	
Valve guide bore diameter—Intake and exhaust valves	0.2761-0.2773 in.	7.0129-7.0434mm
Valves, valve springs and camshaft		
Camshaft journal diameter (No.1-4)	1.7713-1.7720 in.	44.9910-45.0088mm
Camshaft-to-bearing clearance	0.001-0.003 in.	0.0254-0.0762mm
Camshaft thrust clearance	0.001-0.007 in.	0.0254-0.1778mm
Camshaft lobe lift		
Intake and exhaust valves	0.2163 in.	5.4940mm
Camshaft runout	0.005 in.	0.127mm
Camshaft follower (rocker) ratio	1.86:1	
Valve stem diameter		
Intake valves	0.2746-0.2754 in.	6.9748-6.9951mm
Exhaust valves	0.2736-0.2744 in.	6.9494-6.9697mm
Valve guide-to-valve stem clearance		
Intake valves	0.0008-0.0027 in.	0.0203-0.0686mm
Exhaust valves	0.0018-0.0037 in.	0.0457-0.0939mm
Valve face angle limit	44°	
Valve head diameter		
Intake valve	1.730-1.740 in.	43.942-44.196mm
Exhaust valve	1.490-1.510 in.	37.846-38.354mm
Valve head radial runout	0.002 in.	0.0508mm
Valve spring free length (approximate)	2.02 in.	51.308mm
Valve spring preload—Intake and exhaust valves	57-63 lbs. @ 1.56 in.	25.9-28.6 kg @ 39.62mm
Valve spring squareness	0.078 in.	1.9812mm
Valve spring installed height	1.54-1.56 in.	39.116-39.624mm
Engine block		
Engine block-to-cylinder head surface warpage	0.003 in. (6 in. span)	0.0762mm (152.4mm span)
Standard cylinder bore	3.7795-3.7801 in.	95.9993-96.0145mm
Cylinder bore out-of-round and taper	0.0015/0.010	
Cylinder bore-to-piston clearance	.001-.002 in.	.0254-.051mm
Pistons		
Standard piston diameter		
Red	3.7780-3.7785 in.	95.9612-95.9739mm
Blue	3.7785-3.7790 in.	95.9739-95.9866mm
Yellow	3.7790-3.7795 in.	95.9866-95.9993mm
Piston ring groove width		
Top compression ring	0.0600-0.0605 in.	1.524-1.5367mm
Second compression ring	0.0600-0.0605 in.	1.524-1.5367mm
Oil ring	0.1193-0.1203 in.	3.031-3.055mm

89683C51

ENGINE SPECIFICATIONS—2.5L ENGINE

Description	English	Metric
Piston pin diameter	0.9121-0.9122 in.	23.167-23.170mm
Piston rings		
Thickness		
Top compression ring	0.058-0.059 in.	1.46-1.49mm
Second compression ring	0.058-0.059 in.	1.46-1.49mm
Side clearance		
Top compression ring	0.0014-0.0030 in.	0.035-0.076mm
Second compression ring	0.0014-0.0030 in.	0.035-0.076mm
End-gap		
Top compression ring	0.008-0.018 in.	0.20-0.47mm
Second compression ring	0.013-0.023 in.	0.33-0.59mm
Oil ring	0.010-0.035 in.	0.33-0.889mm
Crankshaft and connecting rods		
Crankshaft main journal diameter	2.2051-2.2059 in.	56.0095-56.0298mm
Main bearing-to-journal clearance (oil clearance)	0.0008-0.0026 in.	0.02032-0.06604mm
Crankshaft journal out-of-round and taper	0.0006 in.	0.01524mm
Crankshaft thrust play	0.003-0.008 in.	0.0762-0.2032mm
Crankshaft runout	0.005 in.	0.127mm
Flywheel runout	0.005 in.	0.127mm
Connecting rod journal diameter	2.0464-2.0472 in.	51.9786-51.9989mm
Connecting rod journal-to-connecting rod clearance	0.0008-0.0026 in.	0.02032-0.06604mm
Connecting rod small end bore inside diameter	0.9096-0.9112 in.	23.104-23.144mm
Connecting rod journal out-of-round and taper	0.0004 in.	0.01016mm
Connecting rod big end side clearance	0.0035-0.0115 in.	0.0889-0.2921mm
Connecting rod twist	0.003 in.	0.0762mm
Connecting rod bend	0.0015 in.	0.0381mm

89683C52

ENGINE SPECIFICATIONS—2.9L ENGINE

Description	English	Metric
Pistons		
Standard piston diameter	3.6605-3.6615 in.	92.9767-93.0021mm
Piston ring groove width		
Top compression ring	0.0803-0.0811 in.	2.0396-2.0599mm
Second compression ring	0.1197-0.1205 in.	3.0404-3.0607mm
Oil control ring	0.1579-0.1587 in.	4.0107-4.0310mm
Piston pin diameter	0.9446-0.9450 in.	23.993-24.003mm
Piston rings		
Thickness		
Top compression ring	0.0778-0.0783 in.	1.9761-1.9888mm
Second compression ring	0.1172-0.1177 in.	2.9769-2.9896mm
Side clearance		
Top compression ring	0.0020-0.0033 in.	0.0508-0.08382mm
Second compression ring	0.0020-0.0033 in.	0.0508-0.08382mm
End-gap		
Top compression ring	0.015-0.023 in.	0.381-0.584mm
Second compression ring	0.015-0.023 in.	0.381-0.584mm
Oil ring	0.015-0.055 in.	0.381-1.397mm
Crankshaft and connecting rods		
Crankshaft main journal diameter	2.2433-2.2441 in.	56.9798-57.0001mm
Main bearing-to-journal clearance (oil clearance)	0.0005-0.0019 in.	0.0127-0.0483mm
Crankshaft journal out-of-round and taper	0.0006 in.	0.01524mm
Crankshaft thrust play	0.004-0.008 in.	0.1016-0.2032mm
Crankshaft runout	0.005 in.	0.127mm
Flywheel runout	0.005 in.	0.127mm
Connecting rod journal diameter	2.1252-2.1260 in.	53.9801-54.0004mm
Connecting rod journal-to-connecting rod clearance	0.0005-0.0022 in.	0.0127-0.0559mm
Connecting rod small end bore inside diameter	0.9450-0.9452 in.	24.003-24.0081mm
Connecting rod journal out-of-round and taper	0.0006 in.	0.01524mm
Connecting rod big end side clearance	0.004-0.011 in.	0.1016-0.2794mm
Connecting rod twist	0.006 in.	0.1524mm
Connecting rod bend	0.002 in.	0.0508mm

89683C04

ENGINE SPECIFICATIONS—2.9L ENGINE

Description	English	Metric
Type	60° V6 Over Head Valve Engine	2.9L (2900cc)
Displacement	177 cu. in.	
Number of Cylinders	6	
Bore	3.66 in.	93mm
Stroke	2.83 in.	72mm
Compression ratio	9.0:1	
Valve lash (clearance)	Hydraulic	
Cylinder head		
Cylinder head-to-engine block surface warpage	0.003 in. (6 in. span)	0.0762mm (152.4mm span)
Valve seat width		
Intake valves	0.060-0.079 in.	1.524-2.0066mm
Exhaust valve	0.060-0.079 in.	1.524-2.0066mm
Valve seat angle—Intake and exhaust valves	45°	
Valve guide bore diameter—Intake and exhaust valves	0.3174-0.3184 in.	8.0619-8.0874mm
Valves, valve springs and camshaft		
Camshaft journal diameter		
No. 1	1.7285-1.7293 in.	43.903-43.923mm
No. 2	1.7135-1.7143 in.	43.522-43.542mm
No. 3	1.6985-1.6992 in.	43.141-43.161mm
No. 4	1.6835-1.6842 in.	42.760-42.780 mm
Camshaft-to-bearing clearance	0.001-0.003 in.	0.0254-0.0762mm
Camshaft thrust clearance	0.0008-0.004 in.	0.0203-0.1016mm
Camshaft lobe lift		
Intake valve	0.246 in.	6.2484mm
Exhaust valve	0.254 in.	6.4516mm
Camshaft runout	0.005 in.	0.127mm
Valve stem diameter		
Intake valves	0.3159-0.3167 in.	8.0239-8.0449mm
Exhaust valves	0.3149-0.3156 in.	7.9985-8.0162mm
Valve guide-to-valve stem clearance		
Intake valves	0.0010-0.0027 in.	0.0254-0.0686mm
Exhaust valves	0.0015-0.0032 in.	0.0381-0.08128mm
Valve face angle limit	44°	
Valve head diameter		
Intake valve	1.78-1.81 in.	45.2-46.2mm
Exhaust valve	1.41-1.42 in.	35.82-36.21mm
Valve head radial runout	0.002 in.	0.0508mm
Valve spring free length (approximate)	1.91 in.	48.514mm
Valve spring preload—Intake and exhaust valves	60-68 lbs. @ 1.58 in.	27.2-30.9 kg @ 40.26mm
Valve spring squareness	0.078 in.	1.9812mm
Valve spring installed height	1.58-1.61 in.	40.132-40.894mm
Rocker arms, shaft and pushrods		
Rocker shaft diameter	0.7799-0.7811 in.	19.8095-19.8399mm
Rocker arm ratio	1.46:1	
Pushrod runout	0.020 in.	0.508mm
Engine block		
Engine block-to-cylinder head surface warpage	0.003 in. (6 in. span)	0.0762mm (152.4mm span)
Standard cylinder bore	3.6614-3.6630 in.	92.9995-93.0402mm
Cylinder bore out-of-round and taper	0.0015/0.010	
Cylinder bore-to-piston clearance	0.0024-0.0034 in.	0.061-0.086mm

89683C03

ENGINE SPECIFICATIONS—3.0L ENGINE

Description	English	Metric
Type	60° V6 Over Head Valve Engine	3.0L (2999cc)
Displacement	183 cu. in.	
Number of Cylinders	6	
Bore	3.50 in.	89mm
Stroke	3.14 in.	80mm
Compression ratio	9.3:1	
Valve lash (clearance)	Hydraulic	
Cylinder head		
Cylinder head-to-engine block surface warpage	0.003 in. (0.0762mm) in a 6.0 in. (152.4mm) span	
Valve seat width		
Intake valves	0.060-0.080 in.	1.524-2.032mm
Exhaust valve	0.060-0.080 in.	1.524-2.032mm
Valve seat angle—Intake and exhaust valves	45°	
Valve guide bore diameter—Intake and exhaust valves	0.3144-0.3154	7.9858-8.0112mm
Valves, valve springs and camshaft		
Camshaft journal diameter No. 1-4	2.0074-2.0084 in.	50.987-51.013mm
Camshaft-to-bearing clearance	0.001-0.003 in.	0.0254-0.0762mm
Camshaft thrust clearance	0.007 in. max	0.1778mm max
Camshaft lobe lift		
Intake valve	0.260 in.	6.604mm
Exhaust valve	0.260 in.	6.604mm
Camshaft runout	0.002 in.	0.0508mm
Valve stem diameter		
Intake valves	0.3126-0.3134 in.	7.940-7.960mm
Exhaust valves	0.3121-0.3129 in.	7.928-7.948mm
Valve guide-to-valve stem clearance		
Intake valves	0.0010-0.0027 in.	0.0254-0.0686mm
Exhaust valves	0.0015-0.0032 in.	0.0381-0.08128mm
Valve face angle limit	44°	
Valve head diameter		
Intake valve	1.57 in.	40.0mm
Exhaust valve	1.30 in.	33.0mm
Valve head radial runout	0.002 in.	0.0508mm
Valve spring free length (approximate)	1.84 in.	46.7mm
Valve spring preload—Intake and exhaust valves	65 lbs. @ 1.58 in.	29.51kg @ 40.1mm
Valve spring installed height	1.58 in.	40.132mm
Rocker arm ratio	1.61:1	
Engine block		
Engine block-to-cylinder head surface warpage	0.003 in. (0.0762mm) in a 6.0 in. (152.4mm) span	
Standard cylinder bore	3.504 in.	89.00mm
Cylinder bore out-of-round and taper	0.002 in.	0.050mm
Cylinder bore-to-piston clearance	0.0012-0.0023	0.030-0.051mm
Pistons		
Standard piston diameter	3.5024-3.5031 in.	88.962-883978mm
Piston ring groove width		
Top compression ring	0.0602-0.0612 in.	1.530-1.555mm
Second compression ring	0.0602-0.0612 in.	1.530-1.555mm
Oil control ring	0.1587-0.1596 in.	4.030-4.055mm
Piston pin diameter	0.9119-0.9124 in.	23.162-23.175mm

89683C05

ENGINE SPECIFICATIONS—3.0L ENGINE

Description	English	Metric
Piston rings		
Thickness		
Top compression ring	0.0575-0.0587 in.	1.460-1.490mm
Second compression ring	0.0575-0.0587 in.	1.460-1.490mm
Oil Control ring	Side seal - Snug fit	
Side clearance		
Top compression ring	0.0016-0.0037 in.	0.040-0.095mm
Second compression ring	0.0016-0.0037 in.	0.040-0.095mm
End-gap		
Top compression ring	0.010-0.020 in.	0.25-0.50mm
Second compression ring	0.010-0.020 in.	0.25-0.50mm
Oil ring	0.010-0.049 in.	0.25-1.25mm
Crankshaft and connecting rods		
Crankshaft journal diameter	2.5190-2.5198 in.	63.983-64.003mm
Bearing-to-journal clearance (oil clearance)	0.0005-0.0023 in.	0.020-0.066mm
Crankshaft journal out-of-round and taper	0.0006 in.	0.01524mm
Crankshaft thrust play	0.004-0.008 in.	0.1016-0.2032mm
Crankshaft runout	0.002 in.	0.050mm
Flywheel runout	0.005 in.	0.127mm
Connecting rod journal diameter	2.1253-2.1261 in.	53.983-54.003mm
Connecting rod journal-to-connecting rod clearance	0.0008-0.0027 in.	0.020-0.066mm
Connecting rod small end bore inside diameter	0.9096-0.9112 in.	23.105-23.145mm
Connecting rod journal out-of-round and taper	0.0006 in.	0.01524mm
Connecting rod big end side clearance	0.006-0.014 in.	0.15-0.35mm
Connecting rod twist	0.003 per in.	0.075 per 25mm
Connecting rod bend	0.016 per in.	0.04 per 25mm

89683C06

ENGINE SPECIFICATIONS—4.0L (VIN E) SOHC ENGINE

Description	English	Metric
Type	60° V6 Single Overhead Cam (SOHC) Engine	4.0L (3996cc)
Displacement	244 cu. in.	
Number of Cylinders	6	
Bore	3.9527 in.	100.4mm
Stroke	3.31 in.	84mm
Compression ratio	9.7:1	
Valve lash (clearance)	Hydraulic	
Cylinder head		
Cylinder head-to-engine block surface warpage	0.003 in. total	0.0762mm total
Valve seat width		
Intake valves	0.060-0.094 in.	1.524-2.404mm
Exhaust valve	0.050-0.083 in.	1.273-2.121mm
Valve seat angle—Intake and exhaust valves	45°	
Valve guide bore diameter—Intake and exhaust valves	0.275-0.276 in.	7.00-7.018mm
Valves, valve springs and camshaft		
Camshaft journal diameter—ALL	1.0998-1.100 in.	27.935-27.96mm
Camshaft-to-bearing clearance	0.001-0.003 in.	0.0254-0.0762mm
Camshaft thrust clearance	0.0029-0.007 in.	.075-.185mm
Camshaft lobe lift		
Intake valve	0.259 in.	6.584mm
Exhaust valve	0.259 in.	6.584mm
Camshaft runout	0.00197 in.	0.05mm
Valve stem diameter		
Intake valves	0.274-0.2748 in.	6.965-6.98mm
Exhaust valves	0.273-0.274 in.	6.95-6.965mm
Valve guide-to-valve stem clearance		
Intake valves	0.0008-0.0021 in.	0.020-0.053mm
Exhaust valves	0.0014-0.0027 in.	0.035-0.068mm
Valve face angle limit	45°	
Valve head diameter		
Intake valve	1.807-1.814 in.	45.9-46.1mm
Exhaust valve	1.531-1.539 in.	38.9-39.1mm
Valve head radial runout	0.0012 in.	0.03mm
Valve spring free length (approximate)	1.696 in.	43.1mm
Valve spring preload—Intake and exhaust valves	203-224 ft. lbs. @ 1.413-1.445 in.	275-305 Nm @ 35.9-36.7mm
Valve spring installed height	1.569-1.601 in.	39.64-40.68mm
Engine block		
Engine block-to-cylinder head surface warpage	0.003 in. total	0.0762mm total
Standard cylinder bore	3.952 in.	100.4mm
Cylinder bore out-of-round and taper	0.001 in.	0.025mm
Cylinder bore-to-piston clearance	0.0011-0.0023 in.	0.030-0.060mm
Pistons		
Standard piston diameter	3.952-3.9527 in.	100.38-100.40mm
Piston ring groove width		
Top compression ring	0.0645-0.0653 in.	1.64-1.66mm
Second compression ring	0.0704-0.0712 in.	1.79-1.81mm
Oil control ring	.1377-.1389 in.	3.50-3.53mm
Piston pin diameter	0.9446-0.94447 in.	23.993-23.997mm

89683C07

ENGINE SPECIFICATIONS—4.0L (VIN E) SOHC ENGINE

Description	English	Metric
Piston rings		
Thickness		
Top compression ring	0.0621-0.0629 in.	1.578-1.598mm
Second compression ring	0.068-0.069 in.	1.728-1.740mm
Side clearance		
Top compression ring	0.0020-0.0033 in.	0.0508-0.08382mm
Second compression ring	0.0020-0.0033 in.	0.0508-0.08382mm
End-gap		
Top compression ring	0.007-0.017 in.	0.20-0.45mm
Second compression ring	0.017-0.028 in.	0.45-0.70mm
Oil ring	Snug fit	
Crankshaft and connecting rods		
Crankshaft main journal diameter	2.2433-2.2441 in.	56.9798-57.0001mm
Main bearing-to-journal clearance (oil clearance)	0.0005-0.0019 in.	0.0127-0.0483mm
Crankshaft journal out-of-round and taper	0.0003 in.	0.00762mm
Crankshaft-to-rear face of block runout	0.005 in.	0.127mm
Crankshaft thrust play	0.002-0.0125 in.	0.05-0.32mm
Crankshaft runout	0.002 in.	0.05mm
Connecting rod journal diameter	2.7252-2.7260 in.	53.98-54.0mm
Connecting rod journal-to-connecting rod clearance	0.0003-0.0024 in.	0.008-0.061mm
Connecting rod small end bore inside diameter	0.943-0.9446 in.	23.958-23.976mm
Connecting rod journal out-of-round and taper	0.0003 in.	0.00762mm
Connecting rod big end side clearance	0.0036-0.0106 in.	0.092-0.268mm
Connecting rod twist	0.0015 per in.	0.038 per 25mm
Connecting rod bend	0.00049 per in.	0.0125 per 25mm

89683C08

ENGINE SPECIFICATIONS—4.0L (VIN X) ENGINE

Description	English	Metric
Type	60° V6 Over Head Valve Engine	
Displacement	241 cu. in.	4.0L (3949cc)
Number of Cylinders	6	
Bore	3.94 in.	100mm
Stroke	3.31 in.	84mm
Compression ratio	9.0:1	
Valve lash (clearance)	Hydraulic	
Cylinder head		
Cylinder head-to-engine block surface warpage	0.003 in. (6 in. span)	0.0762mm (152.4mm span)
Valve seat width		
Intake valves	0.060-0.079 in.	1.524-2.0066mm
Exhaust valve	0.060-0.079 in.	1.524-2.0066mm
Valve seat angle—Intake and exhaust valves	45°	
Valve guide bore diameter—Intake and exhaust valves	0.3174-0.3184 in.	8.0619-8.0874mm
Valves, valve springs and camshaft		
Camshaft journal diameter		
No. 1	1.951-1.952 in.	49.57-49.59mm
No. 2	1.937-1.938 in.	49.21-49.23mm
No. 3	1.922-1.923 in.	48.83-48.85mm
No. 4	1.907-1.908 in.	48.44-48.46mm
Camshaft-to-bearing clearance	0.001-0.003 in.	0.0254-0.0762mm
Camshaft thrust clearance	0.0008-0.004 in.	0.0203-0.1016mm
Camshaft lobe lift		
Intake valve	0.275 in.	6.985mm
Exhaust valve	0.275 in.	6.985mm
Camshaft runout	0.005 in.	0.127mm
Valve stem diameter		
Intake valves	0.3159-0.3167 in.	8.0239-8.0449mm
Exhaust valves	0.3149-0.3156 in.	7.9985-8.0162mm
Valve guide-to-valve stem clearance		
Intake valves	0.0008-0.0025 in.	0.02032-0.0635mm
Exhaust valves	0.0018-0.0035 in.	0.04572-0.0889mm
Valve face angle limit	44°	
Valve head diameter		
Intake valve	1.71 in.	43.5mm
Exhaust valve	1.36 in.	34.5mm
Valve head radial runout	0.002 in.	0.0508mm
Valve spring free length (approximate)	1.91 in.	48.514mm
Valve spring preload—Intake and exhaust valves	60-68 lbs. @ 1.58 in.	27.2-30.9 kg @ 40.26mm
Valve spring squareness	0.078 in.	1.9812mm
Valve spring installed height	1.58-1.61 in.	40.132-40.894mm
Rocker arms, shaft and pushrods		
Rocker shaft diameter	0.7799-0.7811 in.	19.8095-19.8399mm
Rocker arm ratio	1.46:1	
Pushrod runout	0.020 in.	0.508mm
Engine block		
Engine block-to-cylinder head surface warpage	0.003 in. (6 in. span)	0.0762mm (152.4mm span)
Standard cylinder bore	3.9527-3.9543 in.	100.399-100.439mm
Cylinder bore out-of-round and taper	0.0015/0.010	
Cylinder bore-to-piston clearance	0.0008-0.0019 in.	0.02032-0.0483mm

89683C09

ENGINE SPECIFICATIONS—4.0L (VIN X) ENGINE

Description	English	Metric
Pistons		
Standard piston diameter	3.9524-3.9531 in.	100.391-100.4087mm
Piston ring groove width		
Top compression ring	0.0803-0.0811 in.	2.0396-2.0599mm
Second compression ring	0.1197-0.1205 in.	3.0404-3.0607mm
Oil control ring	0.1579-0.1587 in.	4.0107-4.0310mm
Piston pin diameter	0.9446-0.9450 in.	23.993-24.003mm
Piston rings		
Thickness		
Top compression ring	0.0778-0.0783 in.	1.9761-1.9888mm
Second compression ring	0.1172-0.1177 in.	2.9769-2.9896mm
Side clearance		
Top compression ring	0.0020-0.0033 in.	0.0508-0.08382mm
Second compression ring	0.0020-0.0033 in.	0.0508-0.08382mm
End-gap		
Top compression ring	0.015-0.023 in.	0.381-0.584mm
Second compression ring	0.015-0.023 in.	0.381-0.584mm
Oil ring	0.015-0.055 in.	0.381-1.397mm
Crankshaft and connecting rods		
Crankshaft main journal diameter	2.2433-2.2441 in.	56.9798-57.0001mm
Main bearing-to-journal clearance (oil clearance)	0.0005-0.0019 in.	0.0127-0.0483mm
Crankshaft journal out-of-round and taper	0.0006 in.	0.01524mm
Crankshaft thrust play	0.002-0.0125 in.	0.05-0.32mm
Crankshaft runout	0.005 in.	0.127mm
Flywheel runout	0.005 in.	0.127mm
Connecting rod journal diameter	2.1252-2.1260 in.	53.9801-54.0004mm
Connecting rod journal-to-connecting rod clearance	0.0005-0.0022 in.	0.0127-0.0559mm
Connecting rod small end bore inside diameter	0.9217-0.9236 in.	23.41-23.46mm
Connecting rod journal out-of-round and taper	0.0003 in.	0.00762mm
Connecting rod big end side clearance	0.0036-0.0106 in.	0.092-0.268mm
Connecting rod twist	0.006 in.	0.1524mm
Connecting rod bend	0.002 in.	0.0508mm

89683C10

ENGINE SPECIFICATIONS—5.0L ENGINE

Description	English	Metric
Type	90° V8 Overhead Valve Engine	5.0L (4949cc)
Displacement	302 cu. in.	
Number of Cylinders	8	
Bore	4.00 in.	101.6mm
Stroke	3.00 in.	76.2mm
Compression ratio	9.0:1	
Valve lash (clearance)	Hydraulic	
Cylinder head		
Cylinder head-to-engine block surface warpage	0.003 in. (0.0762mm) in a 6.0 in. (152.4mm) span	
Valve seat width		
Intake valves	0.060-0.080 in.	1.524-2.032mm
Exhaust valve	0.060-0.080 in.	1.524-2.032mm
Valve seat angle—Intake and exhaust valves	45°	
Valve guide bore diameter—Intake and exhaust valves	0.3433-0.3443	8.720-8.745mm
Valves, valve springs and camshaft		
Camshaft journal diameter		
No. 1	2.0815 in.	52.8701mm
No. 2	2.0665 in.	52.4891mm
No. 3	2.0515 in.	52.1081mm
No. 4	2.0365 in.	51.7271mm
No. 5	2.0215 in.	51.3461mm
Camshaft-to-bearing clearance	0.001-0.003 in.	0.0254-0.0762mm
Camshaft thrust clearance	0.007 in. max	0.1778mm max
Camshaft lobe lift		
Intake valve	0.2637 in.	6.69798mm
Exhaust valve	0.2801 in.	7.11454mm
Camshaft runout	0.005 in. max	0.127mm
Valve stem diameter		
Intake valves	0.3415-0.3423 in.	8.6741-8.6944mm
Exhaust valves	0.3410-0.3418 in.	8.6614-8.6817mm
Valve guide-to-valve stem clearance		
Intake valves	0.0010-0.0027 in.	0.0254-0.0686mm
Exhaust valves	0.0015-0.0032 in.	0.0381-0.08128mm
Valve face angle limit	44°	
Valve head diameter		
Intake valve	1.837-1.847 in.	46.660-46.914mm
Exhaust valve	1.536-1.546 in.	39.01-39.27mm
Valve head radial runout	0.002 in.	0.0508mm
Valve spring free length (approximate)	1.84 in.	46.7mm
Intake valve spring	2.06 in.	52.324mm
Exhaust valve spring	1.88 in.	47.752mm
Valve spring preload		
Intake valve spring	74-82 lbs. @ 1.78 in.	33.6-37.2kg @ 45.21mm
Exhaust valve spring	76-84 lbs. @ 1.60 in.	34.5-38.1kg @ 40.64mm
Valve spring installed height		
Intake valve spring	1.75-1.81 in.	44.45-45.974mm
Exhaust valve spring	1.58-1.64 in.	40.132-41.656mm
Valve spring out-of-square	0.078 in.	1.9812mm
Rocker arm ratio	1.62:1	
Pushrod runout	0.005 in.	0.127mm

89683C11

ENGINE SPECIFICATIONS—5.0L ENGINE

Description	English	Metric
Engine block		
Engine block-to-cylinder head surface warpage	0.003 in. (0.0762mm) in a 6.0 in. (152.4mm) span	
Standard cylinder bore	4.0000-4.0012 in.	101.6-101.6305mm
Cylinder bore out-of-round and taper	0.0015/0.010 in.	0.0381/0.254mm
Cylinder bore-to-piston clearance	0.0012-0.0020 in.	0.0305-0.0508mm
Pistons		
Standard piston diameter	3.9987-3.9993 in.	101.567-101.5822mm
Piston ring groove width		
Top compression ring	0.0602-0.0612 in.	1.530-1.555mm
Second compression ring	0.0602-0.0612 in.	1.530-1.555mm
Oil control ring	0.1587-0.1596 in.	4.030-4.055mm
Piston pin diameter	0.9121-0.9122 in.	23.1673-23.1699mm
Piston rings		
Thickness		
Top compression ring	0.0575-0.0587 in.	1.460-1.490mm
Second compression ring	0.0575-0.0587 in.	1.460-1.490mm
Oil Control ring	Side seal -Snug fit	
Side clearance		
Top compression ring	0.0013-0.0033 in.	0.0330-0.0838mm
Second compression ring	0.0013-0.0033 in.	0.0330-0.0838mm
End-gap		
Top compression ring	0.010-0.020 in.	0.25-0.50mm
Second compression ring	0.018-0.028 in.	0.4572-0.7112mm
Oil ring	0.010-0.040 in.	0.25-1.016mm
Crankshaft and connecting rods		
Crankshaft main journal diameter	2.2482-2.2490 in.	57.1043-57.1246mm
Main bearing-to-journal clearance (oil clearance)	0.0008-0.0026 in.	0.0203-0.06604mm
Crankshaft journal out-of-round and taper	0.0006 in.	0.01524mm
Crankshaft thrust play	0.004-0.008 in.	0.1016-0.2032mm
Crankshaft runout	0.002 in.	0.050mm
Connecting rod journal diameter	2.1228-2.1236 in.	53.9191-53.9191mm
Connecting rod journal out-of-round and taper	0.0006 in.	0.01524mm
Connecting rod journal-to-connecting rod clearance	0.0007-0.0024 in.	0.01778-0.06096mm
Connecting rod small end and bore inside diameter	0.9097-0.9112 in.	23.1064-23.1445mm
Connecting rod big end side clearance	0.010-0.020 in.	0.254-0.508mm
Connecting rod twist	0.015 in.	0.381mm
Connecting rod bend	0.012 in.	0.3048mm

89683C12

TORQUE SPECIFICATIONS—2.3L ENGINE

Component	Ft. Lbs.	Nm
Alternator bracket-to-engine block	30-40	40-55
Auxiliary/oil pump shaft sprocket bolt	28-40	34-54
Auxiliary shaft thrust plate bolts	6-9	8-12
Camshaft sprocket bolt	50-71	68-96
Camshaft thrust plate bolts	6-9	8-12
Connecting rod cap nuts - torque in two steps		
Step 1	25-30	34-41
Step 2	30-36	41-49
Crankshaft main bearing cap bolts - torque in two steps		
Step 1	50-60	68-81
Step 2	75-85	102-115
Crankshaft pulley bolt	103-133	140-180
Cylinder head bolts - torque following steps below		
1991-93		
Step 1	50-60	68-81
Step 2	80-90	108-122
1994-97		
Step 1: Tighten in sequence to	51	70
Step 2: Loosen all bolts, then re-tighten in sequence to	51	70
Step 3: Turn all bolts in sequence an additional	90-100 degrees	90-100 degrees
Cylinder front cover bolts	6-9	8-12
EGR valve-to-spacer bolts	15-22	19-29
EGR connector tube nuts	18-28	25-35
Exhaust manifold to cylinder head bolt, stud or nut - torque in two steps		
1991-93		
Step 1	178-204 inch lbs.	20-24
Step 2	20-30	27-41
1994-97		
Step 1	15-22	20-30
Step 2	45-59	60-80
Exhaust pipe-to-manifold bolts	25-34	34-46
Flywheel-to-crankshaft bolts	56-64	73-87
Intake manifold-to-cylinder head bolt/nuts - torque in two steps		
1991-94		
Step 1	5-7	7-9
Step 2	14-21	19-28
1995-97		
Step 1	62-88 inch lbs.	7-10
Step 2	19-28	26-38
Oil pump drive housing clamp-to-block bolt		
1991-93 models only	15-20	19-28
Oil pump pick-up tube bolts	15-22	19-29
Oil pump-to-engine block bolts		
1991-93	15-22	19-29
1994-97	88-123 inch lbs.	10-14
Oil drain pan plug-to-pan	15-25	21-33
Oil pan-to-engine block		
1991-94	7.5-10	11-13.5
1995-97	10-12	13-16
Oil filter insert-to-engine block	20-25	28-35
Oil filter-to-engine	1/2 turn after gasket contacts surface	
Power steering pump-to-engine block bolts	16-20	21-28
Rocker arm cover-to-cylinder head bolts		
1991-94	62-97 inch lbs.	7-11
1995-97	80-115 inch lbs.	9-13
Spark plug-to-cylinder head	7-15	9-20
Temperature sending unit-to-engine block	8-18	11-24

TORQUE SPECIFICATIONS—2.3L ENGINE

Component	Ft. Lbs.	Nm
Timing belt cover stud - inner	15-22	19-29
Timing belt cover bolts - outer	6-9	8-12
Timing belt tensioner pivot bolt	28-40	38-54
Timing belt tensioner adjuster bolt	14-21	19-29
Water jacket drain plug-to-engine block	23-28	32-37
Water pump-to-engine block bolts	15-22	19-29
Water outlet bolts	15-22	19-29
Vacuum fitting-to-upper manifold	12-18	16-24

89683C14

89683C13

TORQUE SPECIFICATIONS—2.5L ENGINE

Component	Ft. Lbs.	Nm
Alternator bracket-to-engine block	30-40	40-55
Oil pump shaft sprocket bolt	52-70	70-95
Camshaft sprocket bolt	50-71	68-96
Camshaft thrust plate bolts	6-9	8-12
Connecting rod cap nuts - torque in two steps		
Step 1	Fingertight	
Step 2	25-30	34-41
Step 3	30-36	41-49
Crankshaft main bearing cap bolts - torque in two steps		
Step 1	Fingertight	
Step 2	51-59	68-81
Step 3	76-84	102-115
Crankshaft pulley bolt	93-121	125-165
Cylinder head bolts - torque following steps below		
Step 1: Tighten in sequence to	51	70
Step 2: Loosen all bolts, then re-tighten in sequence to	51	70
Step 3: Turn all bolts in sequence an additional	90-100 degrees	90-100 degrees
Engine front cover bolts	10-12	13-15
EGR connector tube nuts	25-35	34-47
Exhaust manifold to cylinder head bolt, stud or nut - torque in two steps		
Step 1	15-22	20-30
Step 2	45-59	60-80
Exhaust pipe-to-manifold bolts	25-34	34-46
Flywheel-to-crankshaft bolts	56-64	73-87
Intake manifold bolt/nuts - torque in two steps		
Upper and Lower		
Step 1	62-88 inch lbs.	7-10
Step 2	20-28	26-38
Oil pump pick-up tube bolts	15-22	19-29
Oil pump-to-engine block bolts	88-123 inch lbs.	10-14
Oil pan-to-engine block	10-12	13-16
Rocker arm cover-to-cylinder head bolts	80-115 inch lbs.	9-13
Spark plug-to-cylinder head	7-15	9-20
Timing belt cover stud - inner	15-22	19-29
Timing belt cover bolts - outer	6-9	8-12
Timing belt tensioner pivot bolt	30-40	40-55
Timing belt tensioner adjuster bolt	26-33	35-45
Water pump-to-engine block bolts	15-22	19-29
Water outlet bolts	71-106 inch lbs.	8-12

89683C63

TORQUE SPECIFICATIONS—2.9L ENGINE

Component	Ft. Lbs.	Nm
Alternator adjuster bolt	29-40	40-55
Alternator bracket - 10mm bolt	29-40	40-55
Alternator bracket - 8mm bolt	14-22	20-30
Alternator pivot bolt	45-61	61-82
Belt pulley-to-crankshaft pulley	19-28	26-38
Camshaft sprocket bolt	19-28	26-38
Camshaft thrust plate bolts	13-16	17-21
Connecting rod cap nut	19-24	26-33
Crankshaft pulley bolt	85-96	115-130
Cylinder head-to-engine block bolts - torque in sequence in three steps		
Step 1	22	30
Step 2	51-55	70-75
Step 3	90 degrees	90 degrees
EGR valve-to-plenum or EGR plate-to-plenum	15-18	21-25
Exhaust manifold-to-cylinder head bolt/nuts	20-30	27-40
Fan clutch-to-water pump	15-25	21-34
Fan-to-fan clutch	6-8	8-11
Flywheel-to-crankshaft bolts	47-52	64-70
Front cover-to-engine block	13-16	17-21
Fuel pressure regulator-to-rail	7-10	9-13
Fuel rail-to-intake manifold	7-10	9-13
Heat shield manifold stud	50-65 inch lbs.	5-7
Idle air bypass valve-to-plenum	7-10	9-13
Intake manifold stud-to-engine block	10-12	14-16
Lower intake manifold - torque in sequence in five steps		
Step 1	Hand start and snug nuts at position 3 & 4	
Step 2	3-6	4-8
Step 3	6-11	8-15
Step 4	11-15	15-21
Step 5	15-18	21-25
Main bearing cap bolts	65-75	88-102
Oil filter	1/2 turn after gasket contacts sealing surface	
Oil filter adapter-to-engine block bolt	15-30	20-40
Oil level indicator tube-to-manifold nut stud	30-40	40-55
Oil pan drain plug	15-21	21-28
Oil pan-to-engine block	4-6	5-8
Oil pump case	6-10	9-13
Oil pump pick-up tube support-to-main cap nut	12-15	17-21
Oil pump pick-up tube-to-pump	6-10	9-13
Rocker arm cover-to-cylinder head	3-5	4-7
Rocker arm shaft support bolt	43-50	59-67
Spark plug	18-28	25-38
Throttle body-to-upper intake	6-10	9-13
Timing chain guide-to-engine block	7-10	9-13
Timing chain tensioner-to-engine block	7-10	9-13
Timing pointer-to-front cover	5-7	7-9
Upper intake manifold - torque in sequence in two steps		
Step 1	7	10
Step 2	15-18	21-25
Water jacket drain plug	14-18	20-25
Water outlet connection	6-9	9-12
Water pump pulley-to-pump	14-22	20-30
Water pump-to-front cover	7-9	9-12

89683C15

TORQUE SPECIFICATIONS—3.0L ENGINE

Component	Ft. Lbs.	Nm
Alternator pivot bolt	45-57	61-75
Camshaft lifter (tappet) guide plate bolts	7-10	10-14
Camshaft sprocket bolt	41-51	55-70
Camshaft thrust plate bolts	6-8	8-12
Coil bracket-to-cylinder head	12-15	16-20
Connecting rod cap nuts	23-28	31-39
Crankshaft damper bolt	92-122	125-165
Crankshaft main bearing cap bolts	55-62	75-85
Cylinder head bolts - torque in sequence in two steps		
Step 1	33-41	45-55
Step 2	63-73	85-99
Distributor hold-down bolt (1991-93 models only)	14-22	19-30
EGR cover-to-throttle body bolts	15-22	20-30
EGR tube-to-EGR valve nut	26-47	35-65
EGR tube-to-exhaust manifold bolt	15-22	20-30
EGR valve to throttle body	19	25
Engine bracket reinforcement brace-to-engine bracket bolt (damper)	35-49	47-67
Engine bracket reinforcement brace-to-engine bracket nut (damper)	60-79	80-107
Engine front cover-to-block	15-22	20-30
Exhaust manifold-to-cylinder head	15-22	20-30
Flywheel-to-crankshaft bolts	54-64	73-87
Fuel rail-to-intake manifold	6-9	8-12
Idler bracket-to-alternator top attaching flange bolt	24-34	33-46
Idler front lower bracket attaching bolt	30-40	40-55
Idler front upper bracket attaching bolt	52-70	70-95
Idler pulley adv. bolts (2-places)	30-40	40-55
Idler top bracket bolt	30-40	40-55
Intake manifold (lower - upper portion is called the throttle body) - torque in two steps		
Step 1	11	15
Step 2	19-24	26-32
Oil dipstick tube bracket-to-exhaust manifold	12-14	16-20
Oil filter	1/2 turn after gasket contacts block surface	
Oil filter insert-to-engine block	20-29	27-40
Oil pan drain plug	10	14
Oil pan-to-engine block	7-10	10-14
Oil pump-to-rear main cap bolt	30-40	40-55
Rocker arm fulcrum bolts	19-28	26-38
Spark plug	7-14	9-20
Thermostat housing-to-intake manifold	15-22	20-30
Throttle body-to-intake manifold (upper manifold)	15-22	20-30
Valve/rocker arm cover	7-10	10-14
Water pump-to-front cover	6-8	8-12

89683C16

TORQUE SPECIFICATIONS—4.0L (VIN X) ENGINE

Component	Ft. Lbs.	Nm
A/C compressor bolts	17-20	22-28
A/C compressor mounting brace and bracket-to-engine bolts	30-40	40-55
Alternator mounting bolts	30-40	40-55
Alternator mounting bracket bolts	30-40	40-55
Camshaft sprocket bolts	44-50	60-68
Camshaft thrust plate bolts	7-10	9-13
Connecting rod cap nuts	18-24	25-32
Crankshaft damper/pulley bolt	30-37	40-50
Crankshaft main bearing cap bolts	66-77	90-104
Crankshaft oil baffle nuts	13-15	17-21
Cylinder head bolts - torque in sequence in three steps		
Step 1	44	60
Step 2	59	80
Step 3	Turn an additional 80-85 degrees	
Drive belt tensioner bolt	30-40	30-40
EGR valve bolts	15-22	20-30
EGR valve tube stud-to-intake manifold	30-40	40-55
EGR valve tube-to-exhaust manifold nuts	26-35	34-48
Engine front cover-to-block	13-15	17-21
Exhaust manifold-to-cylinder head bolts	20	27
Exhaust pipe-to-manifold nuts	20	27
Flywheel-to-crankshaft bolts - cross-tighten in two steps		
Step 1	9-11	12-15
Step 2	50-55	68-74
Ignition coil bracket-to-engine bolts	19-24	26-32
Lower intake manifold bolts - torque in sequence in five steps		
Step 1	Hand-tight	
Step 2	3-6	4-8
Step 3	6-11	8-15
Step 4	11-15	15-21
Step 5	15-18	21-25
Oil filter adapter through bolt	26-30	35-40
Oil pan bolts and nuts	5-7	7-10
Oil pan stud	35 inch lbs.	4
Oil pan-to-transmission bolts	28-38	38-51
Oil pump drive assembly hold-down bolt	13-15	17-21
Oil pump pick-up-to-pump bolts	7-10	9-13
Oil pump-to-engine block bolts	13-15	17-21
Power steering mounting bolts	30-40	40-55
Rocker arm shaft/stand bolts	46-52	62-70
Spark plugs	7-15	9-20
Thermostat housing bolts	7-10	9-13
Timing chain guide bolts	7-9	10-12
Timing chain tensioner bolts	7-8	9-11
Upper intake manifold nuts - torque in sequence in two steps		
Step 1	7	9
Step 2	15-18	20-25
Valve/rocker covers	4.5-5.9	6-8
Water pump pulley bolts	17-20	22-28
Water pump-to-front cover	6-9	8.5-12

89683C17

TORQUE SPECIFICATIONS—4.0L SOHC (VIN E) ENGINE

Component	Ft. Lbs.	Nm
A/C bracket nut	12.5-17	17-23
Accelerator cable bracket bolt	19-25 inch lbs.	2.1-2.9
Accelerator control splash shield bolts	27.5-38 inch lbs.	3.1-4.3
Accessory drive bracket bolts	33.5-36	45.5-49.5
Alternator bracket bolts	30-40	40-45
Balance shaft bolts	6.5-8	9-11
Balance shaft chain guide bolts		
Balance shaft tensioner bolts	20.5-22	28-30
Camshaft bearing cap bolts - torque in sequence in two steps		
Step 1	53.5 inch lbs.	6
Step 2	11-12.5	15-17
Camshaft sprocket bolt	62.5	85
Cassette retaining bolt - left-hand	7-10	10-14
Cassette retaining bolt - right-hand	6.6-8	9-11
Cassette-to-engine block retaining bolt	7.3-10.2	10-14
Connecting rod cap nuts - torque-to-yield bolts, do not re-use the old bolts. Tighten in two steps		
Step 1	15	20
Step 2	Turn an additional 90 degrees (1/4 turn)	
Crankshaft damper bolt - torque in two steps. Never re-use the old bolt		
Step 1	44	60
Step 2	Turn an additional 80-90 degrees (1/4 turn)	
Crankshaft main bearing caps	67-74	90-104
Crankshaft pulley-to-damper bolts	20-28	26-38
Cylinder head bolts - torque in three steps		
Step 1	26	35
Step 2	Turn an additional 90 degrees (1/4 turn)	
Step 3	Turn an additional 90 degrees (1/4 turn)	
EGR bracket bolt	6-8	8-11
EGR valve tube fittings	25-34	34-47
Engine front cover bolts	12.5-15.4	17-21
Engine lifting eye bolts	26-29	35-39
Engine mount bracket-to-engine bolts	44-59	60-80
Engine mount bracket-to-insulator nuts	65-97	88-132
Engine support insulator nuts (motor mount)	51-67	68-92
Exhaust manifold nuts	15-18	20-25
Exhaust pipe-to-manifold bolts	25-32	34-46
Flywheel-to-crankshaft bolts - torque in sequence in two steps		
Step 1	19-25	25-35
Step 2	Turn an additional 90 degrees (1/4 turn)	
Fuel injection supply manifold retaining bolts	14-19	20-26
Fuel line bracket bolts	6.6-8	9-11
Hydraulic camshaft tensioner - left-hand	35-39	47-53
Hydraulic camshaft tensioner - right-hand	30-33	41-45
Intake manifold bolts - lower	8.8-10.3	12-14
Intake manifold bolts - upper	53-62 inch lbs.	6-7
Jackshaft front sprocket bolt - torque in two steps		
Step 1	32-35	43-47
Step 2	Turn an additional 65-75 degrees	
Jackshaft rear sprocket bolt	46-49	63-67
Jackshaft thrust plate bolts	6.6-9.6	9-13
Ladder frame bolts (oil pan-to-block)		
Center bolts - torque in two steps		
Step 1	9.6-12.5	13-17
Step 2	22.5-26.5	30-36
Circumference bolts	5-7.4	8-10
Oil filter adaptor bolt	25.7-28.7	35-39
Oil level indicator tube bracket bolt	15-22	20-30

89683C18

TORQUE SPECIFICATIONS—4.0L SOHC (VIN E) ENGINE

Component	Ft. Lbs.	Nm
Oil pan bolts (ladder frame cover)	6-7.4	8-10
Oil pan drain plug	17-22	22-30
Oil pump bolts	12.5-15.4	17-21
Oil pump pick-up tube bolts	6.6-9.6	9-13
Thermostat housing bolts	6.6-9.6	9-13
Valve cover bolts	6-7.4	8-10
Water pump bolts	6-8	8-11

89683C19

TORQUE SPECIFICATIONS—5.0L ENGINE

Component	Ft. Lbs.	Nm
A/C compressor bolts	16-21	21-29
Accelerator cable bracket bolts	71-106 inch lbs.	8-12
Accessory drive belt tensioner bolts	15-22	20-30
Air cleaner tube clamps	18-26 inch lbs.	2-3
Bell housing bolts	51-64	68-88
Camshaft sprocket bolt	40-45	54-61
Camshaft thrust plate bolts	9-12	13-16
Connecting rod cap nuts	19-24	26-33
Crankshaft thrust main bearing cap bolts	60-70	82-95
Cylinder head bolts - torque in sequence in three steps		
Step 1	25-35	34-47
Step 2	45-55	61-75
Step 3	Turn an additional 85-95 degrees (1/4 turn)	
EGR spacer bolts and nuts	12-18	16-25
Engine front cover bolts	12-18	16-25
Engine mount nuts	95-125	129-170
Exhaust manifold bolts	26-32	35-44
Exhaust pipe-to-manifold bolts	26-33	34-46
Fan clutch-to-water pump	35-46	47-63
Fan shroud bolts	12-18	16-25
Fan-to-fan clutch bolts	14-19	19-26
Flywheel-to-crankshaft bolts	75-85	102-115
Fuel supply rail-to-manifold	71-106 inch lbs.	8-12
Hot water tube nut and fitting	12-18	16-25
Idler pulley	30-40	40-55
Ignition coil bracket nuts	12-18	16-25
Intake cover screws	27-44 inch lbs.	3-5
Lower intake manifold bolts and studs - torque in sequence in two steps		
Step 1	5-10	6-14
Step 2	23-25	31-34
Oil cooler bolt	40-65	54-89
Oil level indicator tube nut	12-18	16-25
Oil pan-to-engine block end bolts	12-18	16-25
Oil pan-to-engine block side bolts	110-144 inch lbs.	13-16
Oil pressure sensor	12-18	16-25
Oil pump bolts	22-31	29-43
Oil pump plate-to-pump body bolts	22-31	29-43
Oil pump screen cover and tube bolt - upper	12-18	16-25
Oil pump screen cover and tube nut	23-31	30-43
Power steering and A/C bracket bolts	40-53	53-72
Power steering cooler nuts	50-68	68-92
Power steering pump bolts	16-21	21-29
Rocker arm bolts	18-25	24-34
Spark plug	7-15	9-20
Starter bolts	17-20	22-28
Throttle lever snow shield	71-106 inch lbs.	8-12
Torque converter nuts	20-34	27-46
Transmission inspection shield bolts	12-16	16-22
Upper intake manifold bolts	12-18	16-25
Valve cover bolts and studs	12-15	16-21
Valve lifter (tappet) guide plate retaining bolts	71-106 inch lbs.	8-12
Vibration damper bolt	110-130	149-177
Water pump bolts	15-21	20-28

89683C20

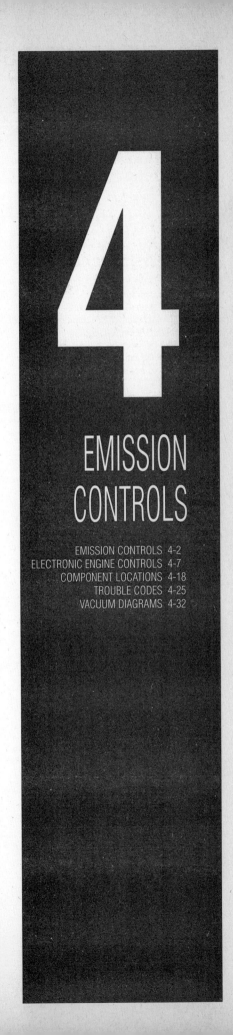

4

EMISSION CONTROLS

EMISSION CONTROLS

Positive Crankcase Ventilation (PCV) System

OPERATION

♦ See Figure 1

The PCV valve system vents crankcase gases into the engine air intake where they are burned with the fuel and air mixture. The PCV valve system keeps pollutants from being released into the atmosphere, and also helps to keep the engine oil clean, by ridding the crankcase of moisture and corrosive fumes. The PCV valve system consists of the PCV valve, it's mounting grommet, the nipple in the air intake and the connecting hoses. On some engine applications, the PCV valve system is connected with the evaporative emission system.

The PCV valve controls the amount of vapors pulled into the intake manifold from the crankcase and acts as a check valve by preventing air flow from entering the crankcase in the opposite direction. The PCV valve also prevents combustion backfiring from entering the crankcase in order to prevent detonation of the accumulated crankcase gases.

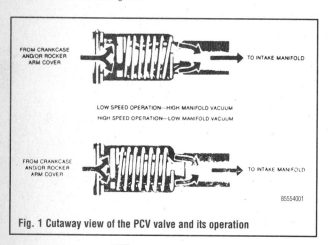

Fig. 1 Cutaway view of the PCV valve and its operation

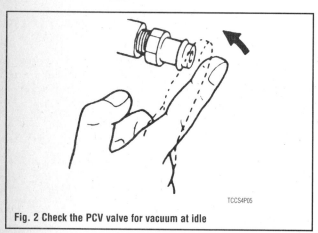

Fig. 2 Check the PCV valve for vacuum at idle

TESTING

1. Remove the PCV valve from the valve cover or engine block mounting grommet. The PCV valve for the 2.3L and 2.5L engine is mounted in the crankcase oil vent separator in a rubber grommet, or its ventilation hose before the connection to the throttle body. The PCV valve for the 3.0L and 4.0L engines is also mounted in a rubber grommet, which is installed towards the rear of the left-hand valve cover. On the 5.0L engine, the PCV valve is located on top of the block by the firewall.

2. Shake the PCV valve. If the valve rattles when shaken, reinstall it and proceed to Step 3. If the valve does not rattle, it is sticking and must be replaced.

3. Start the engine and bring it to normal operating temperature.

4. Disconnect the closure (fresh air) hose from the air inlet tube (connects the air cleaner housing to the throttle body).

5. Place a stiff piece of paper over the hose end and wait 1 minute.

   a. If vacuum holds the paper in place, the system is OK; reconnect the hose.

   b. If the paper is not held in place, check for loose hose connections, vacuum leaks or blockage. Correct as necessary.

REMOVAL & INSTALLATION

♦ See Figures 3, 4 and 5

1. Disconnect the vacuum hose from the PCV valve.

2. Remove the PCV valve from its mounting grommet.

3. To install, attach the PCV vacuum hose to the PCV valve, then insert the valve into its mounting grommet.

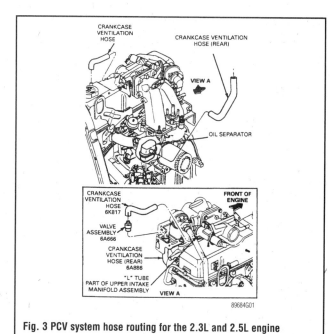

Fig. 3 PCV system hose routing for the 2.3L and 2.5L engine

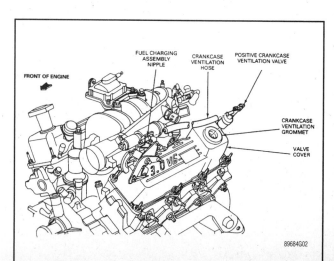

Fig. 4 PCV system hose routing for the 3.0L engine—2.9L engine is similar

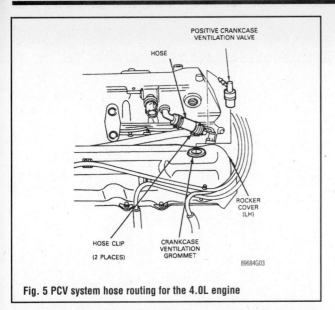

Fig. 5 PCV system hose routing for the 4.0L engine

Evaporative Emission Control System

OPERATION

Fuel vapors trapped in the sealed fuel tank are vented through the orifice vapor valve assembly in the top of the tank. The vapors leave the valve assembly through a single vapor line and continue to the carbon canister for storage until they are purged to the engine for burning.

Purging the carbon canister removes the fuel vapor stored in the carbon canister. The fuel vapor is purged via a CANister Purge (CANP) solenoid or vacuum controlled purge valve. Purging occurs when the engine is at normal operating temperature and off idle.

The evaporative emission control system consists of the following components: fuel vapor (charcoal) canister, orificed vapor valve, fuel vapor CANister Purge (CANP) solenoid, pressure/vacuum relief fuel tank filler cap, as well as, the fuel tank and fuel tank filler pipe, vapor tube and fuel vapor hoses.

Fuel Vapor (Charcoal) Canister

➡**The fuel vapor canister is referred to as the evaporative emissions canister on 1995–99 models.**

The fuel vapors from the fuel tank are stored in the fuel vapor canister until the vehicle is operated, at which time, the vapors will purge from the canister into the engine for consumption. The fuel vapor canister contains activated carbon, which absorbs the fuel vapor. The canister is located in the engine compartment or along the frame rail.

Orificed Vapor Valve

➡**This component is also known as the evaporative emission valve on 1995–99 models.**

Fuel vapor in the fuel tank is vented to the carbon canister through the vapor valve assembly. The valve is mounted in a rubber grommet at a central location in the upper surface of the fuel tank. A vapor space between the fuel level and the tank upper surface is combined with a small orifice and float shut-off valve in the vapor valve assembly to prevent liquid fuel from passing to the carbon canister. The vapor space also allows for thermal expansion of the fuel.

CANP Solenoid

The CANP solenoid is inline with the carbon canister and controls the flow of fuel vapors out of the canister. It is normally closed. When the engine is shut **OFF**, the vapors from the fuel tank flow into the canister. After the engine is started, the solenoid is engaged and opens, purging the vapors into the engine. With the solenoid open, vapors from the fuel tank are routed directly into the engine.

Pressure/Vacuum Relief Fuel Tank Filler Cap

The fuel cap contains an integral pressure and vacuum relief valve. The vacuum valve acts to allow air into the fuel tank to replace the fuel as it is used, while preventing vapors from escaping the tank through the atmosphere. The vacuum relief valve opens after a vacuum of −0.25 psi (1.7 kPa). The pressure valve acts as a backup pressure relief valve in the event the normal venting system is overcome by excessive generation of internal pressure or restriction of the normal venting system. The pressure relief is 2 psi (14 kPa). Fill cap damage or contamination that stops the pressure vacuum valve from working may result in deformation of the fuel tank.

COMPONENT TESTING

◆ **See Figures 6 thru 11**

Fuel Vapor Canister

Generally, the only testing done to the vapor canister is a visual inspection. Look the canister over and replace it with a new one if there is any evidence of cracks or other damage.

➡**Do not try to check the fuel saturation of the canister by weighing it or by the intensity of the fuel odor from the canister. These methods are unreliable and inhaling gasoline fumes can be toxic.**

CANP Solenoid

1991–1994 MODELS

1. Remove the CANP solenoid.
2. Using an external voltage source, apply 9–14 DC volts to the CANP solenoid electrical terminals. Then, use a hand-held vacuum pump and apply 16 in. Hg (53 kPa) vacuum to the manifold side nipple of the CANP solenoid.
    a. If the solenoid opens and allows air to freely pass through it, the solenoid is working properly.
    b. If the solenoid does not allow air to pass freely while energized, replace the solenoid with a new one.

1995–99 MODELS

1. Remove the CANP solenoid.
2. Measure the resistance between the two CANP terminals.
    a. If the resistance is between 30–90 ohms, proceed to the Step 3.
    b. If the resistance is not between 30–90 ohms, replace the CANP solenoid.
3. Attach a hand-held vacuum pump to the intake manifold vacuum side of the CANP solenoid, then apply 16 in. Hg (53 kPa) of vacuum to the solenoid.
    a. If the solenoid will not hold vacuum for at least 20 seconds replace it with a new one.
    b. If the solenoid holds vacuum, proceed to Step 4. Keep the vacuum applied to the solenoid.
4. Using an external voltage source, apply 9–14 DC volts to the CANP solenoid electrical terminals.
    a. If the solenoid opens and the vacuum drops, the solenoid is working properly.
    b. If the solenoid does not open and the vacuum remains, replace the solenoid with a new one.

REMOVAL & INSTALLATION

Fuel Vapor Canister

➡**The fuel vapor canister is referred to as the evaporative emissions canister on 1995–99 models.**

1. Disconnect the vapor hoses from the canister.
2. Remove the mounting screws, then remove the canister.
To install:
3. Position the canister in place, then install the mounting screws.
4. Attach all of the vapor hoses to the canister.

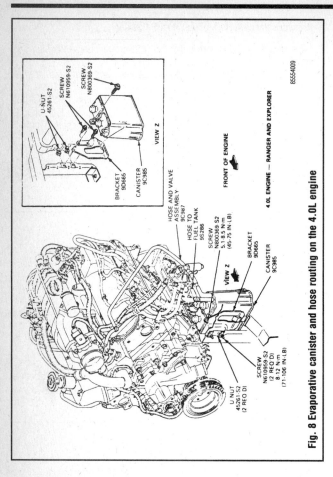

Fig. 8 Evaporative canister and hose routing on the 4.0L engine

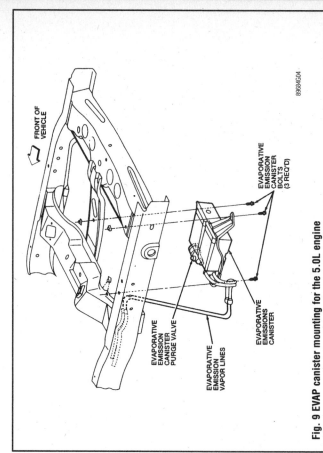

Fig. 9 EVAP canister mounting for the 5.0L engine

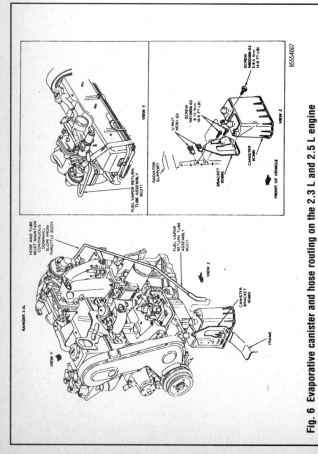

Fig. 6 Evaporative canister and hose routing on the 2.3 L and 2.5 L engine

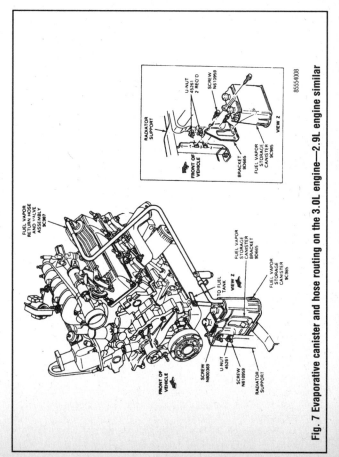

Fig. 7 Evaporative canister and hose routing on the 3.0L engine—2.9L engine similar

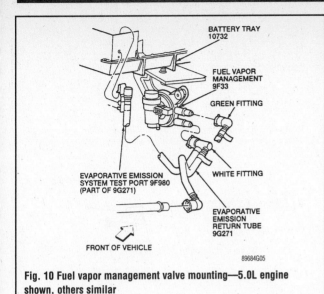

Fig. 10 Fuel vapor management valve mounting—5.0L engine shown, others similar

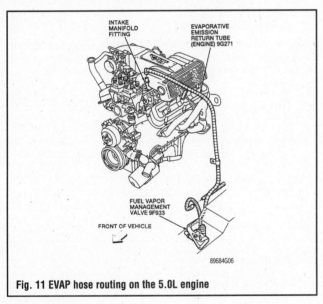

Fig. 11 EVAP hose routing on the 5.0L engine

Fuel Vapor Valve

➡️**This component is also known as the evaporative emission valve on 1995–99 models.**

1. Disconnect the negative battery cable.
2. Relieve the fuel system pressure.
3. Remove the fuel tank.
4. Remove the fuel vapor valve from the fuel tank.

To install:

5. Install the fuel vapor valve into the fuel tank.
6. Install the fuel tank in the vehicle.
7. Connect the negative battery cable.

CANP Solenoid

1. Disconnect the vapor hoses from the CANP solenoid.
2. Unplug the electrical connector from the CANP solenoid.
3. Remove the purge solenoid valve from the vehicle.

To install:

4. Install the CANP solenoid, then attach the engine wiring harness connector to the solenoid.
5. Connect the vapor hoses to the solenoid.

Pressure/Vacuum Relief Fuel Tank Filler Cap

1. Unscrew the fuel filler cap. The cap has a pre-vent feature that allows the tank to vent for the first ¾ turn before unthreading.
2. Remove the screw retaining the fuel cap tether and remove the fuel cap.

To install:

3. Position the end of the tether against its mounting boss, then install and tighten the tether screw.
4. Thread the filler cap into the fuel tank filler tube, making sure to turn it clockwise until the ratchet mechanism gives off 3 or more loud clicks.

Exhaust Gas Recirculation (EGR) System

OPERATION

➡️ **See Figure 12**

The Exhaust Gas Recirculation (EGR) system is designed to reintroduce exhaust gas into the combustion chambers, thereby lowering combustion temperatures and reducing the formation of Oxides of Nitrogen (NO_x).

The amount of exhaust gas that is reintroduced into the combustion cycle is determined by several factors, such as: engine speed, engine vacuum, exhaust system backpressure, coolant temperature, throttle position. All EGR valves are vacuum operated. The EGR vacuum diagram for your particular vehicle is displayed on the Vehicle Emission Control Information (VECI) label.

The EGR system is a Pressure Feedback EGR (PFE) or Differential PFE (DPFE) system, controlled by the Powertrain Control Module (PCM) and composed of the following components: PFE or DPFE sensor (also referred to as the backpressure transducer), EGR Vacuum Regulator (EVR) solenoid, EGR valve, and assorted hoses and tubing.

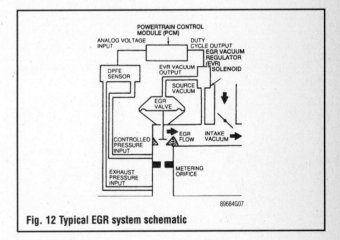

Fig. 12 Typical EGR system schematic

COMPONENT TESTING

➡️ **See Figures 13, 14 and 15**

System Integrity Inspection

Check the EGR system hoses and connections for looseness, pinching, leaks, splitting, blockage, etc. Ensure that the EGR valve mounting bolts are not loose, or that the flange gasket is not damaged. If the system appears to be in good shape, proceed to the EGR vacuum test, otherwise repair the damaged components.

EGR System Vacuum Test

➡️**The EVR solenoid has a constant internal leak; this is normal. There may be a small vacuum signal, however, it should be less than 1.0 in. Hg (3.4 kPa) of vacuum.**

Start the engine and allow it to run until normal operating temperature is reached. With the engine running at idle, detach the vacuum supply hose from

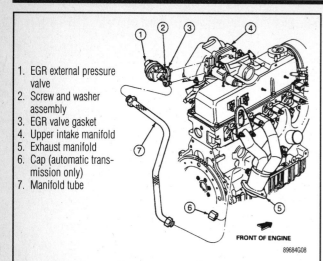

1. EGR external pressure valve
2. Screw and washer assembly
3. EGR valve gasket
4. Upper intake manifold
5. Exhaust manifold
6. Cap (automatic transmission only)
7. Manifold tube

FRONT OF ENGINE

89684G08

Fig. 13 Exploded view of the EGR system and related components for the 2.3L and 2.5L engine

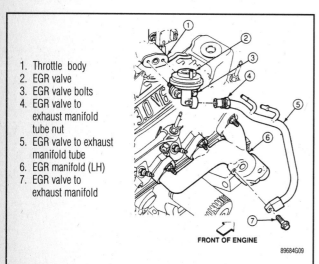

1. Throttle body
2. EGR valve
3. EGR valve bolts
4. EGR valve to exhaust manifold tube nut
5. EGR valve to exhaust manifold tube
6. EGR manifold (LH)
7. EGR valve to exhaust manifold

FRONT OF ENGINE

89684G09

Fig. 14 Exploded view of the EGR system and related components for the 3.0L engine

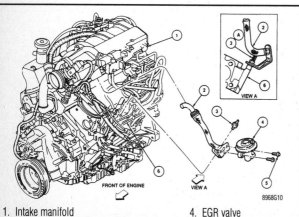

1. Intake manifold
2. Intake manifold to EGR valve tube
3. Intake manifold to EGR valve tube stud
4. EGR valve
5. EGR valve bolts
6. Cylinder head

FRONT OF ENGINE

VIEW A

8968G10

Fig. 15 Exploded view of the EGR system and related components for the 4.0L engine

the EGR valve and install a vacuum gauge to the hose. The vacuum reading should be less than 1.0 in. Hg (3.4 kPa) of vacuum. If the vacuum is greater than that specified, the problem may lie with the EVR solenoid.

EVR Solenoid Test

1. Remove the EVR solenoid.
2. Attempt to lightly blow air into the EVR solenoid.
   a. If air blows through the solenoid, replace the solenoid with a new one.
   b. If air does not pass freely through the solenoid, continue with the test.
3. Apply battery voltage (approximately 12 volts) and a ground to the EVR solenoid electrical terminals. Attempt to lightly blow air, once again, through the solenoid.
   a. If air does not pass through the solenoid, replace the solenoid with a new one.
   b. If air does not flow through the solenoid, the solenoid is OK.

EGR Valve Function Test

1. Install a tachometer on the engine, following the manufacturer's instructions.
2. Detach the engine wiring harness connector from the Idle Air Control (IAC) solenoid.
3. Disconnect and plug the vacuum supply hose from the EGR valve.
4. Start the engine, then apply the parking brake, block the rear wheels and position the transmission in Neutral.
5. Observe and note the idle speed.

➡️If the engine will not idle with the IAC solenoid disconnected, provide an air bypass to the engine by slightly opening the throttle plate or by creating an intake vacuum leak. Do not allow the idle speed to exceed typical idle rpm.

6. Using a hand-held vacuum pump, slowly apply 5–10 in. Hg (17–34 kPa) of vacuum to the EGR valve nipple.
   a. If the idle speed drops more than 100 rpm with the vacuum applied and returns to normal after the vacuum is removed, the EGR valve is OK.
   b. If the idle speed does not drop more than 100 rpm with the vacuum applied and return to normal after the vacuum is removed, inspect the EGR valve for a blockage; clean it if a blockage is found. Replace the EGR valve if no blockage is found, or if cleaning the valve does not remedy the malfunction.

REMOVAL & INSTALLATION

PFE/DPFE Sensor

➡️This component is found on all engines, and is also referred to as the backpressure transducer.

1. Disconnect the negative battery cable.
2. Detach and label the wiring harness connector from the PFE/DPFE sensor.
3. Disconnect all of the hoses from the sensor.

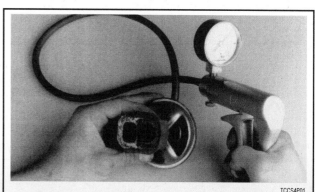

TCCS4P01

Some EGR valves may be tested using a vacuum pump by watching for diaphragm movement

4. Remove the mounting nuts, then separate the sensor from the mounting bracket.

5. If necessary, remove the EVR solenoid and the PFE/DPFE mounting bracket from the upper intake manifold.

To install:

6. If removed, install the EVR solenoid and mounting bracket onto the upper intake manifold.

7. If applicable, install the EGR tube heat shield.

8. Position the PFE/DPFE sensor on the mounting bracket, then install and tighten the mounting nuts until snug.

9. Attach all necessary hoses and wiring to the sensor.

10. Connect the negative battery cable.

EGR Vacuum Regulator (EVR) Solenoid

➡**The EVR solenoid is mounted either on the same bracket as the PFE/DPFE sensor, attached to the upper intake manifold, or near the EGR valve on its own bracket.**

1. Disconnect the negative battery cable.

2. Label and detach the wiring harness connector from the EVR solenoid.

3. Detach the main emission vacuum control connector from the solenoid.

4. Remove the retaining nuts, then separate the solenoid from the mounting bracket.

To install:

5. Position the solenoid on its mounting bracket and install the retaining nuts.

6. Attach the main emission vacuum control connector and the wiring harness connector to the EVR solenoid.

7. Connect the negative battery cable.

EGR Valve

▶ **See Figures 16 and 17**

1. Disconnect the negative battery cable.

2. If necessary, remove the air inlet tube from the throttle body and air cleaner housing.

3. Label and detach all vacuum hoses from the EGR valve.

4. Label and detach any electrical wiring harness connectors from the EGR valve.

5. Disconnect the EGR valve-to-exhaust manifold tube from the EGR valve.

6. Remove the EGR valve mounting fasteners, then separate the valve from the upper intake manifold.

7. Remove and discard the old EGR valve gasket, and clean the gasket mating surfaces on the valve and the intake manifold.

To install:

8. Install the EGR valve, along with a new gasket, on the upper intake manifold, then install and tighten the mounting bolts to 15–22 ft. lbs. (20–30 Nm) on 3.8L engines, or to 106–159 inch lbs. (12–18 Nm) on 5.0L engines.

9. Connect the EGR valve-to-exhaust manifold tube to the valve, then tighten the tube nut to 30 ft. lbs. (41 Nm).

10. Connect all wiring or hoses to the EGR valve.

11. Install the air inlet tube.

12. Connect the negative battery cable.

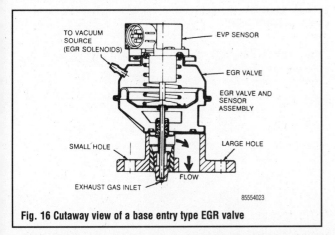

Fig. 16 Cutaway view of a base entry type EGR valve

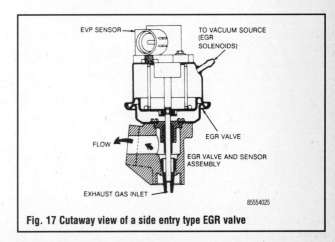

Fig. 17 Cutaway view of a side entry type EGR valve

ELECTRONIC ENGINE CONTROLS

Electronic Engine Control (EEC)

All Sequential Fuel Injection (SFI) systems use the EEC system. The heart of the EEC system is a micro-processor called the Powertrain Control Module (PCM). The PCM receives data from a number of sensors and other electronic components (switches, relay, etc.). Based on information received and information programmed in the PCM's memory, it generates output signals to control various relay, solenoids and other actuators. The PCM in the EEC system has calibration modules located inside the assembly that contain calibration specifications for optimizing emissions, fuel economy and drive ability. The calibration module is called a PROM.

The following are the electronic engine controls used by 1991–99 Ranger/Explorer and Mountaineers:

- Powertrain Control Module (PCM)
- Throttle Position (TP) sensor
- Mass Air Flow (MAF) sensor
- Intake Air Temperature (IAT) sensor
- Idle Air Control (IAC) valve
- Engine Coolant Temperature (ECT) sensor
- Heated Oxygen Sensor (HO2S)
- Camshaft Position (CMP) sensor
- Knock Sensor (KS)

- Vehicle Speed Sensor (VSS)
- Crankshaft Position (CKP) sensor

The MAF sensor (a potentiometer) senses the position of the airflow in the engine's air induction system and generates a voltage signal that varies with the amount of air drawn into the engine. The IAT sensor (a sensor in the area of the MAF sensor) measures the temperature of the incoming air and transmits a corresponding electrical signal. Another temperature sensor (the ECT sensor) inserted in the engine coolant tells if the engine is cold or warmed up. The TP sensor, a switch that senses throttle plate position, produces electrical signals that tell the PCM when the throttle is closed or wide open. A special probe (the HO2S) in the exhaust manifold measures the amount of oxygen in the exhaust gas, which is in indication of combustion efficiency, and sends a signal to the PCM. The sixth signal, camshaft position information, is transmitted by the CMP sensor, installed in place of the distributor (engines with distributorless ignition), or integral with the distributor.

The EEC microcomputer circuit processes the input signals and produces output control signals to the fuel injectors to regulate fuel discharged to the injectors. It also adjusts ignition spark timing to provide the best balance between driveability and economy, and controls the IAC valve to maintain the proper idle speed.

➡**Because of the complicated nature of the Ford system, special tools and procedures are necessary for testing and troubleshooting.**

Powertrain Control Module (PCM)

OPERATION

The Powertrain Control Module (PCM) performs many functions on your car. The module accepts information from various engine sensors and computes the required fuel flow rate necessary to maintain the correct amount of air/fuel ratio throughout the entire engine operational range.

Based on the information that is received and programmed into the PCM's memory, the PCM generates output signals to control relays, actuators and solenoids. The PCM also sends out a command to the fuel injectors that meters the appropriate quantity of fuel. The module automatically senses and compensates for any changes in altitude when driving your vehicle.

REMOVAL & INSTALLATION

▶ **See Figure 18**

1991–92 Models

▶ **See Figure 19**

1. Disconnect the negative battery cable.
2. Remove the inside, lower cowl trim panel from the passenger's side of the vehicle to expose the PCM.
3. Disengage the wiring harness connector from the PCM by loosening the connector retaining bolt, then pulling the connector from the module.
4. Remove the PCM from the bracket by pulling the unit downward.

To install:

5. Install the PCM in the mounting bracket.
6. Attach the wiring harness connector to the module, then tighten the connector retaining bolt.
7. Install the right cowl trim panel.
8. Connect the negative battery cable.

1993–99 Models

▶ **See Figures 20 and 21**

The module is mounted under the hood on the firewall. On 1993–94 models, it is mounted low on the firewall, near the left-hand fender (drivers side). On 1995–99 models, it is mounted high on the firewall offset to the right-hand side of center.

1. Disconnect the negative battery cable.
2. Disengage the wiring harness connector from the PCM by loosening the connector retaining bolt, then pulling the connector from the module.
3. Remove the two nuts and the PCM cover.
4. Remove the PCM from the bracket by pulling the unit outward.

To install:

5. Install the PCM in the mounting bracket.

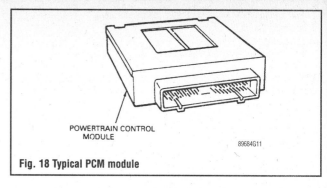

Fig. 18 Typical PCM module

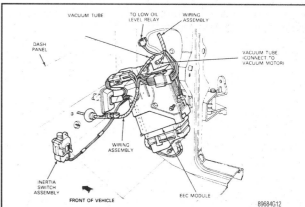

Fig. 19 View of the right-hand kick panel PCM mounting for 1991–92 models

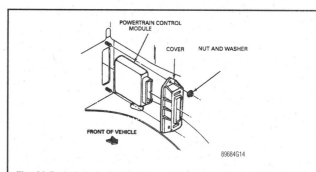

Fig. 20 Exploded view of the firewall PCM mounting for 1993–94 models

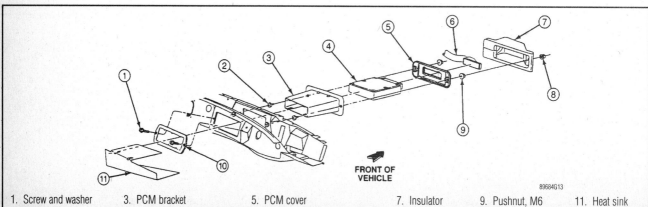

1. Screw and washer	3. PCM bracket	5. PCM cover
2. Stud, M6 x 1	4. Powertrain control module	6. Engine control sensor wiring

7. Insulator	9. Pushnut, M6	11. Heat sink
8. Pushnut	10. Seal	

Fig. 21 Exploded view of the firewall PCM mounting for 1995–99 models

6. Install the PCM cover and tighten the two nuts.
7. Attach the wiring harness connector to the module, then tighten the connector retaining bolt.
8. Connect the negative battery cable.

Heated Oxygen Sensors (HO2S)

OPERATION

▶ **See Figures 22 and 23**

The oxygen sensor supplies the computer with a signal which indicates a rich or lean condition during engine operation. The input information assists the computer in determining the proper air/fuel ratio. A low voltage signal from the sensor indicates too much oxygen in the exhaust (lean condition) and, conversely, a high voltage signal indicates too little oxygen in the exhaust (rich condition).

The oxygen sensors are threaded into the exhaust manifold and/or exhaust pipes on all vehicles. Heated oxygen sensors are used on all models to allow the engine to reach the closed loop faster.

TESTING

✳✳ WARNING

Do not pierce the wires when testing this sensor; this can lead to wiring harness damage. Back probe the connector to properly read the voltage of the HO2S.

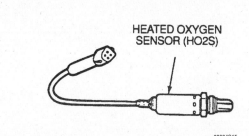

HEATED OXYGEN
SENSOR (HO2S)

89684G15

Fig. 22 Typical Heated Oxygen Sensor (H2OS)—most vehicles are equipped with multiple sensors

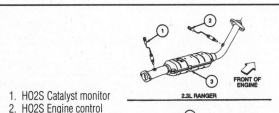

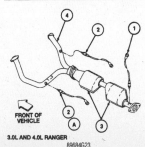

1. HO2S Catalyst monitor
2. HO2S Engine control
3. Catalytic converters
4. Exhaust inlet

2.3L RANGER

FRONT OF ENGINE

FRONT OF VEHICLE

3.0L AND 4.0L RANGER

89684G23

Fig. 23 Typical Heated Oxygen (HO2S) sensor mounting locations— Ranger shown, other models are similar

1. Disconnect the HO2S.
2. Measure the resistance between PWR and GND terminals of the sensor. If the reading is approximately 6 ohms at 68°F (20°C). the sensor's heater element is in good condition.
3. With the HO2S connected and engine running, measure the voltage with a Digital Volt-Ohmmeter (DVOM) between terminals **HO2S** and **SIG RTN** (GND) of the oxygen sensor connector. If the voltage readings are swinging rapidly between 0.01–1.1 volts, the sensor is probably okay.

REMOVAL & INSTALLATION

➡**1996–99 Explorer/Mountaineers use four heated oxygen sensors (HO2S), and V6 equipped Rangers use three HO2Sís, and 2.3L and 2.5L engines use two HO2Sís for the engine control system. The heated sensors are located before and after the dual converters in the exhaust pipes. On 5.0L and 1991–95 engines V6 engines, there are two sensors, one is located in the left exhaust manifold and the other in the dual converter Y-pipe. 1991–95 2.3L engines use only one sensor.**

1. Disconnect the negative battery cable.
2. Raise and safely support the vehicle on jackstands.
3. Disconnect the HO2S from the engine control sensor wiring.

➡**If excessive force is needed to remove the sensors, lubricate the sensor with penetrating oil prior to removal.**

4. Remove the sensors with a sensor removal tool, such as Ford Tool T94P-9472-A.
   To install:
5. Install the sensor in the mounting boss, then tighten it to 27–33 ft. lbs. (37–45 Nm).
6. Reattach the sensor electrical wiring connector to the engine wiring harness.
7. Lower the vehicle.
8. Connect the negative battery cable.

89684P01

From underneath, locate the oxygen sensor (arrow), which is screwed into an exhaust component

89684P02

Using the proper wrench, loosen the oxygen sensor. Ensure that the wire and connector are unplugged

Idle Air Control (IAC) Valve

OPERATION

▶ **See Figure 24**

The Idle Air Control (IAC) valve controls the engine idle speed and dashpot functions. The valve is located on the side of the throttle body. This valve allows air, determined by the Powertrain Control Module (PCM) and controlled by a duty cycle signal, to bypass the throttle plate in order to maintain the proper idle speed.

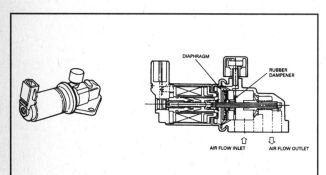

Fig. 24 Typical Idle Air Control (IAC) valve which is mounted to the throttle body—cutaway view shows air bypass direction

TESTING

▶ **See Figure 25**

1. Turn the ignition switch to the **OFF** position.
2. Disengage the wiring harness connector from the IAC valve .
3. Using an ohmmeter, measure the resistance between the terminals of the valve.

➡**Due to the diode in the solenoid, place the ohmmeter positive lead on the VPWR terminal and the negative lead on the ISC terminal.**

4. If the resistance is not 7–13 ohms, replace the IAC valve.

REMOVAL & INSTALLATION

1. Disconnect the negative battery cable.
2. Disengage the wiring harness connector from the IAC valve.
3. Remove the two retaining screws, then remove the IAC valve and discard the old gasket.
   To install:
4. Clean the IAC valve mounting surface on the throttle body of old gasket material.

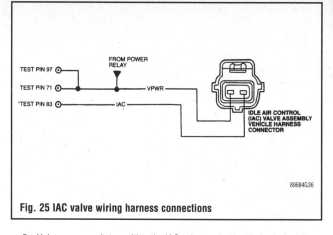

Fig. 25 IAC valve wiring harness connections

5. Using a new gasket, position the IAC valve on the throttle body. Install and tighten the retaining screws to 71–106 inch lbs. (8–12 Nm).
6. Attach the wiring harness connector to the IAC valve.
7. Connect the negative battery cable.

Engine Coolant Temperature (ECT) Sensor

OPERATION

The engine coolant temperature sensor resistance changes in response to engine coolant temperature. The sensor resistance decreases as the surrounding temperature increases. This provides a reference signal to the PCM, which indicates engine coolant temperature.

The ECT sensor is mounted on the lower intake manifold near the water outlet/thermostat housing, except on 2.3L and 2.5L engines. On the 2.3L and 2.5L engine the ECT is mounted on the water outlet/thermostat housing.

TESTING

▶ **See Figures 26 and 27**

1. Disengage the engine wiring harness connector from the ECT sensor.
2. Connect an ohmmeter between the ECT sensor terminals, and set the ohmmeter scale on 200,000 ohms.
3. With the engine cold and the ignition switch in the **OFF** position, measure and note the ECT sensor resistance. Attach the engine wiring harness connector to the sensor.
4. Start the engine and allow the engine to warm up to normal operating temperature.
5. Once the engine has reached normal operating temperature, turn the engine **OFF**
6. Once again, detach the engine wiring harness connector from the ECT sensor.
7. Measure and note the ECT sensor resistance, then compare the cold and hot ECT sensor resistance measurements with the accompanying chart.

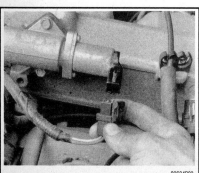

To remove the IAC valve, first disconnect the negative battery cable, then the IAC wire harness plug

Next, remove the two IAC valve attaching bolts . . .

. . . and pull the valve from the intake manifold

When installing the valve, always discard the old gasket and install it using a new one

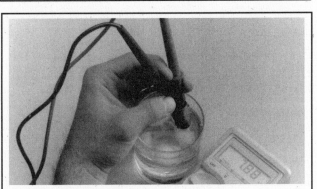

Submerge the end of the temperature sensor in cold or hot water and check resistance

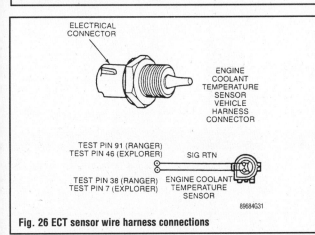

ELECTRICAL CONNECTOR

ENGINE COOLANT TEMPERATURE SENSOR VEHICLE HARNESS CONNECTOR

TEST PIN 91 (RANGER)
TEST PIN 46 (EXPLORER)

SIG RTN

TEST PIN 38 (RANGER)
TEST PIN 7 (EXPLORER)

ENGINE COOLANT TEMPERATURE SENSOR

89684G31

Fig. 26 ECT sensor wire harness connections

IAT/ECT SENSOR VOLTAGE AND RESISTANCE SPECIFICATIONS

Temperature		Engine Coolant/Intake Air Temperature Sensor Values	
°C	°F	Voltage (volts)	Resistance (K ohms)
120	248	0.27	1.18
110	230	0.35	1.55
100	212	0.46	2.07
90	194	0.60	2.80
80	176	0.78	3.84
70	158	1.02	5.37
60	140	1.33	7.70
50	122	1.70	10.97
40	104	2.13	16.15
30	86	2.60	24.27
20	68	3.07	37.30
10	50	3.51	58.75

89684G37

Fig. 27 IAT and ECT sensor specifications chart

8. Replace the ECT sensor if the readings do not approximate those in the chart, otherwise reattach the engine wiring harness connector to the sensor.

REMOVAL & INSTALLATION

1. Partially drain the engine cooling system until the coolant level is below the ECT sensor mounting hole.
2. Disconnect the negative battery cable.
3. Detach the wiring harness connector from the ECT sensor.
4. Using an open-end wrench, remove the coolant temperature sensor from the intake manifold.
   To install:
5. Thread the sensor into the intake manifold by hand, then tighten it securely.
6. Connect the negative battery cable.
7. Refill the engine cooling system.
8. Start the engine, check for coolant leaks and top off the cooling system.

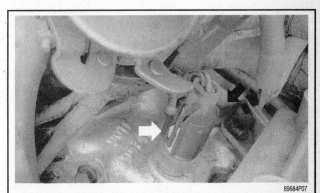

Most ECT sensors (arrow) can be found on the intake manifold, near the water outlet housing

Intake Air Temperature (IAT) Sensor

OPERATION

The Intake Air Temperature (IAT) sensor resistance changes in response to the intake air temperature. The sensor resistance decreases as the surrounding air temperature increases. This provides a signal to the PCM indicating the temperature of the incoming air charge.

Most engines mount the IAT sensor in the air cleaner-to-throttle body supply tube. However, some earlier engines have it mounted to the upper intake manifold.

TESTING

▶ **See Figure 28**

Turn the ignition switch **OFF**.
1. Disengage the wiring harness connector from the IAT sensor.
2. Using a Digital Volt-Ohmmeter (DVOM), measure the resistance between the two sensor terminals.
3. Compare the resistance reading with the accompanying chart. If the reading for a given temperature is approximately that shown in the table, the IAT sensor is okay.
4. Attach the wiring harness connector to the sensor.

REMOVAL & INSTALLATION

1. Disconnect the negative battery cable.
2. Disengage the wiring harness connector from the IAT sensor.
3. Remove the sensor from the air cleaner outlet tube.
   To install:
4. Wipe down the air cleaner outlet tube and IAT sensor mounting boss to clean the sensor area of all dirt and grime.
5. Install the sensor into the air cleaner outlet tube securely.

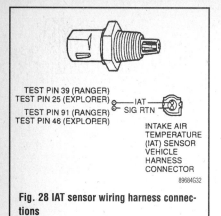

TEST PIN 39 (RANGER)
TEST PIN 25 (EXPLORER)
TEST PIN 91 (RANGER)
TEST PIN 46 (EXPLORER)

IAT
SIG RTN

INTAKE AIR
TEMPERATURE
(IAT) SENSOR
VEHICLE
HARNESS
CONNECTOR

89684G32

Fig. 28 IAT sensor wiring harness connections

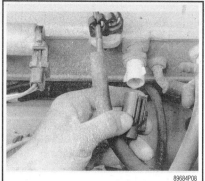

To remove the IAT sensor, disconnect the wire harness plug . . .

. . . then loosen and remove the sensor from its mounting boss

6. Attach the wiring harness connector to the IAT sensor.
7. Connect the negative battery cable.

Mass Air Flow (MAF) Sensor

OPERATION

▶ **See Figure 29**

The Mass Air Flow (MAF) sensor directly measures the amount of the air flowing into the engine. The sensor is mounted between the air cleaner assembly and the air cleaner outlet tube.

The sensor utilizes a hot wire sensing element to measure the amount of air entering the engine. The sensor does this by sending a signal, generated by the sensor when the incoming air cools the hot wire down, to the PCM. The signal is used by the PCM to calculate the injector pulse width, which controls the air/fuel ratio in the engine. The sensor and plastic housing are integral and must be replaced if found to be defective.

The sensing element (hot wire) is a1 thin platinum wire wound on a ceramic bobbin and coated with glass. This hot wire is maintained at 392°F (200°C) above the ambient temperature as measured by a constant ìcold wire".

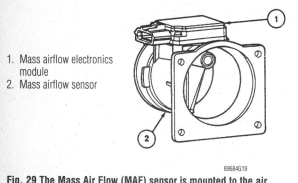

1. Mass airflow electronics module
2. Mass airflow sensor

89684G19

Fig. 29 The Mass Air Flow (MAF) sensor is mounted to the air cleaner housing

TESTING

▶ **See Figure 30**

1. With the engine running at idle, use a DVOM to verify there is at least 10.5 volts between terminals **A** and **B** of the MAF sensor connector. This indicates the power input to the sensor is correct. Then, measure the voltage between MAF sensor connector terminals **C** and **D**. If the reading is approximately 0.34–1.96 volts, the sensor is functioning properly.

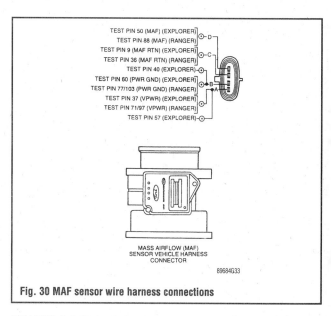

TEST PIN 50 (MAF) (EXPLORER)
TEST PIN 88 (MAF) (RANGER)
TEST PIN 9 (MAF RTN) (EXPLORER)
TEST PIN 36 (MAF RTN) (RANGER)
TEST PIN 40 (EXPLORER)
TEST PIN 60 (PWR GND) (EXPLORER)
TEST PIN 77/103 (PWR GND) (RANGER)
TEST PIN 37 (VPWR) (EXPLORER)
TEST PIN 71/97 (VPWR) (RANGER)
TEST PIN 57 (EXPLORER)

MASS AIRFLOW (MAF)
SENSOR VEHICLE HARNESS
CONNECTOR

89684G33

Fig. 30 MAF sensor wire harness connections

REMOVAL & INSTALLATION

> ✳✳ **CAUTION**

The mass air flow sensor hot wire sensing element and housing are calibrated as a unit and must be serviced as a complete assembly. Do not damage the sensing element or possible failure of the sensor may occur.

1. Disconnect the negative battery cable.
2. Disengage the wiring harness connector from the MAF sensor, and if necessary, the IAT sensor.
3. Loosen the engine air cleaner outlet tube clamps, then remove the tube from the engine.
4. Remove the MAF sensor from the air cleaner assembly by disengaging the retaining clips.
To install:
5. Install the MAF sensor to the air cleaner assembly and ensure that the retaining clips are fully engaged.
6. Install the air cleaner outlet tube, then tighten the outlet tube clamps until snug.
7. Attach the engine wiring harness connectors to the IAT and MAF sensors.
8. Connect the negative battery cable.

To remove the MAF sensor, first disconnect the wire harness plug . . .

. . . then remove the air cleaner-to-throttle body air tube

Remove the four MAF sensor attaching screws . . .

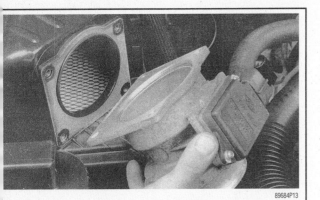

. . . then remove the sensor from the air cleaner housing

Throttle Position (TP) Sensor

OPERATION

See Figure 31

The Throttle Position (TP) sensor is a potentiometer that provides a signal to the PCM that is directly proportional to the throttle plate position. The TP sensor is mounted on the side of the throttle body and is connected to the throttle plate shaft. The TP sensor monitors throttle plate movement and position, and transmits an appropriate electrical signal to the PCM. These signals are used by the PCM to adjust the air/fuel mixture, spark timing and EGR operation according to engine load at idle, part throttle, or full throttle. The TPS is not adjustable.

TESTING

▶ See Figure 32

1. Disconnect the negative battery cable.
2. Disengage the wiring harness connector from the TP sensor.
3. Using a Digital Volt-Ohmmeter (DVOM) set on ohmmeter function, probe the terminals, which correspond to the Brown/White and the Gray/White connector wires, on the TP sensor. Do not measure the wiring harness connector terminals, rather the terminals on the sensor itself.
4. Slowly rotate the throttle shaft and monitor the ohmmeter for a continuous, steady change in resistance. Any sudden jumps, or irregularities (such as jumping back and forth) in resistance indicates a malfunctioning sensor.
5. Reconnect the negative battery cable.
6. Turn the DVOM to the voltmeter setting.

✳✳ WARNING

Ensuring the DVOM is on the voltmeter function is vitally important, because if you measure circuit resistance (ohmmeter function) with the battery cable connected, your DVOM will be destroyed.

7. Detach the wiring harness connector from the PCM (located behind the lower right-hand kick panel in the passengers' compartment), then install a break-out box between the wiring harness connector and the PCM connector.
8. Turn the ignition switch **ON** and using the DVOM on voltmeter function, measure the voltage between terminals 89 and 90 of the breakout box. The specification is 0.9 volts.
9. If the voltage is outside the standard value or if it does not change smoothly, inspect the circuit wiring and/or replace the TP sensor.

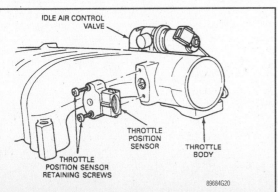

Fig. 31 Typical Throttle Position (TP) sensor mounting on the throttle body

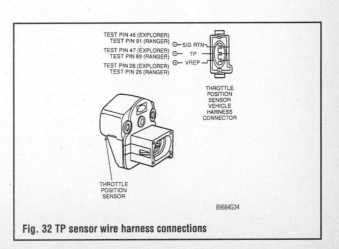

Fig. 32 TP sensor wire harness connections

REMOVAL & INSTALLATION

1. Disconnect the negative battery cable.
2. Disengage the wiring harness connector from the TP sensor.
3. Remove the two TP sensor mounting screws, then pull the TP sensor out of the throttle body housing.

To install:

4. Position the TP sensor against the throttle body housing, ensuring that the mounting screw holes are aligned. When positioning the TP sensor against the throttle body, slide the sensor straight onto the housing.
5. Install and tighten the sensor mounting screws until snug.
6. Attach the wiring harness connector to the sensor, then connect the negative battery cable.

➡**The TP sensor is not adjustable.**

Camshaft Position (CMP) Sensor

OPERATION

▶ **See Figures 33 and 34**

The CMP sensor provides the camshaft position information, called the CMP signal, which is used by the Powertrain Control Module (PCM) for fuel synchronization.

➡**1991–93 2.3L and 1991–95 4.0L (VIN X) engines did not use CMP sensors.**

1994 2.3L California only and 1995–99 2.3L and 2.5L engines utilize CMP sensors. The 1994 CMP is located on the oil pump drive assembly, on the left-hand lower side of the engine block. 1995–99 models CMP sensor is located and triggered by the auxiliary shaft drive sprocket.

On the 1991–94 2.9L and 3.0L engine, the distributor stator is the Camshaft Position (CMP) sensor, and it is a Hall effect magnetic switch. On the 1995–99 3.0L engine, the CMP is mounted on the oil pump drive assembly, located towards the rear of the block. it is also a single hall effect magnetic switch and it is activated by a single vane, and is driven by the camshaft.

On the 4.0L SOHC engine (VIN E), the Camshaft Position (CMP) sensor is a variable reluctance sensor, which is triggered by the high-point mark on the left-hand camshaft. It is mounted to the valve cover.

The 4.0L and 5.0L engines use a separate CMP sensor mounted to the oil pump drive. The drive assembly is located toward the rear of the engine on the 4.0L, and towards the front on the 5.0L engine.

TESTING

Three Wire Sensors

▶ **See Figure 35**

1. With the ignition **OFF**, disconnect the CMP sensor. With the ignition **ON** and the engine **OFF**, measure the voltage between sensor harness connector **VPWR** and **PWR GND** terminals (refer to the accompanying illustration). If the reading is greater than 10.5 volts, the power circuit to the sensor is okay.
2. With the ignition **OFF**, install break-out box between the CMP sensor and the PCM. Using a Digital Volt-Ohmmeter (DVOM) set to the voltage function (scale set to monitor less than 5 volts), measure voltage between break-out box terminals **24** and **40** with the engine running at varying RPM. If the voltage reading varies more than 0.1 volt, the sensor is okay.

Two Wire Sensors

▶ **See Figure 36**

1. With the ignition **OFF**, install a break-out box between the CMP sensor and PCM.
2. Using a Digital Volt-Ohmmeter (DVOM) set to the voltage function (scale set to monitor less than 5 volts), measure the voltage between break-out box terminals **24** and **46** with the engine running at varying RPM. If the voltage reading varies more than 0.1 volt AC, the sensor is okay.

To remove the TP sensor, first disconnect the wire harness plug from the sensor

If the mounting holes of the sensor are slotted, mark its position. Note: factory sensors are not slotted

Remove the two attaching screws . . .

. . . then remove the sensor from the throttle body by lifting straight up to disengage the throttle blade (arrow)

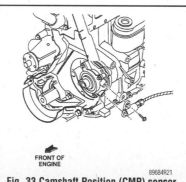

Fig. 33 Camshaft Position (CMP) sensor used on the 2.3L and 2.5L engine—except 1994 California

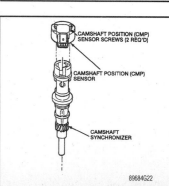

Fig. 34 Oil pump drive mounted CMP sensor used on 3.0L, 4.0L and 5.0L engines and 1994 California 2.3L engines

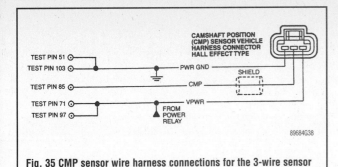

TEST PIN 51

TEST PIN 103 ———— PWR GND

TEST PIN 85 ———— CMP

TEST PIN 71

TEST PIN 97 ———— VPWR ———— FROM POWER RELAY

CAMSHAFT POSITION (CMP) SENSOR VEHICLE HARNESS CONNECTOR HALL EFFECT TYPE

SHIELD

89684G38

Fig. 35 CMP sensor wire harness connections for the 3-wire sensor

*TEST PIN 85 ———— CMP

TEST PIN 91 ———— SIG RTN

SHIELD

CAMSHAFT POSITION (CMP) SENSOR VEHICLE HARNESS CONNECTOR VARIABLE RELUCTANCE (VR) TYPE

*TEST PINS LOCATED ON BREAKOUT BOX
ALL HARNESS CONNECTORS VIEWED INTO MATING SURFACE

89684G39

Fig. 36 CMP sensor wire harness connections for the 2-wire sensor

REMOVAL & INSTALLATION

1995–97 2.3L and 1998–99 2.5L Engines

➡According to the manufacturer, the A/C system, if equipped, must be discharged for this procedure. Have your A/C system refrigerant reclaimed by an MVAC certified repair shop. However, there may be enough flex or slack in the A/C lines to allow you to support the compressor off to the side without disconnecting the lines.

1. Disconnect the negative battery cable.
2. Remove the accessory drive belt.
3. Remove the four bolts securing the A/C compressor to the mounting bracket and set aside.
4. Remove the three compressor/power steering bracket retaining bolts.
5. Pull the bracket, with the power steering pump attached, away from the engine and position it aside.
6. Disconnect the engine control sensor wiring from the camshaft position sensor.
7. Remove the two CMP mounting bolts and then pull the sensor from the oil pump.

To install:

8. Install the CMP sensor to the oil pump and tighten the two mounting screws to 45–61 inch lbs. (5–7 Nm).
9. Reconnect the engine control sensor wiring to the sensor.
10. Position the bracket, with the power steering pump attached, to the engine.
11. Install the three compressor/power steering bracket retaining bolts and tighten securely.
12. Install the A/C compressor to the mounting bracket and tighten the four mounting bolts.
13. Install the accessory drive belt.
14. Connect the negative battery cable. Start the engine and check for leaks.

1991–94 2.9L and 3.0L Engines

Refer to Section 2 in this manual for distributor removal and installation.

1995–99 3.0L, 4.0L (VIN X), 5.0L and 1994 California only 2.3L Engines

▶ See Figures 37, 38, 39 and 40

➡If the camshaft position sensor housing does not contain a plastic locator cover tool, a special service tool such as T89P-12200-A, or equivalent, must be obtained prior to installation. Failure to follow this procedure

may result in improper stator alignment. This will result in the fuel system being out of time with the engine, possibly causing engine damage.

1. Disconnect the negative battery cable.
2. Remove the ignition coil, radio capacitor and ignition coil bracket.
3. Disengage the wiring harness connector from the CMP sensor.

➡Prior to removing the camshaft position sensor, set the No. 1 cylinder to 10° After Top Dead Center (ATDC) of the compression stroke. Note the position of the sensor electrical connection. When installing the sensor, the connection must be in the exact same position.

4. Position the No. 1 cylinder at 10° ATDC, then matchmark the CMP sensor terminal connector position with the engine assembly.
5. Remove the camshaft position sensor retaining screws and sensor.
6. Remove the retaining bolt and hold-down clamp.

➡The oil pump intermediate shaft should be removed with the camshaft sensor housing.

7. Remove the CMP sensor housing from the front engine cover.

To install:

8. If the plastic locator cover is not attached to the replacement camshaft position sensor, attach a synchro positioning tool, such as Ford Tool T89P-12200-A or equivalent. To do so, perform the following:

   a. Engage the sensor housing vane into the radial slot of the tool.
   b. Rotate the tool on the camshaft sensor housing until the tool boss engages the notch in the sensor housing.

➡The cover tool should be square and in contact with the entire top surface of the camshaft position sensor housing.

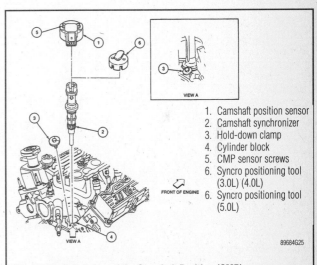

1. Camshaft position sensor
2. Camshaft synchronizer
3. Hold-down clamp
4. Cylinder block
5. CMP sensor screws
6. Syncro positioning tool (3.0L) (4.0L)
6. Syncro positioning tool (5.0L)

89684G25

Fig. 37 Exploded view of the Camshaft Position (CMP) sensor mounting for the 3.0L engine—4.0L and 5.0L engines are similar

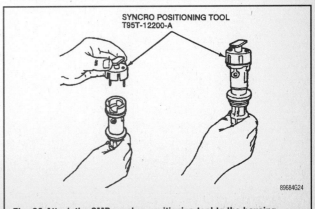

SYNCRO POSITIONING TOOL T95T-12200-A

89684G24

Fig. 38 Attach the CMP synchro positioning tool to the housing

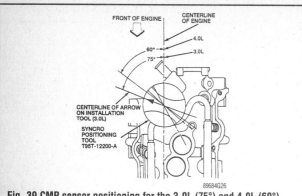

Fig. 39 CMP sensor positioning for the 3.0L (75°) and 4.0L (60°) engines

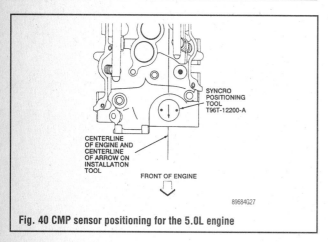

Fig. 40 CMP sensor positioning for the 5.0L engine

9. Transfer the oil pump intermediate shaft from the old camshaft position sensor housing to the replacement sensor housing.

10. Install the camshaft sensor housing so that the drive gear engagement occurs when the arrow on the locator tool is pointed approximately 30° counter-clockwise (the sensor terminal connector should be aligned with its match-marks) from the face of the cylinder block.

11. Install the hold-down clamp and bolt, then tighten the bolt to 15–22 ft. lbs. (20–30 Nm).

12. Remove the synchro positioning tool.

✻✻ CAUTION

If the sensor connector is positioned correctly, DO NOT reposition the connector by rotating the sensor housing. This will result in the fuel system being out of time with the engine. This could possibly cause engine damage. Remove the sensor housing and repeat the installation procedure beginning with step one.

13. Install the sensor and retaining screws, tighten the screws to 22–31 inch lbs. (2–4 Nm).

14. Attach the engine control sensor wiring connector to the sensor.

15. Install the ignition coil bracket, radio ignition capacitor and ignition coil.

16. Connect the negative battery cable.

4.0L SOHC Engine (VIN E)

1. Disconnect the negative battery cable.

2. Disconnect the engine control sensor wiring from the camshaft position sensor.

3. Remove the sensor retaining screw and the sensor from the left-hand valve cover.

To install:

4. Make sure the camshaft position sensor mounting surface is clean and the O-ring is positioned correctly.

5. Position the sensor, then install the retaining screw and tighten it to 71–106 inch lbs. (8–12 Nm).

✻✻ WARNING

Do not overtighten the screw; you may damage the sensor if the retaining screw is overtightened

6. Engage the wiring harness connector to the CMP sensor.

7. Connect the negative battery cable.

Crankshaft Position (CKP) Sensor

OPERATION

The Crankshaft Position (CKP) sensor, located on the front cover (near the crankshaft pulley) is used to determine crankshaft position and crankshaft rpm. The CKP sensor is a reluctance sensor which senses the passing of teeth on a sensor ring because the teeth disrupt the magnetic field of the sensor. This disruption creates a voltage fluctuation, which is monitored by the PCM.

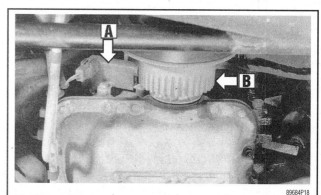

The CKP sensor (A) is triggered by the teeth which are machined into the crankshaft damper (B)

TESTING

♦ **See Figures 41 and 42**

Using a DVOM set to the DC scale to monitor less than 5 volts, measure the voltage between the sensor Cylinder Identification (CID) terminal and ground by backprobing the sensor connector. If the connector cannot be backprobed, fabricate or purchase a test harness. The sensor is okay if the voltage reading varies more than 0.1 volt with the engine running at varying RPM.

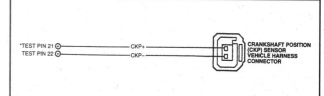

Fig. 41 CKP sensor wire harness connections for all engines except the 4.0L (VIN X and E) engines

REMOVAL & INSTALLATION

♦ **See Figures 43, 44 and 45**

1. Disconnect the negative battery cable.

2. Disengage the wiring harness connector from the CKP sensor.

3. Loosen the CKP sensor mounting stud/bolts, then separate the sensor form the engine front cover.

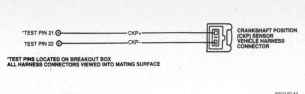

Fig. 42 CKP sensor wire harness connections for the 4.0L (VIN X and E) engines

To install:

→When installing a new sensor on the 4.0L (VIN X and E), position the sensor against the crankshaft damper. There are small rub tabs which wear off and allow the sensor to be perfectly spaced from the damper.

4. Position the sensor against the engine front cover, then install the mounting stud/bolts. Tighten them until snug.
5. Install the CKP sensor cover and retaining nuts; tighten the nuts until snug.
6. Reattach the wiring harness connector to the CKP sensor.
7. Connect the negative battery cable.

Vehicle Speed Sensor (VSS)

OPERATION

The Vehicle Speed Sensor (VSS) is a magnetic pick-up that sends a signal to the Powertrain Control Module (PCM). The sensor measures the rotation of the transmission and the PCM determines the corresponding vehicle speed.

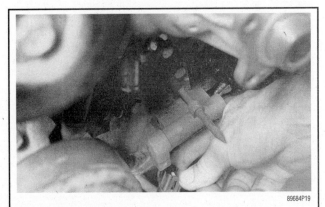

To remove the CKP sensor, first disconnect the wire harness plug . . .

TESTING

▶ **See Figure 46**

1. Turn the ignition switch to the **OFF** position.
2. Disengage the wiring harness connector from the VSS.
3. Using a Digital Volt-Ohmmeter (DVOM), measure the resistance (DVOM ohmmeter function) between the sensor terminals. If the resistance is 190–250 ohms, the sensor is okay.

. . . then unbolt the sensor and pull it away from the engine—crankshaft damper removed for clarity

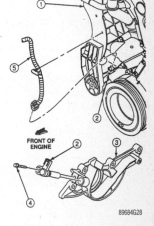

1. Generator mounting bracket (front)
2. Crankshaft position sensor
3. Engine front cover
4. Crankshaft position sensor bolt
5. Engine control sensor wiring

Fig. 43 Exploded view of the 2.3L and 2.5L Crankshaft Position (CKP) sensor

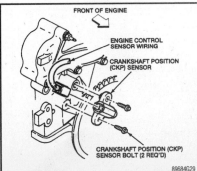

Fig. 44 Exploded view of the 3.0L Crankshaft Position (CKP) sensor—5.0L engine is similar

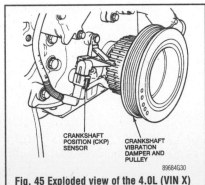

Fig. 45 Exploded view of the 4.0L (VIN X) Crankshaft Position (CKP) sensor—4.0L SOHC (VIN E) engine is similar

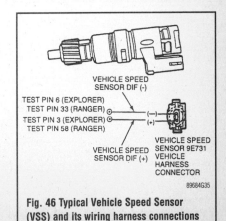

Fig. 46 Typical Vehicle Speed Sensor (VSS) and its wiring harness connections

REMOVAL & INSTALLATION

The VSS is located half-way down the right-hand side of the transmission assembly.

1. Apply parking brake, block the rear wheels, then raise and safely support the front of the vehicle on jackstands.

2. From under the right-hand side of the vehicle, disengage the wiring harness connector from the VSS.

3. Loosen the VSS hold-down bolt, then pull the VSS out of the transmission housing.

To install:

4. If a new sensor is being installed, transfer the driven gear retainer and gear to the new sensor.

5. Ensure that the O-ring is properly seated in the VSS housing.

6. For ease of assembly, engage the wiring harness connector to the VSS, then insert the VSS into the transmission assembly.

7. Install and tighten the VSS hold-down bolt to 62–88 inch lbs. (7–10 Nm).

8. Lower the vehicle and remove the wheel blocks.

COMPONENT LOCATIONS

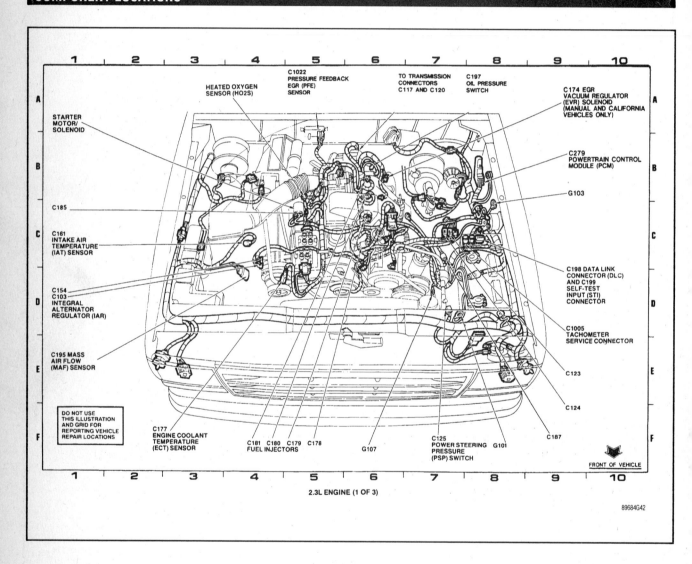

2.3L ENGINE (1 OF 3)

89684G42

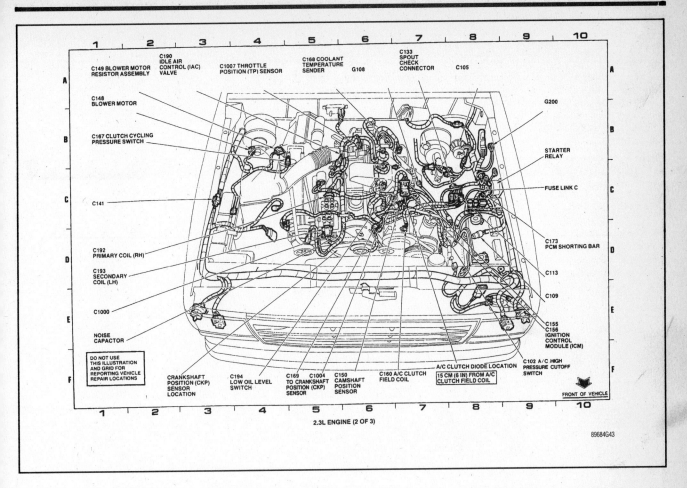

C149 BLOWER MOTOR RESISTOR ASSEMBLY

C190 IDLE AIR CONTROL (IAC) VALVE

C1007 THROTTLE POSITION (TP) SENSOR

C168 COOLANT TEMPERATURE SENDER

G108

C133 SPOUT CHECK CONNECTOR

C105

C148 BLOWER MOTOR

G200

C167 CLUTCH CYCLING PRESSURE SWITCH

STARTER RELAY

FUSE LINK C

C141

C173 PCM SHORTING BAR

C192 PRIMARY COIL (RH)

C113

C193 SECONDARY COIL (LH)

C109

C1000

C155 C156 IGNITION CONTROL MODULE (ICM)

NOISE CAPACTOR

DO NOT USE THIS ILLUSTRATION AND GRID FOR REPORTING VEHICLE REPAIR LOCATIONS

CRANKSHAFT POSITION (CKP) SENSOR LOCATION

C194 LOW OIL LEVEL SWITCH

C169 TO CRANKSHAFT POSITION (CKP) SENSOR

C1004

C150 CAMSHAFT POSITION SENSOR

C160 A/C CLUTCH FIELD COIL

A/C CLUTCH DIODE LOCATION 15 CM (6 IN) FROM A/C CLUTCH FIELD COIL

C102 A/C HIGH PRESSURE CUTOFF SWITCH

FRONT OF VEHICLE

2.3L ENGINE (2 OF 3)

89684G43

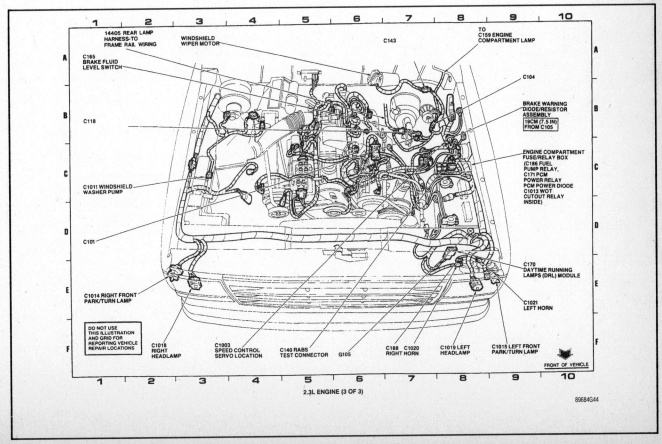

14405 REAR LAMP HARNESS-TO FRAME RAIL WIRING

WINDSHIELD WIPER MOTOR

C143

TO C159 ENGINE COMPARTMENT LAMP

C165 BRAKE FLUID LEVEL SWITCH

C104

BRAKE WARNING DIODE/RESISTOR ASSEMBLY 19CM (7.5 IN) FROM C105

C118

ENGINE COMPARTMENT FUSE/RELAY BOX (C186 FUEL PUMP RELAY, C171 PCM POWER RELAY PCM POWER DIODE C1013 WOT CUTOUT RELAY INSIDE)

C1011 WINDSHIELD WASHER PUMP

C101

C170 DAYTIME RUNNING LAMPS (DRL) MODULE

C1014 RIGHT FRONT PARK/TURN LAMP

C1021 LEFT HORN

DO NOT USE THIS ILLUSTRATION AND GRID FOR REPORTING VEHICLE REPAIR LOCATIONS

C1018 RIGHT HEADLAMP

C1003 SPEED CONTROL SERVO LOCATION

C140 RABS TEST CONNECTOR

G105

C188 C1020 RIGHT HORN

C1019 LEFT HEADLAMP

C1015 LEFT FRONT PARK/TURN LAMP

FRONT OF VEHICLE

2.3L ENGINE (3 OF 3)

89684G44

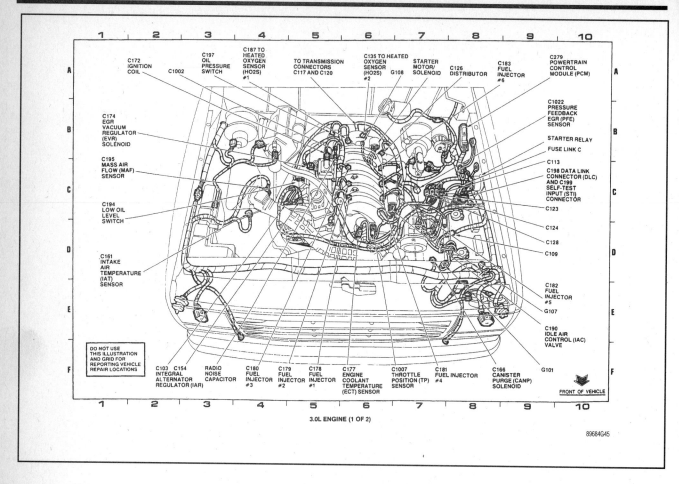

3.0L ENGINE (1 OF 2)

89684G45

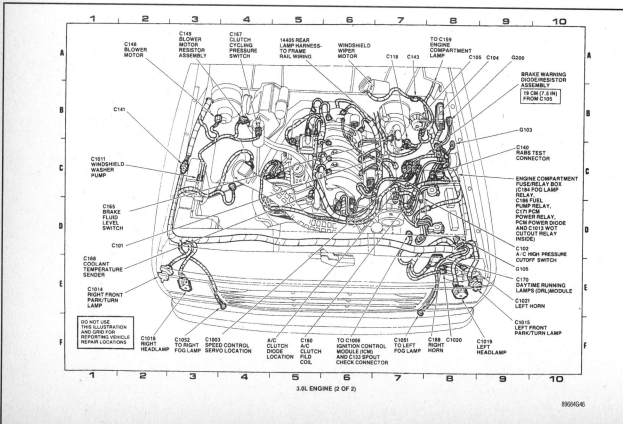

3.0L ENGINE (2 OF 2)

89684G46

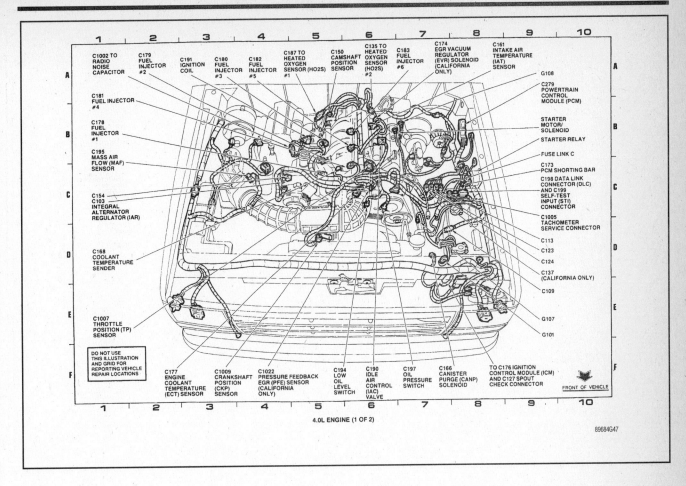

C1002 TO RADIO NOISE CAPACITOR
C179 FUEL INJECTOR #2
C191 IGNITION COIL
C180 FUEL INJECTOR #3
C182 FUEL INJECTOR #5
C187 TO HEATED OXYGEN SENSOR (HO2S) #1
C150 CAMSHAFT POSITION SENSOR
C135 TO HEATED OXYGEN SENSOR (HO2S) #2
C183 FUEL INJECTOR #6
C174 EGR VACUUM REGULATOR (EVR) SOLENOID (CALIFORNIA ONLY)
C161 INTAKE AIR TEMPERATURE (IAT) SENSOR

C181 FUEL INJECTOR #4

C178 FUEL INJECTOR #1

C195 MASS AIR FLOW (MAF) SENSOR

C154 C103 INTEGRAL ALTERNATOR REGULATOR (IAR)

C168 COOLANT TEMPERATURE SENDER

C1007 THROTTLE POSITION (TP) SENSOR

DO NOT USE THIS ILLUSTRATION AND GRID FOR REPORTING VEHICLE REPAIR LOCATIONS

G108

C279 POWERTRAIN CONTROL MODULE (PCM)

STARTER MOTOR/ SOLENOID

STARTER RELAY

FUSE LINK C

C173 PCM SHORTING BAR

C198 DATA LINK CONNECTOR (DLC) AND C199 SELF-TEST INPUT (STI) CONNECTOR

C1005 TACHOMETER SERVICE CONNECTOR

C113
C123
C124
C137 (CALIFORNIA ONLY)
C109

G107

G101

C177 ENGINE COOLANT TEMPERATURE (ECT) SENSOR
C1009 CRANKSHAFT POSITION (CKP) SENSOR
C1022 PRESSURE FEEDBACK EGR (PFE) SENSOR (CALIFORNIA ONLY)
C194 LOW OIL LEVEL SWITCH
C190 IDLE AIR CONTROL (IAC) VALVE
C197 OIL PRESSURE SWITCH
C166 CANISTER PURGE (CANP) SOLENOID
TO C176 IGNITION CONTROL MODULE (ICM) AND C127 SPOUT CHECK CONNECTOR

FRONT OF VEHICLE

4.0L ENGINE (1 OF 2)

89684G47

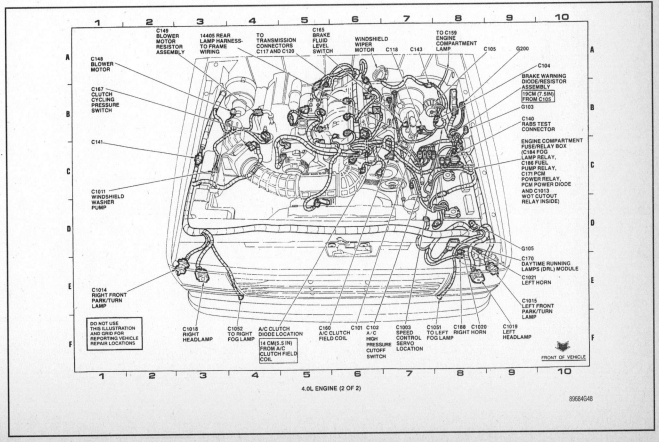

C148 BLOWER MOTOR

C167 CLUTCH CYCLING PRESSURE SWITCH

C141

C1011 WINDSHIELD WASHER PUMP

C1014 RIGHT FRONT PARK/TURN LAMP

DO NOT USE THIS ILLUSTRATION AND GRID FOR REPORTING VEHICLE REPAIR LOCATIONS

C149 BLOWER MOTOR RESISTOR ASSEMBLY
14405 REAR LAMP HARNESS-TO FRAME WIRING
TO TRANSMISSION CONNECTORS C117 AND C120
C165 BRAKE FLUID LEVEL SWITCH
WINDSHIELD WIPER MOTOR
C118
C143
TO C159 ENGINE COMPARTMENT LAMP
C105
G200

C104
BRAKE WARNING DIODE/RESISTOR ASSEMBLY
19CM (7.5IN) FROM C105
G103

C140 RABS TEST CONNECTOR

ENGINE COMPARTMENT FUSE/RELAY BOX (C184 FOG LAMP RELAY, C186 FUEL PUMP RELAY, C171 PCM POWER RELAY, PCM POWER DIODE AND C1013 WOT CUTOUT RELAY INSIDE)

G105

C170 DAYTIME RUNNING LAMPS (DRL) MODULE

C1021 LEFT HORN

C1015 LEFT FRONT PARK/TURN LAMP

C1019 LEFT HEADLAMP

C1018 RIGHT HEADLAMP
C1052 TO RIGHT FOG LAMP
A/C CLUTCH DIODE LOCATION 14 CM(5.5 IN) FROM A/C CLUTCH FIELD COIL
C160 A/C CLUTCH FIELD COIL
C101
C102 A/C HIGH PRESSURE CUTOFF SWITCH
C1003 SPEED CONTROL SERVO LOCATION
C1051 TO LEFT FOG LAMP
C188 RIGHT HORN
C1020 LEFT HORN

FRONT OF VEHICLE

4.0L ENGINE (2 OF 2)

89684G48

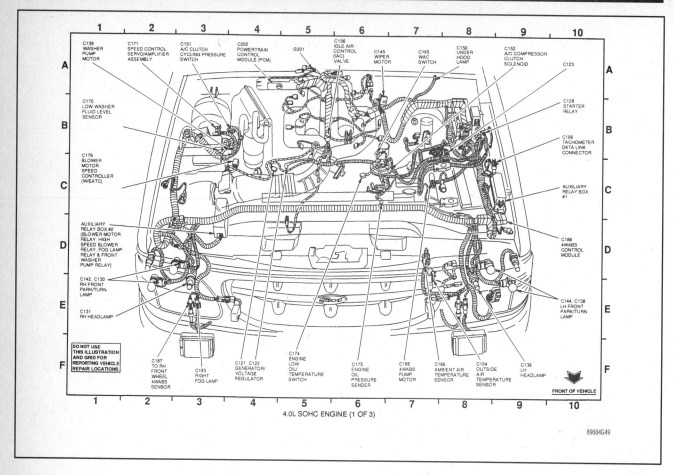

4.0L SOHC ENGINE (1 OF 3)

89684G49

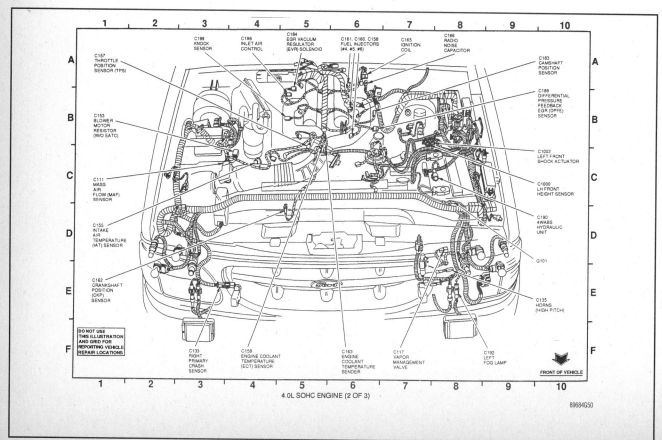

4.0L SOHC ENGINE (2 OF 3)

89684G50

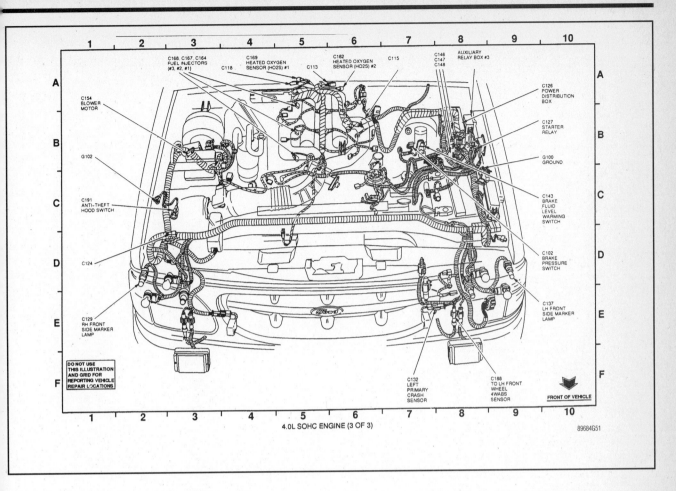

4.0L SOHC ENGINE (3 OF 3)

89684G51

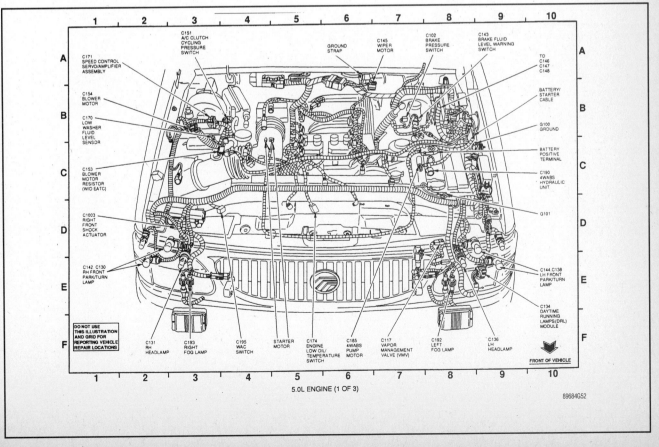

5.0L ENGINE (1 OF 3)

89684G52

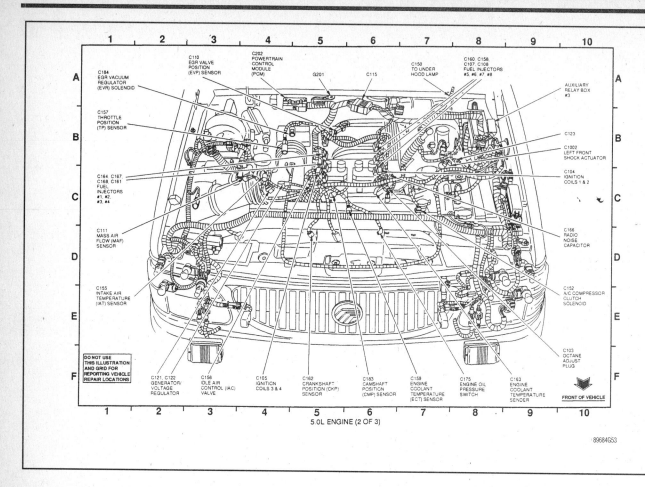

C184
EGR VACUUM
REGULATOR
(EVR) SOLENOID

C110
EGR VALVE
POSITION
(EVP) SENSOR

C202
POWERTRAIN
CONTROL
MODULE
(PCM)

G201

C115

C150
TO UNDER
HOOD LAMP

C160, C158,
C107, C108
FUEL INJECTORS
#5, #6, #7, #8

AUXILIARY
RELAY BOX
#3

C157
THROTTLE
POSITION
(TP) SENSOR

C123

C1002
LEFT FRONT
SHOCK ACTUATOR

C164, C167,
C168, C161
FUEL
INJECTORS
#1, #2,
#3, #4

C104
IGNITION
COILS 1 & 2

C111
MASS AIR
FLOW (MAF)
SENSOR

C166
RADIO
NOISE
CAPACITOR

C155
INTAKE AIR
TEMPERATURE
(IAT) SENSOR

C152
A/C COMPRESSOR
CLUTCH
SOLENOID

C103
OCTANE
ADJUST
PLUG

DO NOT USE
THIS ILLUSTRATION
AND GRID FOR
REPORTING VEHICLE
REPAIR LOCATIONS

C121, C122
GENERATOR/
VOLTAGE
REGULATOR

C156
IDLE AIR
CONTROL (IAC)
VALVE

C105
IGNITION
COILS 3 & 4

C162
CRANKSHAFT
POSITION (CKP)
SENSOR

C183
CAMSHAFT
POSITION
(CMP) SENSOR

C159
ENGINE
COOLANT
TEMPERATURE
(ECT) SENSOR

C175
ENGINE OIL
PRESSURE
SWITCH

C163
ENGINE
COOLANT
TEMPERATURE
SENDER

FRONT OF VEHICLE

5.0L ENGINE (2 OF 3)

89684G53

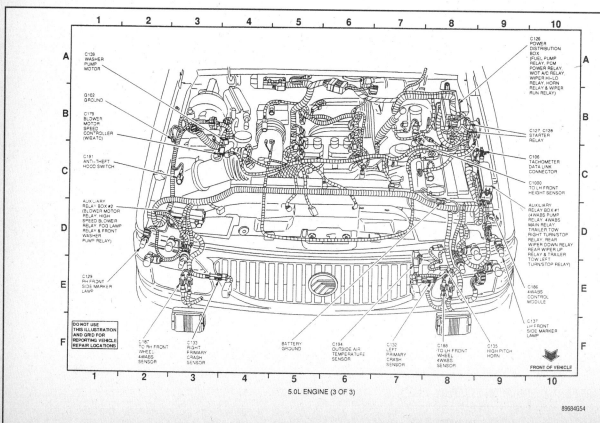

C139
WASHER
PUMP
MOTOR

C126
POWER
DISTRIBUTION
BOX
(FUEL PUMP
RELAY, PCM
POWER RELAY,
WOT A/C RELAY,
WIPER HI-LO
RELAY, HORN
RELAY & WIPER
RUN RELAY)

G102
GROUND

C179
BLOWER
MOTOR
SPEED
CONTROLLER
(W/EATC)

C127, C128
STARTER
RELAY

C106
TACHOMETER
DATA LINK
CONNECTOR

C191
ANTI-THEFT
HOOD SWITCH

C1000
TO LH FRONT
HEIGHT SENSOR

AUXILIARY
RELAY BOX #2
(BLOWER MOTOR
RELAY, HIGH
SPEED BLOWER
RELAY, FOG LAMP
RELAY & FRONT
WASHER
PUMP RELAY)

AUXILIARY
RELAY BOX #1
(4WABS PUMP
RELAY, 4WABS
MAIN RELAY,
TRAILER TOW
RIGHT TURN/STOP
RELAY, REAR
WIPER DOWN RELAY,
REAR WIPER UP
RELAY & TRAILER
TOW LEFT
TURN/STOP RELAY)

C129
RH FRONT
SIDE MARKER
LAMP

C186
4WABS
CONTROL
MODULE

C137
LH FRONT
SIDE MARKER
LAMP

DO NOT USE
THIS ILLUSTRATION
AND GRID FOR
REPORTING VEHICLE
REPAIR LOCATIONS

C187
TO RH FRONT
WHEEL
4WABS
SENSOR

C133
RIGHT
PRIMARY
CRASH
SENSOR

BATTERY
GROUND

C194
OUTSIDE AIR
TEMPERATURE
SENSOR

C132
LEFT
PRIMARY
CRASH
SENSOR

C188
TO LH FRONT
WHEEL
4WABS
SENSOR

C135
HIGH PITCH
HORN

FRONT OF VEHICLE

5.0L ENGINE (3 OF 3)

89684G54

TROUBLE CODES

General Description

Ford Ranger/Explorer and Mountaineer vehicles employ the Electronic Engine Control (EEC) system, to manage fuel, ignition and emissions on vehicle engines.

The Powertrain Control Module (PCM) is given responsibility for the operation of the emission control devices, cooling fans, ignition and advance and in some cases, automatic transmission functions. Because the EEC oversees both the ignition timing and the fuel injector operation, a precise air/fuel ratio will be maintained under all operating conditions. The PCM is a microprocessor or small computer which receives electrical inputs from several sensors, switches and relays on and around the engine.

Based on combinations of these inputs, the PCM controls outputs to various devices concerned with engine operation and emissions. The engine control assembly relies on the signals to form a correct picture of current vehicle operation. If any of the input signals is incorrect, the PCM reacts to what ever picture is painted for it. For example, if the coolant temperature sensor is inaccurate and reads too low, the PCM may see a picture of the engine never warming up. Consequently, the engine settings will be maintained as if the engine were cold. Because so many inputs can affect one output, correct diagnostic procedures are essential on these systems.

One part of the PCM is devoted to monitoring both input and output functions within the system. This ability forms the core of the self-diagnostic system. If a problem is detected within a circuit, the controller will recognize the fault, assign it an identification code, and store the code in a memory section. Depending on the year and model, the fault code(s) may be represented by two or three digit numbers. The stored code(s) may be retrieved during diagnosis.

While the EEC system is capable of recognizing many internal faults, certain faults will not be recognized. Because the computer system sees only electrical signals, it cannot sense or react to mechanical or vacuum faults affecting engine operation. Some of these faults may affect another component which will set a code. For example, the PCM monitors the output signal to the fuel injectors, but cannot detect a partially clogged injector. As long as the output driver responds correctly, the computer will read the system as functioning correctly. However, the improper flow of fuel may result in a lean mixture. This would, in turn, be detected by the oxygen sensor and noticed as a constantly lean signal by the PCM. Once the signal falls outside the pre-programmed limits, the engine control assembly would notice the fault and set an identification code.

Additionally, the EEC system employs adaptive fuel logic. This process is used to compensate for normal wear and variability within the fuel system. Once the engine enters steady-state operation, the engine control assembly watches the oxygen sensor signal for a bias or tendency to run slightly rich or lean. If such a bias is detected, the adaptive logic corrects the fuel delivery to bring the air/fuel mixture towards a centered or 14.7:1 ratio. This compensating shift is stored in a non-volatile memory which is retained by battery power even with the ignition switched **OFF**. The correction factor is then available the next time the vehicle is operated.

➡ **If the battery cable(s) is disconnected for longer than 5 minutes, the adaptive fuel factor will be lost. After repair it will be necessary to drive the truck at least 10 miles to allow the processor to relearn the correct factors. The driving period should include steady-throttle open road driving if possible. During the drive, the vehicle may exhibit driveability symptoms not noticed before. These symptoms should clear as the PCM computes the correction factor. The PCM will also store Code 19 indicating loss of power to the controller.**

FAILURE MODE EFFECTS MANAGEMENT (FMEM)

The engine controller assembly contains back-up programs which allow the engine to operate if a sensor signal is lost. If a sensor input is seen to be out of range—either high or low—the FMEM program is used. The processor substitutes a fixed value for the missing sensor signal. The engine will continue to operate, although performance and driveability may be noticeably reduced. This function of the controller is sometimes referred to as the limp-in or fail-safe mode. If the missing sensor signal is restored, the FMEM system immediately returns the system to normal operation. The dashboard warning lamp will be lit when FMEM is in effect.

HARDWARE LIMITED OPERATION STRATEGY (HLOS)

This mode is only used if the fault is too extreme for the FMEM circuit to handle. In this mode, the processor has ceased all computation and control; the entire system is run on fixed values. The vehicle may be operated but performance and driveability will be greatly reduced. The fixed or default settings provide minimal calibration, allowing the vehicle to be carefully driven in for service. The dashboard warning lamp will be lit when HLOS is engaged. Codes cannot be read while the system is operating in this mode.

MALFUNCTION INDICATOR LAMP (MIL)

The CHECK ENGINE or SERVICE ENGINE SOON dashboard warning lamp is referred to as the Malfunction Indicator Lamp (MIL). The lamp is connected to the engine control assembly and will alert the driver to certain malfunctions within the EEC system. When the lamp is lit, the PCM has detected a fault and stored an identity code in memory. The engine control system will usually enter either FMEM or HLOS mode and driveability will be impaired.

The light will stay on as long as the fault causing it is present. Should the fault self-correct, the MIL will extinguish but the stored code will remain in memory.

Under normal operating conditions, the MIL should light briefly when the ignition key is turned **ON**. As soon as the PCM receives a signal that the engine is cranking, the lamp will be extinguished. The dash warning lamp should remain out during the entire operating cycle.

Diagnostic Connector

To read Diagnostic Trouble Codes (DTCís) the test connector for the EEC system must be used. This connector is known as the Assembly Line Diagnostic Link (ALDL) connector on vehicles with EEC-IV ignition equipped engines, or the Data Link Connector (DLC) on all other models (EEC-V), is located in the passenger compartment. It is attached either to the underside of the instrument panel, and is accessible from the driverís side of the vehicle, or it is under the hood near the power distribution box.

The connector is trapezoidal in shape and can accommodate up to 16 terminals.

Reading Codes

EEC-V EQUIPPED ENGINES

The EEC-V equipped engines utilize On Board Diagnostic II (OBD-II) Diagnostic Trouble Codes (DTCís), which are alpha-numeric (they use letters and numbers). The letters in the OBD-II DTCís make it highly difficult to convey the codes through the use of anything but a scan tool. Therefore, to read the OBD-II DTCís on these vehicles it is necessary to utilize an OBD-II compatible scan tool.

1. Ensure that the ignition switch is in the **OFF** position.
2. Apply the parking brake.
3. Ensure that transmission gearshift is in either Park (automatic transmissions) or Neutral (manual transmissions).
4. Block the rear wheels.
5. Turn off all electrical loads, such as the heater blower motor, the radio, the rear defroster, etc.
6. Connect the scan tool to the Data Link Connector (DLC—3.8L and 4.6L engines) or the Assembly Line Diagnostic Link (ALDL—5.0L engine). Make certain the test button on the scan tool is unlatched or up.
7. Turn the ignition switch to the **ON** position without starting the engine (KOEO).
8. Using the scan tool, retrieve and record any continuous memory DTCís.
9. Turn the ignition switch to the **OFF** position.
10. Start the engine and run it until normal operating temperature is reached.
11. Turn the engine **OFF** and wait 10 seconds.
12. Turn the ignition switch **ON** but do not start the engine.
13. Activate the KOEO self-test. Retrieve and record any KOEO DTCís after the KOEO test is complete.

➡ **Ignore DTC 1000.**

14. If any DTCís were present, refer to the accompanying OBD-II charts to locate the problem(s).

To access the diagnostic connector, unfasten it from its protective cover, which is labeled EEC TEST

89684P21

Inexpensive scan tools, such as this Auto Xray®, are available to interface with your Ford vehicle

TCCS4P11

When using a scan tool, make sure to follow all of the manufacturers instructions carefully to ensure proper diagnosis

TCCS4P08

OBD-II DIAGNOSTIC TROUBLE CODE (DTC) APPLICATIONS

DTC	Applicable System or Component
Constant Memory Trouble Codes	
P0102	MAF sensor reference signal voltage too low
P0103	MAF sensor reference signal too high
P0112	IAT or ECT intermittent fault
P0113	IAT or ECT intermittent fault
P0117	IAT or ECT intermittent fault
P0118	IAT or ECT intermittent fault
P0121	TP sensor fault
P0122	TP sensor reference signal voltage too low
P0123	TP sensor reference signal voltage too high
P0125	ECT sensor fault
P0131	Heated Oxygen Sensor (HO2S) produced negative reference signal voltage
P0133	Fuel control system fault
P0135	HO2S circuit shorted to ground, open or shorted to VPWR circuit
P0136	HO2S fault
P0141	HO2S circuit shorted to ground, open or shorted to VPWR circuit
P0151	Heated Oxygen Sensor (HO2S) produced negative reference signal voltage
P0153	Fuel control system fault
P0155	HO2S circuit shorted to ground, open or shorted to VPWR circuit
P0156	HO2S fault
P0161	HO2S circuit shorted to ground, open or shorted to VPWR circuit
P0171	Air/fuel ratio is too lean or rich for PCM to correct
P0172	Air/fuel ratio is too lean or rich for PCM to correct
P0174	Air/fuel ratio is too lean or rich for PCM to correct
P0175	Air/fuel ratio is too lean or rich for PCM to correct
P0222	Traction Control (TC) system fault
P0223	TC system TP-B circuit voltage fault
P0230	Fuel pump primary circuit fault
P0231	Fuel pump relay and system fault
P0232	Fuel pump relay and system fault
P0300	Misfire detection monitor and/or circuit fault
P0301	Misfire detection monitor and/or circuit fault
P0302	Misfire detection monitor and/or circuit fault
P0303	Misfire detection monitor and/or circuit fault
P0304	Misfire detection monitor and/or circuit fault
P0305	Misfire detection monitor and/or circuit fault
P0306	Misfire detection monitor and/or circuit fault
P0307	Misfire detection monitor and/or circuit fault
P0308	Misfire detection monitor and/or circuit fault
P0320	Ignition engine speed input circuit fault
P0325	Knock Sensor (KS) and/or circuit fault
P0326	Knock Sensor (KS) and/or circuit fault
P0330	Knock Sensor (KS) and/or circuit fault
P0331	Knock Sensor (KS) and/or circuit fault
P0340	Camshaft Position (CMP) sensor and/or circuit fault
P0350	Ignition coil primary circuit fault
P0351	Ignition coil primary circuit fault
P0352	Ignition coil primary circuit fault
P0353	Ignition coil primary circuit fault

89684C04

OBD-II DIAGNOSTIC TROUBLE CODE (DTC) APPLICATIONS

DTC	Applicable System or Component
	Constant Memory Trouble Codes (continued)
P0354	Ignition coil primary circuit fault
P0401	Insufficient EGR flow detected
P0402	EGR flow at idle fault
P0411	Electric air pump hose fault
P0412	Secondary Air Injection (AIR) system fault
P0413	AIR injection VPWR circuit voltage fault
P0414	AIR injection VPWR circuit voltage fault
P0416	AIR injection VPWR circuit voltage fault
P0417	AIR injection VPWR circuit voltage fault
P0420	Catalyst efficiency monitor and/or exhaust system fault
P0430	Catalyst efficiency monitor and/or exhaust system fault
P0442	Evaporative Emission (EVAP) system leak detected
P0443	Intermittent EVAP canister purge valve fault
P0446	EVAP system Fuel Tank Pressure (FTP) sensor fault
P0452	FTP sensor circuit input signal too low
P0453	FTP sensor circuit input signal too high
P0455	Evaporative Emission (EVAP) system leak detected
P0460	Fuel level input circuit fault
P0500	Vehicle Speed Sensor (VSS) and/or circuit fault
P0501	Vehicle Speed Sensor (VSS) and/or circuit fault
P0503	Intermittent VSS and/or circuit fault
P0552	Power Steering Pressure (PSP) sensor and/or circuit fault
P0553	Power Steering Pressure (PSP) sensor and/or circuit fault
P0703	BOO switch input signal fault
P0704	CPP or PNP switch fault, or CPP or PNP switch voltage is too high or open when it should be low or closed
P0707	Manual transmission fault
P0708	Manual transmission fault
P0712	Manual transmission fault
P0713	Manual transmission fault
P0715	Manual transmission fault
P0720	Manual transmission fault
P0721	Manual transmission fault
P0731	Manual transmission fault
P0732	Manual transmission fault
P0733	Manual transmission fault
P0734	Manual transmission fault
P0735	Manual transmission fault
P0736	Manual transmission fault
P0741	Manual transmission fault
P0743	Manual transmission fault
P0746	Manual transmission fault
P0750	Manual transmission fault
P0751	Manual transmission fault
P0755	Manual transmission fault
P0756	Manual transmission fault
P0760	Manual transmission fault
P0761	Manual transmission fault
P0765	Manual transmission fault

89684C05

OBD-II DIAGNOSTIC TROUBLE CODE (DTC) APPLICATIONS

DTC	Applicable System or Component
	Constant Memory Trouble Codes (continued)
P0781	Manual transmission fault
P0782	Manual transmission fault
P0783	Manual transmission fault
P0784	Manual transmission fault
P1000	All OBD-II monitors not yet successfully tested
P1100	MAF sensor reference signal voltage out of specifications
P1112	IAT or ECT intermittent fault
P1117	IAT or ECT intermittent fault
P1120	TP sensor reference voltage out of specifications
P1121	TP sensor reference signal inconsistent with MAF sensor reference signal
P1125	TP sensor reference voltage out of specifications
P1130	HO2S fault
P1131	HO2S fault
P1132	HO2S fault
P1150	HO2S fault
P1151	HO2S fault
P1152	HO2S fault
P1220	TC system series throttle system fault
P1224	Series throttle assembly fault
P1232	Low speed fuel pump primary circuit fault
P1233	Fuel pump driver module and/or system circuit fault
P1234	Fuel pump driver module and/or system circuit fault
P1235	Fuel pump circuit, fuel pump driver module or PCM fault
P1236	Fuel pump circuit, fuel pump driver module or PCM fault
P1237	Fuel pump driver module circuit fault
P1238	Fuel pump driver module circuit fault
P1260	Anti-theft system detected a break-in
P1270	Engine and/or vehicle speed exceeded calibrated limits during vehicle operation
P1285	Engine overheat condition was sensed by PCM
P1289	Intermittent CHT sensor and/or circuit fault
P1290	Intermittent CHT sensor and/or circuit fault
P1299	Engine overheat condition was sensed by PCM
P1309	CMP sensor output signal fault
P1400	Exhaust Gas Recirculation (EGR) system fault
P1401	EVP sensor signal voltage fault
P1405	Upstream pressure hose connection fault
P1406	Downstream pressure hose connection fault
P1409	EGR vacuum regulator solenoid fault
P1411	AIR injection is not being diverted when requested
P1413	AIR injection solid state relay voltage fault
P1414	AIR injection EAIR monitor circuit fault
P1442	Evaporative Emission (EVAP) system leak detected
P1443	Evaporative purge flow sensor fault
P1444	PF circuit input signal too low
P1445	PF circuit input signal too high
P1450	EVAP system unable to bleed fuel tank vacuum fault
P1451	EVAP system Canister Vent (CV) solenoid fault
P1452	EVAP system unable to bleed fuel tank vacuum fault

89684C06

OBD-II DIAGNOSTIC TROUBLE CODE (DTC) APPLICATIONS

DTC	Applicable System or Component
Constant Memory Trouble Codes (continued)	
P1455	EVAP system fault
P1460	Wide Open Throttle A/C (WAC) circuit fault occurred during vehicle operation
P1461	Air Conditioning Pressure (ACP) sensor and/or circuit fault
P1462	ACP sensor reference signal too low
P1463	ACP sensor did not detect a pressure change in A/C system when activated
P1469	Frequent A/C compressor clutch cycling detected
P1474	Fan control circuit failure detected during vehicle operation
P1479	Fan control circuit failure detected during vehicle operation
P1483	Power-to-cooling fan circuit exceeded normal current draw when fan was activated
P1484	Variable load control module (VLCM) and/or circuit fault
P1500	Intermittent VSS reference signal fault
P1504	Idle Air Control (IAC) valve and/or circuit fault
P1505	IAC valve and/or circuit fault
P1506	IAC valve overspeed fault
P1507	Idle Air Control (IAC) valve and/or circuit fault
P1512	Intake Manifold Runner Control (IMRC) fault
P1513	Intake Manifold Runner Control (IMRC) fault
P1516	Intake Manifold Runner Control (IMRC) fault
P1517	Intake Manifold Runner Control (IMRC) fault
P1518	Intake Manifold Runner Control (IMRC) fault
P1519	Intake Manifold Runner Control (IMRC) fault
P1520	Intake Manifold Runner Control (IMRC) fault
P1530	Power-to-A/C clutch circuit open or short to power
P1537	Intake Manifold Runner Control (IMRC) fault
P1538	Intake Manifold Runner Control (IMRC) fault
P1539	Power-to-A/C clutch circuit exceeded normal current draw when A/C was activated
P1549	IMT valve and/or circuit fault
P1550	Power Steering Pressure (PSP) sensor and/or circuit fault
P1625	Open battery supply voltage to VLCM fan or A/C circuit detected
P1626	Open battery supply voltage to VLCM fan or A/C circuit detected
P1651	Power Steering Pressure (PSP) switch and/or circuit fault
P1701	Manual transmission fault
P1714	Manual transmission fault
P1715	Manual transmission fault
P1716	Manual transmission fault
P1717	Manual transmission fault
P1719	Manual transmission fault
P1728	Manual transmission fault
P1741	Manual transmission fault
P1742	Manual transmission fault
P1743	Manual transmission fault
P1744	Manual transmission fault
P1746	Manual transmission fault
P1747	Manual transmission fault
P1749	Manual transmission fault
P1751	Manual transmission fault
P1754	Manual transmission fault
P1756	Manual transmission fault

89684C07

OBD-II DIAGNOSTIC TROUBLE CODE (DTC) APPLICATIONS

DTC	Applicable System or Component
Constant Memory Trouble Codes (continued)	
P1760	Manual transmission fault
P1761	Manual transmission fault
P1762	Manual transmission fault
P1767	Manual transmission fault
P1783	Manual transmission fault
P1784	Manual transmission fault
P1785	Manual transmission fault
P1786	Manual transmission fault
P1787	Manual transmission fault
P1788	Manual transmission fault
P1789	Manual transmission fault
U1020	PCM-to-VLCM two-way communication fault
U1021	Manual transmission fault
U1039	Manual transmission fault
U1051	Manual transmission fault
U1073	PCM-to-VLCM two-way communication fault
U1135	Manual transmission fault
U1256	PCM-to-VLCM two-way communication fault
U1451	Manual transmission fault
Key On, Engine Off (KOEO) Trouble Codes	
135P0	HO2S circuit shorted to ground, open or shorted to VPWR circuit
P0103	MAF sensor reference signal too high
P0112	IAT or ECT sensor reference signal voltage too low
P0113	IAT or ECT sensor reference signal voltage too high
P0117	Cylinder Head Temperature (CHT) sensor and/or circuit fault
P0118	IAT or ECT sensor reference signal voltage too high
P0122	TP sensor reference signal voltage too low
P0123	TP sensor reference signal voltage too high
P0141	HO2S circuit shorted to ground, open or shorted to VPWR circuit
P0155	HO2S circuit shorted to ground, open or shorted to VPWR circuit
P0161	HO2S circuit shorted to ground, open or shorted to VPWR circuit
P0222	Traction Control (TC) system fault
P0223	TC system TP-B circuit voltage fault
P0230	Fuel pump relay fault
P0231	Fuel pump secondary circuit fault
P0232	Fuel pump FPM circuit voltage too high
P0411	Electric air pump hose fault
P0412	Secondary Air Injection (AIR) system fault
P0413	AIR injection VPWR circuit voltage fault
P0414	AIR injection VPWR circuit voltage fault
P0416	AIR injection VPWR circuit voltage fault
P0417	AIR injection VPWR circuit voltage fault
P0443	Evaporative Emission (EVAP) system fault
P0452	FTP sensor circuit input signal too low
P0453	FTP sensor circuit input signal too high
P0460	Fuel level input circuit fault
P0603	Keep Alive Power (KAPWR) circuit and/or PCM fault
P0605	Defective PCM, replace the PCM

89684C08

OBD-II DIAGNOSTIC TROUBLE CODE (DTC) APPLICATIONS

DTC	Applicable System or Component
	Key On, Engine Off (KOEO) Trouble Codes (continued)
P0704	CPP or PNP switch fault, or CPP or PNP switch voltage is too high or open when it should be low or closed
P0705	Manual transmission fault
P0712	Manual transmission fault
P0713	Manual transmission fault
P0743	Manual transmission fault
P0750	Manual transmission fault
P0755	Manual transmission fault
P0760	Manual transmission fault
P1000	DTC 1000 should be ignored; continue with other codes
P1101	Manifold Air Flow (MAF) sensor output voltage fault
P1116	Intake Air Temperature (IAT) or Engine Coolant Temperature (ECT) sensor fault
P1124	TP sensor reference voltage out of specifications
P1151	Throttle Position (TP) reference voltage out of specifications
P1151	HO2S fault
P1220	TC system series throttle system fault
P1224	Series throttle assembly fault
P1232	Low speed fuel pump primary circuit fault
P1233	Fuel pump driver module and/or system circuit fault
P1234	Fuel pump driver module and/or system circuit fault
P1235	Fuel pump circuit, fuel pump driver module or PCM fault
P1236	Fuel pump circuit, fuel pump driver module or PCM fault
P1237	Fuel pump driver module circuit fault
P1238	Fuel pump driver module circuit fault
P1288	Cylinder Head Temperature (CHT) sensor fault
P1289	CHT sensor reference signal too high
P1290	CHT sensor reference signal too low
P1390	Octane Adjust (OCT ADJ) system fault
P1400	Exhaust Gas Recirculation (EGR) system fault
P1401	EVP sensor signal voltage fault
P1409	EGR vacuum regulator solenoid fault
P1411	AIR injection is not being diverted when requested
P1413	AIR injection solid state relay voltage fault
P1414	AIR injection EAIR monitor circuit fault
P1451	EVAP system Canister Vent (CV) solenoid fault
P1460	Wide Open Throttle A/C (WAC) circuit fault
P1461	Air Conditioning Pressure (ACP) sensor and/or circuit fault
P1462	ACP sensor reference signal too low
P1464	ACCS input signal too high
P1473	Power-to-cooling fan circuit open or short to power
P1474	Fan control relay and/or circuit fault
P1479	Fan control relay and/or circuit fault
P1483	Power-to-cooling fan circuit exceeded normal current draw when fan was activated
P1484	Variable load control module (VLCM) and/or circuit fault
P1504	Idle Air Control (IAC) valve and/or circuit fault
P1505	IAC valve and/or circuit fault
P1516	Intake Manifold Runner Control (IMRC) fault
P1517	Intake Manifold Runner Control (IMRC) fault
P1518	Intake Manifold Runner Control (IMRC) fault

89684C09

OBD-II DIAGNOSTIC TROUBLE CODE (DTC) APPLICATIONS

DTC	Applicable System or Component
	Key On, Engine Off (KOEO) Trouble Codes (continued)
P1519	Intake Manifold Runner Control (IMRC) fault
P1520	Intake Manifold Runner Control (IMRC) fault
P1530	Power-to-A/C clutch circuit open or short to power
P1537	Intake Manifold Runner Control (IMRC) fault
P1538	Intake Manifold Runner Control (IMRC) fault
P1539	Power-to-A/C clutch circuit exceeded normal current draw when A/C was activated
P1549	IMT valve and/or circuit fault
P1625	Battery voltage to VLCM fan or A/C circuit not detected
P1626	Battery voltage to VLCM fan or A/C circuit not detected
P1650	Power Steering Pressure (PSP) switch and/or circuit fault
P1703	Signal from Brake On/Off (BOO) switch detected when brake pedal is not applied
P1705	Park/Neutral Position (PNP)/Clutch Pedal Position (CPP) switches and/or circuit fault
P1709	Manual transmission fault
P1711	Manual transmission fault
P1746	Manual transmission fault
P1747	Manual transmission fault
P1754	Manual transmission fault
P1760	Manual transmission fault
P1767	Manual transmission fault
P1788	Manual transmission fault
P1789	Manual transmission fault
U1021	PCM-to-VLCM two-way communication fault
U1073	PCM-to-VLCM two-way communication fault
U1256	PCM-to-VLCM two-way communication fault

89684C10

EEC-IV EQUIPPED ENGINES

The EEC-IV equipped engines use an older diagnostic system to monitor and report engine related malfunctions. This older system is known as On Board Diagnostics (OBD-I). The Diagnostic Trouble Codes (DTCís) are two or three digit numbers, and can be read through the use of a scan tool, an analog voltmeter, or with the Malfunction Indicator Lamp (MIL) located on the instrument cluster. Use the accompanying OBD-I DTC charts to decipher the DTCís for the identification of the malfunctioning component or circuit.

Scan Tool Method

1. Connect the scan tool to the self-test connectors. Make certain the test button is unlatched or up.
2. Start the engine and run it until normal operating temperature is reached.
3. Turn the engine **OFF** and wait 10 seconds.
4. Activate the test button on the STAR tester.
5. Turn the ignition switch **ON** but do not start the engine.
6. The codes will be transmitted. Six to nine seconds after the last code, a single separator pulse will be transmitted. Six to nine seconds after this pulse, the codes from the Continuous Memory will be transmitted.
7. Record all service codes displayed. Do not depress the throttle during the test.
8. Afdter the test, compare the DTCís retrieved with the accompanying OBD-I code identification charts.

Analog Voltmeter Method

In the absence of a scan tool, an analog voltmeter may be used to retrieve stored fault codes. Set the meter range to read DC 0–15 volts. Connect the positive lead of the meter to the battery positive terminal and connect the negative lead of the meter to the Self-Test Output (STO) pin of the diagnostic connector.

Follow the directions given previously for performing the scan tool procedure. To activate the procedure, use a jumper wire to connect the signal return pin on the diagnostic connector to the self-test input connector. The self-test input line is the separate wire and connector with or near the diagnostic connector.

The codes will be transmitted as groups of needle sweeps. This method may be used to read either 2 or 3 digit codes. The Continuous Memory codes are separated from the other codes by 6 seconds, a single sweep and another 6 second delay.

1. After the test, compare the DTCís retrieved with the accompanying OBD-I code identification charts.

Malfunction Indicator Lamp (MIL) Method

The Malfunction Indicator Lamp (MIL) on the dashboard may also be used to retrieve the stored codes. This method displays only the stored codes and does not allow any system investigation. It should only be used in field conditions where a quick check of stored codes is needed.

Follow the directions given previously for performing the scan tool procedure. To activate the tests, use a jumper wire to connect the signal return pin on the diagnostic connector to the Self-Test Input (STO) connector. The self-test input line is the separate wire and connector with or near the diagnostic connector.

Codes are transmitted by place value with a pause between the digits; Code 32 would be sent as 3 flashes, a pause and 2 flashes. A slightly longer pause divides codes from each other. Be ready to count and record codes; the only way to repeat a code is to recycle the system. This method may be used to read either 2 or 3 digit codes. The Continuous Memory codes are separated from the other codes by 6 seconds, a single flash and another 6 second delay.

OBD-I DIAGNOSTIC TROUBLE CODE (DTC) APPLICATIONS

DTC	Applicable System or Component
2-Digit Trouble Codes	
11	System pass
12	RPM unable to achieve upper test limit
13	RPM unable to achieve lower test limit
14	PIP circuit failure
15	PCM Keep Alive Memory (KAM) and/or Read Only Memory (ROM) test failed
16	Idle too low to perform EGO test
18	SPOUT circuit open or grounded, spark angle word failure, or IDA circuit failure
19	PCM internal voltage failure
21	ECT out of self-test range
23	TP sensor out of self-test range
24	IAT sensor out of self-test range
25	Knock not sensed during dynamic test
26	MAF out of self-test range
29	Insufficient input from VSS
31	PFE, EVP or EVR circuit below minimum voltage
32	EVP voltage below closed limit
33	EGR valve opening not detected
34	EVP voltage above closed limit
35	PFE or EVP circuit above maximum voltage
41	HEGO sensor circuit indicates system lean, or no HEGO switching detected (right)
42	HEGO sensor circuit indicates system rich (right)
44	Thermactor air system inoperative (right)
45	Thermactor air upstream during self-test
46	Thermactor air not bypassed during self-test
51	ECT or IAT reads -40°F, or circuit open
53	TP sensor circuit above maximum voltage
54	IAT sensor circuit open
56	MAF circuit above maximum voltage
61	ECT reads 254°F, or circuit is grounded
63	TP sensor circuit below minimum voltage
64	IAT sensor input below test minimum, or grounded
66	MAF sensor input below test minimum, or grounded
67	Neutral/Drive switch open, or A/C is on
74	Brake On/Off (BOO) switch failure, or not actuated
75	BOO switch circuit closed, or PCM input open
77	No Wide Open Throttle (WOT) seen in self-test, or operator error
79	A/C or defroster on during the self-test
81	Air management 2 circuit failure
84	EGR vacuum solenoid circuit failure
85	Canister purge solenoid circuit failure
87	Fuel pump primary circuit failure
91	HEGO sensor circuit indicates system lean, or no HEGO switching detected (left)
92	HEGO sensor circuit indicates system rich (left)
94	Thermactor air system inoperative (left)
95	Fuel pump secondary circuit failure, PCM to ground
96	Fuel pump secondary circuit failure, battery to PCM
98	Hard fault present

OBD-I DIAGNOSTIC TROUBLE CODE (DTC) APPLICATIONS

DTC	Applicable System or Component
3-Digit Trouble Codes	
111	System pass
112	IAT sensor circuit grounded or reads 254°F
113	IAT sensor circuit open, or reads –40°F
114	IAT outside test limits during KOEO test
116	ECT outside limits during KOEO test
117	ECT sensor circuit grounded
118	ECT sensor circuit above maximum voltage, or reads –40°F
121	Closed throttle voltage higher or lower than expected
122	TP sensor circuit below minimum voltage
123	TP sensor circuit above maximum voltage
124	TP sensor voltage higher than expected, but with specified range
125	TP sensor voltage lower than expected, but with specified range
129	Insufficient MAF sensor change during Dynamic Response test
136	HEGO shows system always lean (left)
137	HEGO shows system always rich (left)
139	No HEGO switching (left)
144	No HEGO switching (right)
157	MAF sensor circuit below minimum voltage
158	MAF sensor circuit above maximum voltage
159	MAF sensor higher or lower than expected during KOEO test
167	Insufficient TP sensor change during Dynamic Response test
172	No HEGO switching detected, indicates lean (right)
173	HEGO shows system always rich (rear) or no HEGO switching detected, indicates rich
174	HEGO switching time is slow (right)
175	No HEGO switching, system at adaptive limit (left)
177	HEGO shows system always lean (left)
178	HEGO switching time is slow (left)
179	System at lean adaptive limit at part throttle, system rich (right)
181	System at rich adaptive limit at part throttle, system rich (right)
182	System at lean adaptive limit at idle, system rich (right)
183	System at rich adaptive limit at idle, system rich (right)
184	MAF higher than expected
185	MAF lower than expected
186	Injector pulse width higher than expected
187	Injector pulse width lower than expected
188	System at lean adaptive limit at part throttle, system rich (left)
189	System at rich adaptive limit at part throttle, system rich (left)
191	System at lean adaptive limit at idle, system rich (left)
192	System at rich adaptive limit at idle, system rich (left)
211	PIP circuit fault
212	Loss of IDM input to PCM or SPOUT circuit grounded
213	SPOUT circuit open
311	Thermactor air system inoperative (right)
313	Thermactor air not bypassed during self-test
314	Thermactor air system inoperative (left)
327	EVP or DPFE circuit below minimum voltage
328	EGR closed voltage lower than expected

OBD-I DIAGNOSTIC TROUBLE CODE (DTC) APPLICATIONS

DTC	Applicable System or Component
3-Digit Trouble Codes (continued)	
332	Insufficient EGR flow detected
334	EGR closed voltage higher than expected
337	EVP or DPFE circuit above maximum voltage
452	Insufficient input from VSS
511	EEC processor ROM test failed
512	Keep Alive Memory test failed
513	Failure in EEC processor internal voltage
522	Vehicle not in Park or Neutral during KOEO test
539	A/C or defroster on during KOEO test
542	Fuel pump secondary circuit failure, PCM to ground
543	Fuel pump secondary circuit failure, battery to PCM
552	Air management 1 circuit failed
556	Fuel pump primary circuit failure `
558	EGR vacuum regulator circuit failure
565	Canister purge circuit failure
998	Hard fault present

89684C03

Clearing Codes

CONTINUOUS MEMORY CODES

These codes are retained in memory for 40 warm-up cycles. To clear the codes for the purposes of testing or confirming repair, perform the code reading procedure. When the fault codes begin to be displayed, de-activate the test by either disconnecting the jumper wire (meter, MIL or message center) or releasing the test button on the hand scanner. Stopping the test during code transmission will erase the Continuous Memory. Do not disconnect the negative battery cable to clear these codes; the Keep Alive memory will be cleared and a new code, 19, will be stored for loss of PCM power.

KEEP ALIVE MEMORY

The Keep Alive Memory (KAM) contains the adaptive factors used by the processor to compensate for component tolerances and wear. It should not be routinely cleared during diagnosis. If an emissions related part is replaced during repair, the KAM must be cleared. Failure to clear the KAM may cause severe driveability problems since the correction factor for the old component will be applied to the new component.

To clear the Keep Alive Memory, disconnect the negative battery cable for at least 5 minutes. After the memory is cleared and the battery reconnected, the vehicle must be driven at least 10 miles so that the processor may relearn the needed correction factors. The distance to be driven depends on the engine and vehicle, but all drives should include steady-throttle cruise on open roads. Certain driveability problems may be noted during the drive because the adaptive factors are not yet functioning.

VACUUM DIAGRAMS

Following are vacuum diagrams for most of the engine and emissions package combinations covered by this manual. Because vacuum circuits will vary based on various engine and vehicle options, always refer first to the vehicle emission control information label, if present. Should the label be missing, or should vehicle be equipped with a different engine from the vehi-cle's original equipment, refer to the diagrams below for the same or similar configuration.

If you wish to obtain a replacement emissions label, most manufacturers make the labels available for purchase. The labels can usually be ordered from a local dealer.

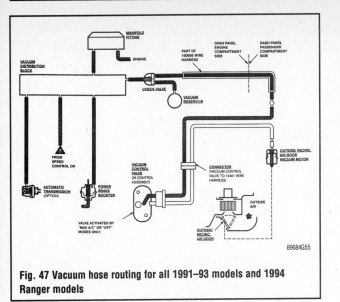

Fig. 47 Vacuum hose routing for all 1991–93 models and 1994 Ranger models

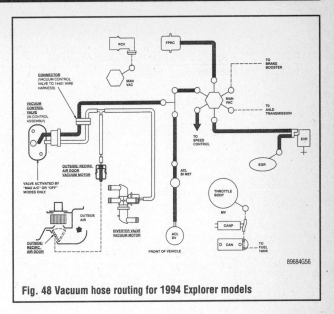

Fig. 48 Vacuum hose routing for 1994 Explorer models

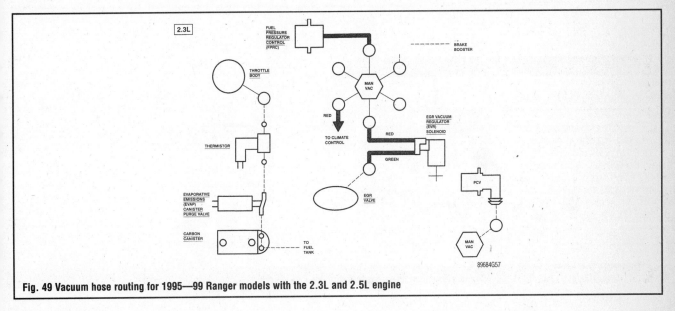

Fig. 49 Vacuum hose routing for 1995—99 Ranger models with the 2.3L and 2.5L engine

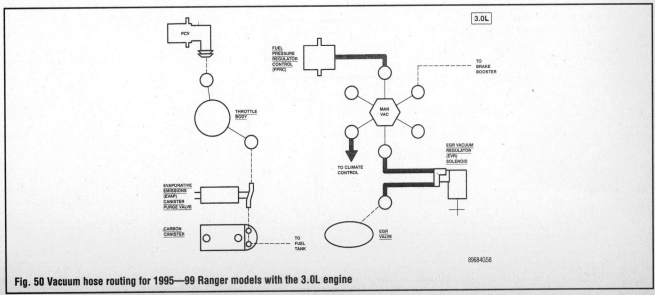

Fig. 50 Vacuum hose routing for 1995—99 Ranger models with the 3.0L engine

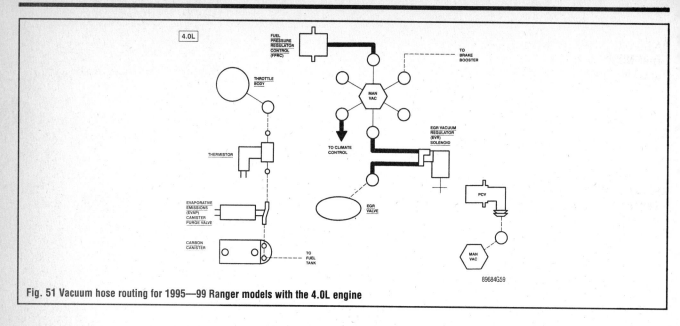

Fig. 51 Vacuum hose routing for 1995—99 Ranger models with the 4.0L engine

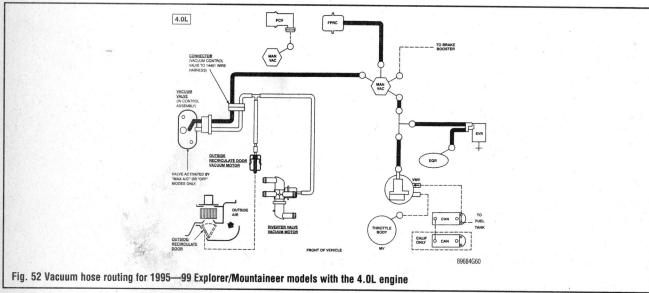

Fig. 52 Vacuum hose routing for 1995—99 Explorer/Mountaineer models with the 4.0L engine

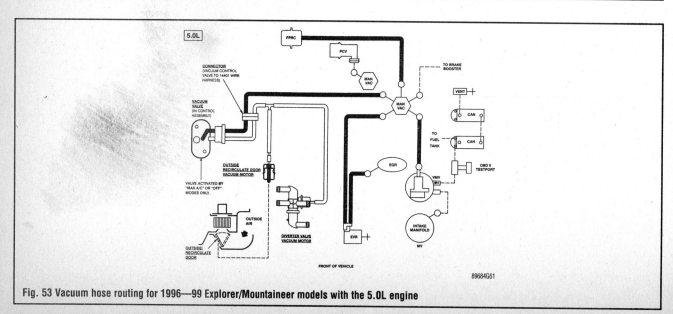

Fig. 53 Vacuum hose routing for 1996—99 Explorer/Mountaineer models with the 5.0L engine

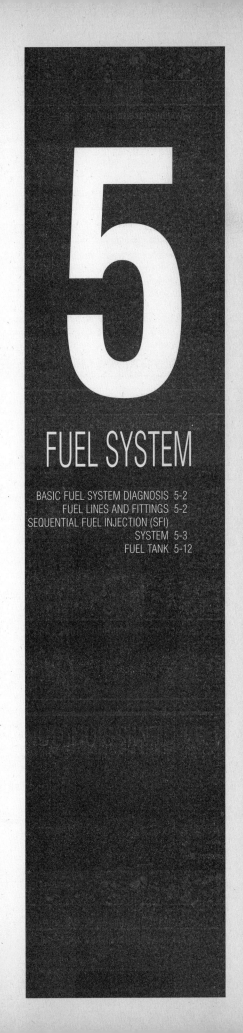

5

FUEL SYSTEM

BASIC FUEL SYSTEM DIAGNOSIS

When there is a problem starting or driving a vehicle, two of the most important checks involve the ignition and the fuel systems. The questions most mechanics attempt to answer first, "is there spark?" and "is there fuel?" will often lead to solving most basic problems. For ignition system diagnosis and testing, please refer to the information on engine electrical components and ignition systems found earlier in this manual. If the ignition system checks out (there is spark), then you must determine if the fuel system is operating properly (is there fuel?).

FUEL LINES AND FITTINGS

General Information

➡**Quick-connect (push type) fuel line fittings must be disconnected using proper procedure or the fitting may be damaged. There are two types of retainers used on the push connect fittings. Line sizes of ⅜ and ⁵⁄₁₆ in. diameter use a hairpin clip retainer. The ¼ in. diameter line connectors use a duck-bill clip retainer. In addition, some engines use spring-lock connections, secured by a garter spring, which require Ford Tool T81P-19623-G (or equivalent) for removal.**

Hairpin Clip Fitting

REMOVAL & INSTALLATION

▸ **See Figures 1 and 2**

1. Clean all dirt and grease from the fitting. Spread the two clip legs about ⅛ in. (3mm) each to disengage from the fitting and pull the clip outward from the fitting. Use finger pressure only; do not use any tools.
2. Grasp the fitting and hose assembly and pull away from the steel line. Twist the fitting and hose assembly slightly while pulling, if the assembly sticks.
3. Inspect the hairpin clip for damage, replacing the clip if necessary. Reinstall the clip in position on the fitting.
4. Inspect the fitting and inside of the connector to ensure freedom from dirt or obstruction. Install the fitting into the connector and push together. A click will be heard when the hairpin snaps into the proper connection. Pull on the line to insure full engagement.

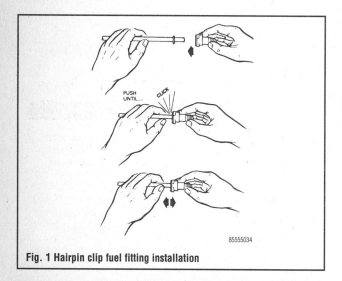

Fig. 1 Hairpin clip fuel fitting installation

Duckbill Clip Fitting

REMOVAL & INSTALLATION

▸ **See Figures 2 and 3**

1. A special tool is available from Ford and other manufacturers for removing the retaining clips. Use Ford Tool T82L-9500-AH or equivalent. If the tool is not on hand, go onto step 2. Align the slot on the push connector

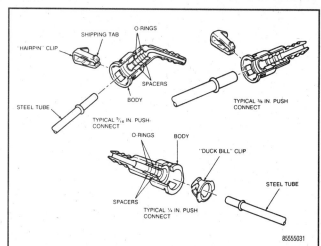

Fig. 2 Exploded views of the hairpin and duckbill clip type fuel fittings

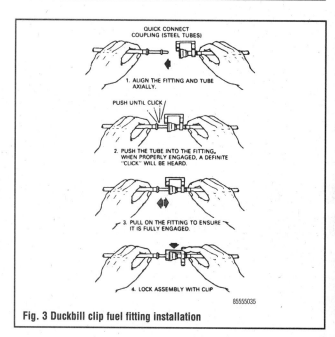

Fig. 3 Duckbill clip fuel fitting installation

disconnect tool with either tab on the retaining clip. Pull the line from the connector.
2. If the special clip tool is not available, use a pair of narrow 6-inch slip-jaw pliers with a jaw width of 0.2 in (5mm) or less. Align the jaws of the pliers with the openings of the fitting case and compress the part of the retaining clip that engages the case. Compressing the retaining clip will release the fitting, which may be pulled from the connector. Both sides of the clip must be compressed at the same time to disengage.
3. Inspect the retaining clip, fitting end and connector. Replace the clip if any damage is apparent.
4. Push the line into the steel connector until a click is heard, indicating the clip is in place. Pull on the line to check engagement.

Spring Lock Coupling

REMOVAL & INSTALLATION

♦ See Figures 4 and 5

The spring lock coupling is held together by a garter spring inside a circular cage. When the coupling is connected together, the flared end of the female fit-

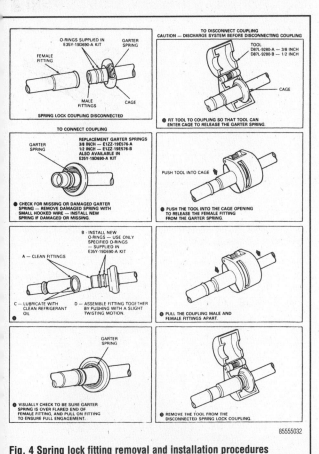

Fig. 4 Spring lock fitting removal and installation procedures

FOR 1/2" FITTING
N805528-S190
BLACK

FOR 3/8" FITTING
N805526-S190
SILVER

FUEL COUPLING
SAFETY CLIP

GARTER
SPRING

PULL ON COUPLING
TO INSURE PROPER
INSTALLATION

SPRING LOCK COUPLING – FOR FUEL LINE TO ENGINE FUEL RAIL CONNECTIONS

INSTALL SAFETY
CLIP – THIS END FIRST

THEN POSITION
CLAMP END
AND SNAP SHUT

Fig. 5 Spring lock horseshoe-shaped retaining clip installation

ting slips behind the garter spring inside the cage of the male fitting. The garter spring and cage then prevent the flared end of the female fitting from pulling out of the cage. As an additional locking feature, most vehicles have a horseshoe-shaped retaining clip that improves the retaining reliability of the spring lock coupling.

SEQUENTIAL FUEL INJECTION (SFI) SYSTEM

General Information

The Sequential Fuel Injection (SFI) system includes a high pressure, inline electric fuel pump mounted in the fuel tank, a fuel supply manifold, a throttle body (meters the incoming air charge for the correct mixture with the fuel), a pressure regulator, fuel filters and both solid and flexible fuel lines. The fuel supply manifold includes 4, 6 or 8 electronically-controlled fuel injectors, each mounted directly above an intake port in the lower intake manifold. Each injector fires once every other crankshaft revolution, in sequence with the engine firing order.

The fuel pressure regulator maintains a constant pressure drop across the injector nozzles. The regulator is referenced to intake manifold vacuum and is connected in parallel to the fuel injectors; it is positioned on the far end of the fuel rail. Any excess fuel supplied by the fuel pump passes through the regulator and is returned to the fuel tank via a return line.

➡**The pressure regulator reduces fuel pressure to 39–40 psi under normal operating conditions. At idle or high manifold vacuum condition, fuel pressure is further reduced to approximately 30 psi.**

The fuel pressure regulator is a diaphragm-operated relief valve, in which the inside of the diaphragm senses fuel pressure and the other side senses mani-

fold vacuum. Normal fuel pressure is established by a spring preload applied to the diaphragm. Control of the fuel system is maintained through the Powertrain Control Module (PCM), although electrical power is routed through the fuel pump relay and an inertia switch. The fuel pump relay is normally located in the power distribution box, under the hood, and the inertia switch is located on the toe-board, to the right of the transmission hump, in the passenger-side footwell. The inline fuel pump is usually mounted in the fuel tank. Tank-mounted pumps can be either high- or low-pressure, depending on the model.

The inertia switch opens the power circuit to the fuel pump in the event of a collision. Once tripped, the switch must be reset manually by pushing the reset button on the assembly.

➡**Check that the inertia switch is reset before diagnosing power supply problems to the fuel pump.**

The fuel injectors used with SFI system are electro-mechanical (solenoid) type, designed to meter and atomize fuel delivered to the intake ports of the engine. The injectors are mounted in the lower intake manifold and positioned so that their spray nozzles direct the fuel charge in front of the intake valves. The injector body consists of a solenoid-actuated pintle and needle-valve assembly. The control unit sends an electrical impulse that activates the solenoid, causing the pintle to move inward off the seat and allow the fuel to flow. The amount of fuel delivered is controlled by the length of time the injector is energized (pulse width), since the fuel flow orifice is fixed and the fuel pressure drop across the injector tip is constant. Correct atomization is achieved by contouring the pintle at the point where the fuel enters the pintle chamber.

➡**Exercise care when handling fuel injectors during service. Be careful not to lose the pintle cap and always replace O-rings to assure a tight seal. Never apply direct battery voltage to test a fuel injector.**

The injectors receive high-pressure fuel from the fuel supply manifold (fuel rail) assembly. The complete assembly includes a single, pre-formed tube with four, six or eight connectors, the mounting flange for the pressure regulator, mounting attachments to locate the manifold and provide the fuel injector retainers and a Schrader® quick-disconnect fitting used to perform fuel pressure tests.

The fuel manifold is normally removed with the fuel injectors and pressure regulator attached. Fuel injector electrical connectors are plastic and have locking tabs that must be released when disconnecting the wiring harness.

FUEL SYSTEM SERVICE PRECAUTIONS

Safety is the most important factor when performing not only fuel system maintenance, but any type of maintenance. Failure to conduct maintenance and repairs in a safe manner may result in serious personal injury or death. Work on a vehicle's fuel system components can be accomplished safely and effectively by adhering to the following rules and guidelines.

• To avoid the possibility of fire and personal injury, always disconnect the negative battery cable unless the repair or test procedure requires that battery voltage by applied.

• Always relieve the fuel system pressure prior to disconnecting any fuel system component (injector, fuel rail, pressure regulator, etc.) fitting or fuel line connection. Exercise extreme caution whenever relieving fuel system pressure to avoid exposing skin, face and eyes to fuel spray. Please be advised that fuel under pressure may penetrate the skin or any part of the body that it contacts.

• Always place a shop towel or cloth around the fitting or connection prior to loosening to absorb any excess fuel due to spillage. Ensure that all fuel spillage is quickly remove from engine surfaces. Ensure that all fuel-soaked cloths or towels are deposited into a flame-proof waste container with a lid.

• Always keep a dry chemical (Class B) fire extinguisher near the work area.

• Do not allow fuel spray or fuel vapors to come into contact with a spark or open flame.

• Always use a second wrench when loosening or tightening fuel line connections fittings. This will prevent unnecessary stress and torsion to fuel piping. Always follow the proper torque specifications.

• Always replace worn fuel fitting O-rings with new ones. Do not substitute fuel hose where rigid pipe is installed.

Relieving Fuel System Pressure

All SFI fuel injected engines are equipped with a pressure relief valve located on the fuel supply manifold. Remove the fuel tank cap and attach fuel pressure gauge T80L-9974-B, or equivalent, to the valve to release the fuel pressure. Be sure to drain the fuel into a suitable container and to avoid gasoline spillage. If a pressure gauge is not available, disconnect the vacuum hose from the fuel pressure regulator and attach a hand-held vacuum pump. Apply about 25 in. Hg (84 kPa) of vacuum to the regulator to vent the fuel system pressure into the

fuel tank through the fuel return hose. Note that this procedure will remove the fuel pressure from the lines, but not the fuel. Take precautions to avoid the risk of fire and use clean rags to soak up any spilled fuel when the lines are disconnected.

An alternate method of relieving the fuel system pressure involves disconnecting the inertia switch. Follow the procedures outlined later in this Section.

Inertia Switch

GENERAL INFORMATION

This switch shuts off the fuel pump in the event of a collision. Once the switch has been tripped, it must be reset manually in order to start the engine.

The inertia switch is located on the toe-board, to the right of the transmission hump, in the passenger-side footwell.

RESETTING THE SWITCH

▶ **See Figures 6 and 7**

1. Turn the ignition switch **OFF**.
2. Ensure that there is no fuel leaking in the engine compartment, along any of the lines or at the tank. There should be no odor of fuel as well.
3. If no leakage and/or odor is apparent, reset the switch by pushing the reset button on the top of the switch.

➡**You may need to pull the carpet down and away from the instrument panel in order to access the switch.**

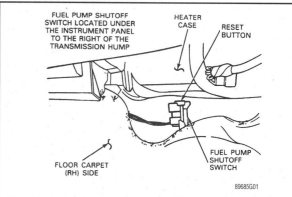

Fig. 6 Fuel pump inertia switch and reset button location

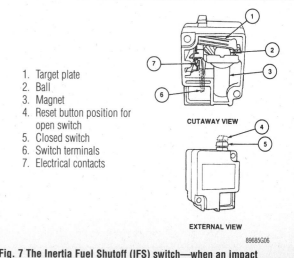

1. Target plate
2. Ball
3. Magnet
4. Reset button position for open switch
5. Closed switch
6. Switch terminals
7. Electrical contacts

Fig. 7 The Inertia Fuel Shutoff (IFS) switch—when an impact occurs, the ball breaks loose from the magnet and strikes the target plate which opens the electrical contacts

The fuel pressure relief valve (A) is located on the fuel supply manifold

4. Cycle the ignition switch from the **ON** to **OFF** positions several times, allowing five seconds at each position, to build fuel pressure within the system.

5. Again, check the fuel system for leaks. There should be no odor of fuel as well.

6. If there is no leakage and/or odor of fuel, it is safe to operate the vehicle. However, it is recommended that the entire system be checked by a professional, especially if the vehicle was in an accident severe enough to trip the inertia switch.

Fuel Pump

REMOVAL & INSTALLATION

▶ **See Figures 8, 9 and 10**

➡**To gain access to the fuel pump, it is necessary to remove the fuel tank.**

1. Depressurize the fuel system and remove the fuel tank from the vehicle.

2. Remove any dirt that has accumulated around the fuel pump attaching flange, to prevent it from entering the tank during service.

3. Turn the fuel pump locking ring counterclockwise using a locking ring removal tool and remove the locking ring.

4. Remove the fuel pump and bracket assembly.

5. Remove the seal gasket and discard it.

To install:

6. Put a light coating of heavy grease on a new seal ring to hold it in place during assembly. Install it in fuel tank ring groove.

7. Insert the fuel pump assembly into the fuel tank, then secure it in place with the locking ring. Tighten the ring until secure.

8. Install the tank in the vehicle.

9. Install a minimum of 10 gallons of fuel and check for leaks.

10. Install a pressure gauge on the throttle body valve and turn the ignition **ON** for 3 seconds. Turn the key **OFF**, then repeat the key cycle five to ten times until the pressure gauge shows at least 30 psi. Reinspect for leaks at the fittings.

11. Remove the pressure gauge. Start the engine and check for fuel leaks.

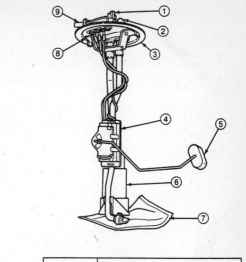

Item	Description
1	Electrical Connector
2	Fuel Return Tube
3	Flange
4	Fuel Gauge Sender Assembly
5	Sender Float
6	Fuel Pump
7	Inlet Filter Sock
8	Fuel Gauge Sender to Electrical Connector-Spade Connection
9	Fuel Supply Tube

89685G03

Fig. 9 Fuel pump and sending unit used on the Super Cab Ranger pick-up

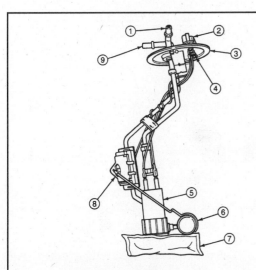

Item	Description
1	Fuel Supply Tube
2	Electrical Connector
3	Flange
4	Fuel Gauge Sender to Electrical Connector-Spade Connection
5	Fuel Pump
6	Sender Float
7	Inlet Filter Sock
8	Fuel Gauge Sender Assembly
9	Fuel Return Tube

89685G02

Fig. 8 Fuel pump and sending unit used on the Regular Cab Ranger pick-up

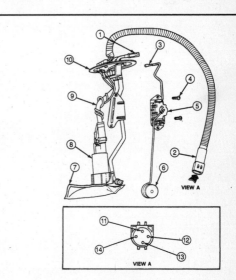

Item	Description
1	Fuel Return Tube
2	Electrical Connector
3	Fuel Gauge Sender to Electrical Connector-Spade Connection
4	Screw
5	Fuel Gauge Sender Assembly
6	Sender Float
7	Inlet Filter Sock
8	Fuel Pump
9	Fuel Supply Tube
10	Flange
11	Pump Positive Terminal
12	Sender Ground Terminal
13	Pump Ground Terminal
14	Sender Positive Terminal

89685G04

Fig. 10 Fuel pump and sending unit used on the Explorer and Mountaineer

TESTING

▶ **See Figures 11, 12, 13 and 14**

✳✳ CAUTION

Fuel pressure must be relieved before attempting to disconnect any fuel lines.

The diagnostic pressure valve (Schrader valve) is located on the fuel supply manifold (rail). This valve provides a convenient point for service personnel to monitor fuel pressure, release the system pressure prior to maintenance, and to bleed out air which may become trapped in the system during pressure replacement. A pressure gauge with an adapter is required to perform pressure tests.

If the pressure tap is not installed or an adapter is not available, use a T-fitting to install the pressure gauge between the fuel filter line and the throttle body fuel inlet or fuel rail.

To test the fuel pump, follow the accompanying diagnostic charts. Testing fuel pressure requires the use of a special pressure gauge (Ford Tool T80L-

TCCS4P04

Fig. 11 Fuel pressure can be checked using an inexpensive pressure/vacuum gauge

FUEL PRESSURE TEST — TEST A

TEST STEP	RESULT	▶	ACTION TO TAKE
A1 CHECK STATIC FUEL PRESSURE • Check for adequate fuel supply. • Key off. • Install fuel pressure gauge. • Install test lead to Fuel Pump (FP) lead of VIP test connector. [diagram: VIP CONNECTOR / FP LEAD (SHORT END OF CONNECTOR) / V8526-A] • Turn key to RUN position. • Ground test lead to run fuel pump. • Check if pressure is within acceptable limits, 240-310 kPa (35-45 psi).	Yes No	▶ ▶	GO to A10. GO to A2.
A2 FUEL LINE CHECK • Check for low pressure but greater than 21 kPa (3 psi) (indicates fuel pump is running but not enough pressure).	Yes No	▶ ▶	GO to A3. GO to A6.
A3 FUEL LINE AND FILTER CHECK • Check for plugged or restricted fuel lines and filter. • Do components check OK?	Yes No	▶ ▶	GO to A4. REPAIR or REPLACE as required. GO to A1.
A4 PUMP VOLTAGE CHECK • Check the voltage to the fuel pump at the connector. • Is the voltage within 0.5 volts of battery voltage? (Measured relative to battery ground).	Yes No	▶ ▶	GO to A5. SERVICE wiring to fuel pump as required. GO to A1.
A5 PRESSURE REGULATOR CHECK • Disconnect the fuel return line. • Is fuel being returned during low pressure condition?	Yes No	▶ ▶	SERVICE or REPLACE the pressure regulator as required. GO to A1. REPLACE the fuel pump. GO to A1.
A6 INERTIA SWITCH CHECK • Check the inertia switch for continuity. • Does switch check OK?	Yes No	▶ ▶	GO to A7. RESET switch as required. GO to A1.
A7 FUEL PUMP / TANK CONNECTOR CHECK • Check if the wiring at the fuel pump / tank connector is loose or open. • Does the wiring check OK?	Yes No	▶ ▶	GO to A8. SERVICE wiring as required. GO to A1.
A8 FUEL PUMP RELAY CHECK • Key in RUN. • Ground FP (test) lead. • Does fuel pump relay energize?	Yes No	▶ ▶	GO to A9. SERVICE or REPLACE relay as required. GO to A1.

89685G16

Fig. 12 Fuel pressure test chart–part 1

FUEL PRESSURE TEST — TEST A (Continued)

TEST STEP	RESULT	▶	ACTION TO TAKE
A9 PCM RELAY CHECK • Key in RUN. • Does PCM relay energize?	Yes No	▶ ▶	REPLACE fuel pump. GO to A1. SERVICE or REPLACE PCM relay as required. GO to A1.
A10 CHECK VALVE TEST • Remove ground from test lead and note pressure on gauge. • Does the pressure remain within 14 kPa (2 psi) for 3 minutes after the ground is removed?	Yes No	▶ ▶	GO to A14. GO to A11.
A11 FUEL LINE AND CONNECTOR LEAK CHECK • Check all fuel lines and connectors for leaks. • Do lines and connectors check OK?	Yes No	▶ ▶	GO to A12. SERVICE or REPLACE fuel lines and connectors as required. GO to A1.
A12 CHECK VALVE TEST, RETURN LINE PLUGGED • Disconnect the return line and plug engine side. • Ground test lead to momentarily activate the fuel pump. • Raise pressure to normal operating pressure, 240-310 kPa (35-45 psi). • Remove ground from test lead and note pressure on gauge. • Does the pressure remain within 14 kPa (2 psi) for 3 minutes after the ground is removed?	Yes No	▶ ▶	If pressure holds, REPLACE regulator and REPEAT last two parts of Test Step. REPLACE the fuel pump. GO to A1.
A13 CHECK VALVE TEST, REGULATOR REPLACED • With the return line still disconnected and regulator plugged, ground the test lead to momentarily activate the fuel pump. • Raise the pressure to normal operating pressure, 240-310 kPa (35-45 psi). • Remove ground from test lead and note pressure on gauge. • Does the pressure remain within 14 kPa (2 psi) for 3 minutes after the ground is removed?	Yes No	▶ ▶	GO to A1. REPLACE fuel pump and GO to A10. If unit still fails Step A10, there may be a leaking fuel injector or fuel rail. Correct these concerns and GO to A10.
A14 ENGINE ON TEST • Disconnect and plug the vacuum line connected to the pressure regulator. • Key ON, engine running at idle. • Is fuel pressure 240-310 kPa (35-45 psi)?	Yes No	▶ ▶	GO to A18. GO to A15.
A15 FUEL LINE AND FILTER CHECK • Check for plugged or restricted fuel lines and filter. • Do components check OK?	Yes No	▶ ▶	GO to A16. REPAIR or REPLACE as required. GO to A1.
A16 PUMP VOLTAGE CHECK • Check the voltage to the fuel pump at the connector. • Is the voltage within 0.5 volts of battery voltage? (Measured relative to battery ground).	Yes No	▶ ▶	GO to A17. SERVICE wiring to fuel pump as required. CHECK for poor or dirty connections on ground side of pump. GO to A1.
A17 PRESSURE REGULATOR CHECK • Disconnect the fuel return line. • Is fuel being returned during low pressure condition?	Yes No	▶ ▶	SERVICE or REPLACE the pressure regulator as required. GO to A1. REPLACE the fuel pump. GO to A1.

89685G17

Fig. 13 Fuel pressure test chart–part 2

FUEL PRESSURE TEST — TEST A (Continued)

TEST STEP	RESULT	▶	ACTION TO TAKE
A18 HIGH SPEED TEST • With engine running at idle and vacuum line disconnected, note fuel rail pressure. • Rapidly accelerate the engine and note the fuel pressure. • Does the pressure remain within 5 psi of the starting pressure? NOTE: Road testing the vehicle while monitoring the pressure may give a better test under load conditions.	Yes No	▶ ▶	Fuel pump is OK. GO to A15.

89685G18

Fig. 14 Fuel pressure test chart–part 3

9974-B, Rotunda Fuel Pressure Testing Kit 014–00447, or equivalent) that attaches to the diagnostic pressure tap fitting. To perform the fuel system test a scan tool is necessary to access the different test modes.

➡ **Depressurize the fuel system before disconnecting any lines.**

Throttle Body Assembly

REMOVAL & INSTALLATION

▶ **See Figures 15, 16, 17, 18 and 19**

➡ The 3.0L engine's throttle body is a 1 piece casting which includes the upper intake manifold. In order to remove the throttle body, the entire upper manifold must be removed. Refer to Section 3 for the proper procedures.

1. Loosen the air inlet tube clamps, then separate the tube from the throttle body and air cleaner housing. Remove the tube from the vehicle.
2. If equipped, remove the throttle linkage shield.

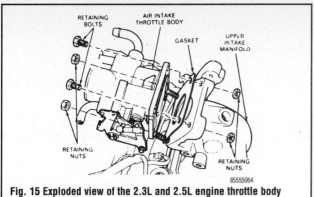

Fig. 15 Exploded view of the 2.3L and 2.5L engine throttle body assembly

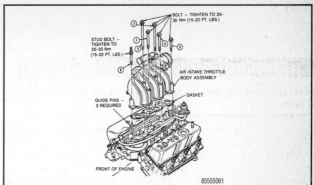

Fig. 17 Exploded view of the 3.0L engine throttle body/upper intake manifold assembly

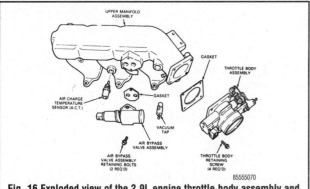

Fig. 16 Exploded view of the 2.9L engine throttle body assembly and related components

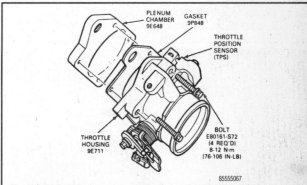

Fig. 18 Exploded view of the 4.0L engine throttle body assembly and related components

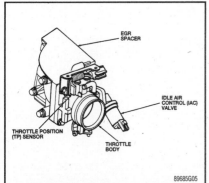

Fig. 19 View of the 5.0L engine throttle body assembly and related components

To remove the throttle body, first remove the air intake hose, then the linkage shield

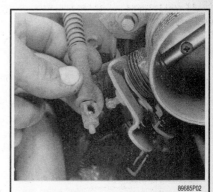

Next, disconnect the throttle control cable(s) from the throttle body . . .

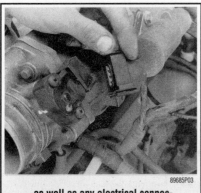

. . . as well as any electrical connections. . .

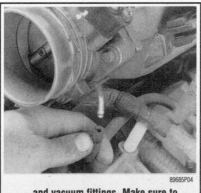

. . . and vacuum fittings. Make sure to label them to assure proper installation

Remove the throttle body-to-upper intake attaching bolts . . .

. . . then remove the throttle body assembly

Remove the old gasket and thoroughly clean the mating surfaces of both pieces

3. Detach the accelerator and speed control (if equipped) cables from the throttle body lever.

4. Label and disengage the engine wiring harness connectors from the Throttle Position (TP) sensor and the Idle Air Control (IAC) valve; both are mounted on the throttle body.

5. Remove the four mounting nuts, then carefully separate the throttle body from the upper intake manifold.

6. Remove and discard the old throttle body-to-intake manifold gasket.

To install:

➡If scraping is necessary to clean the remaining gasket material off of the mating surfaces, take care to avoid scratching or gouging the soft aluminum.

7. Clean the gasket mating surfaces of any residual gasket material.

8. Install the throttle body, along with a new gasket, onto the upper intake manifold. Install and tighten the mounting nuts in a crisscross pattern to specifications.

9. Engage the TP sensor and IAC valve wiring connectors and remove the temporary labels.

10. Reattach the accelerator and speed control cables, if applicable, to the throttle body lever.

11. If removed, install the throttle linkage shield.

12. Install the air inlet tube between the air cleaner housing and the throttle body. Tighten the tube clamps until snug.

Fuel Supply Manifold and Injectors

REMOVAL & INSTALLATION

◆ **See Figures 20 thru 25**

1. Remove the upper intake manifold. Be sure to depressurize the fuel system before disconnecting any fuel lines.

2. Disconnect the fuel supply and return line retaining clips.

3. Detach the vacuum line from the fuel pressure regulator.

4. Disconnect the fuel chassis inlet and outlet fuel hoses from the fuel supply manifold.

5. Label and disconnect the fuel injector wire harness plugs.

6. On the 2.3L and 2.5L engine, remove the two fuel supply manifold retaining bolts.

7. On the 4.0L (VIN X) engine, remove the six upper intake manifold attaching studs.

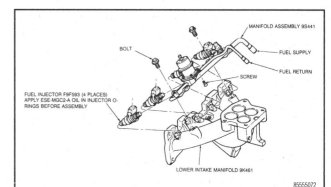

Fig. 20 Exploded view of the 2.3L and 2.5L engine fuel supply rail and injectors

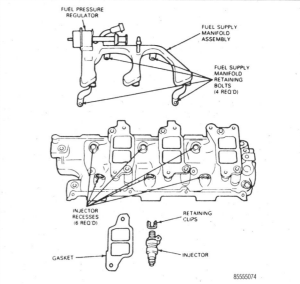

Fig. 21 Exploded view of the 2.9L engine fuel supply rail and injectors

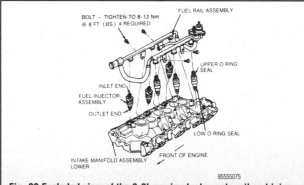

Fig. 22 Exploded view of the 3.0L engine fuel supply rail and injectors

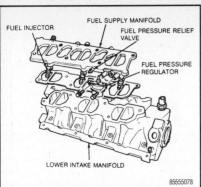

Fig. 23 Exploded view of the 4.0L engine fuel supply rail and injectors

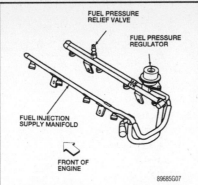

Fig. 24 Exploded view of the 5.0L engine fuel supply rail

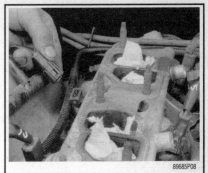

For fuel supply manifold removal, unbolt the upper intake, then disconnect the injector wire harness plugs

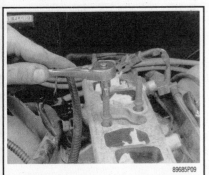

On the 4.0L (VIN X) engine, remove the 6 manifold mounting studs which retain the supply manifold

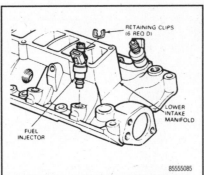

Fig. 25 Some models use small retaining clips to secure the injectors in the supply manifold

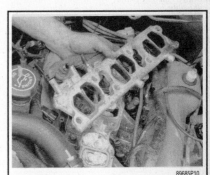

Lift upwards with a rocking motion to disengage the injectors, then remove the supply manifold

On the 4.0L engine, remove the old fuel supply manifold gasket and clean the mating surfaces

Remove the injectors from the engine by gently rocking it while pulling upwards

The injector has O-rings at the nozzle (A) and at the fuel supply manifold (B). Replace any damaged seals

8. On all other engines, remove the four fuel supply manifold retaining bolts.

9. Carefully disengage the fuel rail assembly from the fuel injectors by lifting and gently rocking the rail.

10. Remove the fuel injectors from the intake manifold by lifting while gently rocking them from side to side

11. Place all removed components on a clean surface to prevent contamination by dirt or grease.

➡Never use silicone grease; it will clog the injector. All injectors and the fuel rail must be handled with extreme care to prevent damage to sealing areas and sensitive fuel metering orifices.

12. Examine the injector O-rings for deterioration damage, replacing them as needed.

13. Make sure the injector caps are clean and free from contamination or damage.

To install:

14. Lubricate all O-rings with clean engine oil, then install the injectors into the fuel rail using a light twisting/pushing motion.

15. On the 4.0L (VIN X) engine, position a new fuel rail gasket to the lower intake manifold.

16. Carefully install the fuel rail assembly and injectors into the lower intake manifold. Make certain to correctly position the insulators. Push down on the fuel rail to make sure the O-rings are seated.

17. Hold the fuel rail assembly in place and install the retaining bolts finger tight. Then tighten the bolts to specifications.

18. Connect the fuel supply and return lines.

19. Attach the vacuum hose to the fuel pressure regulator.

20. Connect the fuel injector wiring harness at the injectors.

21. Connect the vacuum line to the fuel pressure regulator, if removed.

22. Install the air intake and throttle body assembly.

23. Run the engine and check for fuel leaks.

TESTING

The fuel injectors can be tested with a Digital Volt-Ohmmeter (DVOM). To test an injector, detach the engine wiring harness connector from it. This may require removing the upper intake manifold or other engine components.

Once access to the injector is gained and the wiring is disconnected from it, set the DVOM to measure resistance (ohms). Measure the resistance of the injector by probing one terminal with the positive DVOM lead and the other injector terminal with the negative lead. The resistance measured should be between 11–18 ohms. If the resistance is not within this range, the fuel injector is faulty and must be replaced with a new one.

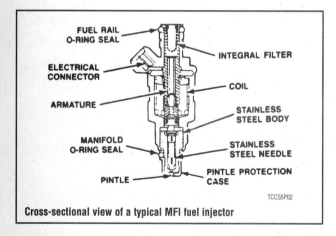

A noid light can be attached to the fuel injector harness in order to test for injector pulse

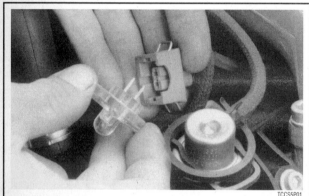

Cross-sectional view of a typical MFI fuel injector

Fuel Pressure Regulator

REMOVAL & INSTALLATION

▶ See Figure 26

Except the 4.0L SOHC (VIN E) Engine

▶ See Figures 27, 28 and 29

1. Depressurize the fuel system; remove shielding as needed.
2. Remove the vacuum line at the pressure regulator.
3. If necessary, disconnect the fuel return line from the regulator.

➡**Some engines use two standard hex head bolts to retain the regulator instead of the Allen® head screws.**

4. Remove the three Allen® head retaining screws from the regulator housing.
5. Remove the pressure regulator assembly, gasket and O-ring. Discard the gasket and check the O-ring for signs of cracks or deterioration.

1. Engine vacuum reference tube
2. Ball seat
3. Spring
4. Upper housing
5. Diaphram
6. Lower housing
7. Fuel outlet tube
8. Fuel inlet tube (supply)
9. O-ring groove
10. Mounting plate
11. Fuel filter screen
12. Spring seat
13. Valve assembly

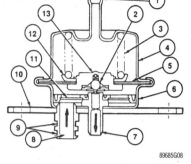

Fig. 26 Cutaway view of the fuel pressure regulator

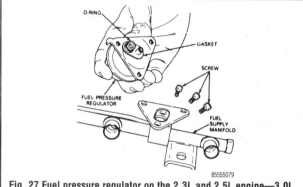

Fig. 27 Fuel pressure regulator on the 2.3L and 2.5L engine—3.0L and 5.0L engines are similar

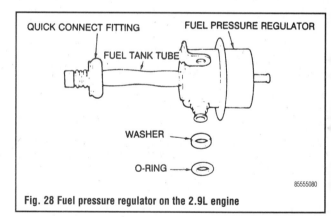

Fig. 28 Fuel pressure regulator on the 2.9L engine

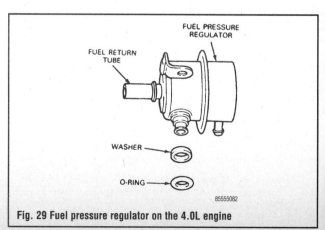

Fig. 29 Fuel pressure regulator on the 4.0L engine

To remove the fuel pressure regulator, first remove the vacuum line from the regulator . . .

. . . then loosen the fuel return line fitting . . .

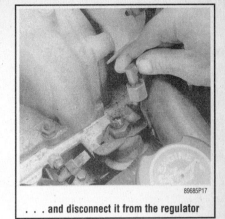

. . . and disconnect it from the regulator

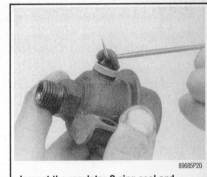

Remove the regulator attaching bolts . . .

. . . then pull the regulator from the supply manifold using a slight rocking motion to unseat the O-ring seal

Inspect the regulator O-ring seal and replace it if needed. A small pick will aid in removing the old seal

To install:

6. Clean the gasket mating surfaces. If scraping is necessary, be careful not to damage the fuel pressure regulator or supply line gasket mating surfaces.

7. Lubricate the pressure regulator O-ring with light engine oil. Do not use silicone grease; it will clog the injectors.

8. Install the O-ring and a new gasket on the pressure regulator.

9. Install the pressure regulator on the fuel manifold and tighten the retaining screws to 27–40 inch lbs. (3–4 Nm) for all engines except the 4.0L (VIN X) engine, which is tightened to 70–97 inch lbs. (8–11 Nm).

➡On the 2.3L and 2.5L engine, install the fuel manifold shield and tighten the bolts to 15–22 ft. lbs. (20–30 Nm).

10. Install the vacuum line at the pressure regulator.

11. If removed, connect the fuel return line.

12. Build fuel pressure in the system by turning the ignition **ON** and **OFF** (without starting the engine) at least five times. Leave the ignition **ON** at least 5 seconds each time. Check for fuel leaks.

4.0L SOHC (VIN E) Engine

▶ See Figures 30 and 31

➡On the 4.0L SOHC (VIN E) engine, the fuel pressure regulator is integral with the supply and return lines that are routed on the engine.

1. Depressurize the fuel system; remove shielding as needed.
2. Remove the upper intake manifold.
3. Disconnect the fuel pressure regulator vacuum line.
4. Disconnect the fuel supply and return lines.
5. Remove the bolts and the fuel supply and return lines at the injection manifold.
6. Unbolt the upper fuel line support bracket from the valve cover.
7. Remove the fuel supply and return line assembly from the vehicle with the regulator assembly attached.

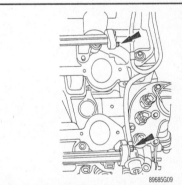

Fig. 30 Remove the four bolts (arrows) that attach the regulator/fuel lines to the supply manifold

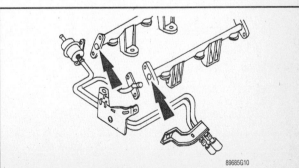

Fig. 31 Position the fuel pressure regulator assembly to the supply manifold (arrows)

To install:

8. Clean the gasket mating surfaces. If scraping is necessary, be careful not to damage the fuel pressure regulator or supply line gasket mating surfaces.

9. Lubricate the pressure regulator O-ring with light engine oil. Do not use silicone grease; it will clog the injectors.

10. Install the O-ring and a new gasket on the pressure regulator.

11. Install the fuel supply and return line assembly.

12. Fasten the upper fuel line support bracket to the valve cover.

13. Install the bolts that fasten the fuel supply and return lines to the injector manifold.

14. Connect the fuel supply and return lines.

15. Connect the vacuum line to the pressure regulator.

16. Install the upper intake manifold.

17. Build fuel pressure in the system by turning the ignition **ON** and **OFF** (without starting the engine) at least five times. Leave the ignition **ON** at least 5 seconds each time. Check for fuel leaks.

FUEL TANK

Tank Assembly

REMOVAL & INSTALLATION

▶ **See Figures 32, 33, 34, 35 and 36**

1. Disconnect the negative battery cable and relieve the fuel system pressure.

2. Siphon or pump as much fuel as possible out through the fuel filler pipe.

➡ **Fuel injected vehicles have reservoirs inside the fuel tank to maintain fuel near the fuel pick-up during cornering or low-fuel operation. These reservoirs could block siphon hoses or tubes from reaching the bottom of the fuel tank. Repeated attempts, using different hose orientations, can overcome this obstacle.**

3. Raise and safely support the vehicle.

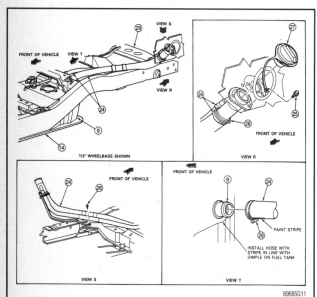

9. Tank assembly, fuel
14. Shield and skid plate assembly
24. Pipe assembly, fuel fill
25. Screw
26. Screw
27. Cap assembly, fuel tank fill
28. Clamp, fuel fill pipe
29. Frame assembly

Fig. 32 Exploded view of the Explorer/Mountaineer fuel filler assembly

Pressure Relief Valve

REMOVAL & INSTALLATION

➡ **The fuel pressure relief valve cap on the valve must be removed.**

1. If the fuel supply manifold is installed on the engine, remove the fuel tank filler cap and relieve fuel system pressure.

2. Using a deep socket or an open-end wrench, remove the valve from the fuel supply manifold.

To install:

3. Install and tighten the pressure relief valve to 69 inch lbs. (7.75 Nm).

4. Build fuel pressure in the system by turning the ignition **ON** and **OFF** (without starting the engine) at least five times. Leave the ignition **ON** at least 5 seconds each time. Check for fuel leaks.

5. Install the pressure relief valve cap and tighten it until snug.

4. If equipped, remove the skid plate attaching bolts, then lower the plate and remove it.

➡ **On Explorer/Mountaineer models, the front fuel tank strap is bolted to the skid plate and will be disconnected when the plate is removed.**

5. Disconnect the fuel fill and vent hoses connecting the filler pipe to the tank.

6. On vehicles equipped with a metal retainer fastening the filler pipe to the fuel tank, remove the screw holding the retainer to the fuel tank flange.

7. Disengage the fuel lines and the electrical connections to the fuel tank sending unit/fuel pump assembly. On some vehicles, these are inaccessible on top of the tank. In this case, they must be disconnected when the tank is partially lowered.

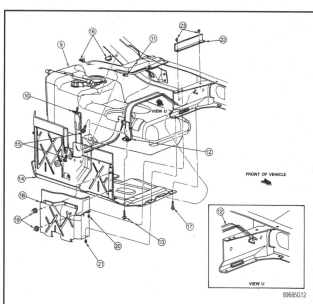

9. Tank assembly, fuel
10. Strap assembly, fuel tank rear
11. U-nut
12. Strap assembly, fuel tank front
13. Bolt
14. Shield and skid plate assembly, fuel tank
15. Bolt
16. U-nut
17. Screw and washer
18. Shield assembly, fuel tank heat front
19. Nut
20. Screw
21. Screw and washer
22. Extension, fuel heat tank shield front

Fig. 33 Exploded view of the Explorer/Mountaineer fuel tank assembly

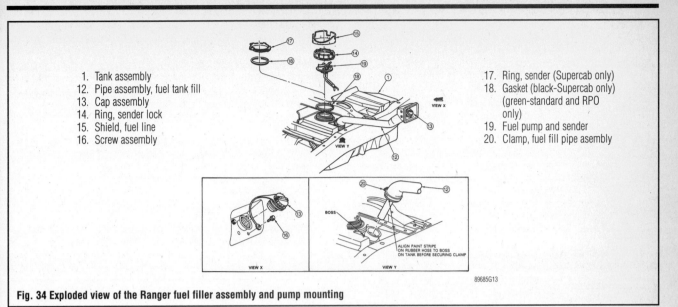

1. Tank assembly
12. Pipe assembly, fuel tank fill
13. Cap assembly
14. Ring, sender lock
15. Shield, fuel line
16. Screw assembly

17. Ring, sender (Supercab only)
18. Gasket (black-Supercab only) (green-standard and RPO only)
19. Fuel pump and sender
20. Clamp, fuel fill pipe asembly

Fig. 34 Exploded view of the Ranger fuel filler assembly and pump mounting

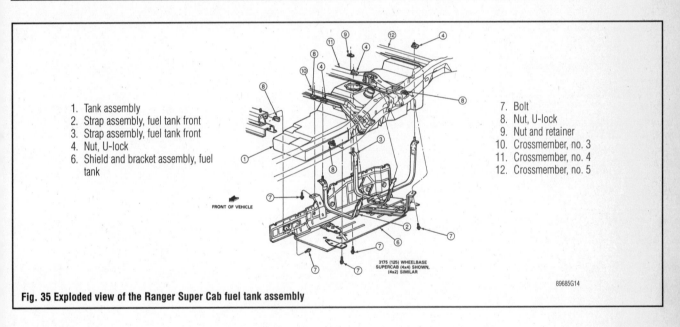

1. Tank assembly
2. Strap assembly, fuel tank front
3. Strap assembly, fuel tank front
4. Nut, U-lock
6. Shield and bracket assembly, fuel tank

7. Bolt
8. Nut, U-lock
9. Nut and retainer
10. Crossmember, no. 3
11. Crossmember, no. 4
12. Crossmember, no. 5

Fig. 35 Exploded view of the Ranger Super Cab fuel tank assembly

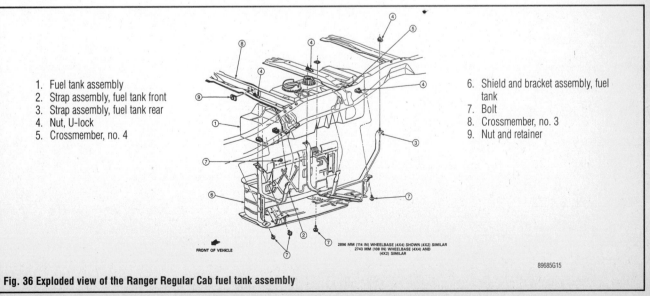

1. Fuel tank assembly
2. Strap assembly, fuel tank front
3. Strap assembly, fuel tank rear
4. Nut, U-lock
5. Crossmember, no. 4

6. Shield and bracket assembly, fuel tank
7. Bolt
8. Crossmember, no. 3
9. Nut and retainer

Fig. 36 Exploded view of the Ranger Regular Cab fuel tank assembly

8. Place a safety support (such as a floor jack) under the fuel tank and remove the bolts from the fuel tank straps. Allow the straps to swing out of the way. Be careful not to deform the fuel tank.

➡**On Ranger vehicles, the rear fuel tank strap has two connections which must be unbolted.**

9. Lower the tank a few inches, then detach the fuel lines and electrical connection from the sending unit/fuel pump assembly, if required.

10. Remove the tank from the vehicle.

To install:

11. Before installation, it would be wise to perform the following:

   a. Double-check the tightness of the sending unit/fuel pump locking ring. If it is already loose, now would be a good time to remove it and check the condition of the gasket underneath.

   b. Ensure that all metal shields are reinstalled in their original positions and that the fasteners are secure.

   c. Be sure that the fuel vapor valve is completely installed on top of the fuel tank.

   d. Make all necessary fuel line or wiring connections which will be inaccessible after the fuel tank is installed.

12. Raise the fuel tank into position in the vehicle. If necessary, attach the fuel lines and sending unit electrical connector before the tank is in its final position.

13. Lubricate the fuel filler pipe with a water-based lubricant. Install the tank onto the filler pipe, then bring the tank into final position. Be careful not to deform the tank.

14. Position the tank straps around the tank and start the retaining nut or bolt. Align the tank with the straps. If equipped, be sure the fuel tank shields are installed with the straps and are positioned correctly.

15. Check the hoses and wiring on top of the tank. Make sure they are correctly routed and will not be pinched between the tank and body.

16. Tighten the fuel tank strap retaining nuts or bolts to 20–30 ft. lbs. (28–41 Nm).

17. If not already attached, connect the fuel hoses and lines. Make sure the fuel supply, fuel return (if present) and the vapor vent attachments are made properly. If not already attached, connect the sending unit.

18. If removed, install the fuel tank skid plate.

19. Lower the vehicle.

20. Fill the tank with fuel and check all connections for leaks.

Sending Unit

REMOVAL & INSTALLATION

Please refer to the fuel pump removal and installation procedure in this section.

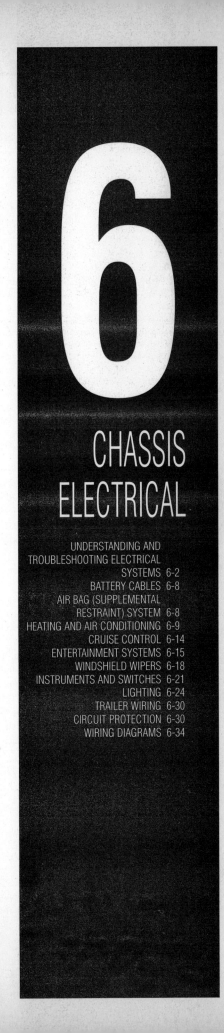

6

CHASSIS
ELECTRICAL

UNDERSTANDING AND TROUBLESHOOTING ELECTRICAL SYSTEMS

Basic Electrical Theory

♦ See Figure 1

For any 12 volt, negative ground, electrical system to operate, the electricity must travel in a complete circuit. This simply means that current (power) from the positive (+) terminal of the battery must eventually return to the negative (−) terminal of the battery. Along the way, this current will travel through wires, fuses, switches and components. If, for any reason, the flow of current through the circuit is interrupted, the component fed by that circuit will cease to function properly.

Perhaps the easiest way to visualize a circuit is to think of connecting a light bulb (with two wires attached to it) to the battery—one wire attached to the negative (−) terminal of the battery and the other wire to the positive (+) terminal. With the two wires touching the battery terminals, the circuit would be complete and the light bulb would illuminate. Electricity would follow a path from the battery to the bulb and back to the battery. It's easy to see that with longer wires on our light bulb, it could be mounted anywhere. Further, one wire could be fitted with a switch so that the light could be turned on and off.

The normal automotive circuit differs from this simple example in two ways. First, instead of having a return wire from the bulb to the battery, the current travels through the frame of the vehicle. Since the negative (−) battery cable is attached to the frame (made of electrically conductive metal), the frame of the vehicle can serve as a ground wire to complete the circuit. Secondly, most automotive circuits contain multiple components which receive power from a single circuit. This lessens the amount of wire needed to power components on the vehicle.

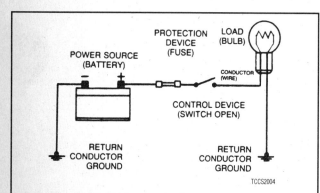

TCCS2004

Fig. 1 This example illustrates a simple circuit. When the switch is closed, power from the positive (+) battery terminal flows through the fuse and the switch, and then to the light bulb. The light illuminates and the circuit is completed through the ground wire back to the negative (ñ) battery terminal. In reality, the two ground points shown in the illustration are attached to the metal frame of the vehicle, which completes the circuit back to the battery

HOW DOES ELECTRICITY WORK: THE WATER ANALOGY

Electricity is the flow of electrons—the subatomic particles that constitute the outer shell of an atom. Electrons spin in an orbit around the center core of an atom. The center core is comprised of protons (positive charge) and neutrons (neutral charge). Electrons have a negative charge and balance out the positive charge of the protons. When an outside force causes the number of electrons to unbalance the charge of the protons, the electrons will split off the atom and look for another atom to balance out. If this imbalance is kept up, electrons will continue to move and an electrical flow will exist.

Many people have been taught electrical theory using an analogy with water. In a comparison with water flowing through a pipe, the electrons would be the water and the wire is the pipe.

The flow of electricity can be measured much like the flow of water through a pipe. The unit of measurement used is amperes, frequently abbreviated as amps (a). You can compare amperage to the volume of water flowing through a pipe. When connected to a circuit, an ammeter will measure the actual amount of cur-

rent flowing through the circuit. When relatively few electrons flow through a circuit, the amperage is low. When many electrons flow, the amperage is high.

Water pressure is measured in units such as pounds per square inch (psi); The electrical pressure is measured in units called volts (v). When a voltmeter is connected to a circuit, it is measuring the electrical pressure.

The actual flow of electricity depends not only on voltage and amperage, but also on the resistance of the circuit. The higher the resistance, the higher the force necessary to push the current through the circuit. The standard unit for measuring resistance is an ohm. Resistance in a circuit varies depending on the amount and type of components used in the circuit. The main factors which determine resistance are:

• Material—some materials have more resistance than others. Those with high resistance are said to be insulators. Rubber materials (or rubber-like plastics) are some of the most common insulators used in vehicles as they have a very high resistance to electricity. Very low resistance materials are said to be conductors. Copper wire is among the best conductors. Silver is actually a superior conductor to copper and is used in some relay contacts, but its high cost prohibits its use as common wiring. Most automotive wiring is made of copper.

• Size—the larger the wire size being used, the less resistance the wire will have. This is why components which use large amounts of electricity usually have large wires supplying current to them.

• Length—for a given thickness of wire, the longer the wire, the greater the resistance. The shorter the wire, the less the resistance. When determining the proper wire for a circuit, both size and length must be considered to design a circuit that can handle the current needs of the component.

• Temperature—with many materials, the higher the temperature, the greater the resistance (positive temperature coefficient). Some materials exhibit the opposite trait of lower resistance with higher temperatures (negative temperature coefficient). These principles are used in many of the sensors on the engine.

OHM'S LAW

There is a direct relationship between current, voltage and resistance. The relationship between current, voltage and resistance can be summed up by a statement known as Ohm's law.

Voltage (E) is equal to amperage (I) times resistance (R): $E = I \times R$

Other forms of the formula are $R = E/I$ and $I = E/R$

In each of these formulas, E is the voltage in volts, I is the current in amps and R is the resistance in ohms. The basic point to remember is that as the resistance of a circuit goes up, the amount of current that flows in the circuit will go down, if voltage remains the same.

The amount of work that the electricity can perform is expressed as power. The unit of power is the watt (w). The relationship between power, voltage and current is expressed as:

Power (w) is equal to amperage (I) times voltage (E): $W = I \times E$

This is only true for direct current (DC) circuits; The alternating current formula is a tad different, but since the electrical circuits in most vehicles are DC type, we need not get into AC circuit theory.

Electrical Components

POWER SOURCE

Power is supplied to the vehicle by two devices: The battery and the alternator. The battery supplies electrical power during starting or during periods when the current demand of the vehicle's electrical system exceeds the output capacity of the alternator. The alternator supplies electrical current when the engine is running. Just not does the alternator supply the current needs of the vehicle, but it recharges the battery.

The Battery

In most modern vehicles, the battery is a lead/acid electrochemical device consisting of six 2 volt subsections (cells) connected in series, so that the unit is capable of producing approximately 12 volts of electrical pressure. Each subsection consists of a series of positive and negative plates held a short distance apart in a solution of sulfuric acid and water.

The two types of plates are of dissimilar metals. This sets up a chemical reaction, and it is this reaction which produces current flow from the battery when its positive and negative terminals are connected to an electrical load. The power removed from the battery is replaced by the alternator, restoring the battery to its original chemical state.

The Alternator

On some vehicles there isn't an alternator, but a generator. The difference is that an alternator supplies alternating current which is then changed to direct current for use on the vehicle, while a generator produces direct current. Alternators tend to be more efficient and that is why they are used.

Alternators and generators are devices that consist of coils of wires wound together making big electromagnets. One group of coils spins within another set and the interaction of the magnetic fields causes a current to flow. This current is then drawn off the coils and fed into the vehicles electrical system.

GROUND

Two types of grounds are used in automotive electric circuits. Direct ground components are grounded to the frame through their mounting points. All other components use some sort of ground wire which is attached to the frame or chassis of the vehicle. The electrical current runs through the chassis of the vehicle and returns to the battery through the ground (−) cable; if you look, you'll see that the battery ground cable connects between the battery and the frame or chassis of the vehicle.

➡️**It should be noted that a good percentage of electrical problems can be traced to bad grounds.**

PROTECTIVE DEVICES

♦ See Figure 2

It is possible for large surges of current to pass through the electrical system of your vehicle. If this surge of current were to reach the load in the circuit, the

surge could burn it out or severely damage it. It can also overload the wiring, causing the harness to get hot and melt the insulation. To prevent this, fuses, circuit breakers and/or fusible links are connected into the supply wires of the electrical system. These items are nothing more than a built-in weak spot in the system. When an abnormal amount of current flows through the system, these protective devices work as follows to protect the circuit:

- Fuse—when an excessive electrical current passes through a fuse, the fuse "blows" (the conductor melts) and opens the circuit, preventing the passage of current.
- Circuit Breaker—a circuit breaker is basically a self-repairing fuse. It will open the circuit in the same fashion as a fuse, but when the surge subsides, the circuit breaker can be reset and does not need replacement.
- Fusible Link—a fusible link (fuse link or main link) is a short length of special, high temperature insulated wire that acts as a fuse. When an excessive electrical current passes through a fusible link, the thin gauge wire inside the link melts, creating an intentional open to protect the circuit. To repair the circuit, the link must be replaced. Some newer type fusible links are housed in plug-in modules, which are simply replaced like a fuse, while older type fusible links must be cut and spliced if they melt. Since this link is very early in the electrical path, it's the first place to look if nothing on the vehicle works, yet the battery seems to be charged and is properly connected.

✳✳ CAUTION

Always replace fuses, circuit breakers and fusible links with identically rated components. Under no circumstances should a component of higher or lower amperage rating be substituted.

SWITCHES & RELAYS

♦ See Figures 3 and 4

Switches are used in electrical circuits to control the passage of current. The most common use is to open and close circuits between the battery and the various electric devices in the system. Switches are rated according to the amount of amperage they can handle. If a sufficient amperage rated switch is not used in a circuit, the switch could overload and cause damage.

Some electrical components which require a large amount of current to operate use a special switch called a relay. Since these circuits carry a large amount of current, the thickness of the wire in the circuit is also greater. If this large wire were connected from the load to the control switch, the switch would have to carry the high amperage load and the fairing or dash would be twice as large to accommodate the increased size of the wiring harness. To prevent these problems, a relay is used.

Relays are composed of a coil and a set of contacts. When the coil has a current passed though it, a magnetic field is formed and this field causes the contacts

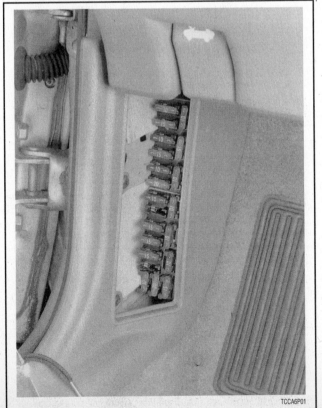

Fig. 2 Most vehicles use one or more fuse panels. This one is located on the driver's side kick panel

TCCA6P01

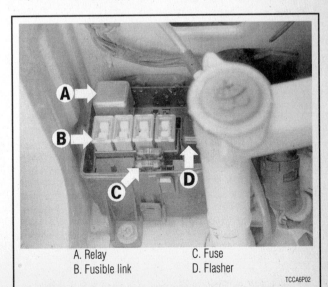

A. Relay   C. Fuse
B. Fusible link   D. Flasher

TCCA6P02

Fig. 3 The underhood fuse and relay panel usually contains fuses, relays, flashers and fusible links

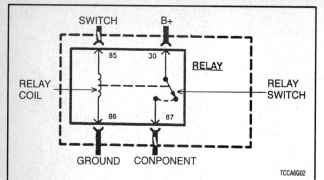

Fig. 4 Relays are composed of a coil and a switch. These two components are linked together so that when one operates, the other operates at the same time. The large wires in the circuit are connected from the battery to one side of the relay switch (B+) and from the opposite side of the relay switch to the load (component). Smaller wires are connected from the relay coil to the control switch for the circuit and from the opposite side of the relay coil to ground

to move together, completing the circuit. Most relays are normally open, preventing current from passing through the circuit, but they can take any electrical form depending on the job they are intended to do. Relays can be considered "remote control switches." They allow a smaller current to operate devices that require higher amperages. When a small current operates the coil, a larger current is allowed to pass by the contacts. Some common circuits which may use relays are the horn, headlights, starter, electric fuel pump and other high draw circuits.

LOAD

Every electrical circuit must include a "load" (something to use the electricity coming from the source). Without this load, the battery would attempt to deliver its entire power supply from one pole to another. This is called a "short circuit." All this electricity would take a short cut to ground and cause a great amount of damage to other components in the circuit by developing a tremendous amount of heat. This condition could develop sufficient heat to melt the insulation on all the surrounding wires and reduce a multiple wire cable to a lump of plastic and copper.

WIRING & HARNESSES

The average vehicle contains meters and meters of wiring, with hundreds of individual connections. To protect the many wires from damage and to keep them from becoming a confusing tangle, they are organized into bundles, enclosed in plastic or taped together and called wiring harnesses. Different harnesses serve different parts of the vehicle. Individual wires are color coded to help trace them through a harness where sections are hidden from view.

Automotive wiring or circuit conductors can be either single strand wire, multi-strand wire or printed circuitry. Single strand wire has a solid metal core and is usually used inside such components as alternators, motors, relays and other devices. Multi-strand wire has a core made of many small strands of wire twisted together into a single conductor. Most of the wiring in an automotive electrical system is made up of multi-strand wire, either as a single conductor or grouped together in a harness. All wiring is color coded on the insulator, either as a solid color or as a colored wire with an identification stripe. A printed circuit is a thin film of copper or other conductor that is printed on an insulator backing. Occasionally, a printed circuit is sandwiched between two sheets of plastic for more protection and flexibility. A complete printed circuit, consisting of conductors, insulating material and connectors for lamps or other components is called a printed circuit board. Printed circuitry is used in place of individual wires or harnesses in places where space is limited, such as behind instrument panels.

Since automotive electrical systems are very sensitive to changes in resistance, the selection of properly sized wires is critical when systems are repaired. A loose or corroded connection or a replacement wire that is too small for the circuit will add extra resistance and an additional voltage drop to the circuit.

The wire gauge number is an expression of the cross-section area of the conductor. Vehicles from countries that use the metric system will typically describe the wire size as its cross-sectional area in square millimeters. In this

method, the larger the wire, the greater the number. Another common system for expressing wire size is the American Wire Gauge (AWG) system. As gauge number increases, area decreases and the wire becomes smaller. An 18 gauge wire is smaller than a 4 gauge wire. A wire with a higher gauge number will carry less current than a wire with a lower gauge number. Gauge wire size refers to the size of the strands of the conductor, not the size of the complete wire with insulator. It is possible, therefore, to have two wires of the same gauge with different diameters because one may have thicker insulation than the other.

It is essential to understand how a circuit works before trying to figure out why it doesn't. An electrical schematic shows the electrical current paths when a circuit is operating properly. Schematics break the entire electrical system down into individual circuits. In a schematic, usually no attempt is made to represent wiring and components as they physically appear on the vehicle; switches and other components are shown as simply as possible. Face views of harness connectors show the cavity or terminal locations in all multi-pin connectors to help locate test points.

CONNECTORS

♦ **See Figures 5 and 6**

Three types of connectors are commonly used in automotive applications—weatherproof, molded and hard shell.

• Weatherproof—these connectors are most commonly used where the connector is exposed to the elements. Terminals are protected against moisture and dirt by sealing rings which provide a weathertight seal. All repairs require the use of a special terminal and the tool required to service it. Unlike standard blade type terminals, these weatherproof terminals cannot be straightened once

Fig. 5 Hard shell (left) and weatherproof (right) connectors have replaceable terminals

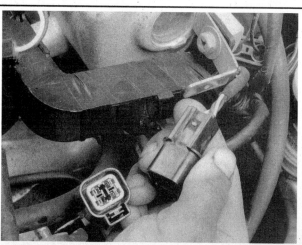

Fig. 6 Weatherproof connectors are most commonly used in the engine compartment or where the connector is exposed to the elements

they are bent. Make certain that the connectors are properly seated and all of the sealing rings are in place when connecting leads.

• Molded—these connectors require complete replacement of the connector if found to be defective. This means splicing a new connector assembly into the harness. All splices should be soldered to insure proper contact. Use care when probing the connections or replacing terminals in them, as it is possible to create a short circuit between opposite terminals. If this happens to the wrong terminal pair, it is possible to damage certain components. Always use jumper wires between connectors for circuit checking and NEVER probe through weatherproof seals.

• Hard Shell—unlike molded connectors, the terminal contacts in hard-shell connectors can be replaced. Replacement usually involves the use of a special terminal removal tool that depresses the locking tangs (barbs) on the connector terminal and allows the connector to be removed from the rear of the shell. The connector shell should be replaced if it shows any evidence of burning, melting, cracks, or breaks. Replace individual terminals that are burnt, corroded, distorted or loose.

Test Equipment

Pinpointing the exact cause of trouble in an electrical circuit is most times accomplished by the use of special test equipment. The following describes different types of commonly used test equipment and briefly explains how to use them in diagnosis. In addition to the information covered below, the tool manufacturer's instructions booklet (provided with the tester) should be read and clearly understood before attempting any test procedures.

JUMPER WIRES

✳✳ CAUTION

Never use jumper wires made from a thinner gauge wire than the circuit being tested. If the jumper wire is of too small a gauge, it may overheat and possibly melt. Never use jumpers to bypass high resistance loads in a circuit. Bypassing resistances, in effect, creates a short circuit. This may, in turn, cause damage and fire. Jumper wires should only be used to bypass lengths of wire or to simulate switches.

Jumper wires are simple, yet extremely valuable, pieces of test equipment. They are basically test wires which are used to bypass sections of a circuit. Although jumper wires can be purchased, they are usually fabricated from lengths of standard automotive wire and whatever type of connector (alligator clip, spade connector or pin connector) that is required for the particular application being tested. In cramped, hard-to-reach areas, it is advisable to have insulated boots over the jumper wire terminals in order to prevent accidental grounding. It is also advisable to include a standard automotive fuse in any jumper wire. This is commonly referred to as a "fused jumper". By inserting an in-line fuse holder between a set of test leads, a fused jumper wire can be used for bypassing open circuits. Use a 5 amp fuse to provide protection against voltage spikes.

Jumper wires are used primarily to locate open electrical circuits, on either the ground (–) side of the circuit or on the power (+) side. If an electrical component fails to operate, connect the jumper wire between the component and a good ground. If the component operates only with the jumper installed, the ground circuit is open. If the ground circuit is good, but the component does not operate, the circuit between the power feed and component may be open. By moving the jumper wire successively back from the component toward the power source, you can isolate the area of the circuit where the open is located. When the component stops functioning, or the power is cut off, the open is in the segment of wire between the jumper and the point previously tested.

You can sometimes connect the jumper wire directly from the battery to the "hot" terminal of the component, but first make sure the component uses 12 volts in operation. Some electrical components, such as fuel injectors or sensors, are designed to operate on about 4 to 5 volts, and running 12 volts directly to these components will cause damage.

TEST LIGHTS

▶ See Figure 7

The test light is used to check circuits and components while electrical current is flowing through them. It is used for voltage and ground tests. To use a

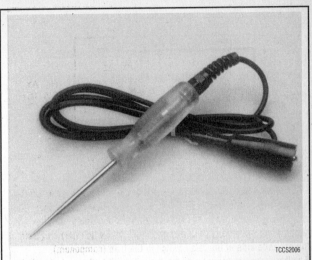

Fig. 7 A 12 volt test light is used to detect the presence of voltage in a circuit

12 volt test light, connect the ground clip to a good ground and probe wherever necessary with the pick. The test light will illuminate when voltage is detected. This does not necessarily mean that 12 volts (or any particular amount of voltage) is present; it only means that some voltage is present. It is advisable before using the test light to touch its ground clip and probe across the battery posts or terminals to make sure the light is operating properly.

✳✳ WARNING

Do not use a test light to probe electronic ignition, spark plug or coil wires. Never use a pick-type test light to probe wiring on computer controlled systems unless specifically instructed to do so. Any wire insulation that is pierced by the test light probe should be taped and sealed with silicone after testing.

Like the jumper wire, the 12 volt test light is used to isolate opens in circuits. But, whereas the jumper wire is used to bypass the open to operate the load, the 12 volt test light is used to locate the presence of voltage in the circuit. If the test light illuminates, there is power up to that point in the circuit; if the test light does not illuminate, there is an open circuit (no power). Move the test light in successive steps back toward the power source until the light in the handle illuminates. The open is between the probe and a point which was previously probed.

The self-powered test light is similar in design to the 12 volt test light, but contains a 1.5 volt penlight battery in the handle. It is most often used in place of a multimeter to check for open or short circuits when power is isolated from the circuit (continuity test).

The battery in a self-powered test light does not provide much current. A weak battery may not provide enough power to illuminate the test light even when a complete circuit is made (especially if there is high resistance in the circuit). Always make sure that the test battery is strong. To check the battery, briefly touch the ground clip to the probe; if the light glows brightly, the battery is strong enough for testing.

➡**A self-powered test light should not be used on any computer controlled system or component. The small amount of electricity transmitted by the test light is enough to damage many electronic automotive components.**

MULTIMETERS

Multimeters are an extremely useful tool for troubleshooting electrical problems. They can be purchased in either analog or digital form and have a price range to suit any budget. A multimeter is a voltmeter, ammeter and ohmmeter (along with other features) combined into one instrument. It is often used when testing solid state circuits because of its high input impedance (usually 10 megaohms or more). A brief description of the multimeter main test functions follows:

• **Voltmeter**—the voltmeter is used to measure voltage at any point in a circuit, or to measure the voltage drop across any part of a circuit. Voltmeters usually have various scales and a selector switch to allow the reading of different voltage ranges. The voltmeter has a positive and a negative lead. To avoid damage to the meter, always connect the negative lead to the negative (–) side of the circuit (to ground or nearest the ground side of the circuit) and connect the positive lead to the positive (+) side of the circuit (to the power source or the nearest power source). Note that the negative voltmeter lead will always be black and that the positive voltmeter will always be some color other than black (usually red).

• **Ohmmeter**—the ohmmeter is designed to read resistance (measured in ohms) in a circuit or component. Most ohmmeters will have a selector switch which permits the measurement of different ranges of resistance (usually the selector switch allows the multiplication of the meter reading by 10, 100, 1,000 and 10,000). Some ohmmeters are "auto-ranging" which means the meter itself will determine which scale to use. Since the meters are powered by an internal battery, the ohmmeter can be used like a self-powered test light. When the ohmmeter is connected, current from the ohmmeter flows through the circuit or component being tested. Since the ohmmeter's internal resistance and voltage are known values, the amount of current flow through the meter depends on the resistance of the circuit or component being tested. The ohmmeter can also be used to perform a continuity test for suspected open circuits. In using the meter for making continuity checks, do not be concerned with the actual resistance readings. Zero resistance, or any ohm reading, indicates continuity in the circuit. Infinite resistance indicates an opening in the circuit. A high resistance reading where there should be none indicates a problem in the circuit. Checks for short circuits are made in the same manner as checks for open circuits, except that the circuit must be isolated from both power and normal ground. Infinite resistance indicates no continuity, while zero resistance indicates a dead short.

❋❋ WARNING

Never use an ohmmeter to check the resistance of a component or wire while there is voltage applied to the circuit.

• **Ammeter**—an ammeter measures the amount of current flowing through a circuit in units called amperes or amps. At normal operating voltage, most circuits have a characteristic amount of amperes, called "current draw" which can be measured using an ammeter. By referring to a specified current draw rating, then measuring the amperes and comparing the two values, one can determine what is happening within the circuit to aid in diagnosis. An open circuit, for example, will not allow any current to flow, so the ammeter reading will be zero. A damaged component or circuit will have an increased current draw, so the reading will be high. The ammeter is always connected in series with the circuit being tested. All of the current that normally flows through the circuit must also flow through the ammeter; if there is any other path for the current to follow, the ammeter reading will not be accurate. The ammeter itself has very little resistance to current flow and, therefore, will not affect the circuit, but it will measure current draw only when the circuit is closed and electricity is flowing. Excessive current draw can blow fuses and drain the battery, while a reduced current draw can cause motors to run slowly, lights to dim and other components to not operate properly.

Troubleshooting Electrical Systems

When diagnosing a specific problem, organized troubleshooting is a must. The complexity of a modern automotive vehicle demands that you approach any problem in a logical, organized manner. There are certain troubleshooting techniques, however, which are standard:

• Establish when the problem occurs. Does the problem appear only under certain conditions? Were there any noises, odors or other unusual symptoms? Isolate the problem area. To do this, make some simple tests and observations, then eliminate the systems that are working properly. Check for obvious problems, such as broken wires and loose or dirty connections. Always check the obvious before assuming something complicated is the cause.

• Test for problems systematically to determine the cause once the problem area is isolated. Are all the components functioning properly? Is there power going to electrical switches and motors. Performing careful, systematic checks will often turn up most causes on the first inspection, without wasting time checking components that have little or no relationship to the problem.

• Test all repairs after the work is done to make sure that the problem is fixed. Some causes can be traced to more than one component, so a careful verification of repair work is important in order to pick up additional malfunctions that may cause a problem to reappear or a different problem to arise. A blown fuse, for example, is a simple problem that may require more than another fuse to repair. If you don't look for a problem that caused a fuse to blow, a shorted wire (for example) may go undetected.

Experience has shown that most problems tend to be the result of a fairly simple and obvious cause, such as loose or corroded connectors, bad grounds or damaged wire insulation which causes a short. This makes careful visual inspection of components during testing essential to quick and accurate troubleshooting.

Testing

OPEN CIRCUITS

▶ **See Figure 8**

This test already assumes the existence of an open in the circuit and it is used to help locate the open portion.

1. Isolate the circuit from power and ground.
2. Connect the self-powered test light or ohmmeter ground clip to the ground side of the circuit and probe sections of the circuit sequentially.
3. If the light is out or there is infinite resistance, the open is between the probe and the circuit ground.
4. If the light is on or the meter shows continuity, the open is between the probe and the end of the circuit toward the power source.

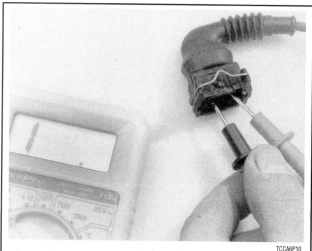

TCCA6P10

Fig. 8 The infinite reading on this multimeter indicates that the circuit is open

SHORT CIRCUITS

➡ **Never use a self-powered test light to perform checks for opens or shorts when power is applied to the circuit under test. The test light can be damaged by outside power.**

1. Isolate the circuit from power and ground.
2. Connect the self-powered test light or ohmmeter ground clip to a good ground and probe any easy-to-reach point in the circuit.
3. If the light comes on or there is continuity, there is a short somewhere in the circuit.
4. To isolate the short, probe a test point at either end of the isolated circuit (the light should be on or the meter should indicate continuity).
5. Leave the test light probe engaged and sequentially open connectors or switches, remove parts, etc. until the light goes out or continuity is broken.
6. When the light goes out, the short is between the last two circuit components which were opened.

VOLTAGE

This test determines voltage available from the battery and should be the first step in any electrical troubleshooting procedure after visual inspection. Many electrical problems, especially on computer controlled systems, can be caused by a low state of charge in the battery. Excessive corrosion at the battery cable terminals can cause poor contact that will prevent proper charging and full battery current flow.

1. Set the voltmeter selector switch to the 20V position.
2. Connect the multimeter negative lead to the battery's negative (−) post or terminal and the positive lead to the battery's positive (+) post or terminal.
3. Turn the ignition switch **ON** to provide a load.
4. A well charged battery should register over 12 volts. If the meter reads below 11.5 volts, the battery power may be insufficient to operate the electrical system properly.

VOLTAGE DROP

⬥ **See Figure 9**

When current flows through a load, the voltage beyond the load drops. This voltage drop is due to the resistance created by the load and also by small resistances created by corrosion at the connectors and damaged insulation on the wires. The maximum allowable voltage drop under load is critical, especially if there is more than one load in the circuit, since all voltage drops are cumulative.

1. Set the voltmeter selector switch to the 20 volt position.
2. Connect the multimeter negative lead to a good ground.
3. Operate the circuit and check the voltage prior to the first component (load).
4. There should be little or no voltage drop in the circuit prior to the first component. If a voltage drop exists, the wire or connectors in the circuit are suspect.
5. While operating the first component in the circuit, probe the ground side of the component with the positive meter lead and observe the voltage readings. A small voltage drop should be noticed. This voltage drop is caused by the resistance of the component.
6. Repeat the test for each component (load) down the circuit.
7. If a large voltage drop is noticed, the preceding component, wire or connector is suspect.

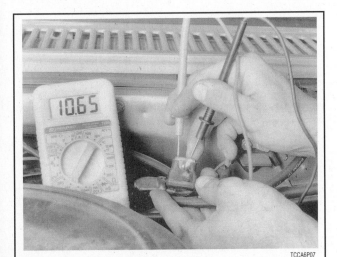

Fig. 9 This voltage drop test revealed high resistance (low voltage) in the circuit

RESISTANCE

⬥ **See Figures 10 and 11**

Fig. 10 Checking the resistance of a coolant temperature sensor with an ohmmeter. Reading is 1.04 kilohms

1. Isolate the circuit from the vehicle's power source.
2. Ensure that the ignition key is **OFF** when disconnecting any components or the battery.
3. Where necessary, also isolate at least one side of the circuit to be checked, in order to avoid reading parallel resistances. Parallel circuit resistances will always give a lower reading than the actual resistance of either of the branches.
4. Connect the meter leads to both sides of the circuit (wire or component) and read the actual measured ohms on the meter scale. Make sure the selector

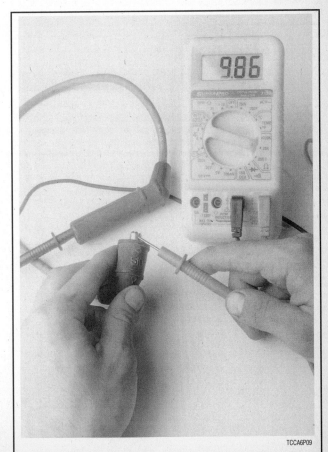

Fig. 11 Spark plug wires can be checked for excessive resistance using an ohmmeter

switch is set to the proper ohm scale for the circuit being tested, to avoid mis-reading the ohmmeter test value.

Wire and Connector Repair

Almost anyone can replace damaged wires, as long as the proper tools and parts are available. Wire and terminals are available to fit almost any need. Even the specialized weatherproof, molded and hard shell connectors are now available from aftermarket suppliers.

Be sure the ends of all the wires are fitted with the proper terminal hardware and connectors. Wrapping a wire around a stud is never a permanent solution and will only cause trouble later. Replace wires one at a time to avoid confusion. Always route wires exactly the same as the factory.

➡**If connector repair is necessary, only attempt it if you have the proper tools. Weatherproof and hard shell connectors require special tools to release the pins inside the connector. Attempting to repair these connectors with conventional hand tools will damage them.**

BATTERY CABLES

Disconnecting the Cables

When working on any electrical component on the vehicle, it is always a good idea to disconnect the negative (-) battery cable. This will prevent potential damage to many sensitive electrical components such as the Powertrain Control Module (PCM), radio, alternator, etc.

➡**Any time you disengage the battery cables, it is recommended that you disconnect the negative (-) battery cable first. This will prevent your accidentally grounding the positive (+) terminal to the body of the vehicle when disconnecting it, thereby preventing damage to the above mentioned components.**

Before you disconnect the cable(s), first turn the ignition to the **OFF** position. This will prevent a draw on the battery which could cause arcing (electric-ity trying to ground itself to the body of a vehicle, just like a spark plug jumping the gap) and, of course, damaging some components such as the alternator diodes.

When the battery cable(s) are reconnected (negative cable last), be sure to check that your lights, windshield wipers and other electrically operated safety components are all working correctly. If your vehicle contains an Electronically Tuned Radio (ETR), don't forget to also reset your radio stations. Ditto for the clock.

Also, Ford reports that anytime the battery cables have been disconnected and then reconnected, some abnormal drive symptoms could occur. The is due to the PCM losing the memory voltage and its learned adaptive strategy. The vehicle will need to be driven for 10 miles (16Km) or more until the PCM relearns its adaptive strategy, and acclimates the engine and transmission functions to your driving style.

AIR BAG (SUPPLEMENTAL RESTRAINT) SYSTEM

General Information

▶ **See Figure 12**

The 1995–99 Ranger, Explorer and Mountaineer vehicles are available with an air bag Supplemental Restraint System (SRS). The SRS is designed to work in conjunction with the standard three-point safety belts to reduce injury in a head-on collision.

❊❊ WARNING

The SRS can actually cause physical injury or death if the safety belts are not used, or if the manufacturer's warnings are not followed. The manufacturer's warnings can be found in your owner's manual, or, in some cases, on your sun visors.

The SRS is comprised of the following components:
• Driver's side air bag module
• Passenger's side air bag module
• Right-hand and left-hand primary crash front air bag sensors
• Air bag diagnostic monitor computer
• Electrical wiring

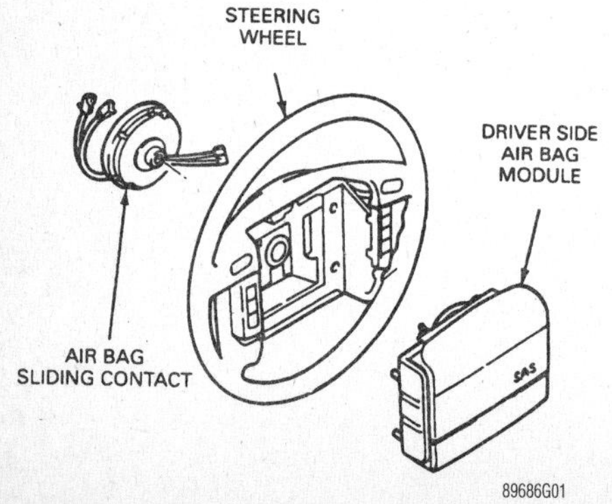

The SRS primary crash front air bag sensors are hard-wired to the air bag modules and determine when the air bags are deployed. During a frontal collision, the sensors quickly inflate the two air bags to reduce injury by cushioning the driver and front passenger from striking the dashboard, windshield, steering wheel and any other hard surfaces. The air bag inflates so quickly (in a fraction of a second) that in most cases it is fully inflated before you actually start to move during an automotive collision.

Since the SRS is a complicated and essentially important system, its components are constantly being tested by a diagnostic monitor computer, which illuminates the air bag indicator light on the instrument cluster for approximately 6 seconds when the ignition switch is turned to the **RUN** position when the SRS is functioning properly. After being illuminated for the 6 seconds, the indicator light should then turn off.

If the air bag light does not illuminate at all, stays on continuously, or flashes at any time, a problem has been detected by the diagnostic monitor computer.

❊❊ WARNING

If at any time the air bag light indicates that the computer has noted a problem, have your vehicle's SRS serviced immediately by a qualified automotive technician. A faulty SRS can cause severe physical injury or death.

SERVICE PRECAUTIONS

Whenever working around, or on, the air bag supplemental restraint system, ALWAYS adhere to the following warnings and cautions.
• Always wear safety glasses when servicing an air bag vehicle and when handling an air bag module.
• Carry a live air bag module with the bag and trim cover facing away from your body, so that an accidental deployment of the air bag will have a small chance of personal injury.
• Place an air bag module on a table or other flat surface with the bag and trim cover pointing up.
• Wear gloves, a dust mask and safety glasses whenever handling a deployed air bag module. The air bag surface may contain traces of sodium hydroxide, a by-product of the gas that inflates the air bag and which can cause skin irritation.
• Ensure to wash your hands with mild soap and water after handling a deployed air bag.

STEERING WHEEL

DRIVER SIDE AIR BAG MODULE

AIR BAG SLIDING CONTACT

89686G01

Fig. 12 Exploded view of the SRS air bag module and related components

• All air bag modules with discolored or damaged cover trim must be replaced, not repainted.

• All component replacement and wiring service must be made with the negative and positive battery cables disconnected from the battery for a minimum of one minute prior to attempting service or replacement.

• NEVER probe the air bag electrical terminals. Doing so could result in air bag deployment, which can cause serious physical injury.

• If the vehicle is involved in a fender-bender which results in a damaged front bumper or grille, have the air bag sensors inspected by a qualified automotive technician to ensure that they were not damaged.

• If at any time, the air bag light indicates that the computer has noted a problem, have your vehicle's SRS serviced immediately by a qualified automotive technician. A faulty SRS can cause severe physical injury or death.

DISARMING THE SYSTEM

1. Disconnect the negative battery cable from the battery.
2. Disconnect the positive battery cable from the battery.

3. Wait one minute. This time is required for the back-up power supply in the air bag diagnostic monitor to completely drain. The system is now disarmed.

If you are disarming the system with the intent of testing the system, do not! The SRS is a sensitive, complex system and should only be tested or serviced by a qualified automotive technician. Also, specific tools are needed for SRS testing.

ARMING THE SYSTEM

1. Connect the positive battery cable.
2. Connect the negative battery cable.
3. Stand outside the vehicle and carefully turn the ignition to the **RUN** position. Be sure that no part of your body is in front of the air bag module on the steering wheel, to prevent injury in case of an accidental air bag deployment.
4. Ensure the air bag indicator light turns off after approximately 6 seconds. If the light does not illuminate at all, does not turn off, or starts to flash, have the system tested by a qualified automotive technician. If the light does turn off after 6 seconds and does not flash, the SRS is working properly.

HEATING AND AIR CONDITIONING

Blower Motor

REMOVAL & INSTALLATION

◊ **See Figures 13 and 14**

Without Air Conditioning

1. Disconnect the negative battery cable.
2. Remove the air cleaner or air inlet duct, as necessary.
3. If necessary, Remove the speed control module and the washer fluid reservoir.
4. Disconnect the wire harness connector from the blower motor by pushing down on the connector tabs and pulling the connector off of the motor.
5. Disconnect the blower motor cooling tube at the blower motor.
6. Remove the 3 screws attaching the blower motor and wheel to the heater blower assembly.
7. Holding the cooling tube aside, pull the blower motor and wheel from the heater blower assembly and remove it from the vehicle.
8. Remove the blower wheel push-nut and/or clamp from the motor shaft and pull the blower wheel from the motor shaft.
   To install:
9. Install the blower wheel on the blower motor shaft.
10. Install the hub clamp and/or push-nut.
11. Holding the cooling tube aside, position the blower motor and wheel on the heater blower assembly and install the 3 attaching screws.

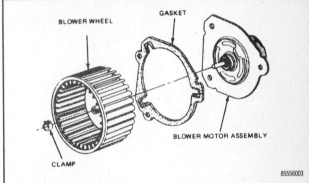

Fig. 14 Exploded view of the blower motor and wheel (fan) assembly

12. Connect the blower motor cooling tube and the wire harness connector.
13. Install the vacuum reservoir on the hoses with the 2 screws.
14. If removed, install the speed control module and the washer fluid reservoir.
15. Install the air cleaner or air inlet duct, as necessary.
16. Connect the negative battery cable and check the system for proper operation.

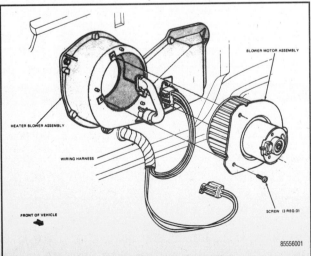

Fig. 13 Exploded view of the blower motor mounting

To remove the blower motor, first disconnect the electrical wire harness plug . . .

. . . then remove the blower motor cooling tube from the motor

Remove the blower motor attaching screws and the washer fluid reservoir . .

. . . then slide the blower motor from the housing. Take care to not damage the blower wheel (arrow)

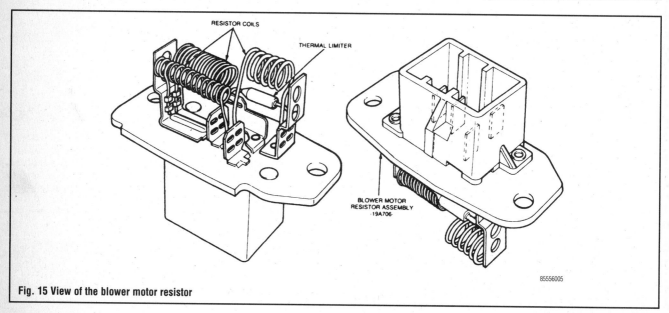

Fig. 15 View of the blower motor resistor

With Air Conditioning

1. Disconnect the negative battery cable.
2. In the engine compartment, disconnect the wire harness from the motor by pushing down on the tab while pulling the connection off at the motor.
3. Remove the air cleaner or air inlet duct, as necessary.
4. If necessary, remove the solenoid box cover retaining bolts and the solenoid box cover.
5. Disconnect the blower motor cooling tube from the blower motor.
6. Remove the blower motor mounting plate attaching screws and remove the motor and wheel assembly from the evaporator assembly blower motor housing.
7. Remove the blower motor hub clamp from the motor shaft and pull the blower wheel from the shaft.

To install:

8. Install the blower motor wheel on the blower motor shaft and install a new hub clamp.
9. Install a new motor mounting seal on the blower housing before installing the blower motor.
10. Position the blower motor and wheel assembly in the blower housing and install the attaching screws.
11. Connect the blower motor cooling tube.
12. Connect the electrical wire harness hard shell connector to the blower motor by pushing into place.
13. If removed, position the solenoid box cover into place and install the 3 retaining screws.
14. Install the air cleaner or air inlet duct, as necessary.
15. Connect the negative battery cable and check the blower motor in all speeds for proper operation.

Blower Motor Resistor

REMOVAL & INSTALLATION

▶ **See Figure 15**

1. Disconnect the negative battery cable.
2. Disconnect the wire connector from the resistor assembly.
3. Remove the 2 screws attaching the resistor assembly to the blower or evaporator case and remove the resistor.
4. Installation is the reverse of the removal procedure. Check the blower motor for proper operation in all blower speeds.

Heater Core

REMOVAL & INSTALLATION

1991–94 Models

▶ **See Figure 16**

1. Disconnect the negative battery cable. Allow the engine to cool down. Drain the cooling system to a level below the heater core fittings on the firewall.

❄❄ CAUTION

When draining the coolant, keep in mind that cats and dogs are attracted by the ethylene glycol antifreeze, and are quite likely to

drink any that is left in an uncovered container or in puddles on the ground. This will prove fatal in sufficient quantity. Always drain the coolant into a sealable container. Coolant should be reused unless it is contaminated or several years old.

2. Disconnect the heater hoses from the heater core tubes and plug hoses.

3. In the passenger compartment, remove the four screws attaching the heater core access cover to the plenum assembly and remove the access cover.

4. Pull the heater core rearward and down, removing it from the plenum assembly.

To install:

5. Position the heater core and seal in the plenum assembly.

6. Install the heater core access cover to the plenum assembly and secure with four screws.

7. Install the heater hoses to the heater core tubes at the dash panel in the engine compartment. Do not over-tighten hose clamps.

8. Check the coolant level and add coolant as required. Connect the negative battery cable.

9. Start the engine and check the system for coolant leaks.

1995–99 Models

▶ See Figure 17

1. Disconnect the negative battery cable. Allow the engine to cool down. Drain the cooling system to a level below the heater core fittings on the firewall.

✸✸ CAUTION

When draining the coolant, keep in mind that cats and dogs are attracted by the ethylene glycol antifreeze, and are quite likely to drink any that is left in an uncovered container or in puddles on the ground. This will prove fatal in sufficient quantity. Always drain the coolant into a sealable container. Coolant should be reused unless it is contaminated or several years old.

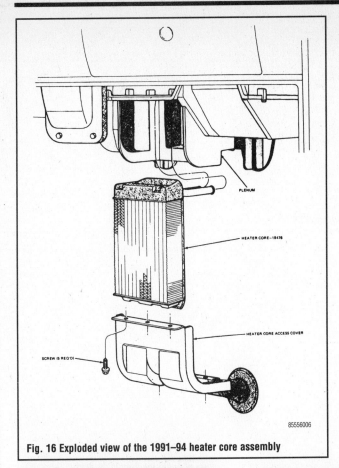

Fig. 16 Exploded view of the 1991–94 heater core assembly

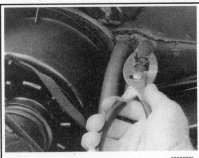

From inside the engine compartment, disconnect the heater hoses from the core fittings . . .

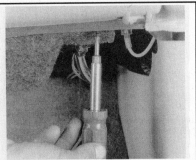

. . . then, in the passenger compartment, remove the under dash cover retaining screws . . .

. . . and allow the cover to drop down. If necessary, you can remove the cover if it is in your way

Remove the heater core access panel attaching screws . . .

. . . then remove the cover by pulling downward and straight back to disengage the drain tube (arrow)

Pull the heater core rearward and down to remove it from the plenum assembly

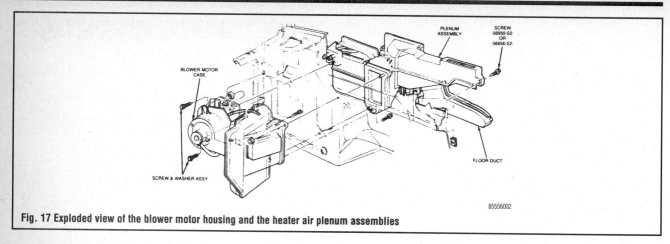

Fig. 17 Exploded view of the blower motor housing and the heater air plenum assemblies

2. Disconnect the heater hoses from the heater core tubes and plug hoses.

3. Remove the five nuts that secure the blower motor housing to the firewall.

4. Pull the housing away from the firewall. Disconnect any wire harness plugs which inhibit the housing.

5. Remove the remaining nuts which secure the heater air plenum (inside the passenger compartment) to the firewall.

6. In the passenger compartment, remove the instrument panel. Refer to Section 10.

7. Pull the heater air plenum rearward from the firewall and remove it from the vehicle.

8. Remove the heater core from the heater air plenum.

9. Inspect all air seals on the components and firewall and replace any that are damaged.

To install:

10. Install the heater core into the air plenum chamber.

11. Position the heater air plenum against the firewall from the passenger compartment.

12. Under the hood, install the plenum retaining nuts.

13. Install the blower motor housing to the firewall and install the attaching nuts.

14. Connect the heater hoses to the heater core tubes at the dash panel in the engine compartment. Do not over-tighten the hose clamps.

15. Install the instrument panel.

16. Check the coolant level and add coolant as required. Connect the negative battery cable.

17. Start the engine and check the system for coolant leaks.

Control Head

▶ **See Figure 18**

REMOVAL & INSTALLATION

▶ **See Figures 19 and 20**

1. Disconnect the negative battery cable.

2. On 1991–94 models, open the ash tray and remove the 2 screws that hold the ash tray drawer slide to the instrument panel. Remove the ash tray and drawer slide bracket from the instrument panel.

3. On 1995–99 models, remove the radio.

4. Gently pull the finish panel away from the instrument panel and the cluster. The finish panel pops straight back for approximately 1 inch (25.4mm), then up to remove. Be careful not to trap the finish panel around the steering column.

➡**If equipped with the electronic 4x4 shift-on-the-fly module, disconnect the wire from the rear of the 4x4 transfer switch before trying to remove the finish panel from the instrument panel.**

5. Remove the 4 screws attaching the control assembly to the instrument panel.

6. Pull the control through the instrument panel opening far enough to allow removal of the electrical connections from the blower switch and control assembly illumination lamp. Using a suitable tool, remove the vacuum harness from the vacuum switch on the side of the control.

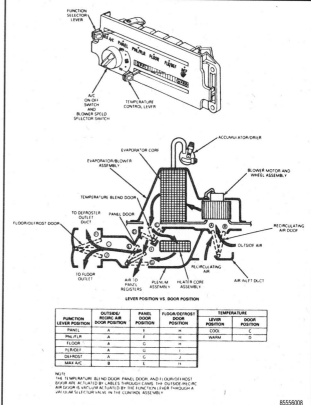

Fig. 18 Example of the control head and the air flow paths in the plenum assembly (with A/C)

FUNCTION LEVER POSITION	OUTSIDE/ RECIRC AIR DOOR POSITION	PANEL DOOR POSITION	FLOOR/DEFROST DOOR POSITION	TEMPERATURE	
				LEVER POSITION	DOOR POSITION
PANEL	A	E	H	COOL	C
PNL/FLR	A	E	H	WARM	D
FLOOR	A	G	H		
FLR/DEF	A	G	H		
DEFROST	A	G	J		
MAX A/C	B	E	H		

NOTE:
THE TEMPERATURE BLEND DOOR, PANEL DOOR, AND FLOOR/DEFROST DOOR ARE ACTUATED BY CABLES THROUGH CAMS. THE OUTSIDE/RECIRC AIR DOOR IS VACUUM ACTUATED BY THE FUNCTION LEVER THROUGH A VACUUM SELECTOR VALVE IN THE CONTROL ASSEMBLY.

7. If equipped with cables, perform the following:

a. At the rear of the control, using a suitable tool, release the temperature and function cable snap-in flags from the white control bracket.

b. On the bottom side of the control, remove the temperature cable from the control by rotating the cable until the T-pin releases the cable. The temperature cable is black with a blue snap-in flag.

c. Pull enough cable through the instrument panel opening until the function cable can be held vertical to the control, then remove the control cable from the function lever. The function cable is white with a black snap-in flag.

8. Remove the control assembly from the instrument panel.

To install:

9. If equipped with control cables, perform the following:

a. Pull the control cables through the control assembly opening in the instrument panel for a distance of approximately 8 in. (203mm).

b. Hold the control assembly up to the instrument panel with its face directed toward the floor of the vehicle. This will locate the face of the control in a position that is 90 degrees out of its installed position.

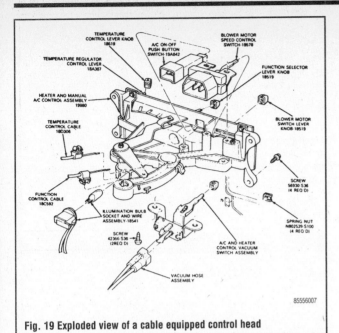

Fig. 19 Exploded view of a cable equipped control head

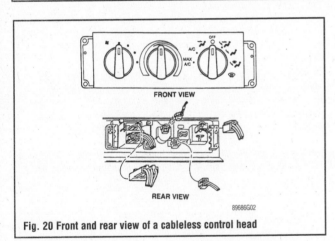

Fig. 20 Front and rear view of a cableless control head

c. Carefully bend and attach the function cable that has a white color code and a black snap-in terminal to the white plastic lever on the control assembly. Rotate the control assembly back to its normal position for installation, then snap the black cable flag into the control assembly bracket.

d. On the opposite side of the control assembly, attach the black temperature control cable with the blue plastic snap-in flag to the blue plastic lever on the control. Make sure the end of the cable is seated securely with the T-top pin on the control. Rotate the cable to its operating position and snap the blue cable flag into the control assembly bracket.

10. Connect the wiring harness to the blower switch and the illumination lamp to its receptacle on the control assembly. Connect the terminal on the vacuum hose to the vacuum switch on the control assembly.

11. Position the control assembly into the instrument panel opening and install the 4 mounting screws.

12. If equipped, reconnect the 4x4 electric shift harness on the rear of the cluster finish panel.

13. Install the cluster finish panel with integral push-pins. Make sure that all pins are fully seated around the rim of the panel.

14. On 1991–94 models, reinsert the ash tray slide bracket and reconnect the illumination connection circuit. Reinstall the 2 screws that retain the ash tray retainer bracket and the finish panel. Replace the ash tray and reconnect the cigarette lighter.

15. On 1995–99 models, reinstall the radio.

16. Connect the negative battery cable and check the heater system for proper control assembly operation.

Control Cables

ADJUSTMENT

Function Selector and Temperature Selector Control Cable

To check the temperature cable adjustment, move the temperature control lever all the way to the left, then move it all the way to the right. At the extreme ends of lever travel, the door should be heard to firmly seat, indicated by a loud thumping sound, allowing either maximum or no air flow through the heater core. To check the function cable adjustment, see that the function lever will reach the detents at the far left and right of its travel. In addition, check that the air flow is correct when the function lever is moved through each detent provided in the control assembly. If cable adjustment is needed, proceed as follows:

1. Disengage the glove compartment door by squeezing its sides together. Allow the door to hang free.

2. Working through the glove compartment opening, remove the cable jacket from the metal attaching clip on the top of the plenum by depressing the clip tab and pulling the cable out of the clip.

➡ **The adjustable end should remain attached to the door cams.**

3. To adjust the temperature control cable, set the temperature lever at COOL and hold. With the cable end attached to the temperature door cam, push gently on the cable jacket to seat the blend door. Push until resistance is felt. Reinstall the cable to the clip by pushing the cable jacket into the clip from the top until it snaps in.

4. To adjust the function control cable, set the function selector lever in the DEFROST detent and hold. With the cable end attached to the function cam, pull on the cam jacket until cam travel stops. Reinstall the cable to the clip by pushing the cable jacket into the clip from the top until it snaps in place.

5. Install the glove compartment.

6. Run the system blower on HIGH and actuate the levers, checking for proper adjustment.

REMOVAL & INSTALLATION

♦ **See Figures 21 and 22**

Temperature and Function Cables

1. Disconnect the negative battery cable.

2. Remove the control assembly from the instrument panel.

3. Disengage the glove compartment door by squeezing the sides together and allowing the door to hang free.

4. Working through the glove compartment and/or control opening, remove the temperature and function cable jackets from their clips on top of the plenum by compressing the clip tans and pulling the cables upward.

5. Reach through the glove compartment opening and disconnect the function and temperature cables from their separate cams. The cable ends are secured to the cams under a retention finger.

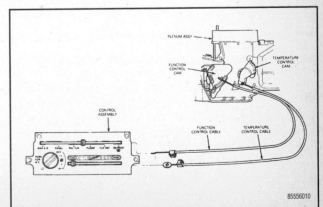

Fig. 21 Control cable connections at the head and the air plenum

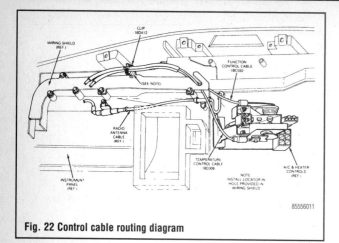

Fig. 22 Control cable routing diagram

6. The cables are routed inside the instrument panel with 2 routing aids. Remove the cables from these devices. Reaching through the control opening, pull the cables upward out of the wiring shield cut-out. Reaching through the glove box opening, pull the cables out of the plastic clip up inside the instrument panel.

7. Pull the cables from the instrument panel through the control assembly opening.

To install:

8. Working through the glove compartment opening and the control opening in the instrument panel, feed the end of the cables to the cam area. Feed the cables in from the glove compartment opening, making sure the coiled end of the white function cable and the round hole diecast end of the temperature cable go in first.

9. Attach the coiled end of the function cable to the function cam, making sure the cable is routed under the cable hold-down feature on the cam assembly. The pigtail coil may be facing either up or down.

10. Attach the diecast end of the temperature cable to the temperature cam

making sure the cable is routed under the cable hold-down feature on the cam assembly.

11. Route the control end of the cable through the instrument panel until the ends stick out of the control opening. It is not necessary to insert the cable into any routing devices previously used. The routing aids are only necessary when the entire instrument panel is removed and reinstalled.

12. Attach the function and temperature cables to the control. Install the control assembly in the instrument panel.

13. Adjust the cables in their clips on top of the plenum.

➡ **Make sure the radio antenna cable does not become disengaged from its mounting and fall into the plenum cam area where it could cause an increase in control assembly operating effort or a faulty selection of system functions.**

14. Connect the negative battery cable and make a final check of the system for proper control cable operation.

Air Conditioning Components

REMOVAL & INSTALLATION

Repair or service of air conditioning components is not covered by this manual, because of the risk of personal injury or death, and because of the legal ramifications of servicing these components without the proper EPA certification and experience. Cost, personal injury or death, environmental damage, and legal considerations (such as the fact that it is a federal crime to vent refrigerant into the atmosphere), dictate that the A/C components on your vehicle should be serviced only by a Motor Vehicle Air Conditioning (MVAC) trained, and EPA certified automotive technician.

➡ **If your vehicle's A/C system uses R-12 refrigerant and is in need of recharging, the A/C system can be converted over to R-134a refrigerant (less environmentally harmful and expensive). Refer to Section 1 for additional information on R-12 to R-134a conversions, and for additional considerations dealing with your vehicle's A/C system.**

CRUISE CONTROL

Vacuum Controlled Systems

▶ **See Figure 23**

The vacuum controlled cruise control system consists of the following components:
- Control switches
- Servo (throttle actuator)
- Speed sensor
- Clutch switch (manual transmissions)
- Stoplamp switch
- Vacuum dump valve
- Amplifier assembly

The throttle actuator is mounted in the engine compartment and is connected to the throttle linkage with an actuator cable. The speed control amplifier regulates the throttle actuator to keep the requested speed. When the brake pedal is

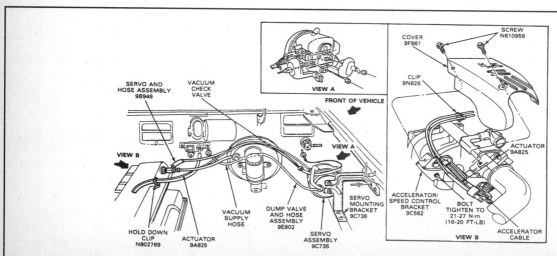

Fig. 23 Vacuum controlled cruise control system components

depressed, an electrical signal from the stoplamp switch returns the system to stand-by mode. The vacuum dump valve also mechanically releases the vacuum in the throttle actuator, thus releasing the throttle independently of the amplifier control. This feature is used as a safety backup.

Electronic Systems

▶ See Figure 24

The electronic cruise control system consists of the following components:

- Control switches
- Servo/control unit (throttle actuator)
- Speed sensor
- Stoplamp and deactivator switches

The throttle actuator/control unit is mounted in the engine compartment and is connected to the throttle linkage with an actuator cable. The control unit regulates the throttle actuator to keep the requested speed. When the brake pedal is depressed, an electrical signal from the stoplamp and deactivator switches return the system to stand-by mode. This system operates independently of engine vacuum, therefore no vacuum lines are required.

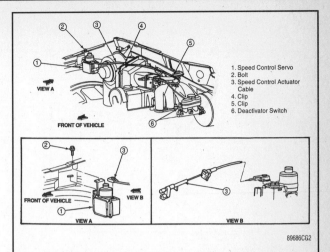

1. Speed Control Servo
2. Bolt
3. Speed Control Actuator Cable
4. Clip
5. Clip
6. Deactivator Switch

89686CG2

Fig. 24 Electronic cruise control system components—2.3L Ranger shown, others similar

CRUISE CONTROL TROUBLESHOOTING

Problem	Possible Cause
Will not hold proper speed	Incorrect cable adjustment
	Binding throttle linkage
	Leaking vacuum servo diaphragm
	Leaking vacuum tank
	Faulty vacuum or vent valve
	Faulty stepper motor
	Faulty transducer
	Faulty speed sensor
	Faulty cruise control module
Cruise intermittently cuts out	Clutch or brake switch adjustment too tight
	Short or open in the cruise control circuit
	Faulty transducer
	Faulty cruise control module
Vehicle surges	Kinked speedometer cable or casing
	Binding throttle linkage
	Faulty speed sensor
	Faulty cruise control module
Cruise control inoperative	Blown fuse
	Short or open in the cruise control circuit
	Faulty brake or clutch switch
	Leaking vacuum circuit
	Faulty cruise control switch
	Faulty stepper motor
	Faulty transducer
	Faulty speed sensor
	Faulty cruise control module

Note: Use this chart as a guide. Not all systems will use the components listed.

TCCA6C01

ENTERTAINMENT SYSTEMS

Radio Receiver/Tape Player

REMOVAL & INSTALLATION

▶ See Figures 25 and 26

1. Disconnect the negative battery cable.
2. On 1991–92 models, remove the finish panel from around the radio assembly.

3. Insert the radio removal tool T87P-19061-A or equivalent, into the radio face.
4. Press in 1 inch (25.4mm) to release the retaining clips, then using the tool as handles, pull the radio out of the instrument panel.
5. Disconnect the antenna and wiring connectors from the radio.

To install:

6. Connect the wiring and slide the radio into the instrument panel. Ensure that the rear mounting bracket is engaged on the mounting track in the panel.
7. If removed, install the finish panel
8. Connect the battery cable.
9. Check the operation of the radio.

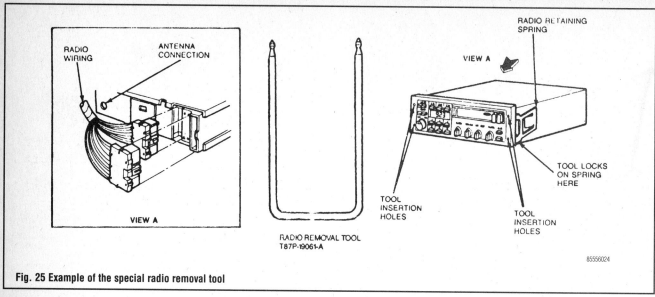

Fig. 25 Example of the special radio removal tool

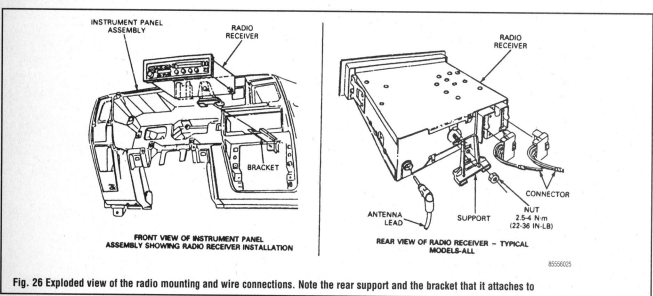

Fig. 26 Exploded view of the radio mounting and wire connections. Note the rear support and the bracket that it attaches to

To remove the radio, insert the removal tool prongs into the release clip access holes (arrows)

Push in approximately 1 inch (25.4mm) to release the retainer clips, then pull straight out to remove

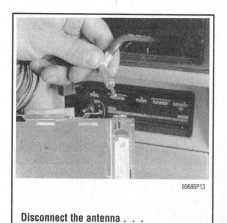

Disconnect the antenna . . .

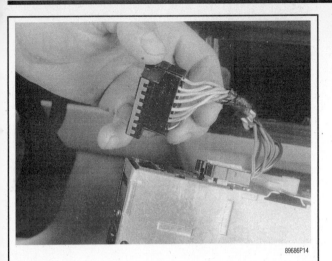

. . . and the electrical wire harness plugs from the back of the radio

Speakers

REMOVAL & INSTALLATION

⁂ WARNING

Never operate the radio with one of the speaker disconnected. Damage to the radio can occur.

Door Mounted Speakers

1. Remove the door trim panel.
2. Remove the four speaker attaching screws.
3. Pull the speaker out from the door frame and disconnect the wire harness plug.
4. Installation is the reverse of the removal procedure.

Body Mounted Rear Speakers

1. On Ranger models, remove the four speaker grille attaching screws and remove the grille.

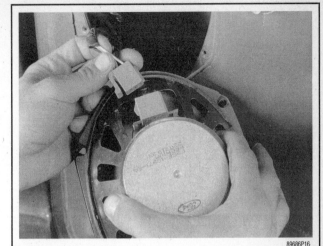

Pull out gently on the speaker and disconnect the wire harness plug from it

To remove a body mounted speaker, first remove the grille attaching screws . . .

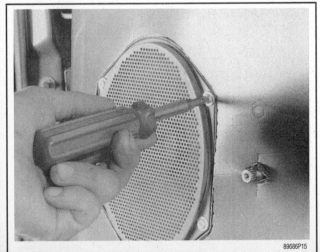

To remove a door mounted speaker, first remove the door trim panel, then the four speaker attaching screws

. . . then pull the grille from the trim panel

Remove the four speaker mounting screws . . .

. . . then pull the speaker out . . .

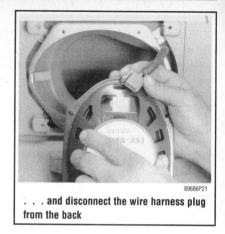

. . . and disconnect the wire harness plug from the back

2. On Explorer/Mountaineer models, gently pry the speaker grille from the trim panel.

3. On SuperCab models, Remove the four speaker mounting screws.

4. Pull the speaker out from the trim panel and disconnect the wire harness plug.

5. Installation is the reverse of the removal procedure.

WINDSHIELD WIPERS

Wiper Arm And Blade

REMOVAL & INSTALLATION

Front Wipers

▶ See Figure 27

1. Raise the blade end of the arm off of the windshield.

2. Move the slide latch away from the pivot shaft. The wiper arm can now be removed from the shaft without the use of any tools.

To install:

3. Be sure the wipers are in the parked position, and the blade assembly is in its correct position.

4. Push the main head over the pivot shaft.

5. Hold the main arm head onto the pivot shaft while raising the blade end of the wiper arm and push the slide latch into the lock under the pivot shaft head.

6. Lower the blade to the windshield. If the blade does not lower to the windshield, the slide latch is not completely in place.

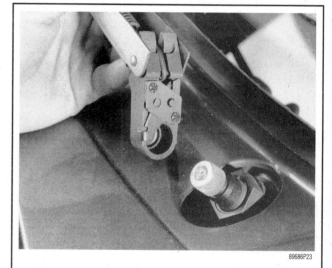

. . . then lift it straight up and off of the shaft to remove

While holding the wiper arm off of the windshield, slide the latch out and away from the pivot shaft . . .

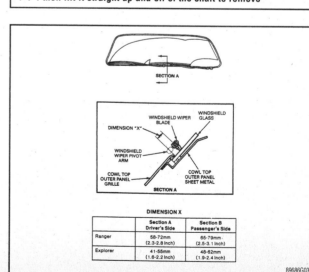

Fig. 27 Windshield wiper arm positioning for the Ranger, Explorer and Mountaineer models

	Section A Driver's Side	Section B Passenger's Side
Ranger	58-72mm (2.3-2.8 Inch)	65-79mm (2.5-3.1 Inch)
Explorer	41-55mm (1.6-2.2 Inch)	48-62mm (1.9-2.4 Inch)

DIMENSION X

Rear Wiper

▶ See Figure 28

✳✳ WARNING

Use a towel or similar device to protect the vehicle finish when performing this procedure.

1. Raise the windshield wiper blade/arm off of the glass and place it into the service position.
2. Using a small, flat bladed prytool, release the retaining clip at the base of the windshield wiper pivot arm.
3. Carefully pry the wiper arm from the shaft.

To install:
4. Ensure that the wiper motor pivot shaft is in the park position.
5. Position the wiper arm over the shaft and firmly push it on until it stops.
6. Lower the wiper blade/arm against the glass.

➥The blade is properly positioned when it firmly contacts the windshield wiper arm stop. If it does not, remove the arm again and reposition it so that it does.

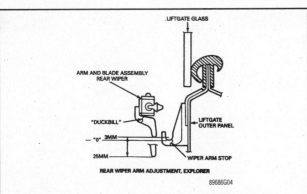

Fig. 28 Rear windshield wiper arm positioning for the Explorer and Mountaineer models

Windshield Wiper Motor

REMOVAL & INSTALLATION

Front Wiper Motor

▶ See Figure 29

1. Turn the wiper switch on. Turn the ignition switch on until the blades are straight up and then turn ignition off to keep them there.
2. Remove the right wiper arm and blade.

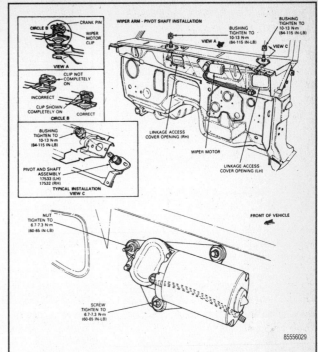

Fig. 29 Typical view of the front wiper motor and linkage assemblies

3. Remove the negative battery cable.
4. Remove the right pivot nut and allow the linkage to drop into the cowl.
5. Remove the linkage access cover, located on the right side of the dash panel near the wiper motor.
6. Reach through the access cover opening and unsnap the wiper motor clip.
7. Push the clip away from the linkage until it clears the nib on the crank pin. Then, push the clip off the linkage.
8. Remove the wiper linkage from motor crank pin.
9. Disconnect the wiper motor's wiring connector.
10. Remove the wiper motor's three attaching screws and remove the motor.

To install:
11. Install the motor and attach the three attaching screws. Tighten to 60–65 inch lbs. (6.7–7.3 Nm).
12. Connect the wiper motor's wiring connector.
13. Install the clip completely on the right linkage. Make sure the clip is completely on.
14. Install the left linkage on the wiper motor crank pin.
15. Install the right linkage on the wiper motor crank pin and pull the linkage on to the crank pin until it snaps.

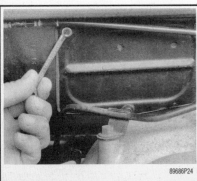

Remove the linkage access cover retaining screws . . .

. . . and remove the cover

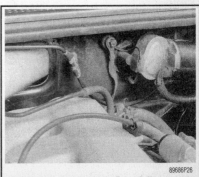

Reach into the access hole and disconnect the wiper motor linkage clip from the motor shaft

Remove the clip. Also, remove the linkages from the wiper motor shaft

Disconnect the wiper motorís wiring harness plug . . .

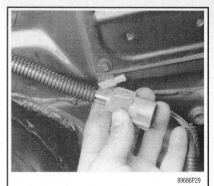

. . . and remove the harness from any holding clips

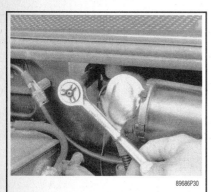

Remove the ground wire retaining nut . . .

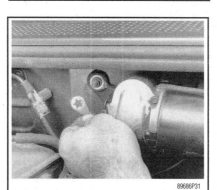

. . . and the ground wire from the wiper motor attaching stud

Remove the three wiper motor-to-firewall attaching screws . . .

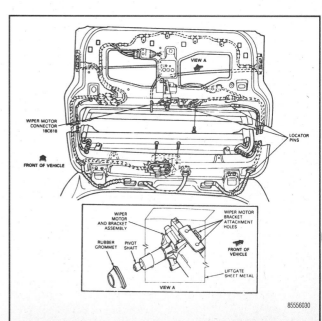

. . . then withdraw the wiper motor and crank assembly from the firewall

➡ **The clip is properly installed if the nib is protruding through the center of the clip.**

16. Reinstall the right wiper pivot shaft and nut.
17. Reconnect the battery and turn the ignition **ON**. Turn the wiper switch off so the wiper motor will park, then turn the ignition **OFF**. Replace the right linkage access cover.
18. Install the right wiper blade and arm.
19. Check the system for proper operation.

Rear Window Wiper Motor

◊ **See Figure 30**

1. Disconnect the negative battery cable.
2. Remove the wiper arm and blade.

Fig. 30 Rear wiper motor assembly and related components

3. Remove the liftgate interior trim.

4. Remove the motor attaching bolts (3). Disconnect the electrical leads.

5. Remove the wiper motor from the vehicle.

To install:

6. Install the wiper motor in position and connect the electrical leads.

7. Install the liftgate trim. Connect the negative battery cable.

Windshield Washer Motor

REMOVAL & INSTALLATION

Front and/or Rear

▶ See Figures 31, 32 and 33

✴✴ WARNING

Never operate the washer fluid pump without fluid in the reservoir. Repeatedly running the reservoir dry will ruin the pump.

➡The front washer fluid reservoir is connected to the coolant overflow tank, which will be removed as an assembly.

1. Disconnect the electrical plug and hose from the washer fluid reservoir. Also, if removing the front washer pump, disconnect the coolant overflow hose from its reservoir.

2. Remove the reservoir attaching screws and lift the assembly from the vehicle.

3. Drain and discard the contents of the washer fluid reservoir.

4. Using a small prytool, pry out the pump retaining ring.

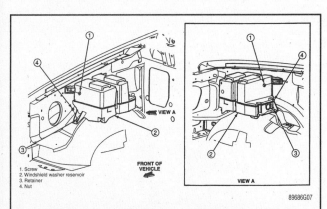

1. Screw
2. Windshield washer reservoir
3. Retainer
4. Nut

Fig. 31 Windshield washer fluid reservoir mounting for 1993–99 models—1991–92 models similar but different location

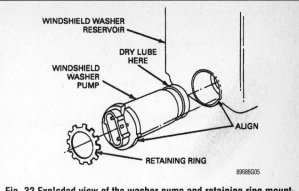

Fig. 32 Exploded view of the washer pump and retaining ring mounting

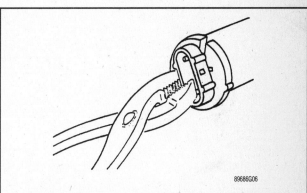

Fig. 33 Pull the washer pump from the reservoir using a pair of pliers as shown

5. Use a pair of pliers and grasp the pump on one wall around the electrical terminals. Pull out the motor and seal from the reservoir.

To install:

6. Thoroughly clean the reservoir pump chamber and ensure that there is no foreign material in it.

7. Lubricate the outside of the pump seal with a dry lubricant, such as graphite powder.

8. If equipped, align the small tab on the motor with the notch on the reservoir.

9. Install the motor so that the seal seats against the bottom of the chamber.

10. Use a 1 inch (25.4mm) socket, preferable a 12-point socket, hand press the retaining ring securely against the motor end plate.

11. Install the reservoir assembly.

12. Connect the hoses and electrical harness plug.

13. Fill the reservoir and operate the washer system. Check for leaks.

INSTRUMENTS AND SWITCHES

Instrument Cluster

REMOVAL & INSTALLATION

1991–94 Models

▶ See Figures 34, 35 and 36

1. Disconnect the negative battery cable.

2. Open the ash tray and remove the two retaining screws. Remove the ash tray assembly from the dash.

3. If necessary, remove the left and right A/C register vents from the dash.

4. Unsnap the instrument cluster trim panel by pulling rearwards around the edge of the panel. Depress the hazard warning switch (4-way flashers) and remove the trim panel.

5. Remove the four screws securing the instrument cluster to the dash mounting.

6. On vehicles equipped with an automatic transmission, perform the following:

a. Remove the two screws attaching the PRNDL indicator to the cluster.

b. If necessary for clearance, block the wheels and apply the parking brake, then turn the ignition switch to unlock the steering wheel and pull the gear select lever into the Low (L) range.

7. Pull the cluster assembly rearward to gain access to the speedometer cable.

➡If there is insufficient slack in the cable for gaining access, disconnect the cable from the transmission. Once disconnected pull the cluster out gently until enough clearance is gained.

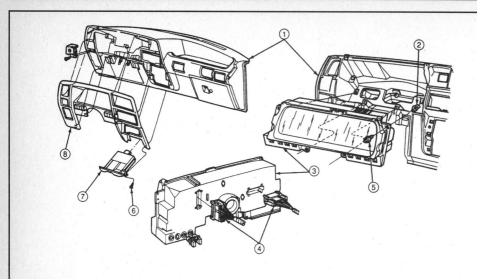

Fig. 34 Exploded views of the 1991–94 instrument cluster and trim panel assemblies

1. Instrument panel
2. Nut
3. Instrument cluster
4. Wire harness connectors
5. Cluster retaining screws
6. Screws
7. Ash tray assembly
8. Instrument cluster trim panel

89686G08

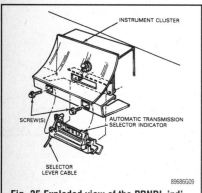

Fig. 35 Exploded view of the PRNDL indicator mounting

89686G09

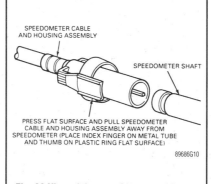

Fig. 36 View of the speedometer cable end at the instrument cluster

89686G10

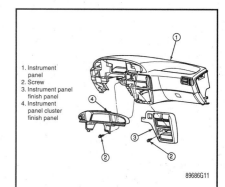

1. Instrument panel
2. Screw
3. Instrument panel finish panel
4. Instrument panel cluster finish panel

Fig. 37 Exploded view of the 1995–99 instrument cluster trim panels

89686G11

8. Disconnect the speedometer cable from the cluster. The cable connection has a flat surface clip; press the clip inward and pull the cable from the cluster.

9. Disconnect the wire harness plugs from the cluster and remove it from the dash.

To install:

10. Apply approximately ³⁄₁₆ inch (4.8mm) diameter ball of silicone dielectric grease in the drive hole of the speedometer head.

11. Position the instrument cluster near its opening and attach the electrical plugs to it.

12. Connect the speedometer cable to the speedometer head. If necessary, reconnect the speedometer cable to the transmission.

13. If removed, install the two PRNDL indicator retaining screws.

14. Insert the cluster into the dash and install the four attaching screws.

15. Ensure that the hazard warning switch is depressed and install the cluster trim panel.

16. Connect the negative battery cable. Start the vehicle and check all gauges, lamps and signals for proper operation.

1995–99 Models

▶ **See Figures 35, 37, 38 and 39**

1. Disconnect the negative battery cable.
2. Remove the radio.
3. Remove the center finish panel to access and remove the lower trim and knee bolster attaching screws.
4. Remove the lower trim and knee bolster.
5. Remove the cluster finish panel and unplug the headlamp and dimmer switch harnesses from it.
6. Remove the four instrument cluster retaining screws.

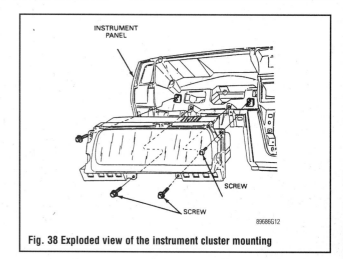

Fig. 38 Exploded view of the instrument cluster mounting

89686G12

7. If equipped with an automatic transmission, remove the two PRNDL indicator attaching screws and remove the indicator by sliding it straight down.

8. Disconnect the electrical wire harness plugs and remove the cluster.

To install:

9. Connect the electrical wire harness plugs and install the instrument cluster.

10. If equipped with an automatic transmission, install the two PRNDL indicator attaching screws and remove the indicator by sliding it straight down.

11. Install the four instrument cluster retaining screws.

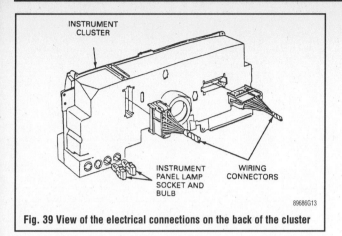

Fig. 39 View of the electrical connections on the back of the cluster

12. Connect the headlamp and dimmer switch harnesses to the cluster finish panel then install it.

13. Install the lower trim and knee bolster panels and the attaching screws.

14. Install the center finish panel.

15. Install the radio.

16. Connect the negative battery cable. Start the vehicle and check all gauges, lamps and signals for proper operation.

Fuel, Oil Pressure, Voltage and Coolant Temperature Gauges

REMOVAL & INSTALLATION

▶ See Figure 40

Each of the gauges can be removed in the same manner, once the instrument cluster is removed.

1. Disconnect the negative battery cable.

2. Remove the instrument cluster assembly.

3. Remove the lens from the instrument cluster.

4. Pull the gauge from the cluster.

To install:

5. Install the gauge, by pushing it firmly into position.

6. Install the cluster lens and install the cluster into the instrument panel.

Rear Wiper Switch

REMOVAL & INSTALLATION

▶ See Figure 41

1. Disconnect the negative battery cable.

2. Remove the instrument cluster finish panel.

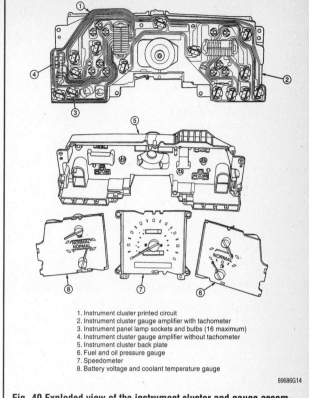

1. Instrument cluster printed circuit
2. Instrument cluster gauge amplifier with tachometer
3. Instrument panel lamp sockets and bulbs (16 maximum)
4. Instrument cluster gauge amplifier without tachometer
5. Instrument cluster back plate
6. Fuel and oil pressure gauge
7. Speedometer
8. Battery voltage and coolant temperature gauge

Fig. 40 Exploded view of the instrument cluster and gauge assemblies

3. Remove the switch from the instrument panel, by carefully prying upward.

4. Disconnect the electrical lead from the switch.

To install:

5. Connect the wiring and install the switch in the instrument panel.

6. Install the cluster finish panel.

7. Connect the negative battery cable. Check the operation of the switch.

Headlight Switch

REMOVAL & INSTALLATION

▶ See Figures 41, 42 and 43

1. Disconnect the battery ground cable.

2. On 1991–94 models, perform the following:
   a. Remove the ash tray assembly and the finish panel (snaps off).

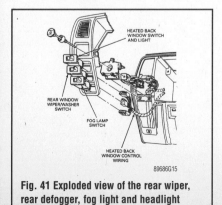

Fig. 41 Exploded view of the rear wiper, rear defogger, fog light and headlight switch assemblies

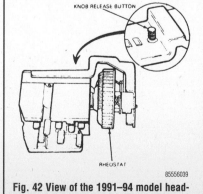

Fig. 42 View of the 1991–94 model headlight switch control knob release button

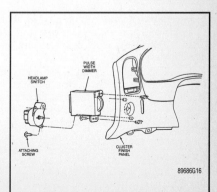

Fig. 43 Exploded view of the 1995–99 model headlight switch components

b. On the Explorer, remove the rear window wiper and heated backlite switch assembly (snaps out).

c. On the Ranger, remove the storage bin (snaps out).

d. Pull the headlight switch knob to the headlight on position. Depress the shaft release button and remove the knob and shaft assembly.

3. On 1995–99 models, remove the instrument panel finish panel.

4. Unscrew the mounting nut and remove the switch from the instrument panel, then remove the wiring connector from the switch.

To install:

5. Connect the wiring connector to the headlamp switch, position the switch in the instrument panel and install the mounting nut.

6. On 1995–99 models, install the instrument panel finish panel.

7. On 1991–94 models, perform the following:

a. Install the headlamp switch knob and shaft assembly by pushing the shaft into the switch until it locks into position.

b. On the Explorer, install the rear window wiper and heated backlite switch assembly.

c. On the Ranger, install the storage bin.

d. Install the finish panel and the ash tray assembly.

8. Connect the battery ground cable, and check the operation of the headlight switch.

Back-up Light Switch

The back-up light switch used on the automatic transmissions is also the neutral safety switch. Refer to Section 7 for the proper procedures.

Ford used two different manual transmissions, the Mitsubishi and the Mazda made 5-speed OverDrive (OD) transmissions. The back-up light switch is located on the right side of the transmission on the Mitsubishi, and on the left side shift cover on the Mazda.

Manual Transmissions

▶ **See Figures 44 and 45**

1. Apply the parking brake and place the gear shift lever in any position other than Neutral (N) or Reverse (R).

2. Raise and safely support the vehicle.

➡**According to the manufacturer, no fluid will leak from the transmission when the switch is removed, but as a precautionary measure, bring a drain pan under the vehicle with you.**

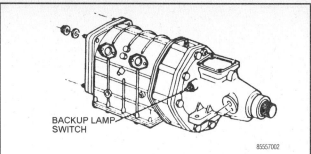

Fig. 44 Location of the back-up light switch on the Mazda transmission

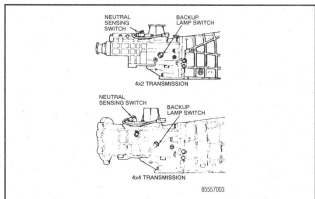

Fig. 45 Location of the back-up light switch on the Mitsubishi transmission

3. Disconnect the electrical wire harness plug from the transmission back-up light switch.

4. Remove the switch from the transmission.

5. Installation is the reverse of the removal procedure. If necessary, or since your there, check the transmission fluid level and top-off as needed.

LIGHTING

Headlights

REMOVAL & INSTALLATION

▶ **See Figures 46 and 47**

1. Open the vehicle's hood and secure it in an upright position.

2. If necessary, open the bulb access panel by depressing the latch then lifting.

3. Unfasten the locking ring which secures the bulb and wire harness plug assembly, then withdraw the assembly rearward.

4. Disconnect the electrical wire harness plug from the bulb and remove the locking ring as well.

To install:

5. Before connecting a light bulb to the wire harness plug, ensure that all electrical contact surfaces are free of corrosion or dirt.

6. Install the locking ring onto the bulb, then line up the replacement headlight bulb with the harness plug. Firmly push the bulb onto the plug until the spring clip latches over the bulb's projection.

❈❈ WARNING

Do not touch the glass bulb with your fingers. Oil from your fingers can severely shorten the life of the bulb. If necessary, wipe off any dirt or oil from the bulb with rubbing alcohol before completing installation.

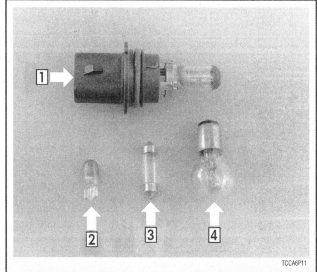

1. Halogen headlight bulb
2. Side marker light bulb
3. Dome light bulb
4. Turn signal/brake light bulb

Examples of various types of automotive light bulbs

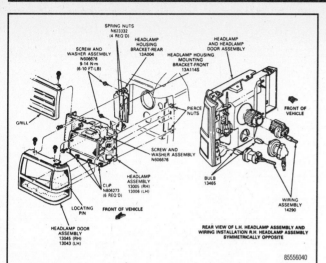

Fig. 46 Exploded view of the front headlight assembly and related components

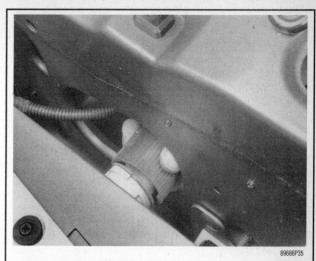

To remove the bulb, grasp the retainer and rotate it counterclockwise to unlock it . . .

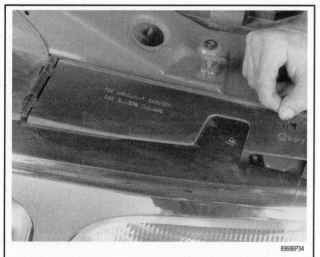

If equipped, open the headlight access panel by sliding the latch and lifting the panel upwards

. . . then withdraw the bulb from the headlight lens housing

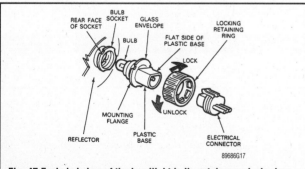

Fig. 47 Exploded view of the headlight bulb, retainer and wire harness plug

7. Position the headlight bulb and secure it with the locking ring.

8. To ensure that the replacement bulb functions properly, activate the applicable switch to illuminate the bulb which was just replaced. (If this is a combination low and high beam bulb, be sure to check both intensities.) If the replacement light bulb does not illuminate, either it too is faulty or there is a problem in the bulb circuit or switch. Correct if necessary.

9. Close the bulb access panel and the vehicle's hood.

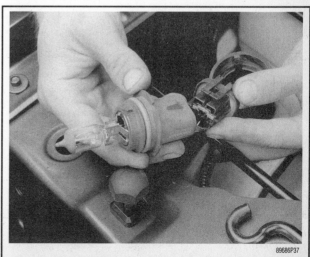

Unplug the wire harness from the bulb and either slide the retainer over the plug, or remove it from the bulb

AIMING THE HEADLIGHTS

▶ **See Figures 48, 49 and 50**

The headlights must be properly aimed to provide the best, safest road illumination. The lights should be checked for proper aim and adjusted as necessary. Certain state and local authorities have requirements for headlight aiming; these should be checked before adjustment is made.

✳✳ CAUTION

About once a year, when the headlights are replaced or any time front end work is performed on your vehicle, the headlight should be accurately aimed by a reputable repair shop using the proper equipment. Headlights not properly aimed can make it virtually impossible to see and may blind other drivers on the road, possibly causing an accident. Note that the following procedure is a temporary fix, until you can take your vehicle to a repair shop for a proper adjustment.

Headlight adjustment may be temporarily made using a wall, as described below, or on the rear of another vehicle. When adjusted, the lights should not glare in oncoming car or truck windshields, nor should they illuminate the passenger compartment of vehicles driving in front of you. These adjustments are rough and should always be fine-tuned by a repair shop which is equipped with headlight aiming tools. Improper adjustments may be both dangerous and illegal.

For most of the vehicles covered by this manual, horizontal and vertical aiming of each sealed beam unit is provided by two adjusting screws which move the retaining ring and adjusting plate against the tension of a coil spring. There is no adjustment for focus; this is done during headlight manufacturing.

➡**Because the composite headlight assembly is bolted into position, no adjustment should be necessary or possible. Some applications, however, may be bolted to an adjuster plate or may be retained by adjusting screws. If so, follow this procedure when adjusting the lights, BUT always have the adjustment checked by a reputable shop.**

Before removing the headlight bulb or disturbing the headlamp in any way, note the current settings in order to ease headlight adjustment upon reassembly. If the high or low beam setting of the old lamp still works, this can be done using the wall of a garage or a building:

1. Park the vehicle on a level surface, with the fuel tank about ½ full and with the vehicle empty of all extra cargo (unless normally carried). The vehicle should be facing a wall which is no less than 6 feet (1.8m) high and 12 feet (3.7m) wide. The front of the vehicle should be about 25 feet from the wall.

2. If aiming is to be performed outdoors, it is advisable to wait until dusk in order to properly see the headlight beams on the wall. If done in a garage, darken the area around the wall as much as possible by closing shades or hanging cloth over the windows.

3. Turn the headlights **ON** and mark the wall at the center of each light's low beam, then switch on the brights and mark the center of each light's high beam. A short length of masking tape which is visible from the front of the vehicle may be used. Although marking all four positions is advisable, marking one position from each light should be sufficient.

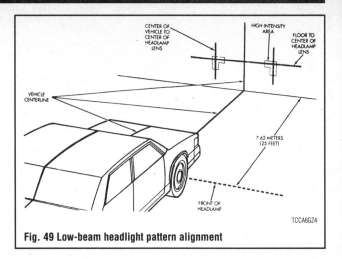
Fig. 49 Low-beam headlight pattern alignment

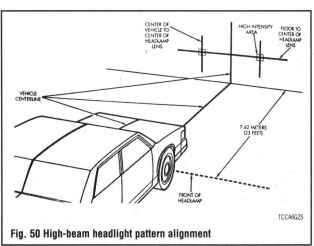
Fig. 50 High-beam headlight pattern alignment

4. If neither beam on one side is working, and if another like-sized vehicle is available, park the second one in the exact spot where the vehicle was and mark the beams using the same-side light. Then switch the vehicles so the one to be aimed is back in the original spot. It must be parked no closer to or farther away from the wall than the second vehicle.

5. Perform any necessary repairs, but make sure the vehicle is not moved, or is returned to the exact spot from which the lights were marked. Turn the headlights **ON** and adjust the beams to match the marks on the wall.

6. Have the headlight adjustment checked as soon as possible by a reputable repair shop.

Signal and Marker Lights

REMOVAL & INSTALLATION

Front Marker and Turn Signal

1991–92 RANGER AND 1991–94 EXPLORER MODELS

▶ **See Figure 51**

1. Remove the screws retaining the headlight and trim assembly. On Explorer, remove the grille.

2. Carefully rotate the headlight and trim assembly away from the vehicle, rotating the inboard side away from the vehicle.

3. Remove the side marker, parking and turn signal bulbs and sockets from the headlamp and trim assembly. They can be removed by turning them.

4. If replacing a lens, remove the retaining screws for the lens to be changed and remove it from the headlight door.

To install:

5. If removed, install the removed lens assembly

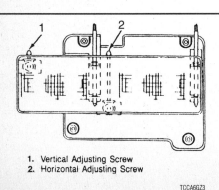

1. Vertical Adjusting Screw
2. Horizontal Adjusting Screw

Fig. 48 Example of headlight adjustment screw location for composite headlamps

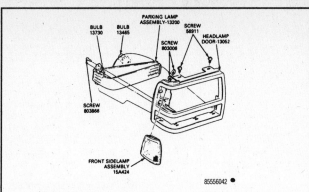

Fig. 51 1991–92 Ranger and Explorer (up to 1994) front turn signal and side marker lens assembly

6. Install the bulbs and sockets.
7. Install the headlight and trim assembly.
8. Check the operation of the lights.

1993–99 RANGER AND 1995–99 EXPLORER/MOUNTAINEER MODELS

▶ See Figure 52

1. Remove the marker/turn signal lens retaining screws or nut.
2. Gently pull outward on the lens assembly to disengage the barbed retainers.

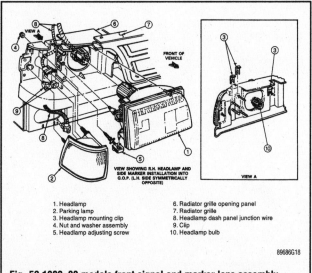

1. Headlamp
2. Parking lamp
3. Headlamp mounting clip
4. Nut and washer assembly
5. Headlamp adjusting screw
6. Radiator grille opening panel
7. Radiator grille
8. Headlamp dash panel junction wire
9. Clip
10. Headlamp bulb

Fig. 52 1993–99 models front signal and marker lens assembly

3. Twist the lamp socket and remove it from the lens.
4. Pull the bulb from the socket.

To install:

5. Install the bulb into the lamp socket.
6. Install the lamp socket to the lens and twist it to lock it in position.
7. Position the lens assembly, ensure that the barbed retainers are aligned with their mounting clips, and press the assembly until fully seated.
8. Install the marker/turn signal lens retaining screws or nut.
9. Check the operation of the lights.

Rear marker and Rear Lamps

▶ See Figures 53 and 54

1. Remove the 2 (Explorer/Mountaineer models) or 4 (Ranger models) screws retaining the lamp assembly to the vehicle.

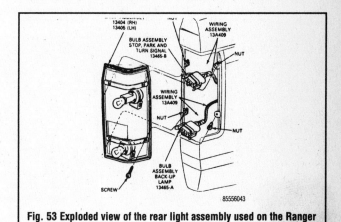

Fig. 53 Exploded view of the rear light assembly used on the Ranger model

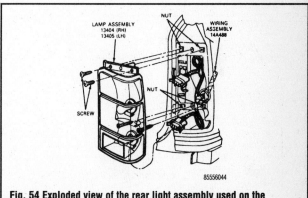

Fig. 54 Exploded view of the rear light assembly used on the Explorer/Mountaineer models

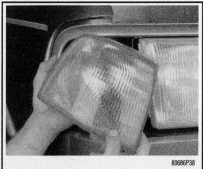

To change a turn signal/marker bulb, first unfasten the lens from the body, the reach behind the lens . . .

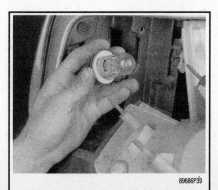

. . . and grasp the lamp socket. Twist then pull the socket from the lens

To remove the bulb from the socket, simply pull it straight out

To change a rear brake, signal or back-up bulb, on the Ranger, first remove the two outer screws . . .

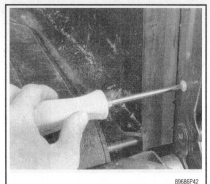

. . . then lower the tail gate and remove the two inner retaining screws

The Explorer/Mountaineer models only use two upper lens retaining screws, the bottom use barbed push pins

Pull the lens assembly out from the vehicle body to access the bulb sockets

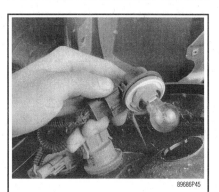

Grasp the bulb socket then twist and pull it out of the lens assembly

Remove the bulb from the socket by pulling it straight out

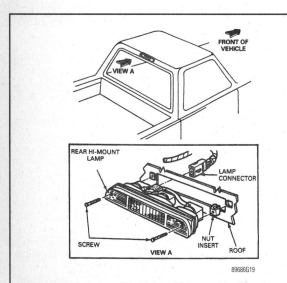

Fig. 55 Exploded view of the Ranger high mount brake and cargo light assembly–Explorer/Mountaineer models are similar, but without cargo light

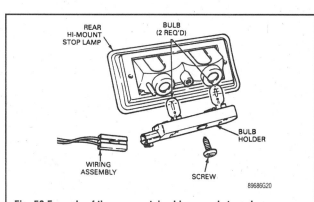

Fig. 56 Example of the screw retained lamp socket used on some high mount brake light assemblies

2. Remove the lamp assembly from the vehicle by pulling it outward. On the Explorer/Mountaineer models, make sure the 2 barbed retainers at the bottom of the assembly release.

3. Remove the lamp sockets from the lens housing by twisting it, then pulling outward.

4. Remove the bulb from the socket by pulling it straight outward.

To install:

5. Install the bulb into the lamp socket.

6. Install the lamp socket to the lens and twist it to lock it in position.

7. Position the lens assembly to the body. On Explorer/Mountaineer models, ensure that the barbed retainers are aligned with their mounting clips, and press the assembly until fully seated.

8. Install the lens assembly retaining screws (four screws used on the Ranger and 2 on the Explorer/Mountaineer).

9. Check the operation of the lights.

High Mount Brake Light

▶ **See Figures 55 and 56**

1. Remove the screws retaining the lamp to the liftgate (Explorer/Mountaineer models) or the cab (Ranger models).

2. Pull the lamp away from the vehicle and disconnect the wiring connector.

➡**Some later models retain the lamp socket to the lens with a screw. Remove the screw and pull the lamp socket away from the lens to access the bulbs.**

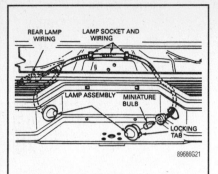

Fig. 57 Exploded view of the rear license plate light assembly—step bumper shown, other styles are similar

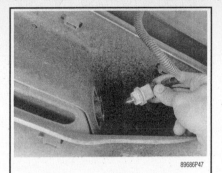

To change the license plate bulb, first remove the socket from the lens housing by twisting then pulling

Next, remove the bulb from the socket by pulling it straight out

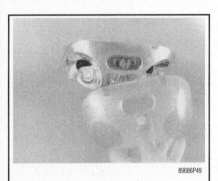

To change a dome or map light, first reach up and remove the dome light lens from the housing

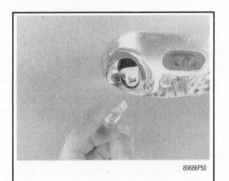

Then simply pull either the map light bulb out of the housing socket . . .

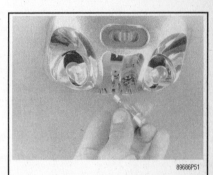

. . . or the area light bulb from its retaining clips/contacts

3. If there is no retaining screw, remove the lamp socket from the lens by twisting it and pulling outward.

4. Pull the bulb straight out from the lamp socket to remove it.

To install:

5. Install the bulb into the lamp socket.

6. Install the lamp socket to the lens and either twist it to lock it in position or install its retaining screw.

7. Position the lens assembly to the body.

8. Install the lens assembly retaining screws.

9. Check the operation of the lights.

License Plate Light

▶ See Figure 57

1. From underneath the rear of the vehicle, grasp the lamp socket and rotate it ¼ turn.

2. Pull the lamp socket from the lens.

3. Pull the bulb from the socket

4. Installation is the reverse of the removal procedure.

Dome and Map Lights

1. Remove the plastic cover.

2. Pull the map and/or area bulb from the dome light assembly.

3. Installation is the reverse of the removal procedure.

Cargo Light

The Ranger has a rear cargo light which illuminates the pick-up bed. It is incorporated with the high mount brake light. For removal & installation procedures refer to the high mount brake light procedures earlier in this Section and remove the cargo lamp socket and bulb instead of the brake lamp components.

Fog/Driving Lights

REMOVAL & INSTALLATION

▶ See Figures 58, 59, 60 and 61

1. Lift up on the locking tab which retains the lens to the lamp housing. Take care not to drop the lens.

2. Remove the lens from the lamp housing and turn it to gain access to the rear of the lens.

3. Disconnect the electrical harness plug from the pigtail connector.

4. Remove the rubber boot from the back of the lens assembly.

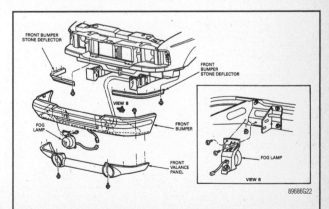

Fig. 58 Exploded view of the fog lamps and related components—Ranger shown, Explorer similar

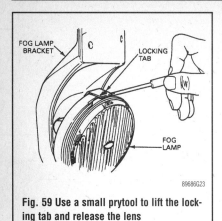

Fig. 59 Use a small prytool to lift the locking tab and release the lens

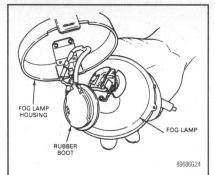

Fig. 60 Pull the lens out of the housing, then slide the rubber boot off and out of the way

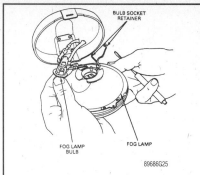

Fig. 61 Release the bulb retainer, then remove the bulb from the lens and unplug it from the wire harness

5. Release the bulb socket retainer from its locking tab.
6. Remove the bulb and socket from the lens and pull the bulb from the socket.

❊❊ WARNING

Never touch the bulb with your bare hands. The naturals oils from your skin will remain on the bulb, causing a localized hot-spot and premature failure. Wipe the bulb with rubbing alcohol before install it into the lens assembly.

To install:

7. Install the bulb into the lamp socket. Follow the warning above.
8. Position the lamp socket into the lens and install the retaining clip.
9. Reposition the rubber boot.
10. Connect the electrical harness plug and position the lens assembly into the lamp housing.
11. Engage the lens retaining tab. Ensure that the lens is securely held in the lamp housing.
12. Check the light for proper operation.

TRAILER WIRING

Wiring the vehicle for towing is fairly easy. There are a number of good wiring kits available and these should be used, rather than trying to design your own.

All trailers will need brake lights and turn signals as well as tail lights and side marker lights. Most areas require extra marker lights for overwide trailers. Also, most areas have recently required back-up lights for trailers, and most trailer manufacturers have been building trailers with back-up lights for several years.

Additionally, some Class I, most Class II and just about all Class III trailers will have electric brakes. Add to this number an accessories wire, to operate trailer internal equipment or to charge the trailer's battery, and you can have as many as seven wires in the harness.

Determine the equipment on your trailer and buy the wiring kit necessary. The kit will contain all the wires needed, plus a plug adapter set which includes the female plug, mounted on the bumper or hitch, and the male plug, wired into, or plugged into the trailer harness.

When installing the kit, follow the manufacturer's instructions. The color coding of the wires is usually standard throughout the industry. One point to note: some domestic vehicles, and most imported vehicles, have separate turn signals. On most domestic vehicles, the brake lights and rear turn signals operate with the same bulb. For those vehicles with separate turn signals, you can purchase an isolation unit so that the brake lights won't blink whenever the turn signals are operated, or, you can go to your local electronics supply house and buy four diodes to wire in series with the brake and turn signal bulbs. Diodes will isolate the brake and turn signals. The choice is yours. The isolation units are simple and quick to install, but far more expensive than the diodes. The diodes, however, require more work to install properly, since they require the cutting of each bulb's wire and soldering in place of the diode.

One, final point, the best kits are those with a spring loaded cover on the vehicle mounted socket. This cover prevents dirt and moisture from corroding the terminals. Never let the vehicle socket hang loosely; always mount it securely to the bumper or hitch.

CIRCUIT PROTECTION

Fuses

▶ **See Figures 62 thru 69**

REPLACEMENT

Fuse Panel

Located inside the passenger compartment, under the drivers-side of the instrument panel.
1. Turn the ignition switch **OFF**.
2. Remove the fuse panel access cover.
3. If equipped, remove the fuse puller tool from the cover.
4. Grasp the push-in type fuse with the provided tool, or a pair of needle-nose pliers.
5. Look through the side of the fuse body to determine if the fuse element is blown.
   To install:
6. Check the amperage rating of the fuse which was removed and obtain a new fuse of the same rating.

❊❊ WARNING

Never replace a blown fuse with a new fuse of a higher rating. Severe electrical damage, as well as possible electrical fire could result.

7. Align the fuse with its mounting position and push it into place until fully seated in the panel.
8. Turn the ignition switch on and operate the accessory that was protected by that fuse.

❊❊ WARNING

If the fuse continues to blow, inspect and test the wire harness and component or components which are protected by that fuse.

Power Distribution Box

Located under the hood, in the engine compartment. It houses the fuses and relays for most of the under hood components which are not controlled by a

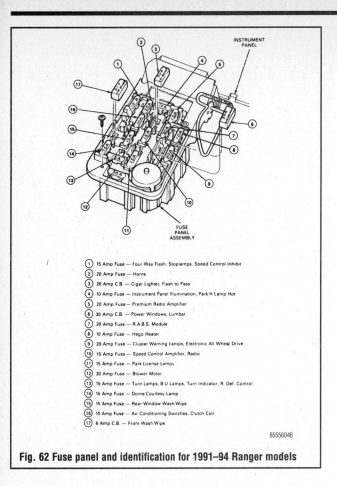

1. 15 Amp Fuse — Four-Way Flash, Stoplamps, Speed Control Inhibit
2. 20 Amp Fuse — Horns
3. 20 Amp C.B. — Cigar Lighter, Flash to Pass
4. 10 Amp Fuse — Instrument Panel Illumination, Park H Lamp Hot
5. 20 Amp Fuse — Premium Radio Amplifier
6. 30 Amp C.B. — Power Windows, Lumbar
7. 20 Amp Fuse — R.A.B.S. Module
8. 10 Amp Fuse — Hego Heater
9. 20 Amp Fuse — Cluster Warning Lamps, Electronic All Wheel Drive
10. 15 Amp Fuse — Speed Control Amplifier, Radio
11. 15 Amp Fuse — Park License Lamps
12. 30 Amp Fuse — Blower Motor
13. 15 Amp Fuse — Turn Lamps, B U Lamps, Turn Indicator, R. Def. Control
14. 15 Amp Fuse — Dome/Courtesy Lamp
15. 15 Amp Fuse — Rear Window Wash/Wipe
16. 10 Amp Fuse — Air Conditioning Switches, Clutch Coil
17. 6 Amp C.B. — Front Wash Wipe

85556046

Fig. 62 Fuse panel and identification for 1991–94 Ranger models

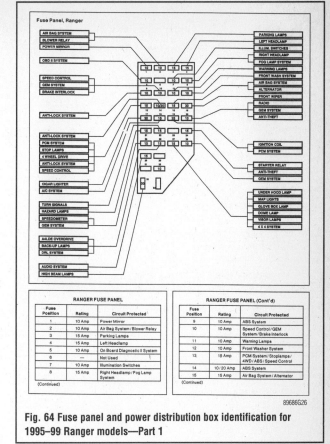

Fig. 64 Fuse panel and power distribution box identification for 1995–99 Ranger models—Part 1

RANGER FUSE PANEL

Fuse Position	Rating	Circuit Protected
1	10 Amp	Power Mirror
2	10 Amp	Air Bag System / Blower Relay
3	15 Amp	Parking Lamps
4	15 Amp	Left Headlamp
5	10 Amp	On Board Diagnostic II System
6	—	Not Used
7	10 Amp	Illumination Switches
8	15 Amp	Right Headlamp / Fog Lamp System

(Continued)

RANGER FUSE PANEL (Cont'd)

Fuse Position	Rating	Circuit Protected
9	10 Amp	ABS System
10	10 Amp	Speed Control / GEM System / Brake Interlock
11	10 Amp	Warning Lamps
12	10 Amp	Front Washer System
13	15 Amp	PCM System / Stoplamps / 4WD / ABS / Speed Control
14	10/20 Amp	ABS System
15	15 Amp	Air Bag System / Alternator

(Continued)

89686G26

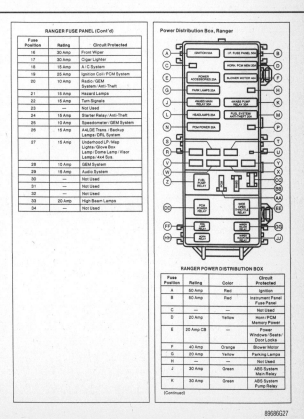

RANGER FUSE PANEL (Cont'd)

Fuse Position	Rating	Circuit Protected
16	30 Amp	Front Wiper
17	30 Amp	Cigar Lighter
18	15 Amp	A/C System
19	25 Amp	Ignition Coil / PCM System
20	10 Amp	Radio / GEM System / Anti-Theft
21	15 Amp	Hazard Lamps
22	15 Amp	Turn Signals
23	—	Not Used
24	15 Amp	Starter Relay / Anti-Theft
25	10 Amp	Speedometer / GEM System
26	15 Amp	A4LDE Trans. / Backup Lamps / DRL System
27	15 Amp	Underhood LP / Map Lights / Glove Box Lamp / Dome Lamp / Visor Lamps / 4x4 Sys.
28	10 Amp	GEM System
29	15 Amp	Audio System
30	—	Not Used
31	—	Not Used
32	—	Not Used
33	20 Amp	High Beam Lamps
34	—	Not Used

RANGER POWER DISTRIBUTION BOX

Fuse Position	Rating	Color	Circuit Protected
A	50 Amp	Red	Ignition
B	50 Amp	Red	Instrument Panel Fuse Panel
C	—	—	Not Used
D	20 Amp	Yellow	Horn / PCM Memory Power
E	20 Amp CB		Power Windows / Seats / Door Locks
F	40 Amp	Orange	Blower Motor
G	20 Amp	Yellow	Parking Lamps
H	—	—	Not Used
J	30 Amp	Green	ABS System Main Relay
K	30 Amp	Green	ABS System Pump Relay

(Continued)

89686G27

Fig. 65 Fuse panel and power distribution box identification for 1995–99 Ranger models—Part 2

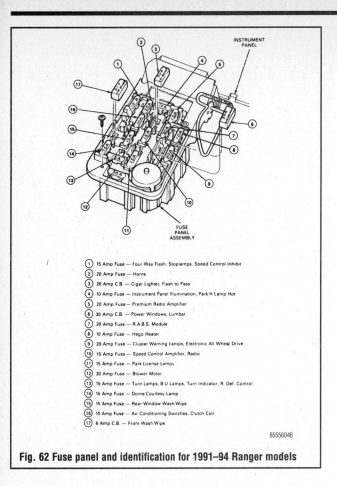

1. 15 AMP FUSE — FOUR-WAY FLASH, STOPLAMPS, SPEED CONTROL INHIBIT
2. 20 AMP FUSE — HORNS
3. 20 AMP C.B. — CIGAR LIGHTER, FLASH TO PASS, POWER LUMBAR, MULTI-FUNCTION SWITCH
4. 10 AMP FUSE — INSTRUMENT PANEL ILLUMINATION
5. 20 AMP FUSE — PREMIUM RADIO AMPLIFIER, TRAILER TOW
6. 30 AMP C.B. — POWER WINDOWS
7. 20 AMP FUSE — R.A.B.S. MODULE
8. 10 AMP FUSE — HEGO HEATER
9. 15 AMP FUSE — CLUSTER WARNING LAMPS, ELECTRONIC ALL WHEEL DRIVE
10. 15 AMP FUSE — SPEED CONTROL AMPLIFIER, RADIO
11. 15 AMP FUSE — PARK/LICENSE LAMPS
12. 30 AMP FUSE — BLOWER MOTOR
13. 15 AMP FUSE — TURN LAMPS, B/U LAMPS, TURN INDICATOR, R. DEF. CONTROL
14. 15 AMP FUSE — DOME/COURTESY LAMP
15. 15 AMP FUSE — REAR WINDOW WASH/WIPE
16. 10 AMP FUSE — AIR CONDITIONING SWITCHES, CLUTCH COIL
17. 6 AMP C.B. — FRONT WASH/WIPE

85556047

Fig. 63 Fuse panel and identification for 1991–94 Explorer models

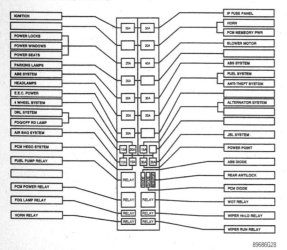

RANGER POWER DISTRIBUTION BOX (Cont'd)

Fuse Position	Rating	Color	Circuit Protected
L	20 Amp	Yellow	Headlamps
M	20 Amp	Yellow	Fuel System / Anti-Theft System
N	30 Amp	Green	PCM Power
P	—	—	Not Used
R	15 Amp	Blue	Daylight Running Lamps / Fog Lamps
S	20 Amp	Yellow	Four-Wheel Drive System
T	15 Amp	Blue	Alternator
U	—	—	Not Used
V	10 Amp	Red	Air Bag System
W	15 Amp	Blue	PCM HO2S System

(Continued)

RANGER POWER DISTRIBUTION BOX (Cont'd)

Fuse Position	Rating	Color	Circuit Protected
X	30 Amp	Green	Power Point
Y	30 Amp	Green	JBL System
Z	Relay	—	Fuel Pump
AA	Diode	—	PCM
BB	Diode	—	Rear ABS
CC	Resistor	—	RABS / Low Fluid
DD	Relay	—	PCM Power
EE	Relay	—	W.A.C.
FF	Relay	—	Fog Lamp
GG	Relay	—	Wiper Hi-Low
HH	Relay	—	Horn
JJ	Relay	—	Wiper Run / Park

Power Distribution Box Configuration, Ranger

89686G28

Fig. 66 Fuse panel and power distribution box identification for 1995–99 Ranger models—Part 3

EXPLORER FUSE PANEL (Cont'd)

Fuse Position	Rating	Circuit Protected
14	10 Amp	Anti-Lock System
15	15 Amp	Air Bag System / Alternator
16	30 Amp	Front Wiper
17	30 Amp	Cigar Lighter
18	15 Amp	A / C System
19	25 Amp	Ignition Coil / PCM System
20	10 Amp	Radio / Power Ant. / GEM Sys. / Anti-Theft / Cell. Phone
21	15 Amp	Hazard Lamps
22	15 Amp	Turn Signals
23	15 Amp	Rear Wiper System
24	15 Amp	Starter Relay / Anti-Theft
25	10 Amp	Speedometer / GEM System
26	15 Amp	A4LDE Trans / DRL Sys. / Backup Lamps / 4WD / Rear Defroster
27	15 Amp	Under Hood LP / Map Lights / Glove Box Lamp / Dome Lamp / Visor Lamps / Accessory Delay / DR Switch Illum. / 4x4 System
28	10 Amp	Memory Seat / GEM System
29	15 Amp	Audio System
30	—	Not Used
31	10 Amp	Aux. Blower System
32	10 Amp	Heated Mirrors / Heated Backlite
33	20 Amp	High Beam Lamps
34	10 Amp	Audio System / Power Antenna
35	—	Not Used
36	—	Not Used

Power Distribution Box, Explorer

EXPLORER POWER DISTRIBUTION BOX

Fuse Position	Rating	Color	Circuit Protected
A	60 Amp	Blue	Ignition
B	60 Amp	Blue	Instrument Panel Fuse Panel
C	50 Amp	Red	Automatic Ride Control Suspension
D	20 Amp	Yellow	Horn / PCM Memory
E	30 Amp CB	—	Power Windows / Seats / Door Locks
F	50 Amp	Red	Blower Motor
G	20 Amp	Yellow	Parking Lamps
H	20 Amp	Yellow	Trailer Park / Stoplamps
J	30 Amp	Green	ABS System

(Continued)

89686G30

Fig. 68 Fuse panel and power distribution box identification for 1995–99 Explorer/Mountaineer models—Part 2

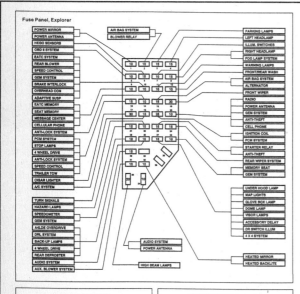

Fuse Panel, Explorer

EXPLORER FUSE PANEL

Fuse Position	Rating	Circuit Protected
1	10 Amp	Power Mirrors / Antenna
2	10 Amp	Air Bag / Blower Relay
3	15 Amp	Parking Lamps
4	15 Amp	Left Headlamp
5	10 Amp	On Board Diagnostic II System
6	15 Amp	HO2S Sensors
7	10 Amp	Illumination Switches
8	15 Amp	Right Headlamp / Fog Lamp System

(Continued)

EXPLORER FUSE PANEL (Cont'd)

Fuse Position	Rating	Circuit Protected
9	10 Amp	EATC Mem. / Seat Mem. / Mess. Ctr. / Cell. Phone
10	10 Amp	EATC Sys. / Rear Blower / Spd. Control / GEM Sys. / Brake Interlock / OH Console Adapt. Susp.
11	10 Amp	Warning Lamps
12	10 Amp	Front and Rear Washers
13	15 Amp	PCM Sys. / Stoplamps / 4WD / ABS / Spd. Control / Trailer Tow

(Continued)

89686G29

Fig. 67 Fuse panel and power distribution box identification for 1995–99 Explorer/Mountaineer models—Part 1

EXPLORER POWER DISTRIBUTION BOX (Cont'd)

Fuse Position	Rating	Color	Circuit Protected
K	30 Amp	Green	ABS System
L	20 Amp	Yellow	Headlamps
M	20 Amp	Yellow	Anti-Theft / Fuel System
N	30 Amp	Green	PCM Power
P	30 Amp	Green	Heated Backlite
R	15 Amp	Blue	Daylight Running Lamps / Fog Lamps
S	20 Amp	Yellow	4-Wheel Drive
T	15 Amp	Blue	Alternator
U	15 Amp	Blue	Automatic Ride Control System
V	10 Amp	Red	Air Bag System

(Continued)

EXPLORER POWER DISTRIBUTION BOX (Cont'd)

Fuse Position	Rating	Color	Circuit Protected
W	30 Amp	Green	Power Point
X	15 Amp	Blue	Rear Wiper System
Y	30 Amp	Green	Lux. Stereo
Z	Relay	—	Fuel Pump
AA	Diode	—	PCM Diode
BB	Diode	—	ABS Diode
CC	—	—	Not Used
DD	Relay	—	PCM Power
EE	Relay	—	WOT
FF	Relay	—	Fog Lamp
GG	Relay	—	Wiper Hi-Low
HH	Relay	—	Horn
JJ	Relay	—	Wiper Run / Park

Power Distribution Box Configuration, Explorer

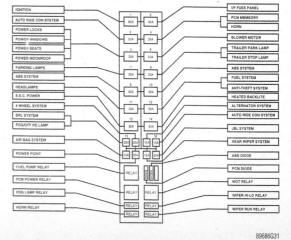

EXPLORER POWER DISTRIBUTION BOX CONFIGURATION

89686G31

Fig. 69 Fuse panel and power distribution box identification for 1995–99 Explorer/Mountaineer models—Part 3

To access the fuses, remove the fuse panel cover. Note the spare fuses (A) and provided fuse puller tool (B)

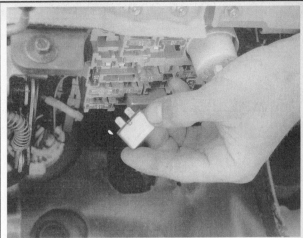

Circuit breakers can be replaced as if it were a fuse, simply grasp hold of it and pull it from the panel

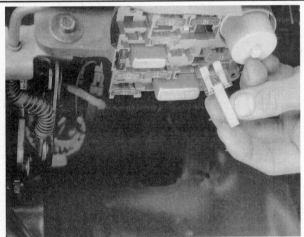

Using the provided tool or a pair of pliers, grasp the fuse and pull it from the panel

dash mounted switch (such as the alternator, fuel pump, ECM, etc.). The fuses and relays are replaced in the same manner as the fuse panel inside the vehicle. The power distribution box cover is hinged on one end and utilizes a retaining latch on the other. Simply release the latch and lift the cover up to gain access to the fuses and relays.

Fusible Links

The fusible link is a short length of special, Hypalon (high temperature) insulated wire, integral with the engine compartment wiring harness and should not be confused with standard wire. It is several wire gauges smaller than the circuit which it protects. Under no circumstances should a fuse link replacement repair be made using a length of standard wire cut from bulk stock or from another wiring harness.

The fusible links are located near the starter solenoid and shares the terminal with the battery-to-starter solenoid cable.

Circuit Breakers

The Ranger, Explorer and Mountaineer models use circuit breakers for components which have a high start-up amperage pull (such as power windows). All breakers will automatically reset if they have been tripped. The circuit breakers are replaceable (should one go bad or not reset) and can be found on the fuse panel.

REPLACEMENT

The circuit breakers are replaced in the same manner as a fuse. Simply pull the breaker from the fuse panel to remove.

Turn Signal and Hazard Flasher Locations

Both the turn signal flasher and the hazard warning flasher are mounted on the fuse panel on the truck. To gain access to the fuse panel, remove the cover from the lower edge of the instrument panel below the steering column. First remove the two fasteners from the lower edge of the cover. Then pull the cover downward until the spring clips disengage from the instrument panel.

The turn signal flasher unit is mounted on the front of the fuse panel, and the hazard warning flasher is mounted on the rear of the fuse panel.

WIRING DIAGRAMS

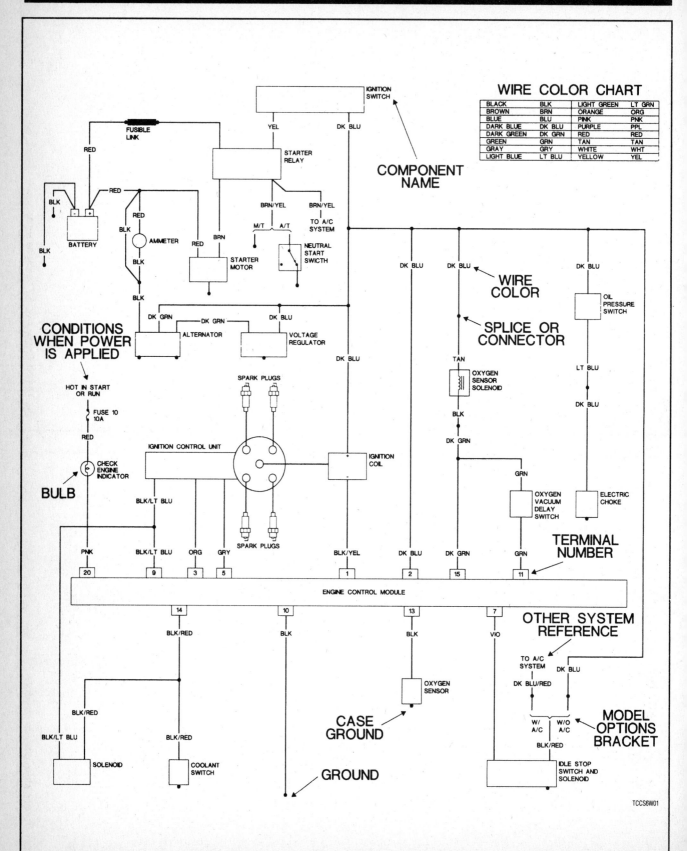

Fig. 70 Sample diagram—how to read and interpret wiring

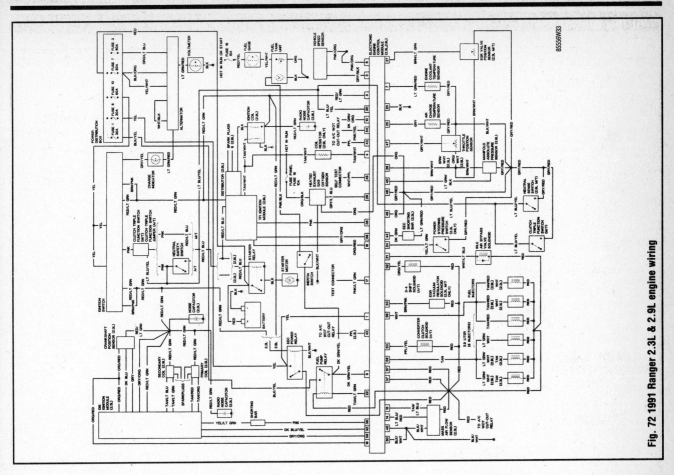

Fig. 72 1991 Ranger 2.3L & 2.9L engine wiring

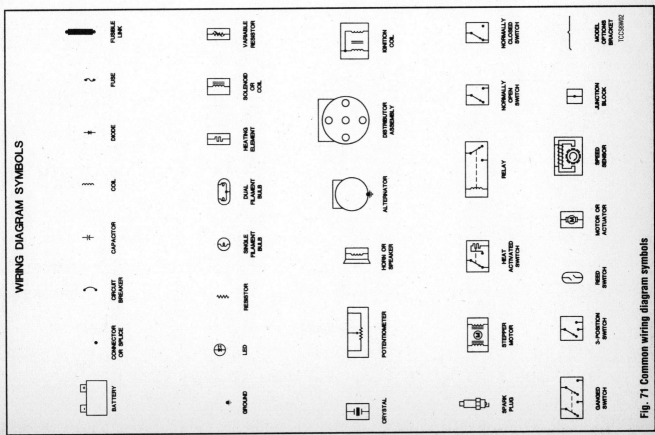

Fig. 71 Common wiring diagram symbols

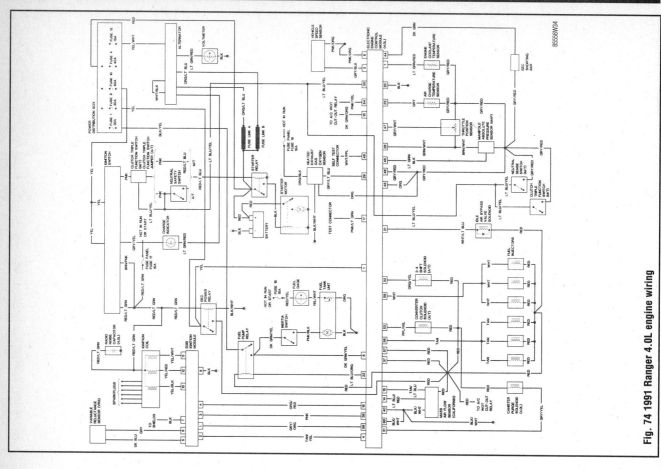

Fig. 74 1991 Ranger 4.0L engine wiring

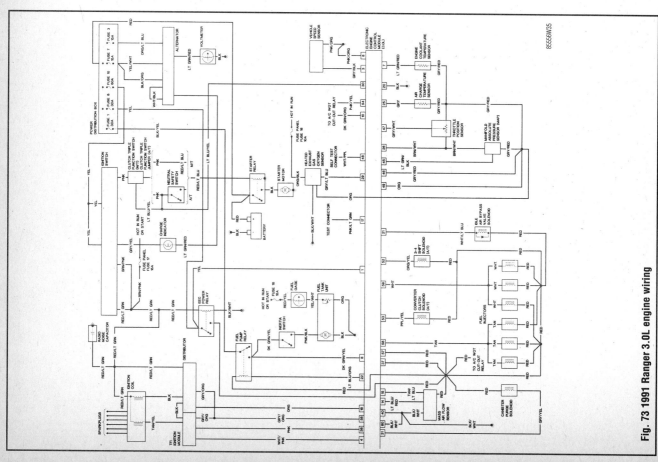

Fig. 73 1991 Ranger 3.0L engine wiring

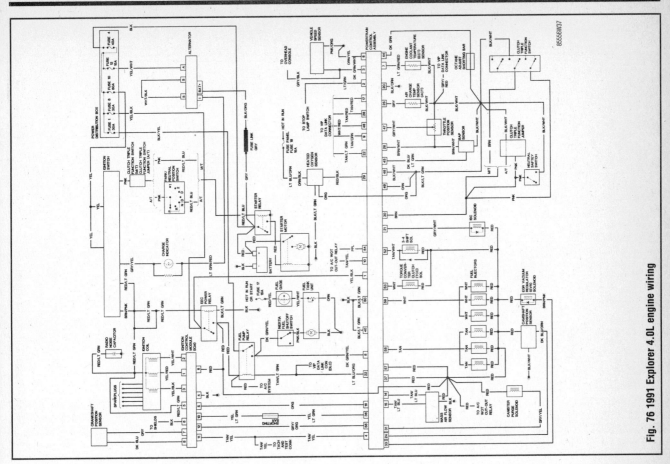

Fig. 76 1991 Explorer 4.0L engine wiring

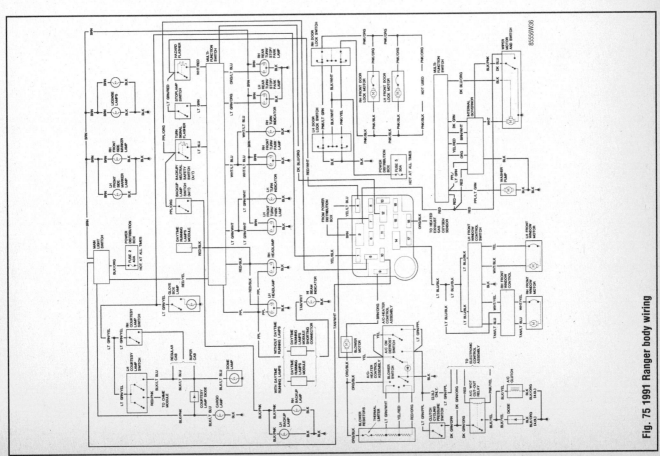

Fig. 75 1991 Ranger body wiring

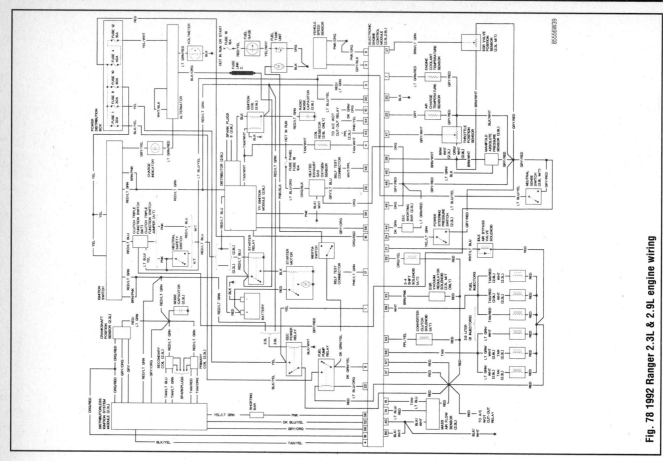

Fig. 78 1992 Ranger 2.3L & 2.9L engine wiring

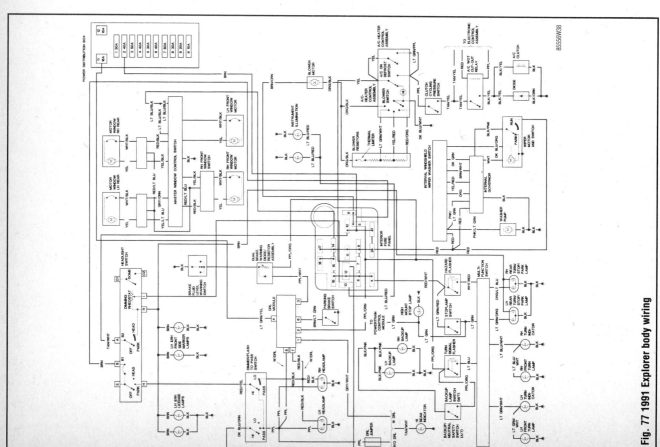

Fig. 77 1991 Explorer body wiring

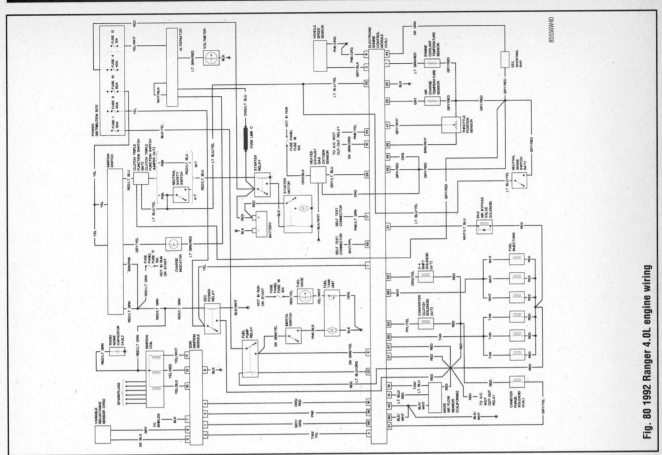

Fig. 80 1992 Ranger 4.0L engine wiring

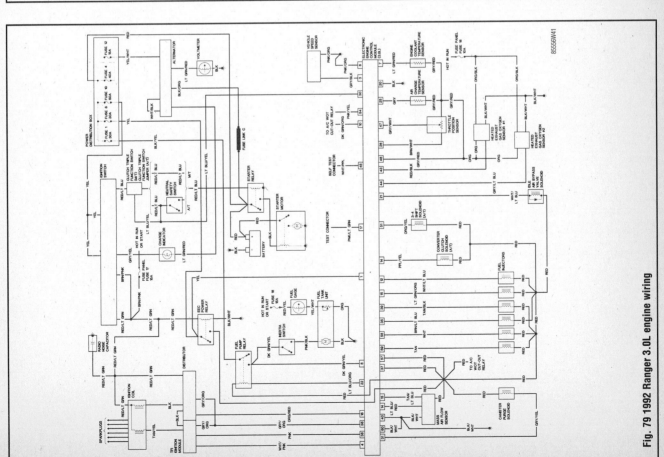

Fig. 79 1992 Ranger 3.0L engine wiring

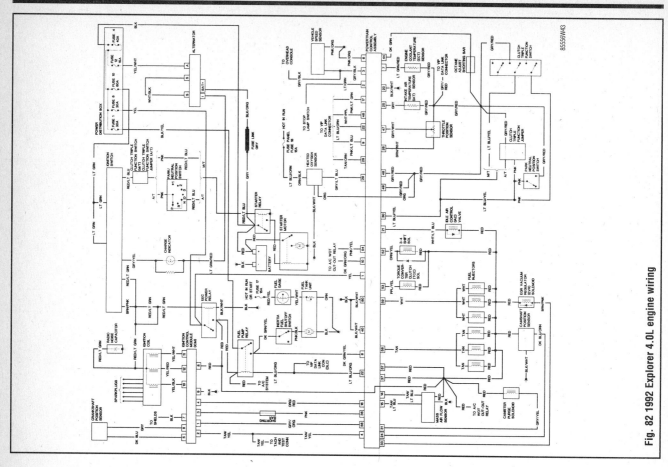

Fig. 82 1992 Explorer 4.0L engine wiring

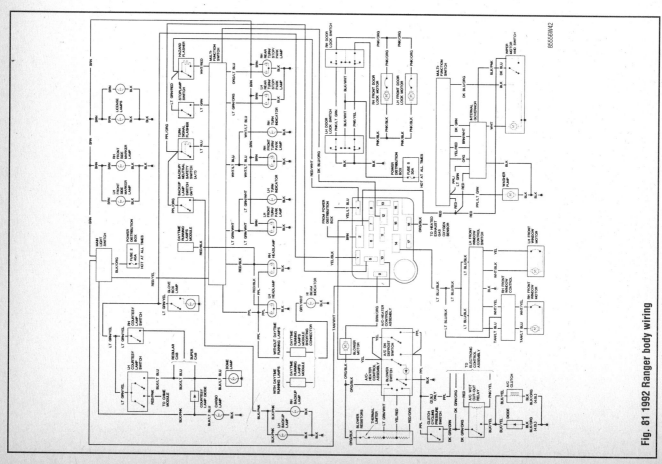

Fig. 81 1992 Ranger body wiring

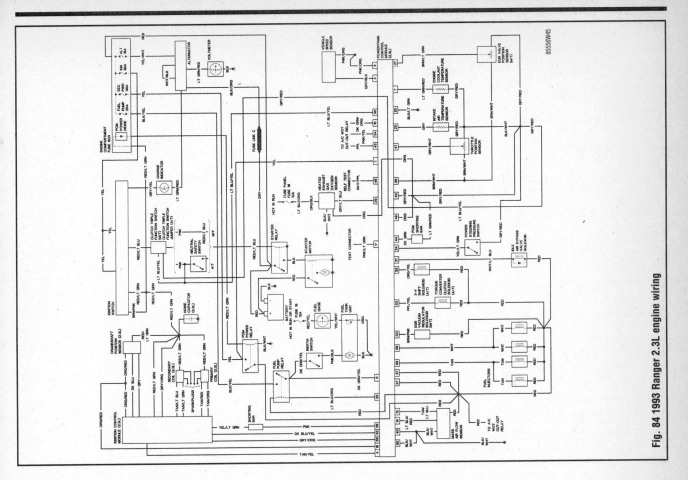

Fig. 84 1993 Ranger 2.3L engine wiring

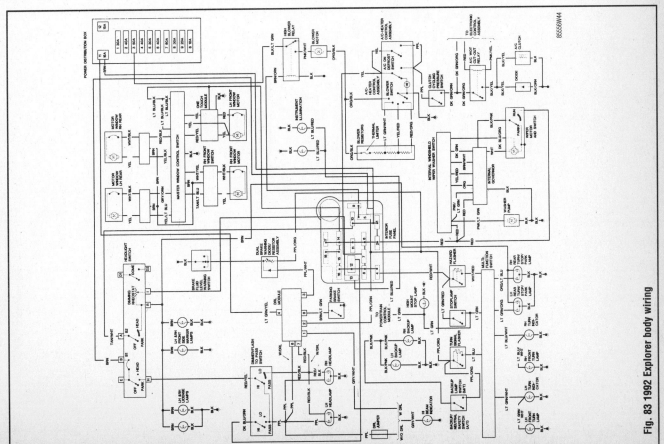

Fig. 83 1992 Explorer body wiring

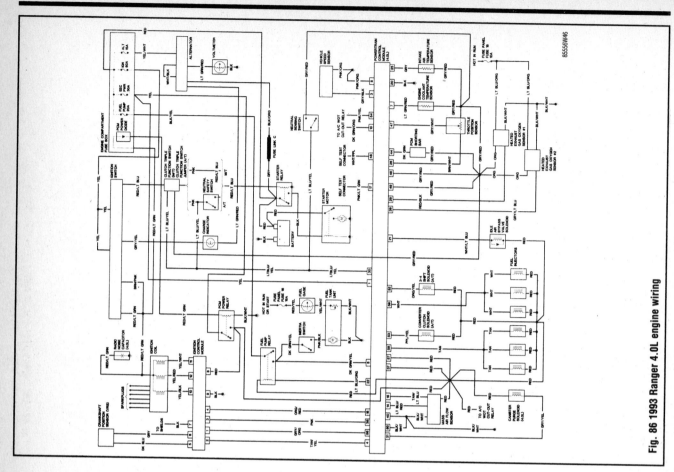

Fig. 86 1993 Ranger 4.0L engine wiring

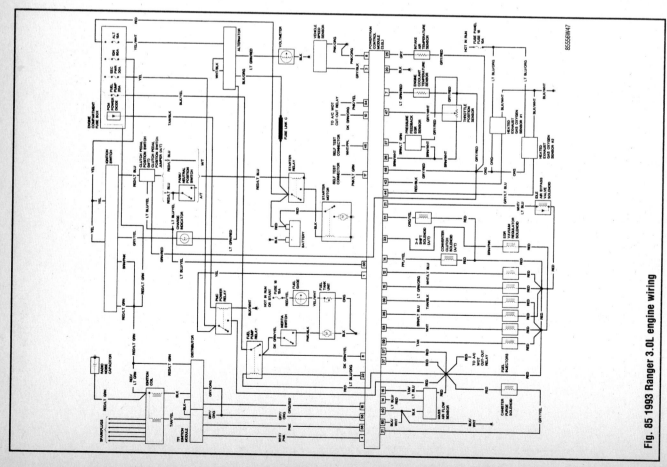

Fig. 85 1993 Ranger 3.0L engine wiring

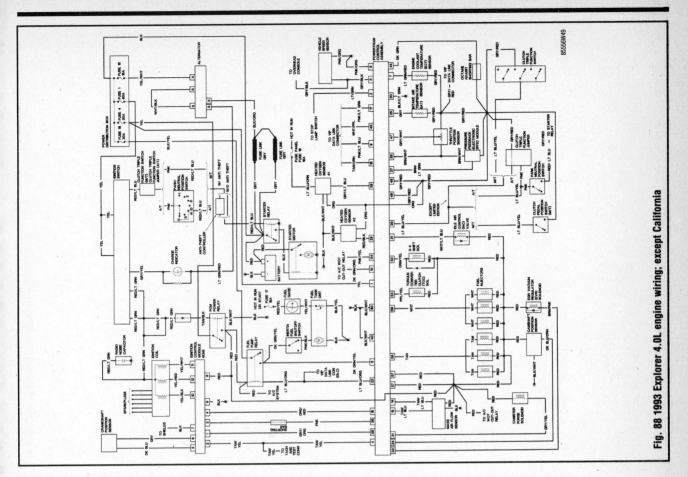

Fig. 88 1993 Explorer 4.0L engine wiring; except California

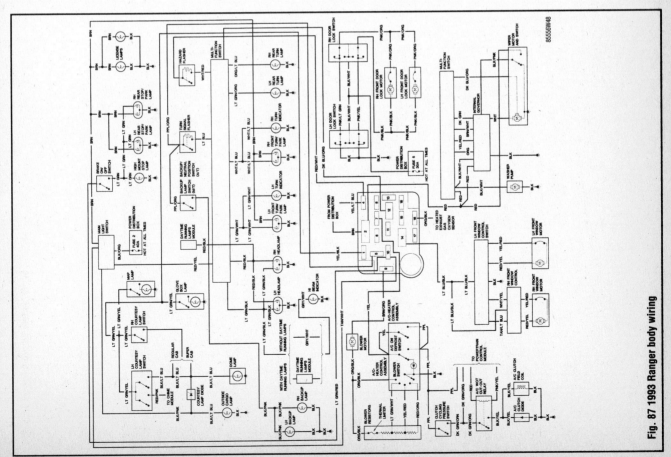

Fig. 87 1993 Ranger body wiring

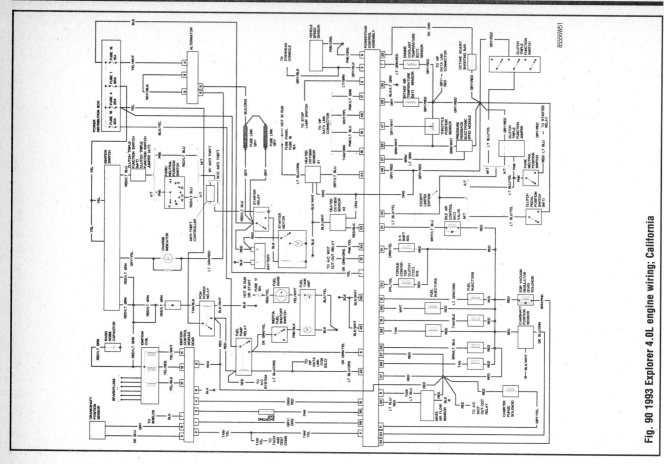

Fig. 90 1993 Explorer 4.0L engine wiring; California

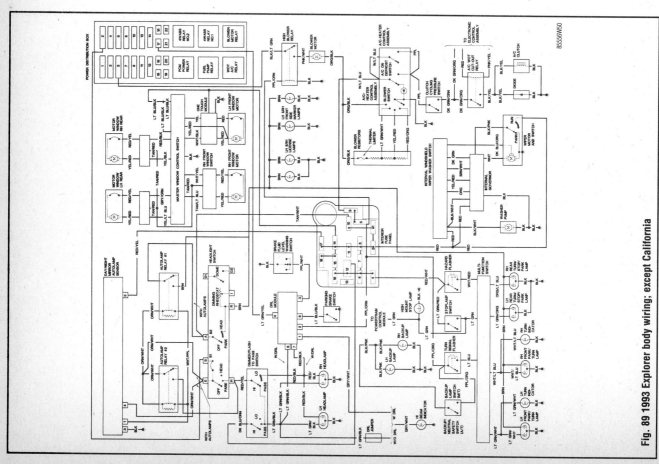

Fig. 89 1993 Explorer body wiring; except California

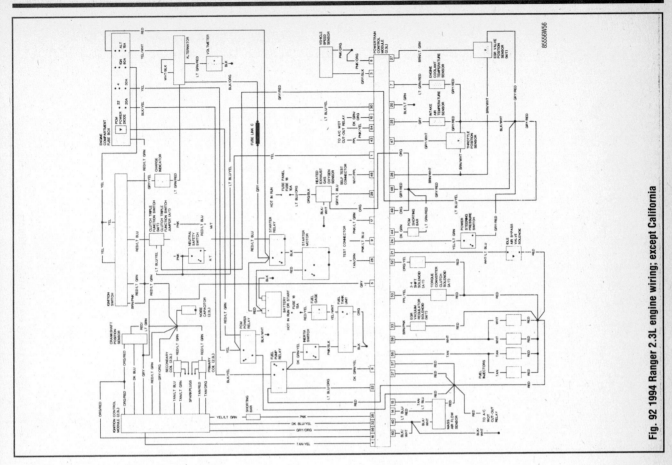

Fig. 92 1994 Ranger 2.3L engine wiring; except California

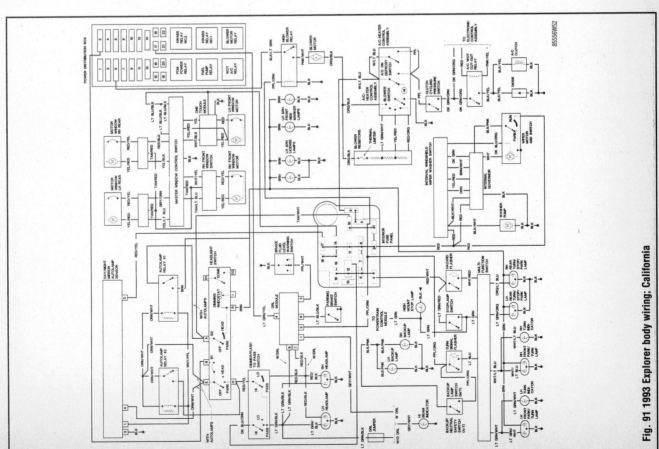

Fig. 91 1993 Explorer body wiring; California

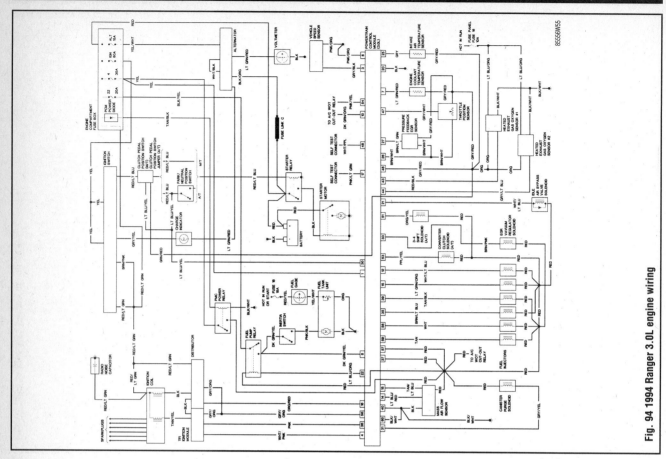

Fig. 94 1994 Ranger 3.0L engine wiring

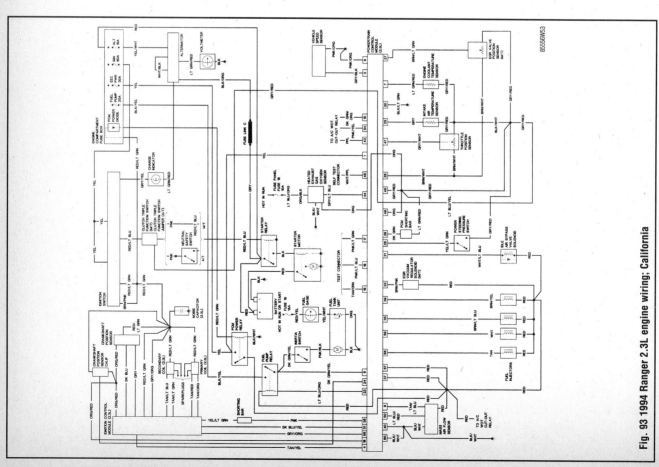

Fig. 93 1994 Ranger 2.3L engine wiring; California

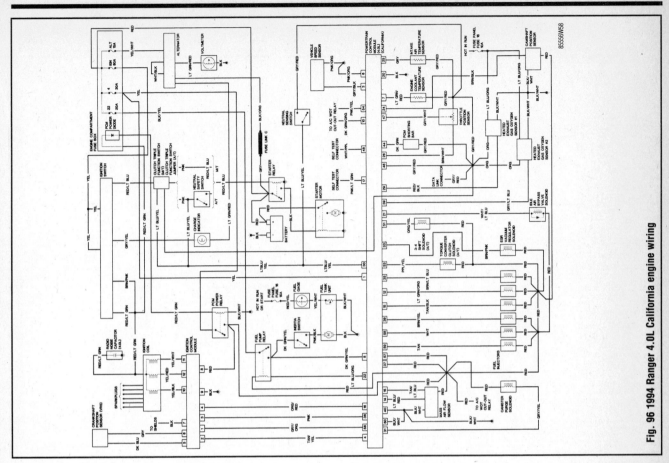

Fig. 96 1994 Ranger 4.0L California engine wiring

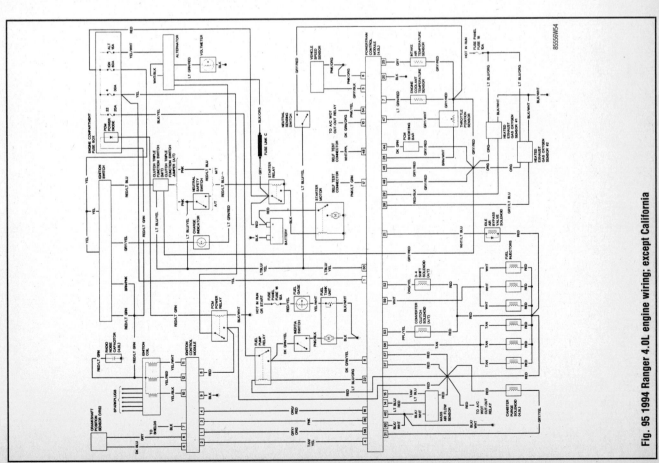

Fig. 95 1994 Ranger 4.0L engine wiring; except California

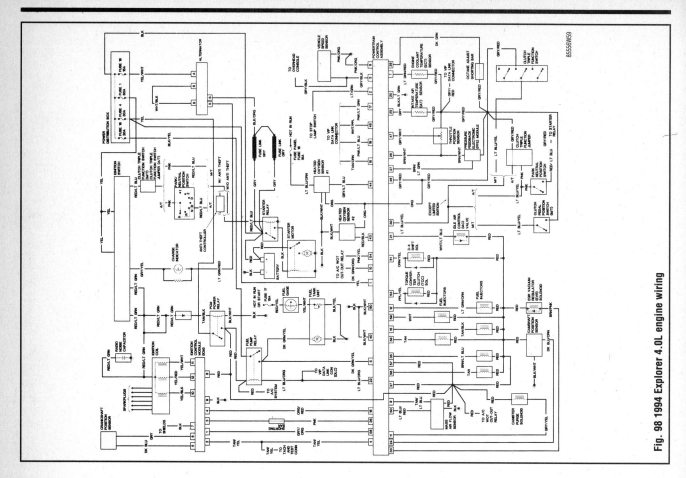

Fig. 98 1994 Explorer 4.0L engine wiring

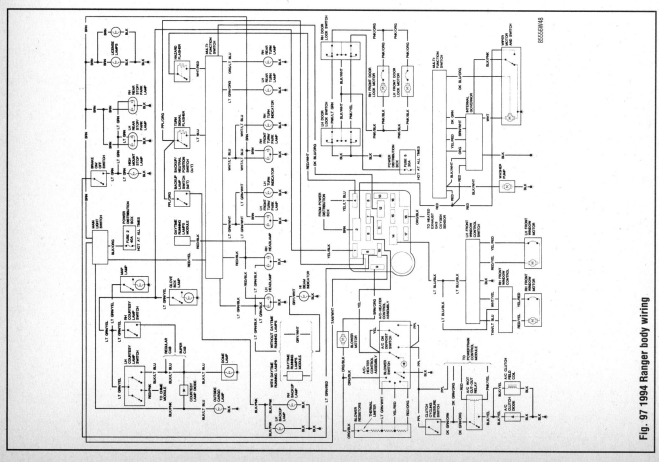

Fig. 97 1994 Ranger body wiring

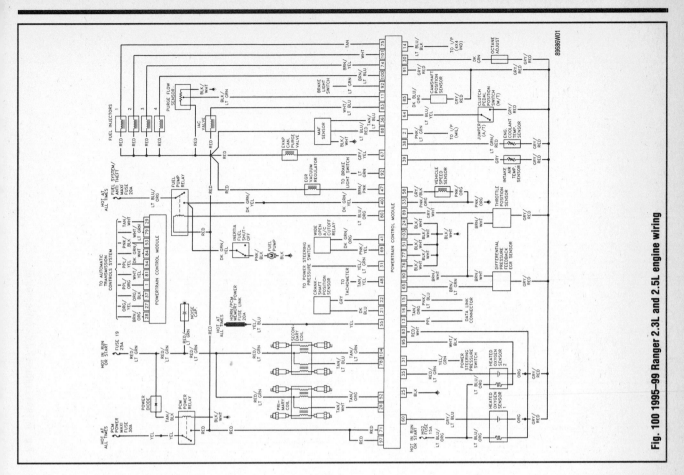

Fig. 100 1995–99 Ranger 2.3L and 2.5L engine wiring

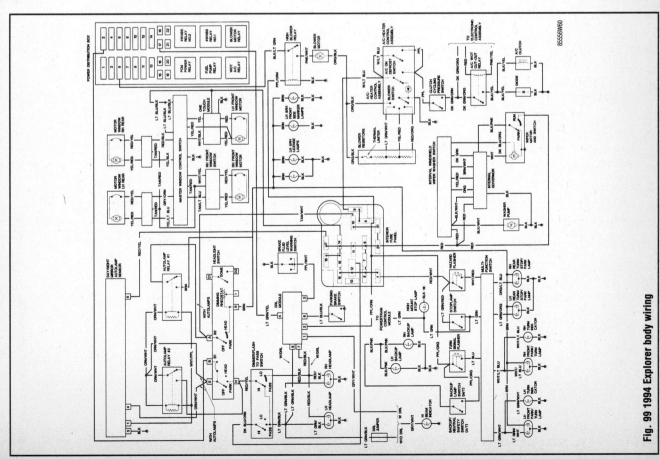

Fig. 99 1994 Explorer body wiring

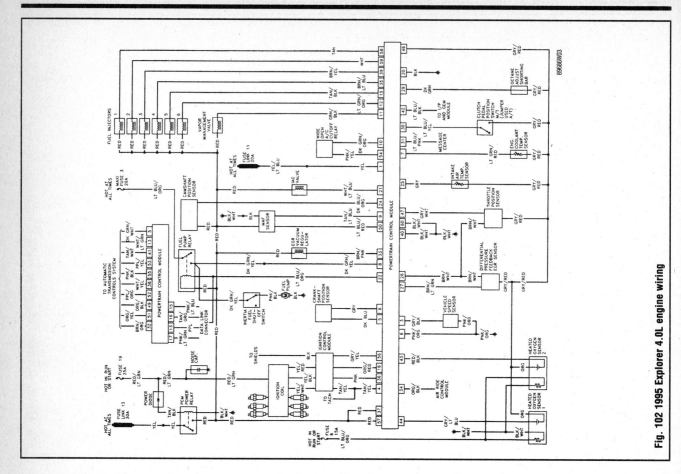

Fig. 102 1995 Explorer 4.0L engine wiring

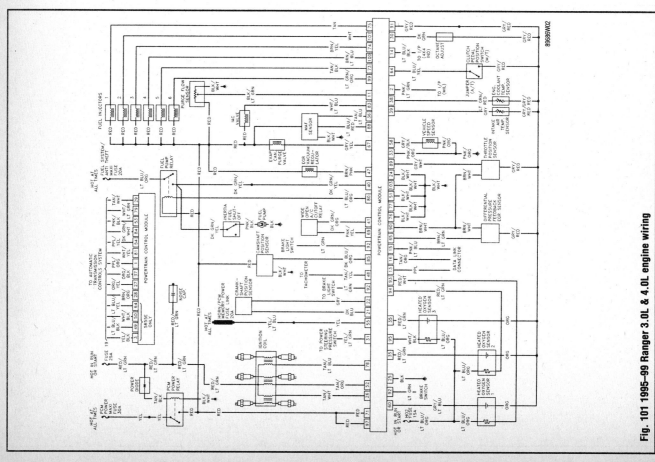

Fig. 101 1995–99 Ranger 3.0L & 4.0L engine wiring

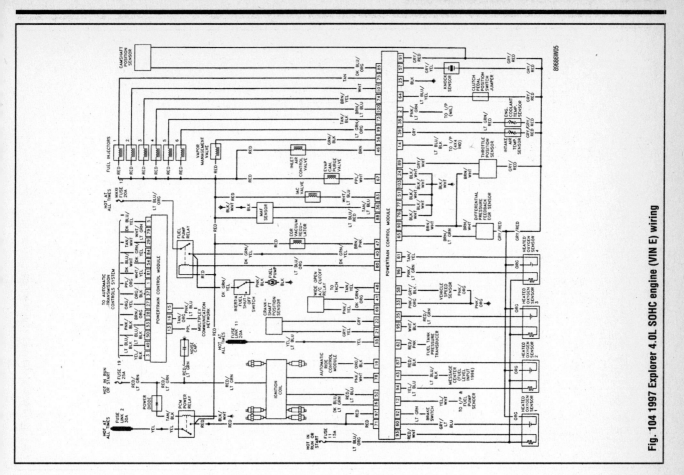

Fig. 104 1997 Explorer 4.0L SOHC engine (VIN E) wiring

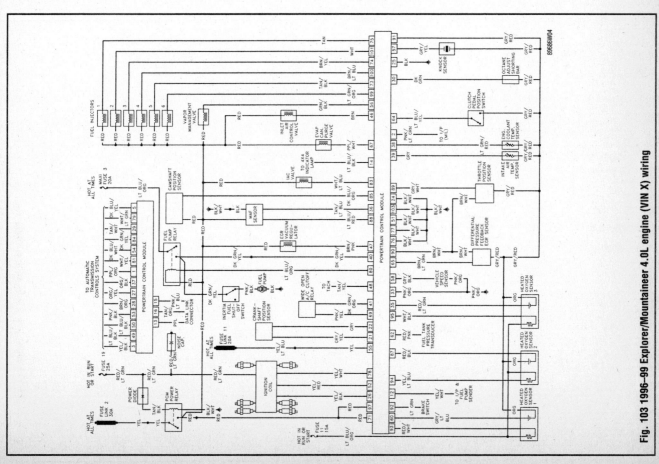

Fig. 103 1996–99 Explorer/Mountaineer 4.0L engine (VIN X) wiring

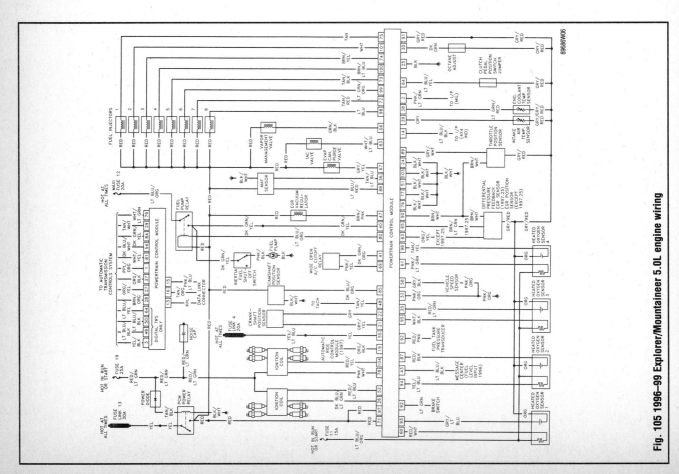

Fig. 106 1995–99 Ranger, Explorer & Mountaineer body wiring

Fig. 105 1996–99 Explorer/Mountaineer 5.0L engine wiring

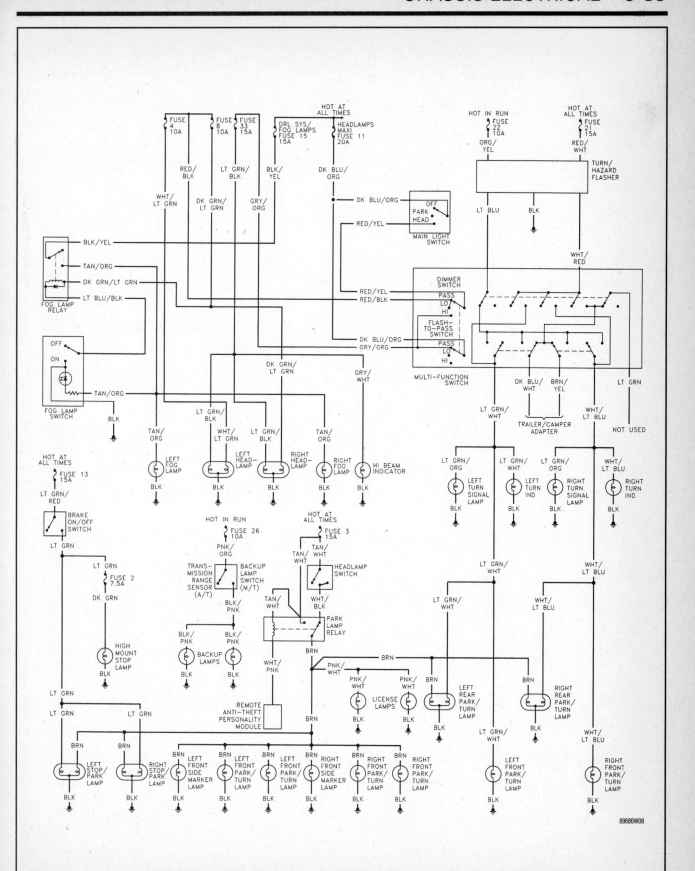

Fig. 107 1995–99 Ranger body wiring

89686W08

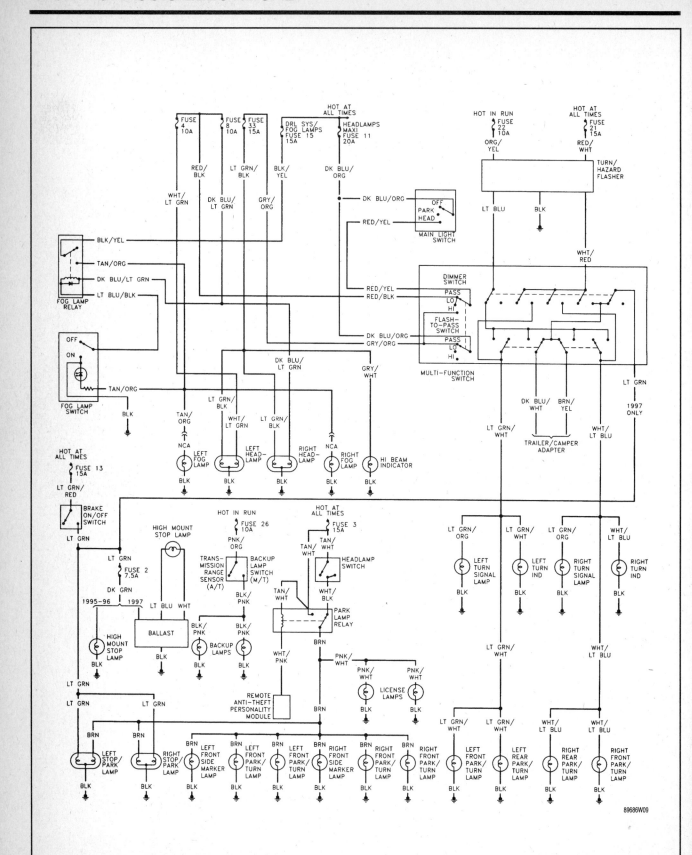

Fig. 108 1995–99 Explorer & Mountaineer body wiring

89686W09

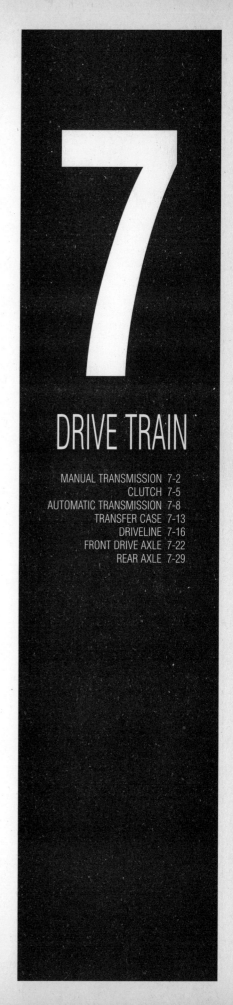

7

DRIVE TRAIN

MANUAL TRANSMISSION

Understanding the Manual Transmission

Because of the way an internal combustion engine breathes, it can produce torque (or twisting force) only within a narrow speed range. Most overhead valve pushrod engines must turn at about 2500 rpm to produce their peak torque. Often by 4500 rpm, they are producing so little torque that continued increases in engine speed produce no power increases.

The torque peak on overhead camshaft engines is, generally, much higher, but much narrower.

The manual transmission and clutch are employed to vary the relationship between engine RPM and the speed of the wheels so that adequate power can be produced under all circumstances. The clutch allows engine torque to be applied to the transmission input shaft gradually, due to mechanical slippage. The vehicle can, consequently, be started smoothly from a full stop.

The transmission changes the ratio between the rotating speeds of the engine and the wheels by the use of gears. 4-speed or 5-speed transmissions are most common. The lower gears allow full engine power to be applied to the rear wheels during acceleration at low speeds.

The clutch driveplate is a thin disc, the center of which is splined to the transmission input shaft. Both sides of the disc are covered with a layer of material which is similar to brake lining and which is capable of allowing slippage without roughness or excessive noise.

The clutch cover is bolted to the engine flywheel and incorporates a diaphragm spring which provides the pressure to engage the clutch. The cover also houses the pressure plate. When the clutch pedal is released, the driven disc is sandwiched between the pressure plate and the smooth surface of the flywheel, thus forcing the disc to turn at the same speed as the engine crankshaft.

The transmission contains a mainshaft which passes all the way through the transmission, from the clutch to the driveshaft. This shaft is separated at one point, so that front and rear portions can turn at different speeds.

Power is transmitted by a countershaft in the lower gears and reverse. The gears of the countershaft mesh with gears on the mainshaft, allowing power to be carried from one to the other. Countershaft gears are often integral with that shaft, while several of the mainshaft gears can either rotate independently of the shaft or be locked to it. Shifting from one gear to the next causes one of the gears to be freed from rotating with the shaft and locks another to it. Gears are locked and unlocked by internal dog clutches which slide between the center of the gear and the shaft. The forward gears usually employ synchronizers; friction members which smoothly bring gear and shaft to the same speed before the toothed dog clutches are engaged.

Identification

The Ranger and Explorer trucks had two manual transmission available, depending on the engine. The Mazda M5OD 5-speed overdrive transmission came equipped on both the 4x2 and 4x4 versions. The Mitsubishi 5-speed overdrive transmission only came on the 2.9L equipped 4x4 Ranger vehicles from 1991–92.

Adjustments

SHIFTER & LINKAGE ADJUSTMENTS

Both of the 5-speed transmissions are directly controlled with a floor shift mechanism built into the transmission extension housing. There are no adjustments necessary on these transmissions.

Shift Handle

REMOVAL & INSTALLATION

▶ **See Figure 1**

1. Disconnect the negative battery cable.

➡**Do not remove the shift knob, unless the shift knob or boot is to be replaced. Otherwise, remove the shift knob, boot and lever as an assembly.**

2. If necessary, remove the shift lever knob on the Mitsubishi 5-speed transmission as follows:

    a. Remove the plastic shift pattern insert from the shift knob.

    b. Heat the shift lever knob to 140–180°F (60–82°C), using a heat gun.

    c. Position a block of wood beneath the shift lever knob and carefully hammer the knob from the lever. Be careful not to damage the finish on the shift lever.

3. Place the gearshift lever in **N** position.

4. Remove the shifter boot retainer screws and slide the boot up the lever.

5. Remove the shift lever-to-extension housing/transfer case adapter housing retaining bolts. Pull the gearshift lever straight up and away from the gearshift lever retainer.

    To install:

6. Prior to installing the shift lever, lubricate the shift lever ball stud, using C1AZ-19590-B (ESA-M1C75-B) or equivalent.

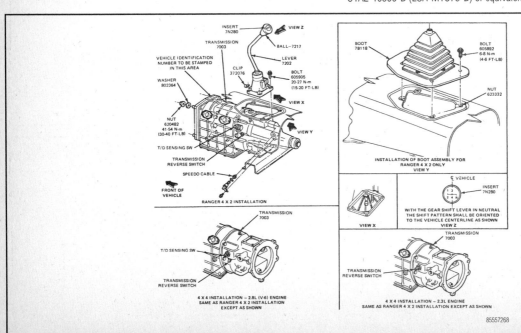

Fig. 1 Exploded view of the transmission shifter lever assembly

85557268

7. Fit the shift lever into place and install the retaining bolts. Tighten the retaining bolts to specifications.

8. Install the rubber boot and retaining screws.

9. If the shift lever knob was removed, heat it to 140°–180°F (60°–82°C), using a heat gun. Tap the knob onto the shift lever, using a 7/16 in. (11mm will work) socket and mallet.

10. Place the shift lever in **N** position. Then, align the shift pattern plastic insert with the vehicle centerline and install it to the shift lever knob.

Neutral Sensing Switch

All manual transmission vehicles are equipped with a neutral sensing switch. The neutral sensing switch signals the vehicle on-board computer, which allows the vehicle to start only when the transmission is in **N**.

REMOVAL & INSTALLATION

▶ **See Figures 2 and 3**

1. Disconnect the negative battery cable.
2. Raise and support the vehicle safely.
3. Place the transmission in any position other than **N**.
4. Clean the area around the switch, then remove the switch.

To install:

5. Install the switch and tighten 8–12 ft. lbs. (11– 16Nm).
6. Reconnect the harness connector to the switch.
7. Lower the vehicle.
8. Reconnect the negative battery cable.

Extension Housing Seal

REMOVAL & INSTALLATION

Two Wheel Drive Models

▶ **See Figures 4 and 5**

1. Disconnect the negative battery cable.

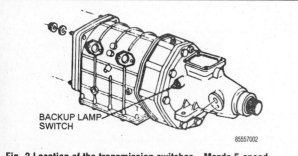

Fig. 2 Location of the transmission switches—Mazda 5-speed

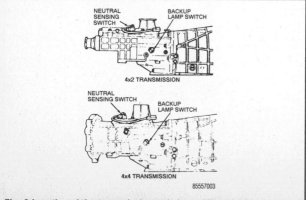

Fig. 3 Location of the transmission switches—Mitsubishi 5-speed

2. Raise and support the vehicle safely.
3. Place a suitable drain pan beneath the extension housing. Clean the area around the extension housing seal.
4. Matchmark the driveshaft to the rear axle flange. Disconnect the driveshaft and pull it rearward from the unit.
5. Remove the extension housing seal using tool T74P-77248-A or equivalent, remove the extension housing seal.

To install:

6. Lubricate the inside diameter of the oil seal and install the seal into the extension housing using tool T74P-77052-A. Check to ensure that the oil seal drain hole faces downward.
7. Install the driveshaft to the extension housing. Connect the driveshaft to the rear axle flange. Make sure the marks made during removal are in alignment. Fit the attaching washer, lockwasher and nuts.
8. Check and adjust the transmission fluid level, using Ford manual transmission lube D8DZ-19C547-A (ESP-M2C83-C) or equivalent.
9. Lower the vehicle.
10. Reconnect the negative battery cable.

Four Wheel Drive Models

Refer to the transfer case procedures for the front and/or rear output shaft seals.

Transmission

REMOVAL & INSTALLATION

▶ **See Figures 6 and 7**

1. Disconnect the negative battery cable.
2. Remove the gearshift lever assembly from the control housing.
3. Cover the opening in the control housing with a cloth to prevent dirt from falling into the unit.
4. Raise the vehicle and support it safely.
5. On 2WD vehicles, matchmark the driveshaft to the rear axle flange. Position a drain pan under the tailend of the transmission. Remove the driveshaft-to-rear axle flange fasteners and pull the driveshaft rearward to disconnect it from the transmission.

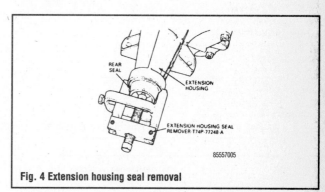

Fig. 4 Extension housing seal removal

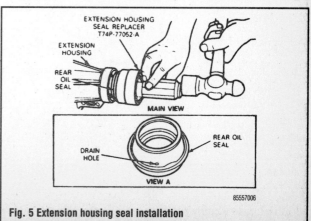

Fig. 5 Extension housing seal installation

6. Disconnect the clutch hydraulic line a the clutch housing. Plug the lines.

7. Disconnect the speedometer from the transfer case/extension housing.

8. Disconnect the starter motor, back-up lamp and, if equipped, neutral sensing switch harness connector.

9. Place a wood block on a service jack and position the jack under the engine oil pan.

10. On 4WD vehicles, remove the transfer case from the vehicle.

11. Remove the starter motor.

12. Position a transmission jack, under the transmission.

13. Remove the transmission-to-engine retaining bolts and washers.

14. Remove the nuts and bolts attaching the transmission mount and damper to the crossmember.

15. Remove the nuts and bolts attaching the crossmember to the frame side rails and remove the crossmember.

16. Lower the engine jack slightly to angle the transmission assembly. Work the clutch housing off the locating dowels and slide the clutch housing and the transmission rearward until the input shaft clears the clutch disc.

17. Lower the transmission jack and remove the transmission from the vehicle.

To install:

18. Check that the mating surfaces of the clutch housing, engine rear and dowel holes are free of burrs, dirt and paint.

19. Place the transmission on the transmission jack. Position the transmis-

sion under the vehicle, then raise it into position. Align the input shaft splines with the clutch disc splines and work the transmission forward into the locating dowels.

20. Install the transmission-to-engine retaining bolts and washers. Tighten the retaining bolts to specifications. Remove the transmission jack.

21. Install the starter motor. Tighten the attaching nuts.

22. Raise the engine and install the rear crossmember, insulator and damper and attaching nuts and bolts. Tighten and torque the bolts to specification.

23. On 4WD vehicles, install the transfer case.

24. On 2WD vehicles, insert the driveshaft into the transmission extension housing and install the center bearing attaching nuts, washers and lockwashers. Connect the driveshaft to the rear axle drive flange.

25. Connect the starter motor, back-up lamp and, if equipped, neutral sensing switch connectors.

26. Connect the hydraulic clutch line and bleed the system.

27. Install the speedometer cable.

28. Check and adjust the fluid level.

29. Lower the vehicle.

30. Install the gearshift lever assembly. Install the boot cover and bolts.

31. Reconnect the negative battery cable.

32. Check for proper shifting and operation of the transmission.

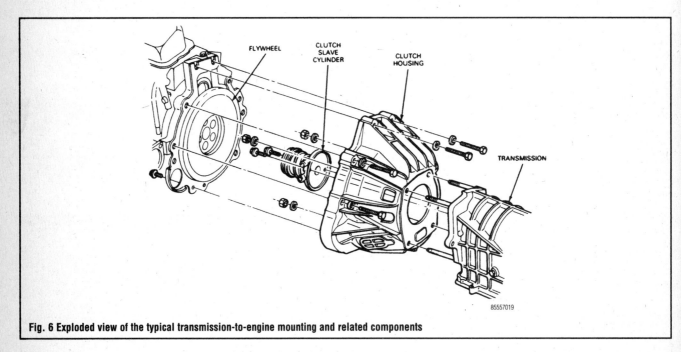

Fig. 6 Exploded view of the typical transmission-to-engine mounting and related components

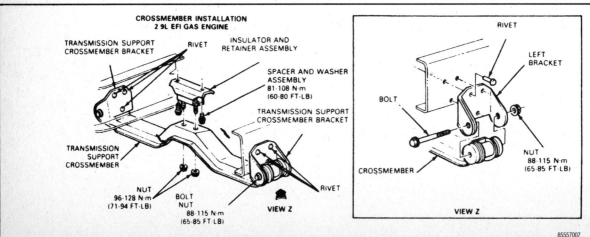

Fig. 7 Exploded view of a 2.9L engine crossmember assembly—other models are similar

CLUTCH

Understanding the Clutch

The purpose of the clutch is to disconnect and connect engine power at the transmission. A vehicle at rest requires a lot of engine torque to get all that weight moving. An internal combustion engine does not develop a high starting torque (unlike steam engines) so it must be allowed to operate without any load until it builds up enough torque to move the vehicle. To a point, torque increases with engine rpm. The clutch allows the engine to build up torque by physically disconnecting the engine from the transmission, relieving the engine of any load or resistance.

The transfer of engine power to the transmission (the load) must be smooth and gradual; if it weren't, drive line components would wear out or break quickly. This gradual power transfer is made possible by gradually releasing the clutch pedal. The clutch disc and pressure plate are the connecting link between the engine and transmission. When the clutch pedal is released, the disc and plate contact each other (the clutch is engaged) physically joining the engine and transmission. When the pedal is pushed in, the disc and plate separate (the clutch is disengaged) disconnecting the engine from the transmission.

Most clutch assemblies consists of the flywheel, the clutch disc, the clutch pressure plate, the throw out bearing and fork, the actuating linkage and the pedal. The flywheel and clutch pressure plate (driving members) are connected to the engine crankshaft and rotate with it. The clutch disc is located between the flywheel and pressure plate, and is splined to the transmission shaft. A driving member is one that is attached to the engine and transfers engine power to a driven member (clutch disc) on the transmission shaft. A driving member (pressure plate) rotates (drives) a driven member (clutch disc) on contact and, in so doing, turns the transmission shaft.

There is a circular diaphragm spring within the pressure plate cover (transmission side). In a relaxed state (when the clutch pedal is fully released) this spring is convex; that is, it is dished outward toward the transmission. Pushing in the clutch pedal actuates the attached linkage. Connected to the other end of this is the throw out fork, which hold the throw out bearing. When the clutch pedal is depressed, the clutch linkage pushes the fork and bearing forward to contact the diaphragm spring of the pressure plate. The outer edges of the spring are secured to the pressure plate and are pivoted on rings so that when the center of the spring is compressed by the throw out bearing, the outer edges bow outward and, by so doing, pull the pressure plate in the same direction — away from the clutch disc. This action separates the disc from the plate, disengaging the clutch and allowing the transmission to be shifted into another gear. A coil type clutch return spring attached to the clutch pedal arm permits full release of the pedal. Releasing the pedal pulls the throw out bearing away from the diaphragm spring resulting in a reversal of spring position. As bearing pressure is gradually released from the spring center, the outer edges of the spring bow outward, pushing the pressure plate into closer contact with the clutch disc. As the disc and plate move closer together, friction between the two increases and slippage is reduced until, when full spring pressure is applied (by fully releasing the pedal) the speed of the disc and plate are the same. This stops all slipping, creating a direct connection between the plate and disc which results in the transfer of power from the engine to the transmission. The clutch disc is now rotating with the pressure plate at engine speed and, because it is splined to the transmission shaft, the shaft now turns at the same engine speed.

The clutch is operating properly if:
1. It will stall the engine when released with the vehicle held stationary.
2. The shift lever can be moved freely between 1st and reverse gears when the vehicle is stationary and the clutch disengaged.

Clutch Interlock Switch

The clutch interlock switch has 3-functions. It is also known as the Clutch Pedal Position (CPP) switch and provides the 3 following functions:
• It requires the clutch pedal to be depressed to the floor in order to start the engine.
• If cuts off the speed control system when the clutch pedal is depressed.
• It provides a fuel control signal to the EEC system.

REMOVAL & INSTALLATION

♦ See Figure 8

1. Disconnect the negative battery cable.
2. Disconnect the connector at the switch by flexing the retaining tab on the switch housing and withdraw the connector.
3. Rotate the switch ½ turn to expose the plastic retainer.
4. Push the tabs together to allow the retainer to slide rearward and separate from the switch.
5. Remove the switch from the pushrod.
To install:
6. Fit the switch to the master cylinder pushrod.
7. Install the plastic retainer.
8. Rotate the switch into the position to attach the clip. Reconnect the switch connector.
9. Reconnect the negative battery cable.

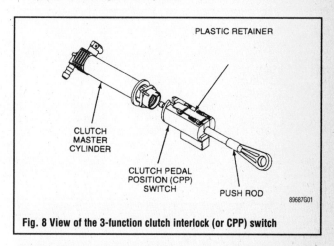

Fig. 8 View of the 3-function clutch interlock (or CPP) switch

Master Cylinder and Reservoir

The hydraulic clutch system operates much like a hydraulic brake system. When you push down (disengage) the clutch pedal, the mechanical clutch pedal movement is converted into hydraulic fluid movement, which is then converted back into mechanical movement by the slave cylinder to actuate the clutch release lever.

The system consists of a combination clutch fluid reservoir/master cylinder assembly, a slave cylinder mounted on the bellhousing, and connecting tubing.

Fluid level is checked at the master cylinder reservoir. The hydraulic clutch system continually remains in adjustment, like a hydraulic disc brake system, so not clutch linkage or pedal adjustment is necessary.

REMOVAL & INSTALLATION

♦ See Figure 9

1. Disconnect the negative battery cable.
2. Disconnect the clutch master cylinder pushrod from the clutch pedal.
3. Remove the switch from the master cylinder assembly, if equipped.
4. Remove the screw retaining the fluid reservoir to the cowl access cover.
5. Disconnect the tube from the slave cylinder and plug both openings.
6. Remove the bolts retaining the clutch master cylinder to the dash panel and remove the clutch master cylinder assembly.
To install:
7. Install the pushrod through the hole in the engine compartment. Make certain it is located on the correct side of the clutch pedal. Place the master

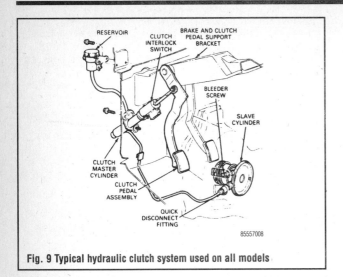

Fig. 9 Typical hydraulic clutch system used on all models

cylinder assembly in position and install the retaining bolts. Tighten to 8–12 ft. lbs. (11–16Nm).

8. Insert the coupling end into the slave cylinder and install the tube into the clips.

9. Fit the reservoir on the cowl access cover and install the retaining screws.

10. Replace the retainer bushing in the clutch master cylinder pushrod if worn or damaged. Install the retainer and pushrod on the clutch pedal pin. Make certain the bushing is fitted correctly with the flange of the bushing against the pedal blade.

11. Install the switch.

12. Bleed the system.

13. Reconnect the negative battery cable.

Slave Cylinder

REMOVAL & INSTALLATION

▶ **See Figures 10 and 11**

➡**Before performing any service that requires removal of the slave cylinder, the master cylinder and pushrod must be disconnected from the clutch pedal. If not disconnected, permanent damage to the master cylinder assembly will occur if the clutch pedal is depressed while the slave cylinder is disconnected.**

1. Disconnect the negative battery cable.

2. Disconnect the coupling at the transmission, using the clutch coupling removal tool T88T-70522-A or equivalent. Slide the white plastic sleeve toward the slave cylinder while applying a slight tug on the tube.

3. Remove the transmission assembly.

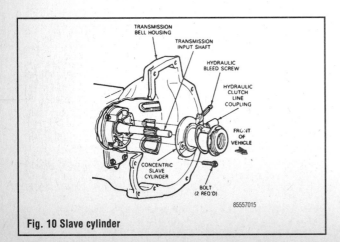

Fig. 10 Slave cylinder

Fig. 11 View of the clutch line coupling removal tool

➡**On the 2.9L (4WD) vehicles, the clutch housing must be removed with the transmission assembly.**

4. Remove the slave cylinder-to-transmission retaining bolts.

5. Remove the slave cylinder from the transmission input shaft.

To install:

6. Fit the slave cylinder over the transmission input shaft with the bleed screws and coupling facing the left side of the transmission.

7. Install the slave cylinder retaining bolts. Torque to 13–19 ft. lbs. (18–26Nm).

8. Install the transmission.

9. Reconnect the coupling to the slave cylinder.

10. Bleed the system.

11. Reconnect the negative battery cable.

BLEEDING THE SYSTEM

The following procedure is recommended for bleeding a hydraulic system installed on the vehicle. The largest portion of the filling is carried out by gravity. It is recommended that the original clutch tube with quick connect be replaced when servicing the hydraulic system because air can be trapped in the quick connect and prevent complete bleeding of the system. The replacement tube does not include a quick connect.

1. Clean the dirt and grease from the dust cap.

2. Remove the cap and diaphragm and fill the reservoir to the top with approved brake fluid C6AZ-19542-AA or BA, (ESA-M6C25-A) or equivalent.

➡**To keep brake fluid from entering the clutch housing, route a suitable rubber tube of appropriate inside diameter from the bleed screw to a container.**

3. Loosen the bleed screw, located in the slave cylinder body, next to the inlet connection. Fluid will now begin to move from the master cylinder down the tube to the slave cylinder.

➡**The reservoir must be kept full at all time during the bleeding operation, to ensure no additional air enters the system.**

4. Notice the bleed screw outlet. When the slave is full, a steady stream of fluid comes from the slave outlet. Tighten the bleed screw.

5. Depress the clutch pedal to the floor and hold for 1–2 seconds. Release the pedal as rapidly as possible. The pedal must be released completely. Pause for 1–2 seconds. Repeat 10 times.

6. Check the fluid level in the reservoir. The fluid should be level with the step when the diaphragm is removed.

7. Repeat Step 5 and 6 five times. Replace the reservoir diaphragm and cap.

8. Hold the pedal to the floor, crack open the bleed screw to allow any additional air to escape. Close the bleed screw, then release the pedal.

9. Check the fluid in the reservoir. The hydraulic system should now be fully bled and should release the clutch.

10. Check the vehicle by starting, pushing the clutch pedal to the floor and selecting reverse gear. There should be no grating of gears. If there is, and the hydraulic system still contains air, repeat the bleeding procedure from Step 5.

Driven Disc and Pressure Plate

❊ CAUTION

The clutch driven disc may contain asbestos, which has been determined to be a cancer causing agent. Never clean clutch surfaces with compressed air! Avoid inhaling any dust from any clutch surface! When cleaning clutch surface, use a commercially available brake cleaning fluid.

REMOVAL & INSTALLATION

▶ **See Figures 12 and 13**

1. Disconnect the negative battery cable.
2. Disconnect the clutch hydraulic system master cylinder from the clutch pedal and remove.
3. Raise the vehicle and support it safely.
4. Remove the starter.
5. Disconnect the hydraulic coupling at the transmission.

➡ **Clean the area around the hose and slave cylinder to prevent fluid contamination.**

6. Remove the transmission from the vehicle.
7. Mark the assembled position of the pressure plate and cover the flywheel, to aid during re-assembly.
8. Loosen the pressure plate and cover attaching bolts evenly until the pressure plate springs are expanded, and remove the bolts.
9. Remove the pressure plate and cover assembly and the clutch disc from the flywheel. Remove the pilot bearing only for replacement.

To install:

10. Position the clutch disc on the flywheel so that the Clutch Alignment Shaft Tool T74P-7137-K or equivalent can enter the clutch pilot bearing and align the disc.
11. When reinstalling the original pressure plate and cover assembly, align the assembly and flywheel according to the marks made during the removal operations. Position the pressure plate and cover assembly on the flywheel, align the pressure plate and disc, and install the retaining bolts that fasten the assembly to the flywheel. Tighten the bolts to 15–25 ft. lbs. (21–35 Nm) in the proper sequence. Remove the clutch disc pilot tool.
12. Install the transmission into the vehicle.
13. Connect the coupling by pushing the male coupling into the slave cylinder.
14. Connect the hydraulic clutch master cylinder pushrod to the clutch pedal.

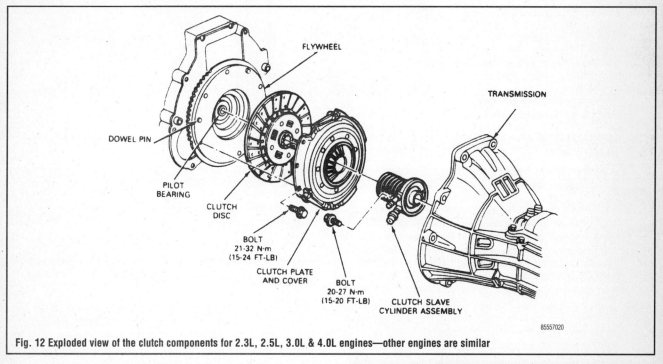

Fig. 12 Exploded view of the clutch components for 2.3L, 2.5L, 3.0L & 4.0L engines—other engines are similar

Fig. 13 Pressure plate bolt torque sequence

Loosen and remove the clutch and pressure plate bolts evenly, a little at a time . . .

. . . then carefully remove the pressure plate and clutch assembly from the flywheel

Check the flywheel surface for flatness and, if necessary, remove it from the engine for truing

Be sure that the flywheel surface is clean before installing the clutch

Typical clutch alignment tool, note how the splines match the transmissionís input shaft

Use the clutch alignment tool to align the clutch disc during assembly.

Be sure to use a torque wrench to tighten all of the bolts

AUTOMATIC TRANSMISSION

Understanding the Automatic Transmission

The automatic transmission allows engine torque and power to be transmitted to the rear wheels within a narrow range of engine operating speeds. It will allow the engine to turn fast enough to produce plenty of power and torque at very low speeds, while keeping it at a sensible rpm at high vehicle speeds (and it does this job without driver assistance). The transmission uses a light fluid as the medium for the transmission of power. This fluid also works in the operation of various hydraulic control circuits and as a lubricant. Because the transmission fluid performs all of these functions, trouble within the unit can easily travel from one part to another.

Identification

There are 5 automatic transmissions used in the Ford Ranger, Explorer and Mountaineer. They may be identified by checking the transmission code on the Safety Standard Certification Label attached to the driver's side door post, in the space marked **Trans.** The transmissions can also be identified by a tag attached to the lower left hand extension attaching bolt. The transmission codes are as follows:

- 1991–94 code T is for the A4LD transmission
- 1995–99 code T is for the 4R44E (2.3L, 2.5L & 3.0L) or 4R55E (4.0L) transmission
- 1996–99 code U is for the 4R70W (5.0L) transmission
- 1997–99 code D is for the 5R55E (5-speed automatic) transmission

All of the automatic transmissions are 4-speed units with a lock-up torque converter, except the 1997–99 5R55E, which is a 5-speed unit with a lock-up torque converter.

Neutral Start Switch/Back-up Switch

REMOVAL & INSTALLATION

A4LD Transmissions

▶ See Figure 14

The Park/Neutral Position (PNP) switch, mounted on the transmission, allows the vehicle to start only in **P** or **N**. The switch has a dual purpose, in that it is also the back-up lamp switch.

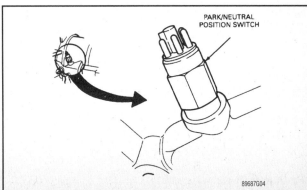

Fig. 14 View of the Park/Neutral Position (PNP) switch used on the A4LD transmission

1. Disconnect the negative battery cable.
2. Raise and support the vehicle safely.
3. Disconnect the harness connector from the neutral start switch.
4. Clean the area around the switch. Remove the switch and O-ring, using a thin wall socket (tool T74P-77247-A or equivalent).

To install:

5. Fit a new O-ring to the switch. Install the switch.
6. Reconnect the harness connector to the switch.
7. Lower the vehicle.
8. Reconnect the negative battery cable.
9. Check the operation of the switch, with the parking brake engaged. The engine should only start in **N** or **P**. The back-up lamps should come ON only in **R**.

Except A4LD Transmissions

♦ **See Figures 15, 16 and 17**

Starting in 1995, the switch was used not only for neutral start sensing and back-up light activation, but also as a gear position range sensor. The Powertrain Control Module reads the sensor to determine which gear position the transmission is in, and adjusts fuel and spark timing accordingly. The new switch is called the Transmission Range (TR) sensor.

➡ **To install the Transmission Range (TR) sensor requires a special Transmission Range Sensor Alignment Tool T97L-70010-AH, or equivalent.**

1. Disconnect the negative battery cable, block the rear wheels and apply the parking brake.
2. Place the transmission shift lever in the Neutral (N) position.
3. Raise and safely support the front of the vehicle
4. Disconnect the shift control cable from the transmission manual control lever.
5. Disconnect the electrical wire harness plug from the TR sensor.

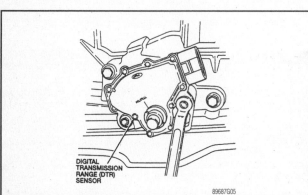

Fig. 15 Remove the two Transmission Range (TR) sensor retaining bolts

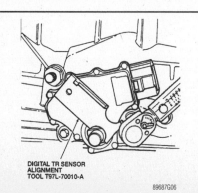

Fig. 16 Align the new sensor with the Digital TR Sensor Alignment Tool

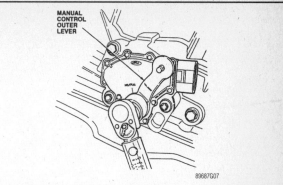

Fig. 17 Install the manual control lever to the sensor and tighten the retaining bolt

6. Remove the manual control lever retaining nut as well as the lever.
7. Remove the two retaining bolts and the sensor.

To install:

8. Ensure that the transmission shift lever is in the Neutral (N) position.
9. Install the TR sensor and loosely install the retaining bolts.
10. Align TR sensor slots using the Transmission Range Sensor Alignment Tool T97L-70010-AH, or equivalent.
11. Tighten the retaining bolts to 7–9 ft. lbs. (9–12 Nm).
12. Install the manual control lever to the sensor and tighten the retaining nut to 22–26 ft. lbs. (30–35 Nm).
13. Connect the TR sensor electrical wire harness plug.
14. Install the shift control cable to the transmission manual control lever.
15. Lower the vehicle and connect the negative battery cable.
16. Ensure that the wheels are still blocked and the parking brake is applied.
17. Check for proper operation of the switch. The engine should only start in Park (P) or Neutral (N).

ADJUSTMENT

A4LD Transmissions

No adjustment is necessary or possible on the A4LD transmission Park Neutral Position (PNP) switch.

Except the A4LD Transmissions

♦ **See Figures 16 and 17**

➡ **To adjust the Transmission Range (TR) sensor requires a special Transmission Range Sensor Alignment Tool T97L-70010-AH, or equivalent.**

1. Raise and safely support the vehicle.
2. Block the rear wheels and apply the parking brake.
3. Place the transmission shift control lever in the Neutral (N) position.
4. Remove the nut securing the transmission control manual lever to the TR sensor.
5. Loosen the two TR sensor retaining bolts.
6. Align the TR sensor slots using the Transmission Range Sensor Alignment Tool T97L-70010-AH, or equivalent.
7. Tighten the TR sensor retaining bolts to 7–9 ft. lbs. (9–12 Nm).
8. Install the nut retaining the transmission manual control lever to the TR sensor. Tighten to 12–16 ft. lbs. (16–22 Nm).
9. Lower the vehicle. Leave the wheels blocked and the parking brake applied.
10. Check the TR sensor operation. The engine should only start in Park (P) or Neutral (N).

Vacuum Diaphragm

Only the A4LD transmissions use a vacuum diaphragm (or modulator). All other models are PCM controlled and do not require vacuum supply from the engine.

REMOVAL & INSTALLATION

A4LD Transmission

♦ **See Figure 18**

1. Disconnect the negative battery cable.
2. Raise and support the vehicle safely.
3. Disconnect the hose from the vacuum diaphragm.
4. Remove the vacuum diaphragm retaining clamp bolt and clamp. Do not pry on the clamp.
5. Pull the vacuum diaphragm from the transmission case and remove the vacuum diaphragm control rod from the transmission case.

To install:

6. Install the vacuum diaphragm control rod from the transmission case.
7. Push the vacuum diaphragm into the case and secure it with the clamp and bolt. Tighten to 80–106 inch lbs. (9–12Nm).
8. Fit the vacuum hose to the diaphragm.
9. Lower the vehicle.
10. Reconnect the negative battery cable.

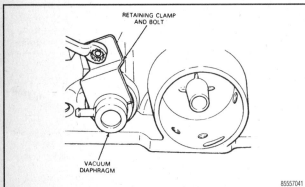

Fig. 18 Remove the vacuum diaphragm retaining clamp and bolt, then pull the diaphragm out of the transmission

Extension Housing Seal

REMOVAL & INSTALLATION

♦ **See Figures 19 and 20**

1. Disconnect the negative battery cable.
2. Raise and support the vehicle safely.
3. Matchmark the driveshaft end yoke and rear axle companion flange to assure proper positioning during assembly. Remove the driveshaft.
4. Remove the oil seal from the extension housing, using seal remover T71P-7657-A or equivalent.

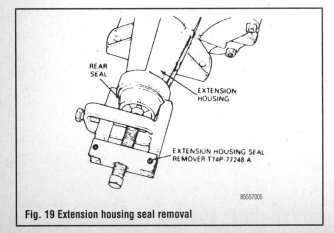

Fig. 19 Extension housing seal removal

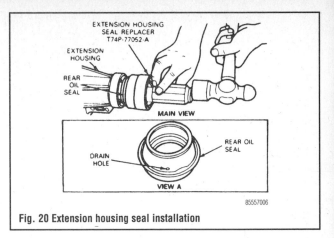

Fig. 20 Extension housing seal installation

To install:

Before install the replacement seal, inspect the sealing surface of the universal joint yoke for scores. If scoring is found, replace the yoke.

5. Install the new seal, using seal installer T74P-77052-A or equivalent. Coat the inside diameter at the end of the rubber boot portion of the seal with long-life lubricant (C1AZ-19590-BA or equivalent).
6. Align the matchmarks and install the driveshaft.
7. Lower the vehicle.
8. Reconnect the negative battery cable.

Transmission Assembly

REMOVAL & INSTALLATION

♦ **See Figures 21, 22, 23, 24 and 25**

1. Disconnect the negative battery cable.
2. Raise the vehicle and support it safely.
3. Position a drain pan under the transmission pan and drain the transmission fluid.
4. Remove the converter access cover from the lower right side of the converter housing on the 3.0L engine. Remove the cover from the bottom of the engine oil pan on the 2.3L and 2.5L engine. Remove a bolt on the access cover of the 2.9L engine and swing the cover open. Remove the access cover and adapter plate bolts from the lower left side of the converter housing on all other applications.
5. Remove the flywheel to converter attaching nuts. Use a socket and breaker bar on the crankshaft pulley attaching bolt. Rotate the pulley clockwise as viewed from the front to gain access to each of the nuts.

➡**On belt driven overhead cam engines, never rotate the pulley in a counterclockwise direction as viewed from the front.**

6. Remove the speedometer cable and/or vehicle speed sensor from the transfer case (4WD) or extension housing (2WD).
7. On 2WD vehicles, scribe a mark indexing the driveshaft to the rear axle flange. Remove the driveshaft.
8. On 4WD vehicles, remove the transfer case.
9. Disconnect the shift rod or cable at the transmission manual lever and retainer bracket.
10. Disconnect the downshift cable from the downshift lever. Depress the tab on the retainer and remove the kickdown cable from the bracket.
11. Disconnect all of the transmission wire harness plugs.
12. Remove the starter mounting bolts and the ground cable. Remove the starter.
13. If equipped, remove the vacuum line from the transmission vacuum modulator.
14. Remove the filler tube from the transmission.
15. Position a transmission jack under the transmission and raise it slightly.
16. Remove the engine rear support to crossmember bolts.
17. Remove the crossmember to frame side support attaching nuts and bolts. Remove the crossmember.
18. Remove the converter housing to engine bolts.

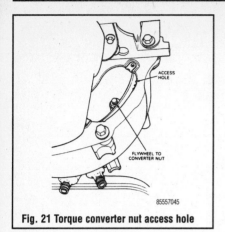

Fig. 21 Torque converter nut access hole

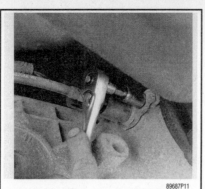

Remove the Vehicle Speed Sensor (VSS) clamp retaining bolt . . .

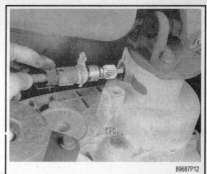

. . . then pull the VSS sensor from the transfer case (4WD) or extension housing (2WD)

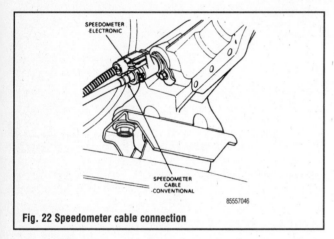

Fig. 22 Speedometer cable connection

19. Slightly lower the jack to gain access to the oil cooler lines. Disconnect the oil cooler lines at the transmission. Plug all openings to keep dirt and contamination out.

20. Move the transmission to the rear so it disengages from the dowel pins and the converter is disengaged from the flywheel. Lower the transmission from the vehicle.

21. If necessary, remove the torque converter from the transmission.

➡If the transmission is to be removed for a period of time, support the engine with a safety stand and wood block.

To install:

⁂ WARNING

Before installing an automatic transmission, always check that the torque converter is fully seated into the transmission. Typically, the

converter has notches or tangs on the hub which must engage the transmission fluid pump. If they are not engaged in the pump, the transmission will not mate to the engine properly, as the converter will be holding it away. Severe damage to the pump, converter or transmission casing can occur if the transmission-to-engine bolts are tightened as if to force the transmission to mate to the engine.

Proper installation of the converter requires full engagement of the converter hub in the pump gear. To accomplish this, the converter must be pushed and at the same time rotated through what feels like 2 notches or bumps. When fully installed, rotation of the converter will usually result in a clicking noise heard, caused by the converter surface touching the housing to case bolts.

This should not be a concern, but an indication of proper converter installation since, when the converter is attached to the engine flywheel, it will be pulled slightly forward away from the bolt heads. Besides the clicking sound, the converter should rotate freely with no binding.

For reference, a properly installed converter will have a distance from the converter pilot nose from face to converter housing outer face of $^{13}/_{32}$–$^{7}/_{16}$ in. (10.5–14.5mm).

22. Install the converter on the transmission.

23. With the converter properly installed, position the transmission on the jack.

24. Rotate the converter so that the drive studs are in alignment with the holes in the flywheel.

25. Move the converter and transmission assembly forward into position, being careful not to damage the flywheel and converter pilot. The converter housing is piloted into position by the dowels in the rear of the engine block.

➡During this move, to avoid damage, do not allow the transmission to get into a nose down position as this will cause the converter to move forward and disengage from the pump gear.

26. Install the converter housing to engine attaching bolts and tighten to specification. The 2 longer bolts are located at the dowel holes.

27. Remove the jack supporting the engine.

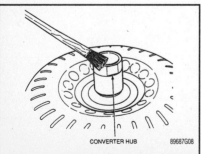

Fig. 23 Lightly lubricate the converter hub with transmission fluid. Note the machined fluid pump drive flat on the very edge of the hub (arrow)

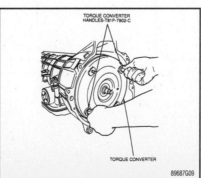

Fig. 24 Handles which thread onto the converter-to-flywheel studs can be use to ease the installation process

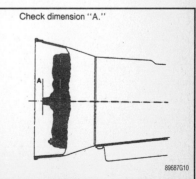

Fig. 25 Check dimension A to ensure that the converter is fully seated into the transmission and pump

28. The rest of the installation procedure is the reverse of removal. Always tighten all fasteners to specifications given. Follow the procedures outlined in Section 1 when filling the transmission with fluid.

ADJUSTMENTS

Shift/Manual Linkage

SHIFT SELECT LEVER

♦ See Figure 26

➡ **Before performing the linkage adjustment, confirm that the shift indicator is properly adjusted.**

1. Turn the vehicle **OFF**, block the rear wheels and engage the parking brake.
2. From inside the vehicle, place the gear shift lever in the overdrive position (shown as a circle with the letter D in the middle). On 1991 vehicles, hang an 8 lb. (3.6Kg) weight on the lever. On 1992–99 vehicles, use a 3 lb. (1.4Kg) weight.
3. Raise and safely support the vehicle.
4. From underneath, use a prytool to remove the shift control cable end from the transmission manual control lever ball stud.
5. Unlock the cable adjuster body by pushing down on the two tangs and releasing the lock tab.
6. Move the shift cable back and forth the full adjustment length four or five times to remove any accumulated dirt. Ensure that the adjuster body moves freely.
7. Move the transmission manual control lever all the way rearward (counterclockwise) to its last position, then move it forward three detent positions. The transmission is now set in the overdrive position.
8. Holding the cable end fitting, push it rearward until the fitting lines up with the lever ball stud. Connect the cable end to the ball stud.
9. Push up on the lock tab to lock the adjuster body into position. Ensure that the locator tab is properly seated.
10. Ensure that the shift cable is properly clipped to the floorpan and that is routed into the tunnel.

11. Lower the vehicle.
12. Remove the weight from the gear select lever.
13. After adjustment, check for Park (P) engagement. Start the engine and check all the lever positions for proper operation.

SHIFT SELECT INDICATOR

♦ See Figures 27, 28, 29 and 30

To test the shift select indicator:
1. Turn the engine **OFF**, apply the parking brake and place the transmission select lever in the OD (overdrive) position.
2. Hang a 3 lb. (1.4Kg) weight on the select lever.
3. Look at the selector indicator on the instrument panel. The pointer should be centered on the D within the overdrive (circle with a letter D in the middle) graphic. If it is not, adjust as follows.
To adjust the indicator:
4. Remove the steering wheel.
5. Remove the lower steering column trim panel from the dash board.
6. Remove the lower steering column shroud by removing the two securing screws.
7. Lift off the upper steering column shroud.
8. On 1996–99 vehicles, remove the ignition switch lock cylinder.
9. With the engine **OFF** and the parking brake set, move the transmission select lever into the overdrive position. Hang a 3 lb. (1.4Kg) weight on the lever.
10. On 1991 vehicles, loosen the indicator cable end screw, then move the cable end to properly position the pointer until it is centered on the overdrive graphic. Tighten the cable end screw.
11. On 1992–99 vehicles, turn the adjuster thumb wheel to properly position the pointer until it is centered on the overdrive graphic.
12. If removed, install the ignition switch lock cylinder.
13. Install the upper and lower steering column shrouds and the steering wheel.
14. Remove the weight from the lever.
15. Operate the shift select lever in all positions and ensure that the indicator pointer aligns with all of the position graphics.

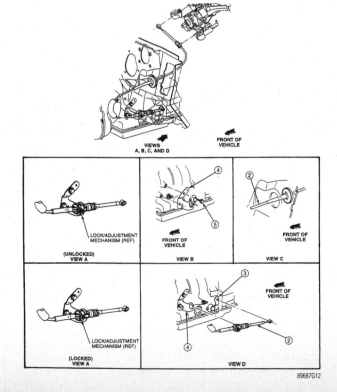

1. Transmission column shift selector tube
2. Shift cable and bracket
3. Manual control lever
4. Transmission shift cable bracket
5. Bolt

Fig. 26 Exploded views of the shift cable assembly and mounting

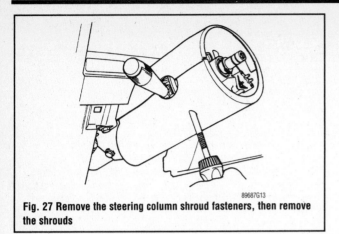

Fig. 27 Remove the steering column shroud fasteners, then remove the shrouds

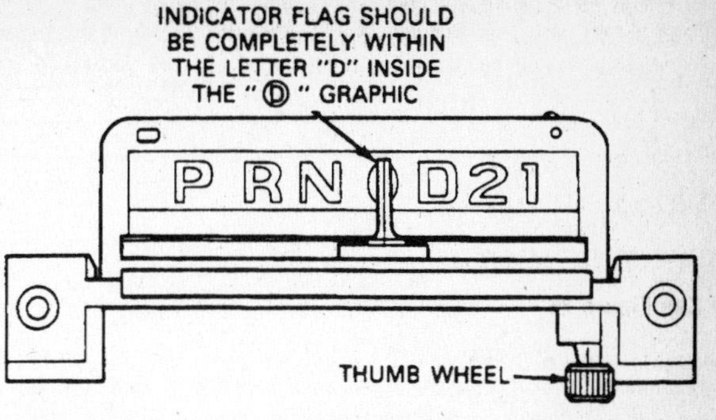

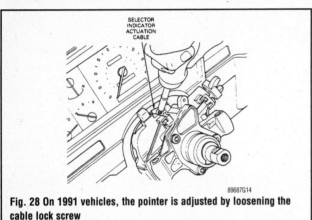

Fig. 28 On 1991 vehicles, the pointer is adjusted by loosening the cable lock screw

INDICATOR FLAG SHOULD BE COMPLETELY WITHIN THE LETTER "D" INSIDE THE "Ⓓ" GRAPHIC

P R N Ⓓ 2 1

THUMB WHEEL

Fig. 29 On 1992 and later vehicles, there are two styles of thumb wheel adjusters. One style is mounted to the indicator assembly . . .

STEERING COLUMN ASSEMBLY

TRANSMISSION SELECTOR LEVER ARM

THUMBWHEEL

TRANSMISSION CONTROL SELECTOR INDICATOR

Fig. 30 . . . the other style is mounted to the underside of the column

KICKDOWN CABLE

▶ **See Figure 31**

The kickdown cable is self-adjusting over a tolerance range of 1 in. (25mm). If the cable requires readjustment, reset the by depressing the semi-circular metal tab on the self-adjuster mechanism and pulling the cable forward (toward the front of the vehicle) to the "Zero" position setting. The cable will then automatically readjust to the proper length when kicked down.

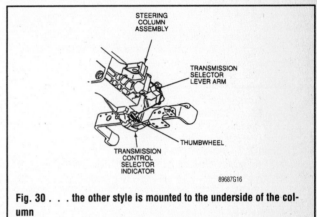

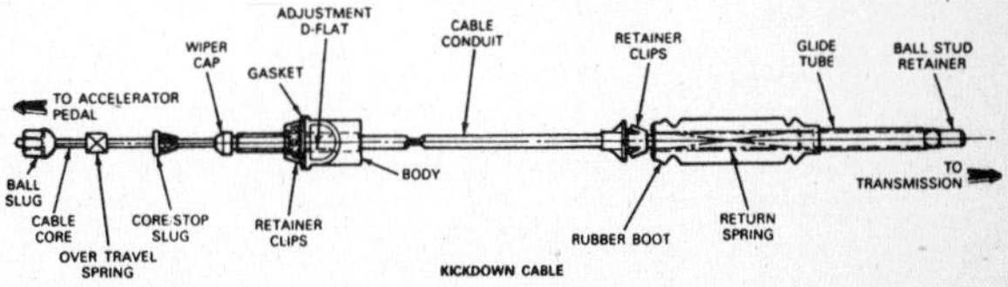

Fig. 31 View of the transmission kickdown cable assemble and its adjusting points

TRANSFER CASE

Identification

▶ **See Figure 32**

There are three transfer cases used on the Ranger, Explorer and Mountaineer. There are 2 versions of the Borg Warner 13-54 (mechanical shift and electronic shift), a Borg Warner 44-05 (Control Trac) and an All Wheel Drive (AWD) transfer case.

The Borg Warner 13-54, mechanical shift transfer case, is a 3-piece aluminum part time unit. It transfers power from the transmission to the rear axle and when actuated, also the front drive axle. The unit is lubricated by a positive displacement oil pump that channels oil flow through drilled holes in the rear output shaft. The pump turns with the rear output shaft and allows towing of the vehicle at maximum legal road speeds for extended distances without disconnecting the front and/or rear driveshaft.

The Borg Warner 13-54, electronic shift transfer case, transfers power from the transmission to the rear axle and also the front drive axle, when electronically actuated.

This system consists of a pushbutton control, an electronic control module, an electric shift motor with an integral shift position sensor and a speed sensor.

The electric shift motor, mounted externally at the rear of the transfer case, drives a rotary helical cam. The cam moves the 2WD-4WD shift fork and 4H-4L reduction shift fork to the selected vehicle drive position. The system has no selectable Neutral (N) setting.

➡**The manufacturer recommends that the Borg Warner 13-54 transfer case equipped vehicles should not be operated in 4WD (whether HI or LOW) mode on dry pavement. Severe driveline torsional wind-up will occur, possibly damaging the drivetrain components.**

The Borg Warner 44-05 transfer case operates in the same manner as the 13-54, except that it also houses a transfer case clutch. This clutch, which is controlled by the Generic Control Module (GEM), enables the vehicle to be driven in 4-wheel drive on dry pavement by cycling the clutch to compensate for different front and rear driveshaft speeds (as in turning). The system has a dealer installable Neutral (N) position mode.

The All Wheel Drive (AWD) transfer case is a 2-piece aluminum, chain driven, viscous clutch type unit. The AWD transfer case is always active in 4-wheel drive, thus producing a full-time engagement. The viscous clutch automatically distributes power to both the front and rear wheels, depending on need.

Rear Output Shaft Seal

REMOVAL & INSTALLATION

▶ **See Figures 33 and 34**

1. Raise and safely support the vehicle.
2. Matchmark the rear driveshaft to the transfer case yoke then disconnect the shaft from the yoke. Wire the driveshaft up and out of the way.
3. Using a 30mm (1.18 in.) thin-wall socket, remove the rear output shaft yoke retaining nut.

➡**Some fluid may dribble out as the yoke is removed, and then again when the seal is removed. While an old rag should suffice for catching the fluid, a small catch can may be better, especially if the vehicle is not parked level.**

4. Remove the output shaft yoke washer, rubber seal and the yoke from the output shaft.
5. Remove the rear output shaft seal by prying and pulling on the curved outer lip of the seal or by using Impact Slide Hammer Tool T50T-100-A and Seal Remover T74P-77248-A or equivalent. Take care to not damage the bearing, bearing cage or case.

To install:

6. Ensure that the output housing bore is free of any dirt, burrs or nicks. Apply premium long-life grease to the seal lip.
7. Position the new seal to the output housing and using an appropriate driver, such as the Output Shaft Seal Replacer T83T-7065-B and Driver Handle T80T-4000-W, press the seal into the housing until fully seated.
8. Install the rear out put shaft yoke, rubber seal and washer.
9. Install the output shaft yoke retaining nut and tighten to 250–280 ft. lbs. (339–381 Nm).
10. Connect the rear driveshaft to the transfer case.
11. Lower the vehicle.
12. Drive the vehicle and check for leaks.

Front Output Shaft Seal

REMOVAL & INSTALLATION

Borg Warner 13-54 and 1995–96 44-05 models

▶ **See Figures 33, 34 and 35**

1. Raise and safely support the vehicle.
2. If equipped, remove the skid plate from the frame.
3. If equipped, remove the damper from the transfer case.
4. Place a drain pan under the transfer case, remove the drain plug and drain the fluid.
5. Matchmark the front driveshaft to the transfer case yoke then disconnect the shaft from the yoke. Wire the driveshaft up and out of the way.
6. Using a 30mm (1.18 in.) thin-wall socket, remove the rear output shaft yoke retaining nut.
7. Remove the output shaft yoke washer, rubber seal and the yoke from the output shaft.
8. Remove the front output shaft seal using Impact Slide Hammer Tool T50T-100-A or equivalent.

To install:

9. Ensure that the output housing bore is free of any dirt, burrs or nicks. Apply premium long-life grease to the seal lip.
10. Position the new seal to the output housing and using an appropriate driver, such as the Output Shaft Seal Replacer T83T-7065-B and Driver Handle T80T-4000-W, press the seal into the housing until fully seated.
11. Install the front output shaft yoke, rubber seal and washer.
12. Install the output shaft yoke retaining nut and tighten to 250–280 ft. lbs. (339–381 Nm).
13. Connect the front driveshaft to the transfer case.
14. If removed, install the damper.

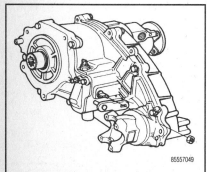

Fig. 32 View of the Borg-Warner model 13-54 with mechanical shift. Electronic shift and model 44-05 are similar

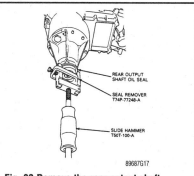

Fig. 33 Remove the rear output shaft seal—slide hammer and seal removal tool shown

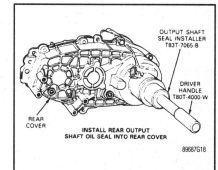

Fig. 34 Drive the new seal into the case housing using the appropriate seal installation tool

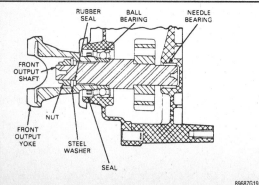

Fig. 35 Cutaway view of the front output shaft, seal and yoke assembly—rear components are similar

15. Remove the oil fill plug and add the proper amount of Dexron/Mercon® automatic transmission fluid.
16. If removed, install the skid plate.
17. Lower the vehicle.
18. Drive the vehicle and check for leaks.

AWD and 1997–99 Borg Warner 44-05 Models

In order to replace the front output shaft seal on the AWD and 1997–99 Borg Warner 44-05 transfer cases, they must be removed from the vehicle and their cases must be split. The output shaft is retained internally by a snapring. Consult a professional repair shop as specialized knowledge of transfer cases is required.

Transfer Case Assembly

REMOVAL & INSTALLATION

▶ **See Figures 36, 37 and 38**

> ☀☀ **CAUTION**
>
> **The catalytic converter is located beside the transfer case. Be careful when working around the catalytic converter because of the extremely high temperatures generated by the converter.**

1. Disconnect the negative battery cable.
2. Raise the vehicle and support it safely.
3. If so equipped, remove the skid plate from frame.
4. Remove the damper from the transfer case, if so equipped.
5. On electronic shift models, remove the wire connector from the feed wire harness at the rear of the transfer case. Be sure to squeeze the locking tabs, then pull the connectors apart.
6. Disconnect the front driveshaft from the axle input yoke.
7. If equipped, loosen the clamp retaining the front driveshaft boot to the transfer case, and pull the driveshaft and front boot assembly out of the transfer case front output shaft.
8. Disconnect the rear driveshaft from the transfer case output shaft yoke.
9. If equipped, disconnect the speedometer driven gear from the transfer case rear cover.

10. If equipped, disconnect the electrical wire harness plug from the Vehicle Speed Sensor (VSS).
11. Disconnect the vent hose from the mounting bracket.
12. On manual shift models, perform the following:
    a. Remove the shift lever retaining nut and remove the lever.
    b. Remove the bolts that retains the shifter to the extension housing. Note the size and location of the bolts to aid during installation. Remove the lever assembly and bushing.
13. If equipped, remove the heat shield from the transfer case.
14. Support the transfer case with a transmission jack.
15. Remove the 5 bolts (6 bolts on the AWD transfer case) retaining the transfer case to the transmission and the extension housing.
16. Slide the transfer case rearward off the transmission output shaft and lower the transfer case from the vehicle. Remove the gasket from between the transfer case and extension housing.

To install:

17. Install the heat shield onto the transfer case, if equipped, and place a new gasket between the transfer case and adapter.
18. Raise the transfer case with a suitable transmission jack or equivalent, raise it high enough so that the transmission output shaft aligns with the splined transfer case input shaft.
19. Slide the transfer case forward on to the transmission output shaft and onto the dowel pin. Install transfer case retaining bolts and torque them to specification.
20. The remainder of the installation procedure is the reverse of removal. Check the fluid level and, if necessary, top off with Dexron/Mercon automatic transmission fluid to achieve the proper level.

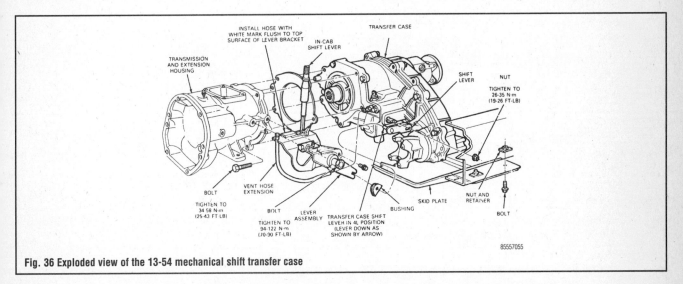

Fig. 36 Exploded view of the 13-54 mechanical shift transfer case

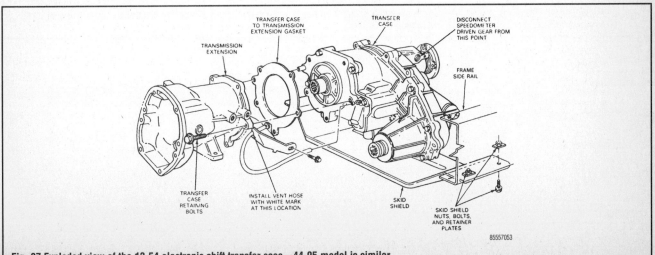

Fig. 37 Exploded view of the 13-54 electronic shift transfer case—44-05 model is similar

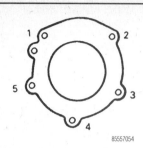

85557054

Fig. 38 Case-to-extension bolt torque sequence for all models except the AWD transfer case

ADJUSTMENTS

Manual Shift Models

▶ **See Figure 39**

The following procedure should be used, if a partial or incomplete engagement of the transfer case shift lever detent is experienced or if the control assembly requires removal.

1. Disconnect the negative battery cable.
2. Raise the shift boot to expose the top surface of the cam plates.
3. Loosen the 1 large and 1 small bolt, approximately 1 turn. Move the transfer case shift lever to the **4L** position (lever down).
4. Move the cam plate rearward until the bottom chamfered corner of the neutral lug just contacts the forward right edge of the shift lever.
5. Hold the cam plate in this position and torque the larger bolt first to 70–90 ft. lbs. (95–122 Nm) and torque the smaller bolt to 31–42 ft. lbs. (42–57 Nm).
6. Move the transfer case in cab shift lever to all shift positions to check for positive engagement. There should be a clearance between the shift lever and the cam plate in the **2H** front and **4H** rear (clearance not to exceed 3.3mm) and **4L** shift positions.
7. Install the shift boot assembly.
8. Reconnect the negative battery cable.

Except Manual Shift Models

Both of the electronic shift and the AWD model transfer cases do not require any linkage adjustments, nor are any possible.

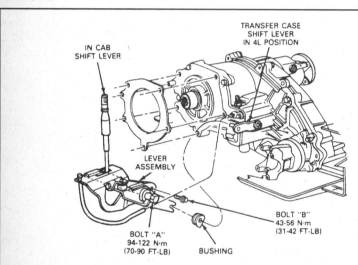

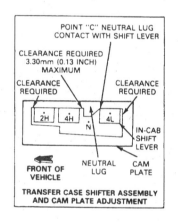

89687G20

Fig. 39 Exploded view of the manual shift transfer case controls

DRIVELINE

General Description

The driveshaft is a steel tubular or aluminum shaft which is used to transfer the torque from the engine, through the transmission output shaft, to the differential in the axle, which in turn transmits torque to the wheels.

The splined slip yoke and transmission output shaft permit the driveshaft to move forward and rearward as the axle moves up and down. This provides smooth performance during vehicle operation.

The front driveshaft connects the power flow from the transfer case to the front drive axle.

Some vehicles may be equipped with a Double Cardan type driveshaft. This driveshaft incorporates 2 U-joints, a centering socket yoke and a center slip at the transfer case end of each shaft. A single U-joint is used at the axle end of the shaft.

The Constant Velocity (CV) type U-joint allows the driveline angel to be adjusted according to the up-and-down movement of the vehicle without disturbing the power flow. The CV U-joint is composed of an outer bearing retainer and flange, spring, cap, circlip, inner bearing assembly and wire ring. The inner bearing assembly is composed of a bearing cage, 6 ball bearings and an inner race.

The driveshafts used on Ranger, Explorer and Mountaineer may be 1 of 3 types. They are as follows:
- Front and rear driveshaft—Single Cardan type U-joint
- Front and rear driveshaft—Double Cardan type U-joint
- Rear driveshaft—CV (Constant Velocity) type U-joint

Single Cardan Type Front Driveshaft

REMOVAL & INSTALLATION

▶ **See Figure 40**

1. Disconnect the negative battery cable.
2. Raise and support the vehicle safely.

➡**The driveshaft is a balanced unit. Before removing the drive shaft, matchmark the driveshaft in relationship to the end yoke so that it may be installed in its original position.**

3. Using a shop cloth or gloves, pull back on the dust slinger to remove the boot from the transfer case slip yoke.

Troubleshooting Basic Driveshaft and Rear Axle Problems

When abnormal vibrations or noises are detected in the driveshaft area, this chart can be used to help diagnose possible causes. Remember that other components such as wheels, tires, rear axle and suspension can also produce similar conditions.

BASIC DRIVESHAFT PROBLEMS

Problem	Cause	Solution
Shudder as car accelerates from stop or low speed	• Loose U-joint • Defective center bearing	• Replace U-joint • Replace center bearing
Loud clunk in driveshaft when shifting gears	• Worn U-joints	• Replace U-joints
Roughness or vibration at any speed	• Out-of-balance, bent or dented driveshaft • Worn U-joints • U-joint clamp bolts loose	• Balance or replace driveshaft • Replace U-joints • Tighten U-joint clamp bolts
Squeaking noise at low speeds	• Lack of U-joint lubrication	• Lubricate U-joint; if problem persists, replace U-joint
Knock or clicking noise	• U-joint or driveshaft hitting frame tunnel • Worn CV joint	• Correct overloaded condition • Replace CV joint

85557057

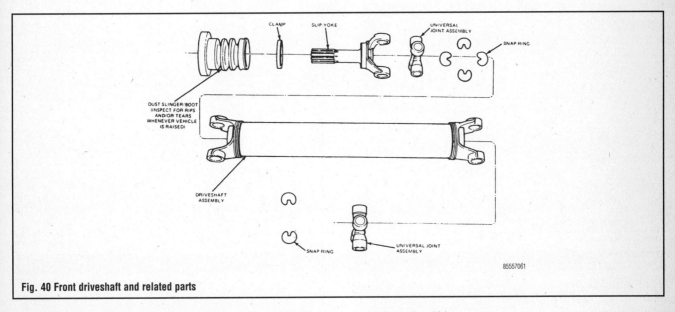

Fig. 40 Front driveshaft and related parts

4. Remove the bolts and straps that retains the driveshaft to the front driving axle yoke. Remove the U-joint assembly from the front driving axle yoke.

5. Slide the splined yoke assembly out of the transfer case and remove the driveshaft assembly.

6. Inspect the boot for rips or tears. Inspect the stud yoke splines for wear or damage. Replace any damage parts.

To install:

7. Apply a light coating of Multi-purpose Long-Life lubricant C1AZ-19490-B or equivalent, to the yoke splines and the edge of the inner diameter of the rubber boot.

8. Slide the driveshaft into the transfer case front output yoke assembly. Make certain the wide tooth splines on the slip yoke are indexed to the output yoke in the transfer case.

9. Position the U-joint assembly in the front drive axle yoke in its original position. Install the retaining bolts and straps. Tighten the bolts to 10–15 ft. lbs. (14–20Nm).

10. Firmly press the dust slinger until the boot is felt to engage the output yoke in the transfer case.

11. Lower the vehicle.

12. Connect the negative battery cable.

➡If replacement of the dust slinger/boot is necessary. Use the following procedure.

DUST SLINGER/BOOT REPLACEMENT

◆ **See Figure 41**

1. Remove the boot clamp using cutter pliers and discard the clamp. Remove the boot from the stud yoke.

2. Install a new dust slinger/boot on the stud yoke making certain the boot is seated in the groove in the yoke.

3. Install a new clamp on the boot. Position the clamp tabs in the slots so each tab fits into a slot. Then, crimp the clamp securely using a pair of clamp pliers T63P-9171-A or equivalent. Do not crimp to the point where the clamp damage the boot.

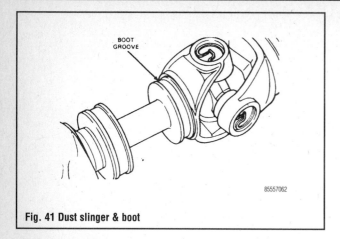

Fig. 41 Dust slinger & boot

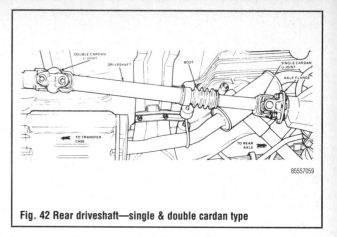

Fig. 42 Rear driveshaft—single & double cardan type

Double Cardan Type Front and Rear Driveshaft

REMOVAL & INSTALLATION

▶ **See Figure 42**

1. Disconnect the negative battery cable.
2. Raise and support the vehicle safely.

➡ **The driveshaft is a balanced unit. Before removing the drive shaft, matchmark the driveshaft in relationship to the axle flange so that it may be installed in its original position.**

3. Remove the bolts retaining the flange to the transfer case. Disconnect the U-joint from the flange at the transfer case.
4. Remove the bolts retaining the flange to the rear axle. Disconnect the U-joint from the flange at the rear axle.
5. Remove the driveshaft.

To install:

6. Position the single U-joint end of the driveshaft to the rear axle and install the retaining bolts. Tighten the bolts to 61–87 ft. lbs. (83–118Nm).
7. Position the double Cardan U-joint to the transfer case and install the retaining bolts. Tighten the bolts to 12–16 ft. lbs. (17–22Nm).
8. Lower the vehicle.
9. Re-connect the negative battery cable.

DISASSEMBLY & ASSEMBLY

▶ **See Figures 43, 44 and 45**

1. Place the driveshaft on a suitable workbench.
2. Matchmark the positions of the spiders, the center yoke and the centering socket yoke as related to the stud yoke which is welded to the front of the driveshaft tube.

➡ **The spiders must be assembled with the bosses in their original position to provide proper clearance.**

3. Remove the snaprings that secure the bearings in the front of the center yoke.
4. Position the U-joint tool, T74P-4635-C or equivalent, on the center yoke. Thread the tool clockwise until the bearing protrudes approximately ⅜ in. (10mm) out of the yoke.
5. Position the bearing in a vice and tap on the center yoke to free it from the bearing. Lift the 2 bearing cups from the spider.
6. Re-position the tool on the yoke and move the remaining bearing in the opposite direction so that it protrudes approximately ⅜ in. (10mm) out of the yoke.
7. Position the bearing in a vice. Tap on the center yoke to free it from the bearing. Remove the spider from the center yoke.
8. Pull the centering socket yoke off the center stud. Remove the rubber seal from the centering ball stud.
9. Remove the snaprings from the center yoke and from the driveshaft yoke.
10. Position the tool on the driveshaft yoke and press the bearing outward

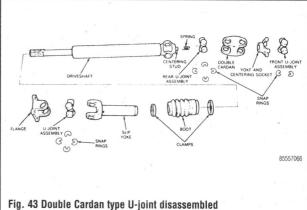

Fig. 43 Double Cardan type U-joint disassembled

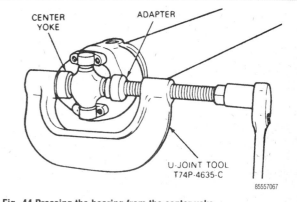

Fig. 44 Pressing the bearing from the center yoke

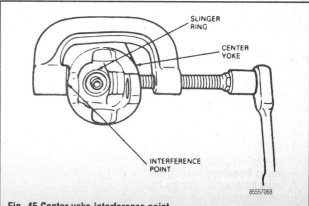

Fig. 45 Center yoke interference point

until the inside of the center yoke almost contacts the slinger ring at the front of the driveshaft yoke. Pressing beyond this point can distort the slinger ring interference point.

11. Clamp the exposed end of the bearing in a vice and drive on the center yoke with a soft-faced hammer to free it from the bearing.

12. Reposition the tool and press on the spider to remove the opposite bearing.

13. Remove the center yoke from the spider. Remove the spider form the driveshaft yoke.

14. Clean all serviceable parts in cleaning solvent. If using a repair kit, install all of the parts supplied in the kit.

15. Remove the clamps on the driveshaft boot seal. Discard the clamps.

16. Note the orientation of the slip yoke to the driveshaft tube for installation during assembly. Mark the position of the slip yoke to the driveshaft tube.

17. Carefully pull the slip yoke from the driveshaft. Be careful not to damage the boot seal.

18. Clean and inspect the spline area of the driveshaft.

To assemble:

19. Lubricate the driveshaft slip splines with Multi-purpose Long-Life lubricant C1AZ-19490-B or equivalent.

20. With the boot loosely installed on the driveshaft tube, install the slip yoke into the driveshaft splines in their original orientation.

21. Using new clamps, install the driveshaft boot in its original position.

22. To assemble the double Cardan joint, position the spider in the driveshaft yoke. Make certain the spider bosses (or lubrication plugs on kits) will be in the same position as originally installed. Press in the bearing using the U-joint tool. Then, install the snaprings.

23. Pack the socket relief and the ball with Multi-purpose Long-Life lubricant C1AZ-19490-B or equivalent, then position the center yoke over the spider ends and press in the bearing. Install the snaprings.

24. Install a new seal on the centering ball stud. Position the centering socket yoke on the stud.

25. Place the front spider in the center yoke. Make certain the spider bosses (or lubrication plugs on kits) are properly positioned.

26. With the spider loosely positioned on the center stop, seat the first pair of bearings into the centering socket yoke. Then, press the second pair into the centering yoke. Install the snaprings.

27. Apply pressure on the centering socket yoke and install the remaining bearing cup.

28. If a kit was used, lubricate the U-joint through the grease fitting, using Multi-purpose Long-Life lubricant C1AZ-19490-B or equivalent.

Single Cardan Type Rear Driveshaft

REMOVAL & INSTALLATION

◆ **See Figures 42 and 46**

Except 4WD Ranger

1. Disconnect the negative battery cable.
2. Raise and support the vehicle safely.

➥The driveshaft is a balanced unit. Before removing the drive shaft, matchmark the driveshaft yoke in relationship to the axle flange so that it may be installed in its original position.

3. On Super Cab vehicles, remove the center bearing assembly-to-frame retaining bolts. Remove the spacers under the center bearing bracket, if installed.

4. Remove the retaining bolts and disconnect the driveshaft from the axle companion flange. Pull the driveshaft rearward until the slip yoke clears the transmission extension housing and seal. Plug the extension housing to prevent lubricant leakage.

To install:

5. Lubricate the slip yoke splines with Multi-purpose Long-Life lubricant C1AZ-19490-B or equivalent. Remove the plug from the extension housing.

6. Inspect the extension housing seal. Replace, if necessary.

7. Install the driveshaft assembly. Do not allow the slip yoke assembly to bottom on the output shaft with excessive force.

8. Install the driveshaft so the index mark on the rear yoke is in line with the

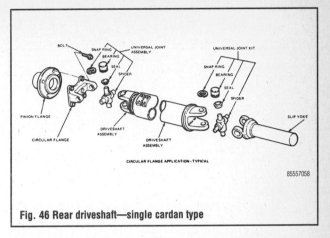

Fig. 46 Rear driveshaft—single cardan type

index mark on the axle companion flange. Tighten all circular flange bolts to 61–87 ft. lbs. (83–118Nm).

9. On Super Cab vehicles, tighten the center bearing retaining bolts to 27–37 ft. lbs. (37–50Nm).

➥**Make certain the center bearing bracket assembly is reinstalled "square" to the vehicle. If the spacers were installed under the center bearing be sure to reinstall them.**

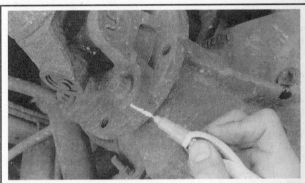

Before unbolting the driveshaft, matchmark the shaft and axle flanges to maintain proper balance . . .

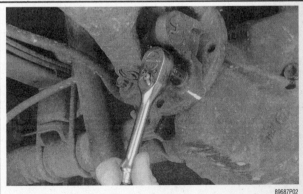

. . . then remove the driveshaft-to-axle flange retaining bolts

4WD Ranger

1. Disconnect the negative battery cable.
2. Raise and support the vehicle safely.

➥**The driveshaft is a balanced unit. Before removing the drive shaft, matchmark the driveshaft yoke in relationship to the axle flange so that it may be installed in its original position.**

3. On Super Cab vehicles, remove the center bearing assembly-to-frame retaining bolts. Remove the spacers under the center bearing bracket, if installed.

4. Remove the retaining bolts and disconnect the driveshaft from the axle companion flange.

5. Remove the retaining bolts that retains the driveshaft to the rear of transfer case.

6. Remove the driveshaft.

To install:

7. Install the driveshaft into the rear of the transfer case. Make certain that the driveshaft is positioned with the slip yoke toward the front of the vehicle. Install the bolts and tighten to 41–55 ft. lbs. (55–74Nm).

8. Install the driveshaft so the index mark on the rear yoke is in line with the index mark on the axle companion flange.

9. On Super Cab vehicles, tighten the center bearing retaining bolts to 27–37 ft. lbs. (37–50Nm).

➡**Make certain the center bearing bracket assembly is reinstalled "square" to the vehicle. If the spacers were installed under the center bearing be sure to reinstall them.**

DISASSEMBLY & ASSEMBLY

◆ **See Figures 47 and 48**

1. Prior to disassembly, mark the position of the driveshaft components relative to the driveshaft tube. All components must be re-assembled in the same relationship to maintain proper balance.

2. Place the driveshaft on a suitable workbench.

3. Remove the snaprings that retain the bearing cups.

4. Position the U-joint removal tool, T74P-4635-C or equivalent, on the slip yoke and press out the bearing. If the bearing cup cannot be pressed all the way out of the slip yoke, remove it with vise grip or channel lock pliers.

5. Reposition the tool 180° to press on the spider and remove the remaining bearing cup from the opposite side.

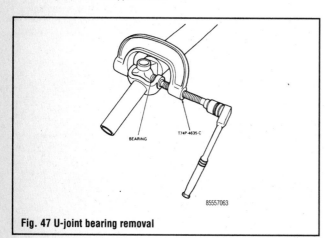

Fig. 47 U-joint bearing removal

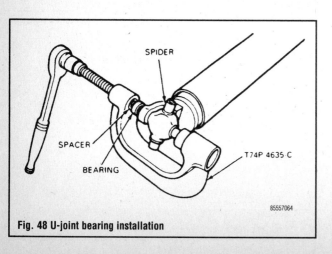

Fig. 48 U-joint bearing installation

6. On 2WD vehicles, remove the slip yoke form the spider. On 4WD vehicles, remove the spider from the driveshaft.

7. Remove the remaining bearing cups and spiders from the driveshaft in the same manner.

8. Clean the yoke area at each end of the driveshaft.

9. Four Wheel Drive (4WD) vehicles only:

a. Remove the clamps on the driveshaft boot seal. Discard the clamp.

b. Note the orientation of the slip yoke to the driveshaft tube for installation during assembly. Mark the position of the slip yoke to the driveshaft tube.

c. Carefully pull the slip yoke from the driveshaft. Be careful not to damage the boot seal.

d. Clean and inspect the spline area of the driveshaft.

To assemble:

10. Four Wheel Drive (4WD) vehicles only:

a. Lubricate the driveshaft slip splines with Multi-purpose Long-Life lubricant C1AZ-19490-B or equivalent.

b. With the boot loosely installed on the driveshaft tube, install the slip yoke into the driveshaft splines in their original orientation.

c. Using new clamps, install the driveshaft boot in its original position.

11. Start a new bearing cup into the yoke at the rear of the driveshaft.

12. Position the new spider in the rear yoke and press the bearing cup ¼ in. (6mm) below the yoke surface, using spacer.

13. Remove the tool and install a new snapring.

14. Start a new bearing cup into the opposite side of the yoke.

15. Position the U-joint tool and press on the bearing cup until the opposite bearing cup contacts the snapring.

16. Remove the tool and install a new snapring. It may be necessary to grind the surface of the snapring to permit easier entry.

17. Reposition the driveshaft and install the remaining bearing cups and spider in the same manner.

18. Check the universal joints for freedom of movement. If binding has resulted from misalignment during assembly, a sharp rap on the yokes with a brass hammer will seat the bearing needles. Be sure to support the shaft end during this procedure and do not strike the bearings themselves. Make certain the universal joints are free to rotate easily without binding before installing the driveshaft.

19. Lubricate the U-joint assemblies with Multi-purpose Long-Life lubricant C1AZ-19490-B or equivalent.

Constant Velocity (CV) Type Rear Driveshaft

REMOVAL & INSTALLATION

◆ **See Figure 49**

1. Disconnect the negative battery cable.

2. Raise and support the vehicle safely.

➡**The driveshaft is a balanced unit. Before removing the drive shaft, matchmark the driveshaft in relationship to the flange on the transfer case and the flange on the rear axle so that it may be installed in its original position.**

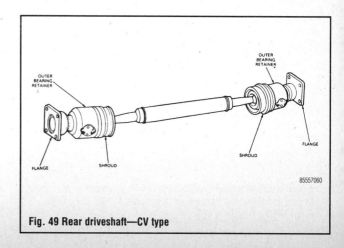

Fig. 49 Rear driveshaft—CV type

3. Remove the bolts retaining the driveshaft to the transfer case.

4. Remove the bolts retaining the driveshaft to the rear axle flange.

5. Remove the driveshaft.

To install:

6. Position the driveshaft to the rear axle flange so that the marks made previously are line up. Install and tighten the retaining bolts to 61–87 ft. lbs. (83–118Nm).

7. Position the driveshaft to the transfer case flange so that the marks made previously are line up. Install and tighten the retaining bolts to 61–87 ft. lbs. (83–118Nm).

8. Lower the vehicle.

9. Reconnect the negative battery cable.

DISASSEMBLY & ASSEMBLY

▶ **See Figures 50, 51, 52 and 53**

1. Place the driveshaft on a suitable workbench.

➡ **The CV joint components are matched. Extreme care should be take not to mix or substitute components.**

2. Remove the clamp retaining the shroud to the outer bearing race and flange assembly.

3. Carefully tap the shroud lightly with a blunt tool and remove the shroud. Be careful not to damage the shroud, dust boot or outer bearing race and flange assembly.

4. Peel the boot upward and away from the outer bearing race and flange assembly.

5. Remove the wire ring that retains the inner race to the outer race.

6. Remove the inner race and shaft assembly from the outer race and flange assembly. Remove the cap and spring from inside the outer retainer.

7. Remove the circlip retaining the inner race assembly to the shaft, using snapring pliers. Discard the clip and remove the inner race assembly.

8. If required, remove the clamp retaining the boot to the shaft and remove the boot.

9. Carefully pry the ball bearings from the cage. Be careful not to scratch or damage the cage, race or ball bearings.

10. Rotate the inner race to align with the cage windows and remove the inner race through the wider end of the cage.

To assemble:

11. Install the inner bearing race in the bearing cage. Install the race through the large end of the cage with the counterbore facing the large end of the cage.

12. Push the race to the top of the cage and rotate the race until all the ball slots are aligned with the windows. This will lock the race to the top of the cage.

13. With the bearing cage and inner race properly aligned, install the ball bearings. The bearings can be pressed through the bearing cage with the heel of the hand. Repeat this step until the remaining ball bearings are installed.

14. If removed, install a new dust boot on the shaft, using a new clamp. Make certain the boot is seated in its groove.

➡ **The clamp is a fixed diameter push-on metal ring.**

15. Install the inner bearing assembly on the shaft. Make certain the circlip is exposed.

16. Install a new circlip on the shaft. Do not over-expand or twist the circlip during installation.

17. Install the spring and cap in the outer bearing retainer and flange.

18. Fill the outer bearing retainer with 3 oz. of Constant Velocity Joint Grease, D8RZ-19590-A or equivalent.

19. Insert the inner race and shaft assembly in the outer bearing retainer and flange.

20. Push the inner race down until the wire spring groove is visible and install the wire ring.

21. Fill the top of the outer bearing retainer with Constant Velocity Joint Grease, D8RZ-19590-A or equivalent. Remove all excess grease from the external surfaces.

22. Pull the dust boot over the retainer. Make certain the boot is seated in the groove and that any air pressure which may have built up in the boot is relieved.

➡ **Insert a dulled screwdriver blade between the boot and outer bearing retainer and allow the trapped air to escape from the boot.**

23. Install the shroud over the boot and retainer and install the clamp.

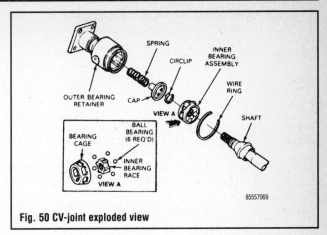

Fig. 50 CV-joint exploded view

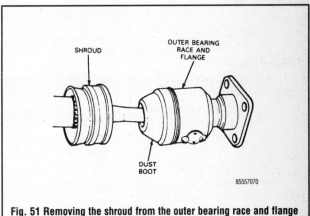

Fig. 51 Removing the shroud from the outer bearing race and flange

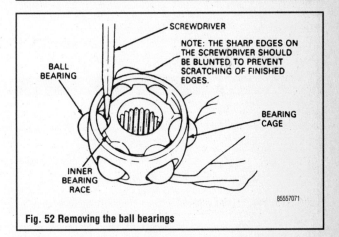

Fig. 52 Removing the ball bearings

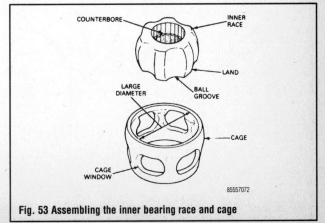

Fig. 53 Assembling the inner bearing race and cage

Center Bearing

REMOVAL & INSTALLATION

▶ See Figure 54

1. Remove the driveshaft from the vehicle.
2. Separate the driveshaft from the coupling shaft maintaining proper orientation.
3. Remove the nut retaining the half round yoke to the coupling shaft and remove the yoke.
4. Check the center bearing support for wear by rotating the outer area while holding the coupling shaft. If any wear or roughness is evident, replace the bearing.
5. Inspect the rubber insulator for evidence of hardness, cracking or deterioration. Replace if damaged in any way.
6. Re-install the coupling shaft yoke.

➡ Be sure the yoke is re-installed on the coupling shaft in the same orientation as it was originally installed. The orientation is critical so that proper driveshaft balance and U-joint phasing is maintained. Tighten the retaining nut to 100–120 ft. lbs. (135–162Nm).

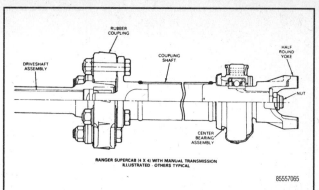

Fig. 54 Cutaway view of the coupling shaft and center support bearing

7. Re-assemble the driveshaft to the coupling shaft, maintaining proper orientation.

FRONT DRIVE AXLE

General Information

The front drive axle on the Ranger, Explorer and Mountaineer can be either the Dana 28 series, or the Dana 35 series. However, there are two versions of the Dana 35 and while both are an Independent Front Suspension (IFS) axle, their differences are drastic.

The Mountaineer, 1995–99 Explorer and 1998–99 Rangers use a centrally mounted front differential with unequal length upper and lower control arms and front axle halfshafts. Also, these axle assemblies do not use hub-locks at the wheel ends. Instead, they use a vacuum operated disconnect system mounted to the axle housing, which locks and unlocks the axles. See Vacuum Disconnect Axle Lock later in this section for service procedures.

All other models use the twin I-beam style front axle assembly with either manual or automatic locking hubs at the wheel ends.

Manual Locking Hubs

REMOVAL & INSTALLATION

▶ See Figure 55

1. Loosen the front wheel lug nuts.
2. Raise and safely support the front of the vehicle.
3. Remove the lug nuts and wheel/tire assembly.
4. If equipped, remove the lug nut retainer washers from the wheel studs.

➡ Some gentle tapping with a soft faced hammer may help to loosen the locking hub if it seems stuck.

5. Remove the manual locking hub assembly from the rotor by pulling straight outward.
6. Inspect the O-ring seal on the back side of the hub assembly and, if damaged, replace it.
7. Installation is the reverse of the removal procedure. Ensure that the rotor mounting face is flat and free of burrs, dirt or grease, especially where the O-ring seal makes contact.

Automatic Locking Hubs

REMOVAL & INSTALLATION

Except Mountaineer, 1995–99 Explorer and 1998–99 Ranger

OUTER HUB COVER

▶ See Figure 56

1. Loosen the front wheel lug nuts.
2. Raise and safely support the front of the vehicle.
3. Remove the lug nuts and wheel/tire assembly.
4. If equipped, remove the lug nut retainer washers from the wheel studs.

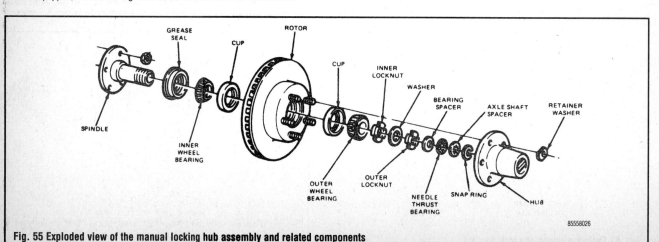

Fig. 55 Exploded view of the manual locking hub assembly and related components

To remove the manual locking hub, remove the wheel and stud retainers (if equipped), then pull the hub off

Turn the hub assembly over . . .

. . . and inspect this rubber O-ring seal for damage. Replace as needed

Fig. 56 Exploded view of the automatic locking hubs and related components

➡ Some gentle tapping with a soft faced hammer may help to loosen the locking hub cover if it seems stuck.

5. Remove the automatic locking hub cover assembly from the rotor by pulling straight outward.

6. Inspect the O-ring seal on the back side of the hub assembly and, if damaged, replace it.

7. Installation is the reverse of the removal procedure. Ensure that the rotor mounting face is flat and free of burrs, dirt or grease, especially where the O-ring seal makes contact.

INNER HUB LOCKING CAM

▶ See Figures 57 and 58

1. Remove the outer hub cover.
2. Remove the snap-ring from the end of the splined axle shaft.
3. Remove the axle shaft spacer(s).

✳✳ WARNING

Do not pry on the locking cam or thrust spacers during removal. Prying may damage the cam or spacers.

4. Pull the locking cam assembly and the two thrust spacers (behind cam assembly) from the wheel bearing adjusting nut.

5. Installation is the reverse of the removal procedure. Make sure to install the two thrust spacers first. Also, when pushing or pressing the locking cam into position, ensure that the key in the cam assembly is aligned with the keyway of the front spindle.

✳✳ WARNING

Extreme care must be taken when aligning the locking cam key with the keyway on the front spindle to prevent damage to the fixed cam.

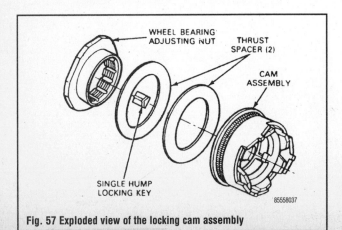

Fig. 57 Exploded view of the locking cam assembly

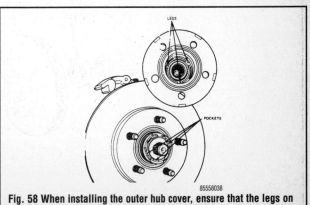

Fig. 58 When installing the outer hub cover, ensure that the legs on the cover seat in the pockets on the locking cam

Mountaineer, 1995–99 Explorer and 1998–99 Ranger

While the Mountaineer, 1995–99 Explorer and 1998–99 Rangers technically have automatic locking hubs, the system is mounted to the axle housing itself and is called a vacuum disconnect axle lock. Refer to the procedures in this section.

Vacuum Disconnect Axle Lock

The vacuum disconnect axle locking system was used on the Mountaineer, 1995–99 Explorer and 1998–99 Ranger models only. The axle locking controls are mounted to the axle housing. All other models use manual or automatic locking hubs at the wheel ends.

REMOVAL & INSTALLATION

▶ **See Figure 59**

1. Raise and safely support the front of the vehicle.

➡ **If possible, support the right side of the vehicle slighly higher than the left. This will minimize the amount of axle fluid lost when the center disconnect shift motor cover is removed.**

2. Position a drain pan beneath the center disconnect shift motor cover.
3. Label and disconnect the vacuum lines at the shift motor.
4. Unplug the electrical wire harness connectors from the shift motor.
5. Remove the four shift motor cover-to-axle housing retaining bolts.
6. Pull the cover and shift motor assembly straight out from the axle housing.
7. To disassemble the shift fork and shift motor from the cover, proceed as follows:
   a. Note the position of the shift fork to assure proper assembly.
   b. Remove the outboard snapring that retains the shift fork to the motor shaft and slide the fork off of the shaft.
   c. Remove the inboard snapring that located the shift fork.
   d. Remove the snapring from the motor shaft where the shaft comes through the cover then slide the motor and shaft out from the cover.
To install:
8. Inspect all gaskets and O-ring seals for damage and replace them as required.
9. Inspect the nylon bushings on the shift fork and if worn, replace them.

10. To assemble the shift motor and fork to the cover, proceed as follows:
   a. Lightly lubricate the O-ring on the motor shaft and slide it into the cover until it is fully seated.
   b. Install the motor shaft-to-cover snapring.
   c. Install the inboard shift fork snapring.
   d. Install the shift fork in the same position as was removed.
   e. Install the outboard shift fork snapring.
11. Ensure that the locking collar inside the axle assembly slides freely back and forth. Position the locking collar so that the shift fork will engage it when installing.
12. Install the center disconnect assembly into the axle housing. Ensure that the shift fork is engaging the locking collar.
13. Install and tighten the four cover retaining bolts.
14. Connect the vacuum fittings and electrical harness plugs to the shift motor assembly.
15. Ensure that the vehicle is level and check the axle fluid level. Top off the fluid as needed.
16. Lower the vehicle, road test and check for leaks.

Spindles and Spindle Bearings

REMOVAL & INSTALLATION

▶ **See Figures 55 and 56**

Except Mountaineer, 1995–99 Explorer and 1998–99 Ranger

1. Loosen the front wheel lug nuts.
2. Raise and support the vehicle safely. Remove the wheel and tire assembly.
3. Remove the disc brake calipers and support the caliper on the vehicle's frame rail.
4. Remove the hub locks and lock nuts.
5. Remove the hub and rotor.
6. Remove the nuts retaining the spindle to the steering knuckle. Tap the spindle with a plastic or rawhide hammer to jar the spindle from the knuckle.
7. Inspect the needle bearings inside the spindle bore. If worn or damaged, replace as follows:
   a. Place the spindle in a vise on the second step of the spindle. Wrap a

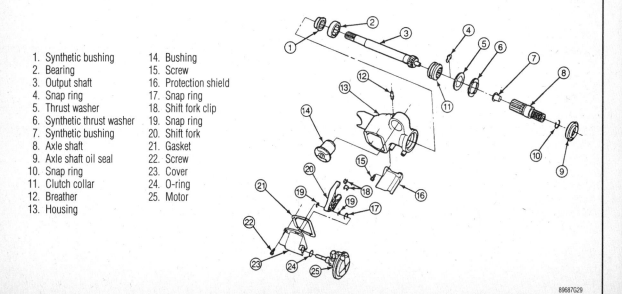

1. Synthetic bushing
2. Bearing
3. Output shaft
4. Snap ring
5. Thrust washer
6. Synthetic thrust washer
7. Synthetic bushing
8. Axle shaft
9. Axle shaft oil seal
10. Snap ring
11. Clutch collar
12. Breather
13. Housing
14. Bushing
15. Screw
16. Protection shield
17. Snap ring
18. Shift fork clip
19. Snap ring
20. Shift fork
21. Gasket
22. Screw
23. Cover
24. O-ring
25. Motor

89687G29

Fig. 59 Exploded view of the vacuum disconnect axle lock assembly on Mountaineer, 1995–99 Explorer and 1998–99 Ranger

shop towel around the spindle or use a brass–jawed vise to protect the spindle.

    b. Remove the oil seal and needle bearing from the spindle with a slide hammer and seal remover tool, 1175–AC or equivalent.

    c. Clean all dirt and grease from the spindle bearing bore. Bearing bore must be free from nicks and burrs.

    d. Place the bearing in the bore with the manufacturer's identification facing outward. Drive the bearing into the bore using spindle bearing replacer tool, T83T–3123–A and drive handle T80T–4000–W or equivalent.

    e. Install the grease seal in the bearing bore with the lip side of the seal facing towards the tool. Drive the seal in the bore using spindle bearing replacer tool, T83T–3123–A and drive handle T80T–4000–W or equivalent. Coat the bearing seal lip with Multi–Purpose Long Life Lubricant C1AZ–19590–B or equivalent.

To install:

    8. Inspect the seal on the axle shaft, and if damaged or worn replace it. Refer to front axle shaft removal & installation procedure in this Section.

    9. Install the splash shield and spindle onto the steering knuckle. Install and tighten the spindle nuts to 35–45 ft. lbs. (47–61Nm).

➡**Since the rotor is removed, check that the wheel bearings are properly greased and that the rotor grease seal is in acceptable condition.**

    10. Install the rotor on the spindle.

    11. Install the wheel bearing, locknut, thrust bearing, snapring and locking hubs.

    12. Install the disc brake calipers. Install the wheel and tire assembly.

    13. Lower the vehicle. Tighten the lug nuts to specification.

Mountaineer, 1995–99 Explorer and 1998–99 Ranger

    The Mountaineer, 1995–99 Explorer and 1998–99 Ranger models do not use spindles. Instead they use an internally splined wheel hub which is pressed into a sealed bearing. If the assembly goes bad, it must be replaced as an entire unit. For removal & installation procedures, refer to Section 8.

Axle Shafts and Seals

REMOVAL & INSTALLATION

Except Mountaineer, 1995–99 Explorer and 1998–99 Ranger

◗ **See Figures 60, 61 and 62**

    1. Loosen the front wheel lug nuts.

    2. Raise and support the vehicle safely. Remove the wheel and tire assembly.

    3. Remove the disc brake calipers and support the caliper on the vehicle's frame rail.

    4. Remove the hub locks and lock nuts.

    5. Remove the hub and rotor.

    6. Remove the nuts retaining the spindle to the steering knuckle. Tap the spindle with a plastic or rawhide hammer to jar the spindle from the knuckle.

    7. Remove the front disc brake rotor shield.

➡**The left-hand axle shaft is engaged inside of the front carrier assembly. Depending on how the truck is sitting (especially if it is not level),**

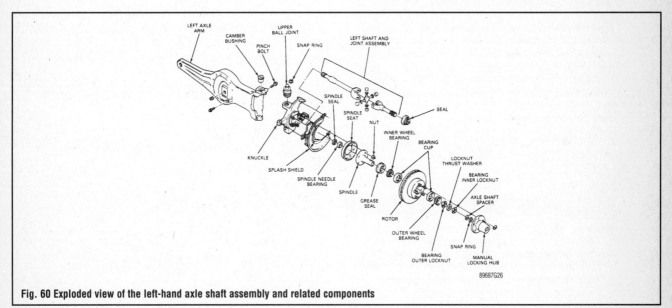

Fig. 60 Exploded view of the left-hand axle shaft assembly and related components

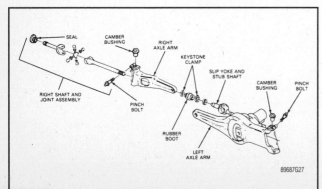

Fig. 61 Exploded view of the right-hand axle shaft assembly and related components

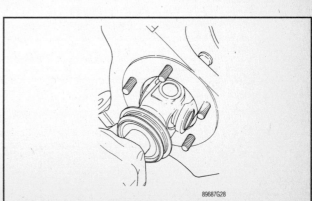

Fig. 62 Pull the axle shaft assemble out through the hole in the steering knuckle

some fluid may leak out of the front carrier assembly. A small drip pan should can be placed underneath the front carrier as a precautionary measure.

8. Remove the left-hand side axle shaft by pulling the assembly out of the carrier and through the hole in the steering knuckle (spindle mount).

9. Remove the right-hand axle shaft by performing the following:

a. Remove and discard the right front axle joint boot clamp from the outer axle assembly.

b. Pull the right-hand axle shaft out of the axle joint boot and stub shaft and through the hole in the steering knuckle (spindle mount).

10. Inspect the seals on the outer axle shaft ends, and replace them if necessary. Replace the seals as follows:

a. Remove the old seal from the axle shaft by driving them off with a hammer.

b. Thoroughly clean the axle seal area of the shaft.

c. Place the shaft in a press and install the new seal using the Spindle/Axle Seal Installer Tool T83T-3132-A, or equivalent.

To install:

11. Install the right-hand axle shaft as follows:

a. Ensure that the rubber boot is properly installed on the carrier stub shaft. Slide a new outer axle shaft boot clamp onto the rubber boot.

➡The model 35 front axle does not use blind, or master, splines. Therefore, special attention should be made to ensure that the yoke ears are in line (in phase) during assembly.

b. Slide the right axle shaft assemble through the hole in the steering knuckle, into the rubber boot and engage the splines of the stub shaft. Ensure the splines are fully engaged.

c. Position the rubber boot and clamp onto the outer axle shaft and crimp the clamp securely on the rubber boot using Keystone Clamp Pliers T63P-9171-A.

12. Install the left-hand axle shaft by sliding it through the hole in the steering knuckle and engaging it into the carrier. Ensure that the shaft is fully seated into the carrier and engage to the splines inside.

13. Install the front disc brake rotor shield, spindle and retaining nuts.

14. Install the front brake rotors, bearings, locknuts and hubs.

15. Install the brake caliper and wheel assembly.

16. Lower the vehicle. Tighten the lug nuts to specification.

Mountaineer, 1995–99 Explorer and 1998–99 Ranger

▶ **See Figures 63, 64, 65, 66 and 67**

✳✳ WARNING

Do not perform this procedure unless a new wheel hub nut and washer assembly and a new axle shaft circlip are available. Once removed, these parts must never be reused during assembly.

1. Loosen the front wheel lug nuts.
2. Raise and safely support the vehicle.
3. Remove the wheels.
4. Remove and discard the center wheel hub nut and washer.

✳✳ WARNING

Never reuse the wheel hub nut and washer. This nut is a torque prevailing design and cannot be reused.

5. Remove the disc brake caliper and position it aside.

➡The hub shaft is a slip fit into the wheel hub and bearing; a press is not normally required.

6. Ensure that the wheel hub shaft can be pushed inwards. If not, assemble a press to the front wheel studs and press the wheel hub shaft inwards slightly to break it loose.

7. Place a jack under the lower control arm to support it.

8. Remove the upper ball joint-to-steering knuckle retaining bolt and separate the joint from the knuckle.

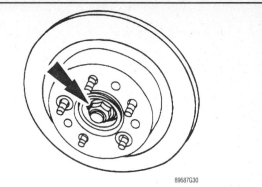

Fig. 63 Remove the wheel hub nut (arrow) and discard it. NEVER reuse the wheel hub nut

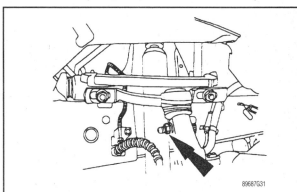

Fig. 64 Remove the upper ball joint-to-steering knuckle retaining bolt

Fig. 65 Rotate the knuckle (1) downward and pull the CV-joint (2) out of the wheel hub by compressing the axle shaft (3) inward

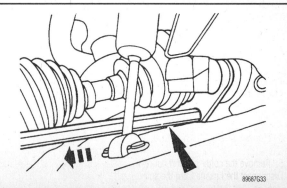

Fig. 66 Using a CV-joint puller (arrow) to remove the inboard joint from the axle housing

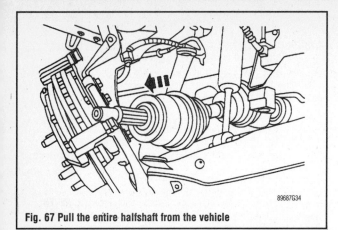

Fig. 67 Pull the entire halfshaft from the vehicle

✵✵ WARNING

Support the steering knuckle and do not allow it to drop or swing downwards. This can overstress the CV-boot and joint, causing damage.

9. Remove the outboard CV-joint from the wheel hub by slightly rotating the steering knuckle down, taking care not to overstress the joint or boot, and pulling the CV-joint out from the hub.

10. Use a CV joint puller and impact slide hammer to pull the inboard CV-joint from the axle housing. You can also use a prytool to carefully pry the CV-joint outward to disengage the internal circlip. Take care to not damage the axle housing seal.

11. Remove the halfshaft from the vehicle. Remove the circlip from the inboard CV-joint end and discard it.

To install:

12. Install a new circlip to the inboard CV-joint end.

13. Position the halfshaft into the vehicle. Slide the inboard CV-joint end into the axle housing until it is fully seated. Ensure that the circlip is engaged in the housing by attempting to pull the joint outwards.

14. Install the outboard CV-joint end into the wheel hub.

15. Position the upper ball joint to the steering knuckle and install the retaining bolt.

16. Install the disc brake caliper back onto the rotor.

17. Install a new wheel hub nut and washer and tighten to 157–213 ft. lbs. (212–288 Nm).

18. Install the wheel and lug nuts.

19. Lower the vehicle and tighten the lug nuts.

Axle Housing

REMOVAL & INSTALLATION

Dana 28

▶ **See Figure 68**

1. Disconnect the negative battery cable.

2. Raise and support the vehicle safely. Remove the wheel and tire assembly.

➡ **Before removing the driveshaft from the front axle yoke, mark the yoke and driveshaft so that they can be reassembled in the same relative position, thus eliminating driveshaft imbalance.**

3. Disconnect the driveshaft from the front axle yoke.

4. Remove the disc brake calipers and support the caliper on the vehicle's frame rail.

5. Remove the cotter pin and nut retaining the steering linkage to the spindle. Disconnect the linkage from the spindle.

➡ **The axle arm assembly must be supported on the jack throughout spring removal and installation and must not be permitted to hang by**

the brake hose. If the length of the brake hose is not sufficient to provide adequate clearance for the removal and installation of the spring, the caliper must be removed.

6. Remove the bolt and nut and disconnect the shock absorber from the radius arm bracket.

7. Remove the stud and bolts that connect the radius arm bracket and radius arm to the axle arm. Remove the bracket and radius arm.

8. Remove the pivot bolt securing the right handle axle arm assembly to the crossmember. Remove the keystone clamps securing the axle shaft boot from the axle shaft slip yoke and axle shaft and slide the rubber boot over. Disconnect the right driveshaft from the slip yoke assembly. Lower the jack and remove the right axle arm assembly.

9. Position another jack under the differential housing. Remove the bolt that connects the left axle arm to the crossmember. Lower the jacks and remove the left axle arm assembly.

To install:

10. Position the under the left axle arm assembly. Raise the axle arm until the arm is in position in the left pivot bracket. Install the nut and bolt and tighten to 120–150 ft. lbs. (163–203Nm).

➡ **Do not remove the jack from under the differential housing at this time.**

11. Place new keystone clamps for the axle shaft boot on the axle shaft assembly. Position the right axle arm on a jack and raise the right axle arm so the right driveshaft slides onto the slip yoke stub shaft and the axle arm is in position in the right pivot bracket. Install the nut and bolt and tighten to 120–150 ft. lbs. (163–203Nm).

➡ **Do not remove the jack from the right axle arm at this time.**

12. Position the radius arm and front bracket on the axle arms. Install a new stud and nut on the top of the axle and radius arm assembly and tighten to 160–220 ft. lbs. (217–298Nm). Install the bolts in the front of the bracket and tighten to 27–37 ft. lbs. (37–50Nm).

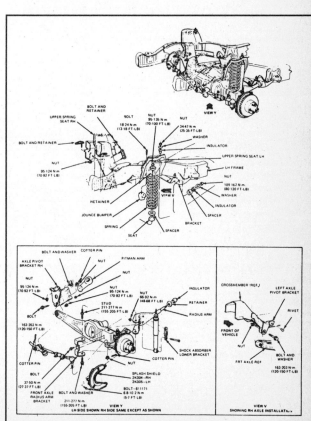

Fig. 68 Exploded view of the Dana 28 front drive axle found on Rangers—other models are similar

13. Install the seat, spacer retainer and coil spring on the stud and nut. Raise the jack to compress the coil spring. Install the nut and tighten to 70–100 ft. lbs. (95–135Nm).

14. Connect the shock absorber to the axle arm assembly. Install the nut and tighten to 42–72 ft. lbs. (57–97Nm).

15. Connect the tie rod ball joint to the spindle. Install the nut and tighten to 50–75 ft. lbs. (68–101Nm).

16. Lower the jacks from the axle arms.

17. Install the disc brake calipers. Install the wheel and tire assembly. Install the lug nuts and tighten to 85–115 ft. lbs. (115–155Nm).

18. Connect the front output shaft to the front axle yoke. Install the U-bolts and tighten to 8–15 ft. lbs. (11–20Nm).

19. Remove the jacks and lower the vehicle.

20. Reconnect the negative battery cable.

Dana 35

EXCEPT MOUNTAINEER, 1995–99 EXPLORER AND 1 998–99 RANGER

▶ **See Figure 69**

1. Disconnect the negative battery cable.

2. Raise and support the vehicle safely. Remove the wheel and tire assembly.

3. Remove the spindle, shaft and joint assembly.

➡ **Before removing the driveshaft from the front axle yoke, mark the yoke and driveshaft so that they can be reassembled in the same relative position, thus eliminating driveshaft imbalance.**

4. Disconnect the driveshaft from the front axle yoke.

5. Remove the cotter pin and nut retaining the steering linkage to the spindle. Disconnect the linkage from the spindle.

6. Remove the left stabilizer bar link lower bolt. Remove the link from the radius arm bracket.

7. Position a jack under the left axle arm assembly ad slightly compress the coil spring.

8. Remove the shock absorber lower nut and disconnect the shock absorber from the radius arm bracket.

9. Remove the nut which retains the lower portion of the spring to the

axle arm. Slowly lower the jack and remove the coil spring, spacer, seat and stud.

➡ **The axle arm assembly must be supported on the jack throughout spring removal and installation and must not be permitted to hang by the brake hose. If the length of the brake hose is not sufficient to provide adequate clearance for the removal and installation of the spring, the caliper must be removed.**

10. Remove the stud and bolts that connect the radius arm bracket and radius arm to the axle arm. Remove the bracket and radius arm.

11. Position another jack under the differential housing. Remove the bolt that connects the left axle arm to the axle pivot bracket. Lower the jacks and remove the left axle arm assembly.

To install:

12. Position the under the left axle arm assembly. Raise the axle arm until the arm is in position in the left pivot bracket. Install the nut and bolt and tighten to 120–150 ft. lbs. (163–203Nm).

➡ **Do not remove the jack from the axle arm at this time.**

13. Position the radius arm and front bracket on the axle arms. Install a new stud and nut on the top of the axle and radius arm assembly and tighten to 190–230 ft. lbs. (258–311Nm). Install the bolts in the front of the bracket and tighten to 27–37 ft. lbs. (37–50Nm).

14. Install the seat, spacer retainer and coil spring on the stud and nut. Raise the jack to compress the coil spring. Install the nut and tighten to 70–100 ft. lbs. (95–135Nm).

15. Connect the shock absorber to the radius arm. Install the nut and tighten to 42–72 ft. lbs. (57–97Nm).

16. Connect the tie rod ball joint to the knuckle. Install the nut and tighten to 50–75 ft. lbs. (68–101Nm). Install the stabilizer bar mounting bracket and tighten to 203–240 ft. lbs. (275–325Nm).

17. Connect the front driveshaft shaft to the front axle yoke. Install the U-bolts and tighten the nuts to 8–15 ft. lbs. (11–20Nm).

➡ **Reassemble the yoke and driveshaft to the marks made during disassembly.**

18. Install the spindle, shaft and joint assemblies.

19. Remove the jacks and lower the vehicle.

20. Reconnect the negative battery cable.

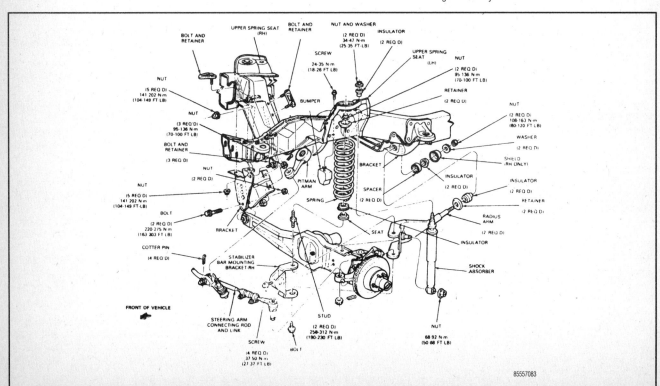

Fig. 69 Exploded view of the Dana 35 front drive axle on Rangers—other models are similar

MOUNTAINEER, 1995–99 EXPLORER AND 1998–99 RANGER

▶ See Figures 70, 71 and 72

➡The manufacturer recommends using new fasteners when installing the front axle. Before beginning this procedure, make sure to acquire new mounting bolts.

1. Remove the front axle halfshafts. Refer to axle shaft and seal procedures earlier in this Section.
2. Matchmark the front driveshaft to the front axle companion flange.
3. Unbolt the front driveshaft retaining straps from the front axle assembly and support it out of the way.

✳✳ WARNING

Do not allow the driveshaft to hang unsupported, damage to the shaft and or U-joint can occur.

4. Disconnect the axle vent tube.
5. Place a jack under the front axle to support it.
6. Remove the left front axle-to-frame attaching bolt.
7. Remove the remaining two axle-to-frame bolts.
8. Lower the axle assembly and remove it from under the vehicle.

To install:

9. Place the axle assembly on a jack and position it under the vehicle.
10. Raise the axle assembly up and align the three mounting holes.
11. Install the three mounting bolts and tighten them to 45–59 ft. lbs. (60–90 Nm).
12. Connect the axle vent tube.
13. Install the front driveshaft to the axle companion flange, aligning the matchmarks made earlier, then install the retaining straps and tighten the bolts.
14. Install the axle halfshafts.

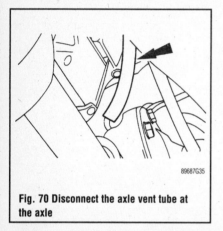

Fig. 70 Disconnect the axle vent tube at the axle

89687G35

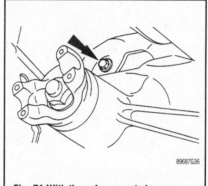

Fig. 71 With the axle supported, remove the left front axle-to-frame bolt first

89687G36

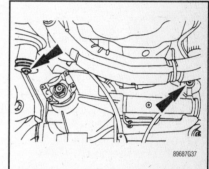

89687G37

Fig. 72 Remove the two remaining axle-to-frame attaching bolts then lower the axle housing

REAR AXLE

Determining Axle Ratio

The drive axle is said to have a certain axle ratio. This number (usually a whole number and a decimal fraction) is actually a comparison of the number of gear teeth on the ring gear and the pinion gear. For example, a 4.11 rear means that theoretically, there are 4.11 teeth on the ring gear and one tooth on the pinion gear or, put another way, the driveshaft must turn 4.11 times to turn the wheels once. Actually, on a 4.11 rear, there might be 37 teeth on the ring gear and 9 teeth on the pinion gear. By dividing the number of teeth on the pinion gear into the number of teeth on the ring gear, the numerical axle ratio (4.11) is obtained. This also provides a good method of ascertaining exactly what axle ratio one is dealing with.

Another method of determining gear ratio is to jack up and support the truck so that both rear wheels are off the ground. Make a chalk mark on the rear wheel and the driveshaft. Put the transmission in neutral. Turn the rear wheel one complete turn and count the number of turns that the driveshaft makes. The number of turns that the driveshaft makes in one complete revolution of the rear wheel is an approximation of the rear axle ratio.

Axle Shaft, Bearing and Seal

REMOVAL & INSTALLATION

▶ See Figures 73, 74 and 75

1. Disconnect the negative battery cable.
2. Raise and support the vehicle safely.

3. Remove the rear wheels and brake drums.
4. Drain the rear axle lubricant.
5. For all axles except 3.73:1 and 4.10:1 ratio:
   a. Remove the differential pinion shaft lock bolt and differential pinion shaft.

➡The pinion gears may be left in place. Once the axle shafts are removed, reinstall the pinion shaft and lock bolt.

   b. Push the flanged end of the axle shafts toward the center of the vehicle and remove the C-lockwasher from the end of the axle shaft.
   c. Remove the axle shafts from the housing. If the seals and/or bearing are not being replaced, be careful not to damage the seals with the axle shaft splines upon removal.
6. For 3.73:1 and 4.10:1 ratio axles:
   a. Remove the pinion shaft lock bolt. Place a hand behind the differential case and push out the pinion shaft until the step contacts the ring gear.
   b. Remove the C-lockwasher from the axle shafts.
   c. Remove the axle shafts from the housing. If the seals and/or bearing are not being replaced, be careful not to damage the seals with the axle shaft splines upon removal.
7. Insert the wheel bearing and seal remover, T85L-1225-AH or equivalent, and a slide hammer into the axle bore and position it behind the bearing so the tanks on the tool engage the bearing outer race. Remove the bearing and seal as a unit.

To install:

8. If removed, lubricate the new bearing with rear axle lubricant and install the bearing into the housing bore. Use axle tube bearing replacer, T78P-1225-A or equivalent.

To remove the axle, first remove the rear axle cover and drain the fluid

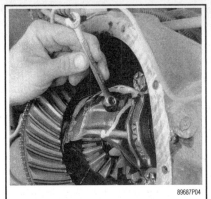

Next, loosen the pinion shaft lock bolt . . .

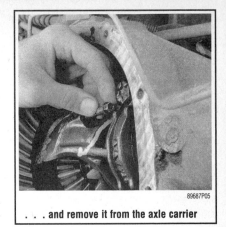

. . . and remove it from the axle carrier

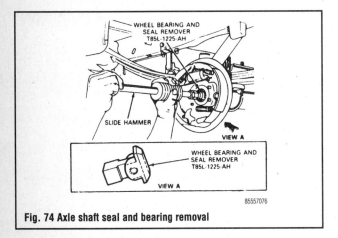

Pull the pinion shaft out of the axle carrier. DO NOT rotate the axle with the pinion shaft removed!

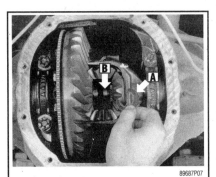

Push in on the axle flange (wheel side) and remove the axle C-lock (A) from the end of the axle (B)

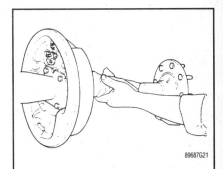

Fig. 73 Slide the axle out of the axle tube. Use care to not damage the bearing or seal

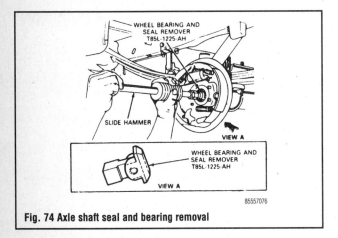

Fig. 74 Axle shaft seal and bearing removal

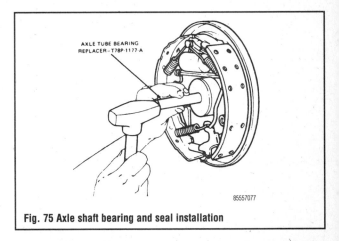

Fig. 75 Axle shaft bearing and seal installation

9. Apply Multi-Purpose Long-Life Lubricant, C1AZ-19590-B or equivalent, between the lips of the axle shaft seal.

10. Install a new axle shaft seal using axle tube seal replacer T78P-1177-A or equivalent.

➡To permit axle shaft installation on 3.73:1 and 4.10:1 ratio axles, make sure the differential pinion shaft contacts the ring gear before performing Step 11.

11. Carefully slide the axle shaft into the axle housing, making sure not to damage the oil seal. Start the splines into the side gear and push firmly until the button end of the axle shaft can be seen in the differential case.

12. Install the C-lockwasher on the end of the axle shaft splines, then pull the shaft outboard until the shaft splines engage the C-lockwasher seats in the counterbore of the differential side gear.

13. Position the differential pinion shaft through the case and pinion gears, aligning the hole in the shaft with the lock screw hole. Install the lock bolt and tighten to 15–22 ft. lbs. (21–29Nm).

14. Clean the gasket mounting surface on the rear axle housing and cover. Apply a continuous bead of Silicone Rubber Sealant ESE-M4G195-A or equivalent to the carrier casting face.

15. Install the cover and tighten the retaining bolts to 25–35 ft. lbs. (20–34Nm).

➡The cover assembly must be installed within 15 minutes of application of the silicone sealant.

16. Add lubricant until it is ¼ in. (6mm) below the bottom of the filler hole in the running position. Install the filler plug and tighten to 15–30 ft. lbs. (20–41Nm).

Pinion Oil Seal

REMOVAL & INSTALLATION

♦ **See Figures 76 and 77**

1. Disconnect the negative battery cable.
2. Raise and support the vehicle safely. Allow the axle to drop to rebound position for working clearance.
3. Remove the rear wheels and brake drums. No drag must be present on the axle.
4. Mark the companion flanges and U-joints for correct reinstallation position.
5. Remove the driveshaft.
6. Using an inch pound torque wrench and socket on the pinion yoke nut measure the amount of torque needed to maintain differential rotation through several clockwise revolutions. Record the measurement.
7. Use a suitable tool to hold the companion flange. Remove the pinion nut.
8. Place a drain pan under the differential. Clean the area around the seal and mark the yoke-to-pinion relation.
9. Use a 2-jawed puller to remove the companion flange.
10. Remove the seal with a small prybar and/or locking pliers and hammer.
To install:
11. Thoroughly clean the oil seal bore.

➡**If you are not absolutely certain of the proper seal installation depth, the proper seal driver must be used. If the seal is misaligned or damaged during installation, it must be removed and a new seal installed.**

12. Drive the new seal into place with a seal driver such as T83T-4676-A. Coat the seal lip with clean, waterproof wheel bearing grease.
13. Coat the splines with a small amount of wheel bearing grease and install the yoke, aligning the matchmarks. Never hammer the yoke onto the pinion!

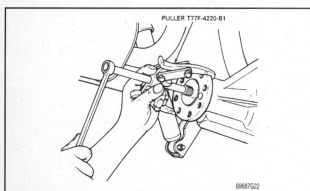

PULLER T77F-4220-B1

89687G22

Fig. 76 Use a 2-jawed puller to remove the driveshaft companion flange

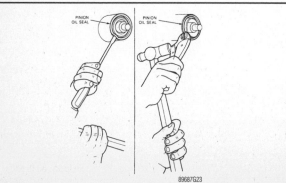

PINION OIL SEAL   PINION OIL SEAL

89687G23

Fig. 77 Remove the seal by either prying it out, or grasping the lip edge with locking pliers and tapping it out of the housing

14. Install a new nut on the pinion.
15. Hold the yoke with a holding tool. Tighten the pinion nut, taking frequent turning torque readings until the original preload reading is attained. If the original preload reading, that you noted before disassembly, is lower than the specified reading of 8–14 inch lbs. for used bearings; 16–29 inch lbs. for new bearings, keep tightening the pinion nut until the specified reading is reached. If the original preload reading is higher than the specified values, torque the nut just until the original reading is reached.

✳✳ WARNING

Under no circumstances should the nut be backed off to reduce the preload reading! If the preload is exceeded, the yoke and bearing must be removed and a new collapsible spacer must be installed. The entire process of preload adjustment must be repeated.

16. Install the driveshaft using the matchmarks. Torque the nuts to 15 ft. lbs.
17. Lower the vehicle.
18. Reconnect the negative battery cable.

Axle Housing

REMOVAL & INSTALLATION

♦ **See Figures 78 and 79**

1. Disconnect the negative battery cable.
2. Raise and support the vehicle safely.
3. Matchmark and disconnect the driveshaft at the axle.
4. Remove the wheels and brake drums.
5. Disengage the brake line from the clips that retain the line to the housing.
6. Disconnect the vent tube from the housing.
7. Remove the axle shafts.
8. Remove the brake backing plate from the housing and support them with wire. Do not disconnect the brake line.
9. If the rear lower shock absorber mounts are integral to the axle housing, disconnect each shock from the mounting bracket.
10. Lower the axle slightly to reduce some of the spring tension. At each rear spring, remove the spring clip (U-bolt) nuts, spring clips and spring seat caps.
11. If the axle housing is mounted on top of the springs, proceed as follows:
   a. Slide the axle housing to the right-side and lower the left-side axle tube end until it clears the leaf spring.
   b. Slide the axle housing to the left-side until the right-side axle tube end will clear the leaf spring.
12. Lower the axle housing and remove it from under the vehicle.
To install:
13. Position the axle housing to the rear springs. Install the spring clips (U-bolts), spring seat clamps and nuts. Tighten the spring clamps evenly to 115 ft. lbs.
14. If a new axle housing is being installed, remove the bolts that attach the brake backing plate and bearing retainer from the old housing flanges. Position the bolts in the new housing flanges to hold the brake backing plates in position. Torque the bolts to 40 ft. lbs.
15. Install the axle shafts.
16. Connect the vent tube to the housing.
17. Position the brake line to the housing and secure it with the retaining clips.
18. Raise the axle housing and springs enough to allow connecting the rear shock absorbers to the mounting bracket studs on the housing. Torque the nuts to 60 ft. lbs.
19. Connect the driveshaft to the axle. Torque the nuts to 8–15 ft. lbs.
20. Install the brake drums and wheels.
21. Lower the vehicle.
22. Reconnect the negative battery cable.

1. Shock absorber
2. Rear spring shackle bracket
3. Rear spring shackle
4. Rear spring
5. Rear spring cap and plate (must be installed as shown)
6. Nut
7. Rear axle assembly
8. U-bolt (4 x 2)
9. Front hanger bracket
10. Spacer, rear spring (LH)
11. Spacer, rear spring (RH)
12. U-bolt (4 x 4)

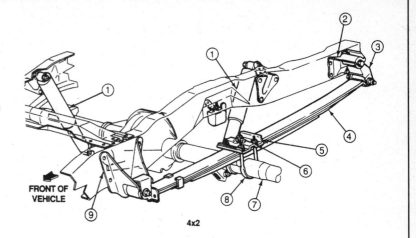

FRONT OF VEHICLE

4x2

89687G24

Fig. 78 View of the under-spring mounted axle assembly

1. Rear spring shackle
2. Rear spring
3. Rear stabilizer bar
4. Rear spring cap and plate
5. Rear spring shackle bracket
6. Shock absorber

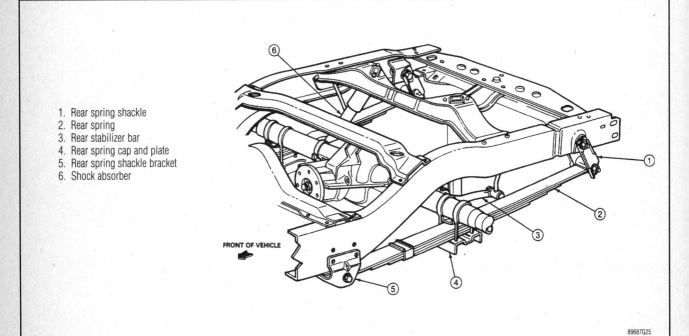

FRONT OF VEHICLE

89687G25

Fig. 79 Example of the over-spring mounted axle assembly

TORQUE SPECIFICATIONS

Component	Ft. Lbs.	Nm
Automatic Transmission		
A4LD		
Control lever nut	30-40	41-54
Converter-to-flywheel attaching nuts	20-34	27-46
Oil pan-to-case	8-10	11-13
Speed sensor retaining bolt	71-97 inch lbs.	8-11
Transmission-to-engine bolts		
2.3L, 2.5L, 2.9L and 4.0L engines	28-38	38-51
3.0L engines	33-44	44-60
Vacuum diaphragm retainer clip-to-case	80-106 inch lbs.	9-12
Vacuum diaphragm retainer clip-to-case stud	106-142 inch lbs.	12-16
4R44E/4R55E		
Control lever nut	30-40	41-54
Converter-to-flywheel attaching nuts	20-34	27-46
Oil pan-to-case	8-10	11-13
Speed sensor retaining bolt	71-97 inch lbs.	8-11
Transmission range sensor-to-case	71-97 inch lbs.	8-11
Transmission-to-engine bolts		
2.3L, 2.5L and 4.0L engines	28-38	38-51
3.0L engines	33-44	44-60
4R70W		
Control lever nut	20-27	26-37
Speed sensor retaining bolt	71-97 inch lbs.	8-11
Torque converter-to-flywheel	20-34	27-46
Transmission linkage-to-control lever adjusting nut	14-19	19-26
Transmission pan-to-case bolts	9-11	12-15
Transmission range sensor-to-case	80-100 inch lbs.	9-11
Transmission support crossmember bolts and nuts	64-81	87-110
Transmission-to-engine bolts	37-50	50-68
5R55E		
Control lever nut	30-40	41-54
Converter-to-flexplate nuts	22-30	30-40
Crossmember-to-frame through bolts	65-85	88-115
Speed sensor retaining bolt	71-97 inch lbs.	8-11
Transmission mount bolts	65-85	88-115
Transmission pan-to-case bolts	115-133 inch lbs.	13-15
Transmission range sensor-to-case	71-97 inch lbs.	8-11
Transmission-to-engine bolts	30-41	40-55
Manual Transmission		
Mitsubishi 5-speed		
Clutch housing-to-engine	28-38	38-51
Clutch housing-to-transmission	30-40	41-54
Crossmember-to-frame	65-85	88-115
Damper-to-insulator on crossmember	71-94	97-127
Drain plug	25-32	35-44
Fill plug	22-25	30-34
Insulator-to-transmission	60-80	81-108
Shift lever plate-to-transmission bolts	6-10	8-14
Mazda 5-speed (M50D)		
Clutch housing-to-engine bolts	28-38	38-51
Drain plug	29-43	40-58
Filler plug	29-43	40-58
Shift lever-to-transmission gear select stub shaft bolt	46-68	63-93
Top plate	12-16	16-22

89687C51

TORQUE SPECIFICATIONS

Component	Ft. Lbs.	Nm
Transfer Case (4x4)		
Borg Warner Model 13-54		
Drain and fill plugs	14-22	19-30
Front and rear output shaft yoke nut	150-180	203-244
Front driveshaft yoke bolts	12-16	16-22
Rear driveshaft flange bolts	61-87	83-118
Shift control bolts - large	70-90	95-122
Shift control bolts - small	31-42	42-57
Shift lever nut	19-26	26-35
Transfer case-to-transmission bolts	25-35	34-48
Borg Warner Model 44-05		
Damper bolts	25-35	34-48
Drain and fill plugs	7-17	9-23
Front driveshaft-to-transfer case bolts	22	30
Rear driveshaft flange bolts	70-95	94-123
Rear output shaft yoke nut	250-275	338-372
Transfer case-to-transmission bolts	25-35	34-48
All Wheel Drive (AWD) Model		
Damper-to-case bolts	16-20	22-28
Drain and fill plugs	7-17	9-23
Front driveshaft-to-transfer case bolts	22	30
Rear driveshaft flange bolts	70-95	94-123
Rear output shaft yoke nut	250-275	338-372
Strut bolts	74-95	100-130
Transfer case-to-transmission bolts	25-35	34-48
Clutch Components		
Fluid reservoir-to-firewall	18-24 inch lbs.	2-3
Master cylinder-to-firewall	15-20	21-27
Pressure plate-to-flywheel	15-24	21-32
Slave cylinder-to-clutch housing	15-20	21-27
Front Drive Axle		
1991–97 Ranger and 1991–94 Explorer		
Axle pivot bolt	120-150	163-200
Axle pivot bracket-to-frame	83-92	113-124
Input shaft yoke nut	200	271
Lower ball joint nut	95-110	129-149
Radius arm front bracket and axle stud	190-230	255-311
Radius arm front bracket front bolts	27	29
Radius arm front bracket lower bolts	190-220	255-298
Shock absorber-to-radius arm nut	39-53	53-72
Shock absorber-to-upper spring seat	25-35	34-46
Spring retainer nut	70-100	95-135
Stabilizer bar end link nuts	30-40	40-55
Stabilizer bar-to-frame retainer bolts	22-30	30-40
Upper ball joint fastener		
1991–92 Dana model 35	85-100	115-136
1991–93 Dana model 28	85-100	115-136
1993 Dana model 35 and all 1994–97 models	65-85	88-115

89687C52

TORQUE SPECIFICATIONS

Component	Ft. Lbs.	Nm
Front Drive Axle (cont.)		
Mountaineer, 1995–97 Explorer AND 1998–99 Ranger		
Disc brake caliper bracket-to-steering knuckle	73-97	98-132
Note: Use new bolts or reuse old bolts using threadlocking compound		
Lower control arm-to-frame pivot bolts and nuts	111-148	150-200
Shock absorber-to-lower control arm nuts	15-21	21-29
Shock absorber-to-to upper frame seat	30-40	40-55
Stabilizer bar-to-frame retainer bolts	65-91	88-119
Stabilizer endlink-to-lower control arm nuts	10-13	13-17
Steering knuckle-to-lower ball joint nut	84-113	113-153
Steering knuckle-to-upper ball joint pinch bolt	30-41	40-55
Upper control arm-to-adjusting arm (right-side only)	95-128	128-173
Upper control arm-to-frame bolts and nuts	84-113	113-153
Wheel hub nut and washer - New	157-213	212-288
Rear Drive Axle		
Antilock brake sensor	25-30	34-41
Brake backing plate-to-axle tube	20-40	27-54
Differential rear cover bolt	15-20	21-27
Drive pinion nut (minimum)	160	217
Filler plug	15-30	20-40
Limited slip break-away test toque (minimum)	30	41
Pinion shaft lock bolt	15-30	20-40

89687C53

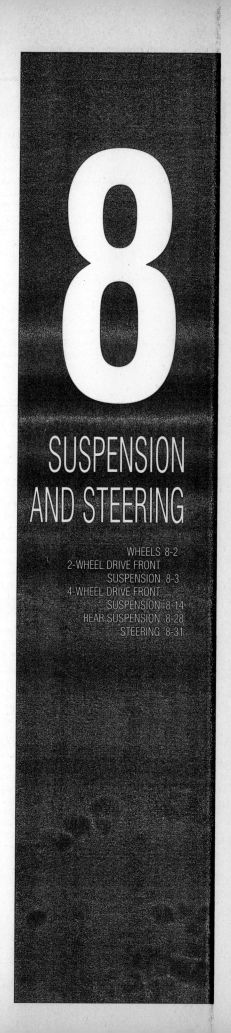

8
SUSPENSION
AND STEERING

WHEELS

Front Wheels

REMOVAL & INSTALLATION

▶ **See Figure 1**

1. Set the parking brake. Block the diagonally opposite wheel.
2. On vehicles with automatic transmission position the selector lever in **P**.
3. On vehicles with manual transmission position the selector lever in **N**.
4. As necessary, remove the hubcap or wheel cover. Loosen the lug nuts, but do not remove them.
5. Raise the vehicle until the wheel and tire assembly clears the floor. Properly support the vehicle.
6. Remove the lug nuts. Remove the tire and wheel assembly from its mounting.

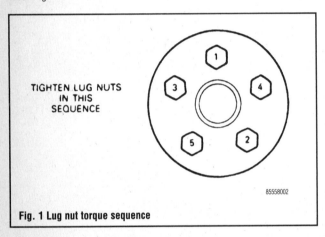

Fig. 1 Lug nut torque sequence

To install:

7. Position the wheel and tire assembly on its mounting.

✳✳ CAUTION

Whenever a wheel is installed be sure to remove any corrosion, dirt or foreign material that may be present on the mounting surfaces of the hub, drum or rotor that contacts the wheel. Installing wheels without proper metal to metal contact at the wheel mounting surfaces can cause the wheel lug nuts to loosen and could allow the wheel to come off while the vehicle is in motion!

8. Install the lug nuts. Be sure that the cone end of the lug nut faces inward.
9. With the lug nuts loosely installed, turn the wheel until one nut is at the top of the bolt circle. Tighten the lug nut until snug.

10. In a crisscross manner tighten the remaining lug nuts until snug in order to minimize run-out.
11. Lower the vehicle. Torque the lug nuts to 100 ft. lbs. in the proper sequence.

✳✳ CAUTION

Retighten the wheel lug nuts to specification after about 500 miles of driving. Failure to do this could result in the wheel coming off while the vehicle is in motion possibly causing loss of vehicle control or collision.

INSPECTION

Replace wheels if they are bent, cracked, leaking air or heavily rusted or if the lug nuts often become loose. Do not use bent wheels that have been straightened or do not use inner tubes in leaking wheels. Do not replace wheels with used wheels. Wheels that have been straightened or are leaking air or are used may have structural damage and could fail without warning.

Front Wheel Lug Studs

REMOVAL & INSTALLATION

Except Mountaineer, 1995–99 Explorer and 1998–99 Ranger

▶ **See Figures 2, 3 and 4**

1. Raise and support the vehicle safely.
2. Remove the tire and wheel assembly.
3. Remove the disc brake rotor. Be sure to properly support the brake caliper to avoid damage to the brake line hose.
4. Position the disc brake rotor in a press so that press ram pressure is not directly exerted on the disc brake rotor surface.
5. Using the proper press stock, press the lug stud from the disc brake rotor. Discard the lug stud. Remove the disc brake rotor from its mounting in the press.

To install:

6. Position a new lug stud in the disc brake rotor hole. Align the serrations of the new stud with the serration marks from the old lug stud.
7. Using a hammer tap the lug stud until the serrations on the stud are started in the hole. Be sure that the lug stud is not installed in an off centered position.
8. Reposition the disc brake rotor in the press so that the rotor is supported on the wheel mounting flange. Be sure to allow enough clearance for the stud to pass through the hole.
9. Do not apply ram pressure directly to the rotor surface. Using the proper press stock, press the lug stud in position until the stud is flush against the inner surface of the disc brake rotor hub.

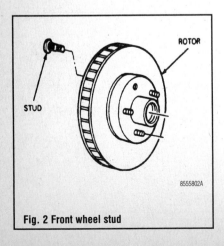

Fig. 2 Front wheel stud

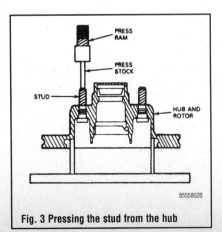

Fig. 3 Pressing the stud from the hub

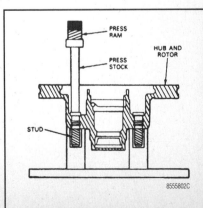

Fig. 4 Pressing the new stud into the hub

10. Install the disc brake rotor. Reposition the brake caliper. Install the tire and wheel assembly. Lower the vehicle.

✳✳ CAUTION

Retighten the wheel lug nuts to specification after about 500 miles of driving. Failure to do this could result in the wheel coming off while the vehicle is in motion possibly causing loss of vehicle control or collision.

Mountaineer, 1995–99 Explorer and 1998–99 Ranger

1. Loosen the wheel lug nuts.
2. Raise and safely support the vehicle.
3. Remove the wheel.
4. Remove the brake caliper, bracket and rotor.
5. Use a wheel stud removal tool, such as C-clamp Assembly Tool T74P-3044-A1, and press the wheel stud out of the hub flange. A C-clamp and socket may also be used.

To install:
6. Insert the new wheel stud through the hole in the hub flange. Rotate the new stud slowly and ensure that the serrations are aligned with those made by the original stud.
7. Place four flat washers over the outside end of the stud and thread the lug nut onto the stud with the flat side against the washers.

✳✳ WARNING

Do not use air tools as the serrations may be stripped from the wheel stud.

8. Tighten the lug nut until the wheel stud head seat against the back side of the flange.
9. Remove the lug nut and washers.
10. Install the brake rotor, bracket and caliper.
11. Install the wheel and snug all of the lug nuts.
12. Lower the vehicle then tighten the wheel lug nuts to specification.

INSPECTION

Replace wheels if they are bent, cracked, leaking air or heavily rusted or if the lug nuts often become loose. Do not use bent wheels that have been straightened or do not use inner tubes in leaking wheels. Do not replace wheels with used wheels. Wheels that have been straightened or are leaking air or are used may have structural damage and could fail without warning.

Rear Wheel Lug Studs

REMOVAL & INSTALLATION

▶ **See Figures 5 and 6**

1. Raise and support the vehicle safely.
2. Remove the tire and wheel assembly.
3. Except on Mountaineer and 1995–99 Explorer, remove the brake drum.
4. On Mountaineer and 1995–99 Explorer, remove the rear disc brake caliper, bracket and rotor.
5. Using wheel stud removal tool T74P-3044-A1 or equivalent, press the lug stud from its seat in the hub.

2-WHEEL DRIVE FRONT SUSPENSION

▶ **See Figures 7 and 8**

All vehicles, except the Mountaineer, 1995–99 Explorer and 1998–99 Ranger, use a twin I-beam front suspension which utilizes coil springs to support the vehicle and radius rods to locate the I-beam.

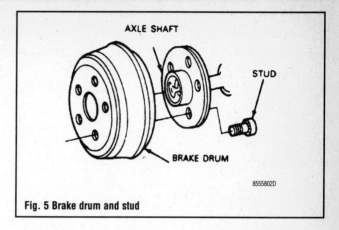

Fig. 5 Brake drum and stud

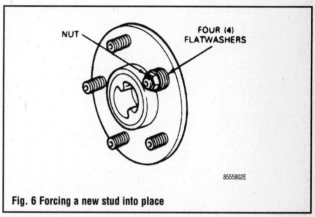

Fig. 6 Forcing a new stud into place

✳✳ WARNING

Never use a hammer to remove the lug stud, as damage to the hub or bearing may result.

To install:
6. Insert the new lug stud in the hole in the hub. Rotate the stud slowly to assure the serrations are aligned with those made by the old lug nut stud.
7. Place 4 flat washers over the outside end of the lug nut stud and thread the wheel lug nut with the flat washer side against the washers.
8. Tighten the wheel nut until the stud head seats against the back side of the hub. Do not use air tools as the serrations may be stripped from the stud.
9. Remove the wheel lug nut and washers.
10. Except on Mountaineer and 1995–99 Explorer, install the brake drum.
11. On Mountaineer and 1995–99 Explorer, install the rear disc brake rotor, bracket and caliper.
12. Install the tire and wheel assembly and snug the lug nuts.
13. Lower the vehicle and tighten the wheel lug nuts to specification.

✳✳ CAUTION

Retighten the wheel lug nuts to specification after about 500 miles of driving. Failure to do this could result in the wheel coming off while the vehicle is in motion possibly causing loss of vehicle control or collision.

Mountaineer, 1995–99 Explorer and 1998–99 Ranger models use unequal length control arms (Short/Long Arm—SLA) which utilize torsion bars to support the vehicle.

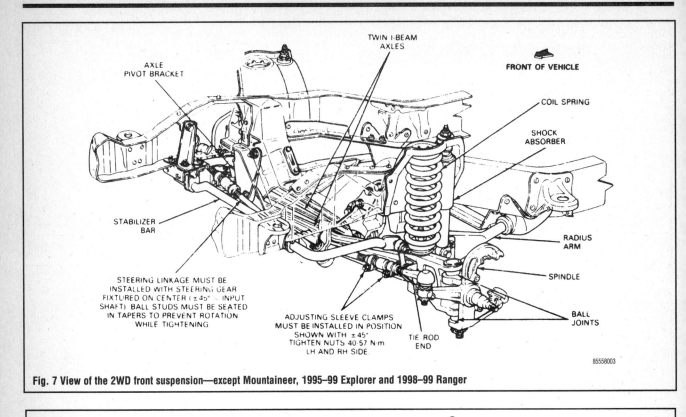

Fig. 7 View of the 2WD front suspension—except Mountaineer, 1995–99 Explorer and 1998–99 Ranger

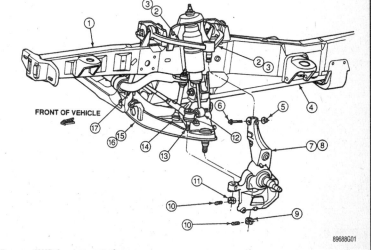

1. Frame
2. Front suspension arm bushing joint (LH shown)
3. Front suspension arm bushing joint (RH)
4. Torsion bar
5. Nut
6. Bolt
7. Front wheel spindle (RH)
8. Front wheel spindle (LH)
9. Nut
10. Cotter pin
11. Nut
12. Front shock absorber
13. Tie rod end
14. Front stabilizer bar link
15. Front suspension lower arm (RH)
16. Front suspension lower arm (LH)
17. Front stabilizer bar

Fig. 8 View of the Mountaineer, 1995–99 Explorer and 1998–99 Ranger 2WD front suspension

Coil Springs

All models except the Mountaineer, 1995–99 Explorer and 1998–99 Ranger use coil springs.

REMOVAL & INSTALLATION

▶ See Figure 9

1. Raise the front of the vehicle and place jackstands under the frame and a jack under the axle.

❋❋ WARNING

The axle must not be permitted to hang by the brake hose. If the length of the brake hoses is not sufficient to provide adequate clearance for removal and installation of the spring, the disc brake caliper must be removed from the spindle. A Strut Spring Compressor, T81P-5310-A or equivalent may be used to compress the spring sufficiently, so that the caliper does not have to be removed. After removal, the caliper must be placed on the frame or otherwise supported to prevent suspending the caliper from the caliper hose. These precautions are absolutely necessary to prevent serious damage to the tube portion of the caliper hose assembly!

2. Disconnect the shock absorber at the lower shock stud. Remove the nut securing the lower retainer to spring seat. Remove the lower retainer.

3. Lower the axle as far as it will go without stretching the brake hose and tube assembly. The axle should now be unsupported without hanging by the brake hose. If not, then either remove the caliper or use Strut Spring Compressor Tool, T81P-5310-A or equivalent. Remove the spring.

4. If there is a lot of slack in the brake hose assembly, a pry bar can be used to lift the spring over the bolt that passes through the lower spring seat.

5. Rotate the spring so the built-in retainer on the upper spring seat is cleared.

6. Remove the spring from the vehicle.

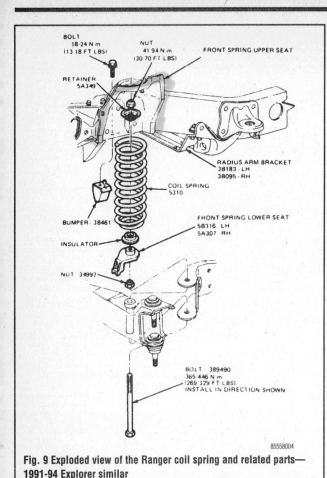

Fig. 9 Exploded view of the Ranger coil spring and related parts—1991-94 Explorer similar

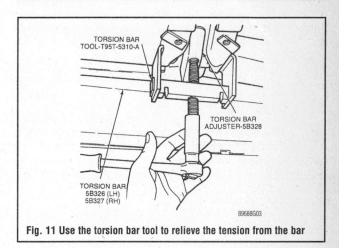

1. Frame
2. Nut
3. Bolt
4. Torsion bar protector
5. Torsion bar (LH)
6. Torsion bar (RH)
7. Adjuster
8. Adjuster bolt
9. Torsion bar support nut

FRONT OF VEHICLE

Fig. 10 Exploded view of the torsion bar rear mounting components

Fig. 11 Use the torsion bar tool to relieve the tension from the bar

To install:

7. If removed, install the bolt in the axle arm and install the nut all the way down. Install the spring lower seat and lower insulator. On the 1991–94 Explorer, also install the stabilizer bar mounting bracket and spring spacer.

8. With the axle in the lowest position, install the top of the spring in the upper seat. Rotate the spring into position.

9. Lift the lower end of the spring over the bolt.

10. Raise the axle slowly until the spring is seated in the lower spring upper seat. Install the lower retainer and nut.

11. Connect the shock absorber to the lower shock stud.

12. Remove the jack and jackstands and lower vehicle.

Torsion Bars

· Only the Mountaineer, 1995–99 Explorer and 1998–99 Ranger models use torsion bars.

REMOVAL & INSTALLATION

▶ **See Figures 10 and 11**

➡**A special tool (Torsion Bar Tool T95T-5310-A) is required for removing the torsion bar. Also, anytime the torsion bar or its adjuster is removed, the vehicle ride height must be checked.**

1. Raise and safely support the front of the vehicle. Place the jackstands so as to support the frame of the vehicle. Do not position the jackstands under the lower control arms and do not use car ramps. The lower control arms must be free to hang unhindered.

2. Remove the torsion bar protector/skid plate from the frame.

3. Remove the torsion bar adjuster bolt from the support nut. Count the number of turns required to remove the bolt and record it for installation.

4. Use Torsion Bar Tool T95T-5310-A, or equivalent, to raise the adjuster lever.

5. Remove the support nut then lower the adjuster lever completely.

6. Slide the torsion bar forward, into the lower control arm, to allow the adjuster lever to be removed.

7. Lower the torsion bar and pull it from the lower control arm.

➡**Ensure that you do not mix up the right and left-hand torsion bars. They must be installed to the side they were originally removed. If installing a new torsion bar, ensure to order the bar for the proper side of the vehicle.**

To install:

8. Raise the torsion bar and slide it forward into the lower control arm.

9. Slide the torsion bar rearward and engage it into the adjuster lever.

10. Use Torsion Bar Tool T95T-5310-A, or equivalent, to raise the adjuster lever.

11. Install the support nut and remove the tool.

12. Lubricate the tip of the adjuster bolt and start it into the support nut.

13. Tighten the adjuster the same number of turns you recorded earlier, then rotate two additional turns.

14. Install the torsion bar protector/skid plate. Tighten the bolts securely.

15. Lower the vehicle and check the ride height adjustment.

RIDE HEIGHT ADJUSTMENT

➡**To perform the ride height check and adjustment requires the use of special slip plates under the front wheels. These plates allow the front suspension to properly settle by bypassing the tires adhesion to the ground.**

1. Raise and support the vehicle. If equipped with ARC suspension, disconnect the front and rear air lines at the shock absorbers.

2. Position frictionless slip plates under the tires then lower the vehicle onto the slip plates.

3. Bounce the vehicles front and rear suspensions several times to normalize the vehicle static ride height.

4. Measure the distance between the center of the lower control arm bushing bolt and the ground. Record the measurement as dimension A.

5. Measure the distance between the lowest point of the steering knuckle (but not the ball joint) and the ground. Record the measurement as dimension B.

6. Subtract dimension B from dimension A for ride height.

7. For vehicles without ARC suspension, ride height should be 4.33–4.56 in. (110–116mm).

8. For vehicles with ARC suspension, ride height should be 3.26–3.50 in. (83–89mm).

9. To increase the ride height, raise the vehicle and tighten the torsion bar adjuster bolt. Recheck the ride height.

10. To decrease the ride height, raise the vehicle and loosen the torsion bar adjuster bolt. Recheck the ride height.

11. Once proper ride height is established, raise and support the vehicle.

12. If equipped with ARC suspension, connect the front and rear air lines at the shocks.

13. Remove the slip plates from under the wheels.

14. Lower the vehicle.

Shock Absorbers

REMOVAL & INSTALLATION

➡ **Low pressure gas shocks are charged with Nitrogen gas. Do not attempt to open, puncture or apply heat to them. Prior to installing a new shock absorber, hold it upright and extend it fully. Invert it and fully compress and extend it at least 3 times. This will bleed trapped air.**

Except Mountaineer, 1995–99 Explorer and 1998–99 Ranger

▶ **See Figure 12**

1. Raise the vehicle, as required to provide additional access and remove the nut attaching the shock absorber to the lower mounting stud on the radius arm.

2. Slide the lower shock absorber end off of the stud.

3. Remove the nut, washer and insulator from the upper shock absorber mount at the frame bracket and remove the shock absorber.

➡ **A second wrench may be needed to hold the shock absorber from turning while removing the upper attaching nut.**

To install:

4. Position the washer and insulator on the shock absorber rod and position the shock absorber to the upper frame bracket mount.

5. Position the insulator and washer on the shock absorber rod and install the attaching nut loosely.

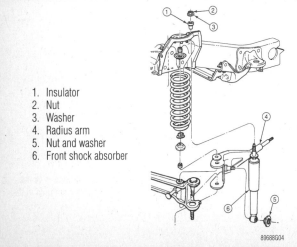

1. Insulator
2. Nut
3. Washer
4. Radius arm
5. Nut and washer
6. Front shock absorber

89688G04

Fig. 12 Exploded view of the front shock absorber—except Mountaineer, 1995–99 Explorer and 1998–99 Ranger

6. Position the shock absorber to the lower mounting stud and install the attaching nut loosely.

7. Tighten the lower shock attaching bolts to 39–53 ft. lbs. (53–72 Nm), and the upper shock attaching bolts to 25–34 ft. lbs. (34–46 Nm).

Mountaineer, 1995–99 Explorer and 1998–99 Ranger

▶ **See Figure 13**

1. Raise the front of the vehicle and place jackstands under the lower control arms. Ensure that the lower shock attaching nuts do not become obstructed by the jackstands.

2. Remove the upper shock-to-frame attaching nut, washer and insulator assembly.

3. Remove the two lower shock-to-control arm attaching nuts.

4. Slightly compress the shock absorber by hand and remove it from the vehicle.

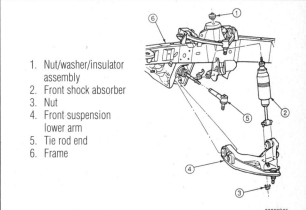

1. Nut/washer/insulator assembly
2. Front shock absorber
3. Nut
4. Front suspension lower arm
5. Tie rod end
6. Frame

89688G05

Fig. 13 Exploded view of the Mountaineer, 1995–99 Explorer and 1998–99 Ranger front shock absorber

To install:

5. Position the lower washer and insulator on the shock absorber rod and position the shock absorber to the upper frame bracket mount.

6. Position the upper insulator and washer on the shock absorber rod and install the attaching nut loosely.

7. Position the lower shock absorber mounting studs into the control arm and install the attaching nuts loosely.

8. Tighten the lower shock attaching nuts to 15–21 ft. lbs. (21–29 Nm), and the upper shock attaching bolts to 30–40 ft. lbs. (40–55 Nm).

TESTING

The purpose of the shock absorber is simply to limit the motion of the spring during compression and rebound cycles. If the vehicle is not equipped with these motion dampers, the up and down motion would multiply until the vehicle

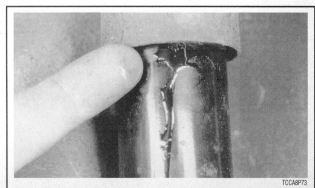

TCCA8P73

When fluid is seeping out of the shock absorber, it's time to replace it

was alternately trying to leap off the ground and to pound itself into the pavement.

Countrary to popular rumor, the shocks do not affect the ride height of the vehicle. This is controlled by other suspension components such as springs and tires. Worn shock absorbers can affect handling; if the front of the vehicle is rising or falling excessively, the ìfootprintî of the tires changes on the pavement and steering is affected.

The simplest test of the shock absorber is simply push down on one corner of the unladen vehicle and release it. Observe the motion of the body as it is released. In most cases, it will come up beyond it original rest position, dip back below it and settle quickly to rest. This shows that the damper is controlling the spring action. Any tendency to excessive pitch (up-and-down) motion or failure to return to rest within 2-3 cycles is a sign of poor function within the shock absorber. Oil-filled shocks may have a light film of oil around the seal, resulting from normal breathing and air exchange. This should NOT be taken as a sign of failure, but any sign of thick or running oil definitely indicates failure. Gas filled shocks may also show some film at the shaft; if the gas has leaked out, the shock will have almost no resistance to motion.

While each shock absorber can be replaced individually, it is recommended that they be changed as a pair (both front or both rear) to maintain equal response on both sides of the vehicle. Chances are quite good that if one has failed, its mate is weak also.

Ball Joints

INSPECTION

▶ **See Figure 14**

1. Check and adjust the front wheel bearings. Raise and support the vehicle.
2. Have a helper grasp the lower edge of the tire and move the wheel assembly in and out.
3. While the wheel is being moved, observe the lower spindle arm and the lower part of the axle jaw.
4. A 1⁄32 in. (0.8mm) or greater movement between the lower part of the axle jaw and the lower spindle arm indicates that the lower ball joint must be replaced
5. To check the upper ball joints, while the wheel is being moved, observe the upper spindle arm and the upper part of the axle jaw.
6. A 1⁄32 in. (0.8mm) or greater movement between the upper part of the axle jaw and the upper spindle arm indicates that the upper ball joint must be replaced

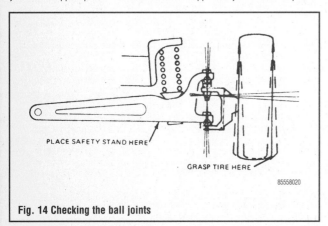

Fig. 14 Checking the ball joints

REMOVAL & INSTALLATION

Except Mountaineer, 1995–99 Explorer and 1998–99 Ranger

▶ **See Figures 15 and 16**

➡**The ball joints are arranged such that if the upper ball joint is to be removed, the lower ball joint must be removed first. Conversely, the upper ball joint must be installed first, before the lower ball joint. Failure to install the upper ball joint before the lower, will result in a lack of clearance for the installation tool.**

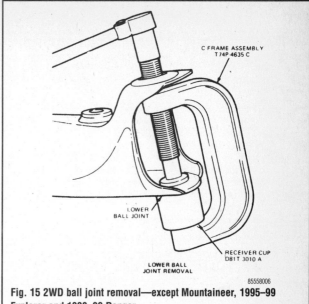

Fig. 15 2WD ball joint removal—except Mountaineer, 1995–99 Explorer and 1998–99 Ranger

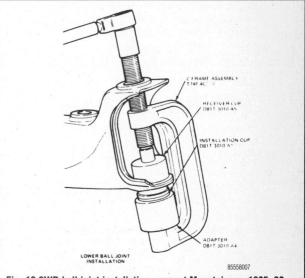

Fig. 16 2WD ball joint installation—except Mountaineer, 1995–99 Explorer and 1998–99 Ranger

1. Remove the steering knuckle.
2. Place knuckle in vise and remove snapring from bottom ball joint socket if so equipped.
3. Assemble the C-frame, T74P-4635-C, forcing screw, D79T-3010-AE and ball joint remover T83T-3050-A or equivalent on the lower ball joint.
4. Turn forcing screw clockwise until the lower ball joint is removed from the steering knuckle.
5. Repeat the previous steps for the upper ball joint.

➡**Always remove the lower ball joint first**

To install:
6. Clean the steering knuckle bore and insert lower ball joint in knuckle as straight as possible. The lower ball joint doesn't have a cotter pin hole in the stud.
7. Assemble the C-frame, T74P-4635-C, forcing screw, D790T-3010-AE, ball joint installer, T83T-3050-A and receiver cup T80T-3010-A3 or equivalent tools, to install the upper ball joint.
8. Turn the forcing screw clockwise until the upper ball joint is firmly seated.

➡If the ball joint cannot be installed to the proper depth, realignment of the receiver cup and ball joint installer will be necessary.

9. Repeat the previous steps for the upper ball joint. Install the snapring on the lower ball joint.

10. Install the steering knuckle.

Mountaineer, 1995–99 Explorer and 1998–99 Ranger

The ball joints on the Mountaineer, 1995–99 Explorer and 1998–99 Ranger are integral with the control arm. If the ball joint is defective, the entire control arm must be replaced. Refer to the appropriate control arm removal and installation procedures later in the section.

Knuckle and Spindle

REMOVAL & INSTALLATION

Except Mountaineer, 1995–99 Explorer and 1998–99 Ranger

▶ See Figure 17

1. Raise the front of the vehicle and install jackstands.
2. Remove the wheel and tire assembly.
3. Remove the caliper assembly from the rotor and hold it out of the way with wire.
4. Remove the dust cap, cotter pin, nut, nut retainer, washer, and outer bearing, and remove the rotor from the spindle.
5. Remove brake dust shield.
6. Disconnect the steering linkage from the spindle and spindle arm by removing the cotter pin and nut.
7. With Tie Rod removal tool 3290-D or equivalent remove the tie rod end from the spindle arm.
8. If equipped, unbolt the front wheel ABS sensor and wire harness from the steering knuckle.
9. Remove the cotter pin and the castellated nut from the lower ball joint stud.
10. Remove the axle clamp bolt from the axle. Remove the camber adjuster from the upper ball joint stud and axle beam.
11. Strike the area inside the top of the axle to pop the lower ball joint loose from the axle beam.

✳✳ WARNING

Do not use a ball joint fork to separate the ball joint from the spindle, as this will damage the seal and the ball joint socket!

12. Remove the spindle and the ball joint assembly from the axle.

To install:

➡A 3 step sequence for tightening ball joint stud nuts must be followed to avoid excessive turning effort of spindle about axle.

13. Prior to assembly of the spindle, make sure the upper and lower ball joints seals are in place.

14. Place the spindle and the ball joint assembly into the axle.
15. Install the camber adjuster in the upper over the upper ball joint. If camber adjustment is necessary, special adapters must be installed.
16. Tighten the lower ball joint stud to 104–146 ft. lbs. (141–198 Nm) for 1991–94 models and 89–133 ft. lbs. (120–180 Nm) for 1995–99 models. Continue tightening the castellated nut until it lines up with the hole in the ball joint stud. Install the cotter pin. Install the dust shield.
17. If removed, install the front wheel ABS sensor and wire harness to the steering knuckle.
18. Install the hub and rotor on the spindle.
19. Install the outer bearing cone, washer, and nut. Adjust bearing end-play and install the cotter pin and dust cap.
20. Install the caliper.
21. Connect the steering linkage to the spindle. Tighten the nut to 52–74 ft. lbs. (70–100 Nm) and advance the nut as required for installation of the cotter pin.
22. Install the wheel and tire assembly. Lower the vehicle. Check, and if necessary, adjust the toe setting.

Mountaineer, 1995–99 Explorer and 1998–99 Ranger

▶ See Figure 18

➡The steering knuckle and spindle are an integral assembly.

1. Position the steering wheel to the on-center position.
2. Loosen the wheel lug nuts then raise and safely support the front of the vehicle.
3. Remove the wheels.
4. Remove the front disc brake caliper, bracket and rotor. Also remove the rotor splash shield.
5. Remove the cotter pin and nut retaining the tie rod end to the steering knuckle.
6. Disconnect the tie rod end from the steering knuckle using a jawed puller, such as Pitman Arm Puller T64P-3590-F, or equivalent.
7. If equipped, unbolt the front wheel ABS sensor and wire harness from the steering knuckle.
8. Unload the torsion bar. Follow the torsion bar removal procedures, but do not remove the bar.
9. Support the lower control arm with a jack. Remove the cotter pin and loosen the nut retaining the lower ball joint to the steering knuckle.
10. Disconnect the lower ball joint from the steering knuckle using a jawed puller, such as Pitman Arm Puller T64P-3590-F, or equivalent.
11. Remove the lower ball joint retaining nut and slowly raise the lower control arm until the ball joint stud is disengaged from the steering knuckle.
12. Remove the upper ball joint retaining bolt and nut from the steering knuckle then disconnect the joint from the knuckle.
13. Remove the steering knuckle/spindle assembly from the vehicle.

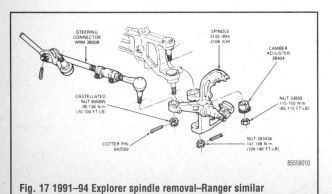

Fig. 17 1991–94 Explorer spindle removal–Ranger similar

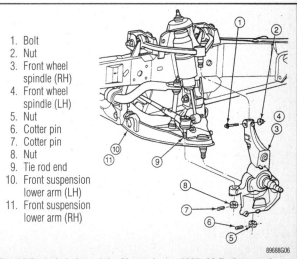

1. Bolt
2. Nut
3. Front wheel spindle (RH)
4. Front wheel spindle (LH)
5. Nut
6. Cotter pin
7. Cotter pin
8. Nut
9. Tie rod end
10. Front suspension lower arm (LH)
11. Front suspension lower arm (RH)

Fig. 18 Exploded view of the Mountaineer, 1995–99 Explorer and 1998–99 Ranger steering knuckle

To install:

14. Inspect the upper and lower ball joints and seals for damage and replace as needed.

15. Position the steering knuckle onto the upper ball joint and install the retaining bolt and nut. Tighten the bolt to 30–41 ft. lbs. (40–55 Nm).

16. Install the lower ball joint stud into the steering knuckle until the stud protrudes through the knuckle.

17. Install the retaining nut to the lower ball joint stud and tighten to 84–113 ft. lbs. (113–153 Nm). Install the cotter pin, advancing (tightening) the nut as needed. Never loosen the ball joint nut in order to install the cotter pin.

18. Connect the tie rod end to the steering knuckle and install the retaining nut. Tighten to 57–77 ft. lbs. (77–104 Nm) and install the cotter pin, advancing (tightening) the nut as needed. Never loosen the ball joint nut in order to install the cotter pin.

19. Install the front disc brake splash shield, rotor, bracket and caliper.

20. Install the wheel and snug all of the lug nuts.

21. Reload the torsion bar pressure. Refer to the torsion bar installation procedures. Check and, if necessary, set the vehicle ride height.

22. Lower the vehicle and tighten the wheel lug nuts to 100 ft. lbs. (135 Nm).

Radius Arm

Radius arms are not found on Mountaineer, 1995–99 Explorer and 1998–99 Ranger models.

REMOVAL & INSTALLATION

▶ **See Figure 19**

1. Raise the front of the vehicle, place jackstands under the frame. Place a jack under the axle.

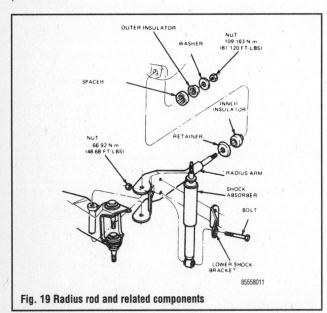

Fig. 19 Radius rod and related components

❊❊❊ WARNING

The axle must be supported on the jack throughout spring removal and installation, and must not be permitted to hang by the brake hose. If the length of the brake hose is not sufficient to provide adequate clearance for removal and installation of the spring, the disc brake caliper must be removed from the spindle. After removal, the caliper must be placed on the frame or otherwise supported to prevent suspending the caliper from the caliper hose. These precautions are absolutely necessary to prevent serious damage to the tube portion of the caliper hose assembly.

2. Disconnect the lower end of the shock absorber from the shock lower bracket (bolt and nut).

3. Remove the front spring. Loosen the axle pivot bolt.

4. Remove the spring lower seat from the radius arm, and then remove the bolt and nut that attaches the radius arm to the axle and front bracket.

5. Remove the nut, rear washer and insulator from the rear side of the radius arm rear bracket.

6. Remove the radius arm from the vehicle, and remove the inner insulator and retainer from the radius arm stud.

To install:

7. Position the front end of the radius arm to the axle. Install the attaching bolt from underneath, and install the nut finger tight.

8. Install the retainer and inner insulator on the radius arm stud and insert the stud through the radius arm rear bracket.

9. Install the rear washer, insulator and nut on the arm stud at the rear side of the arm rear bracket. Tighten the nut to 82–113 ft. lbs. (113–153 Nm).

10. Tighten the nut on the radius arm-to-axle bolt to 188–254 ft. lbs. (255–345 Nm).

11. Install the spring lower seat and spring insulator on the radius arm so that the hole in the seat goes over the arm-to-axle bolt.

12. Install the front spring.

13. Connect the lower end of the shock absorber to the stud on the radius arm with the retaining nut and tighten to specifications.

Stabilizer Bar

REMOVAL & INSTALLATION

Ranger

1. As required, raise and support the vehicle safely.

2. Remove the nuts and bolts retaining the stabilizer bar to the end links.

3. Remove the retainers and the stabilizer bar and bushings from the vehicle.

To install:

4. Position the stabilizer bar to the axles and brackets.

5. Install the retainer and the end link bolts.

6. Torque the retainer bolts to 35–50 ft. lbs. (47–67 Nm) on 1991–94 models and 22–30 ft. lbs. (30–40 Nm) on 1995–99 models. Torque the end link nuts to 30–41 ft. lbs. (40–55 Nm).

1991–94 Explorer

▶ **See Figure 20**

1. As required, raise and support the vehicle safely.

2. Remove the nuts and washer and disconnect the stabilizer link assembly from the front I-beam axle.

3. Remove the mounting bolts and remove the stabilizer bar retainers from the stabilizer bar assembly.

4. Remove the stabilizer bar from the vehicle.

To install:

5. Place stabilizer bar in position on the frame mounting brackets.

6. Install retainers and tighten retainer bolt to 35–50 ft. lbs. (47–67 Nm). If removed, install the stabilizer bar link assembly to the stabilizer bar. Install the nut and washer and tighten to 30–41 ft. lbs. (40–55 Nm).

7. Position the stabilizer bar link in the I-beam mounting bracket. Install the bolt and tighten to 30–41 ft. lbs. (40–55 Nm).

Mountaineer, 1995–99 Explorer and 1998–99 Ranger

▶ **See Figure 21**

1. Raise and safely support the vehicle.

2. Remove the nut, washer and bushing (on underside of the lower control arm) linking the stabilizer bar end to the lower control arm.

3. Lift up on the bar and remove the remaining bushings and the spacer and bolt assembly (called the end link) from the stabilizer bar end.

4. Remove the bar mounting bracket-to-frame bolts.

5. Remove the stabilizer bar from the vehicle. If necessary, remove the mounting brackets and insulators from the bar.

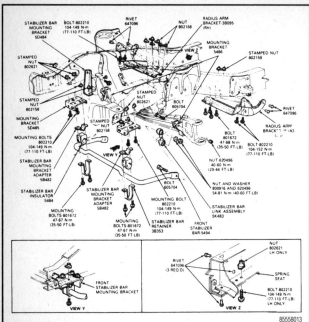

Fig. 20 Exploded view of the 1991–94 Explorer stabilizer bar and related parts—Ranger similar

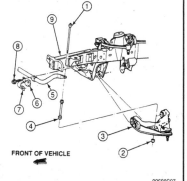

1. Front stabilizer bar link bolt and bushing assembly
2. Nut and washer
3. Front suspension lower arm
4. Front stabilizer bar link
5. Front stabilizer bar
6. Front stabilizer bar bushing
7. Stabilizer bar bracket
8. Bolt
9. Frame

Fig. 21 Exploded view of the Mountaineer, 1995–99 Explorer and 1998–99 Ranger stabilizer bar mounting

To install:

6. Inspect all of the stabilizer bar mounting and end link bushings. Replace any that are cracked, squashed, swollen or damaged.

7. Position the stabilizer bar mounting brackets to the frame and install the retaining bolts loosely.

8. Install the end link assembly to the bar end and the lower control arm. Install the end link retaining bolt loosely.

9. Tighten the mounting bracket bolts to 65–91 ft. lbs. (88–119 Nm).

➡The end link assembly must be tightened with the vehicle weight on the front wheels.

10. Lower the vehicle then tighten the end link retaining nut to 10–13 ft. lbs. (13–17 Nm).

I-Beam Axle

REMOVAL & INSTALLATION

♦ **See Figure 22**

1. Raise and safely support the vehicle. Remove the front wheel spindle. Remove the front spring. Remove the front stabilizer bar, if equipped.

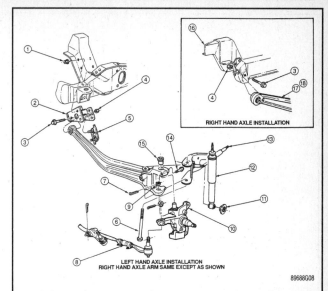

1. Nut
2. Right front axle pivot bracket
3. Bolt
4. Nut
5. Bolt and retainer
6. Bolt
7. Cotter pin
8. Steering connecting arm
9. Nut
10. Front wheel spindle
11. Nut and washer assembly
12. Front shock absorber
13. Radius arm
14. Bolt
15. Camber adjuster
16. Crossmember reference
17. Front right hand axle
18. Left axle

Fig. 22 Exploded view of the front I-beam axle assembly

2. Remove the spring lower seat from the radius arm, and then remove the bolt and nut that attaches the stabilizer bar bracket, if equipped, and the radius arm to the (I-Beam) front axle.

3. Remove the axle-to-frame pivot bracket bolt and nut.

To install:

4. Position the axle to the frame pivot bracket and install the bolt and nut finger tight.

5. Position the opposite end of the axle to the radius arm, install the attaching bolt from underneath through the bracket, the radius arm and the axle. Install the nut and tighten to 188–254 ft. lbs. (255–345 Nm).

6. Install the spring lower seat on the radius arm so that the hole in the seat indexes over the arm-to-axle bolt.

7. Install the front spring.

➡Lower the vehicle on its wheels or properly support the vehicle at the front springs before tightening the axle pivot bolt and nut.

8. Tighten the axle-to-frame pivot bracket bolt to 111–148 ft. lbs. (150–200 Nm).

9. Install the front wheel spindle.

Upper Control Arm

Only the Mountaineer, 1995–99 Explorer and 1998–99 Ranger models have control arms.

REMOVAL & INSTALLATION

♦ **See Figure 23**

➡After performing this procedure, it will be necessary to have the wheel alignment checked and adjusted by a professional shop.

1. Position the steering wheel to the on-center position. Loosen the wheel lug nuts.

2. Raise and safely support the vehicle. Position the jack stands under the lower control arms.

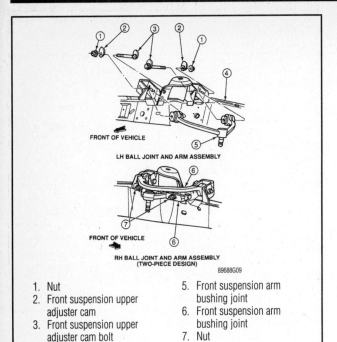

1. Nut
2. Front suspension upper adjuster cam
3. Front suspension upper adjuster cam bolt
4. Frame
5. Front suspension arm bushing joint
6. Front suspension arm bushing joint
7. Nut

Fig. 23 Exploded views of the right and left upper control arms

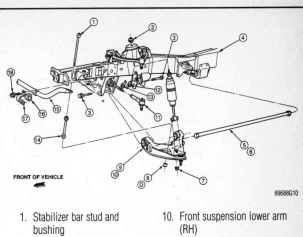

1. Stabilizer bar stud and bushing
2. Nut, washer, and insulator assembly
3. Bolt
4. Frame
5. Torsin bar (LH)
6. Torsion bar (RH)
7. Nut
8. Nut and washer
9. Front suspension lower arm (LH)
10. Front suspension lower arm (RH)
11. Tie rod end
12. Nut
13. Nut
14. Front stabilizer bar link
15. Front stabilizer bar
16. Front stabilizer bar bushing
17. Stabilizer bar bracket
18. Bolt

Fig. 24 Exploded view of the lower control arm assembly

3. Remove the wheel lug nuts and wheel.

➡**Before removing the steering knuckle-to-upper ball joint retaining (pinch) bolt, secure the steering knuckle from tilting.**

4. Remove the steering knuckle-to-upper ball joint retaining (pinch) bolt and separate the two components.
5. Make alignment marks on the control arm pivot bolt cam assemblies.
6. To remove the left side control arm proceed as follows:
   a. Remove the nuts and cam bolts from the control arm pivot points.
   b. Pull the control arm from the vehicle frame.
7. To remove the right side control arm, proceed as follows:
   a. If only the ball joint is to be removed, make alignment marks on the control arm and ball joint assembly then remove the two retaining nuts and the ball joint. Skip to the installation procedures.
   b. Remove the nuts and cam bolts from the control arm pivot points.
   c. Pull the control arm from the vehicle frame.

To install:
8. For right-side control arm, if removed, install the ball joint assembly and retaining nuts to the control arm and tighten the nuts to 95–128 ft. lbs. (128–173 Nm).
9. Install the control arm pivot points into the frame pockets.
10. Install the cam bolts and nuts, align the matchmarks and tighten the nuts to 84–113 ft. lbs. (113–153 Nm).
11. Connect the upper ball joint shaft to the steering knuckle. Install the retaining (pinch) bolt and tighten to 30–41 ft. lbs. (40–55 Nm).
12. Install the wheel and snug the lug nuts.
13. Lower the vehicle and tighten the lug nuts to 100 ft. lbs. (135 Nm).
14. Have the alignment checked by a professional repair shop.

Lower Control Arm

Only the Mountaineer, 1995–99 Explorer and 1998–99 Ranger models have control arms.

REMOVAL & INSTALLATION

♦ **See Figure 24**

➡**To remove the lower control arm, the torsion bar must be removed. Anytime the torsion bar is disturbed, the ride height must be checked and adjusted.**

1. Position the steering wheel to the on-center position. Loosen the wheel lug nuts.
2. Raise and safely support the vehicle.
3. Remove the wheel lug nuts and wheel.
4. Disconnect the stabilizer bar link bolt from the lower control arm.
5. Remove the front shock absorber.
6. Remove the torsion bar.
7. Remove the lower ball joint retaining nut cotter pin and loosen the nut but do not remove it.
8. Disconnect the lower ball joint stud from the steering knuckle using a jawed puller, such as Pitman Arm Puller T64P-3590-F, or equivalent.

✳✳ WARNING

Fasten a support, either out of a block of wood or wire wrapped around the frame, and support the weight of the steering knuckle/brake assembly. Do not allow the steering knuckle/brake assembly to hang from the upper ball joint as this may damage the joint.

9. Position a jack under the lower control arm then remove the lower ball joint retaining nut.
10. Raise the lower control arm until the lower ball joint stud is free from the steering knuckle.
11. Remove the two nuts and bolts retaining the lower arm pivot points to the frame crossmember.
12. Remove the lower control arm from the frame pockets. Some careful prying may ease the removal of the arm.

To install:
13. Inspect the lower ball joint, boot and pivot bushings. If any inspected components are worn or damaged, the entire control arm must be replaced.

➡**Do not tighten the lower control arm mounting bolts to the final torque until the end of the installation procedure.**

14. Position the lower control arm pivot points into the frame and crossmember pockets. Install the bolts and nuts and snug the bolts.
15. Position a jack under the lower control arm.
16. Install the torsion bar.
17. Raise the lower control arm to allow the lower ball joint stud to be inserted into the steering knuckle.

18. Lower the control arm assembly and ensure that the lower ball joint stud protrudes through the steering knuckle bore.

19. Install the lower ball joint attaching nut and tighten to 83–113 ft. lbs. (113–153 Nm). Install a new cotter pin, advancing (tightening) the nut as required. Never loosen the retaining nut in order to install the cotter pin.

20. Install the shock absorber.

21. Install the wheel and snug the lug nuts.

22. Lower the vehicle and tighten the lug nuts to 100 ft. lbs. (135 Nm).

➡**The lower control arm-to-frame bolts must be tightened with the weight of the vehicle resting on the wheels. If clearance permits, allow the vehicle to sit on the ground while tightening the bolts.**

23. If necessary, raise the vehicle again and position either car ramps under the wheels or jackstands on the lower control arms, as close to the wheels as possible.

24. Tighten the control arm-to-frame bolts to 111–148 ft. lbs. (150–200 Nm).

25. Lower the vehicle.

26. Check and adjust the ride height.

27. While it should not be necessary, have the wheel alignment checked by a professional shop.

Front Wheel Bearings

REMOVAL & INSTALLATION

1. Raise and support the vehicle safely. Remove the tire and wheel assembly from the hub and rotor.

2. Remove the caliper from its mounting and position it to the side with mechanics wire in order to prevent damage to the brake line hose.

3. Remove the grease cap from the hub. Remove the cotter pin, retainer, adjusting nut and flatwasher from the spindle.

4. Remove the outer bearing cone and roller assembly from the hub. Remove the hub and rotor from the spindle.

5. Using seal removal tool 1175-AC or equivalent remove and discard the grease seal. Remove the inner bearing cone and roller assembly from the hub.

6. Clean the inner and outer bearing assemblies in solvent. Inspect the bearings and the cones for wear and damage. Replace defective parts, as required.

7. If the cups are worn or damaged, remove them with front hub remover tool T81P-1104-C and tool T77F-1102-A or equivalent.

8. Wipe the old grease from the spindle. Check the spindle for excessive wear or damage. Replace defective parts, as required.

To install:

9. If the inner and outer cups were removed, use bearing driver handle tool T80-4000-W or equivalent and replace the cups. Be sure to seat the cups properly in the hub.

10. Use a bearing packer tool and properly repack the wheel bearings with the proper grade and type grease. If a bearing packer is not available work as much of the grease as possible between the rollers and cages. Also, grease the cone surfaces.

11. Position the inner bearing cone and roller assembly in the inner cup. A light film of grease should be included between the lips of the new grease retainer (seal).

12. Install the retainer using the proper installer tool. Be sure that the retainer is properly seated.

13. Install the hub and rotor assembly onto the spindle. Keep the hub centered on the spindle to prevent damage to the spindle and the retainer.

14. Install the outer bearing cone and roller assembly and flatwasher on the spindle. Install the adjusting nut. Adjust the wheel bearings.

15. Install the retainer, a new cotter pin and the grease cap. Install the caliper.

16. Lower the vehicle and tighten the lug nuts to 100 ft. lbs. Before driving the vehicle pump the brake pedal several times to restore normal brake pedal travel.

TCCS8028

Remove the nut and washer from the spindle . . .

TCCS8029

. . . then remove the outer bearing

TCCS8030

Pull the hub and rotor assembly from the spindle

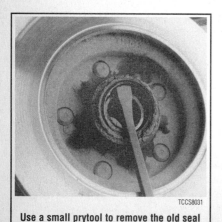

TCCS8031

Use a small prytool to remove the old seal

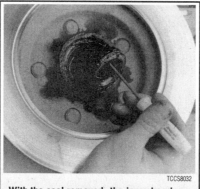

TCCS8032

With the seal removed, the inner bearing may be withdrawn from the hub

TCCS8033

Thoroughly pack the bearing with fresh, high temperature wheel bearing grease

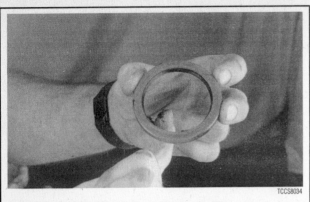
Apply a thin coat of fresh grease to the new seal lip

Use a suitably sized driver to install the inner bearing seal to the hub

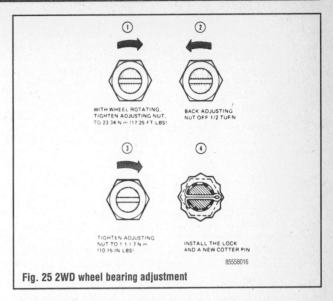
Fig. 25 2WD wheel bearing adjustment

❈❈ **CAUTION**

Retighten the wheel lug nuts to specification after about 500 miles of driving. Failure to do this could result in the wheel coming off while the vehicle is in motion possibly causing loss of vehicle control or collision.

ADJUSTMENT

▶ **See Figure 25**

1. Raise and support the vehicle safely. Remove the wheel cover. Remove the grease cap from the hub.
2. Wipe the excess grease from the end of the spindle. Remove the cotter pin and retainer. Discard the cotter pin.
3. Loosen the adjusting nut 3 turns.

❈❈ **WARNING**

Obtain running clearance between the disc brake rotor surface and shoe linings by rocking the entire wheel assembly in and out several times in order to push the caliper and brake pads away from the rotor. An alternate method to obtain proper running clearance is to tap lightly on the caliper housing. Be sure not to tap on any other area that may damage the disc brake rotor or the brake lining surfaces. Do not pry on the phenolic caliper piston. The running clearance must be maintained throughout the adjustment procedure. If proper clearance cannot be maintained, the caliper must be removed from its mounting.

4. While rotating the wheel assembly, tighten the adjusting nut to 17–25 ft. lbs. in order to seat the bearings. Loosen the adjusting nut a half turn. Retighten the adjusting nut 18–20 inch lbs.
5. Place the retainer on the adjusting nut. The castellations on the retainer must be in alignment with the cotter pin holes in the spindle. Once this is accomplished install a new cotter pin and bend the ends to insure its being locked in place.
6. Check for proper wheel rotation. If correct, install the grease cap and wheel cover. If rotation is noisy or rough recheck your work and correct as required.
7. Lower the vehicle and tighten the lug nuts to 100 ft. lbs., if the wheel was removed. Before driving the vehicle pump the brake pedal several times to restore normal brake pedal travel.

❈❈ **CAUTION**

If the wheel was removed, retighten the wheel lug nuts to specification after about 500 miles of driving. Failure to do this could result in the wheel coming off while the vehicle is in motion possibly causing loss of vehicle control or collision.

Wheel Alignment

If the tires are worn unevenly, if the vehicle is not stable on the highway or if the handling seems uneven in spirited driving, the wheel alignment should be checked. If an alignment problem is suspected, first check for improper tire inflation and other possible causes. These can be worn suspension or steering components, accident damage or even unmatched tires. If any worn or damaged components are found, they must be replaced before the wheels can be properly aligned. Wheel alignment requires very expensive equipment and involves minute adjustments which must be accurate; it should only be performed by a trained technician. Take your vehicle to a properly equipped shop.

Following is a description of the alignment angles which are adjustable on most vehicles and how they affect vehicle handling. Although these angles can apply to both the front and rear wheels, usually only the front suspension is adjustable.

CASTER

▶ **See Figure 26**

Looking at a vehicle from the side, caster angle describes the steering axis rather than a wheel angle. The steering knuckle is attached to a control arm or strut at the top and a control arm at the bottom. The wheel pivots around the line between these points to steer the vehicle. When the upper point is tilted back, this is described as positive caster. Having a positive caster tends to make the wheels self-centering, increasing directional stability. Excessive positive caster makes the wheels hard to steer, while an uneven caster will cause a pull to one side. Overloading the vehicle or sagging rear springs will affect caster, as will raising the rear of the vehicle. If the rear of the vehicle is lower than normal, the caster becomes more positive.

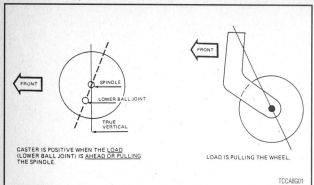

Fig. 26 Caster affects straight-line stability. Caster wheels used on shopping carts, for example, employ positive caster

CAMBER

▶ See Figure 27

Looking from the front of the vehicle, camber is the inward or outward tilt of the top of wheels. When the tops of the wheels are tilted in, this is negative camber; if they are tilted out, it is positive. In a turn, a slight amount of negative camber helps maximize contact of the tire with the road. However, too much negative camber compromises straight-line stability, increases bump steer and torque steer.

TOE

▶ See Figure 28

Looking down at the wheels from above the vehicle, toe angle is the distance between the front of the wheels, relative to the distance between the back of the wheels. If the wheels are closer at the front, they are said to be toed-in or to have negative toe. A small amount of negative toe enhances directional stability and provides a smoother ride on the highway.

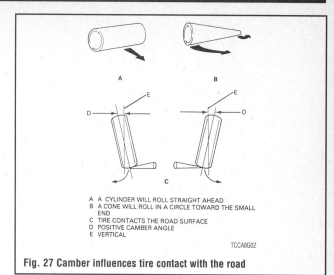

A A CYLINDER WILL ROLL STRAIGHT AHEAD
B A CONE WILL ROLL IN A CIRCLE TOWARD THE SMALL END
C TIRE CONTACTS THE ROAD SURFACE
D POSITIVE CAMBER ANGLE
E VERTICAL

Fig. 27 Camber influences tire contact with the road

Fig. 28 With toe-in, the distance between the wheels is closer at the front than at the rear

4-WHEEL DRIVE FRONT SUSPENSION

▶ See Figures 29 and 30

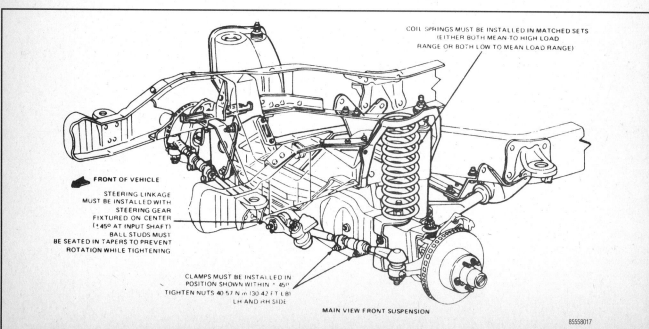

COIL SPRINGS MUST BE INSTALLED IN MATCHED SETS
(EITHER BOTH MEAN-TO-HIGH LOAD
RANGE OR BOTH LOW TO MEAN LOAD RANGE)

FRONT OF VEHICLE
STEERING LINKAGE MUST BE INSTALLED WITH STEERING GEAR FIXTURED ON CENTER (±45° AT INPUT SHAFT) BALL STUDS MUST BE SEATED IN TAPERS TO PREVENT ROTATION WHILE TIGHTENING

CLAMPS MUST BE INSTALLED IN POSITION SHOWN WITHIN ±45°
TIGHTEN NUTS 40-57 N·m (30-42 FT LB)
LH AND RH SIDE

MAIN VIEW FRONT SUSPENSION

85558017

Fig. 29 4WD front suspension—except Mountaineer, 1995–99 Explorer and 1998–99 Ranger

FRONT SUSPENSION COMPONENT LOCATIONS

1. Lower ball joint & steering knuckle
2. Shock absorber
3. Radius arm
4. I-beam
5. Outer tie rod end
6. Adjusting sleeve
7. Drag link
8. Stabilizer bar
9. Stabilizer bar end link

8968P00

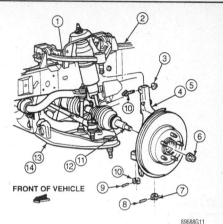

1. Front suspension arm bushing joint
2. Frame
3. Nut
4. Front wheel hub and spindle (RH)
5. Front wheel hub and spindle (LH)
6. Hub washer and nut assembly
7. Nut
8. Cotter pin
9. Cotter pin
10. Nut
11. Front wheel driveshaft and joint (RH)
12. Front wheel driveshaft and joint (RH)
13. Front suspension lower arm (RH)
14. Front suspension lower arm (LH)

FRONT OF VEHICLE

89688G11

Fig. 30 Exploded view of the 4WD Mountaineer, 1995–99 Explorer and 1998–99 Ranger front suspension

Coil Springs

All models except the Mountaineer, 1995–99 Explorer and 1998–99 Ranger use coil springs.

REMOVAL & INSTALLATION

♦ **See Figure 31**

1. Raise the vehicle and install jackstands under the frame. Position a jack beneath the spring under the axle. Raise the jack and compress the spring.
2. Remove the nut retaining the shock absorber to the radius arm. Slide the shock out from the stud.
3. Remove the nut that retains the spring to the axle and radius arm. Remove the retainer.
4. Slowly lower the axle until all spring tension is released and adequate clearance exists to remove the spring from its mounting.
5. Remove the spring by rotating the upper coil out of the tabs in the upper spring seat. Remove the spacer and the seat.

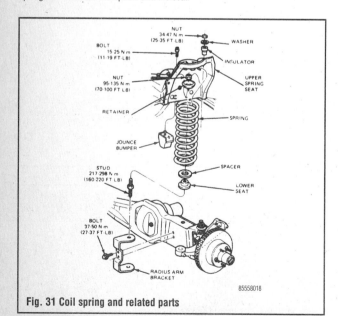

Fig. 31 Coil spring and related parts

✳✳ WARNING

The axle must be supported on the jack throughout spring removal and installation, and must not be permitted to hang by the brake hose. If the length of the brake hose is not sufficient to provide adequate clearance for removal and installation of the spring, the disc

brake caliper must be removed from the spindle. After removal, the caliper must be placed on the frame or otherwise supported to prevent suspending the caliper from the brake line hose. These precautions are absolutely necessary to prevent serious damage to the tube portion of the caliper hose assembly!

6. If required, remove the stud from the axle assembly.
To install:
7. If removed, install the stud on the axle and torque to 190–230 ft. lbs. Install the lower seat and spacer over the stud.
8. Place the spring in position and slowly raise the front axle. Ensure springs are positioned correctly in the upper spring seats.
9. Position the spring lower retainer over the stud and lower seat and torque the attaching nut to 70–100 ft. lbs.
10. Position the shock absorber to the lower stud and install the attaching nut. Tighten the nut to 41–63 ft. lbs. Lower the vehicle.

Torsion Bars

Only the Mountaineer, 1995–99 Explorer and 1998–99 Ranger models use torsion bars.

REMOVAL & INSTALLATION

♦ **See Figures 32 and 33**

✳✳ WARNING

If equipped, always turn off the Automatic Ride Control (ARC) service switch before lifting the vehicle off of the ground. Failure to do so could damage the ARC system components. Refer to Section 1 for jacking procedures.

➡A special tool (Torsion Bar Tool T95T-5310-A) is required for removing the torsion bar. Also, anytime the torsion bar or its adjuster is removed, the vehicle ride height must be checked.

1. Raise and safely support the front of the vehicle. Place the jackstands so as to support the frame of the vehicle. Do not position the jackstands under the lower control arms and do not use car ramps. The lower control arms must be free to hang unhindered.
2. Remove the torsion bar protector/skid plate from the frame.
3. Remove the torsion bar adjuster bolt from the support nut. Count the number of turns required to remove the bolt and record it for installation.
4. Use Torsion Bar Tool T95T-5310-A, or equivalent, to raise the adjuster lever.
5. Remove the support nut then lower the adjuster lever completely.
6. Slide the torsion bar forward, into the lower control arm, to allow the adjuster lever to be removed.
7. Lower the torsion bar and pull it from the lower control arm.

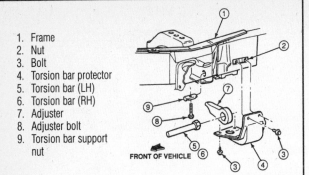

1. Frame
2. Nut
3. Bolt
4. Torsion bar protector
5. Torsion bar (LH)
6. Torsion bar (RH)
7. Adjuster
8. Adjuster bolt
9. Torsion bar support nut

FRONT OF VEHICLE

89688G02

Fig. 32 Exploded view of the torsion bar rear mounting components

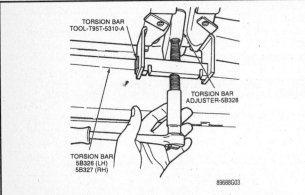

TORSION BAR
TOOL-T95T-5310-A

TORSION BAR
ADJUSTER-5B328

TORSION BAR
5B326 (LH)
5B327 (RH)

89688G03

Fig. 33 Use the torsion bar tool to relieve the tension from the bar

➡Ensure that you do not mix up the right and left-hand torsion bars. They must be installed to the side they were originally removed. If installing a new torsion bar, ensure to order the bar for the proper side of the vehicle.

To install:

8. Raise the torsion bar and slide it forward into the lower control arm.
9. Slide the torsion bar rearward and engage it into the adjuster lever.
10. Use Torsion Bar Tool T95T-5310-A, or equivalent, to raise the adjuster lever.
11. Install the support nut and remove the tool.
12. Lubricate the tip of the adjuster bolt and start it into the support nut.
13. Tighten the adjuster the same number of turns you recorded earlier, then rotate two additional turns.
14. Install the torsion bar protector/skid plate. Tighten the bolts securely.
15. Lower the vehicle and check the ride height adjustment.

RIDE HEIGHT ADJUSTMENT

➡To perform the ride height check and adjustment requires the use of special slip plates under the front wheels. These plates allow the front suspension to properly settle by bypassing the tires adhesion to the ground.

1. Raise and support the vehicle. If equipped with ARC suspension, disconnect the front and rear air lines at the shock absorbers.
2. Position frictionless slip plates under the tires then lower the vehicle onto the slip plates.
3. Bounce the vehicles front and rear suspensions several times to normalize the vehicle static ride height.
4. Measure the distance between the center of the lower control arm bushing bolt and the ground. Record the measurement as dimension A.
5. Measure the distance between the lowest point of the steering knuckle (but not the ball joint) and the ground. Record the measurement as dimension B.
6. Subtract dimension B from dimension A for ride height.

7. For vehicles without ARC suspension, ride height should be 4.33–4.56 in. (110–116mm).
8. For vehicles with ARC suspension, ride height should be 3.26–3.50 in. (83–89mm).
9. To increase the ride height, raise the vehicle and tighten the torsion bar adjuster bolt. Recheck the ride height.
10. To decrease the ride height, raise the vehicle and loosen the torsion bar adjuster bolt. Recheck the ride height.
11. Once proper ride height is established, raise and support the vehicle.
12. If equipped with ARC suspension, connect the front and rear air lines at the shocks.
13. Remove the slip plates from under the wheels.
14. Lower the vehicle.

Shock Absorbers

REMOVAL & INSTALLATION

Except Mountaineer, 1995–99 Explorer and 1998–99 Ranger

▶ See Figure 34

1. Raise the vehicle, as required to provide additional access and remove the nut attaching the shock absorber to the lower mounting stud on the radius arm.
2. Slide the lower shock absorber end off of the stud.
3. Remove the nut, washer and insulator from the upper shock absorber mount at the frame bracket and remove the shock absorber.

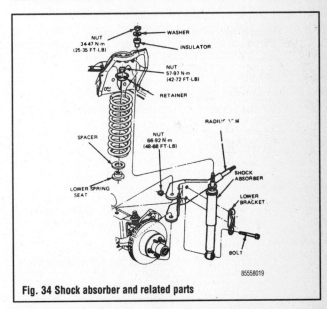

NUT
34-47 N·m
(25-35 FT-LB)

WASHER

INSULATOR

NUT
57-97 N·m
(42-72 FT-LB)

RETAINER

SPACER

RADIUS ARM

NUT
66-92 N·m
(48-68 FT-LB)

SHOCK ABSORBER

LOWER SPRING SEAT

LOWER BRACKET

BOLT

85558019

Fig. 34 Shock absorber and related parts

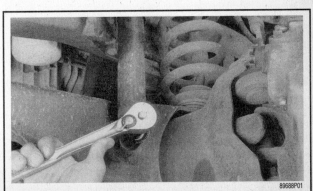

89688P01

To remove the front shock absorber, remove the lower radius arm shock retaining nut . . .

. . . then pull the lower shock mount from the stud

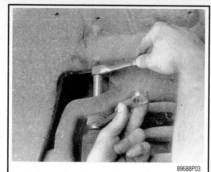

Next, unbolt the upper shock mount using a second wrench on the mount stud to keep it from spinning . . .

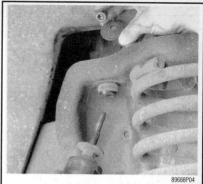

. . . then pull the shock assembly from the upper spring mount

➡A second wrench may be needed to hold the shock absorber from turning while removing the upper attaching nut.

To install:

4. Position the washer and insulator on the shock absorber rod and position the shock absorber to the upper frame bracket mount.

5. Position the insulator and washer on the shock absorber rod and install the attaching nut loosely.

6. Position the shock absorber to the lower mounting stud and install the attaching nut loosely.

7. Tighten the lower shock attaching bolts to 39–53 ft. lbs. (53–72 Nm), and the upper shock attaching bolts to 25–34 ft. lbs. (34–46 Nm).

Mountaineer, 1995–99 Explorer and 1998–99 Ranger

WITHOUT AUTOMATIC RIDE CONTROL (ARC)

▶ **See Figure 35**

1. Raise the front of the vehicle and place jackstands under the lower control arms. Ensure that the lower shock attaching nuts do not become obstructed by the jackstands.

2. Remove the upper shock-to-frame attaching nut, washer and insulator assembly.

3. Remove the two lower shock-to-control arm attaching nuts.

4. Slightly compress the shock absorber by hand and remove it from the vehicle.

To install:

5. Position the lower washer and insulator on the shock absorber rod and position the shock absorber to the upper frame bracket mount.

6. Position the upper insulator and washer on the shock absorber rod and install the attaching nut loosely.

7. Position the lower shock absorber mounting studs into the control arm and install the attaching nuts loosely.

8. Tighten the lower shock attaching nuts to 15–21 ft. lbs. (21–29 Nm), and the upper shock attaching bolts to 30–40 ft. lbs. (40–55 Nm).

WITH AUTOMATIC RIDE CONTROL (ARC)

▶ **See Figure 36**

✳✳ WARNING

Always turn off the Automatic Ride Control (ARC) service switch before lifting the vehicle off of the ground. Failure to do so could damage the ARC system components. Refer to Section 1 for jacking procedures.

1. Place the vehicle in two-wheel drive.

2. Raise the front of the vehicle and place jackstands under the lower control arms. Ensure that the lower shock attaching nuts do not become obstructed by the jackstands.

3. Unplug the vehicle wire harness connector from the shock absorber pig tail plug. Disconnect the pig tail frame retainers.

4. Disconnect the air line from the shock absorber. Push in and hold the plastic ring on the shock. While holding the ring, pull the air line out firmly.

5. If removing the left front shock, disconnect the front height sensor from the upper bracket. Release the spring clip and pull the sensor from the upper ball stud.

6. Remove the upper shock-to-frame attaching nut, washer and insulator assembly.

7. Remove the two lower shock-to-control arm attaching nuts.

8. Slightly compress the shock absorber by hand and remove it from the vehicle.

To install:

9. Position the lower washer and insulator on the shock absorber rod and position the shock absorber to the upper frame bracket mount.

10. Position the upper insulator and washer on the shock absorber rod and install the attaching nut loosely.

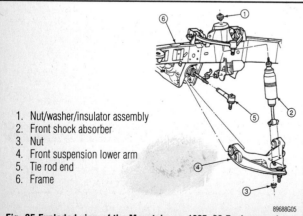

1. Nut/washer/insulator assembly
2. Front shock absorber
3. Nut
4. Front suspension lower arm
5. Tie rod end
6. Frame

Fig. 35 Exploded view of the Mountaineer, 1995–99 Explorer and 1998–99 Ranger front shock absorber

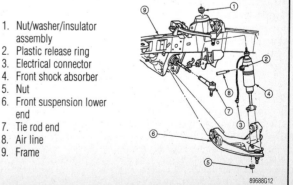

1. Nut/washer/insulator assembly
2. Plastic release ring
3. Electrical connector
4. Front shock absorber
5. Nut
6. Front suspension lower end
7. Tie rod end
8. Air line
9. Frame

Fig. 36 Exploded view of the ARC suspension shock absorber

11. Position the lower shock absorber mounting studs into the control arm and install the attaching nuts loosely.

12. Tighten the lower shock attaching nuts to 15–21 ft. lbs. (21–29 Nm), and the upper shock attaching bolts to 30–40 ft. lbs. (40–55 Nm).

13. If removed, connect the front height sensor to the upper bracket.

14. Connect the air line to the shock absorber. Push in and hold the plastic ring on the shock. While holding the ring, push the air line in firmly.

15. Plug-in the vehicle wire harness connector to the shock absorber pig tail. Install the pig tail frame retainers.

16. Lower the vehicle, then turn on the ARC service switch. Check the ARC system for normal operation by switching the 4-wheel drive selector lever and observing vehicle movement.

TESTING

Please refer to the shock absorber testing procedure found in the 2-wheel drive section.

Ball Joints

INSPECTION

▶ See Figure 37

1. Check and adjust the front wheel bearings. Raise and support the vehicle.

2. Have a helper grasp the lower edge of the tire and move the wheel assembly in and out.

3. While the wheel is being moved, observe the lower spindle arm and the lower part of the axle jaw.

4. A 1/32 in. (0.8mm) or greater movement between the lower part of the axle jaw and the lower spindle arm indicates that the lower ball joint must be replaced

5. To check the upper ball joints, while the wheel is being moved, observe the upper spindle arm and the upper part of the axle jaw.

6. A 1/32 in. (0.8mm) or greater movement between the upper part of the axle jaw and the upper spindle arm indicates that the upper ball joint must be replaced

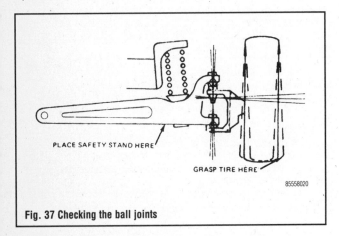

PLACE SAFETY STAND HERE
GRASP TIRE HERE
85558020

Fig. 37 Checking the ball joints

REMOVAL & INSTALLATION

Except Mountaineer, 1995–99 Explorer and 1998–99 Ranger

➡The ball joints are arranged such that if the upper ball joint is to be removed, the lower ball joint must be removed first. Also, when installing the upper ball joint, the lower ball joint must be installed first. Failure to install the lower ball joint before the upper, will result in a lack of clearance for the installation tool.

1. Remove the steering knuckle.

2. Place knuckle in vise and remove snapring from bottom ball joint socket if so equipped.

3. Assemble the C-frame, T74P-4635-C, forcing screw, D79T-3010-AE and ball joint remover T83T-3050-A or equivalent on the lower ball joint.

4. Turn forcing screw clockwise until the lower ball joint is removed from the steering knuckle.

5. Repeat the previous steps for the upper ball joint.

➡Always remove and install the lower ball joint first

To install:

6. Clean the steering knuckle bore and insert lower ball joint in knuckle as straight as possible. The lower ball joint doesn't have a cotter pin hole in the stud.

7. Assemble the C-frame, T74P-4635-C, forcing screw, D790T-3010-AE, ball joint installer, T83T-3050-A and receiver cup T80T-3010-A3 or equivalent tools, to install the lower ball joint.

8. Turn the forcing screw clockwise until the lower ball joint is firmly seated. Install the snapring on the lower ball joint.

➡If the ball joint cannot be installed to the proper depth, realignment of the receiver cup and ball joint installer will be necessary.

9. Repeat the previous steps for the upper ball joint.

10. Install the steering knuckle.

Mountaineer, 1995–99 Explorer and 1998–99 Ranger

The ball joints on the Mountaineer, 1995–99 Explorer and 1998–99 Ranger are integral with the control arms. If the ball joint is defective, the entire control arm must be replaced. Refer to the appropriate control arm removal & installation procedures later in the section.

Steering Knuckle

REMOVAL & INSTALLATION

Except Mountaineer, 1995–99 Explorer and 1998–99 Ranger

1. Raise the vehicle and support on jackstands.

2. Remove the wheel and tire assembly.

3. Remove the caliper.

4. Remove hub locks and locknuts.

5. Remove the hub and rotor. Ensure that the wheel bearings do not fall out.

6. Remove the nuts retaining the spindle to the steering knuckle. Tap the spindle with a plastic or rawhide hammer to jar the spindle from the knuckle. Remove the splash shield.

7. Remove the axle shaft for the side of the vehicle you are working on. Refer to Section 7 for axle shaft removal procedures.

8. Remove the cotter pin from the tie rod nut and then remove the nut. Tap on the tie rod stud to free it from the steering arm.

9. Remove the upper ball joint cotter pin and nut. Loosen the lower ball joint nut to the end of the stud.

10. Strike the inside of the spindle near the upper and lower ball joints to break the spindle loose from the ball joint studs.

11. Remove the camber adjuster sleeve. If required, use pitman arm puller, T64P-3590-F or equivalent to remove the adjuster out of the spindle. Remove the lower ball joint nut.

12. Remove the steering knuckle from the I-beam end.

To install:

13. Install the steering knuckle to the I-beam end, engaging both upper and lower ball joints studs in their respective holes.

14. Install the camber adjuster into the support arm. Position the slot in its original position.

✳✳ CAUTION

The following torque sequence must be followed exactly when securing the spindle. Excessive spindle turning effort may result in reduced steering returnability if this procedure is not followed.

15. Install a new nut on the bottom of the ball joint stud and torque to 90 ft. lbs. (minimum). Tighten to align the nut to the next slot in the nut with the hole in the ball joint stud. Install a new cotter pin.

16. Install the snapring on the upper ball joint stud. Install the upper ball joint pinch bolt and torque the nut to 48–65 ft. lbs.

➡**The camber adjuster will seat itself into the knuckle at a predetermined position during the tightening sequence. Do not attempt to adjust this position.**

17. Install the axle shaft or shafts that were removed.
18. Install the splash shield and spindle onto the steering knuckle. Install and tighten the spindle nuts to 40–50 ft. lbs.
19. Install the rotor on the spindle and push the outer wheel bearing inwards to seat it..
20. Install the locknuts and adjust the wheel bearings. Install the remainder of the locking hub assemblies.

Mountaineer, 1995–99 Explorer and 1998–99 Ranger

✱✱✱ WARNING

Do not perform this procedure unless a new wheel hub nut and washer assembly is available. Once removed, these parts must never be reused during assembly.

1. Position the steering wheel to the on-center position.

✱✱✱ WARNING

If equipped, always turn off the Automatic Ride Control (ARC) service switch before lifting the vehicle off of the ground. Failure to do so could damage the ARC system components. Refer to Section 1 for jacking procedures.

2. Loosen the wheel lug nuts then raise and safely support the front of the vehicle.
3. Remove the wheels.
4. Remove the front disc brake caliper, bracket and rotor. Also remove the rotor splash shield.
5. If equipped, unbolt the front wheel ABS sensor and wire harness from the steering knuckle.
6. Remove the front wheel hub nut and washer.

✱✱✱ WARNING

Never reuse the wheel hub nut and washer. This nut is a torque prevailing design and cannot be reused.

7. Remove the cotter pin and nut retaining the tie rod end to the steering knuckle.
8. Disconnect the tie rod end from the steering knuckle using a jawed puller, such as Pitman Arm Puller T64P-3590-F, or equivalent.
9. Unload the torsion bar. Follow the torsion bar removal procedures, but do not remove the bar.
10. Support the lower control arm with a jack. Remove the cotter pin and loosen the nut retaining the lower ball joint to the steering knuckle.
11. Disconnect the lower ball joint from the steering knuckle using a jawed puller, such as Pitman Arm Puller T64P-3590-F, or equivalent.
12. Remove the lower ball joint retaining nut and slowly raise the lower control arm until the ball joint stud is disengaged from the steering knuckle.

➡**The hub shaft is a slip fit into the wheel hub and bearing; a press is not normally required.**

13. Ensure that the wheel hub shaft can be pushed inwards. If not, assemble a press to the front wheel studs and press the wheel hub shaft inwards slightly to break it loose.
14. Remove the upper ball joint retaining bolt and nut from the steering knuckle then disconnect the joint from the knuckle.
15. Remove the steering knuckle/spindle assembly from the vehicle.
To install:
16. Inspect the upper and lower ball joints and seals for damage and replace as needed.
17. Position the steering knuckle onto the upper ball joint, while aligning

the axle shaft with the wheel hub, and install the retaining bolt and nut. Tighten the bolt to 30–41 ft. lbs. (40–55 Nm).
18. Install the lower ball joint stud into the steering knuckle until the stud protrudes through the knuckle.
19. Install the retaining nut to the lower ball joint stud and tighten to 84–113 ft. lbs. (113–153 Nm). Install the cotter pin, advancing (tightening) the nut as needed. Never loosen the ball joint nut in order to install the cotter pin.
20. Connect the tie rod end to the steering knuckle and install the retaining nut. Tighten to 57–77 ft. lbs. (77–104 Nm) and install the cotter pin, advancing (tightening) the nut as needed. Never loosen the ball joint nut in order to install the cotter pin.
21. If removed, install the ABS sensor to the wheel hub.
22. Install the hub washer and nut then tighten to 157–213 ft. lbs. (212–288 Nm).
23. Install the front disc brake splash shield, rotor, bracket and caliper.
24. Install the wheel and snug all of the lug nuts.
25. Reload the torsion bar pressure. Refer to the torsion bar installation procedures. Check and, if necessary, set the vehicle ride height.
26. Lower the vehicle and tighten the wheel lug nuts to 100 ft. lbs. (135 Nm).

Radius Arm

Radius arms are not used on Mountaineer, 1995–99 Explorer and 1998–99 Ranger models.

REMOVAL & INSTALLATION

⬥ **See Figure 38**

1. Raise the front of the vehicle, place jackstands under the frame. Place a jack under the axle.

✱✱✱ WARNING

The axle must be supported on the jack throughout spring removal and installation, and must not be permitted to hang by the brake hose. If the length of the brake hose is not sufficient to provide adequate clearance for removal and installation of the spring, the disc brake caliper must be removed from the spindle. After removal, the caliper must be placed on the frame or otherwise supported to prevent suspending the caliper from the caliper hose. These precautions are absolutely necessary to prevent serious damage to the tube portion of the caliper hose assembly.

2. Disconnect the lower stud. Remove the front spring from the vehicle.
3. Remove the spring lower seat and stud from the radius arm. Remove the bolts that attach the radius arm to the axle and front bracket.
4. Remove the nut, rear washer and insulator from the rear side of the radius arm rear bracket.
5. Remove the radius arm from the vehicle. Remove the inner insulator and retainer from the radius arm stud.

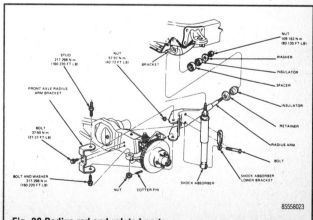

Fig. 38 Radius rod and related parts

To install:

6. Position the front end of the radius arm from bracket to axle. Install the retaining bolts and stud in the bracket finger tight.

7. Install the retainer and inner insulator on the radius arm stud and insert the stud through the radius arm rear bracket.

8. Install the rear washer, insulator and nut on the arm stud at the rear side of the arm rear bracket. Tighten the nut to 80–120 ft. lbs.

9. Tighten the stud to 190–230 ft. lbs. Tighten the front bracket to axle bolts to 37–50 ft. lbs. and the lower bolt and washer to 190–230 ft. lbs.

10. Install the spring lower seat and spring insulator on the radius arm so that the hole in the seat goes over the arm to axle bolt. Tighten the axle pivot bolt to 120–150 ft. lbs.

11. Install the front spring. Connect the lower stud of the radius arm and torque the retaining nut to 39–53 ft. lbs. on 1991–94 vehicles.

Stabilizer Bar

REMOVAL & INSTALLATION

Ranger

1. As required, raise and support the vehicle safely.
2. Remove the nuts and bolts retaining the stabilizer bar to the end links.
3. Remove the retainers and the stabilizer bar and bushings from the vehicle.

To install:

4. Position the stabilizer bar to the axles and brackets.
5. Install the retainer and the end link bolts.
6. Torque the retainer bolts to 35–50 ft. lbs. (47–67 Nm) on 1991–94 models and 22–30 ft. lbs. (30–40 Nm) on 1995–99 models. Torque the end link nuts to 30–41 ft. lbs. (40–55 Nm).

1991–94 Explorer

1. As required, raise and support the vehicle safely.
2. Remove the nuts and washer and disconnect the stabilizer link assembly from the front I-beam axle.
3. Remove the mounting bolts and remove the stabilizer bar retainers from the stabilizer bar assembly.
4. Remove the stabilizer bar from the vehicle.

To install:

5. Place stabilizer bar in position on the frame mounting brackets.
6. Install retainers and tighten retainer bolt to 35–50 ft. lbs. (47–67 Nm). If removed, install the stabilizer bar link assembly to the stabilizer bar. Install the nut and washer and tighten to 30–41 ft. lbs. (40–55 Nm).
7. Position the stabilizer bar link in the I-beam mounting bracket. Install the bolt and tighten to 30–41 ft. lbs. (40–55 Nm).

Mountaineer, 1995–99 Explorer and 1998–99 Ranger

1. Raise and safely support the vehicle.
2. Remove the nut, washer and bushing (on underside of the lower control arm) linking the stabilizer bar end to the lower control arm.

3. Lift up on the bar and remove the remaining bushings and the spacer and bolt assembly (called the end link) from the stabilizer bar end.

4. Remove the bar mounting bracket-to-frame bolts.

5. Remove the stabilizer bar from the vehicle. If necessary, remove the mounting brackets and insulators from the bar.

To install:

6. Inspect all of the stabilizer bar mounting and end link bushings. Replace any that are cracked, squashed, swollen or damaged.

7. Position the stabilizer bar mounting brackets to the frame and install the retaining bolts loosely.

8. Install the end link assembly to the bar end and the lower control arm. Install the end link retaining bolt loosely.

9. Tighten the mounting bracket bolts to 65–91 ft. lbs. (88–119 Nm).

➡The end link assembly must be tightened with the vehicle weight on the front wheels.

10. Lower the vehicle then tighten the end link retaining nut to 10–13 ft. lbs. (13–17 Nm).

I-Beam Axle

The I-beam axle is part of the front drive axle assembly. Refer to Section 7 for front drive axle housing removal and installation procedures.

Upper Control Arm

Only the Mountaineer, 1995–99 Explorer and 1998–99 Ranger models have control arms.

REMOVAL & INSTALLATION

♦ **See Figure 39**

➡After performing this procedure, it will be necessary to have the wheel alignment checked and adjusted by a professional shop.

1. Position the steering wheel to the on-center position. Loosen the wheel lug nuts.
2. Raise and safely support the vehicle. Position the jack stands under the lower control arms.
3. Remove the wheel lug nuts and wheel.

➡Before removing the steering knuckle-to-upper ball joint retaining (pinch) bolt, secure the steering knuckle from tilting.

4. Remove the steering knuckle-to-upper ball joint retaining (pinch) bolt and separate the two components.
5. Make alignment marks on the control arm pivot bolt cam assemblies.
6. To remove the left side control arm proceed as follows:
   a. Remove the nuts and cam bolts from the control arm pivot points.
   b. Pull the control arm from the vehicle frame.
7. To remove the right side control arm, proceed as follows:
   a. If only the ball joint is to be removed, make alignment marks on the

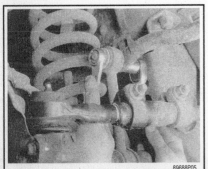

To remove the stabilizer bar, first unbolt the stabilizer bar end-to-radius arm links . . .

89688P05

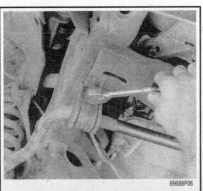

. . . then remove the bar retainer strap bolts followed by the bar and its bushings

89688P06

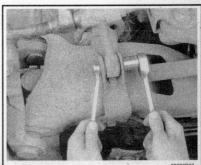

If necessary, remove the end link-to-radius arm mounting bolts to remove the end links

89688P07

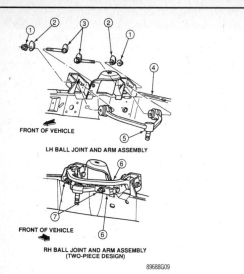

FRONT OF VEHICLE

LH BALL JOINT AND ARM ASSEMBLY

FRONT OF VEHICLE

**RH BALL JOINT AND ARM ASSEMBLY
(TWO-PIECE DESIGN)**

89688G09

1. Nut
2. Front suspension upper adjuster cam
3. Front suspension upper adjuster cam bolt
4. Frame
5. Front suspension arm bushing joint
6. Front suspension arm bushing joint
7. Nut

Fig. 39 Exploded view of the left and right upper control arms

control arm and ball joint assembly then remove the two retaining nuts and the ball joint. Skip to the installation procedures.

   b. Remove the nuts and cam bolts from the control arm pivot points.

   c. Pull the control arm from the vehicle frame.

To install:

  8. For right-side control arm, if removed, install the ball joint assembly and retaining nuts to the control arm and tighten the nuts to 95–128 ft. lbs. (128–173 Nm).

  9. Install the control arm pivot points into the frame pockets.

  10. Install the cam bolts and nuts, align the matchmarks and tighten the nuts to 84–113 ft. lbs. (113–153 Nm).

  11. Connect the upper ball joint shaft to the steering knuckle. Install the retaining (pinch) bolt and tighten to 30–41 ft. lbs. (40–55 Nm).

12. Install the wheel and snug the lug nuts.
13. Lower the vehicle and tighten the lug nuts to 100 ft. lbs. (135 Nm).
14. Have the alignment checked by a professional repair shop.

Lower Control Arm

Only the Mountaineer, 1995–99 Explorer and 1998–99 Ranger models have control arms.

REMOVAL & INSTALLATION

▶ **See Figure 40**

➡**To remove the lower control arm, the torsion bar must be removed. Anytime the torsion bar is disturbed, the ride height must be checked and adjusted.**

  1. Position the steering wheel to the on-center position. Loosen the wheel lug nuts.

  2. Raise and safely support the vehicle.

  3. Remove the wheel lug nuts and wheel.

  4. Disconnect the stabilizer bar link bolt from the lower control arm.

  5. Remove the front shock absorber.

  6. Remove the torsion bar.

  7. Remove the lower ball joint retaining nut cotter pin and loosen the nut but do not remove it.

  8. Disconnect the lower ball joint stud from the steering knuckle using a jawed puller, such as Pitman Arm Puller T64P-3590-F, or equivalent.

✶✶ WARNING

Fasten a support, either out of a block of wood or wire wrapped around the frame, and support the weight of the steering knuckle/brake assembly. Do not allow the steering knuckle/brake assembly to hang from the upper ball joint as this may damage the joint.

  9. Position a jack under the lower control arm then remove the lower ball joint retaining nut.

  10. Raise the lower control arm until the lower ball joint stud is free from the steering knuckle.

  11. Remove the two nuts and bolts retaining the lower arm pivot points to the frame crossmember.

  12. Remove the lower control arm from the frame pockets. Some careful prying may ease the removal of the arm.

1. Stabilizer bar stud and bushing
2. Nut, washer, and insulator assembly
3. Bolt
4. Frame
5. Torsion bar (LH)
6. Torsion bar (RH)
7. Nut
8. Nut and washer
9. Front suspension lower arm (LH)
10. Front suspension lower arm (RH)
11. Tie rod end
12. Nut
13. Nut
14. Front stabilizer bar link
15. Front stabilizer bar
16. Front stabilizer bar bushing
17. Stabilizer bar bracket
18. Bolt

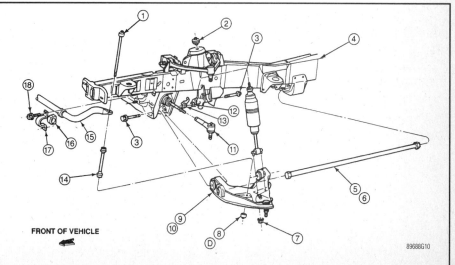

FRONT OF VEHICLE

89688G10

Fig. 40 Exploded view of the lower control arm

To install:

13. Inspect the lower ball joint, boot and pivot bushings. If any inspected components are worn or damaged, the entire control arm must be replaced.

➡**Do not tighten the lower control arm mounting bolts to the final torque until the end of the installation procedure.**

14. Position the lower control arm pivot points into the frame and cross-member pockets. Install the bolts and nuts and snug the bolts.
15. Position a jack under the lower control arm.
16. Install the torsion bar.
17. Raise the lower control arm to allow the lower ball joint stud to be inserted into the steering knuckle.
18. Lower the control arm assembly and ensure that the lower ball joint stud protrudes through the steering knuckle bore.
19. Install the lower ball joint attaching nut and tighten to 83–113 ft. lbs. (113–153 Nm). Install a new cotter pin, advancing (tightening) the nut as required. Never loosen the retaining nut in order to install the cotter pin.
20. Install the shock absorber.
21. Install the wheel and snug the lug nuts.
22. Lower the vehicle and tighten the lug nuts to 100 ft. lbs. (135 Nm).

➡**The lower control arm-to-frame bolts must be tightened with the weight of the vehicle resting on the wheels. If clearance permits, allow the vehicle to sit on the ground while tightening the bolts.**

23. If necessary, raise the vehicle again and position either car ramps under the wheels or jackstands on the lower control arms, as close to the wheels as possible.
24. Tighten the control arm-to-frame bolts to 111–148 ft. lbs. (150–200 Nm).
25. Lower the vehicle.
26. Check and adjust the ride height.
27. While it should not be necessary, have the wheel alignment checked by a professional shop.

Front Wheel Bearings

REMOVAL & INSTALLATION

Except Mountaineer, 1995–99 Explorer and 1998–99 Ranger

▶ **See Figure 41**

WITH MANUAL LOCKING HUBS

▶ **See Figures 42, 43 and 44**

1. Raise the vehicle and install jackstands.
2. Remove the wheel and tire assembly.
3. Remove the retainer washers from the lug nut studs and remove the manual locking hub assembly from the spindle.
4. Remove the snapring and spacer from the end of the spindle shaft.
5. Remove the outer wheel bearing locknut from the spindle using 4 prong spindle nut spanner wrench, T86T-1197-A or equivalent. Make sure the tabs on the tool engage the slots in the locknut.
6. Remove the locknut washer from the spindle.
7. Remove the inner wheel bearing locknut from the spindle using 4 prong spindle nut spanner wrench, T86T-1197-A or equivalent. Make sure the tabs on the tool engage the slots in the locknut.
8. Remove the outer bearing cone and roller assembly from the hub. Remove the hub and rotor from the spindle.
9. Using seal removal tool 1175-AC or equivalent remove and discard the grease seal. Remove the inner bearing cone and roller assembly from the hub.
10. Clean the inner and outer bearing assemblies in solvent. Inspect the bearings and the cones for wear and damage. Replace defective parts, as required.
11. If the cups are worn or damaged, remove them with front hub remover tool T81P-1104-C and tool T77F-1102-A or equivalent.

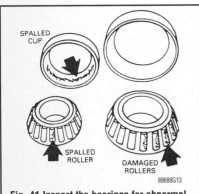

Fig. 41 Inspect the bearings for abnormal wear and/or damage

Before beginning the wheel bearing removal, and after the outer hub is removed, wipe off any excess grease

After the grease is wiped off, remove the axle shaft snapring . . .

. . . then pull the splined spacer from the axle shaft end

Use a 4 pronged socket to loosen the outer wheel bearing locknut . . .

. . . then remove the outer locknut

Remove the lockwasher from behind the outer locknut . . .

. . . then loosen and remove the inner locknut—note the lockwasher engagement pin (arrow)

While pushing inwards on the rotor/hub assembly, remove the outer wheel bearing . . .

. . . then pull the rotor/hub assembly from the spindle, taking care not to scratch the bearing cups in the hub

Pry out the grease seal on the back of the rotor/hub assembly . . .

. . . then remove the inner wheel bearing. Thoroughly clean and inspect all of the parts for wear or damage

After packing the bearing with grease, position a new seal to the rotor/hub assembly . . .

. . . then, using the correct seal installer, drive the seal into the rotor/hub until it is fully seated

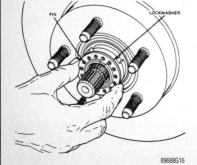

Fig. 42 Ensure that the pin on the inner locknut engages one of the holes of the lock washer

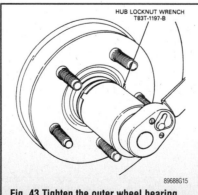

Fig. 43 Tighten the outer wheel bearing locknut to specification

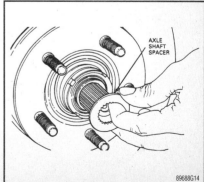

Fig. 44 Install the splined axle shaft spacer then the snapring

12. Wipe the old grease from the spindle. Check the spindle for excessive wear or damage. Replace defective parts, as required.

To install:

13. If the inner and outer cups were removed, use bearing driver handle tool T80-4000-W or equivalent and replace the cups. Be sure to seat the cups properly in the hub.

14. Use a bearing packer tool and properly repack the wheel bearings with the proper grade and type grease. If a bearing packer is not available work as much of the grease as possible between the rollers and cages. Also, grease the cone surfaces.

15. Position the inner bearing cone and roller assembly in the inner cup. A light film of grease should be included between the lips of the new grease seal.

16. Install the grease seal by driving in place with hub seal replacer tool T83T-1175-B and Driver Handle T80T-4000-W.

17. Install the hub and rotor assembly onto the spindle. Keep the hub centered on the spindle to prevent damage to the spindle and the retainer.

18. Install the outer bearing cone and roller assembly

19. Carefully install the rotor onto the spindle. Install the outer wheel bearing in the rotor.

20. Install the inner adjusting nut with the pin facing out. Tighten the inner adjusting nut to 35 ft. lbs. (47 Nm) to seat the bearings.

21. Follow the appropriate wheel bearing adjustment procedures.

WITH AUTOMATIC LOCKING HUBS

▶ See Figures 45, 46 and 47

1. Raise the vehicle and install jackstands.
2. Remove the wheel and tire assembly.
3. Remove the retainer washers from the lug nut studs and remove the automatic locking hub assembly from the spindle.
4. Remove the snapring and spacer from the end of the spindle shaft.
5. Pull the locking cam assembly and the two plastic spacers off of the wheel bearing adjusting nut.
6. Use a magnet and remove the locking key from under the adjusting nut.

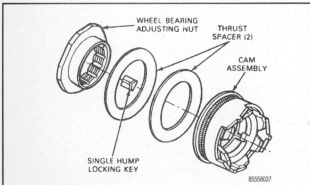

Fig. 45 Exploded view of the locking cam, thrust washers, locking key and bearing adjuster nut

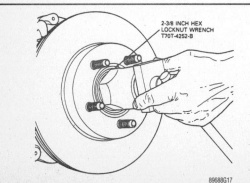

Fig. 46 Remove the wheel bearing adjusting nut after removing the locking key from under it

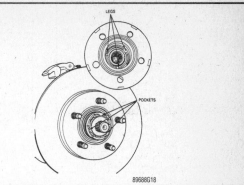

Fig. 47 When installing the outer hub cover, align the cam pockets with the legs on the cover

If required, rotate the adjusting nut slightly to relieve pressure against the locking key.

❊❊ WARNING

To prevent damage to the adjusting nut and spindle threads on vehicles equipped with automatic hubs, look into the spindle keyway under the adjusting nut and remove the separate locking key before removing the adjusting nut.

7. Remove the wheel bearing locknut using a 2-⅜ inch (60.3mm) hex socket, such as Hex Locknut Wrench T70T-4252-B.

8. Remove the outer bearing cone and roller assembly from the hub. Remove the hub and rotor from the spindle.

9. Using seal removal tool 1175-AC or equivalent remove and discard the grease seal. Remove the inner bearing cone and roller assembly from the hub.

10. Clean the inner and outer bearing assemblies in solvent. Inspect the bearings and the cones for wear and damage. Replace defective parts, as required.

11. If the cups are worn or damaged, remove them with front hub remover tool T81P-1104-C and tool T77F-1102-A or equivalent.

12. Wipe the old grease from the spindle. Check the spindle for excessive wear or damage. Replace defective parts, as required.

To install:

13. If the inner and outer cups were removed, use bearing driver handle tool T80-4000-W or equivalent and replace the cups. Be sure to seat the cups properly in the hub.

14. Use a bearing packer tool and properly repack the wheel bearings with the proper grade and type grease. If a bearing packer is not available work as much of the grease as possible between the rollers and cages. Also, grease the cone surfaces.

15. Position the inner bearing cone and roller assembly in the inner cup. A light film of grease should be included between the lips of the new grease seal.

16. Install the grease seal by driving in place with hub seal replacer tool T83T-1175-B and Driver Handle T80T-4000-W.

17. Install the hub and rotor assembly onto the spindle. Keep the hub centered on the spindle to prevent damage to the spindle and the retainer.

18. Install the outer bearing cone and roller assembly.

19. Carefully install the rotor onto the spindle. Install the outer wheel bearing in the rotor.

20. Install the adjusting nut and tighten 35 ft. lbs. (47 Nm) to seat the bearings.

21. Follow the appropriate wheel bearing adjustment procedures.

Mountaineer, 1995–99 Explorer and 1998–99 Ranger

▶ See Figure 48

❊❊ WARNING

If equipped, always turn off the Automatic Ride Control (ARC) service switch before lifting the vehicle off of the ground. Failure to do so could damage the ARC system components. Refer to Section 1 for jacking procedures.

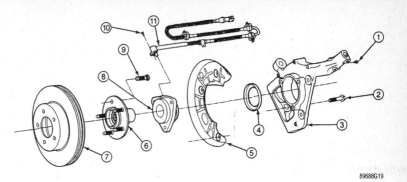

1. Hex tapping screw
2. Flange head screw
3. Steering knuckle
4. Hub oil slinger
5. Brake dust shield
6. Flange hub
7. Rotor
8. Bearing assembly
9. Wheel bolt
10. Front brake anti-lock sensor screw
11. Front brake anti-lock sensor

89688G19

Fig. 48 Exploded view of the Mountaineer, 1995–99 Explorer and 1998–99 Ranger sealed front wheel bearing and related components

1. Loosen the wheel lug nuts then raise and safely support the front of the vehicle.
2. Remove the wheels.
3. Remove the front disc brake caliper, bracket and rotor. Also remove the rotor splash shield.
4. If equipped, unbolt the front wheel ABS sensor and wire harness from the steering knuckle.
5. Remove the front wheel hub nut and washer.

✳✳ WARNING

Never reuse the wheel hub nut and washer. This nut is a torque prevailing design and cannot be reused.

➥The hub shaft is a slip fit into the wheel hub and bearing; a press is not normally required.

6. Ensure that the wheel hub shaft can be pushed inwards. If not, assemble a press to the front wheel studs and press the wheel hub shaft inwards slightly to break it loose.
7. Remove the three wheel hub/bearing to steering knuckle retaining bolts. Remove the hub and bearing assembly.

To install:
8. Install the ABS sensor to the wheel hub then position the hub to the front axle shaft and steering knuckle.
9. Install the three retaining bolts and tighten them to 70–80 ft. lbs. (95–108 Nm).
10. Install the hub washer and nut and tighten to 157–213 ft. lbs. (212–288 Nm).

11. Install the ABS sensor retaining bolt.
12. Install the front brake rotor shield, rotor, bracket and caliper.
13. Install the wheel and snug the lug nuts.
14. Lower the vehicle and tighten the lug nuts to 100 ft. lbs. (135 Nm).

ADJUSTMENT

Except Mountaineer, 1995–99 Explorer and 1998–99 Ranger

WITH MANUAL LOCKING HUBS

◆ See Figure 49

1. Raise the vehicle and install jackstands.
2. Remove the wheel and tire assembly.
3. Remove the retainer washers from the lug nut studs and remove the manual locking hub assembly from the spindle.
4. Remove the snapring and spacer from the end of the spindle shaft.
5. Remove the outer wheel bearing locknut from the spindle using 4 prong spindle nut spanner wrench, T86T-1197-A or equivalent. Make sure the tabs on the tool engage the slots in the locknut.
6. Remove the locknut washer from the spindle.
7. Loosen the inner wheel bearing locknut using 4 prong spindle nut spanner wrench, tool T86T-1197-A or equivalent. Make sure that the tabs on the tool engage the slots in the locknut and that the slot in the tool is over the pin on the locknut.
8. Tighten the inner locknut to 35 ft. lbs. (47 Nm) to seat the bearings.
9. Spin the rotor and back off the inner locknut ¼ turn. Install the lockwasher on the spindle. Retighten the inner locknut to 16 inch lbs. (1.8 Nm). It

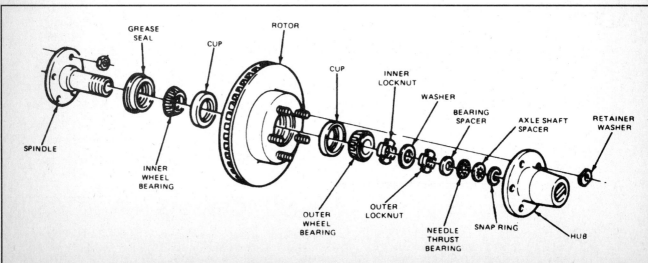

Fig. 49 Exploded view of the manual locking hubs and wheel bearings

85558026

may be necessary to turn the inner locknut slightly so that the pin on the locknut aligns with the closest hole in the lockwasher.

10. Install the outer wheel bearing locknut using 4 prong spindle nut spanner wrench, tool T86T-1197-A or equivalent. Tighten locknut to 150 ft. lbs.

11. Install the axle shaft spacer.

12. Clip the snapring onto the end of the spindle.

13. Install the manual hub assembly over the spindle. Install the retainer washers.

14. Install the wheel and tire assembly. Install and torque lug nuts to specification.

15. Check the end-play of the wheel and tire assembly on the spindle. End-play should be 0.001–0.003 in. (0.025–0.076mm) and the maximum torque to rotate the hub should be 25 inch lbs. (2.8Nm).

WITH AUTOMATIC LOCKING HUBS

▶ See Figure 50

1. Raise the vehicle and install jackstands.

2. Remove the wheel and tire assembly.

3. Remove the retainer washers from the lug nut studs and remove the automatic locking hub assembly from the spindle.

4. Remove the snapring and spacer from the end of the spindle shaft.

5. Pull the locking cam assembly and the two plastic spacers off of the wheel bearing adjusting nut.

6. Use a magnet and remove the locking key from under the adjusting nut. If required, rotate the adjusting nut slightly to relieve pressure against the locking key.

✳✳ WARNING

To prevent damage to the adjusting nut and spindle threads on vehicles equipped with automatic hubs, look into the spindle keyway under the adjusting nut and remove the separate locking key before removing the adjusting nut.

7. Loosen the wheel bearing locknut using a 2-⅜ inch (60.3mm) hex socket, such as Hex Locknut Wrench T70T-4252-B.

8. Tighten the inner locknut to 35 ft. lbs. (47 Nm) to seat the bearings.

9. Spin the rotor and back off the inner locknut ¼ turn (90°). Retighten the locknut to 16 inch lbs. (1.8 Nm).

10. Align the closest lug in the bearing adjusting nut with the center of the spindle keyway slot. Advance the nut to the next if required.

11. Install the separate locking key in the spindle keyway under the adjusting nut.

✳✳ CAUTION

Extreme care must be taken when aligning the adjusting nut with the center of the spindle keyway slot to prevent damage to the separate locking key. The wheel and tire assembly may come off while the vehicle is in motion if the key is damaged.

12. Install the two plastic thrust spacers and push or press the cam assembly onto the adjusting nut by lining up the keyway in the cam assembly with the separate locking key.

✳✳ WARNING

Do not damage the locking key when installing the cam assembly.

13. Install the axle shaft spacer.

14. Clip the snapring onto the end of the spindle.

15. Install the manual hub assembly over the spindle. Install the retainer washers.

16. Install the wheel and tire assembly. Install and torque lug nuts to specification.

17. Check the endplate of the wheel and tire assembly on the spindle. End-play should be 0.001–0.003 in. (0.025–0.076mm) and the maximum torque to rotate the hub should be 25 inch lbs. (2.8Nm).

Mountaineer, 1995–99 Explorer and 1998–99 Ranger

The Mountaineer, 1995–99 Explorer and 1998–99 Ranger use non-adjustable wheel bearings. If the endplate is not within specifications, the wheel bearings must be replaced. End-play should be 0.000–0.003 in. (0.00–0.08mm).

Wheel Alignment

Please refer to 2-wheel drive front suspension wheel alignment, earlier in this section.

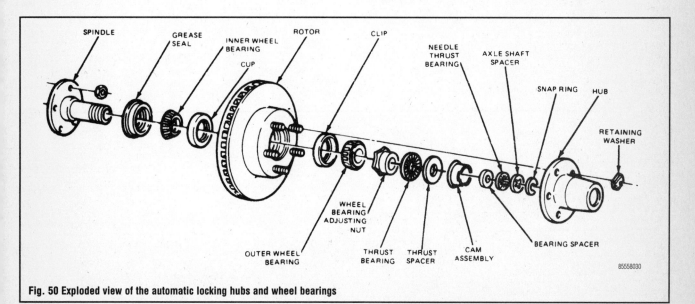

Fig. 50 Exploded view of the automatic locking hubs and wheel bearings

85558030

REAR SUSPENSION

▶ See Figure 51

REAR SUSPENSION COMPONENT LOCATIONS

1. Leaf spring
2. Stabilizer bar end link
3. Stabilizer bar
4. Shock absorber
5. Spring shackle

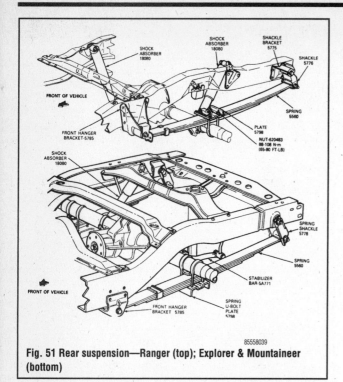

Fig. 51 Rear suspension—Ranger (top); Explorer & Mountaineer (bottom)

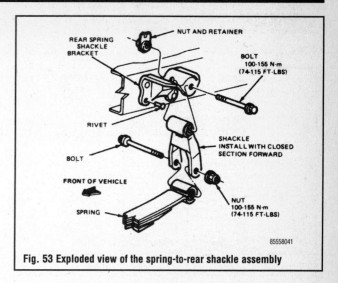

Fig. 53 Exploded view of the spring-to-rear shackle assembly

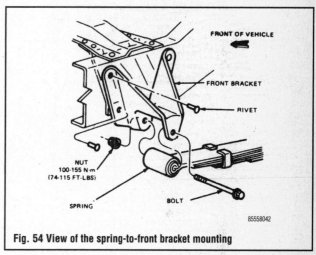

Fig. 54 View of the spring-to-front bracket mounting

Leaf Springs

REMOVAL & INSTALLATION

▶ See Figures 52, 53 and 54

✶✶ WARNING

If equipped, always turn off the Automatic Ride Control (ARC) service switch before lifting the vehicle off of the ground. Failure to do so could damage the ARC system components. Refer to Section 1 for jacking procedures.

1. Raise the vehicle and install jackstands under the frame. The vehicle must be supported in such a way that the rear axle hangs free with the tires still touching the ground.
2. Remove the nuts from the spring U-bolts and drive the U-bolts from the U-bolt plate.
3. Remove the spring to bracket nut and bolt at the front of the spring.

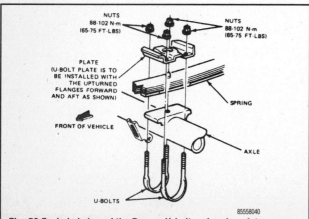

Fig. 52 Exploded view of the Ranger U-bolt and spring plate assembly—Explorer/Mountaineer similar

4. Remove the shackle upper and lower nuts and bolts at the rear of the spring.
5. Remove the spring and shackle assembly from the rear shackle bracket.
To install:
6. Position the spring in the shackle. Install the upper shackle spring bolt and nut with the bolt head facing outward.
7. Position the front end of the spring in the bracket and install the bolt and nut.
8. Position the shackle in the rear bracket and install the nut and bolt.
9. Position the spring on top of the axle with the spring tie bolt centered in the hole provided in the seat.
10. Lower the vehicle to the floor. Torque the spring U-bolt nuts to 65–75 ft. lbs. Torque the front spring bolt to 75–115 ft. lbs. Torque the rear shackle nuts and bolts to 75–115 ft. lbs.

Shock Absorbers

REMOVAL & INSTALLATION

Without Automatic Ride Control (ARC)

▶ See Figures 55 and 56

1. Raise the vehicle and position jackstands under the axle or wheel, in order to take the load off of the shock absorber.
2. Remove the shock absorber lower retaining nut and bolt. Swing the lower end free of the mounting bracket on the axle housing.

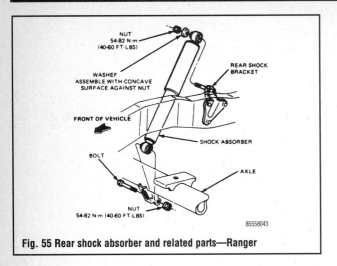

Fig. 55 Rear shock absorber and related parts—Ranger

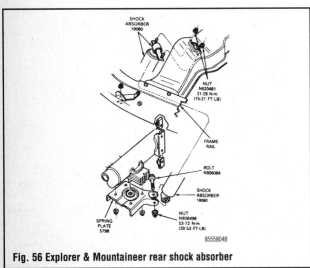

Fig. 56 Explorer & Mountaineer rear shock absorber

3. Remove the retaining nut(s) from the upper shock absorber mounting.
4. Remove the shock absorber from the vehicle.
5. Installation is the reverse of the removal procedure. Torque the lower shock absorber retaining bolt to 39–53 ft. lbs.
6. On the Ranger torque the upper shock absorber mounting nut to 39–53 ft. lbs. On the Explorer/Mountaineer torque the upper shock absorber retaining nuts to 15–21 ft. lbs.

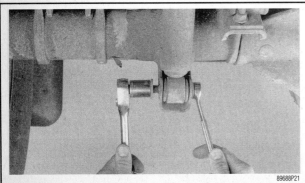

To remove the rear shock absorber, first unbolt the lower shock mounting from the drive axle . . .

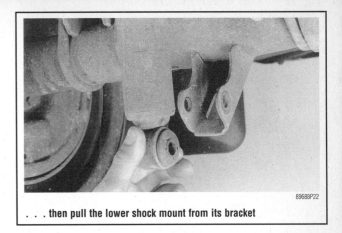

. . . then pull the lower shock mount from its bracket

Finally, unbolt the upper shock mount and remove the shock from the vehicle

With Automatic Ride Control (ARC)

▶ See Figure 57

✳✳ WARNING

If equipped, always turn off the Automatic Ride Control (ARC) service switch before lifting the vehicle off of the ground. Failure to do so could damage the ARC system components. Refer to Section 1 for jacking procedures.

1. Place the vehicle in two wheel drive.
2. Turn off the ARC control service switch.

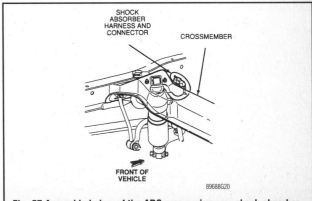

Fig. 57 Assembled view of the ARC suspension rear shock absorber

3. Raise the rear of the vehicle and place the jackstands under the rear axle assembly.

4. Pry the rear shock absorber electrical connector retainer from the cross member then disconnect the plug.

5. Disconnect the air line at the shock absorber by pushing in and holding the plastic ring while firmly pulling outward on the air line.

6. Remove the lower shock absorber mounting nut and bolt assembly and swing the shock out of the bracket.

7. Remove the two upper shock attaching nuts from the top of the cross-member then remove the shock.

8. Installation is the reverse of the removal procedure. Tighten the upper attaching nuts to 15–21 ft. lbs. (21–29 Nm) and the lower attaching bolt to 39–53 ft. lbs. (53–72 Nm).

TESTING

1. Visually check the shock absorbers for the presence of fluid leakage. A thin film of fluid is acceptable. Anything more than that means that the shock absorber must be replaced.

2. Disconnect the lower end of the shock absorber. Compress and extend the shock fully as fast as possible. If the action is not smooth in both directions, or there is no pressure resistance, replace the shock absorber. Shock absorbers should be replaced in pairs. In the case of relatively new shock absorbers, where one has failed, that one, alone, may be replaced.

Stabilizer Bar

REMOVAL & INSTALLATION

▶ See Figure 58

❊❊ WARNING

If equipped, always turn off the Automatic Ride Control (ARC) service switch before lifting the vehicle off of the ground. Failure to do so could damage the ARC system components. Refer to Section 1 for jacking procedures.

1. As required, raise and support the vehicle.
2. Remove the nuts, bolts and washers and disconnect the stabilizer bar from the links.
3. Remove the U-bolts and nuts from the mounting bracket and retainers. Remove the mounting brackets, retainers and stabilizer bars.

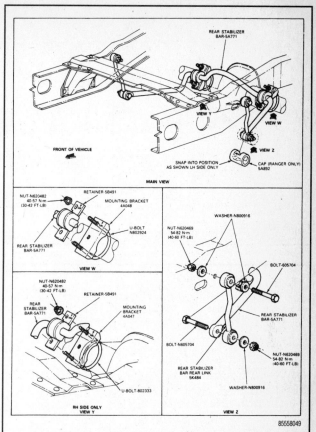

Fig. 58 Common rear stabilizer bar mounting—Ranger shown, other models are similar

To install:
4. Position the U-bolts and mounting brackets on the axle with the brackets having the **UP** marking in the proper position.
5. Install the stabilizer bar and retainers on the mounting brackets with the retainers having the **UP** marking in the proper position.
6. Connect the stabilizer bar to the rear links. Install the nuts, bolts, and washers and tighten.
7. Tighten the mounting bracket U-bolt nuts to 30–42 ft. lbs.

STEERING

Steering Wheel

REMOVAL & INSTALLATION

1991–94 Models

1. Disconnect the negative battery cable.
2. Center the steering wheel to the straight ahead position.
3. From the underside of the steering wheel, remove the screws that hold the steering wheel pad to the steering wheel spokes.
4. Lift up the steering wheel pad and disconnect the horn wires from the steering wheel pad by pulling the spade terminal from the blade connectors.
5. Remove the steering wheel pad. Loosen the bolt 2 or 3 turns from the steering shaft.

❊❊ CAUTION

Tilt columns have a compression spring under the steering wheel that can unexpectantly "pop up" the steering wheel if the bolt is removed completely.

6. Using the proper steering wheel removal tool, loosen the steering wheel on the steering column.

To remove the steering wheel, first remove the horn pad retaining screws from the backside of the wheel

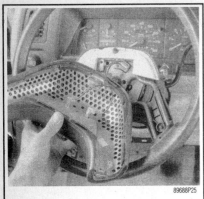

Next, lift up and turn over the horn pad . . .

. . . then disconnect the horn pad electrical plug from the column

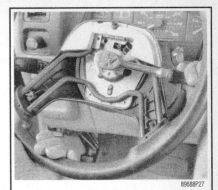

Loosen the steering wheel-to-shaft retaining bolt a couple of turns . . .

. . . then assemble a puller to the wheel and loosen the wheel from the shaft

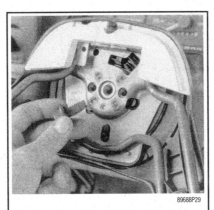

Finally, remove the retaining bolt

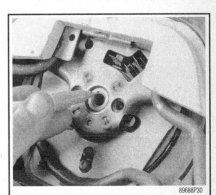

Before pulling the wheel from the shaft, make a matchmark on the shaft and wheel

Finish by pulling the steering wheel from the column shaft

✳ WARNING

Do not hammer on the steering wheel or the steering shaft or use a knock off type steering wheel puller as damage to the steering column will occur.

7. Remove the tool and the steering wheel retaining bolt then lift off the steering wheel.

8. Installation is the reverse of the removal procedure. Be sure that the steering wheel is properly aligned before installing the lock bolt. Torque the steering wheel lock bolt to 23–33 ft. lbs. (31–45 Nm).

1995–99 Models

▶ See Figures 59, 60 and 61

✳ CAUTION

Whenever working on a vehicle equipped with an air bag, always refer to Section 6 for disarming procedures. Follow the procedures outlined or severe injury, or even death may occur.

➡The manufacturer recommends installing the steering wheel using a new wheel-to-shaft retaining bolt. Before beginning this procedure, obtain a new bolt.

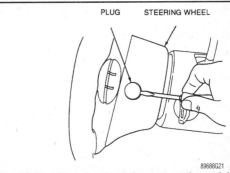

Fig. 59 After disarming the air bag, pry out the retaining screw covers on the sides of the steering wheel

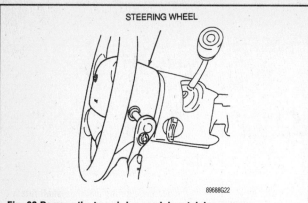

Fig. 60 Remove the two air bag module retaining screws

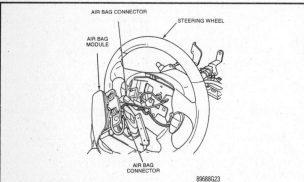

Fig. 61 Pull the module away from the steering wheel and disconnect all of the wire harness plugs

1. Follow the procedures in Section 6 and disarm the air bag.
2. Pry out the two plugs covering the drivers side air bag module screws on the sides of the steering wheel.
3. Remove the two air bag module retaining screws and carefully lift the module away from the steering wheel.
4. Disconnect the air bag electrical harness plug at the sliding contact. Also unplug the horn and, if equipped, cruise control wire harness connectors.

✳✳ CAUTION

Always carry the air bag with the horn pad facing away from your body.

5. Remove the air bag module and set it on a clean, dry and stable bench with the horn pad facing upwards.

✳✳ CAUTION

Tilt columns have a compression spring under the steering wheel that can unexpectanly ìpop upî the steering wheel if the bolt is removed completely.

6. Loosen but do not remove the steering wheel retaining bolt approximately 2 to 3 turns.
7. Using the proper steering wheel removal tool, loosen the steering wheel on the steering column.

✳✳ WARNING

Do not hammer on the steering wheel or the steering shaft or use a knock off type steering wheel puller as damage to the steering column will occur.

8. Remove the tool and the steering wheel retaining bolt. Discard the steering wheel retaining bolt.

✳✳ WARNING

Ensure that the air bag sliding contact wire harness does not get caught on the steering wheel assembly when lifting the wheel from the shaft.

9. Remove the steering wheel while routing the wire harness through the wheel opening.
To install:
10. Ensure that the vehicleís front wheels are in the straight-ahead position.
11. Route the air bag sliding contact wire harnesses through the steering wheel opening (at the 3 oíclock position).
12. Align the steering wheel and shaft and press the wheel onto the shaft. Ensure that the sliding contact wire harness does not get pinched by the wheel.
13. Install the new lock bolt and tighten to 25–34 ft. lbs. (34–46 Nm).
14. Position the air bag module and connect all of the wire harness plugs to it.
15. Carefully install the module to the wheel and loosely install the side retaining bolts.
16. Hold the module in position while tightening the retaining bolts to 67–92 inch lbs. (7.6–10.4 Nm).
17. Install the two cover plugs by snapping them into the holes on the side of the steering wheel.
18. Arm the air bag system by following the procedures in Section 6.

Combination Switch

REMOVAL & INSTALLATION

▶ **See Figures 62 and 63**

1. Disconnect the negative battery cable. Remove the steering wheel.
2. On vehicles equipped with tilt wheel, remove the tilt lever.
3. On vehicles equipped with tilt wheel, remove the steering column collar by pressing on the collar from the top and bottom while removing the collar.
4. Remove the instrument panel trim cover retaining screws. Remove the trim cover.
5. Remove the 2 screws from the bottom of the steering column shroud. Remove the bottom half of the shroud by pulling the shroud down and toward the rear of the vehicle.
6. If the vehicle is equipped with automatic transmission, move the shift lever as required to aid in removal of the shroud. Lift the top half of the shroud from the column.
7. On 1991 automatic transmission equipped models, disconnect the selector indicator actuation cable by removing the screw from the column casting and the plastic plug at the end of the cable.
8. Remove the 2 self tapping screws that retain the combination switch to the steering column casting. Disengage the switch from the casting.
9. Disconnect the 3 electrical connectors, using caution not to damage the locking tabs. Be sure not to damage the PRNDL cable.

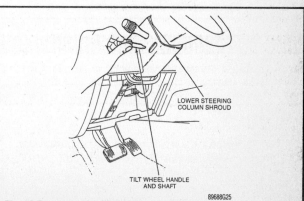

Fig. 62 To remove the tilt column control lever, simply rotate it counterclockwise until removed

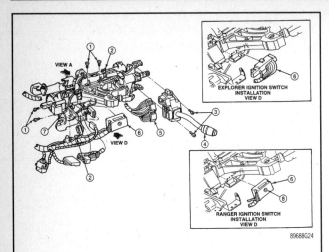

1. Screw
2. Transmission control selector lever assembly
3. Screw
4. Multi-function switch
5. Multi-function switch connector
6. Ignition switch connector
7. Brake shift interlock switch
8. Screw

Fig. 63 Exploded view of the combination switch mounting and column related wire harness connectors

10. Installation is the reverse of the removal procedure. Torque the combination switch retaining screws to 18–27 inch lbs. (2–3 Nm).

Ignition Switch

REMOVAL & INSTALLATION

♦ **See Figure 63**

1. Disconnect the negative battery cable.
2. Remove the steering wheel.
3. As necessary, remove all under dash panels in order to gain access to the ignition switch.
4. As necessary, lower the steering column to gain working clearance.
5. Disconnect the ignition switch electrical connectors.
6. Remove the ignition switch retaining screws from the studs. Disengage the ignition switch from switch rod. Remove the switch from the vehicle.

To install:

7. Position the lock cylinder in the **LOCK** position.
8. To set the switch, position a wire in the opening in the outer surface of the switch through its positions until the wire drops down into the slot.

➡**The slot is in the bottom of the switch where the rod must be inserted to allow full movement through the switch positions.**

9. Position the ignition switch on the column studs and over the actuating rod. Torque the retaining nuts to 40–64 inch lbs. (4.5–7.2 Nm).
10. Remove the wire from the slot in the housing. Continue the installation in the reverse order of the removal procedure.

Ignition Lock Cylinder Assembly

REMOVAL & INSTALLATION

♦ **See Figure 64**

1. Disconnect the negative battery cable. Remove the steering wheel.
2. On vehicles equipped with tilt wheel, remove the tilt lever.
3. On vehicles equipped with tilt wheel, remove the steering column collar by pressing on the collar from the top and bottom while removing the collar.
4. Remove the instrument panel trim cover retaining screws. Remove the trim cover.

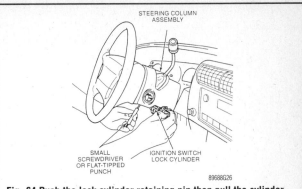

Fig. 64 Push the lock cylinder retaining pin then pull the cylinder from the column

5. Remove the 2 screws from the bottom of the steering column shroud. Remove the bottom half of the shroud by pulling the shroud down and toward the rear of the vehicle.
6. Turn the lock cylinder with the ignition key in it to the **ON** position. On vehicles equipped with automatic transmission be sure that the selector lever is in the **P** position.
7. Push up on the lock cylinder retaining pin with a ⅛ in. (3mm) diameter wire pin or small punch. Pull the lock cylinder from the column housing. Disconnect the lock cylinder wiring plug from the horn brush wiring connector.

To install:

8. Prior to installation of the lock cylinder, lubricate the cylinder cavity, including the drive gear, with Lubriplate® or equivalent.
9. To install the lock cylinder, turn the lock cylinder to the **ON** position, depress the retaining pin. Insert the lock cylinder housing into its housing in the flange casting. Be sure that the tab at the end of the cylinder aligns with the slot in the ignition drive gear.
10. Turn the key to the **OFF** position. This action will permit the cylinder retaining pin to extend into the cylinder casting housing hole.
11. Using the ignition key rotate the lock cylinder to ensure correct mechanical operation in all positions. Connect the key warning wire plug.
12. Install the steering column lower shroud. Install the steering wheel.
13. Check for proper vehicle operation in **P** and **N**. Also be sure that the start circuit cannot be actuated in **D** or **R**.

Steering Column

REMOVAL & INSTALLATION

♦ **See Figure 65**

※ **CAUTION**

Whenever working on a vehicle equipped with an air bag, always refer to Section 6 for disarming procedures. Follow the procedures outlined or severe injury, or even death may occur.

1. Disconnect the negative battery cable. If equipped with an airbag, refer to Section 6 to disable the system.
2. Set the parking brake. If equipped with automatic transmission position the selector lever in **N**.
3. Remove the bolt that holds the intermediate shaft to the steering column shaft.
4. Using the proper tool, compress the intermediate shaft until it is clear of the steering column shaft.
5. Remove the nuts from the studs and remove the shift cable bracket from the steering column bracket, if the vehicle is equipped with automatic transmission.
6. If the vehicle is equipped with automatic transmission disconnect the shift cable from the column lever. Remove the steering wheel.

➡**If the vehicle is equipped with tilt wheel, be sure that the steering wheel is in the fall up position before removing it.**

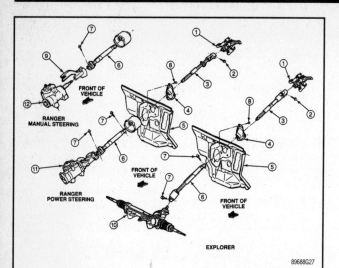

1. Steering column
2. Bolt, M10-1.5 x 35
3. Steering gear intermediate shaft
4. Steering column open weather seal
5. Dash panel
6. Steering gear lower shaft
7. Bolt, M10-1.5 x 35
8. Screw, M6-1 x 20
9. Steering shaft U-joint
10. Steering gear (Explorer)
11. Steering gear (Ranger—Power)
12. Steering gear (Ranger—Manual)

Fig. 65 Exploded view of the typical steering column assemblies and related components

7. On vehicles equipped with tilt wheel, remove the tilt lever.

8. On vehicles equipped with tilt wheel, remove the steering column collar by pressing on the collar from the top and bottom while removing the collar.

9. Remove the instrument panel trim cover retaining screws. Remove the trim cover.

10. Remove the 2 screws from the bottom of the steering column shroud. Remove the bottom half of the shroud by pulling the shroud down and toward the rear of the vehicle.

11. If the vehicle is equipped with automatic transmission, move the shift lever as required to aid in removal of the shroud. Lift the top half of the shroud from the column.

12. If the vehicle is equipped with automatic transmission, disconnect the selector indicator actuation cable by removing the screw from the column casting and the plastic plug at the end of the cable.

13. To remove the plastic plug from the shift lever socket casting push on the nose of the plug until the head clears the casting and pull the plug from the casting.

14. Remove the plastic clip that retains the combination switch wiring to the steering column bracket.

15. Remove the 2 screws form the multi function switch. Remove the switch from the column and leave the wiring connectors attached to the switch. Position the switch and the wiring out of the way.

16. Disconnect the key warning buzzer wire from the horn brush wire. Remove the screw that holds the horn brush connector to the column. Remove the connector.

17. Remove the 5 screws that hold the toe plate to the dash panel. Loosen the toe plate clamp bolt.

18. Support the steering column assembly. Remove the bolts that hold the breakaway bracket to the pedal support bracket.

19. Pry apart the locking tabs and disconnect the ignition switch wiring harness. Carefully remove the steering from the vehicle.

20. If the vehicle is equipped with automatic transmission, remove the shift cable bracket from the column.

To install:

21. If the vehicle is equipped with automatic transmission, install the shift cable bracket from the column. Torque the cable bracket bolts to 13–22 ft. lbs. (17–31 Nm).

22. Position the steering column in the hole in the vehicle floor.

23. Connect the ignition switch wiring harness to the column connector. Install the column breakaway bolts, but do not tighten.

24. Install and torque the toe plate bolts to 5–8 ft. lbs. Torque the toe plate clamp bolt to 62–97 inch lbs. (7–11 Nm)

25. Torque the steering column breakaway bolts to 19–27 ft. lbs. (25–36 Nm).

26. Continue the installation in the reverse order of the removal procedure. Torque the steering column shaft to the intermediate shaft U-joint pinch bolt to 25–34 ft. lbs. (34–46 Nm).

Steering Linkage

▶ **See Figure 66**

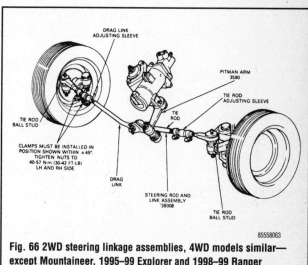

Fig. 66 2WD steering linkage assemblies, 4WD models similar—except Mountaineer, 1995–99 Explorer and 1998–99 Ranger

REMOVAL & INSTALLATION

Except Mountaineer, 1995–99 Explorer and 1998–99 Ranger

PITMAN ARM

1. As required, raise and safely support the vehicle using jackstands.

2. Remove the cotter pin and nut from the drag link ball stud at the pitman arm.

3. Remove the drag link ball stud from the pitman arm using pitman arm removal tool T64P-3590-F or equivalent.

4. Remove the pitman arm retaining nut and washer. Remove the pitman arm from the steering gear sector shaft using tool T64P-3590-F or equivalent.

To install:

5. Installation is the reverse of the removal procedure. Torque the pitman arm attaching washer and nut to 170–228 ft. lbs. (230–310 Nm). Torque the drag link ball stud nut to 51–73 ft. lbs. (70–100 Nm) and install a new cotter pin.

6. Check and adjust front end alignment, as required.

TIE ROD

1. Raise and support the vehicle using jackstands. Be sure that the front wheels are in the straight ahead position.

2. Remove the nut and cotter pin from the ball stud on the drag link. Remove the ball stud from the drag link using pitman arm removal tool T64P-3590-F or equivalent.

3. Loosen the bolts on the tie rod adjusting sleeve. Be sure to count and record the number of turns it takes to remove the tie rod from the tie rod adjusting sleeve. Remove the tie rod from the vehicle.

To install:

4. Install the tie rod in the tie rod sleeve in the same number of turns it took to remove it. Torque the tie rod adjusting sleeve nuts to 30–42 ft. lbs. (40–57 Nm).

5. Be sure that the adjusting sleeve clamps are pointed down ±45°. Tighten

To remove the tie rod end, first remove the cotter pin and discard it. A new pin will be used for installation

Loosen and remove the tie rod end retaining nut . . .

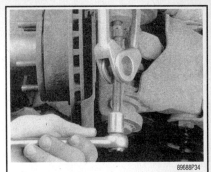

. . . then, using a jawed puller, loosen the tie rod stud-to-steering knuckle connection

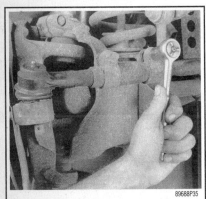

Loosen the tie rod sleeve clamp bolts . . .

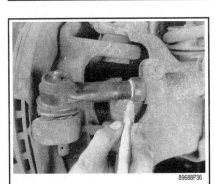

. . . and before unthreading the tie rod from the sleeve, make an installation mark on the threads

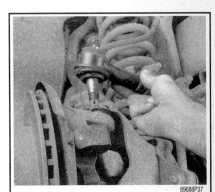

Lift the tie rod end out of the steering knuckle bore . . .

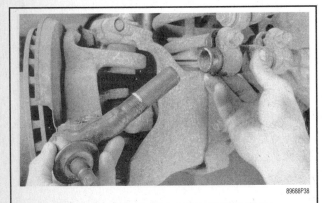

. . . and unthread the tie rod end from the adjusting sleeve

the tie rod ball stud to drag link retaining bolt to 51–73 ft. lbs. (70–100 Nm). Install a new cotter pin.

6. Check and adjust front end alignment, as required.

DRAG LINK

1. Raise and support the vehicle using jackstands. Be sure that the front wheels are in the straight ahead position.
2. Remove the nuts and cotter pins from the ball stud at the pitman arm and steering tie rod. Remove the ball studs from the linkage using pitman arm removal tool T64P-3590-F or equivalent.
3. Loosen the bolts on the drag link adjusting sleeve. Be sure to count and record the number of turns it takes to remove the drag link.

To install:

4. Install the drag link in the same number of turns it took to remove it. Tighten the adjusting sleeve nuts to 30–42 ft. lbs. (40–57 Nm). Be sure that the adjusting sleeve clamps are pointed down ±45°.

5. Position the drag link ball stud in the pitman arm. Position the steering tie rod ball stud in the drag link. With the vehicle wheels in the straight ahead position install and torque the nuts to 51–73 ft. lbs. (70–100 Nm). Install a new cotter pin.

6. Check and adjust front end alignment, as required.

Mountaineer, 1995–99 Explorer and 1998–99 Ranger

✳✳ WARNING

If equipped, always turn off the Automatic Ride Control (ARC) service switch before lifting the vehicle off of the ground. Failure to do so could damage the ARC system components. Refer to Section 1 for jacking procedures.

OUTER TIE ROD END

1. Position the front wheels in the straight ahead position.
2. Raise and safely support the vehicle, as necessary.
3. Remove and discard the outer tie rod end retaining nut cotter pin.
4. Remove the nut and install a puller to separate the tie rod end from the steering knuckle.
5. Hold the tie rod end with a wrench and loosen the jam nut.
6. Mark the exact position of the outer tie rod on the inner tie rod threads. Grip the tie rod end with a pair of pliers and unscrew the outer end from the inner tie rod.

To install:

7. Ensure that the inner tie rod threads are clean.
8. Thread the outer tie rod end onto the inner tie rod to the same location as marked earlier.
9. Install the out tie rod end stud into the steering knuckle then install and tighten the attaching nut to 57–77 ft. lbs. (77–104 Nm). Install new cotter pins, advancing (tightening) the nut as required. NEVER loosen the nut to install the cotter pin.

10. Tighten the jam nut, while holding the outer tie rod, to 50–68 ft. lbs. (68–92 Nm).

11. Have the toe alignment checked and adjusted by a professional shop.

INNER TIE ROD END

▶ See Figure 67

1. Unlock the steering column, engage the parking brake then raise and safely support the vehicle.
2. Clean away and loose dirt or oil from the steering rack housing.
3. Loosen the jam nut but keep it flush with the outer tie rod end.
4. Remove the outer tie rod end, then remove the jam nut from the inner tie rod end.
5. Remove the steering rack housing from the vehicle.
6. Clean the areas around the boots where they attach to the steering rack housing.
7. Remove the clamps from the boots (both the small outer and large inner clamps) then remove the boots from the housing, separating the vent tube while doing so. Note the location of the vent tube ends at the boots.
8. Turn the input shaft as required to expose the flat at the outer end of the rack teeth. Ensure that enough of the flat is exposed to engage an adjustable wrench to it.

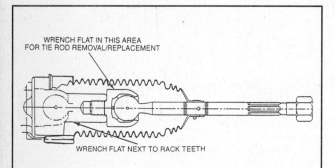

Fig. 67 Cutaway view of the Mountaineer, 1995–99 Explorer and 1998–99 Ranger inner tie rod assembly

✳✳ WARNING

The torque required to break the inner tie rod loose could exceed 100 ft. lbs. (136 Nm). If this force is reacted against the pinion teeth, sufficient damage may be incurred to affect the smoothness of operation.

9. Use a large wrench on the inner tie rod socket flats and an adjustable wrench on the rack teeth flats and remove the tie rod.

To install:

10. Install the inner tie rod end to the rack and using the two wrenches as per removal, tighten the tie rod end to 81–95 ft. lbs. (110–130 Nm).
11. Apply 1 cu. in. (1639 cu. mm) of wheel bearing grease evenly around the large end of a new boot and half as much grease to the small end. Install the new boots, working the vent tube onto its fittings, and align them to their original positions.
12. Install new inner (large) clamps and reinstall the outer clamps.
13. Install the locknuts and outer tie rod ends.
14. Install the steering rack housing back into the vehicle.
15. Lower the vehicle. Have the front wheel alignment checked and adjusted by a professional shop.

Manual Steering Gear

ADJUSTMENTS

▶ See Figure 68

Preload and Meshload

INSPECTION

1. Raise and support the front of the vehicle on jackstands.
2. Disconnect the pitman arm at the ball stud.
3. Lubricate the wormshaft seal with a drop of automatic transmission fluid.
4. Remove the horn pad from the steering wheel.
5. Turn the steering wheel slowly to one stop.
6. Using an inch-pound torque wrench on the steering wheel nut, check the amount of torque needed to rotate the steering wheel through a 1½ turn cycle. The preload should be 2–6 inch lbs. If correct, proceed with the rest of the steps. If not perform preload and mesh adjustment.
7. Rotate the steering wheel from stop-to-stop, counting the total number of turns. Using that figure, center the steering wheel (½ the total turns).
8. Using the inch-pound torque wrench, rotate the steering wheel 90° to either side of center, noting the highest torque reading over center. The meshload should be 4–10 inch lbs., or at least 2 inch lbs. more than the preload figure.

ADJUSTMENT

1. Remove the steering gear from the vehicle.
2. Torque the sector cover bolts on the gear to 32–40 ft. lbs.
3. Loosen the preload adjuster nut and tighten the worm bearing adjuster nut until all end-play has been removed. Lubricate the wormshaft seal with a few drops of automatic transmission fluid.
4. Using an $11\frac{1}{16}$ in., 12-point socket and an inch lbs. torque wrench, carefully turn the wormshaft all the way to the right.
5. Turn the shaft back to the left and measure the torque over a 1½ turn cycle. This is the preload reading.
6. Tighten or loosen the adjuster nut to bring the preload into range (5–6 inch lbs.).
7. Hold the adjuster nut while torqueing the locknut to 166–187 ft. lbs.
8. Rotate the wormshaft stop-to-stop counting the total number of turns and center the shaft (½ the total turns).
9. Using the torque wrench and socket, measure the torque required to turn the shaft 90° to either side of center.
10. Turn the sector shaft adjusting screw as needed to bring the meshload

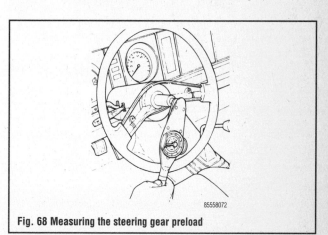

Fig. 68 Measuring the steering gear preload

torque within the 9–11 inch lbs. range, or at least 4 inch lbs. higher than the preload torque.

11. Hold the adjusting screw while tightening the locknut to 14–25 ft. lbs.
12. Install the gear.

REMOVAL & INSTALLATION

▶ See Figure 69

1. Raise and safely support the vehicle using jackstands. Disengage the flex coupling shield from the steering gear input shaft shield and slide it up the intermediate shaft.
2. Remove the bolt that retains the flex coupling to the steering gear.
3. Remove the steering gear input shaft shield.
4. Remove the nut and washer that secures the pitman arm to the sector shaft. Remove the pitman arm using pitman arm puller tool, T64P-3590-F or equivalent. Do not hammer on the end of the puller as this can damage the steering gear.
5. Remove the bolts and washers that attach the steering gear to the side rail. Remove the gear.

To install:
6. Rotate the gear input shaft (wormshaft) from stop to stop, counting the total number of turns. Then turn back exactly half-way, placing the gear on center.
7. Slide the steering gear input shaft shield on the steering gear input shaft.
8. Position the flex coupling on the steering gear input shaft. Ensure that the flat on the gear input shaft is facing straight up and aligns with the flat on the flex coupling. Install the steering gear to side rail with bolts and washers. Torque the bolts to 66 ft. lbs. (89 Nm).
9. Place the pitman arm on the sector shaft and install the attaching washer and nut. Align the 2 blocked teeth on the Pitman arm with 4 missing teeth on the steering gear sector shaft. Tighten the nut to 170–228 ft. lbs. (230–310 Nm).
10. Install the flex coupling to steering gear input shaft attaching bolt and tighten to 50–62 ft. lbs. (68–84 Nm).
11. Snap the flex coupling shield to the steering gear input shield.
12. Check the system to ensure equal turns from center to each lock position.

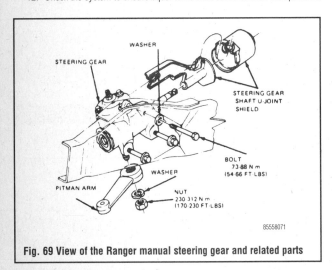

Fig. 69 View of the Ranger manual steering gear and related parts

Power Steering Gear

ADJUSTMENTS

Meshload

▶ See Figure 68

1. As required, raise and support the vehicle using jackstands.
2. Disconnect the pitman arm from the sector shaft using tool T64P-3590-F or equivalent.

3. Disconnect and cap the fluid return line at the reservoir return line pipe.
4. Place the end of the return line in a clean container and turn the steering wheel from stop to stop several times to discharge the fluid from the gear. Discard the used fluid.
5. Turn the steering gear 45° from the right stop.
6. Remove the steering wheel hub cover. Attach an inch lb. torque wrench to the steering wheel nut and determine the torque required to rotate the shaft slowly about ⅛ turn from the 45° position toward center.
7. Turn the steering wheel back to center and determine the torque required to rotate the shaft back and forth across the center position.
8. Specification for vehicles under 5000 miles is 12–24 inch lbs. If the vehicle has over 5000 miles, reset the meshload measured while rocking the input shaft over center is less than 10 inch lbs. greater than torque 45° from the right stop.
9. If reset is required loosen the adjuster locknut and turn the sector shaft adjuster screw until the reading is the specified value greater than the torque at 45° from the stop. Hold the sector shaft screw in place and tighten the locknut.

REMOVAL & INSTALLATION

▶ See Figure 70

1. Disconnect the pressure and return lines from the steering gear. Plug the lines and the ports in the gear to prevent entry of dirt.
2. Remove the upper and lower steering gear shaft U-joint shield from the flex coupling. Remove the bolts that secure the flex coupling to the steering gear and to the column steering shaft assembly.
3. Raise the vehicle and remove the pitman arm attaching nut and washer.
4. Remove the pitman arm from the sector shaft using tool T64P-3590-F. Remove the tool from the pitman arm. Do not damage the seals.
5. Support the steering gear, and remove the steering gear attaching bolts.
6. Work the steering gear free of the flex coupling. Remove the steering gear from the vehicle.

To install:
7. Install the lower U-joint shield onto the steering gear lugs. Slide the upper U-joint shield into place on the steering shaft assembly.
8. Slide the flex coupling into place on the steering shaft assembly. Turn the steering wheel so that the spokes are in the horizontal position. Center the steering gear input shaft.
9. Slide the steering gear input shaft into the flex coupling and into place on the frame side rail. Install the attaching bolts and tighten to 50–62 ft. lbs. (68–84 Nm). Tighten the flex coupling bolt 30–40 ft. lbs. (41–54 Nm).
10. Be sure the wheels are in the straight ahead position, then install the pitman arm on the sector shaft. Install the pitman arm attaching washer and nut. Tighten nut to 170–228 ft. lbs. (230–310 Nm).
11. Connect and tighten the pressure and the return lines to the steering gear.
12. Disconnect the coil wire. Fill the reservoir. Turn on the ignition and turn the steering wheel from left to right to distribute the fluid.
13. Recheck fluid level and add fluid, if necessary. Connect the coil wire, start the engine and turn the steering wheel from side to side. Inspect for fluid leaks.

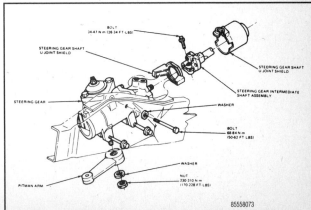

Fig. 70 View of the power steering gear and related parts used on Ranger and 1991–94 Explorer

Power Rack and Pinion Steering Gear

REMOVAL & INSTALLATION

▶ See Figures 71 and 72

❊❊ WARNING

If equipped, always turn off the Automatic Ride Control (ARC) service switch before lifting the vehicle off of the ground. Failure to do so could damage the ARC system components. Refer to Section 1 for jacking procedures.

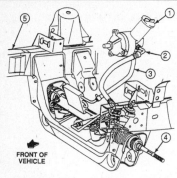

89688G29

1. Power steering pump
2. Power steering pressure hose
3. Power steering cooler and hose assembly
4. Steering gear
5. Frame

Fig. 71 View of the power steering hose connections for the power rack and pinion steering gear

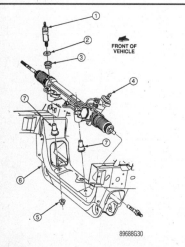

FRONT OF VEHICLE

89688G30

1. Bolt
2. Washer
3. Steering gear mounting housing insulator
4. Steering gear
5. Nut
6. Front crossmember
7. Steering gear insulator

Fig. 72 Exploded view of the power rack and pinion steering gear mounting

1. Raise and safely support the front of the vehicle, block the rear wheels and apply the parking brake.
2. Start the engine then rotate the steering wheel from lock-to-lock and record the number of rotations.
3. Divide the number of rotations by two. This gives the number of rotations to achieve true center of the steering. Turn the wheel in one direction to the full lock.
4. Turn the wheel in the opposite direction the number of turns equal to true steering (lock-to-lock number divided by two).

❊❊ WARNING

Do not rotate the steering wheel when the shaft is disconnected from the steering gear as damage to the clock spring could occur.

5. Remove the bolt retaining the lower steering column shaft to the steering gear input shaft and disconnect the two.
6. Remove the stabilizer bar.
7. Unscrew the quick-connect fittings for the power steering pressure and return hoses at the steering gear housing.
8. Plug the ends of the lines and the fitting in the rack to avoid dirt contamination.
9. Remove the two nuts securing the power steering cooler and remove the cooler.
10. Remove the outer tie rod ends.
11. Remove the two nuts, bolts and washer assemblies retaining the steering gear housing to the front crossmember.

To install:

12. Position the steering gear to the front crossmember and install the nuts, bolts and washer assemblies. Tighten to 94–127 ft. lbs. (128–172 Nm).
13. Install the power steering cooler and two retaining bolts.
14. Connect the power steering lines to the steering gear housing and tighten the fittings to 20–25 ft. lbs. (27–34 Nm).
15. Install the outer tie rod ends.
16. Ensure that the steering shaft or gear input shaft has not been rotated, then connect the two.
17. Install the intermediate shaft-to-steering input shaft retaining (pinch) bolt and tighten to 30–42 ft. lbs. (41–56 Nm).
18. Lower the vehicle and refill the power steering pump reservoir.
19. Bleed the air from the power steering system. Follow the procedures in this Section.
20. Ensure that there are no leaks and the fluid is maintained at the proper level.
21. Have the alignment checked and adjusted by a professional repair shop.

Power Steering Pump

REMOVAL & INSTALLATION

▶ See Figures 73, 74 and 75

1. Disconnect the negative battery cable.
2. Remove some power steering fluid from the reservoir by disconnecting the fluid return line hose at the reservoir. Drain the fluid into a container and discard it.
3. Remove the pressure hose from the pump. If equipped, disconnect the power steering pump pressure switch.
4. On the 2.3L, 2.5L and 3.0L engines, loosen the idler pulley assembly pivot and adjusting bolts to slacken the belt tension.
5. On the 2.9L engine loosen the adjusting nut and the slider bolts on the pump support to slacken belt tension.
6. On the 4.0L engine, slacken belt tension by lifting the tensioner pulley in a clockwise direction. Remove the drive belt from under the tensioner pulley and slowly lower the pulley to its stop.
7. Remove the drive belt from the pulley. If necessary, remove the oil dipstick tube.
8. If equipped, remove the power steering pump bracket support brace.
9. Install power steering pump pulley removal tool T69L-10300-B or equivalent. Hold the pump and rotate the tool counterclockwise to remove the pulley. Do not apply in and out pressure to the pump shaft, as internal pump damage will occur.

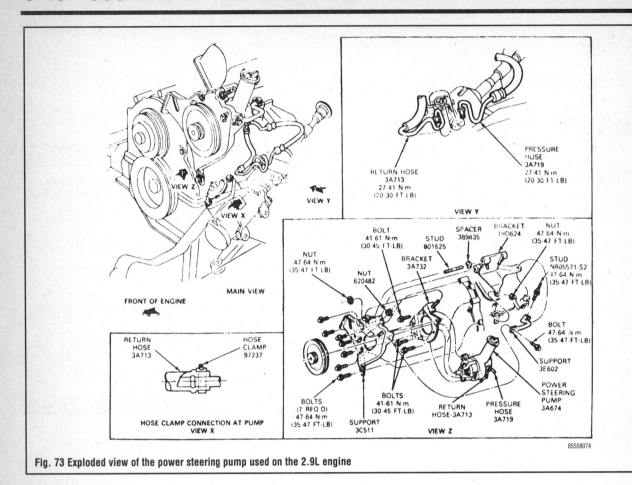

Fig. 73 Exploded view of the power steering pump used on the 2.9L engine

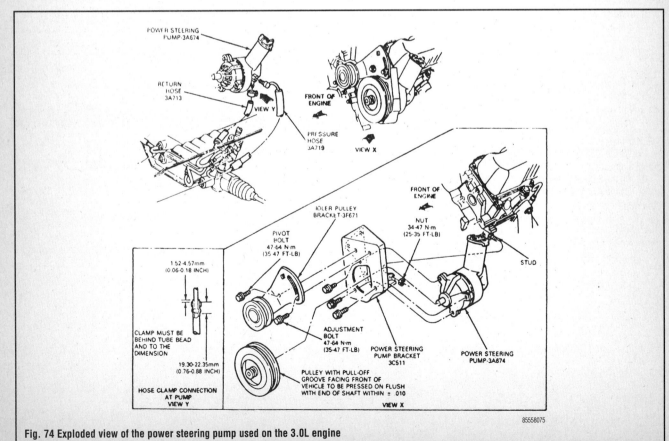

Fig. 74 Exploded view of the power steering pump used on the 3.0L engine

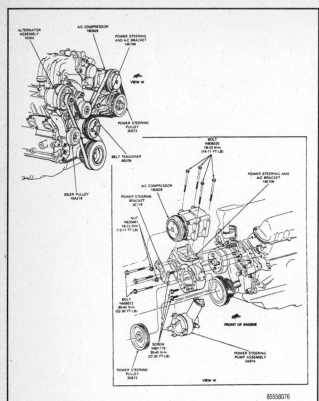

Fig. 75 Exploded view of the power steering pump used on the 4.0L engine

10. Remove the power steering retaining bolts. Remove the power steering pump from the vehicle.

To install:

11. Position the pump on the bracket. Install and tighten the retaining bolts.

12. Install the pulley removal tool and install the power steering pump pulley to the power steering pump.

➡**Fore and aft location of the pulley on the power steering pump shaft is critical. Incorrect belt alignment may cause belt squeal or chirp. Be sure that the pull off groove on the pulley is facing front and flush with the end of the shaft ± 0.010 in. (0.25mm).**

13. Continue the installation in the reverse order of the removal procedure. Adjust the belt tension to specification.

14. On the 2.3L, 2.5L and 3.0L engines torque the idler pivot pulley bolts 30–40 ft. lbs. for the 2.3L, 2.5L engine and 35–47 ft. lbs. for the 3.0L engine

15. On the 2.9L engine torque the slider bolts to 35–47 ft. lbs.

16. On the 4.0L while lifting the tensioner pulley in a clockwise direction, slide the belt under the tensioner pulley and lower the pulley to the belt.

BLEEDING

1. Disconnect the coil wire.
2. Crank the engine and continue adding fluid until the level stabilizes.

3. Continue to crank the engine and rotate the steering wheel about 30° to either side of center.

4. Check the fluid level and add as required.

5. Connect the coil wire and start the engine. Allow it to run for several minutes.

6. Rotate the steering wheel from stop to stop.

7. Shut of the engine and check the fluid level. Add fluid as necessary.

QUICK-CONNECT PRESSURE LINE

◗ **See Figure 76**

If a leak occurs between the tubing and the tube nut, replace the hose assembly. If a leak occurs between the tube nut and the pump outlet replace the plastic washer.

1. Check the fitting to determine whether the leak is between the tube and tube nut or between the tube nut and pump outlet.

2. If the leak is between the tube nut and pump outlet check to be sure the nut is tightened to 30–40 ft. lbs. Do not overtighten this nut.

3. If the leak continues or if the leak is between the tube and tube nut, remove the line.

4. Unscrew the tube nut and inspect the plastic seal washer. Replace the plastic seal washer when the line is removed.

5. To aid in the assembly of the new plastic seal washer, a tapered shaft may be required to stretch the washer so that it may be slipped over the tube nut threads.

6. If the rubber O-ring is damaged it cannot be serviced and the hose assembly will have to be replaced.

7. Connect the tube nut and torque to 30–40 ft. lbs.

✳✳ CAUTION

The quick connect fitting may disengage if not fully assembled, if the snapring is missing or if the tube nut or hose end is not machined properly. If the fitting disengages replace the hose assembly. The fitting is fully engaged when the hose will not pull out. To test for positive engagement the system should be properly filled, the engine started and the steering wheel turned from stop to stop.

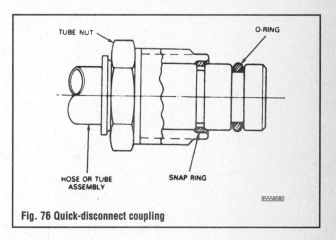

Fig. 76 Quick-disconnect coupling

TORQUE SPECIFICATIONS

Component	Ft. Lbs.	Nm
4x2 Front Suspension - 1991–97 Ranger and 1991–94 Explorer		
ABS sensor bolt	67-93 inch lbs.	7.5-10.5
Axle arm pivot-to-frame bracket bolt	111-148	150-200
Axle-to-radius arm bolt	188-254	255-345
Lower ball joint stud nut		
1991-94 Ranger and Explorer	104-146	141-198
1995-97 Ranger	89-133	120-180
Lower spring retainer nut	70-100	95-135
Radius arm-to-frame bracket nut	82-113	113-153
Shock absorber to upper spring seat (upper mount)	25-34	34-46
Shock absorber-to-radius arm nut (lower mount)	39-53	53-72
Stabilizer bar end link-to-axle arm bolt	30-41	40-55
Stabilizer bar-to-end link	30-41	40-55
Suspension bumper-to-spring seat bolts	18-26	25-35
Upper ball joint axle clamp bolt	50-68	68-92
Wheel lug nuts	100	135
4x2 Front Suspension - Mountaineer, 1995–99 Explorer and 1998–99 Ranger		
Disc brake caliper bracket-to-steering knuckle	73-97	98-132
Note: Use new bolts or reuse old bolts using threadlocking compound		
Lower control arm-to-frame pivot bolts and nuts	111-148	150-200
Shock absorber-to-lower control arm nuts	15-21	21-29
Shock absorber-to-to upper frame seat	30-40	40-55
Stabilizer bar-to-frame retainer bolts	65-91	88-119
Stabilizer endlink-to-lower control arm nuts	10-13	13-17
Steering knuckle-to-lower ball joint nut	84-113	113-153
Steering knuckle-to-upper ball joint pinch bolt	30-41	40-55
Upper control arm-to-adjusting arm (right-side only)	95-128	128-173
Upper control arm-to-frame bolts and nuts	84-113	113-153
4x4 Front Suspension - All Models		
Refer to the Drive Train Section 7 torque specification charts		
Rear Suspension		
Rear shackle-to-spring nut and shackle-to-frame bracket bolt		
Mountaineer, Explorer and 1991–94 Ranger	74-115	100-155
1995–99 Ranger	65-87	88-118
Shock absorber upper mounting bolt	41-53	55-72
Shock lower absorber mounting bolt	39-41	53-56
Spring U-bolt-to-plate nut		
Ranger	65-87	88-118
Mountaineer and Explorer	88-108	119-146
Spring-to-front frame bracket bolt		
Mountaineer, Explorer and 1991–94 Ranger	74-115	100-155
1995–99 Ranger	65-87	88-118
Stabilizer bar end link-to-bar	50-59	68-80
Stabilizer end link-to-frame bolt	50-59	68-80
Stabilizer-to-mounting bar bracket	30-34	40-46
Steering Components		
Air bag module-to-steering wheel	67-92 inch lbs.	7.6-10.4
Drag link-to-pitman arm nut	51-73	70-100
Drag link-to-tie rod end nut	51-73	70-100
Pitman arm-to-steering gear nut	170-228	230-310
Power steering gear mounting bolts	50-62	68-84
Power steering hose fitting	22-30	30-40
Steering column intermediate shaft connector bolts	25-34	34-46
Steering column mounting bolts	19-27	26-36
Steering wheel-to-column mounting bolt	25-33	34-46
Tie rod adjusting sleeve clamp bolts	30-42	40-57
Tie rod end-to-steering knuckle	52-74	70-100

89688C51

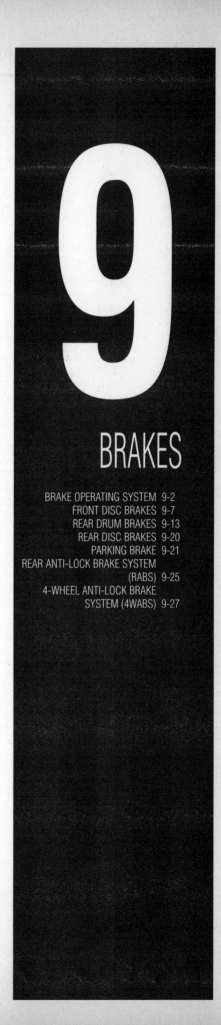

9

BRAKES

BRAKE OPERATING SYSTEM

Basic Operating Principles

Hydraulic systems are used to actuate the brakes of all modern automobiles. The system transports the power required to force the frictional surfaces of the braking system together from the pedal to the individual brake units at each wheel. A hydraulic system is used for two reasons.

First, fluid under pressure can be carried to all parts of an automobile by small pipes and flexible hoses without taking up a significant amount of room or posing routing problems.

Second, a great mechanical advantage can be given to the brake pedal end of the system, and the foot pressure required to actuate the brakes can be reduced by making the surface area of the master cylinder pistons smaller than that of any of the pistons in the wheel cylinders or calipers.

The master cylinder consists of a fluid reservoir along with a double cylinder and piston assembly. Double type master cylinders are designed to separate the front and rear braking systems hydraulically in case of a leak. The master cylinder coverts mechanical motion from the pedal into hydraulic pressure within the lines. This pressure is translated back into mechanical motion at the wheels by either the wheel cylinder (drum brakes) or the caliper (disc brakes).

Steel lines carry the brake fluid to a point on the vehicle's frame near each of the vehicle's wheels. The fluid is then carried to the calipers and wheel cylinders by flexible tubes in order to allow for suspension and steering movements.

In drum brake systems, each wheel cylinder contains two pistons, one at either end, which push outward in opposite directions and force the brake shoe into contact with the drum.

In disc brake systems, the cylinders are part of the calipers. At least one cylinder in each caliper is used to force the brake pads against the disc.

All pistons employ some type of seal, usually made of rubber, to minimize fluid leakage. A rubber dust boot seals the outer end of the cylinder against dust and dirt. The boot fits around the outer end of the piston on disc brake calipers, and around the brake actuating rod on wheel cylinders.

The hydraulic system operates as follows: When at rest, the entire system, from the piston(s) in the master cylinder to those in the wheel cylinders or calipers, is full of brake fluid. Upon application of the brake pedal, fluid trapped in front of the master cylinder piston(s) is forced through the lines to the wheel cylinders. Here, it forces the pistons outward, in the case of drum brakes, and inward toward the disc, in the case of disc brakes. The motion of the pistons is opposed by return springs mounted outside the cylinders in drum brakes, and by spring seals, in disc brakes.

Upon release of the brake pedal, a spring located inside the master cylinder immediately returns the master cylinder pistons to the normal position. The pistons contain check valves and the master cylinder has compensating ports drilled in it. These are uncovered as the pistons reach their normal position. The piston check valves allow fluid to flow toward the wheel cylinders or calipers as the pistons withdraw. Then, as the return springs force the brake pads or shoes into the released position, the excess fluid reservoir through the compensating ports. It is during the time the pedal is in the released position that any fluid that has leaked out of the system will be replaced through the compensating ports.

Dual circuit master cylinders employ two pistons, located one behind the other, in the same cylinder. The primary piston is actuated directly by mechanical linkage from the brake pedal through the power booster. The secondary piston is actuated by fluid trapped between the two pistons. If a leak develops in front of the secondary piston, it moves forward until it bottoms against the front of the master cylinder, and the fluid trapped between the pistons will operate the rear brakes. If the rear brakes develop a leak, the primary piston will move forward until direct contact with the secondary piston takes place, and it will force the secondary piston to actuate the front brakes. In either case, the brake pedal moves farther when the brakes are applied, and less braking power is available.

All dual circuit systems use a switch to warn the driver when only half of the brake system is operational. This switch is usually located in a valve body which is mounted on the firewall or the frame below the master cylinder. A hydraulic piston receives pressure from both circuits, each circuit's pressure being applied to one end of the piston. When the pressures are in balance, the piston remains stationary. When one circuit has a leak, however, the greater pressure in that circuit during application of the brakes will push the piston to one side, closing the switch and activating the brake warning light.

In disc brake systems, this valve body also contains a metering valve and, in some cases, a proportioning valve. The metering valve keeps pressure from traveling to the disc brakes on the front wheels until the brake shoes on the rear wheels have contacted the drums, ensuring that the front brakes will never be used alone. The proportioning valve controls the pressure to the rear brakes to lessen the chance of rear wheel lock-up during very hard braking.

Warning lights may be tested by depressing the brake pedal and holding it while opening one of the wheel cylinder bleeder screws. If this does not cause the light to go on, substitute a new lamp, make continuity checks, and, finally, replace the switch as necessary.

The hydraulic system may be checked for leaks by applying pressure to the pedal gradually and steadily. If the pedal sinks very slowly to the floor, the system has a leak. This is not to be confused with a springy or spongy feel due to the compression of air within the lines. If the system leaks, there will be a gradual change in the position of the pedal with a constant pressure.

Check for leaks along all lines and at wheel cylinders. If no external leaks are apparent, the problem is inside the master cylinder.

DISC BRAKES

Instead of the traditional expanding brakes that press outward against a circular drum, disc brake systems utilize a disc (rotor) with brake pads positioned on either side of it. An easily-seen analogy is the hand brake arrangement on a bicycle. The pads squeeze onto the rim of the bike wheel, slowing its motion. Automobile disc brakes use the identical principle but apply the braking effort to a separate disc instead of the wheel.

The disc (rotor) is a casting, usually equipped with cooling fins between the two braking surfaces. This enables air to circulate between the braking surfaces making them less sensitive to heat buildup and more resistant to fade. Dirt and water do not drastically affect braking action since contaminants are thrown off by the centrifugal action of the rotor or scraped off the by the pads. Also, the equal clamping action of the two brake pads tends to ensure uniform, straight line stops. Disc brakes are inherently self-adjusting. There are three general types of disc brake:

1. A fixed caliper.
2. A floating caliper.
3. A sliding caliper.

The fixed caliper design uses two pistons mounted on either side of the rotor (in each side of the caliper). The caliper is mounted rigidly and does not move.

The sliding and floating designs are quite similar. In fact, these two types are often lumped together. In both designs, the pad on the inside of the rotor is moved into contact with the rotor by hydraulic force. The caliper, which is not held in a fixed position, moves slightly, bringing the outside pad into contact with the rotor. There are various methods of attaching floating calipers. Some pivot at the bottom or top, and some slide on mounting bolts. In any event, the end result is the same.

DRUM BRAKES

Drum brakes employ two brake shoes mounted on a stationary backing plate. These shoes are positioned inside a circular drum which rotates with the wheel assembly. The shoes are held in place by springs. This allows them to slide toward the drums (when they are applied) while keeping the linings and drums in alignment. The shoes are actuated by a wheel cylinder which is mounted at the top of the backing plate. When the brakes are applied, hydraulic pressure forces the wheel cylinder's actuating links outward. Since these links bear directly against the top of the brake shoes, the tops of the shoes are then forced against the inner side of the drum. This action forces the bottoms of the two shoes to contact the brake drum by rotating the entire assembly slightly (known as servo action). When pressure within the wheel cylinder is relaxed, return springs pull the shoes back away from the drum.

Most modern drum brakes are designed to self-adjust themselves during application when the vehicle is moving in reverse. This motion causes both shoes to rotate very slightly with the drum, rocking an adjusting lever, thereby causing rotation of the adjusting screw. Some drum brake systems are designed to self-adjust during application whenever the brakes are applied. This on-board adjustment system reduces the need for maintenance adjustments and keeps both the brake function and pedal feel satisfactory.

✳✳ WARNING

Clean, high quality brake fluid is essential to the safe and proper operation of the brake system. You should always buy the highest quality brake fluid that is available. If the brake fluid becomes contaminated, drain and flush the system, then refill the master cylinder with new fluid. Never reuse any brake fluid. Any brake fluid that is removed from the system should be discarded.

Brake Light Switch

REMOVAL & INSTALLATION

▶ See Figure 1

1. Lift the locking tab on the switch connector and disconnect the wiring.
2. Remove the hairpin retainer, slide the stoplamp switch, pushrod and nylon washer off of the pedal. Remove the washer, then the switch by sliding it up or down.

➡On some vehicles equipped with speed control, the spacer washer is replaced by the dump valve adapter washer.

To install:

3. Position it so that the U-shaped side is nearest the pedal and directly over/under the pin.
4. Slide the switch up or down, trapping the master cylinder pushrod and bushing between the switch side plates.
5. Push the switch and pushrod assembly firmly towards the brake pedal arm. Assemble the outside white plastic washer to the pin and install the hairpin retainer.

➡Don't substitute any other type of retainer. Use only the Ford specified hairpin retainer.

6. Assemble the connector on the switch.
7. Check stoplamp operation.

➡Make sure that the stoplamp switch wiring has sufficient travel during a full pedal stroke.

Master Cylinder

REMOVAL & INSTALLATION

▶ See Figure 2

✳✳ WARNING

Vehicles with 4-wheel anti-lock brakes require an Anti-lock Brake Adapter (T90P-50-ALA) and Jumper (T93T-50-ALA) in order to bleed the master cylinder and the Hydraulic Control Unit (HCU). Failure to do so will trap air in the HCU unit, eventually causing a spongy pedal.

➡Before performing this procedure, ensure that you have the tools necessary to bleed the master cylinder and the HCU unit. If the tools are not available, you can still perform the procedure. However, you will need to tow the vehicle to a professional garage capable of bleeding the ABS system.

1. With the engine turned off, push the brake pedal down to expel vacuum from the brake booster system.
2. Disconnect the brake fluid level sensor wire from the reservoir.
3. Disconnect the hydraulic lines (use correct tool, a Line Wrench) from the brake master cylinder.
4. Remove the brake booster-to-master cylinder retaining nuts and lock washers. Remove the master cylinder from the brake booster.

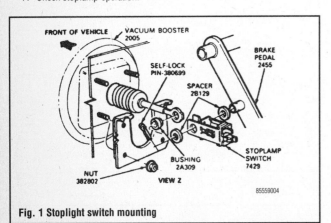

Fig. 1 Stoplight switch mounting

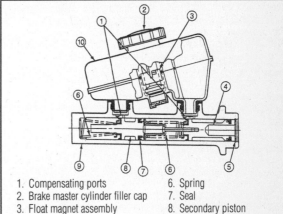

1. Compensating ports
2. Brake master cylinder filler cap
3. Float magnet assembly
4. Primary piston
5. Bore end seal
6. Spring
7. Seal
8. Secondary piston
9. Brake master cylinder
10. Brake master cylinder reservoir

Fig. 2 Cutaway view of the master cylinder assembly

To remove the master cylinder, first disconnect the fluid level sensor wire

Next, loosen the fluid line fittings at the master cylinder with a flarenut wrench . . .

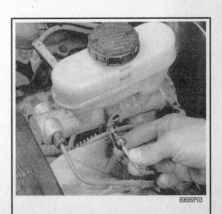

. . . then disconnect the lines

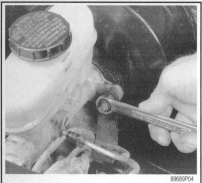

If equipped, remove any bracket retaining nuts . . .

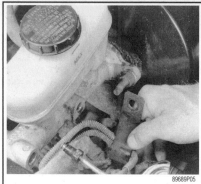

. . . and pull the bracket from the mounting stud

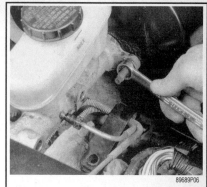

Remove the master cylinder-to-power booster attaching bolts . . .

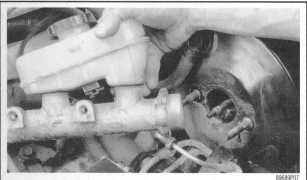

. . . then pull the master cylinder off of the mounting studs and remove it from the vehicle.

To install:

5. Before installing the master cylinder, check the distance from the outer end of the booster assembly push rod to the front face of the brake booster assembly. Turn the push rod adjusting screw in or out as required to obtain the length shown. Refer to illustration in this Section.

6. Position the master cylinder assembly over the booster push rod and onto the 2 studs on the booster assembly. Install the attaching nuts and lockwashers and tighten to 13–25 ft. lbs.

7. Connect the hydraulic brake system lines to the master cylinder.

8. Bleed the hydraulic brake system (refer to procedure in this Section). Centralize the differential valve. Then, fill the dual master cylinder reservoirs with DOT 3 brake fluid to within ¼ in. (6mm) of the top. Install the gasket and reservoir cover. Roadtest the vehicle for proper operation.

When replacing the master cylinder it is best to BENCH BLEED the master cylinder before installing it to the vehicle. Mount the master cylinder into a vise or suitable equivalent (do not damage the cylinder). Fill the cylinder to the correct level with the specified fluid. Block off all the outer brake line holes but one, then, using a long tool such as rod position it in the cylinder to actuate the brake master cylinder. Pump (push tool in and out) the brake master cylinder 3 or 4 times till brake fluid is release out and no air is in the brake fluid. Repeat this procedure until all brake fluid is released out of every hole and no air is expelled.

Power Booster

REMOVAL & INSTALLATION

▶ **See Figures 3, 4, 5, 6 and 7**

➡Make sure that the booster rubber reaction disc is properly installed if the master cylinder push rod is removed or accidentally pulled out. A dislodged disc may cause excessive pedal travel and extreme operation sensitivity. The disc is black compared to the silver colored valve plunger that will be exposed after the push rod and front seal is removed. The booster unit is serviced as an assembly and must be

replaced if the reaction disc cannot be properly installed and aligned, or if it cannot be located within the unit itself.

1. Disconnect the stop lamp switch wiring to prevent running the battery down.

2. Support the master cylinder from the underside with a prop.

3. Remove the master cylinder-to-booster retaining nuts.

4. Loosen the clamp that secures the manifold vacuum hose to the booster check valve, and remove the hose. Remove the booster check valve.

5. Pull the master cylinder off the booster and leave it supported by the prop, far enough away to allow removal of the booster assembly.

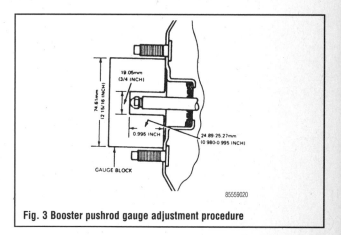

Fig. 3 Booster pushrod gauge adjustment procedure

1. Power brake booster check valve
2. Return spring
3. Tandem power diaphragms
4. Vacuum port closed— brakes on
5. Filter (air inlet)
6. Brake pedal push rod
7. Atmospheric port open— brakes on
8. Master cylinder push rod
9. Check valve grommet

Fig. 4 Cutaway view of the vacuum assisted power brake booster assembly

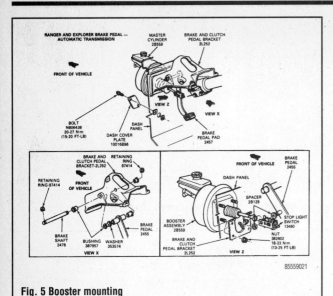

Fig. 5 Booster mounting

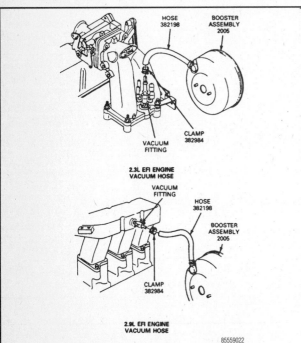

Fig. 6 Booster vacuum hose connections for the 2.3L, 2.5L & 2.9L engines—3.0L engine similar to 2.9L engine

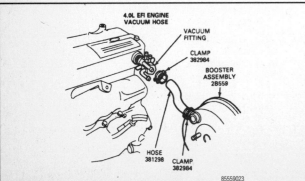

Fig. 7 Booster vacuum hose connections for the 4.0L—5.0L engine similar

6. From inside the cab on vehicles equipped with push rod mounted stop lamp switch, remove the retaining pin and slide the stop lamp switch, push rod, spacers and bushing off the brake pedal arm.

7. From the engine compartment remove the bolts that attach the booster to the dash panel.

To install:

8. Mount the booster assembly on the engine side of the dash panel by sliding the bracket mounting bolts and valve operating rod in through the holes in the dash panel.

➡**Make certain that the booster push rod is positioned on the correct side of the master cylinder to install onto the push pin prior to tightening the booster assembly to the dash.**

9. From inside the cab, install the booster mounting bracket-to-dash panel retaining nuts.

10. Position the master cylinder on the booster assembly, install the retaining nuts, and remove the prop from underneath the master cylinder.

11. Install the booster check valve. Connect the manifold vacuum hose to the booster check valve and secure with the clamp.

12. From inside the cab on vehicles equipped with push rod mounted stop lamp switch, install the bushing and position the switch on the end of the push rod. Then install the switch and rod on the pedal arm, along with spacers on each side, and secure with the retaining pin.

13. Connect the stop lamp switch wiring.

14. Start the engine and check brake operation.

Brake Hoses and Lines

Metal lines and rubber brake hoses should be checked frequently for leaks and external damage. Metal lines are particularly prone to crushing and kinking under the vehicle. Any such deformation can restrict the proper flow of fluid and therefore impair braking at the wheels. Rubber hoses should be checked for cracking or scraping; such damage can create a weak spot in the hose and it could fail under pressure.

Any time the lines are removed or disconnected, extreme cleanliness must be observed. Clean all joints and connections before disassembly (use a stiff bristle brush and clean brake fluid); be sure to plug the lines and ports as soon as they are opened. New lines and hoses should be flushed clean with brake fluid before installation to remove any contamination.

REMOVAL & INSTALLATION

1. Disconnect the negative battery cable.

2. Raise and safely support the vehicle on jackstands.

3. Remove any wheel and tire assemblies necessary for access to the particular line you are removing.

4. Thoroughly clean the surrounding area at the joints to be disconnected.

5. Place a suitable catch pan under the joint to be disconnected.

6. Using two wrenches (one to hold the joint and one to turn the fitting), disconnect the hose or line to be replaced.

7. Disconnect the other end of the line or hose, moving the drain pan if necessary. Always use a back-up wrench to avoid damaging the fitting.

8. Disconnect any retaining clips or brackets holding the line and remove the line from the vehicle.

➡**If the brake system is to remain open for more time than it takes to swap lines, tape or plug each remaining clip and port to keep contaminants out and fluid in.**

To install:

9. Install the new line or hose, starting with the end farthest from the master cylinder. Connect the other end, then confirm that both fittings are correctly threaded and turn smoothly using finger pressure. Make sure the new line will not rub against any other part. Brake lines must be at least 1/2 in. (13mm) from the steering column and other moving parts. Any protective shielding or insulators must be reinstalled in the original location.

❋❋ WARNING

Make sure the hose is NOT kinked or touching any part of the frame or suspension after installation. These conditions may cause the hose to fail prematurely.

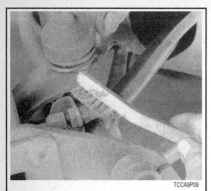

Use a brush to clean the fittings of any debris

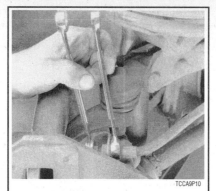

Use two wrenches to loosen the fitting. If available, use flare nut type wrenches

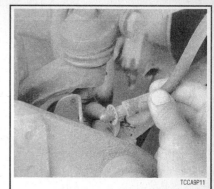

Any gaskets/crush washers should be replaced with new ones during installation

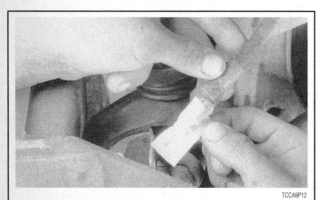

Tape or plug the line to prevent contamination

10. Using two wrenches as before, tighten each fitting.
11. Install any retaining clips or brackets on the lines.
12. If removed, install the wheel and tire assemblies, then carefully lower the vehicle to the ground.
13. Refill the brake master cylinder reservoir with clean, fresh brake fluid, meeting DOT 3 specifications. Properly bleed the brake system.
14. Connect the negative battery cable.

Bleeding The Brakes

✳✳ WARNING

Vehicles with 4-wheel anti-lock brakes require an Anti-lock Brake Adapter (T90P-50-ALA) and Jumper (T93T-50-ALA) in order to bleed the master cylinder and the Hydraulic Control Unit (HCU). Failure to do so will trap air in the HCU unit, eventually causing a spongy pedal. The tools are not required for caliper or wheel cylinder bleeding procedures.

When any part of the hydraulic system has been disconnected for repair or replacement, air may get into the lines and cause spongy pedal action (because air can be compressed and brake fluid cannot). To correct this condition, it is necessary to bleed the hydraulic system after it has been properly connected to be sure all air is expelled from the brake cylinders and lines.

When bleeding the brake system, bleed one brake cylinder at a time, beginning at the cylinder with the longest hydraulic line (farthest from the master cylinder) first. ALWAYS Keep the master cylinder reservoir filled with brake fluid during the bleeding operation. Never use brake fluid that has been drained from the hydraulic system, no matter how clean it is.

It will be necessary to centralize the pressure differential value after a brake system failure has been corrected and the hydraulic system has been bled.

The primary and secondary hydraulic brake systems are individual systems and are bled separately. During the entire bleeding operation, do not allow the reservoir to run dry. Keep the master cylinder reservoir filled with brake fluid.

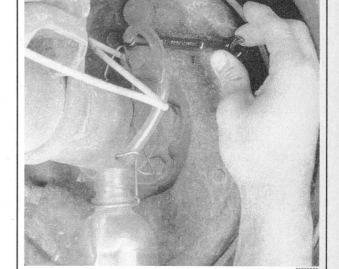

Bleed the rear brakes first, ensuring that no air bubbles remain visible moving through the tubing

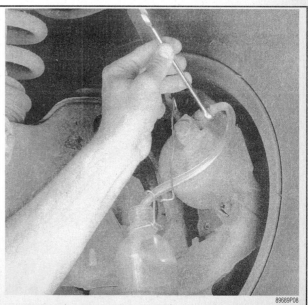

Bleed the caliper until you can see clean, air bubble free brake fluid moving through the tube

1. Clean all dirt from around the master cylinder fill cap, remove the cap and fill the master cylinder with brake fluid until the level is within ¼ in. (6mm) of the top edge of the reservoir.

2. Clean off the bleeder screws at all 4 wheels. The bleeder screws are located on the inside of the brake backing plate, on the backside of the wheel cylinders and on the front brake calipers.

3. Attach a length of rubber hose over the nozzle of the bleeder screw at the wheel to be done first. Place the other end of the hose in a glass jar, submerged in brake fluid.

4. Open the bleeder screw valve ½–¾ turn.

5. Have an assistant slowly depress the brake pedal. Close the bleeder screw valve and tell your assistant to allow the brake pedal to return slowly. Continue this pumping action to force any air out of the system. When bubbles cease to appear at the end of the bleeder hose, close the bleeder valve and remove the hose.

6. Check the master cylinder fluid level and add fluid accordingly. Do this after bleeding each wheel.

7. Repeat the bleeding operation at the remaining 3 wheels, ending with the one closet to the master cylinder. Fill the master cylinder reservoir.

FRONT DISC BRAKES

♦ See Figure 8

Ford used two types of calipers on the Ranger, Explorer and Mountaineer trucks; A single piston caliper was used from 1991–94 and a dual piston caliper was used on 1995–99 models. The single piston caliper is retained by two push pins, which also act as the calipers sliding surface. The outboard pad mounts directly to the single piston caliper. The dual piston caliper is mounted to an anchor plate by two slider bolts. The pads are mounted to the anchor plate rather than the caliper.

Brake Pads

INSPECTION

Replace the front pads when the pad thickness is at the minimum thickness recommended by the Ford Motor Co. which is ⅛₂ in. (0.8mm), or at the minimum allowed by the applicable state or local motor vehicle inspection code. Pad thickness may be checked by removing the wheel and looking through the inspection port in the caliper assembly.

1. Lower caliper pin
2. Outboard brake pad
3. Brake caliper
4. Upper caliper pin
5. Brake rotor splash shield
6. Brake rotor
7. Manual locking hub cover

89689P46

View of the 1991–94 front disc brake components

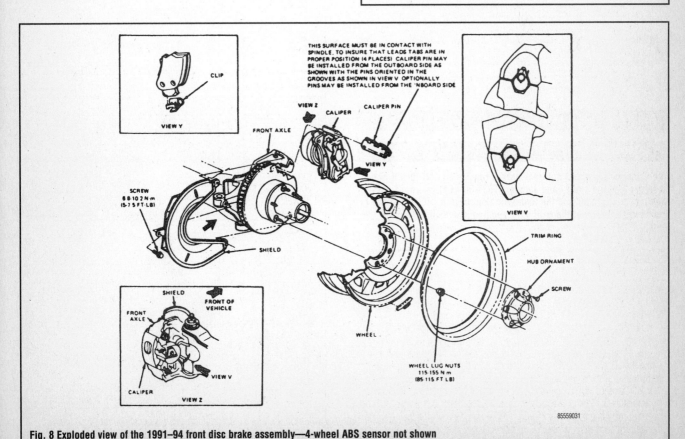

Fig. 8 Exploded view of the 1991–94 front disc brake assembly—4-wheel ABS sensor not shown

REMOVAL & INSTALLATION

Single Piston Caliper

▶ See Figures 9 thru 19

> ❊❊ **CAUTION**
>
> **Always replace all disc pad assemblies on an axle. Never service one wheel only.**

➡Ford recommends that new caliper pins be installed whenever the caliper is removed from the steering knuckle.

> ❊❊ **CAUTION**
>
> **Older brake pads or shoes may contain asbestos, which has been determined to be a cancer causing agent. Never clean the brake surfaces with compressed air! Avoid inhaling any dust from any brake surface! When cleaning brake surfaces, use a commercially available brake cleaning fluid.**

1. To avoid fluid overflow when the caliper piston is pressed into the caliper cylinder bores, remove or siphon part of the brake fluid out of the master cylinder reservoir (connected to the front disc brakes). Discard the removed fluid.

2. Loosen the wheel lug nuts.

3. Raise the vehicle and install jackstands. Remove a front wheel and tire assembly.

4. Place an 8 in. (203mm) C-clamp on the caliper and tighten the clamp slightly to push the caliper piston in its bore. This will ease caliper removal from the rotor. Remove the clamp.

➡Do not use a screwdriver or similar tool to pry piston away from the rotor.

5. There are 3 types of caliper pins used: a single tang type, a double tang type and a split-shell type. The pin removal process is dependent upon how the pin is installed (bolt head direction). Remove the upper caliper pin first.

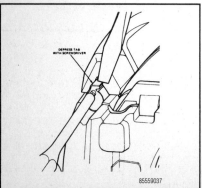
Before beginning the brake pad procedure, remove some fluid from the master cylinder

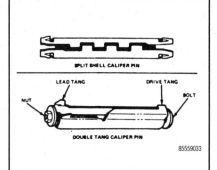
Fig. 9 Two styles of caliper pins used, single tang pin is similar to the double tang

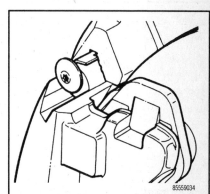
Fig. 10 View of a caliper pin with the bolt head facing the outside of the caliper

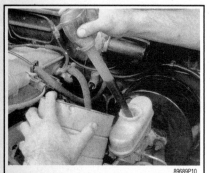
Fig. 11 Use a hacksaw to remove the bolt head from the pin

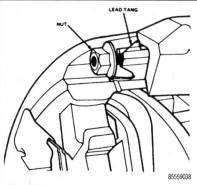
Fig. 12 View of a caliper pin with the nut facing the outside of the caliper

Use a hammer and punch, and drive the caliper pin out from between the caliper and its mount

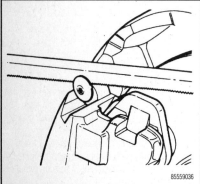
Fig. 13 When removing the pin, you may need to depress the pin tab with a tool

Pull the out from behind the caliper. Repeat the procedure for the lower pin

Slide the caliper assembly off of the rotor

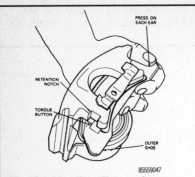

Fig. 14 Holding the caliper as shown, press down then slide the pad out to remove it from the caliper

Remove the outer brake pad from the caliper

If necessary, support the caliper by a length of wire from the frame. Never let it hang by the hose

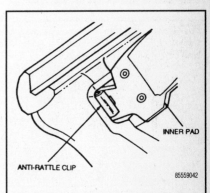

Finally, remove the inner brake pad from the steering knuckle assembly

Place the inner pad's friction material against the caliper piston and press it in with a C-clamp

Fig. 15 Ensure that the anti-rattle clip is installed as shown on the inner pad

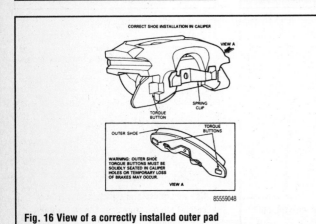

Fig. 16 View of a correctly installed outer pad

➡**On some applications, the pin may be retained by a nut and Torx® head bolt (except the split-shell type).**

  6. If the bolt head is on the outside of the caliper, use the following procedure:

    a. From the inner side of the caliper, tap the bolt within the caliper pin until the bolt head on the outer side of the caliper shows a separation between the bolt head and the caliper pin.

    b. Using a hacksaw or bolt cutter, remove the bolt head from the bolt.

    c. Depress the tab on the bolt head end of the upper caliper pin with a screwdriver, while tapping on the pin with a hammer. Continue tapping until the tab is depressed by the V-slot.

    d. Place one end of a punch, ½ in. (13mm) or smaller, against the end of the caliper pin and drive the caliper pin out of the caliper toward the inside of the vehicle. Do not use a screwdriver or other edged tool to help drive out the caliper pin as the V-grooves may be damage.

✳✳ WARNING

Never reuse caliper pins. Always install new pins whenever a caliper is removed.

  7. If the nut end of the bolt is on the outside of the caliper, use the following procedure:

    a. Remove the nut from the bolt.

    b. Depress the lead tang on the end of the upper caliper pin with a screwdriver while tapping on the pin with a hammer. Continue tapping until the lead tang is depressed by the V-slot.

    c. Place one end of a punch, ½ in. (13mm) or smaller, against the end of the caliper pin and drive the caliper pin out of the caliper toward the inside of the vehicle. Do not use a screwdriver or other edged tool to help drive out the caliper pin as the V-grooves may be damaged.

  8. Repeat the procedure in Step 4 for the lower caliper pin.

  9. Remove the caliper from the rotor.

  10. Remove the outer pad. Remove the anti-rattle clips and remove the inner pad.

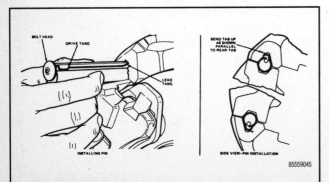

Fig. 17 Install the upper caliper pin with the tang facing up—tangs are installed facing down on the bottom pin

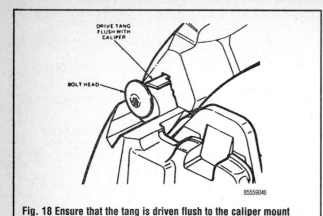

Fig. 18 Ensure that the tang is driven flush to the caliper mount

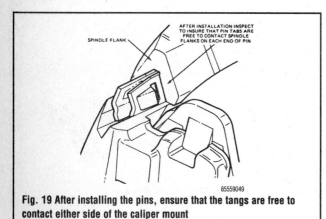

Fig. 19 After installing the pins, ensure that the tangs are free to contact either side of the caliper mount

11. Place the inner pads friction material against the caliper piston and assemble the C-clamp to the caliper again. Tighten the clamp until the caliper piston is fully seated into its bore.

To install:

12. Place a new anti-rattle clip on the lower end of the inner pad. Be sure the tabs on the clip are positioned properly and the clip is fully seated.

13. Position the inner pads and anti-rattle clip in the abutment with the anti-rattle clip tab against the pad abutment and the loop-type spring away from the rotor. Compress the anti-rattle clip and slide the upper end of the pad in position.

14. Install the outer pad, making sure the torque buttons on the pad spring clip are seated solidly in the matching holes in the caliper.

15. Install the caliper on the spindle, making sure the mounting surfaces are free of dirt and lubricate the caliper grooves with Disc Brake Caliper Grease. Install new caliper pins, making sure the pins are installed with the tang in position as shown. The pin must be installed with the lead tang in first, the bolt head facing outward (if equipped) and the pin positioned as shown. Position the lead tang in the V-slot mounting surface and drive in the caliper until the drive tang is flush with the caliper assembly. Install the nut (if equipped) and tighten to 32–47 inch lbs.

⁑⁂ WARNING

Never reuse caliper pins. Always install new pins whenever a caliper is removed.

16. Install the wheel and tire assembly.

17. Remove the jackstands and lower the vehicle. Torque the lug nuts to 100 ft. lbs. (135 Nm).

➡**The first couple of times you apply the brakes, the pedal may go to the floor. Continue to pump the brake pedal until it feels firm.**

18. Check the brake fluid level and fill as necessary. Check the brakes for proper operation before driving the vehicle.

Dual Piston Caliper

◆ See Figures 20, 21 and 22

⁑⁂ CAUTION

Older brake pads or shoes may contain asbestos, which has been determined to be a cancer causing agent. Never clean the brake surfaces with compressed air! Avoid inhaling any dust from any brake surface! When cleaning brake surfaces, use a commercially available brake cleaning fluid.

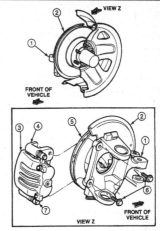

1. Front wheel hub and spindle
2. Front disc brake rotor shield
3. Disc brake caliper
4. Front disc brake caliper anchor plate
5. Front disc brake hub and rotor
6. Bolt, caliper anchor plate
7. Caliper pin bolt

Fig. 20 Exploded view of the 4x4 Ranger front brake caliper assembly—4x2 Ranger similar

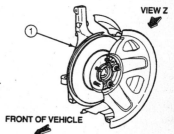

1. Front wheel hub and spindle
2. Disc brake caliper
3. Front disc brake caliper anchor plate
4. Bolt, anchor plate
5. Caliper pin bolt

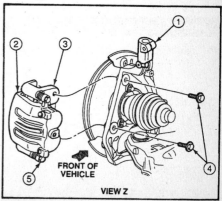

Fig. 21 Exploded view of the 4x4 Explorer/Mountaineer front brake caliper assembly—4x2 models similar

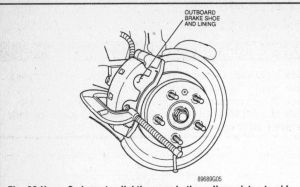

Fig. 22 Use a C-clamp to slightly press in the caliper piston to aid removal

1. To avoid fluid overflow when the caliper piston is pressed into the caliper cylinder bores, remove or siphon part of the brake fluid out of the master cylinder reservoir (connected to the front disc brakes). Discard the removed fluid.

2. Loosen the wheel lug nuts.

3. Raise and safely support the front of the vehicle. Remove the wheel.

4. Place an 8 in. (203mm) C-clamp on the caliper and tighten the clamp to bottom the caliper pistons in their bores. Remove the clamp.

5. Remove the two caliper slide pin bolts and lift the caliper from the anchor plate.

➡**Use care to retain as much of the original caliper slide pin grease as possible.**

6. Position the caliper on a frame member or suspend it with some wire. Do not allow the caliper to hang by the brake hose.

7. Remove the brake pads and, if necessary, the anti-rattle clips from the anchor plate.

8. Remove the shims, if any, from the brake pads for re-use.

To install:

9. If removed, install the anti-rattle clips.

10. Install the brake pads to the anchor plate.

11. Position the caliper over the brake pads and align the slide pin mounting holes.

12. Install the slide pin bolts and tighten them to 21–26 ft. lbs. (30–36 Nm).

13. Install the wheel and snug the lug nuts.

14. Lower the vehicle and tighten the lug nuts to 100 ft. lbs. (135 Nm).

➡**The first couple of times you apply the brakes, the pedal may go to the floor. Continue to pump the brake pedal until it feels firm.**

15. Start the engine and apply the brakes several times to readjust the caliper pistons. Ensure that the pedal feels firm before operating the vehicle.

Calipers

▶ **See Figures 23 and 24**

REMOVAL & INSTALLATION

1. Follow the procedures for pad removal earlier in this section.

2. Remove the brake hose-to-caliper attaching bolt.

3. Discard the brass washers and plug the brake hose and caliper bolt hole.

4. On dual piston caliper models, and if necessary, remove the brake pad anchor plate by removing the two attaching screws from the back of the steering knuckle.

5. Inspect the caliper, piston and rubber seals/boots for damage and replace as necessary.

To install:

6. On dual piston calipers, and if removed, position the anchor plat to the steering knuckle and install the two retaining bolts. Use a threadlocking com-

pound on the old bolts or install new bolts and tighten them to 73–97 ft. lbs. (98–132 Nm).

7. If it was necessary to remove the brake pads, install them to the anchor plate (dual piston) or caliper (single piston).

8. Install the caliper as instructed in the brake pad installation procedures.

➡**Always use new sealing washers when assembling the hose to the brake caliper.**

9. Place a new sealing washer on the brake hose bolt, slide the bolt through the hose fitting and install a second sealing washer to the bolt.

10. Position the hose/bolt to the caliper then tighten the bolt to 22–29 ft. lbs. (30–40 Nm).

11. Bleed the brake system. Check for leaks and proper operation before placing the vehicle into service.

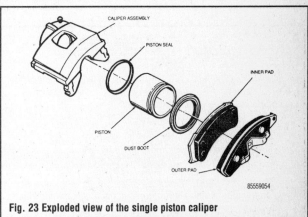

Fig. 23 Exploded view of the single piston caliper

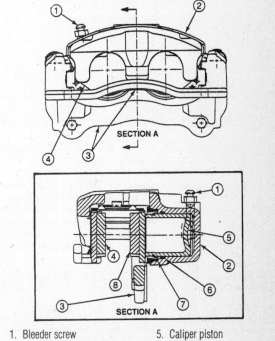

1. Bleeder screw
2. Disc brake caliper housing
3. Front disc brake caliper anchor plate
4. Brake shoe and lining, outboard
5. Caliper piston
6. Piston seal
7. Dust boot
8. Brake shoe and lining, inboard

Fig. 24 Cross-sectional view of the dual piston caliper

Loosen the brake hose-to-caliper retaining bolt . . .

89689P20

. . . then remove it, along with the hose fitting and the sealing washers

89689P21

Always discard the old sealing washers and use new ones when installing the caliper

89689P22

OVERHAUL

▶ See Figures 25 thru 30

➡Some vehicles may be equipped dual piston calipers. The procedure to overhaul the caliper is essentially the same with the exception of multiple pistons, O-rings and dust boots.

1. Remove the caliper from the vehicle and place on a clean work-bench.

✳✳ CAUTION

NEVER place your fingers in front of the pistons in an attempt to catch or protect the pistons when applying compressed air. This could result in personal injury!

➡Depending upon the vehicle, there are two different ways to remove the piston from the caliper. Refer to the brake pad replacement procedure to make sure you have the correct procedure for your vehicle.

2. The first method is as follows:
   a. Stuff a shop towel or a block of wood into the caliper to catch the piston.
   b. Remove the caliper piston using compressed air applied into the caliper inlet hole. Inspect the piston for scoring, nicks, corrosion and/or worn or damaged chrome plating. The piston must be replaced if any of these conditions are found.
3. For the second method, you must rotate the piston to retract it from the caliper.
4. If equipped, remove the anti-rattle clip.
5. Use a prytool to remove the caliper boot, being careful not to scratch the housing bore.

Fig. 25 For some types of calipers, use compressed air to drive the piston out of the caliper, but make sure to keep your fingers clear

TCCA9P01

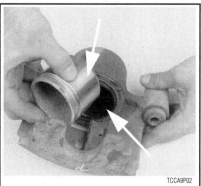

Fig. 26 Withdraw the piston from the caliper bore

TCCA9P02

Fig. 27 Use a prytool to carefully pry around the edge of the boot . . .

TCCSA9P04

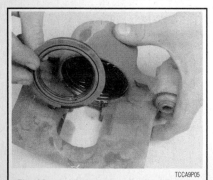

Fig. 28 . . . then remove the boot from the caliper housing, taking care not to score or damage the bore

TCCA9P05

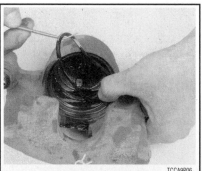

Fig. 29 Use extreme caution when removing the piston seal; DO NOT scratch the caliper bore

TCCA9P06

Fig. 30 Use the proper size driving tool and a mallet to properly seal the boots in the caliper housing

TCCA9P07

6. Remove the piston seals from the groove in the caliper bore.

7. Carefully loosen the brake bleeder valve cap and valve from the caliper housing.

8. Inspect the caliper bores, pistons and mounting threads for scoring or excessive wear.

9. Use crocus cloth to polish out light corrosion from the piston and bore.

10. Clean all parts with denatured alcohol and dry with compressed air.

To assemble:

11. Lubricate and install the bleeder valve and cap.

12. Install the new seals into the caliper bore grooves, making sure they are not twisted.

13. Lubricate the piston bore.

14. Install the pistons and boots into the bores of the calipers and push to the bottom of the bores.

15. Use a suitable driving tool to seat the boots in the housing.

16. Install the caliper in the vehicle.

17. Install the wheel and tire assembly, then carefully lower the vehicle.

18. Properly bleed the brake system.

Brake Rotor (Disc)

REMOVAL & INSTALLATION

Except 1995–99 4-Wheel Drive Models

1. Loosen the wheel lug nuts.

2. Jack up the front of the vehicle and support on jackstands.

3. Remove the wheel and tire.

4. On 1991–94 models, remove the brake caliper assembly as described earlier in this Section, but do not disconnect the brake hose.

5. On 1995–99 models, remove the two anchor plate-to-steering knuckle bolts then slide the assembly off of the rotor.

6. Suspend the caliper assembly by a piece of wire. Do not allow it to hang by the brake hose.

7. Follow the procedure given under wheel bearing removal in Section 7 for models with manual and automatic locking hubs.

➡New rotor assemblies come protected with an anti-rust coating which should be removed with denatured alcohol or degreaser. New hubs must be packed with EP wheel bearing grease.

8. Installation is the reverse of the removal procedure.

REAR DRUM BRAKES

▶ **See Figures 32 and 33**

Brake Drums

REMOVAL & INSTALLATION

❊❊ CAUTION

Older brake pads or shoes may contain asbestos, which has been determined to be a cancer causing agent. Never clean the brake surfaces with compressed air! Avoid inhaling any dust from any brake surface! When cleaning brake surfaces, use a commercially available brake cleaning fluid.

1. Raise the vehicle so that the wheel to be worked on is clear of the floor and install jackstands under the vehicle.

2. Remove the hub cap and the wheel/tire assembly. Remove the 3 retaining nuts and remove the brake drum. It may be necessary to back off the brake shoe adjustment in order to remove the brake drum. This is because the drum might be grooved or worn from being in service for an extended period of time.

1995–99 4-Wheel Drive Models

1. Loosen the wheel lug nuts.

2. Jack up the front of the vehicle and support on jackstands.

3. Remove the wheel and tire.

4. Remove the two anchor plate-to-steering knuckle bolts then slide the assembly off of the rotor.

5. Grasp the rotor and pull it from the wheel hub. Some models may have a small retaining screw holding the rotor to the wheel hub, if so, remove the screw then pull the rotor off.

6. Installation is the reverse of the removal procedure.

INSPECTION

▶ **See Figure 31**

1. Inspect the rotor for cracks, grooves or waviness. Rotors that aren't too badly scored or grooved can be resurfaced by most automotive shops.

2. Measure the rotor thickness using a caliper gauge.

3. Minimum rotor thickness should be 0.81 in. (20.5mm). If refinishing exceeds that, the rotor will have to be replaced.

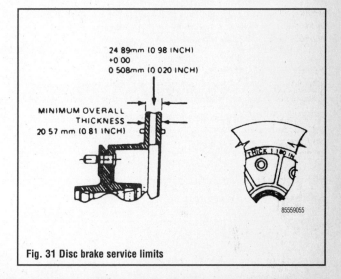

Fig. 31 Disc brake service limits

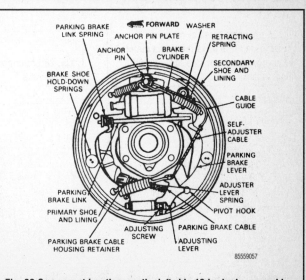

Fig. 32 Component locations on the left side 10 in. brake assembly

REAR DRUM BRAKE COMPONENTS

1. Secondary shoe
2. Adjusting screw assembly
3. Primary shoe
4. Adjuster spring
5. Adjuster lever
6. Hold-down pin
7. Hold-down spring
8. Hold-down assembly
9. Adjuster cable guide
10. Parking brake lever
11. Parking brake link
12. Link spring
13. Primary shoe return spring
14. Anchor pin plate
15. Secondary shoe return spring
16. Adjuster cable

89689P00

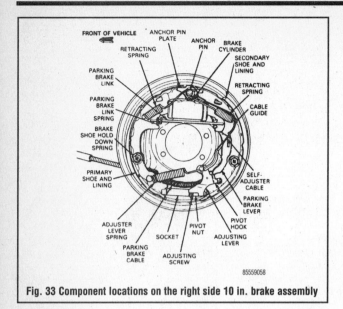

FRONT OF VEHICLE — ANCHOR PIN PLATE — ANCHOR PIN — BRAKE CYLINDER — SECONDARY SHOE AND LINING — RETRACTING SPRING — RETRACTING SPRING — CABLE GUIDE — PARKING BRAKE LINK — PARKING BRAKE LINK SPRING — BRAKE SHOE HOLD DOWN SPRING — PRIMARY SHOE AND LINING — SELF-ADJUSTER CABLE — PARKING BRAKE LEVER — ADJUSTER LEVER SPRING — SOCKET — PIVOT NUT — PIVOT HOOK — ADJUSTING LEVER — PARKING BRAKE CABLE — ADJUSTING SCREW

85559058

Fig. 33 Component locations on the right side 10 in. brake assembly

3. Before installing a new brake drum, be sure and remove any protective coating with carburetor degreaser.

4. Install the brake drum in the reverse order of removal and adjusts the brakes.

INSPECTION

▶ See Figure 34

After the brake drum has been removed from the vehicle, it should be inspected for run-out, severe scoring cracks, and the proper inside diameter.

Minor scores on a brake drum can be removed with fine emery cloth, provided that all grit is removed from the drum before it is installed on the vehicle.

A badly scored, rough, or out-of-round (run-out) drum can be ground or turned on a brake drum lathe. Do not remove any more material from the drum than is necessary to provide a smooth surface for the brake shoe to contact. The maximum diameter of the braking surface is shown on the inside of each brake drum. Brake drums that exceed the maximum braking surface diameter shown on the brake drum, either through wear or refinishing, must be replaced. This is because after the outside wall of the brake drum reaches a certain thickness (thinner than the original thickness) the drum loses its ability to dissipate the heat created by the friction between the brake drum and the brake shoes, when the brakes are applied. Also the brake drum will have more tendency to warp and/or crack.

The maximum braking surface diameter specification, which is shown on each drum, allows for a 0.060 in. (1.5mm) machining cut over the original nominal drum diameter plus 0.030 in. (0.76mm) additional wear before reaching the diameter where the drum must be discarded. Use a brake drum micrometer to measure the inside diameter of the brake drums.

Brake Shoes

REMOVAL & INSTALLATION

▶ See Figures 35, 36, 37 and 38

❊❊ CAUTION

Older brake pads or shoes may contain asbestos, which has been determined to be a cancer causing agent. Never clean the brake surfaces with compressed air! Avoid inhaling any dust from any brake surface! When cleaning brake surfaces, use a commercially available brake cleaning fluid.

1. Raise and support the vehicle and remove the wheel and brake drum from the wheel to be worked on.

89689P18

To remove the rear brake drum, first safely raise the rear of the vehicle and remove the wheel . . .

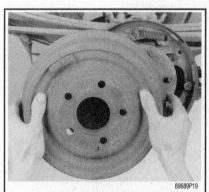

89689P19

. . . then grasp hold of the drum and pull it from the axle flange and brake shoes

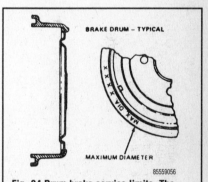

BRAKE DRUM – TYPICAL

MAXIMUM DIAMETER

85559056

Fig. 34 Drum brake service limits. The maximum inside diameter is cast into the drum

89689P23

Clean the brake shoe assemblies with a liquid cleaning solution, NEVER with compressed air

89689P24

To begin remove the brake shoes, pull the adjuster cable towards the shoe . . .

89689P25

. . . and disconnect the pivot hook from the adjusting lever. Wind the starwheel all the way in

➡If you have never replaced the brakes on a car before and you are not too familiar with the procedures involved, only disassemble and assemble one side at a time, leaving the other side intact as a reference during reassembly.

2. Install a clamp over the ends of the wheel cylinder to prevent the pistons of the wheel cylinder from coming out, causing loss of fluid.

3. Contract the brake shoes by pulling the self-adjusting lever away from the starwheel adjustment screw and turn the starwheel up and back until the pivot nut is drawn onto the starwheel as far as it will come.

4. Pull the adjusting lever, cable and automatic adjuster spring down and toward the rear to unhook the pivot hook from the large hole in the secondary shoe web. Do not attempt to pry the pivot hook from the hole.

5. Remove the automatic adjuster spring and the adjusting lever.

6. Remove the primary shoe-to-anchor spring with a brake tool. (Brake tools are very common and are available at auto parts stores). Remove the secondary shoe-to-anchor spring and unhook the cable anchor. Remove the anchor pin plate.

7. Remove the cable guide from the secondary shoe.

8. Remove the shoe hold-down springs, shoes, adjusting screw, pivot nut, and socket. Note the color of each hold-down spring for assembly. To remove the hold-down springs, reach behind the brake backing plate and place one finger on the end of one of the brake hold-down spring mounting pins. Using a pair of pliers, grasp the washer-type retainer on top of the hold-down spring that corresponds to the pin that you are holding. Push down on the pliers and turn them 90° to align the slot in the washer with the head on the spring mounting pin. Remove the spring and washer retainer and repeat this operation on the hold-down spring on the other shoe.

9. Remove the parking brake link and spring. Disconnect the parking brake cable from the parking brake lever.

10. After removing the rear brake secondary shoe, disassemble the parking brake lever from the shoe by removing the retaining clip and spring washer.

To assemble and install the brake shoes:

11. Assemble the parking brake lever to the secondary shoe and secure it with the spring washer and retaining clip.

Disconnect the adjuster lever return spring from the lever . . .

. . . and remove the spring and the lever

Next, using a brake spring removal tool . . .

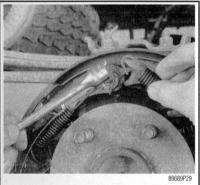
. . . disconnect the primary brake shoe return spring from the anchor pin

Repeat the procedure and remove the secondary return spring, adjuster cable and its guide

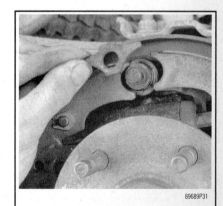
Also remove the anchor pin plate

Pull the bottoms of the shoes apart and remove the adjuster screw assembly

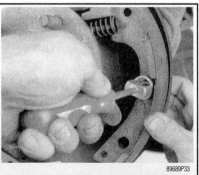
Press in the hold-down springs while holding in on the nail from behind, then turn the cup 90° . . .

. . . and release to remove the hold-down spring. Pull the nail out from the backing plate

Remove the primary (front) brake shoe from the backing plate . . .

. . . and the parking brake strut as well

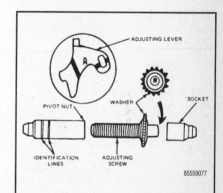

Remove the secondary shoe hold-down, pull the shoe out then press up on the cable spring . . .

. . . and disconnect the parking brake cable from its lever by pulling it from the slot

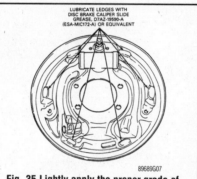

Fig. 35 Lightly apply the proper grade of lubricant to the points shown on the backing plate

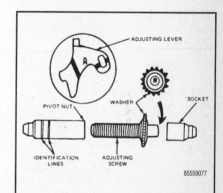

Fig. 36 Exploded view of a typical brake adjuster assembly

Fig. 37 The return spring and adjuster correctly installed

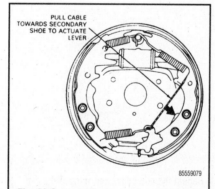

Fig. 38 Correct adjuster cable routing, driver's side shown

View of the rear drum brake shoes completely assembled to the backing plate

12. Apply a light coating of Lubriplate® at the points where the brake shoes contact the backing plate.

13. Position the brake shoes on the backing plate, and install the hold-down spring pins, springs, and spring washer-type retainers. Install the parking brake link, spring and washer. Connect the parking brake cable to the parking brake lever.

14. Install the anchor pin plate, and place the cable anchor over the anchor pin with the crimped side toward the backing plate.

15. Install the primary shoe-to-anchor spring with the brake tool.

16. Install the cable guide on the secondary shoe web with the flanged holes fitted into the hole in the secondary shoe web. Thread the cable around the cable guide groove.

17. Install the secondary shoe-to-anchor (long) spring. Be sure that the cable end is not cocked or binding on the anchor pin when installed. All of the parts should be flat on the anchor pin. Remove the wheel cylinder piston clamp.

18. Apply Lubriplate® to the threads and the socket end of the adjusting starwheel screw. Turn the adjusting screw into the adjusting pivot nut to the limit of the threads and then back off ½ turn.

➡Interchanging the brake shoe adjusting screw assemblies from one side of the vehicle to the other would cause the brake shoes to retract rather than expand each time the automatic adjusting mechanism operated. To prevent this, the socket end of the adjusting screw is stamped with an R or an L for RIGHT or LEFT. The adjusting pivot nuts can be distinguished by the number of lines machined around the body of the nut; one line indicates left hand nut and 2 lines indicates a right hand nut.

19. Place the adjusting socket on the screw and install this assembly between the shoe ends with the adjusting screw nearest to the secondary shoe.

20. Place the cable hook into the hole in the adjusting lever from the backing plate side. The adjusting levers are stamped with an R (right) or an L (left) to indicate their installation on the right or left hand brake assembly.

21. Position the hooked end of the adjuster spring in the primary shoe web and connect the loop end of the spring to the adjuster lever hole.

22. Pull the adjuster lever, cable and automatic adjuster spring down toward the rear to engage the pivot hook in the large hole in the secondary shoe web.

23. After installation, check the action of the adjuster by pulling the section of the cable between the cable guide and the adjusting lever toward the secondary shoe web far enough to lift the lever past a tooth on the adjusting screw starwheel. The lever should snap into position behind the next tooth, and release of the cable should cause the adjuster spring to return the lever to its original position. This return action of the lever will turn the adjusting screw starwheel one tooth. The lever should contact the adjusting screw starwheel one tooth above the center line of the adjusting screw.

If the automatic adjusting mechanism does not perform properly, check the following:

24. Check the cable end fittings. The cable ends should fill or extend slightly beyond the crimped section of the fittings. If this is not the case, replace the cable.

25. Check the cable guide for damage. The cable groove should be parallel to the shoe web, and the body of the guide should lie flat against the web. Replace the cable guide if this is not so.

26. Check the pivot hook on the lever. The hook surfaces should be square with the body on the lever for proper pivoting. Repair or replace the hook as necessary.

27. Make sure that the adjusting screw starwheel is properly seated in the notch in the shoe web.

ADJUSTMENTS

▶ **See Figures 39, 40 and 41**

The drum brakes are self-adjusting and require a manual adjustment only after the brake shoes have been replaced.

➡**Disc brakes are not adjustable.**

To adjust the rear brakes with drums installed, follow the procedure given below:

1. Raise the vehicle and support it with safety stands.
2. Remove the rubber plug from the adjusting slot on the backing plate.
3. Turn the adjusting screw using a Brake Shoe Adjustment Tool or equivalent inside the hole to expand the brake shoes until they drag against the brake drum and lock the drum.

4. Insert a small screwdriver or piece of firm wire (coat hanger wire) into the adjusting slot and push the automatic adjusting lever out and free of the starwheel on the adjusting screw and hold it there.

5. Engage the topmost tooth possible on the starwheel with the brake adjusting spoon. Move the end of the adjusting spoon upward to move the adjusting screw starwheel downward and contract the adjusting screw. Back off the adjusting screw starwheel until the wheel spins FREELY with a minimum of drag about 10 to 12 notches. Keep track of the number of turns that the starwheel is backed off, or the number of strokes taken with the brake adjusting spoon.

6. Repeat this operation for the other side. When backing off the brakes on the other side, the starwheel adjuster must be backed off the same number of turns to prevent side-to-side brake pull.

7. When all drum brakes are adjusted, remove the safety stands and lower the vehicle and make several stops while backing the vehicle, to equalize the brakes at all of the wheels.

8. Road test the vehicle. PERFORM THE ROAD TEST ONLY WHEN THE BRAKES WILL APPLY AND THE VEHICLE CAN BE STOPPED SAFELY!

Wheel Cylinders

REMOVAL & INSTALLATION

1. To remove the wheel cylinder, jack up the vehicle and remove the wheel, hub, and drum.
2. Remove the brake shoe assemblies.
3. Disconnect the brake line at the fitting on the brake backing plate.
4. Remove the screws that hold the wheel cylinder to the backing plate and remove the wheel cylinder from the vehicle.
5. Installation is the reverse of the above removal procedure. After installation bleed and adjust the brakes as described earlier in this Section.

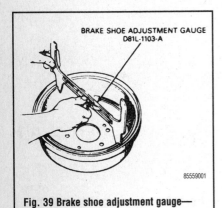

Fig. 39 Brake shoe adjustment gauge—Step 1

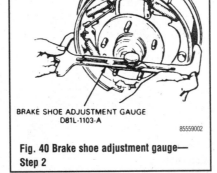

Fig. 40 Brake shoe adjustment gauge—Step 2

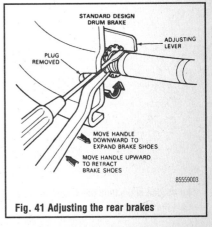

Fig. 41 Adjusting the rear brakes

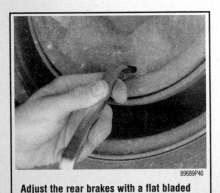

Adjust the rear brakes with a flat bladed tool inserted in the access hole in the backing plate

Remove the brake shoes and the brake line, then remove the bolts and tilt the cylinder inwards . . .

. . . then lift it up and off of the backing plate

OVERHAUL

▶ **See Figures 42 thru 51**

Wheel cylinder overhaul kits may be available, but often at little or no savings over a reconditioned wheel cylinder. It often makes sense with these components to substitute a new or reconditioned part instead of attempting an overhaul.

If no replacement is available, or you would prefer to overhaul your wheel cylinders, the following procedure may be used. When rebuilding and installing wheel cylinders, avoid getting any contaminants into the system. Always use clean, new, high quality brake fluid. If dirty or improper fluid has been used, it will be necessary to drain the entire system, flush the system with proper brake fluid, replace all rubber components, then refill and bleed the system.

1. Remove the wheel cylinder from the vehicle and place on a clean workbench.

2. First remove and discard the old rubber boots, then withdraw the pistons. Piston cylinders are equipped with seals and a spring assembly, all located behind the pistons in the cylinder bore.

3. Remove the remaining inner components, seals and spring assembly. Compressed air may be useful in removing these components. If no compressed air is available, be VERY careful not to score the wheel cylinder bore when removing parts from it. Discard all components for which replacements were supplied in the rebuild kit.

4. Wash the cylinder and metal parts in denatured alcohol or clean brake fluid.

✳✳ WARNING

Never use a mineral-based solvent such as gasoline, kerosene or paint thinner for cleaning purposes. These solvents will swell rubber components and quickly deteriorate them.

Fig. 42 Remove the outer boots from the wheel cylinder

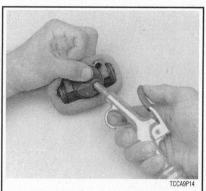
Fig. 43 Compressed air can be used to remove the pistons and seals

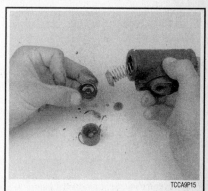
Fig. 44 Remove the pistons, cup seals and spring from the cylinder

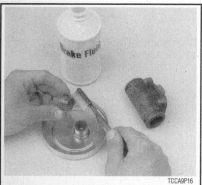
Fig. 45 Use brake fluid and a soft brush to clean the pistons . . .

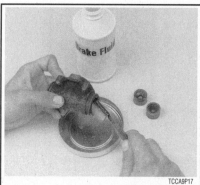
Fig. 46 . . . and the bore of the wheel cylinder

Fig. 47 Once cleaned and inspected, the wheel cylinder is ready for assembly

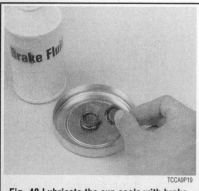
Fig. 48 Lubricate the cup seals with brake fluid

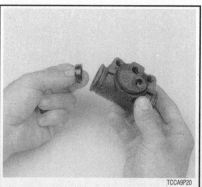
Fig. 49 Install the spring, then the cup seals in the bore

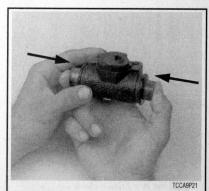
Fig. 50 Lightly lubricate the pistons, then install them

Fig. 51 The boots can now be installed over the wheel cylinder ends

5. Allow the parts to air dry or use compressed air. Do not use rags for cleaning, since lint will remain in the cylinder bore.
6. Inspect the piston and replace it if it shows scratches.
7. Lubricate the cylinder bore and seals using clean brake fluid.
8. Position the spring assembly.
9. Install the inner seals, then the pistons.
10. Insert the new boots into the counterbores by hand. Do not lubricate the boots.
11. Install the wheel cylinder.

REAR DISC BRAKES

General Information

Rear disc brakes were used on all Mountaineers and 1995–99 Explorers. The system utilizes a drum-in-hat type rear brake rotor. The integral drum allows the use of a drum-and-shoe type parking brake system. All other components are similar to their front disc brake components.

Brake Pads

REMOVAL & INSTALLATION

▶ **See Figures 52 and 53**

❊❊ CAUTION

Older brake pads or shoes may contain asbestos, which has been determined to be a cancer causing agent. Never clean the brake surfaces with compressed air! Avoid inhaling any dust from any brake surface! When cleaning brake surfaces, use a commercially available brake cleaning fluid.

1. To avoid fluid overflow when the caliper piston is pressed into the caliper cylinder bores, remove or siphon part of the brake fluid out of the master cylinder reservoir (connected to the front disc brakes). Discard the removed fluid.
2. Loosen the wheel lug nuts then raise and safely support the rear of the vehicle.
3. Remove the wheel.
4. Place an 8 in. (203mm) C-clamp on the caliper and tighten the clamp to bottom the caliper pistons in their bores. Remove the clamp.
5. Remove the two caliper slide pin bolts.

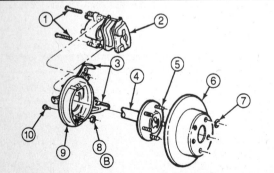

1. Caliper bolt
2. Rear disc brake caliper
3. Shoe slippers
4. Axle shaft
5. Wheel hub bolt
6. Rear disc brake rotor
7. Keeper nut
8. Nut, rear wheel disc brake adapter-to-rear axle flange
9. Rear wheel disc brake adapter
10. Bolt, adapter-to-axle flange

89689G09

Fig. 52 Exploded view of the rear disc brake assembly

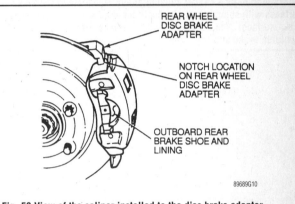

89689G10

Fig. 53 View of the caliper installed to the disc brake adapter

➡ **Use care to retain as much of the original caliper slide pin grease as possible.**

6. Work the rear brake caliper off of the brake pads and adapter mount.
7. Position the caliper on a frame member or suspend it with some wire. Do not allow the caliper to hang by the brake hose.
8. Remove and discard the pad slippers.
9. Remove the outboard brake pad by pressing it in enough to release the locating lug at one end then swing it up to release the other end.
10. Remove the inboard brake pad by tilting it enough to release the retainer spring from the caliper piston.

To install:

11. Inspect the rear brake caliper for damage and wear. Replace as necessary.
12. Position the inboard brake pad in the caliper and press the retainer spring fully into the caliper piston.
13. Start one end of the outboard pad on the brake caliper and rotate it down until the locating lugs and the retainer spring are fully seated.
14. Install new shoe slippers to the caliper mount.
15. Position the brake caliper over the rotor and align the sliding pin mounts.
16. Install the caliper bolts and tighten them to 20 ft. lbs. (27 Nm).
17. Install the wheel and snug the lug nuts.
18. Lower the vehicle and tighten the lug nuts to 100 ft. lbs. (135 Nm).
19. Check the brake fluid level in the master cylinder reservoir and correct as necessary.

➡ **The first couple of times you apply the brakes, the pedal may go to the floor. Continue to pump the brake pedal until it feels firm.**

20. Start the engine and apply the brakes several times to readjust the caliper pistons. Ensure that the pedal feels firm before operating the vehicle.

INSPECTION

1. Loosen the wheel lug nuts.
2. Raise and safely support the vehicle. Remove the wheel.
3. Looking through the rear brake caliper pad inspection hole, measure the pad thickness from the rotor surface to the pads metal backing.

4. Minimum pad thickness is ⅛ in. (3.12mm), however, your local safety inspection laws may supersede this dimension. Contact the appropriate authorities for specific safety requirements.

5. Any pad which is below the minimum allowable thickness will require you to replace all of the pads (both wheels).

Brake Caliper

REMOVAL & INSTALLATION

✳✳ CAUTION

Older brake pads or shoes may contain asbestos, which has been determined to be a cancer causing agent. Never clean the brake surfaces with compressed air! Avoid inhaling any dust from any brake surface! When cleaning brake surfaces, use a commercially available brake cleaning fluid.

1. To avoid fluid overflow when the caliper piston is pressed into the caliper cylinder bores, remove or siphon part of the brake fluid out of the master cylinder reservoir (connected to the front disc brakes). Discard the removed fluid.

2. Loosen the wheel lug nuts then raise and safely support the rear of the vehicle.

3. Remove the wheel.

4. Place an 8 in. (203mm) C-clamp on the caliper and tighten the clamp to bottom the caliper pistons in their bores. Remove the clamp.

5. Remove the rear brake hose-to-caliper attaching bolt. Discard the sealing washers.

6. Remove the two caliper slide pin bolts.

➡**Use care to retain as much of the original caliper slide pin grease as possible.**

7. Work the rear brake caliper off of the brake pads and adapter mount.

8. If necessary, remove the brake pads.

To install:

9. Inspect the rear brake caliper for damage and wear. Replace as necessary.

10. If removed, install the brake pads.

11. Install new shoe slippers to the caliper mount.

12. Position the brake caliper over the rotor and align the sliding pin mounts.

13. Install the caliper bolts and tighten them to 20 ft. lbs. (27 Nm).

14. Install the brake hose attaching bolt, using new sealing washers and tighten to 29 ft. lbs. (40 Nm).

15. Install the wheel and snug the lug nuts.

16. Refill the master cylinder as needed and bleed the brake system.

17. Lower the vehicle and tighten the lug nuts to 100 ft. lbs. (135 Nm).

➡**The first couple of times you apply the brakes, the pedal may go to the floor. Continue to pump the brake pedal until it feels firm.**

18. Start the engine and apply the brakes several times to readjust the caliper pistons. Ensure that the pedal feels firm before operating the vehicle.

OVERHAUL

The rear disc brake caliper is overhauled in the same manner as the front disc brake caliper. Refer to those procedures earlier in this section.

Brake Disc

REMOVAL & INSTALLATION

1. Remove the rear disc brake caliper, but do not disconnect the brake hose.

2. If equipped, remove the press-on keeper nuts from the wheel studs.

3. Remove the rear brake rotor from the axle flange by pulling it straight outwards.

4. If the rotor binds on the rear parking brake shoes, remove the adjuster plug from the back of the axle end then, using a drum brake spoon, adjust the parking brake shoes to release the rotor.

5. Installation is the reverse of the removal procedure. If necessary, check the parking brake shoe adjustment.

INSPECTION

1. Inspect the rotor for cracks, grooves or waviness. Rotors that aren't too badly scored or grooved can be resurfaced by most automotive shops.

2. Measure the rotor thickness using a caliper gauge.

3. Minimum rotor thickness should be 0.409 in. (10.4mm). If refinishing exceeds that, the rotor will have to be replaced.

PARKING BRAKE

Cable

ADJUSTMENT

1991–92 models

PRE-TENSION PROCEDURE

▶ **See Figure 54**

➡**This procedure is to be used when a new Tension Limiter has been installed.**

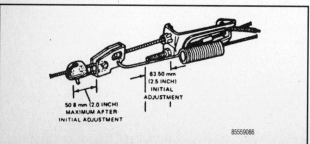

Fig. 54 Pre-tension adjustment

1. Depress the parking brake pedal.

2. Grip the Tension Limiter Bracket to prevent it from spinning and tighten the equalizer nut 2½ in. (63.5mm) up the rod.

3. Check to make sure the cinch strap has slipped less than 1⅜ in. (35mm) remaining.

FINAL ADJUSTMENT

➡**This procedure is to be used to remove the slack from the system if a new Tension Limiter has not been installed.**

1. Make sure the brake drums are cold for correct adjustment.

2. Position the parking brake pedal to the fully depressed position.

3. Grip the threaded rod to prevent it from spinning and tighten the equalizer nut 6 full turns past its original position on the threaded rod.

4. Attach an appropriate cable tension gauge (Rotunda Model 21-0018 or equivalent) behind the equalizer assembly either toward the right or left rear drum assembly and measure cable tension. Cable tension should be 400–600 lbs. with the parking brake pedal fully in the last detent position. If tension is low, repeat Steps 2 and 3.

5. Release parking brake and check for rear wheel drag. The cables should be tight enough to provide full application of the rear brake shoes, when the parking brake lever or foot pedal is placed in the fully applied position, yet loose enough to ensure complete release of the brake shoes when the lever is in the released position.

➡**The Tension Limiter will reset the parking brake tension any time the system is disconnected provided the distance between the bracket and** the cinch strap hook is reduced during adjustment. When the cinch strap contacts the bracket, the system tension will increase significantly and over tensioning may result. If all available adjustment travel has been used, the tension limiter must be replaced.

1993–99 Models

Starting in 1993, all models use a self-adjusting parking brake cable assembly. However, in order to remove any of the cables or components, the following procedures must be followed.

CABLE TENSION RELEASE

▶ See Figure 55

Method 1:
1. Place the parking brake cable control in the released position.
2. Have an assistant pull on the intermediate brake cable while you insert a 5/32 in. (4mm) diameter steel pin (or drill bit) into the hole provided in the parking brake control assembly.
3. To release the cable tension, pull out the lock pin from the control assembly.

Method 2:
For relieving tension from the rear cables only.
1. Pull backwards on the rear cable and conduit about 1.0–2.0 in. (25–50mm) and place a clamp on the parking brake cable and conduit behind the rear crossmember.

> ✳ **WARNING**
>
> **Ensure that you do not damage the nylon coating on the cable.**

2. To release the cable tension, remove the clamp holding the rear cable to the crossmember.

CABLE TENSION RESETTING

▶ See Figures 56, 57, 58 and 59

In the event that one of the cables has broken, or the cable tension release procedures were not followed perform the following procedures:
1. Remove the parking brake control assembly.
2. Engage the coil spring to the tab on the adjusting wheel in the control assembly.
3. Ensure the control assembly is in the released position.
4. Slip a spare front parking brake (or remove you existing one) cable around the pulley and insert the cable end into the pivot hole in the ratchet plate.
5. Position the free end of the parking brake cable on the floor and step on it, or clamp it in a vise.
6. Pull on the control assembly, holding the mounting bracket tightly against the body of the control, until the cable tension rotates the cable track assembly so that the (lock pin) 5/32 in. (4mm) diameter steel pin (or drill bit) can be fully seated through the plate.
7. Insert the lock pin so that the assembly is in the "cable released" position.
8. Install the parking brake control lever.

REMOVAL & INSTALLATION

▶ See Figures 60 and 61

Equalizer-To-Control Cable

1. Raise the vehicle on a hoist and support on jackstands.
2. On 1991–92 models, back off the equalizer nut and remove slug of front cable from the tension limiter.
3. On 1993–99 models, relieve the parking brake cable tension as outlined under cable adjustments.

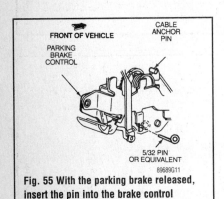

Fig. 55 With the parking brake released, insert the pin into the brake control assembly as shown to lock the cable tension spring

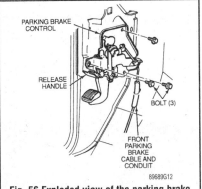

Fig. 56 Exploded view of the parking brake control assembly mounting

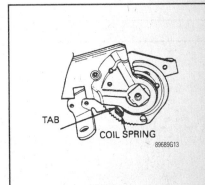

Fig. 57 Engage the coil spring to the tab on the adjusting wheel

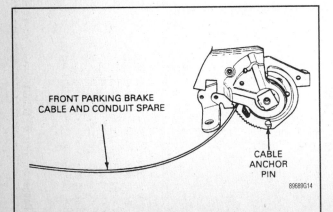

Fig. 58 Slip the front parking brake cable around the pulley and insert the cable end to the ratchet plate

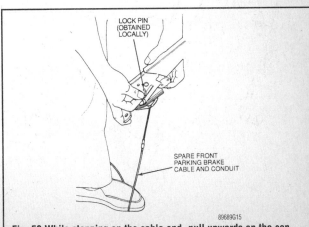

Fig. 59 While stepping on the cable end, pull upwards on the control assembly then install the lock pin when the holes align

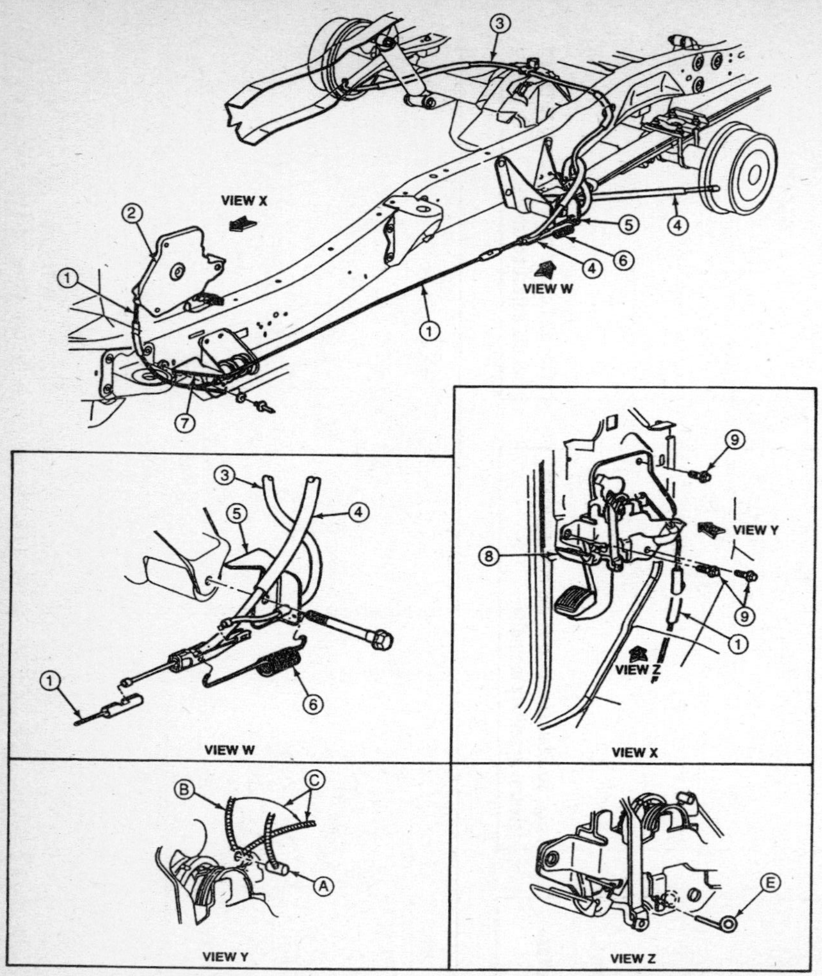

89689617

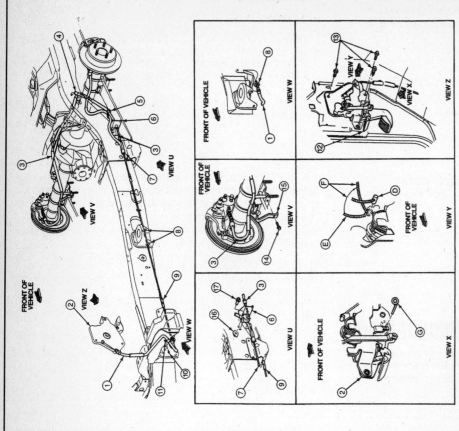

1. Front parking brake cable and conduit
2. Parking brake control
3. Parking brake rear cable and conduit (RH)
4. Rear parking brake rear cable retainer
5. Parking brake cable insulator
6. Parking brake cable bracket
7. Parking brake rear cable and conduit (LH)
8. Grommet
9. Parking brake intermediate cable
10. Bolt, front parking brake cable clamp
11. Bolt, front parking brake cable and conduit
12. Parking brake release handle
13. Bolt, parking brake control-to-cowl side

14. Bolt, parking brake cable retainer clip
15. Parking brake cable retainer clip
16. Nut
17. Bolt, parking brake cable and conduit

A. Parking brake front cable and conduit, before inserting into ratchet plate pivot hole
B. Parking brake front cable and conduit, after inserting into ratchet plate pivot hole
C. Parking brake front cable and conduit, installed
D. Parking brake front cable and conduit, before inserting into ratchet plate pivot hole
E. Parking brake front cable and conduit after inserting into ratchet plate pivot hole
F. Parking brake front cable and conduit, installed
G. 4mm (5/32-inch) steel pin or equivalent size drill bit

Fig. 61 Mountaineer and 1995–99 Explorer parking brake cable routing diagram

89689616

1. Front parking brake cable and conduit
2. Parking brake control
3. Parking brake rear cable and conduit (LH)
4. Parking brake rear cable and conduit (RH)
5. Parking brake cable bracket (rear)
6. Parking brake equalizer cable spring
7. Parking brake cable bracket (front)
8. Parking brake release handle
9. Bolt, parking brake control-to-cowl side

A. Parking brake front cable and conduit, before inserting into ratchet plate pivot hole
B. Parking brake front cable and conduit, after inserting into ratchet plate pivot hole
C. Parking brake front cable and conduit, installed
D. 4mm (5/32-inch) steel pin or equivalent size drill bit

Fig. 60 Ranger and 1991–94 Explorer parking brake cable routing diagram

4. Remove the parking brake cable from the bracket.

5. Remove the jackstands and lower the vehicle. Remove the forward ball end of the parking brake cable from the control assembly clevis.

6. Remove the cable from the control assembly.

7. Using a fishing line wire leader or cord attached to the control lever end of the cable, remove the cable from the vehicle.

To install:

8. Transfer the fish wire or cord to the new cable. Position the cable in the vehicle, routing the cable through the dash panel. Remove the fish wire and secure the cable to the control.

9. Connect the forward ball end of the brake cable to the clevis of the control assembly. Raise the vehicle on a hoist.

10. Route the cable through the bracket.

11. Connect the slug of the cable to the Tension Limiter connector.

12. On 1991–92 models, adjust the parking brake cable at the equalizer using the appropriate procedure shown above.

13. On 1993–99 models, release the cable tension as outlined under cable adjustments.

14. Rotate both rear wheels to be sure that the parking brakes are not dragging.

Equalizer-To-Rear Wheel Cables

EXCEPT REAR DISC BRAKE

▶ **See Figure 62**

1. Raise the vehicle and remove the wheel and brake drum.

2. On 1991–92 models, remove the locknut on the threaded rod and disconnect the cable from the equalizer.

3. On 1993–99 models, relieve the parking brake cable tension as outlined under cable adjustments. Disconnect the left rear cable from the front cable. For the right rear cable, disconnect it from the cable equalizer and rear guide bracket.

4. Use a 7/16 in. (14mm) wrench and compress the prongs that retain the cable housing to the frame bracket, and pull the cable and housing out of the bracket.

5. Working on the wheel side, use a 7/16 in. (14mm) wrench and compress the prongs on the cable retainer so they can pass through the hole in the brake backing plate. Draw the cable retainer out of the hole.

6. With the spring tension off the parking brake lever, lift the cable out of the slot in the lever, and remove the cable through the brake backing plate hole.

To install:

7. Route the right cable behind the right shock and through the hole in the left frame side rail. Route the left cable inboard of the leaf spring. Pull the cable through the brake backing plate until the end of the cable is inserted over the slot in the parking brake lever. Pull the excess slack from the cable and insert the cable housing into the brake backing plate access hole until the retainer prongs expand.

8. Insert the front of the cable housing through the frame crossmember bracket until the prong expands. Insert the ball end of the cable into the key hole slots on the equalizer, rotate the equalizer 90° and recouple the Tension Limiter threaded rod to the equalizer.

9. Install the rear brake drum and wheel, and adjust the rear brake shoes.

10. On 1991–92 models, adjust the parking brake tension using the appropriate procedure shown above.

11. On 1993–99 models, release the cable tension as outlined under cable adjustments.

12. Rotate both rear wheels to be sure that the parking brakes are not dragging.

13. Lower the vehicle and tighten the wheel lug nuts to 100 ft. lbs. (135 Nm).

REAR DISC BRAKE

▶ **See Figure 63**

1. Loosen the rear wheel lug nuts.

2. Raise the rear of the vehicle and remove the wheel.

3. Relieve the parking brake cable tension as outlined under cable adjustments.

4. Disconnect the left rear cable from the front cable. For the right rear cable, disconnect it from the cable equalizer and rear guide bracket.

5. Use a 7/16 in. (14mm) wrench and compress the prongs that retain the cable housing to the frame bracket, and pull the cable and housing out of the bracket.

6. Lift the parking brake rear cable eyelet off of the parking brake lever at the rear disc brake backing plate.

7. Compress the retainer fingers at the caliper adapter bracket with a 1/2 in. (13mm) box end wrench and remove the parking brake cable through the hole in the bracket.

To install:

8. Hook the cable eyelet over the parking brake lever. Push back the spring and put the exposed cable through the slot in the backing plate bracket.

9. Push the cable housing end into the bracket to engage the retainer fingers.

10. Route the cable along its original path.

11. For the right rear cable, insert the cable end through the rear guide bracket until the retainer fingers engage.

12. Connect the rear cables back to their original positions.

13. Release the cable tension as outlined under cable adjustments.

14. Install the wheel and, if necessary, adjust the rear parking brake shoes.

15. Rotate both rear wheels to be sure that the parking brakes are not dragging.

16. Lower the vehicle and tighten the wheel lug nuts to 100 ft. lbs. (135 Nm).

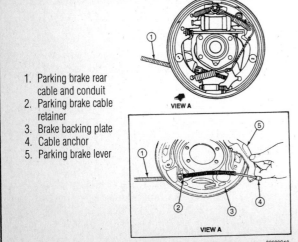

1. Parking brake rear cable and conduit
2. Parking brake cable retainer
3. Brake backing plate
4. Cable anchor
5. Parking brake lever

VIEW A

VIEW A

89689G18

Fig. 62 View of the rear brake cable mounting assembly

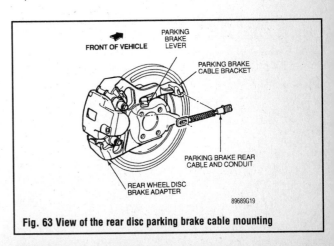

FRONT OF VEHICLE

PARKING BRAKE LEVER

PARKING BRAKE CABLE BRACKET

PARKING BRAKE REAR CABLE AND CONDUIT

REAR WHEEL DISC BRAKE ADAPTER

89689G19

Fig. 63 View of the rear disc parking brake cable mounting

Brake Shoes

Only the Mountaineer and 1995–99 Explorer models use separate parking brake shoes.

REMOVAL & INSTALLATION

▶ **See Figure 64**

1. Remove the rear disc brake rotor.
2. Remove the outboard return spring.
3. Remove the adjusting screw spring.
4. Remove the rear brake shoe hold-down spring and pin.
5. Remove the brake shoe adjusting screw and nut.
6. Remove the front brake shoe hold-down spring and pin.
7. Remove both parking brake shoes and the inboard return spring.
8. Check the parking brake lever for excessive wear and replace as necessary.

To install:

9. Position the front parking brake shoe to the backing plate and install the hold-down pin and spring.
10. Install the rear parking brake shoe with the inboard return spring.
11. Position the brake shoe adjuster screw and nut on the shoes and install the rear shoe hold-down pin and spring.
12. Install the brake shoe adjuster spring.
13. Install the outboard return spring.
14. Adjust the parking brake shoes and install the rotor, caliper and wheel.
15. Lower the vehicle and tighten the wheel lug nuts to 100 ft. lbs. (135 Nm).

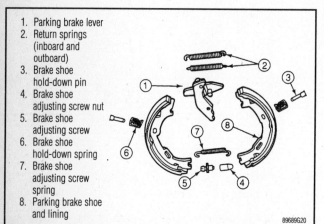

1. Parking brake lever
2. Return springs (inboard and outboard)
3. Brake shoe hold-down pin
4. Brake shoe adjusting screw nut
5. Brake shoe adjusting screw
6. Brake shoe hold-down spring
7. Brake shoe adjusting screw spring
8. Parking brake shoe and lining

89689G20

Fig. 64 Exploded view of the rear disc brake parking brake shoe assembly

ADJUSTMENT

▶ **See Figures 65 and 66**

1. Remove the rear disc brake rotor.
2. Using Brake Adjustment Gauge D81L-1103-A or equivalent, measure the inside diameter of the drum portion of the rear disc brake rotor.
3. Adjust the parking brake adjuster screw until the outside diameter of the parking brake shoes measures 0.020 in. (0.508mm) less than the drum measurement.
4. Install the rear disc brake rotor.

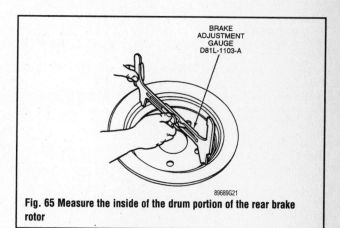

BRAKE ADJUSTMENT GAUGE D81L-1103-A

89689G21

Fig. 65 Measure the inside of the drum portion of the rear brake rotor

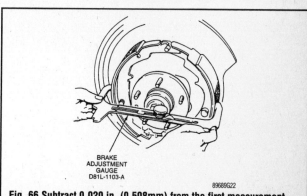

BRAKE ADJUSTMENT GAUGE D81L-1103-A

89689G22

Fig. 66 Subtract 0.020 in. (0.508mm) from the first measurement, adjust the brake shoes to that size

REAR ANTI-LOCK BRAKE SYSTEM (RABS)

Component Location

▶ **See Figure 67**

The RABS consists of the following components:

1. RABS module—located in the dash under the instrument panel mount on a brace, center of panel area.
2. Dual Solenoid Electro-Hydraulic Valve is located 5 in. (127mm) rearward of the No. 1 crossmember on the inboard side of the LH frame rail.
3. Speed Sensor and Exciter Ring—located in the rear differential housing.
4. Yellow REAR ANTI-LOCK Warning Light—located in the instrument cluster.
5. RABS Diagnostic Connector (1991–96)—located on the main wire bundle inside of cab under the dash, slightly rearward driver side.
6. RABS Diagnostic Connector (1997)—located on the forward end of the power distribution box, under the hood.
7. Diode/Resistor Element (1991–96)—located three inches left of the cluster connector takeouts in the instrument panel wiring harness.
8. Diode/Resistor Element (1997)—located in the power distribution box, under the hood.

9. Sensor test Connector—located under the hood slightly rearward the washer bottle.

System Self-Test

▶ **See Figure 68**

The RABS module performs system tests and self-tests during startup and normal operation. The valve, sensor and fluid level circuits are monitored for proper operation. If a fault is found, the RABS will be deactivated and the REAR ANTI LOCK light will be lit until the ignition is turned OFF. When the light is lit, the diagnostic flashout code may be obtained. Under normal operation, the light will stay on for about 2 seconds while the ignition switch is in the ON position and will go out shortly after. A flash code may be obtained only when the yellow light is ON. Before reading the code, drive the vehicle to a level area and place the shift lever in the PARK or NEUTRAL position. Keep the vehicle ignition ON.

➡**Starting in 1993, all vehicles use the RABS II system. The major difference between the two systems is the addition of keep alive memory (codes are stored, even if ignition is turned off), and a code 16 can be set which means the system is operating properly.**

8559099

FLASHOUT CODES CHART

CONDITION	
No Flashout Code	
Yellow REAR ABS Light Flashes 1 Time	This Code Should Not Occur
Yellow REAR ABS Light Flashes 2 Times	Open Isolate Circuit
Yellow REAR ABS Light Flashes 3 Times	Open Dump Circuit
Yellow REAR ABS Light Flashes 4 Times	Red Brake Warning Light Illuminated RABS Valve Switch Closed
Yellow REAR ABS Light Flashes 5 Times	System Dumps Too Many Times in 2WD (2WD and 4WD vehicles). Condition Occurs While Making Normal or Hard Stops. Rear Brake May Lock
Yellow REAR ABS Light Flashes 6 Times	(Sensor Signal Rapidly Cuts In and Out). Condition Only Occurs While Driving
Yellow REAR ABS Light Flashes 7 Times	No Isolate Valve Self Test
Yellow REAR ABS Light Flashes 8 Times	No Dump Valve Self Test
Yellow REAR ABS Light Flashes 9 Times	High Sensor Resistance
Yellow REAR ABS Light Flashes 10 Times	Low Sensor Resistance
Yellow REAR ABS Light Flashes 11 Times	Stoplamp Switch Circuit Defective. Condition Indicated Only When Driving Above 35 mph
Yellow REAR ABS Light Flashes 12 Times	Fluid Level Switch Grounded During a RABS Stop
Yellow REAR ABS Light Flashes 13 Times	Speed Processor Check
Yellow REAR ABS Light Flashes 14 Times	Program Check
Yellow REAR ABS Light Flashes 15 Times	Memory Failure
Yellow REAR ABS Light Flashes 16 Times or More	16 or More Flashes Should Not Occur

NOTE: Refer to Obtaining the Flashout Code in this section for procedure to obtain flashout code.

CAUTION: WHEN CHECKING RESISTANCE IN THE RABS SYSTEM, ALWAYS DISCONNECT THE BATTERY. IMPROPER RESISTANCE READINGS MAY OCCUR WITH THE VEHICLE BATTERY CONNECTED.

Fig. 68 RABS trouble code index

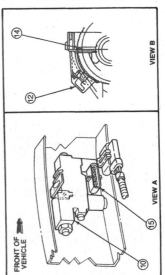

89689G23

1. Anti-lock electronic control module
2. Main wiring
3. J-nut
4. Screw
5. Power distribution box
6. Wire connector cover, RABS
7. RABS test connector
8. Rear wiring
9. RABS valve wiring
10. RABS valve
11. Frame side rail
12. Speed sensor
13. Rear axle housing
14. Speed sensor ring
15. RABS valve connector

Fig. 67 RABS component locations for 1991–96 models

TO OBTAIN THE FLASH CODE:

1. Locate the RABS diagnostic connector (orange/black wire) and attach a jumper wire to it and momentarily (1 to 2 seconds) ground it to the chassis.

2. Quickly remove the ground. When the ground is made and then removed, the RABS light will begin to flash.

3. The code consists of a number of short flashes and ends with a long flash. Count the short flashes and include the following long flash in the count to obtain the code number. Example 3 short flashes and one long flash indicated Code No. 4. The code will continue until the ignition is turned **OFF**. Refer to the flashcode diagnosis charts for further instructions.

Computer (RABS) Module

REMOVAL & INSTALLATION

1. Remove any instrument panel covers to gain access to the module.
2. Disconnect the wiring harness to the module.
3. Remove the retaining screws and remove the module.

To install:

4. Place the module in position against the under dash crossmember. Install and tighten the retaining bolts.
5. Connect the wiring harness to the module.
6. Install any instrument panels which were removed.
7. Check the system for proper operation.

RABS Valve

REMOVAL & INSTALLATION

1. Disconnect the brake lines from the valve and plug the lines.
2. Disconnect the wiring harness at the valve.

3. Remove the 3 nuts retaining the valve to the frame rail and lift out the valve.

4. Installation is the reverse of removal. Don't overtighten the brake lines. Bleed the brakes.

RABS Sensor

TESTING

Remove the RABS sensor from the axle housing.

1. Connect a Digital Volt/Ohm Meter (DVOM) across the two sensor terminals and record the reading.
2. The reading should be between 0.8 and 1.4 k Ohms.
3. If not, replace the sensor.

REMOVAL & INSTALLATION

1. Thoroughly clean the axle housing around the sensor.
2. Disconnect the electrical harness plug from the sensor.
3. Remove the sensor hold-down bolt.
4. Remove the sensor by pulling it straight out of the axle housing.
5. Ensure that the axle surface is and that no dirt can enter the housing.
6. If a new sensor is being installed, lubricate the O-ring with clean engine oil. Carefully push the sensor into the housing aligning the mounting flange hole with the threaded hole in the housing. Torque the hold-down bolt to 30 ft. lbs. If the old sensor is being installed, clean it thoroughly and install a new O-ring coated with clean engine oil.

Exciter Ring

The ring is located on the differential case inside the axle housing. Once it is pressed off the case it cannot be reused. This job should be left to a qualified service technician as it requires the rear differential to be disassembled.

To remove the rear wheel sensor, first disconnect the electrical harness plug . . .

89689P43

. . . then remove the sensor-to-axle housing hold-down bolt

89689P44

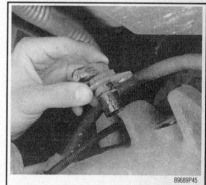

Pull the sensor up and out of the axle housing

89689P45

4-WHEEL ANTI-LOCK BRAKE SYSTEM (4WABS)

This system is used on the Mountaineer and 1993–99 Explorer, it was optional on all 1995–99 4-wheel drive Ranger models.

The 4WABS system consists of the following components:

1. The anti-lock Hydraulic Control Unit (HCU)—mounted to a bracket which is bolted to the left-hand inner fender.
2. The Explorer/Mountaineer 4WABS module—located on the outboard side of the left-hand inner fender, behind the plastic fender liner.
3. The Ranger 4WABS module—located in front and to the right of the battery, on the radiator support.
4. The front wheel sensors – bolted to the steering knuckles (4x2) or, on Explorer/Mountaineer (4x4) they are part of the wheel bearing assembly and on Ranger (4x4) they are part of the front axle assembly.
5. The rear speed sensor—located on the rear axle housing.

6. The front speed sensor indicator rings—located on the front rotor assemblies (4x2) or, on Ranger they are pressed into the front wheel hub and spindle and on Explorer/Mountaineer (4x4) are integral in the front wheel bearing assemblies.
7. The rear speed sensor indicator rings—located on the ring gear inside the rear axle housing.
8. The Explorer/Mountaineer G-switch—located on the left-hand frame rail aft of the No. 2 crossmember.
9. The Ranger G-switch—located on the left-hand frame rail forward of the No. 3 crossmember.
10. The Explorer/Mountaineer main and pump motor relay—located in a four relay box mounted near the battery on the left fender wall.
11. The Ranger main and pump motor relay—located in a two relay box mounted near the master cylinder on the left cowl side.

System Self-Test

♦ **See Figure 69**

The 4WABS module performs system tests and self-tests during startup and normal operation. The valve, sensor and fluid level circuits are monitored for proper operation. If a fault is found, the 4WABS will be deactivated and the amber ANTI LOCK light will be lit until the ignition is turned OFF. When the light is lit, the Diagnostic Trouble Code (DTC) may be obtained. Under normal operation, the light will stay on for about 2 seconds while the ignition switch is in the ON position and will go out shortly after.

The Diagnostic Trouble Codes (DTC) are an alphanumeric code and a scan tool, such as Rotunda NGS Tester 007-00500, is required to retrieve the codes. The DTC code chart has been included.

Hydraulic Control Unit (HCU)

PUMP TESTING

1. Disconnect the HCU pump motor electrical plug.
2. Connect a Digital Volt/Ohm Meter (DVOM) across the two pump terminals and record the reading.
3. The reading should be between 52-68 Ohms
4. If not, replace the pump motor.

REMOVAL & INSTALLATION

♦ **See Figure 70**

1. Disconnect the battery ground cable.

SERVICE CODE INDEX

DTC	Concern	Sets At
B1432	Anti-Lock Brake Control Module Failure	Key On
C1101	Intermittent Valve Failure	Key On
C1185	Main Relay Output Circuit Failure	Key On
B1317	Battery Voltage High	Key On
B1318	Battery Voltage Low	Key On
C1198	LF ISO Valve Coil Circuit Failure	Key On
C1194	LF Dump Valve Coil Circuit Failure	Key On
C1214	RF ISO Valve Coil Circuit Failure	Key On
C1210	RF Dump Valve Coil Circuit Failure	Key On
C1206	R ISO Valve Coil Circuit Failure	Key On
C1202	R Dump Valve Coil Circuit Failure	Key On
C1155	LF Wheel Speed Sensor Input Circuit Failure	Key On
C1158	LF Wheel Speed Sensor Coherency Fault	40 km/h (25 mph)
C1258	LF Wheel Speed Sensor Wheel Speed Comparison Fault	19 km/h (12 mph)
C1233	LF Wheel Speed Sensor Input Missing (Long Term)	>2 Min.
C1145	RF Wheel Speed Sensor Input Circuit Failure	Key On
C1148	RF Wheel Speed Sensor Coherency Fault	40 km/h (25 mph)
C1259	RF Wheel Speed Sensor Wheel Speed Comparison Fault	19 km/h (12 mph)
C1234	RF Wheel Speed Sensor Input Missing (Long Term)	>2 Min.
C1230	RA Wheel Speed Sensor Input Circuit Failure	Key On
C1229	RA Wheel Speed Sensor Coherency Fault	40 km/h (25 mph)
C1260	RA Wheel Speed Sensor Wheel Speed Comparison Fault	19 km/h (12 mph)
C1237	R Wheel Speed Sensor Input Missing (Long Term)	>2 Min.
No Code	Front Left Valve Pair Function Test	—
No Code	Front Right Valve Pair Function Test	—
No Code	Rear Axle Valve Pair Function Test	—
C1096	Pump Motor Triggered but Did Not Run	7 km/h (4 mph)
C1102	G-Switch Failure	See NOTE Below
C1095	Pump Motor Running but Not Triggered	Key On
No Code	No Communication	—

NOTE: DTC C1102 indicates a G-Switch circuit failure. If the yellow ABS warning lamp comes on at key ON, check for a ground short on Pins 30, 31, or 32. If the yellow ABS lamp comes on at approximately 32 km/h (20 mph), there is either: 1) a battery short on Pins 30, 31 or 32; 2) an open on Pins 30 and 31; or 3) an open on Pin 32. If the yellow ABS lamp comes on after driving the vehicle for 2 minutes at approximately 72 km/h (45 mph), check for an open on Pin 30 or 31 (one pin only).

89689G24

Fig. 69 4-Wheel Anti-lock Brake System (4WABS) diagnostic trouble code chart

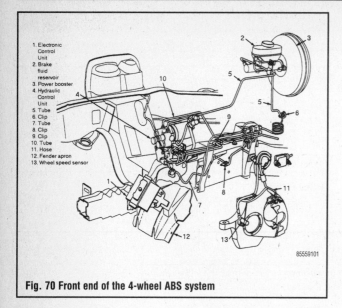

1. Electronic Control Unit
2. Brake fluid reservoir
3. Power booster
4. Hydraulic Control Unit
5. Tube
6. Clip
7. Tube
8. Clip
9. Clip
10. Tube
11. Hose
12. Fender apron
13. Wheel speed sensor

Fig. 70 Front end of the 4-wheel ABS system

2. Unplug the 8-pin connector from the unit, and the 4-pin connector from the pump motor.

3. Disconnect the 5 inlet and outlet tubes from the unit. Immediately plug the ports.

4. Remove the 3 unit attaching nuts and lift out the unit.

5. Installation is the reverse of removal. Torque the mounting nuts to 12-18 ft. lbs. and the tube fittings to 10-18 ft. lbs.

➡**After reconnecting the battery, it may take 10 miles or more of driving for the Powertrain Control Module to relearn its driveability codes.**

6. Bleed the brakes.

Electronic Control Unit

REMOVAL & INSTALLATION

1. Disconnect the battery ground cable.
2. Unplug the wiring from the ECU.
3. Remove the mounting bolts, slide the ECU off its bracket.
4. Installation is the reverse of removal. Torque the mounting screw to 5-6 ft. lbs. and the connector bolt to 4-5 ft. lbs.

➡**After reconnecting the battery, it may take 10 miles or more of driving for the Powertrain Control Module to relearn its driveability codes.**

Front Wheel Speed Sensor

TESTING

1. Disconnect the speed sensor wire harness plug from the sensor or sensor pigtail.

2. Connect a Digital Volt/Ohm Meter (DVOM) across the two sensor terminals and record the reading.

3. The reading should be within the following ranges for the appropiate model and sensor.

Ranger
- Front right sensor—1.0–1.4 k Ohms
- Front left sensor—1.0–1.4 k Ohms

Explorer/Mountaineer—4x4 models only
- Front right sensor—0.270–0.330 k Ohms
- Front left sensor—0.270–0.330 k Ohms

REMOVAL & INSTALLATION

1. Inside the engine compartment, disconnect the sensor from the harness.
2. Unclip the sensor cable from the brake hose clips.
3. Remove the retaining bolt from the spindle and slide the sensor from its hole.
4. Installation is the reverse of removal. Torque the retaining bolt to 40-60 inch lbs.

Rear Speed Sensor

TESTING

1. Remove the rear wheel speed sensor from the axle housing.
2. Connect a Digital Volt/Ohm Meter (DVOM) across the two sensor terminals and record the reading.
3. The reading should be between 0.8 and 1.4 k Ohms.
4. If not, replace the sensor.

REMOVAL & INSTALLATION

▶ **See Figure 71**

1. Disconnect the wiring from the harness.
2. Remove the sensor hold-down bolt and remove the sensor from the axle.

To install:

3. Thoroughly clean the mounting surfaces. Make sure no dirt falls into the axle. Clean the magnetized sensor pole piece. Metal particles can cause sensor problems. Replace the O-ring.

4. Coat the new O-ring with clean engine oil.

5. Position the new sensor on the axle. It should slide into place easily. Correct installation will allow a gap of 0.005-0.045 in.

6. Torque the hold-down bolt to 25-30 ft. lbs.

7. Connect the wiring.

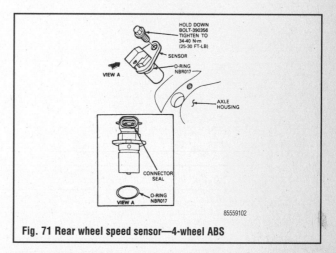

Fig. 71 Rear wheel speed sensor—4-wheel ABS

Front Speed Sensor Ring

REMOVAL & INSTALLATION

▶ **See Figure 72**

1. Raise and support the front end on jackstands.
2. Remove the wheels.
3. Remove the caliper, rotor and hub.
4. Using a 3-jawed puller, remove the ring from the hub. The ring cannot be reused; it must be replaced.

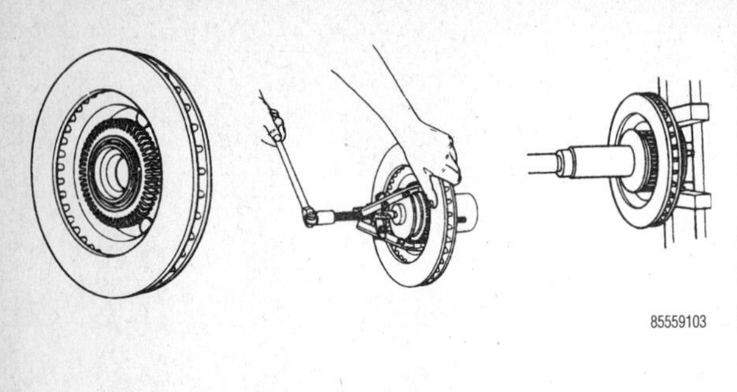

Fig. 72 Front wheel sensor ring—4-wheel ABS

To install:

5. Support the hub in a press so that the lug studs do not rest on the work surface.
6. Position the **new** sensor ring on the hub. Using a cylindrical adapter 98mm ID X 106mm OD, press the ring into place. The ring **must** be fully seated!
7. The remainder of installation is the reverse of removal.

Rear Speed Sensor Ring

REMOVAL & INSTALLATION

The ring is located on the differential case inside the axle housing. Once it is pressed off the case it cannot be reused. This job should be left to a qualified service technician as it requires the rear differential to be disassembled.

BRAKE SPECIFICATIONS

All measurements in inches unless noted

Year	Model		Master Cylinder Bore	Brake Disc Original Thickness	Brake Disc Minimum Thickness	Brake Disc Maximum Runout	Brake Drum Diameter Original Inside Diameter	Brake Drum Diameter Max. Wear Limit	Brake Drum Diameter Max. Machine Diameter	Minimum Lining Thickness Front	Minimum Lining Thickness Rear
1991	Ranger	①	0.938	0.850	0.810	0.003	9.00	9.09	9.06	0.062 ⑤	0.030 ⑤
		②	③	0.850	0.810	0.003	10.00	10.09	10.06	0.062 ⑤	0.030 ⑤
	Explorer	①	0.938	0.850	0.810	0.003	9.00	9.09	9.06	0.062 ⑤	0.030 ⑤
		②	③	0.850	0.810	0.003	10.00	10.09	10.06	0.062 ⑤	0.030 ⑤
1992	Ranger	①	0.938	0.850	0.810	0.003	9.00	9.09	9.06	0.062 ⑤	0.030 ⑤
		②	③	0.850	0.810	0.003	10.00	10.09	10.06	0.062 ⑤	0.030 ⑤
	Explorer	①	0.938	0.850	0.810	0.003	9.00	9.09	9.06	0.062 ⑤	0.030 ⑤
		②	③	0.850	0.810	0.003	10.00	10.09	10.06	0.062 ⑤	0.030 ⑤
1993	Ranger	①	0.938	0.850	0.810	0.003	9.00	9.09	9.06	0.062 ⑤	0.030 ⑤
		②	③	0.850	0.810	0.003	10.00	10.09	10.06	0.062 ⑤	0.030 ⑤
	Explorer	①	0.938	0.850	0.810	0.003	9.00	9.09	9.06	0.062 ⑤	0.030 ⑤
		②	③	0.850	0.810	0.003	10.00	10.09	10.06	0.062 ⑤	0.030 ⑤
1994	Ranger	①	0.938	0.850	0.810	0.003	9.00	9.09	9.06	0.062 ⑤	0.030 ⑤
		②	③	0.850	0.810	0.003	10.00	10.09	10.06	0.062 ⑤	0.030 ⑤
	Explorer	①	0.938	0.850	0.810	0.003	9.00	9.09	9.06	0.062 ⑤	0.030 ⑤
		②	③	0.850	0.810	0.003	10.00	10.09	10.06	0.062 ⑤	0.030 ⑤
1995	Ranger	①	0.938	1.023	④	0.003	9.00	9.09	9.06	0.062 ⑤	0.030 ⑤
		②	③	1.023	④	0.003	10.00	10.09	10.06	0.062 ⑤	0.030 ⑤
	Explorer	Front	0.938	1.023	④	0.003	—	—	—	0.062 ⑤	—
		Rear	0.938	0.472	0.409	0.003	—	—	—	—	0.125 ⑤
1996	Ranger	①	0.938	1.023	④	0.003	9.00	9.09	9.06	0.062 ⑤	0.030 ⑤
		②	③	1.023	④	0.003	10.00	10.09	10.06	0.062 ⑤	0.030 ⑤
	Explorer	Front	0.938	1.023	④	0.003	—	—	—	0.062 ⑤	—
		Rear	0.938	0.472	0.409	0.003	—	—	—	—	0.125 ⑤
1997	Ranger	①	0.938	1.023	④	0.003	9.00	9.09	9.06	0.062 ⑤	0.030 ⑤
		②	③	1.023	④	0.003	10.00	10.09	10.06	0.062 ⑤	0.030 ⑤
	Explorer	Front	0.938	1.023	④	0.003	—	—	—	0.062 ⑤	—
		Rear	0.938	0.472	0.409	0.003	—	—	—	—	0.125 ⑤
	Mountaineer	Front	0.938	1.023	0.810	0.003	—	—	—	0.062 ⑤	—
		Rear	0.938	0.472	0.409	0.003	—	—	—	—	0.125 ⑤
1998	Ranger	①	0.938	1.023	④	0.003	9.00	9.09	9.06	0.062 ⑤	0.030 ⑤
		②	③	1.023	④	0.003	10.00	10.09	10.06	0.062 ⑤	0.030 ⑤
	Explorer	Front	0.938	1.023	④	0.003	—	—	—	0.062 ⑤	—
		Rear	0.938	0.472	0.409	0.003	—	—	—	—	0.125 ⑤
	Mountaineer	Front	0.938	1.023	0.810	0.003	—	—	—	0.062 ⑤	—
		Rear	0.938	0.472	0.409	0.003	—	—	—	—	0.125 ⑤
1999	Ranger	①	0.938	1.023	④	0.003	9.00	9.09	9.06	0.062 ⑤	0.030 ⑤
		②	③	1.023	④	0.003	10.00	10.09	10.06	0.062 ⑤	0.030 ⑤
	Explorer	Front	0.938	1.023	④	0.003	—	—	—	0.062 ⑤	—
		Rear	0.938	0.472	0.409	0.003	—	—	—	—	0.125 ⑤
	Mountaineer	Front	0.938	1.023	0.810	0.003	—	—	—	0.062 ⑤	—
		Rear	0.938	0.472	0.409	0.003	—	—	—	—	0.125 ⑤

① 9 inch rear brake drum used on 4x2 vehicles under 4580 lbs. Gross Vehicle Weight Rating (GVWR)
② 10 inch rear brake drum used on vehicles over 4580 lbs. Gross Vehicle Weight Rating (GVWR) or with limited slip rear drive axle
③ 4x2 vehicles use 0.938 in. master cylinder bore
4x4 vehicles use 0.975 in. master cylinder bore
④ 4x2 vehicles have min. thickness of 0.960 in.
4x4 vehicles have min. thickness of 0.810 in.
⑤ If lining is riveted, measurement is for material above the rivet head
If lining is bonded, measurement is for material above the backing plate

89689C51

10

BODY

EXTERIOR

Doors

ADJUSTMENT

➡**Loosen the hinge-to-door bolts for lateral adjustment only. Loosen the hinge-to-body bolts for both lateral and vertical adjustments.**

1. Determine which hinge bolts are to be loosened and back them out just enough to allow movement.

2. To move the door safely, use a padded pry bar. When the door is in the proper position, tighten the bolts to specification and check the door operation. There should be no binding or interference when the door is closed and opened.

3. Door closing adjustment can also be affected by the position of the lock striker plate. Loosen the striker plate bolts and move the striker plate just enough to permit proper closing and locking of the door.

89680P01

Before moving the door lock striker, mark its original position for future reference . . .

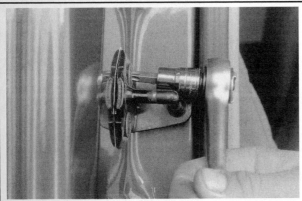

89680P02

. . . then loosen the attaching bolts. Move it to a new position, tighten the bolts and close the door

Hood

ALIGNMENT

1. Open the hood and matchmark the hinge and latch positions.
2. Loosen the hinge-to-hood bolts just enough to allow movement of the hood.

3. Move the hood as required to obtain the proper fit and alignment between the hood and all adjoining body panels. Tighten the bolts securely when satisfactorily aligned.

4. Loosen the 2 latch attaching bolts.

5. Move the latch from side-to-side to align the latch with the striker. Torque the latch bolts.

6. Lubricate the latch and hinges and check the hood fit several times.

Liftgate

ALIGNMENT

♦ **See Figure 1**

➡**On Explorer, the liftgate glass should not be open while the liftgate is open. Make sure the window is closed before opening the liftgate.**

The liftgate can be adjusted slightly in or out and side to side by loosening the hinge-to-header nut or bolt. Some up and down adjustment can be accomplished by loosening the hinge bolts on the liftgate and moving the gate up or down. The liftgate should be adjusted for even and parallel fit with adjoining panels.

The door latch strikers can also be adjusted. Loosen the striker center bolt and move the assembly to a new position. Check that the door latches and unlatches easily.

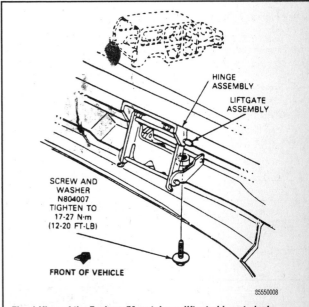

85550008

Fig. 1 View of the Explorer/Mountaineer liftgate hinge to body mounting

Tailgate

REMOVAL & INSTALLATION

♦ **See Figure 2**

1. Remove the tailgate support strap at the pillar T-head pivot.
2. Lift off the tailgate at the right hinge.
3. Pull off the left hinge.
4. Transfer all necessary hardware to the new tailgate if necessary.
5. Installation is the reverse of removal.

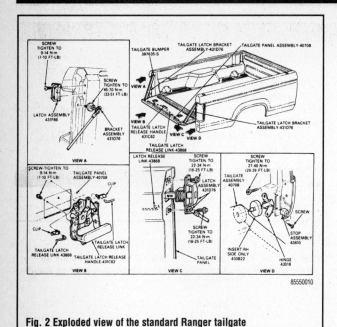

Fig. 2 Exploded view of the standard Ranger tailgate

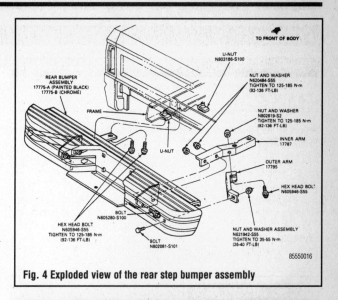

Fig. 4 Exploded view of the rear step bumper assembly

Front and Rear Bumpers

REMOVAL & INSTALLATION

▶ **See Figures 3 and 4**

1. Support the bumper. Disconnect electrical pigtails, if applicable.
2. Remove the nuts and bolts attaching the bumper brackets to the frame. Once the bumper is removed from the truck, remove the brackets from the bumper.
3. Remove the valance panel and rubstrip from the bumper as required.
4. Installation is the reverse of removal. Use a leveling tool to ensure a level installation before tightening the bolts.
5. Support the bumper and torque the bracket-to-frame bolts to specifications.

Grille

REMOVAL & INSTALLATION

▶ **See Figures 5 and 6**

1. Remove all of the plastic retainers across the top of the grille, if equipped.
2. Remove the screws, one at each corner, attaching the grille to the headlight housings.
3. On Mountaineer and 1995–97 Explorer, remove the head light lens assemblies to gain access to the grille retaining screws on the ends.

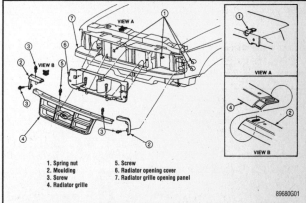

1. Spring nut
2. Moulding
3. Screw
4. Radiator grille
5. Screw
6. Radiator opening cover
7. Radiator grille opening panel

Fig. 5 Exploded view of the 1993–97 Ranger front grille—1991–92 Ranger and 1991–94 Explorer models are similar

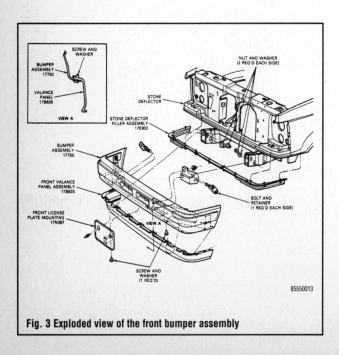

Fig. 3 Exploded view of the front bumper assembly

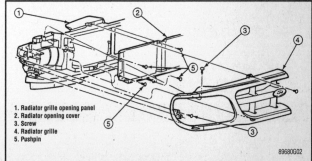

1. Radiator grille opening panel
2. Radiator opening cover
3. Screw
4. Radiator grille
5. Pushpin

Fig. 6 Exploded view of the Mountaineer and 1995–97 Explorer front grille

4. Carefully push inward on the snap-in retainers and disengage the grille from the headlight housings.

5. Installation is the reverse of removal.

Outside Mirrors

REMOVAL & INSTALLATION

♦ See Figure 7

1. Except for 1991–92 Ranger models, the door panel must first be removed to gain access to the mounting nuts. Disconnect the harness connector if equipped with power mirrors.

2. Remove the mounting screws or nuts and lift off the mirror. Remove and discard the gasket.

3. When installing, make sure the gasket is properly positioned before tightening the screws.

4. If equipped with power mirror, plug in the electrical connector and test the operation of the power mirror before installing the door panel.

Antenna

REMOVAL & INSTALLATION

Fixed Mast Antenna

♦ See Figure 8

1. Disconnect the antenna lead-in cable from the cable assembly in-line connector above the glove box.

2. Working under the instrument panel, disengage the cable from its retainers.

➡**On some models, it may be necessary to remove the instrument panel pad to get at the cable.**

3. Unscrew the antenna mast from the base.
4. Outside, unsnap the cap from the antenna base.
5. Remove the 3 screws and lift off the antenna, pulling the cable with it, carefully.
6. Remove and discard the gasket.

To install:

7. Place the gasket in position on the cowl panel.
8. Insert the antenna cable through the hole and seat the antenna base on the cowl. Secure with the 3 screws.
9. Position the cap over the antenna base and snap it into place.
10. Install the antenna mast to the base.
11. Route the cable in exactly the same position as before removal behind the instrument panel.
12. Connect the cable to the in-line connector above the glove box.

Electric Antenna

♦ See Figure 9

1. Ensure that the antenna is in the fully retracted position.
2. Remove the retaining screws for the right-hand front wheel splash shield for access to the lower retaining screw.
3. Remove the lower antenna mounting bracket retaining screw.
4. Unsnap the antenna base cap from the antenna base and remove it.
5. Loosen and remove the antenna-to-base retaining nut.
6. Disconnect the electrical wire harness plug and the antenna lead-in wire at the antenna.

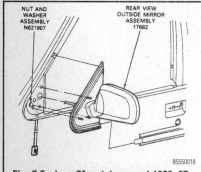

Fig. 7 Explorer/Mountaineer and 1993–97 Ranger outside rear view mirror

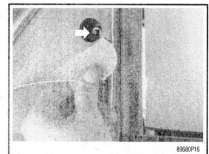

To remove the outside mirror, first remove the door trim panel and peel back the padding to access the nuts (arrow)

With the access holes uncovered, loosen and remove the mirror attaching nuts

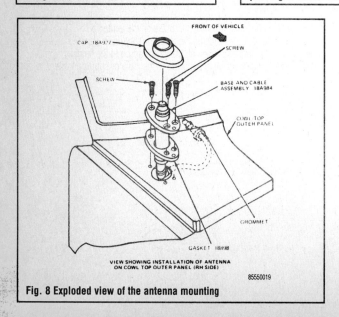

Fig. 8 Exploded view of the antenna mounting

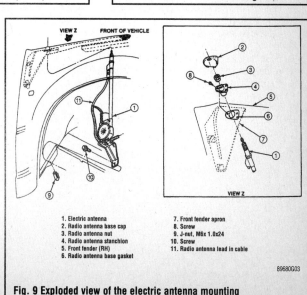

1. Electric antenna
2. Radio antenna base cap
3. Radio antenna nut
4. Radio antenna stanchion
5. Front fender (RH)
6. Radio antenna base gasket
7. Front fender apron
8. Screw
9. J-nut, M6x 1.0x24
10. Screw
11. Radio antenna lead in cable

Fig. 9 Exploded view of the electric antenna mounting

7. Remove the antenna through the fender/splash shield access.
8. Installation is the reverse of the removal procedure.

Fenders

REMOVAL & INSTALLATION

Ranger

▶ See Figures 10 and 11

1. Clean out all dirt from the fender attaching hardware and lubricate them to ease removal.
2. Remove the grille.
3. Remove the bolt attaching the rear lower end of the fender to the lower corner of the cab.
4. From inside the cab, remove the bolt attaching the rear end of the fender to the cowl.
5. Remove the screws around the wheel opening attaching the fender apron.
6. On 1993–97 models remove the bolt attaching the lower rear of the fender to the rocker.
7. Remove the bolts along the top of the apron attaching the fender.
8. Remove the bolt attaching the brace to radiator support assembly.
9. Remove the fender and remove the brace from the fender.

To install:

10. Position the nuts, retainers and brace on the fender.
11. Position the fender on the apron and loosely install the apron retaining bolts.
12. Loosely install the bolt from inside the cab attaching the rear end of fender to the cowl.
13. Loosely install the bolt attaching the rear lower end of the fender to the lower corner of the cab.
14. Loosely install the bolt attaching the brace to the radiator support assembly.
15. Loosely install the 4 bolts along the fender inner body attaching the fender.
16. Adjust the position of the fender and tighten all mounting bolts.
17. Install the grille.
18. Install the apron screws around the wheel opening.

Explorer and Mountaineer

▶ See Figure 11

1. Clean out all dirt from the fender attaching hardware and lubricate them to ease removal.
2. Remove the headlight door and side marker lamp.
3. Remove both bolts attaching the headlight assembly to the fender.
4. From inside the door opening, remove the bolt attaching the rear end of the fender to the cowl.
5. Remove the 4 bolts along the top of the fender inner body attaching the fender.
6. Raise the truck to a convenient height.
7. Remove the bolt attaching the brace to the radiator support assembly.
8. Remove the 4 screws attaching the fender apron to the fender.
9. Remove the 2 bolts attaching the fender to the rocker panel.
10. Lower the vehicle and remove the fender. Remove the brace from the fender.

To install:

11. Install the fender and raise the truck.

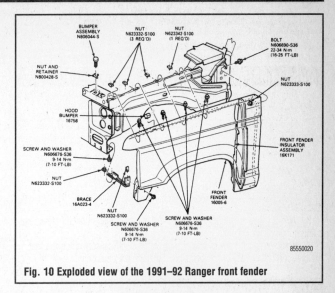

Fig. 10 Exploded view of the 1991–92 Ranger front fender

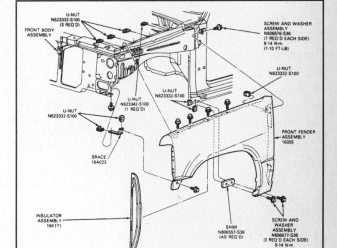

Fig. 11 Exploded view of the Explorer/Mountaineer front fender—1993–97 Ranger is similar

12. Position the nuts, retainers and brace on the fender.
13. Install the 2 bolts attaching the fender to the rocker panel.
14. Install the 4 screws attaching the fender apron to the fender.
15. Install the bolt attaching the brace to the radiator support. Lower the truck.
16. Install the 4 bolts along the top of the fender inner body attaching the fender.
17. Install the bolt attaching the rear end of the fender to the cowl.
18. Install both bolts attaching the headlight assembly to the fender.
19. Install the headlight door and side marker lamp.

INTERIOR

Door Panels

REMOVAL & INSTALLATION

1991–92 Ranger

1. Open the window. Remove the armrest.
2. Remove the door handle screw and pull off the handle.
3. If equipped with manual windows, remove the window regulator handle screw and pull off the handle.

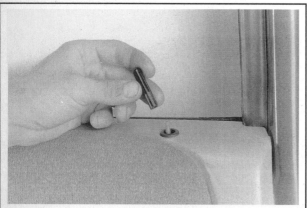

To remove the door trim panel, first open the window and unscrew the door lock knob

a. If equipped with power windows, remove the power window switch housing.
b. If equipped with manual door locks, remove the door lock control.
c. If equipped with power door locks, remove the power door lock switch housing.
4. If equipped with electric outside rear view mirrors, remove the power mirror switch housing.
5. Using a flat wood spatula, insert it carefully behind the panel and slide it along to find the push-pins. When you encounter a pin, pry the pin outward. Do this until all the pins are out. NEVER PULL ON THE PANEL TO REMOVE THE PINS!
6. Installation is the reverse of removal.

Explorer/Mountaineer and 1993–97 Ranger

1. Open the window.
2. Unscrew the door lock knob.
3. On Explorer/Mountaineer, remove the 2 screws retaining the trim panel located above the door handle.
4. On Ranger, remove the two screws in the armrest and remove it.
5. If equipped with manual window crank handles, pull off the handle cover, then remove the attaching screw.
6. Remove the trim cup behind (Explorer/Mountaineer) or around (Ranger) the door handle using a small prying tool. Retention nibs will flex for ease of removal.
7. If equipped with power accessories, use the notch at the lower end of the plate and pry the plate off. Remove the plate from the trim panel and pull the wiring harness from behind the panel. Disconnect the harness from the switches.
8. Remove any retaining screws uncovered by the removed trim pieces.
9. Using a flat wood spatula, insert it carefully behind the panel and slide it along to find the push-pins. When you encounter a pin, pry the pin outward. Do this until all the pins are out. NEVER PULL ON THE PANEL TO REMOVE THE PINS!

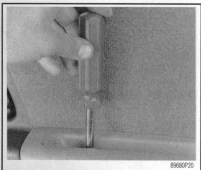

Next, on Ranger models, remove the two screws from the armrest and remove the armrest

If equipped with manual window crank handles, pull back the handle cover . . .

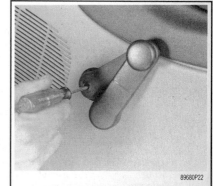

. . . and remove the crank handle retaining screw . . .

. . . then remove the handle by pulling it from the window crankshaft

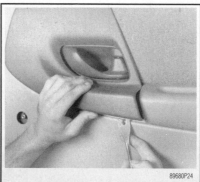

Carefully pry under the trim panel around the door handle . . .

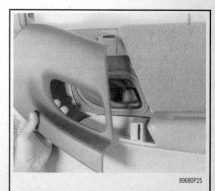

. . . and remove it, then remove any uncovered screws

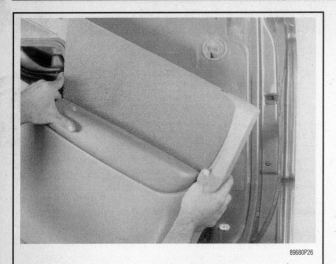

Pry out the trim panel-to-door frame retaining clips, then lift up and pull the panel free

10. Lift slightly to disengage the panel from the flange at the top of the door.

11. Disconnect the door courtesy lamp and remove the panel completely. Replace any damaged or bent attaching clips.

12. Installation is the reverse of removal.

Instrument Panel

REMOVAL & INSTALLATION

▶ See Figures 12 and 13

1. Disconnect the negative battery cable.

2. Disconnect the instrument panel wiring connectors in the engine compartment.

3. Remove the 2 screws retaining the lower steering column cover and remove the cover.

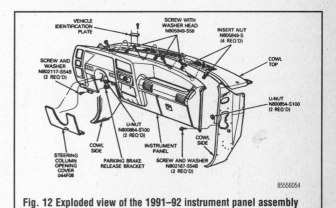

Fig. 12 Exploded view of the 1991–92 instrument panel assembly

1. Instrument panel defroster opening grille
2. Passenger air bag opening cover assembly (Explorer)
3. Screw
4. Screw
5. Instrment panel assembly
6. Glove box
7. Pushpin
8. Rivet
9. Instrument panel sound insulation
10. Screw
11. Instrument panel finish center bracket
12. Screw
13. Nut
14. Instrument panel brace
15. Screw
16. Instrument panel ash receptacle
17. Screw
18. Instrument panel finish panel (center)
19. Instrument panel radio opening panel
20. Instrument panel cover access cover
21. Instrument panel steering column cover
22. Instrument panel steering column opening cover reinforcement
23. Nut
24. Instrument panel steering column opening center reinforcement
25. Screw
26. Transmission control selector indicator
27. Instrument cluster
28. Instrument panel fuse panel opening door
29. Instrument panel finish panel (cluster)

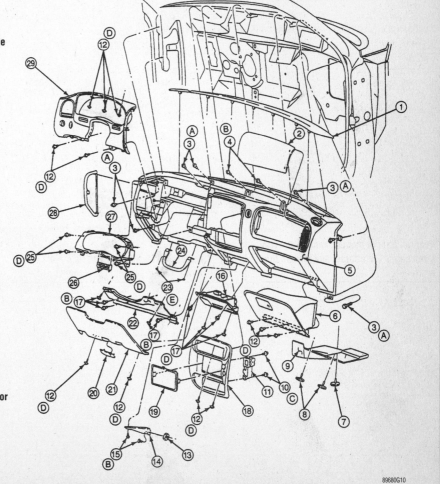

Fig. 13 Exploded view of the 1993–97 instrument panel assembly

4. Remove the ashtray and retainer.

5. Remove the upper and lower steering column shrouds.

6. Remove the instrument cluster finish panel. Remove the radio assembly and equalizer, if equipped.

7. Remove the screws retaining the instrument cluster. Remove the cluster, making sure to disconnect the electrical leads.

8. Remove the screw that attaches the instrument panel to the brake and clutch pedal support.

9. Disconnect the wiring from the switches on the steering column.

10. Remove the front inside pillar mouldings.

11. Remove the right side cowl trim cover.

12. Remove the lower right insulator from under the instrument panel.

13. Remove the 2 bolts retaining the instrument panel to the lower right side of the cowl.

14. Remove the 2 screw retaining the instrument panel to the parking brake bracket, on the drivers side.

15. Remove the 4 screw retaining the top of the instrument panel.

16. Reach through the openings in the instrument panel and disconnect any remaining electrical connectors. Disconnect the heater/air conditioning controls.

➡**Removing the instrument panel will be much easier with the help of an assistant, as it is extremely bulky and difficult to maneuver.**

17. Carefully tilt the instrument panel forward and remove it from the vehicle. Work the instrument panel around the steering wheel.

To install:

18. If the instrument panel is being replaced, transfer all mounting brackets and switches to the new panel.

19. Position the instrument panel inside the vehicle and install the 4 screw that retain it along the top.

20. Install the retaining screws on the left and right sides. Make sure the instrument panel is properly mounted.

➡**Making sure the instrument panel is positioned correctly at this point, will avoid problems with fit and rattles, after its installed. Also check for pinched or cut wires.**

21. Install the mouldings and the trim panels.

22. Connect the heater/air conditioning controls and all of the instrument panel switches.

23. Connect the wiring to the steering column switches.

24. Install the instrument cluster, radio and ashtray assemblies.

25. Install the instrument cluster finish panel.

26. Install the steering column shrouds.

27. Reconnect all wiring connectors in the engine compartment.

28. Connect the negative battery cable.

29. Check the operation of ALL accessories.

Center Console

REMOVAL & INSTALLATION

◆ **See Figures 14 and 15**

1. Remove the small arm rest screw covers.

2. Remove the 4 arm rest retaining bolts.

3. Remove the 2 rear arm rest retaining screws and the 2 screws in the front utility tray.

4. Remove the entire assembly, by lifting it from its mounting bracket.

5. Install the console in position and install all mounting screws.

Door Locks

REMOVAL & INSTALLATION

Door Latch

◆ **See Figures 16, 17 and 18**

1. Remove the door trim panel and watershield.

2. Disconnect the rods from the handle and lock cylinder, and from the remote control assembly.

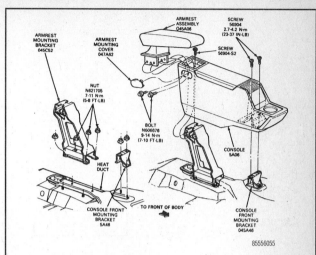

Fig. 14 Exploded view of the standard center console (may have one or two cup holders)

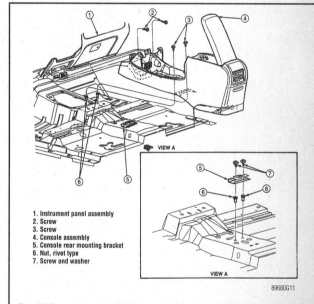

1. Instrument panel assembly
2. Screw
3. Screw
4. Console assembly
5. Console rear mounting bracket
6. Nut, rivet type
7. Screw and washer

Fig. 15 Exploded view of the high-end center console

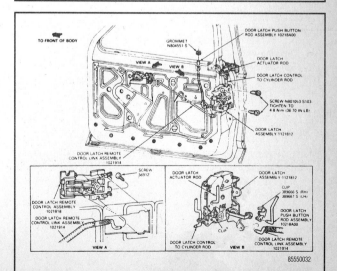

Fig. 16 Door latch assembly—Ranger

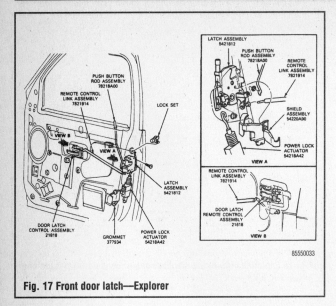

Fig. 17 Front door latch—Explorer

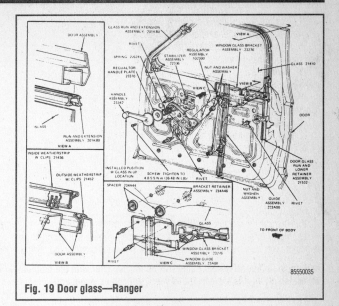

Fig. 19 Door glass—Ranger

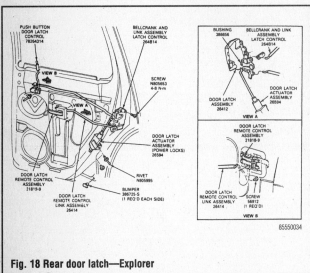

Fig. 18 Rear door latch—Explorer

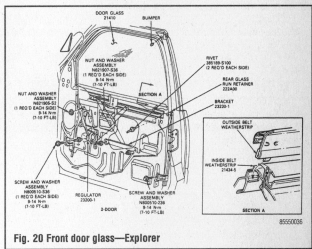

Fig. 20 Front door glass—Explorer

3. Remove the latch assembly attaching screws and remove the latch from the door.

4. Installation is the reverse of removal.

Door Lock Cylinder

1. Open the window.
2. Remove the trim panel and watershield.
3. Disconnect the actuating rod from the lock control link clip.
4. Slide the retainer away from the lock cylinder.
5. Remove the cylinder from the door.
6. Use a new gasket when installing to ensure a watertight fit.
7. Lubricate the cylinder with suitable oil recommended for this application.

Door Glass and Regulator

REMOVAL & INSTALLATION

Glass

▶ **See Figures 19, 20 and 21**

1. Remove the door trim panel and speaker if applicable.
2. Remove the screw from the division bar. Remove the inside belt weatherstrip(s) if equipped.

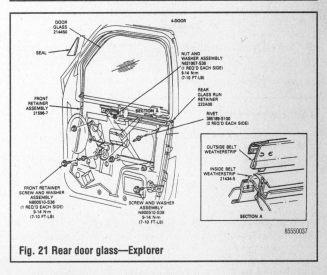

Fig. 21 Rear door glass—Explorer

3. Remove the 2 vent window attaching screws from the front edge of the door.

4. Lower the glass and pull the glass out of the run retainer near the vent window division bar, just enough to allow the removal of the vent window, if equipped.

5. Push the front edge of the glass downward and remove the rear glass run retainer from the door.

6. If equipped with retaining rivets, remove them carefully. Otherwise, remove the glass from the channel using Glass and Channel Removal Tool 2900 (made by the Sommer and Mala Glass Machine Co. of Chicago, ILL., or its equivalent). Remove the glass through the belt opening if possible.

To install:

7. Install the glass spacer and retainer into the retention holes.

8. Install the glass into the door, position on the bracket and align the retaining holes.

9. Carefully install the retaining rivets or equivalent.

10. Raise the glass to the full closed position.

11. Install the rear glass run retainer and glass run. Install the inside belt weatherstrip(s).

12. Check for smooth operation before installing the trim panel.

Regulator

EXCEPT EXPLORER/MOUNTAINEER FRONT DOOR

♦ **See Figure 22**

1. Remove the door trim panel. If equipped with power windows, disconnect the wire from the regulator

2. Support the glass in the full UP position or remove completely.

3. Remove the window guide and glass bracket if equipped.

4. Remove the center pins from the regulator attaching rivets.

5. Drill out the regulator attaching rivets using a ¼ in. (6mm) drill bit.

6. Disengage the regulator arm from the glass bracket and remove the regulator.

7. Installation is the reverse of removal. ¼ in.–20 x ½ in. bolts and nuts may be used in place of the rivets to attach the regulator.

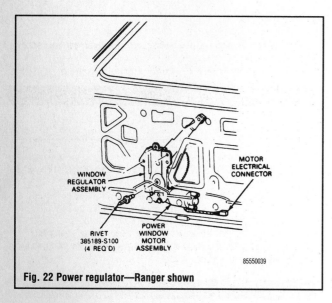

Fig. 22 Power regulator—Ranger shown

EXPLORER/MOUNTAINEER FRONT DOOR

♦ **See Figure 23**

1. Remove the door trim panel and watershield.

2. Remove the inside door belt weatherstrip and glass stabilizer.

3. Remove the door glass.

4. Remove the 2 nuts attaching the equalizer bracket.

5. Remove the rivets attaching the regulator base plate to the door.

6. Remove the regulator and glass bracket as an assembly from the door and transfer to a workbench.

7. Carefully bend the tab flat in order to remove the air slides from the glass bracket C-channel.

8. Install new regulator arm plastic guides into the C-channel and bend the tab back 90°. If the tab is broken or cracked, replace the glass bracket assembly. Make sure the rubber bumper is installed properly on the new glass bracket, if applicable.

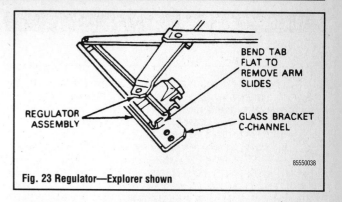

Fig. 23 Regulator—Explorer shown

※※ CAUTION

If the regulator counterbalance spring is to be removed, make sure the regulator arms are in a fixed position prior to removal. This will prevent possible injury when the C-spring unwinds.

To install:

9. Assemble the glass bracket and regulator assembly.

10. Install the assembly in the door. Set the regulator base plate to the door using the base plate locator tab as a guide.

11. Attach the regulator to the door using new rivets. ¼ in.–20 x ½ in. bolts and nuts may be used in place of the rivets to attach the regulator.

12. Install the equalizer bracket, door belt weatherstrip and glass stabilizer.

13. Install the glass and check for smooth operation before installing the door trim panel.

Electric Window Motor

REMOVAL & INSTALLATION

Ranger

1. Disconnect the negative battery cable.

2. Open the window. Remove the trim panel and watershield and support the window.

3. Disconnect the power window motor connector.

4. There may be a drill dimple in the door panel, opposite the concealed motor retaining bolt. Drill out the dimple to gain access to the bolt. Be careful to avoid damage to the wires. Remove the motor mounting bolts and remove the motor and regulator assembly.

5. Separate the motor and drive from the regulator on a workbench.

6. Installation is the reverse of removal.

7. Check for smooth operation before installing the trim panel.

Except Ranger

1. Raise the window fully if possible. If not, you will have to support the window during this procedure. Disconnect the battery ground.

2. Remove the door trim panel.

3. Disconnect the window motor wiring harness.

4. There may be a drill dimple in the door panel, opposite the concealed motor retaining bolt. Drill out the dimple to gain access to the bolt. Be careful to avoid damage to the wires.

5. Remove the motor mounting bolts (front door) or rivets(rear door).

6. Push the motor towards the outside of the door to disengage it from the gears. You'll have to support the window glass once the motor is disengaged.

7. Remove the motor from the door.

8. Installation is the reverse of removal. To avoid rusting in the drilled areas, prime and paint the exposed metal, or, cover the holes with waterproof body tape. Make sure that the motor works properly before installing the trim panel.

Windshield and Fixed Glass

REMOVAL & INSTALLATION

If your windshield, or other fixed window, is cracked or chipped, you may decide to replace it with a new one yourself. However, there are two main reasons why replacement windshields and other window glass should be installed only by a professional automotive glass technician: safety and cost.

The most important reason a professional should install automotive glass is for safety. The glass in the vehicle, especially the windshield, is designed with safety in mind in case of a collision. The windshield is specially manufactured from two panes of specially-tempered glass with a thin layer of transparent plastic between them. This construction allows the glass to "give" in the event that a part of your body hits the windshield during the collision, and prevents the glass from shattering, which could cause lacerations, blinding and other harm to passengers of the vehicle. The other fixed windows are designed to be tempered so that if they break during a collision, they shatter in such a way that there are no large pointed glass pieces. The professional automotive glass technician knows how to install the glass in a vehicle so that it will function optimally during a collision. Without the proper experience, knowledge and tools, installing a piece of automotive glass yourself could lead to additional harm if an accident should ever occur.

Cost is also a factor when deciding to install automotive glass yourself. Performing this could cost you much more than a professional may charge for the same job. Since the windshield is designed to break under stress, an often life saving characteristic, windshields tend to break VERY easily when an inexperienced person attempts to install one. Do-it-yourselfers buying two, three or even four windshields from a salvage yard because they have broken them during installation are common stories. Also, since the automotive glass is designed to prevent the outside elements from entering your vehicle, improper installation can lead to water and air leaks. Annoying whining noises at highway speeds from air leaks or inside body panel rusting from water leaks can add to your stress level and subtract from your wallet. After buying two or three windshields, installing them and ending up with a leak that produces a noise while driving and water damage during rainstorms, the cost of having a professional do it correctly the first time may be much more alluring. We here at Chilton, therefore, advise that you have a professional automotive glass technician service any broken glass on your vehicle.

WINDSHIELD CHIP REPAIR

➡**Check with your state and local authorities on the laws for state safety inspection. Some states or municipalities may not allow chip repair as a viable option for correcting stone damage to your windshield.**

Although severely cracked or damaged windshields must be replaced, there is something that you can do to prolong or even prevent the need for replacement of a chipped windshield. There are many companies which offer windshield chip repair products, such as Loctite's® Bullseye™ windshield repair kit. These kits usually consist of a syringe, pedestal and a sealing adhesive. The syringe is mounted on the pedestal and is used to create a vacuum which pulls the plastic layer against the glass. This helps make the chip transparent. The adhesive is then injected which seals the chip and helps to prevent further stress cracks from developing

➡**Always follow the specific manufacturer's instructions.**

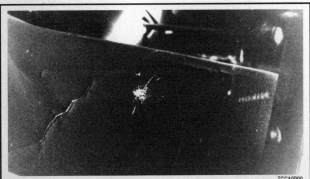

TCCA0P00

Small chips on your windshield can be fixed with an aftermarket repair kit, such as the one from Loctite®

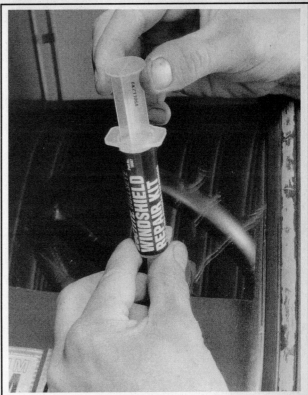

TCCA0P09

Hold the syringe with one hand while pulling the plunger back with the other hand

Inside Rear View Mirror

REMOVAL & INSTALLATION

The mirror is held in place with a single setscrew. Loosen the screw and lift the mirror off. Don't forget to unplug the electrical connector if the truck has an electric Day/Night mirror.

Repair kits for damaged mirrors are available and most auto parts stores. The most important part of the repair is the beginning. Mark the outside of the windshield to locate the pad, then scrape the old adhesive off with a razor blade. Clean the remaining adhesive off with chlorine-based window cleaner (not petroleum-based solvent) as thoroughly as possible. Follow the manufacturers instructions exactly to complete the repair.

Seats

REMOVAL & INSTALLATION

Bench Seat

♦ **See Figure 24**

1. On the right side, remove the seat track insulator.
2. Remove 4 seat track-to-floor retaining screws (2 each side) and lift the seat and track assembly from vehicle.
3. To remove the tracks from the seat, place the seat upside-down on a clean bench.
4. Disconnect the track latch tie rod assembly from latch lever and hook in the center of the cushion assembly.
5. Remove 4 track-to-seat cushion retaining screws (2 each side) and remove the tracks from the cushion assembly.
   To install:
6. Position the track to the cushion assembly. Install the 4 track-to-seat retaining screws and tighten.

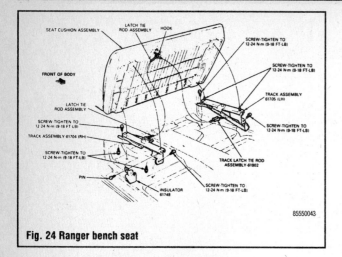

Fig. 24 Ranger bench seat

7. Connect the track latch tie rod assembly to the latch lever and hook in center of cushion.
8. Position the seat and track assembly in the vehicle.
9. Install the 4 seat track-to-floor retaining screws and tighten to specification.
10. On the right side, install the seat track insulator.

Bucket and 60/40 Seats

♦ **See Figures 25, 26 and 27**

1. Remove the seat track insulator (Ranger passenger seat only).
2. Remove the 4 seat track-to-floorpan screws (2 each side) and lift the seat and track assembly from the vehicle.
3. To remove the seat tracks from the seat cushion, position the seat upside down on a clean bench.

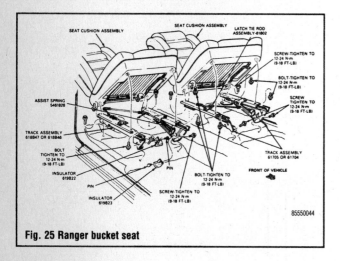

Fig. 25 Ranger bucket seat

4. Disconnect the latch tie rod assembly and assist spring from the tracks.
5. Remove 4 track-to-seat cushion screws (2 each side) from the track assemblies. Remove the tracks from seat cushion.

To install:

6. Position the tracks to the seat cushion. Install the 4 track-to-seat cushion screws (2 each side) and tighten.
7. Connect the latch tie rod assembly and assist spring to the tracks.
8. Position the seat and track assembly in the vehicle.
9. Install 4 track-to-floorpan screws and tighten to specification.
10. Install the seat track insulators (Ranger passenger seat only).

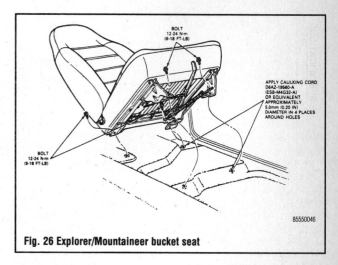

Fig. 26 Explorer/Mountaineer bucket seat

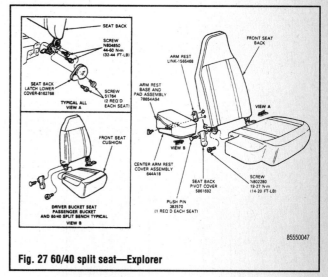

Fig. 27 60/40 split seat—Explorer

TORQUE SPECIFICATIONS

Component	Ft. Lbs.	Nm
Doors		
Door hinge-to-body	18-25	24-34
Door hinge-to-door	18-25	24-34
Latch-to-door screws	36-70 inch lbs.	4-8
Striker-to-body		
1991-92	24-32	33-44
1993-97	17-28	22-28
Fenders		
Fender-to-body bolts	8-10	10-14
Splash shield-to-fender bolts	8-9	10-13.5
Hood		
Hinge-to-body (if removable)	62-97 inch lbs.	7-11
Hood latch screws		
Explorer/Mountaineer	7-10	9-14
Ranger	9-10	11-14
Hood-to-hinge bolts	62-97 inch lbs.	7-11
Mirrors (outside)		
Conventional		
1991-92 Ranger	24-40 inch lbs.	2.7-4.5
All other models	35-53 inch lbs.	4-6
Western style		
Mirror-to-bracket	16-25	22-34
Bracket-to-door	25-40 inch lbs.	2.7-4.5
Upper bracket		
Lower bracket	35-70 inch lbs.	4-8
Pick-up box		
Box-to-frame bolts		
1991-93	40-56	54-76
1994-97	40-70	54-95
Outer-to-inner panel screws	89-115 inch lbs.	10-13
Upper outside moulding strips	89-124 inch lbs.	10-14
Wheel housing splash shield	27-35 inch lbs.	3-4
Rear door window		
Power window motor	25-50 inch lbs.	3-6
Regulator replacement bolts	36-60 inch lbs.	4-7
Rear lift gate - Explorer and Mountaineer		
Hinge-to-body bolts	13-20	17-27
Latch-to-liftgate	7-10	9-14
Striker-to-body	24-32	33-44
Seat belts		
All fasteners	22-32	30-43

89680C01

TORQUE SPECIFICATIONS

Component	Ft. Lbs.	Nm
Seats		
Front		
Bench		
Track-to-floor	9-18	12-24
Track-to-seat	9-18	12-24
Bucket		
Arm rest bracket	9-18	12-24
Track-to-floor	9-18	12-24
Track-to-seat	9-18	12-24
Reclining seat		
Pivot bolt	15-20	20-27
Recliner mechanism-to-seat back	16-23	22-32
Recliner mechanism-to-seat cushion	32-44	44-60
Seat back latch		
Support-to-seat back	15-20	20-27
Support-to-seat cushion	15-30	20-43
Rear		
Mountaineer/Explorer		
Rear bench - all fasteners	22-34	30-46
Ranger Super Cab - rear folding		
Seat-to-floor	13-20	17-27
Tailgate - Composite		
Cable		
Hinge bolts	16-25	22-34
Retainer-to-tailgate	20-29	27-40
Striker-to-body bolts	53-89 inch lbs.	6-10
1991-93	24-33	33-45
1994-97	20-25	26-43
Tailgate - Steel		
Hinge screws	20-29	27-40
Latch bolts		
1991-93	16-25	22-34
1994-97	91-122 inch lbs.	10-14
Striker-to-body bolts	7-10	9-14
Support bracket bolts	33-51	45-70

89680C02

GLOSSARY

AIR/FUEL RATIO: The ratio of air-to-gasoline by weight in the fuel mixture drawn into the engine.

AIR INJECTION: One method of reducing harmful exhaust emissions by injecting air into each of the exhaust ports of an engine. The fresh air entering the hot exhaust manifold causes any remaining fuel to be burned before it can exit the tailpipe.

ALTERNATOR: A device used for converting mechanical energy into electrical energy.

AMMETER: An instrument, calibrated in amperes, used to measure the flow of an electrical current in a circuit. Ammeters are always connected in series with the circuit being tested.

AMPERE: The rate of flow of electrical current present when one volt of electrical pressure is applied against one ohm of electrical resistance.

ANALOG COMPUTER: Any microprocessor that uses similar (analogous) electrical signals to make its calculations.

ARMATURE: A laminated, soft iron core wrapped by a wire that converts electrical energy to mechanical energy as in a motor or relay. When rotated in a magnetic field, it changes mechanical energy into electrical energy as in a generator.

ATMOSPHERIC PRESSURE: The pressure on the Earth's surface caused by the weight of the air in the atmosphere. At sea level, this pressure is 14.7 psi at 32°F (101 kPa at 0°C).

ATOMIZATION: The breaking down of a liquid into a fine mist that can be suspended in air.

AXIAL PLAY: Movement parallel to a shaft or bearing bore.

BACKFIRE: The sudden combustion of gases in the intake or exhaust system that results in a loud explosion.

BACKLASH: The clearance or play between two parts, such as meshed gears.

BACKPRESSURE: Restrictions in the exhaust system that slow the exit of exhaust gases from the combustion chamber.

BAKELITE: A heat resistant, plastic insulator material commonly used in printed circuit boards and transistorized components.

BALL BEARING: A bearing made up of hardened inner and outer races between which hardened steel balls roll.

BALLAST RESISTOR: A resistor in the primary ignition circuit that lowers voltage after the engine is started to reduce wear on ignition components.

BEARING: A friction reducing, supportive device usually located between a stationary part and a moving part.

BIMETAL TEMPERATURE SENSOR: Any sensor or switch made of two dissimilar types of metal that bend when heated or cooled due to the different expansion rates of the alloys. These types of sensors usually function as an on/off switch.

BLOWBY: Combustion gases, composed of water vapor and unburned fuel, that leak past the piston rings into the crankcase during normal engine operation. These gases are removed by the PCV system to prevent the buildup of harmful acids in the crankcase.

BRAKE PAD: A brake shoe and lining assembly used with disc brakes.

BRAKE SHOE: The backing for the brake lining. The term is, however, usually applied to the assembly of the brake backing and lining.

BUSHING: A liner, usually removable, for a bearing; an anti-friction liner used in place of a bearing.

CALIPER: A hydraulically activated device in a disc brake system, which is mounted straddling the brake rotor (disc). The caliper contains at least one piston and two brake pads. Hydraulic pressure on the piston(s) forces the pads against the rotor.

CAMSHAFT: A shaft in the engine on which are the lobes (cams) which operate the valves. The camshaft is driven by the crankshaft, via a belt, chain or gears, at one half the crankshaft speed.

CAPACITOR: A device which stores an electrical charge.

CARBON MONOXIDE (CO): A colorless, odorless gas given off as a normal byproduct of combustion. It is poisonous and extremely dangerous in confined areas, building up slowly to toxic levels without warning if adequate ventilation is not available.

CARBURETOR: A device, usually mounted on the intake manifold of an engine, which mixes the air and fuel in the proper proportion to allow even combustion.

CATALYTIC CONVERTER: A device installed in the exhaust system, like a muffler, that converts harmful byproducts of combustion into carbon dioxide and water vapor by means of a heat-producing chemical reaction.

CENTRIFUGAL ADVANCE: A mechanical method of advancing the spark timing by using flyweights in the distributor that react to centrifugal force generated by the distributor shaft rotation.

CHECK VALVE: Any one-way valve installed to permit the flow of air, fuel or vacuum in one direction only.

CHOKE: A device, usually a moveable valve, placed in the intake path of a carburetor to restrict the flow of air.

CIRCUIT: Any unbroken path through which an electrical current can flow. Also used to describe fuel flow in some instances.

CIRCUIT BREAKER: A switch which protects an electrical circuit from overload by opening the circuit when the current flow exceeds a predetermined level. Some circuit breakers must be reset manually, while most reset automatically.

COIL (IGNITION): A transformer in the ignition circuit which steps up the voltage provided to the spark plugs.

COMBINATION MANIFOLD: An assembly which includes both the intake and exhaust manifolds in one casting.

COMBINATION VALVE: A device used in some fuel systems that routes fuel vapors to a charcoal storage canister instead of venting them into the atmosphere. The valve relieves fuel tank pressure and allows fresh air into the tank as the fuel level drops to prevent a vapor lock situation.

COMPRESSION RATIO: The comparison of the total volume of the cylinder and combustion chamber with the piston at BDC and the piston at TDC.

CONDENSER: 1. An electrical device which acts to store an electrical charge, preventing voltage surges. 2. A radiator-like device in the air conditioning system in which refrigerant gas condenses into a liquid, giving off heat.

CONDUCTOR: Any material through which an electrical current can be transmitted easily.

CONTINUITY: Continuous or complete circuit. Can be checked with an ohmmeter.

COUNTERSHAFT: An intermediate shaft which is rotated by a mainshaft and transmits, in turn, that rotation to a working part.

CRANKCASE: The lower part of an engine in which the crankshaft and related parts operate.

CRANKSHAFT: The main driving shaft of an engine which receives reciprocating motion from the pistons and converts it to rotary motion.

CYLINDER: In an engine, the round hole in the engine block in which the piston(s) ride.

CYLINDER BLOCK: The main structural member of an engine in which is found the cylinders, crankshaft and other principal parts.

CYLINDER HEAD: The detachable portion of the engine, usually fastened to the top of the cylinder block and containing all or most of the combustion chambers. On overhead valve engines, it contains the valves and their operating parts. On overhead cam engines, it contains the camshaft as well.

DEAD CENTER: The extreme top or bottom of the piston stroke.

DETONATION: An unwanted explosion of the air/fuel mixture in the combustion chamber caused by excess heat and compression, advanced timing, or an overly lean mixture. Also referred to as "ping".

DIAPHRAGM: A thin, flexible wall separating two cavities, such as in a vacuum advance unit.

DIESELING: A condition in which hot spots in the combustion chamber cause the engine to run on after the key is turned off.

DIFFERENTIAL: A geared assembly which allows the transmission of motion between drive axles, giving one axle the ability to turn faster than the other.

DIODE: An electrical device that will allow current to flow in one direction only.

DISC BRAKE: A hydraulic braking assembly consisting of a brake disc, or rotor, mounted on an axle, and a caliper assembly containing, usually two brake pads which are activated by hydraulic pressure. The pads are forced against the sides of the disc, creating friction which slows the vehicle.

DISTRIBUTOR: A mechanically driven device on an engine which is responsible for electrically firing the spark plug at a predetermined point of the piston stroke.

DOWEL PIN: A pin, inserted in mating holes in two different parts allowing those parts to maintain a fixed relationship.

DRUM BRAKE: A braking system which consists of two brake shoes and one or two wheel cylinders, mounted on a fixed backing plate, and a brake drum, mounted on an axle, which revolves around the assembly.

DWELL: The rate, measured in degrees of shaft rotation, at which an electrical circuit cycles on and off.

ELECTRONIC CONTROL UNIT (ECU): Ignition module, module, amplifier or igniter. See Module for definition.

ELECTRONIC IGNITION: A system in which the timing and firing of the spark plugs is controlled by an electronic control unit, usually called a module. These systems have no points or condenser.

END-PLAY: The measured amount of axial movement in a shaft.

ENGINE: A device that converts heat into mechanical energy.

EXHAUST MANIFOLD: A set of cast passages or pipes which conduct exhaust gases from the engine.

FEELER GAUGE: A blade, usually metal, or precisely predetermined thickness, used to measure the clearance between two parts.

FIRING ORDER: The order in which combustion occurs in the cylinders of an engine. Also the order in which spark is distributed to the plugs by the distributor.

FLOODING: The presence of too much fuel in the intake manifold and combustion chamber which prevents the air/fuel mixture from firing, thereby causing a no-start situation.

FLYWHEEL: A disc shaped part bolted to the rear end of the crankshaft. Around the outer perimeter is affixed the ring gear. The starter drive engages the ring gear, turning the flywheel, which rotates the crankshaft, imparting the initial starting motion to the engine.

FOOT POUND (ft. lbs. or sometimes, ft.lb.): The amount of energy or work needed to raise an item weighing one pound, a distance of one foot.

FUSE: A protective device in a circuit which prevents circuit overload by breaking the circuit when a specific amperage is present. The device is constructed around a strip or wire of a lower amperage rating than the circuit it is designed to protect. When an amperage higher than that stamped on the fuse is present in the circuit, the strip or wire melts, opening the circuit.

GEAR RATIO: The ratio between the number of teeth on meshing gears.

GENERATOR: A device which converts mechanical energy into electrical energy.

HEAT RANGE: The measure of a spark plug's ability to dissipate heat from its firing end. The higher the heat range, the hotter the plug fires.

HUB: The center part of a wheel or gear.

HYDROCARBON (HC): Any chemical compound made up of hydrogen and carbon. A major pollutant formed by the engine as a byproduct of combustion.

HYDROMETER: An instrument used to measure the specific gravity of a solution.

INCH POUND (inch lbs.; sometimes in.lb. or in. lbs.): One twelfth of a foot pound.

INDUCTION: A means of transferring electrical energy in the form of a magnetic field. Principle used in the ignition coil to increase voltage.

INJECTOR: A device which receives metered fuel under relatively low pressure and is activated to inject the fuel into the engine under relatively high pressure at a predetermined time.

INPUT SHAFT: The shaft to which torque is applied, usually carrying the driving gear or gears.

INTAKE MANIFOLD: A casting of passages or pipes used to conduct air or a fuel/air mixture to the cylinders.

JOURNAL: The bearing surface within which a shaft operates.

KEY: A small block usually fitted in a notch between a shaft and a hub to prevent slippage of the two parts.

MANIFOLD: A casting of passages or set of pipes which connect the cylinders to an inlet or outlet source.

MANIFOLD VACUUM: Low pressure in an engine intake manifold formed just below the throttle plates. Manifold vacuum is highest at idle and drops under acceleration.

MASTER CYLINDER: The primary fluid pressurizing device in a hydraulic system. In automotive use, it is found in brake and hydraulic clutch systems and is pedal activated, either directly or, in a power brake system, through the power booster.

MODULE: Electronic control unit, amplifier or igniter of solid state or integrated design which controls the current flow in the ignition primary circuit based on input from the pick-up coil. When the module opens the primary circuit, high secondary voltage is induced in the coil.

NEEDLE BEARING: A bearing which consists of a number (usually a large number) of long, thin rollers.

OHM: (Ω) The unit used to measure the resistance of conductor-to-electrical flow. One ohm is the amount of resistance that limits current flow to one ampere in a circuit with one volt of pressure.

OHMMETER: An instrument used for measuring the resistance, in ohms, in an electrical circuit.

OUTPUT SHAFT: The shaft which transmits torque from a device, such as a transmission.

OVERDRIVE: A gear assembly which produces more shaft revolutions than that transmitted to it.

OVERHEAD CAMSHAFT (OHC): An engine configuration in which the camshaft is mounted on top of the cylinder head and operates the valve either directly or by means of rocker arms.

OVERHEAD VALVE (OHV): An engine configuration in which all of the valves are located in the cylinder head and the camshaft is located in the cylinder block. The camshaft operates the valves via lifters and pushrods.

OXIDES OF NITROGEN (NOx): Chemical compounds of nitrogen produced as a byproduct of combustion. They combine with hydrocarbons to produce smog.

OXYGEN SENSOR: Use with the feedback system to sense the presence of oxygen in the exhaust gas and signal the computer which can reference the voltage signal to an air/fuel ratio.

PINION: The smaller of two meshing gears.

PISTON RING: An open-ended ring with fits into a groove on the outer diameter of the piston. Its chief function is to form a seal between the piston and cylinder wall. Most automotive pistons have three rings: two for compression sealing; one for oil sealing.

PRELOAD: A predetermined load placed on a bearing during assembly or by adjustment.

PRIMARY CIRCUIT: the low voltage side of the ignition system which consists of the ignition switch, ballast resistor or resistance wire, bypass, coil, electronic control unit and pick-up coil as well as the connecting wires and harnesses.

PRESS FIT: The mating of two parts under pressure, due to the inner diameter of one being smaller than the outer diameter of the other, or vice versa; an interference fit.

RACE: The surface on the inner or outer ring of a bearing on which the balls, needles or rollers move.

REGULATOR: A device which maintains the amperage and/or voltage levels of a circuit at predetermined values.

RELAY: A switch which automatically opens and/or closes a circuit.

RESISTANCE: The opposition to the flow of current through a circuit or electrical device, and is measured in ohms. Resistance is equal to the voltage divided by the amperage.

RESISTOR: A device, usually made of wire, which offers a preset amount of resistance in an electrical circuit.

RING GEAR: The name given to a ring-shaped gear attached to a differential case, or affixed to a flywheel or as part of a planetary gear set.

ROLLER BEARING: A bearing made up of hardened inner and outer races between which hardened steel rollers move.

ROTOR: 1. The disc-shaped part of a disc brake assembly, upon which the brake pads bear; also called, brake disc. 2. The device mounted atop the distributor shaft, which passes current to the distributor cap tower contacts.

SECONDARY CIRCUIT: The high voltage side of the ignition system, usually above 20,000 volts. The secondary includes the ignition coil, coil wire, distributor cap and rotor, spark plug wires and spark plugs.

SENDING UNIT: A mechanical, electrical, hydraulic or electro-magnetic device which transmits information to a gauge.

SENSOR: Any device designed to measure engine operating conditions or ambient pressures and temperatures. Usually electronic in nature and designed to send a voltage signal to an on-board computer, some sensors may operate as a simple on/off switch or they may provide a variable voltage signal (like a potentiometer) as conditions or measured parameters change.

SHIM: Spacers of precise, predetermined thickness used between parts to establish a proper working relationship.

SLAVE CYLINDER: In automotive use, a device in the hydraulic clutch system which is activated by hydraulic force, disengaging the clutch.

SOLENOID: A coil used to produce a magnetic field, the effect of which is to produce work.

SPARK PLUG: A device screwed into the combustion chamber of a spark ignition engine. The basic construction is a conductive core inside of a ceramic insulator, mounted in an outer conductive base. An electrical charge from the spark plug wire travels along the conductive core and jumps a preset air gap to a grounding point or points at the end of the conductive base. The resultant spark ignites the fuel/air mixture in the combustion chamber.

SPLINES: Ridges machined or cast onto the outer diameter of a shaft or inner diameter of a bore to enable parts to mate without rotation.

TACHOMETER: A device used to measure the rotary speed of an engine, shaft, gear, etc., usually in rotations per minute.

THERMOSTAT: A valve, located in the cooling system of an engine, which is closed when cold and opens gradually in response to engine heating, controlling the temperature of the coolant and rate of coolant flow.

TOP DEAD CENTER (TDC): The point at which the piston reaches the top of its travel on the compression stroke.

TORQUE: The twisting force applied to an object.

TORQUE CONVERTER: A turbine used to transmit power from a driving member to a driven member via hydraulic action, providing changes in drive ratio and torque. In automotive use, it links the driveplate at the rear of the engine to the automatic transmission.

TRANSDUCER: A device used to change a force into an electrical signal.

TRANSISTOR: A semi-conductor component which can be actuated by a small voltage to perform an electrical switching function.

TUNE-UP: A regular maintenance function, usually associated with the replacement and adjustment of parts and components in the electrical and fuel systems of a vehicle for the purpose of attaining optimum performance.

TURBOCHARGER: An exhaust driven pump which compresses intake air and forces it into the combustion chambers at higher than atmospheric pressures. The increased air pressure allows more fuel to be burned and results in increased horsepower being produced.

VACUUM ADVANCE: A device which advances the ignition timing in response to increased engine vacuum.

VACUUM GAUGE: An instrument used to measure the presence of vacuum in a chamber.

VALVE: A device which control the pressure, direction of flow or rate of flow of a liquid or gas.

VALVE CLEARANCE: The measured gap between the end of the valve stem and the rocker arm, cam lobe or follower that activates the valve.

VISCOSITY: The rating of a liquid's internal resistance to flow.

VOLTMETER: An instrument used for measuring electrical force in units called volts. Voltmeters are always connected parallel with the circuit being tested.

WHEEL CYLINDER: Found in the automotive drum brake assembly, it is a device, actuated by hydraulic pressure, which, through internal pistons, pushes the brake shoes outward against the drums.

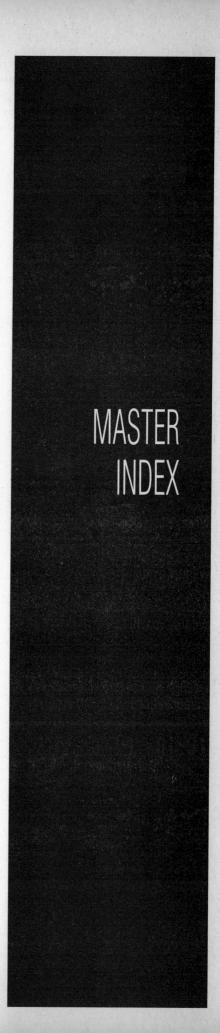

MASTER

INDEX